THE WORKS OF JONATHAN EDWARDS

VOLUME 2

Perry Miller, General Editor

PREVIOUSLY PUBLISHED

Paul Ramsey, ed., *Freedom of the Will* 1957

JONATHAN EDWARDS

Religious Affections

EDITED BY JOHN E. SMITH

PROFESSOR OF PHILOSOPHY, YALE UNIVERSITY

"The affections are no other than the more vigorous and sensible exercises of the inclination and will of the soul."
J. E.

New Haven

YALE UNIVERSITY PRESS, 1959

Set in Baskerville type and

Printed in the United States of America

Library of Congress catalog card number: 59-12702

A

TREATISE

Concerning

Religious Affections,

In Three PARTS;

PART I. Concerning the Nature of the *Affections*, and their Importance in *Religion*.

PART II. Shewing what are *no certain Signs* that *religious Affections* are *gracious*, or that they are *not*.

PART III. Shewing what *are distinguishing Signs* of truly gracious and *holy Affections*.

By *Jonathan Edwards*, A.M.

And Pastor of the *first* Church in *Northampton*.

Levit. ix. ult. and x. 1, 2. *And there came a Fire out from before the Lord,-----upon the Altar; -----which when all the People saw, they shouted and fell on their Faces. And* Nadab *and* Abihu ----- *offered strange Fire before the Lord, which he commanded them not: And there went out a Fire from the Lord, and devoured them, and they died before the Lord.*

Cant. ii. 12, 13. *The Flowers appear on the Earth, the Time of the Singing of Birds is come, and the Voice of the Turtle is heard in our Land; the Fig-tree putteth forth her green Figs, and the Vines with the tender Grape, give a good Smell.* Ver. 15. *Take us the Foxes, the little Foxes, which spoil the Vines; for our Vines have tender Grapes.*

BOSTON:

Printed for S. KNEELAND and T. GREEN in *Queen-street*, over against the Prison. 1746.

CONTENTS

EDITOR'S INTRODUCTION

ONE sure test of any thinker is the courage and persistence he displays in attacking fundamental questions. Judged by this criterion, Edwards was a thinker of stature. Not only did he produce a formidable answer to the formidable problem of the freedom of the will, but in the present *Treatise Concerning Religious Affections* [1] he struggled with the central question of Puritan Protestantism: How shall the presence of the divine Spirit be discerned? In the *Affections* Edwards dared to see a perennial problem in a parochial situation; dared to believe that religious revivals in eighteenth-century New England would pose a problem as old as religion itself. By what criteria are we to judge genuine from spurious piety? "Believe not every spirit, but try the spirits," the author of the First Epistle of John had warned; Edwards was to teach his contemporaries how to obey the command. To attack this question and to return to it in several treatises demanded a serious spirit, but to believe that so basic a problem could be involved in experiences disdainfully described by some as mere "commotions," buried away in a wilderness, took courage and resolve as well.

The *Affections* was Edwards' most concentrated and persistent attempt to deal with the fundamental question. He had written other pieces about the revivals. In these he had interpreted, criticized, and defended revivalism in a number of ways, but the *Affections* contains his most acute and detailed treatment of the central task of defining the soul's relation to God. To understand and to judge what he wrote we must follow the argument in detail and even underplay the social setting within which it was written. The

1. Throughout the volume *Affections* will be used as a short title for this *Treatise;* other short titles used are the following: *Narrative* for *A Faithful Narrative of the Surprising Work of God; Distinguishing Marks* for *The Distinguishing Marks of a Work of the Spirit of God; Some Thoughts* for *Some Thoughts Concerning the Present Revival of Religion in New England.*

full story of Edwards' brilliant, at times pathetic, defense of "affectionate" religion requires the cooperation of several interests: social and political history must be supplemented by theology and philosophy.[2]

The main purpose of the present edition of the *Affections* is to make available a faithful text of a classic work as well as to supply such information as a modern reader may require concerning the historical setting of the *Affections,* Edwards' idea of signs or tests of "affections," and the meaning, as he saw it, of each sign which points to gracious affections. In this Introduction, therefore, an attempt is made to interpret the main doctrines expressed in the work, and to relate them to the present religious situation. For the reader interested in the general history of Puritanism and especially in the formation of Edwards' mind, accounts of the authors and works quoted by him in his notes are also included. To assist in handling this material, there is a section on his use of sources.[3] In keeping with the practice of the Yale Edition, there is also a concluding note on the history of the text and the sources of the present edition.

1. *Historical Background*

"In this world, so full of darkness and delusion, it is of great importance," wrote Samuel Hopkins in his biography of Edwards, "that all should be able to distinguish between true religion and that which is false." [4] And Hopkins went on to say that no one had taken greater pains or was more successful in his endeavors to deal with the problem than Edwards. This judgment is correct. It points to an interest so basic for Edwards that the whole of his thought might be viewed as one magnificent answer to the question, *What is true religion?*

The period during which he was writing was dominated by the

2. Forming an excellent supplement for study of the Great Awakening is Perry Miller's piece, "Jonathan Edwards and the Great Awakening," first published in *America in Crisis,* ed. Daniel Aaron (New York, Knopf, 1952) and reprinted in *Errand into the Wilderness* (Cambridge, Harvard University Press, 1956), pp. 153–66. The latter is a collection of Miller's essays. See also E. S. Gaustad, *The Great Awakening in New England,* New York, Harper, 1957.

3. In order to avoid filling the text itself with many editor's notes, I have included the bulk of the necessary supplementary information in the Introduction.

4. *The Life and Character of the Late Reverend, Learned, and Pious Mr. Jonathan Edwards* (Edinburgh, 1799), p. iv.

phenomenon known as revivalism, and especially that segment of it which in America we call the Great Awakening. There were in fact a series of awakenings, some great, others small, beginning with Solomon Stoddard's five "harvests" of souls in Northampton between the years 1679 and 1718 and proceeding through the fervor of 1734–35 to the climax of the Great Awakening in the 1740's. Benjamin Trumbull, writing of the situation in the Connecticut Valley prior to 1734, described it as a time in which the doctrines of religion were neglected and in their place was substituted a "lifeless morality." Edwards had also complained of the sorry state of religious feeling in 1729, the time of Stoddard's death. Trumbull wrote, "In this state of general declension and security, it pleased God in sovereign mercy to begin an extraordinary work of conviction and conversion, such as had never been experienced in New England before." [5] He says that it first began in Northampton under Edwards' influence.[6]

5. Benjamin Trumbull, *A Complete History of Connecticut,* 2 vols. New Haven, 1818; the quoted passage is from the New London edition of 1898, 2, 105. See Miller, "Edwards and the Great Awakening," in *Errand into the Wilderness,* p. 163. We may supplement and add support from another direction to Miller's suggestion that the "crisis" character of the Awakening consisted in the inability of the Boston wing to grasp the significance of revivalism, and especially the inadequacy of their standards for judging the interpretation Edwards gave to religion of the heart. Charles Chauncy's criticisms of revivalism, and of JE in particular, though they are often incisive and always honest, show that he did not grasp the subtle—sometimes oversubtle—conception of "affections" which was JE's principal concept in his interpretation of revivalism. Throughout all of Chauncy's writings runs the contrast between "reason" or "judgment" on one side and "emotion" or "imagination" on the other. This contrast is both too sharp and too simple to permit an understanding of what Edwards meant. Affections involve a more intimate relation between an "idea" and a "sense" than the dichotomy of Chauncy permits. We may say that JE's ideas involve a greater sensibility than Chauncy's rationalism could grasp and that his sensibility involves more of idea than the emotionalism of John Davenport could allow. The intimate relation between the two poles brought about by the concept of affections is the real meaning of JE's "middle ground" in the revival disputes. Part of the tragedy is that neither extreme understood the genius of this transcending third position.

6. It is important to notice that the Connecticut valley was where revivalism was principally concentrated. Trumbull says, "In Connecticut the work was more powerful than in Boston" (2, 121). This, though a charming understatement, is substantially true; Boston was not really touched by "heart religion" before the first visit of George Whitefield in 1739. There is little doubt that Whitefield's reputation and preaching is what made revivalism into something

Edwards was in the center of the most important of the eighteenth-century revival activities. He preached "affecting" sermons, including the famous one at Enfield in 1741 (which is erroneously supposed to be more representative of Edwards' thought than it actually is); he filled the pastoral office, helping to interpret the experiences of his parishioners, lending aid in decisions involving "cases of conscience," as they were called,[7] corresponding with ministers abroad, giving counsel and advice concerning religious experiences; and finally—as the theologian and philosopher of this type of piety—publishing, in addition to the *Affections,* three other works aimed at interpreting and defending the work of the Spirit in New England: *A Faithful Narrative of the Surprising Work of God* (1737), *The Distinguishing Marks of a Work of the Spirit of God* (1741), and *Some Thoughts Concerning the Present Revival of Religion in New England* (1742).[8] Each of these works is, in its own way, a

sufficiently important to be taken seriously in Boston; prior to that time affectionate religion appeared to represent all that was subversive of propriety and decorum. Besides Stoddard, Edwards, and Whitefield, the names of Jonathan Dickinson, Gilbert and William Tennent, and Theodore J. Frelinghuysen should be mentioned. These men preached evangelistic religion in New Jersey, and the Tennents founded at Neshaminy, Pa., the famous "Log College" as an evangelical academy for training ministers. See W. W. Sweet, *Revivalism in America,* New York, Scribner's, 1944.

7. It has frequently been said, and not without support from JE's own statements, that he spent less time in pastoral work than other ministers, serving the church instead through his preaching and writing. There is no doubt some truth in this view, but it seems likely that JE did a great deal more pastoral work than has been thought, as his acquaintance with the experience of many different people, recorded in his *Faithful Narrative,* shows. See Miller, "Jonathan Edwards and the Great Awakening," 163.

8. The *Faithful Narrative* was originally a letter dated Nov. 6, 1736, addressed to the Rev. Dr. Benjamin Coleman of Boston. It was published by Isaac Watts and John Guyse in England in the following year, with a preface attached apologizing for JE's parochial examples. JE had decided to illustrate his account by describing the experiences of Abigail Hutchinson, a frail young woman, and Phoebe Bartlett, a child of four. The *Distinguishing Marks* was published at Boston in 1741 and originally consisted of sermons delivered in New Haven; the text as it appeared in the first edition is considerably altered in the Dwight edition (*The Works of President Edwards,* 10 vols. New York, 1829–30) and, in fact, represents the least faithful text in that edition of JE's works. *Some Thoughts* provoked Charles Chauncy's (1705–87) *Seasonable Thoughts on the State of Religion in New England* (1743), which is a severe criticism of revivalism and "enthusiasm," although it must not be taken as an unrelieved attack upon JE. In the same year Chauncy also published, though anonymously, an answer to JE's *Distinguishing Marks* in the form of a "letter

commentary upon revivalism, and each attempts to consider the problem of distinguishing true piety from false and to defend the movement considered in the large as a genuine work of the divine Spirit.

The *Faithful Narrative* [9] is of value for a reader of the *Affections* because it provides a clear and vivid account of the facts to be interpreted and of the religious experiences Edwards was attempting to judge. It shows, moreover, how seriously Edwards took "experimental religion" and how carefully he kept his thought in touch with a core of fact. The empirical bent of his mind is well illustrated in the *Narrative;* it is a trait often cited as characteristic of the early Edwards, but it is clear that his later writings exhibit the same concern for direct experience.

The *Narrative* anticipates the doctrine of the *Affections* in one most basic point: the idea of the *new sense* [1] or the new conviction about the truth of the gospel attained by those who received the gift of the Spirit. People said they had heard the gospel before and that they had even "allowed" (i.e. assented to) its truth, but that with the new sense they could "see" its truth. The experience of "seeing" or of direct apprehension formed, in the language of the empirical philosophy Edwards embraced, the *original* of his idea of "the sense of the heart." [2] The doctrine of conviction which interprets the meaning of this new sense is the major idea of the *Affections.*

The *Distinguishing Marks* (Boston, 1741) [3] provides an excellent introduction to the general problem treated in the *Affections,* and

---

to a friend," entitled, *The Late Commotions in New England Considered.* Chauncy's sermon entitled "Enthusiasm" is also significant in this connection; the revivalism it presupposes is much more characteristic of the sort represented by John Davenport than the revival as interpreted and defended by Edwards.

9. The text is found in the Worcester ed. (*The Works of President Edwards,* 8 vols. Worcester, 1808–09), *3,* 9–82. All citations are from this edition.

1. See esp. Worcester ed., *3,* 48–9.

2. See *Miscellaneous Observations,* No. 782; below, p. 52 n. The sense of the heart as the sense of the "Excellency" of divine things had already been expressed by JE in the sermon of August 1733, "A Divine and Supernatural Light," published in the following year.

3. The Worcester edition, unfortunately, does not contain this work. I am citing it from the Dwight edition, *3,* 559–612. The text in Dwight is considerably altered from that of the first edition (Boston, 1741), but I have chosen it for convenience sake, since it is more readily available and will enable the reader to locate passages easily. Those passages mentioned in the text have been checked with the first edition, and the alterations are not significant for purposes of this Introduction.

it gives the reader his first glimpse of the subtlety displayed by Edwards in evaluating the fruits of the Spirit. In the Preface to the *Affections* we are told[4] that this work differs from the *Distinguishing Marks* in that it treats of the "gracious" operation of the Spirit alone, whereas the earlier work had to do with the Spirit in both its "common and saving operations." Calvinists, it should be remembered, traditionally distinguished within the Spirit common and saving operations; the term "gracious," however, was reserved for the latter alone. The *Affections* in treating only the gracious affections, is narrowed in scope, a fact which made for greater concentration in the analysis. The *Affections* represents a probing of the nature of piety with a finer instrument than Edwards had used in other revival writings.

The *Distinguishing Marks* makes its contribution to an understanding of the *Affections* by introducing us to the idea of a *sign* through which piety is to be judged. Here, as in the *Affections,* Edwards justified his use of signs on the grounds that where counterfeits abound and tares exist among the wheat, it is necessary to have a standard by which to distinguish the false from the true. In addition, the distinction between positive and negative signs used so effectively in the *Affections,* appears clearly in the *Distinguishing Marks.* Its meaning is the same in both instances; negative signs are events or characteristics of events which are *not* to be taken as genuine criteria for judging whether the hand of God is present in revival experiences. As illustrations Edwards singles out various aspects of popular revival experience—the unusual effects upon men's bodies, the fact of "much noise" about religion, excessive imaginings and all manner of misconduct by those supposedly converted—and claims that these cannot be used legitimately for judging genuine from false piety. In calling attention to these signs, Edwards was not only preparing the way for his own positive signs, but also attempting to destroy the arguments of his opponents. Detractors had cited against the authenticity of the revival the very features which to Edwards' mind were inessential. In claiming that they were not valid criteria, he was cutting the ground from beneath those who believed that they could discredit heart religion merely by pointing to its external expressions.

The importance Edwards attached to the problem raised by the negative signs can be seen not only by his devoting an entire section

4. See the Preface, below, p. 89.

to it in the *Affections* but also by the attention he continued to give it in the last of the earlier revival writings, *Some Thoughts Concerning the Present Revival* (Boston, 1742).[5] Here Edwards laid great stress upon the difference between accompanying effects or "occasional causes" connected with an event, and its *proper* or ultimate cause. Occasional causes are insufficient as criteria; from them alone no certain judgment is possible concerning the presence or absence of the divine Spirit. Through this distinction Edwards was able to admit, and even to emphasize, the presence of corruptions in the revival by calling attention to these occasional causes. But he was, at the same time, not willing to admit such causes as a legitimate basis of judgment. "Enthusiasm, superstition and intemperate zeal," he declared, are bound to accompany a time of religious revival, but such corruptions give us no clue to the ultimate cause behind revival experience and hence they must not be used as criteria of judgment. According to the *Affections* only a *proper* cause provides us with a genuine or positive sign for critical judgment; negative signs do not go to the heart of the matter. Those, therefore, who hoped to deny the authenticity of the Awakening by pointing to its corruptions were in error; their standards were inadequate for judgment.

There is a final point in *Some Thoughts* which contributes to an understanding of the *Affections*—the earlier work argues for the identification of the fruits of the Spirit and the affections.[6] This is a crucial step in his argument and is reinforced in the early pages of the *Affections*. In surveying the revival "in general," as Edwards liked to put it, he claimed to discern a certain "uniformity" in the phenomena, and he described this common element as identical with the scriptural picture of true religion. The *peace* of God, the *joy* of believing, the *light of knowledge* of God's glory in Christ, the *love* of God dwelling in the heart—all these fruits are taken from the record of Paul's experience in the New Testament and are set down by Edwards as the sure marks of the divine Spirit. This is a point central to the *Affections;* before Edwards could proceed to

5. The text is found in Worcester ed., *3*, 87–351.

6. Worcester ed., *3*, 141. In this connection it is worth mentioning the great store which JE set upon the widespread character of a phenomenon and the consistency with which it continued to manifest itself in the same form. This is what he meant by the lesson of experience and the need for supplementing biblical rule and precept with empirical fact.

lay down criteria for distinguishing true affections from false he had first to establish their connection with genuine religion. The decisive step was taken when he identified the traditional fruits of the Spirit with affections; he claimed that to pray for the coming of the Spirit is to pray for the affections he described. It is thus no accident that the first part of the *Affections,* prior to the consideration of any criteria for judgment, is given over to showing that the fruits are the affections and that affections must be present if the Spirit is present at all.

2. *The Argument: the "Twelve Signs of Gracious Affections"*

The *Affections* is a masterful treatment of a basic theological problem; it is also a work of remarkable literary power. We are grasped by the earnestness of the author, by his concern that we understand him aright, and by the pains he has taken to capture our imagination. In directing attention to his style, we cannot overlook the fact that many readers have found the *Affections* difficult going, nor should we ignore what is implied in the activity of the many editors who thought it necessary to rewrite the text. It is admittedly an exacting work; it calls forth a reader's best effort. But there are rewards if we are willing to raise ourselves to the level of Edwards' austere standards; nothing is to be gained by bringing him down to a more facile plane in order to make him say what we would like to hear.

Edwards was in tight control of his ideas; he knew exactly what he wanted to say and he said it in an uncompromising way. The result is a meticulous form of expression, a precision in language and an intricacy which reveals a deep and subtle mind. He would not let a subject drop until he had exposed it from every side, nor would he move on to another theme until he had expressed the results of his analysis incisively and arrestingly. A careful reader will be delighted by Edwards' ability to guide him through a long line of argument and he will come to exercise his own ingenuity in anticipating some of the surprising turns in the road.

The most striking features of the *Affections,* then, are the exactitude and vividness of the language. Edwards always sought the right word, the one which exactly expressed his intended meaning. When, for example, he wished to emphasize the need for the heart in genuine religious conviction, he found expressions like "assent" or "allow" too pale and lifeless. A man may "allow," he says, that something is so and he may give assent to it in a merely notional way, but unless he is willing to "profess" that conviction, his heart is not in it. Professing is an affectionate believing and stems from the whole man. If we forget that Edwards chose his language with care and are led to suppose that some other form of expression would have done as well, we shall misunderstand him and lose the fruit of his efforts to make difficult things clear.

The vividness and imaginative power of his style are intimately connected with the fundamental theme of the work; doctrine and style flow together. Edwards was convinced that if religion consists in holy affections, the proclamation of that doctrine must be made in an affecting way. In one of his earlier writings we find him criticizing a minister he had heard for his failure to adapt the form of his expression to the content of his message. Edwards saw incongruity and even contradiction in the attempt to communicate the truth about life in a lifeless way. When we must convey a *sense* of what we say, just because what we say is of no account unless it grasps the sense of the hearer, an affecting style is needed. Edwards never lost sight of this principle in the *Affections*.

Consider, for example, the magnificent comparison between the true saints and those merely puffed up by the experience of vigorous but fleeting emotions. Hypocrites are likened to meteors which flare up suddenly in a blaze of light trailing showers of many sparks but soon falling back to earth, their light dissipated; all is over in a twinkling. The true saints are like the fixed stars; they shine by a light which is steady and sure, a light which continues to show itself over time and through the infinite spaces. Thus is expressed the central doctrine that the true saints have the sense of the heart, a steady and abiding principle in their own natures; something not to be confused with the spectacular emotions and commotions of revivalism.

The affecting style compels the reader to understand by vicarious participation in what is being described. And the remarkable thing is that the result is achieved at the same time that an intricate analysis is taking place. Like Henri Bergson, Edwards had the gift of analyzing an experience in great detail before our eyes at the same time that his language leads us to participate in the experience itself. This gift represents the fusion of the descriptive and evocative functions of language; we are made to see the anatomy of experience at the same time that the language in which the analysis is couched lays hold upon us, making us participate in that experience with all its directness and warmth.

The continuing power of the *Affections* is to be found in the success with which Edwards brought together the essential ingredients of a theological work. It must express a synthesis of clear argument and the quickening spirit of direct experience. If a formula is needed, it must combine information and inspiration. In contrast to devotional writing, a theological work must contain analysis and argument; it must exercise and enlighten the mind. But the nature of its subject requires that it touch the heart and engage the inner man; it cannot be a compendium of doctrine alone. The *Affections* furnishes both; as one follows the line of argument defining the nature of genuine piety, one is led to understand and to feel its power at the same time. Analysis and experience converge.

There has been a tendency among interpreters to view the *Affections* not as a sustained analysis in its own right but as an historian's document pointing beyond itself to the past or to events in Edwards' life that were yet to come. Thus the work has been viewed simply as commentary upon the Great Awakening, or as an indication of the position Edwards was to take in the communion controversy which came to a head in 1750. In both cases the *Affections* is made to appear as an interlude between historical events. Important as the historical setting may have been, the fact remains that Edwards' real story is to be found in the life of the mind. His works must therefore be treated as attempts to answer basic and perennial theological problems. Moreover, the *Affections* has been praised in vague descriptions; it must now be read and analyzed in a way consistent with a work of its stature. The highest praise of a book should proceed not from uncritical acceptance but from a willingness to treat it as important enough to be argued about.

Edwards poses his central problem in the Preface: "What are the distinguishing qualifications of those that are in favor with God, and entitled to his eternal rewards?" In expanding upon his theme he is led to identify this question with a second, "What is the nature of true religion?" Even if he had not told us that this problem had been at the center of his mind "ever since I first entered on the study of divinity," we could still trace it from his earliest writings and sermons to the publication of the *Affections* in 1746. What continued to puzzle and vex him was the mixture of evil with good in the revival and among the saints, and consequently the problem of finding a way to distinguish the one from the other so that the evil might be exposed and rejected and the good retained. He was not blind to the presence of tares among the wheat, nor did he overlook, as Wesley accused him of doing, the mixture of purity and corruption in those genuinely favored of God. Indeed, it was his acknowledgment of counterfeit piety that forced him to find criteria for distinguishing false from true religion.

The *Affections* is especially distinguished by the intensity of its concern with the religious life of the individual; all but essentials are stripped away and a frontal assault is made upon the underlying problem. Edwards had previously described religion as it could be found in the depths of the individual soul, but these discussions had been more concerned with the fates and fortunes of the revival at large than with the gracious operation of the Spirit. He recognized this fact himself; in the *Affections* he was anxious to center attention on the gracious activity of the Spirit in the *individual* soul. This work was, so to speak, a final try at answering the crucial question, and in order to present his position in the clearest light, he concentrated upon the activity of the Spirit in its purity and upon the positive description of the genuine religious life.

Thus far much has been said about affections, but little attention has been paid to exactly what they are. Here, as in all his writings, Edwards was most circumspect; he begins with an account of the nature of affections and a defense of the thesis that they are the substance of true religion. Our first task, therefore, is to understand exactly what he meant by affections, how they arise, what relation they bear to the divine Spirit, and how they stand connected with the understanding and the will. Having answered these questions, we may consider the meaning of signs or criteria for judging the affections. The twelve signs of gracious affections are these criteria. Not only do they serve as tests or standards of genuine piety, but they are themselves the very substance of the religious life.

The first point to be stressed is that Edwards, for all his ability to draw clear distinctions, nevertheless struggled to preserve the unity and integrity of the self and to avoid compartmentalizing the human functions and powers. This means that despite his rather sharp distinction between understanding, affections, and will, we must not overlook the extent to which these initial distinctions are overridden in the course of the argument. The entire discussion shows a moving back and forth between analysis and synthesis; clarity demands distinctions within the self and between its powers, but the integrity of the self requires that its faculties or capacities be related to each other so as to preserve unity.

The starting point of the *Affections* is subtle; Edwards required a biblical picture of true religion as a model, and he found it in a word addressed to the early church during a time of persecution. He assumed that in a time of pressure, when faith is tried in the fire of persecution and disbelief, religion will appear in its true form. Consequently, he chose his text for the opening section (the part of the *Affections* most clearly in sermonic form) from I Peter 1:8: "Whom having not seen, ye love: in whom, though now ye see him not, yet believing, ye rejoice with joy unspeakable, and full of glory." From this text together with the historical context, he derives his conception of true religion as consisting in the affections of love and joy in Christ; the former rests upon a spiritual sight, since the object of love is unseen with ordinary eyes, and the latter is the fruit of faith. The nature of such joy is to be "full of glory" and to Edwards this meant a filling of the mind and the whole being of the believer with a sight, a sense, and a power from beyond nature. He further derives or, as the expression ran, "raises" from the text this doctrine: "True religion, in great part, consists in holy affections";[7] the development of this thesis involves, first, an account of the nature of affections, and secondly, the adducing of those considerations which show "that a great part of true religion lies in the affections."

Edwards' response to his own question about the nature of affections is that they form a class of "vigorous" and "sensible" exercises of will or inclination. The special kind of such exercises entitled to the name "affections" are those that are vigorous enough to carry the self well beyond indifference, to the point where "the motion of the blood and animal spirits begins to be sensibly altered" and some change shows in the "heart."[8] Whether or not we take the physiological trappings seriously, it is clear that Edwards wants to root affections in the inclination or central orientation of the self; affections are signposts indicating the *direction* of the soul, whether it is toward God in love or away from God and toward the world. This becomes clearer when we pay attention to his distinction between the understanding and the inclination or will. He

7. See below, p. 95.
8. Below, pp. 96–7.

refers initially to "two faculties" in man; one "capable of perception and speculation," which is called understanding, and the other, left for the moment without a name, which is said to be the means whereby "the soul does not merely perceive and view things, but is someway inclined with respect to the things it views or considers." [9] On the one hand the soul may be inclined toward something and approve it, or it may be displeased and thus reject it. The judgment or inclination of the self involved in such reactions of attraction or aversion is intimately related to what Edwards meant by the "heart." This fact has been obscured in the past because of a misapprehension according to which the heart is vaguely described as "emotional" and set over against the "head," which is a symbol for reason and knowledge. *Edwards' analysis gives no warrant either for the identification or the opposition.*

The only contrast Edwards sets up is between the understanding as a grasp of meaning unaccompanied by any "inclination" or judgment of approval or disapproval, and the will or inclination as comprising such a reaction. In other words, a line is drawn between understanding and will, where the distinction means the difference between the "neutral observer" and one who "takes sides"; but there is no clear warrant for making this into an opposition between the two terms (and, *a fortiori,* it gives us no reason for opposing understanding and affections). The point almost invariably missed is that in Edwards' view the *inclination* (the faculty initially distinguished from the understanding) involves *both* the will and the mind. When inclination receives overt expression in action it is most commonly called "will," and when inclination is expressed through the mind alone it is called "heart." The latter relationship is central to the *Affections.* Those "more vigorous and sensible exercises" [1] of inclination, i.e. of being inclined and not in a state of indifference, are what Edwards calls "affections." They are thus the expressions of inclination *through the mind.* They stand in a necessary relation to the ideas of the understanding and are also the springs of actions commonly ascribed to the will. Inclination is not a blind affair, since it is based on an apprehension of the idea, the doctrine or the object which the self is attempting to judge. Nor are the affections merely mental in the sense that they have to do with

9. Below, p. 96.

1. Below, p. 97. Cf. p. 98. "But yet, it is not the body but the mind only, that is the proper seat of the affections."

the depths of the soul alone, for the sign to which Edwards attached the greatest importance, the sign of consistent practice, shows that in order to be genuine, affections must manifest themselves in an outward and visible way.[2]

The essential point is that the affections manifest the center and unity of the self; they express the whole man and give insight into the basic orientation of his life. Edwards was aware that the term "affections" does not ordinarily mean all of our "actings" and that it may not even be understood to involve action at all. To understand what he means we must take such phrases as "exercise of the will" and "actings of the inclination and will" to mean choice or judgment in the first instance [3] and overt action secondarily. The crucial point is that in every choice the soul likes or dislikes, and when these "inclinations" are "vigorous" and "lively" the liking or disliking coincides with love and hatred. Affections, then, are *lively* inclinations and choices which show that man is a being with a heart.

There is a further preliminary distinction; and although it occupies but a paragraph,[4] it is of pivotal importance. "The *affections* and *passions,*" he says, "are frequently spoken of as the same," but there are grounds for distinguishing them. Passions he describes as those inclinations whose "effects on the animal spirits are more violent" and in them the mind is overpowered and "less in its own command." The self becomes literally a "patient," seized by the object of a passion. With the affections, however, the situation

2. Try as we may, it is difficult to avoid confusion over the difference between will and affections and their mutual connections. JE is not clear himself, although it is obvious that the problem stems from his attempt to preserve the integrity of the self against the tendency to break it up into "faculties." We are told that "the affections are not essentially distinct from the will," and this point is repeatedly emphasized. On the other hand, will is said to denote *inclination expressed in action* as distinct from the "heart," which points to *inclination expressed in the mind.* Since, however, affections are most often identified with the "heart," it may appear that further identification of will and affections will need some qualification. Perhaps the attempt to be too meticulous here will only lead to confusion. If we stick to the idea that an affection is a "warm" and "fervid" inclination involving judgment, we shall not go wrong.

3. See the introductory discussion of the nature of will in JE's *Freedom of the Will,* ed. Paul Ramsey (New Haven, Yale University Press, 1957), pp. 137–40; cf. pp. 16 ff. The analysis there definitely stresses the element of choice or judgment over that of exertion, and shows JE's insistence upon identifying "volition" and "preference."

4. Below, p. 98.

stands quite otherwise. These require instead a clear understanding and sufficient control of the self to make choice possible. This distinction enabled him to criticize and reject a great many revival phenomena, especially those of a pathological sort, and to dissociate the heart religion he advocated from hysteria, the excesses of bodily effects and enthusiasm. His contemporaries paid insufficient attention to his distinctions. They thought he was defending revivalism in the sense of religious passions at the expense of intellect, whereas he was developing a conception of affections accompanied by understanding.

With this conceptual framework, with the affections separated into two principal kinds—those seeking to possess their object and those seeking to reject their object—Edwards returns to the Bible to establish more securely the thesis that genuine religion "in great part, consists in holy affections." [5] The piety which God requires, the only one he will accept, is one which engages the heart and inclines the self as a whole toward the divine glory in a love which is unmixed. Of all the aspects of human life and experience, religion is the one in which it is least possible to be "lukewarm"; piety which does not include a fixed and fervent inclination touching the heart is no genuine piety. Hearing the Word, as the Bible repeatedly emphasizes, is not enough, nor is it sufficient merely to "allow" that the doctrine may be true. What is needed is that the soul be "moved" and filled with the love of God which ultimately shows itself through right conduct in the world. Neither is possible in Edwards' view unless the soul is "affected" and the will inclined. In this sense affections are motive forces or springs, and the particular change called conversion becomes possible only if the self is affected at the heart. "I am bold to assert," he says, "that there never was any considerable change wrought in the mind or conversation of any one person, by anything of a religious nature, that ever he read, heard or saw, that had not his affections moved." [6]

We must not overlook the duality in Edwards' theory of affections

5. Below, p. 95. It is important to notice that JE does not want to swallow religion in affections; they constitute the most important part of genuine piety and the testing of their character provides a test of piety, but he is most careful to qualify his position by such phrases as "in great part." His full formula is that affections are *necessary for* religion and *constitute a large part* of its nature.

6. Below, p. 102. Here, as in the case throughout the early part of the *Affections,* the connection between affections and will is uppermost; later on, JE stresses much more the place of understanding and the divine light.

rooted in the fact that love is both one of the particular affections and the fountain of all affections. His contention is that the basis of true religion is found in that chief affection which is love to God unmixed; this defines the original relation of the soul to God. Religion, however, includes along with the basic relation to God, life in the world and in the glory to come. This means that as a life and not merely a doctrine it has further content; Edwards' view is that this content itself consists largely in affectionate life. Hope, joy, fear, zeal, compassion and others are frequently referred to in the New Testament as the substance of religion; Edwards describes them as affections and goes on to argue that they make up the religious life. To avoid confusion we must understand that he is defining the basic religious relationship as essentially the affection of love. This is what he means when he says "the essence of all true religion lies in holy love," [7] but at the same time he maintains that the fruits of love are also affections—joy, zeal, peace—which have their proper place in the whole of religion. "For love," he says, "is not only one of the affections, but it is the first and chief of the affections, and the fountain of all the affections." [8] There is thus a basic affection, holy love, which relates the self to God in a decisive way and it has to do with the "first fruit" of the Spirit or "sealing of the Spirit," in biblical phrasing. There are also fruits or further gifts of the Spirit which represent the substance of the religious life in the world. The dual meaning of love running throughout Edwards' analysis need not confuse us if we understand the comprehensiveness with which he uses the term.[9] Love taken as the fountain of affections is the more important sense of the term because it refers not only to the relationship between man and God at the root of all religion but also to the activity of the Holy Spirit in the individual soul. Moreover, when holy love is said to be the essence of genuine religion, it is then possible to explain sin by contrast as that equally basic and ultimate *rejection* of God, symbolized in the Bible as "hardness of

7. Below, p. 107.

8. Below, pp. 107–8.

9. The duality involved is reflected in the ordinary use of the term "affection." In the eighteenth century the term meant the whole class of attitudes and dispositions to which JE refers: love, hope, fear, etc. Because of the centrality of love, the class term "affections" came to be identified with it alone, although it is but one of the affections. The phenomenon is familiar to students of language; a class term has often become identified with one of its members when that member has come to be regarded as more basic than others.

heart." [1] Edwards was most acute in finding biblical support for his position; assuming such hardness and rejection of God to be the very opposite of genuine piety, he sought, among the biblical illustrations of the hard-hearted, evidence to show that what they chiefly lacked was the affection of love. And he argued in the reverse direction, declaring that if the antithesis of genuine piety is to be without holy love, there is further reason for believing that love is a mark of true religion. Those who have such religion overflow with that divine love which Pharaoh, for example, did not have.

The intention of the *Affections* is to test these fruits of the Spirit, not to praise them. Edwards never lost sight of the twofold task that followed: on the one hand, to defend the central importance of the affections against those who would eliminate them from religion; and on the other, to provide criteria for testing them lest religion degenerate into emotional fanaticism and false enthusiasm. Moreover, testing the spirits was no academic exercise; Edwards wanted to give to the individual some basis for judging the state of his own soul. It is essential here that we attend to his subtlety and depth. Simple oppositions and alternatives will not do. They allow for too much or too little. We need an approach more sophisticated than is implied in asking whether Edwards was "for" or "against" affections. Many of his contemporaries approached him in that light; they were bound to be disappointed, simply because no answer of a strict either/or type can be given. The point is that he was "for" the affections, but not in any sense you please; moreover, he was not *uncritically* for them, which is why he was at such pains to explain what they are, how you might know when you had them, and which ones marked the genuine presence of the divine Spirit. His book, consequently, brings together two lines of thought: it identifies the activity of the Holy Spirit with the affections in the soul and at the same time shows how these same affections when properly tested enable us to discriminate genuine from false piety. It is not difficult to understand what a precarious line Edwards marked out for him-

1. It is interesting that instead of describing sin and hardness of heart as "affection" in the direction of hatred, aversion, and rejection, JE refers instead to the hard heart as an "unaffected heart," i.e. as a heart not affected by "virtuous affections." This is a minor inconsistency only, but it is apt to cause confusion. The point is simply that since JE was interested in the genuine religious affections, he identified "affection" with those which are directed toward God, and described the hard heart as devoid of affection.

self. To those who rejected heart religion his analysis of genuine piety in terms of affections was anathema, but he was equally set upon by those who wanted their affections neat, so to speak, and had no time for bothersome inquiries into their grounds and authenticity.

In concluding the opening section of the *Affections,* Edwards proceeds to draw some concrete conclusions from his previous doctrine. He criticizes those who reject all affections because of the excesses of some and the vain zeal of others. He attacks the oscillation from one extreme to the other and he is as outspoken against those who accept all affections uncritically as against those who want to be done with them completely. He did not miss the opportunity to put a vivid biblical construction upon the New England revival experience while also preparing the ground for his own theory of signs and tests. He tells the congregation that he sees the hand of Satan both in the Revival and in those who fight against it. Satan, seeing that people were unlearned in heart religion, sowed tares in the form of false affections and thus misled and confounded many with the belief that they belonged to the Lord's elect. On the other hand, after seeing the reaction that took place after the high tide of affectionate religion, Satan set to work in another direction to establish the belief that affection itself is an evil. In both cases genuine religion is made to suffer. Against this background Edwards' position stands out most clearly: affections are essential, but since there are false as well as true affections, critical tests are required. The main concern of his book is to establish the only valid criteria for making such tests. Testing the spirits is of the essence of "experimental religion."

Edwards devotes his short second section to what were formerly called "negative signs." Here he makes his position more explicit by describing these signs as insufficient to enable us to conclude whether affections are gracious or not. The critical force of negative signs lies in the fact that their insufficiency refutes anyone who rejects all affections, by showing that an excess or exaggeration cannot be taken as conclusive. The argument attempts to demonstrate, both by biblical example and appeal to general experience, that the presence of a given characteristic does not mean either the presence or absence of the divine Spirit in its saving operations. In every case the accidental character of these signs is said to reside in the fact that they can be present without the Spirit's presence. The full extent of their insufficiency becomes apparent only after the positive signs are set forth, but taken by themselves Edwards argues that they are to be found where there is no genuine piety and that they may be absent where genuine piety exists. They cannot, therefore, be taken as necessary conditions.

There is no need to follow Edwards in detail through his discussion of all the negative signs. His analysis is clear enough and is even repetitive of much he had expressed before. There are, however, two points of special importance: the first has to do with the idea that the Spirit is bound to a definite *order* of operation and the second concerns whether it is possible to infer anything about affections from the fact that they come to be accepted by *other people* as signs of saintliness.

As regards the first point, Edwards' thesis is as follows: "Nothing can certainly be determined concerning the nature of affections by this, that comforts and joys seem to follow awakenings and convictions of conscience, in a *certain order*" [2] Before proceeding to his final conclusion, Edwards first calls attention to the fact that God deals with human beings in a way that has a discernible pattern in it. That is to say, there are abundant evidences in the Scripture of God's having first convicted, wounded, distressed, and terrified man by the contrast between his sin and the divine majesty, and then comforted him with glad tidings. "It seems to be," says Edwards, "the natural import of the word 'gospel,' glad tidings, that it is news of deliverance and salvation, after great fear and distress." [3] He concludes that nothing can be said against the authenticity of comforts and joys because they come after terrors and convictions of conscience, for the prevalence of this order of events in so many biblical experiences nullifies any such claim. On the other hand, he is concerned to maintain that comforts and joys cannot be accepted as genuine merely because they succeed great terrors and fears of hell; being afraid of hell is not the same as having genuine convictions of conscience. His argument at this point is apt to be confusing because he speaks of both the *nature* of the states in the soul and their *order*. The argument begins by emphasizing the order of events in the soul, but we soon discover that their nature is involved as well. The fact is, one aspect cannot be separated from the other. The problem of order is made central at this point.

As regards the nature of the states, Edwards wants to say that

2. Below, p. 151. Cf. p. 159, and esp. pp. 161–2.

3. Below, p. 155.

terror or fear is not necessarily the same as conviction of conscience; even granting that terrors and convictions have actually been produced by the Spirit in the soul, this fact by itself does not prove that true comfort *must* follow. The principal reason is revealing; the "unmortified corruption of the heart may quench the Spirit of God," [4] he says, and this can mean only that if grace is not irresistible, the "preparation" or common influences of the Spirit are capable of being resisted or stifled by pride and the claim of a false hope. Satan, moreover is able to counterfeit the operations of the Spirit, but there is an important qualification about his power to do so: Satan can *exactly imitate the order* of affections, but not their nature. "The nature of divine things," says Edwards, "is harder for the devil to imitate, than their order," [5] and from this fact follows the chief problem. It also explains why Edwards fastened upon the concept of order. It Satan can imitate the order exactly, then the order of operation followed by the Spirit *cannot* be a certain and decisive sign; the truly dependable signs are, as we shall see, those which Satan cannot perform. "Therefore," Edwards concludes, "no order or method of operations and experiences, is any certain sign of their divinity." [6]

This point has several far-reaching repercussions. First, Edwards is denying the validity of many Puritan descriptions of salvation as involving a sequential process. There is thus in his thought room for a certain "variety" in religious experience and no conversion by "rule." Secondly, and even more basic, if we confine our attention to the order alone there is no necessary transition from nature to grace. The sharp separation between "common" and "saving" operations comes to the fore; we have no insight into any necessary connection between an order of events in nature and their issuance in grace. The Scripture, Edwards asserts, is silent on this point, and there is no alternative to denying the validity of order as a sign of genuine piety. He is willing to admit only that some awareness or conviction of sin on the part of the believer is necessary, but this necessary condition is not itself a sufficient ground from which to infer the presence of the Spirit.[7] The ultimate basis for Edwards' view is not only the Bible but an appeal to experience. No better

4. Below, p. 157.
5. Below, p. 159.
6. Ibid.
7. See above, p. 18, for the concept of a negative sign.

example of Edwards "the experimental divine" can be found than his appeal to the observations he made in the midst of the Revival to refute the thesis that the Spirit is bound to a single method or order in laying hold of the soul. As a final and telling word he says, "we are often in Scripture expressly directed to try ourselves by the *nature* of the fruits of the Spirit; but nowhere by the Spirit's *method* of producing them." [8]

The second noteworthy point in Part II concerns the attempt to use the "approval of the godly" as a criterion for judging affections. Edwards' contention is of the utmost importance for his entire theory; it means that external judgment, the judgment of one man upon another, is not only unreliable but ultimately impossible. The saints, though they know "experimentally" what true religion is in their own selves, have no power of discerning the *heart* of another. Edwards liked to cite I Sam. 16:7 as an authority: "The Lord seeth not as man seeth; for man looketh on the outward appearance, but the Lord looketh on the heart." There are at least two consequences of the position taken which need to be underlined in any study of Puritan piety. First, the testing of the spirits can ultimately be done only by the self for itself; the external situation may lead a man to seek the counsel and judgment of others but no man can pronounce any final judgment concerning the status of another before God. "It is against the doctrines of Scripture," says Edwards, "which do plainly teach us that the state of others' souls toward God, cannot be known by us." [9] Secondly, there is the consequence that the "public charity" forming the basis of acceptance between the visible saints in the visible church must not imply any *final* judgment by any man about the religious status of his neighbor. This is a touchy point. Edwards in several places argued against making a distinction *within* the visible church between the sheep and the goats. It has sometimes been objected by critics that his refusal to allow this distinction was incompatible with the position he later took in demanding conversion experiences and confession of Christ as conditions for being received into full communion. His position can be made consistent with the principle laid down in the *Affections*. When the congregation accepts a confession based upon conversion experiences, it must not suppose that this acceptance is the same as certain knowledge of the

8. Below, p. 162.
9. Below, p. 189. Cf. esp. p. 181.

confessor's state. This is a subtle line of thought but it is consistent; some credentials are demanded of the believer who presents himself, but their acceptance by others does not mean or imply certain knowledge on their part of the status of another person. The heart of the other is known but to God; the acceptance or approval of others is no certain sign for judging religious affections.

The third and largest part of the *Affections* contains the heart of Edwards' position: the exhaustive account of the twelve signs of gracious affections. This analysis must, of course, stand or fall on its own merits. The reader will be aided greatly in approaching the text, however, if he has clearly in mind several leading ideas. He must understand what Edwards meant by a sign, what basic principle is behind each sign, and the way in which the individual is supposed to use the sign as a test of his own heart.

Since this part of the book contains the bulk of the material quoted by Edwards in defense and illustration of his position, the reader will do well to bear in mind what is said later about his relation to other writers.[1] It would be an error to suppose that Edwards was directly dependent for his own doctrine upon the works cited; his own thought was remarkably self-contained and, furthermore, he firmly believed that his entire theory of affections was rooted in the biblical picture of the true religious life. Consequently, the works of others appear more as illustrations and confirmations of his position than as "influences" from which it might be derived. This remains true even of his use of Stoddard and Shepard, upon whom he relied most.

The positive signs are meant to delineate those affections that are "gracious" or "saving." The entire theory presupposes a distinction in kind (more obvious in the treatment of some signs than others) between "common" and "saving" operations of the Spirit. As Edwards had occasion to point out, the *Affections* is directly concerned only with those operations which are saving, as compared with the *Distinguishing Marks,* which paid more attention to the common workings of God. The whole discussion of the positive signs is prefaced by a re-emphasis upon the closing note of Part II: the signs of gracious affections are not for enabling us to distinguish true from false affections in others. Edwards repeats what he had claimed many times before: "it was never God's design to give us any rules, by which we may know, who of our fellow-

1. Below, pp. 52 ff.

professors are his, and to make a full and clear separation between sheep and goats." [2] Edwards goes even further and allows for uncertainty in the knowledge with which the saints are supposed to know themselves. The signs are neither doubtful nor unavailable, but there are weaknesses in the person (the clouding of the eye of judgment) and seeds of corruption (the cold or carnal "frame"). These work together to make the process of discerning both difficult and uncertain when applied to the experience of a particular individual. The qualification is important; for while Edwards' theory of signs or criteria went considerably beyond what some of his contemporaries believed possible in the discerning of spirits, he claimed no infallibility for their application in a given case. The rules themselves have their own certainty, but the applications always fall short; no biblical principle is on the same level with its application.[3]

Turning to the meaning of sign in the positive sense, we must understand a sign to be a mark through which the presence of the divine Spirit can be known. Edwards does not say that we *infer* the presence of God's grace using the signs as a basis; he does, in fact, leave that relationship vague. It is best to suppose that the sign "points to" the activity of the Spirit, especially when we consider the matter from the side of our human process of knowing. Taken apart from its evidential force, however, a sign must be understood as the very presence of the Spirit, since it is the working of divine grace in the heart of the believer. Not all signs make this point equally evident. As we attempt to discern and judge our state, the signs are viewed by us as pointing to or announcing the presence of the Spirit; considered in themselves, the signs *are* that presence. While all signs perform a common service in critical judgment, they differ on their material side. Thus a sign may be a cause or ground in one case, a quality of life or a relation in another, and even a series of deeds stretching over an extended time. Whatever its particular nature, however, a sign is of no value or interest save as it enables us to assess the nature of piety. Positive signs are the marks of the Spirit.

Since Edwards' main aim is to test affections, every sign refers to them in some specific way. Not every sign, however, fastens upon their inner nature. Some clearly do so, as in the tenth sign which singles out symmetry and proportion. Other signs point instead to

2. Below, p. 193.
3. Below, p. 194.

the ground or stimulus of affections such as the evangelical humiliation at the heart of the sixth sign. Confusion can be avoided if we bear in mind that some signs point to affections themselves, others to their ground, and still others to what issues from them or to their consequences. Whatever aspect is made central, it is affections that are the object of the test; to test affections is to test religion.

It is a curious fact that Edwards nowhere considers the relations between the signs, whether they imply each other, whether some are more basic than others and similar questions. The signs have, to be sure, a natural affinity as belonging to the one integral religious life, but Edwards has not yet told us whether genuine piety must exhibit *all* the signs or whether perhaps one or more might be taken as a sufficient basis for judgment. The one clue we have for answering these questions is given in a principle which is common to every sign. The Spirit in its saving or gracious operation dwells in the believer in its proper form, or, in classical philosophical expression, according to its own kind. Edwards placed great emphasis upon the distinction between the Spirit as *operating on* the self and thus as still externally related to it, and as *dwelling in* the self in its own proper nature.[4] Only the latter form is the presence of the Spirit as *grace;* the former represents the "common work" of the Spirit. All signs as positive indications of gracious affections point back to the saving operation; if this indwelling fails to take place, no genuine signs can appear at all. It so happens that while the indwelling Spirit forms a common background of all signs, the fact is more explicitly stated in some (e.g. the first, fourth, and seventh signs), and we are perhaps justified in taking these as more basic than others.

THE FIRST SIGN

The initial sign is based upon the principle that only those affections arising from influences that are *spiritual, supernatural,* and *divine,* can be regarded as genuine. The exposition and defense consists entirely in showing the biblical meaning of these three terms. By *spiritual* Edwards means "sanctified" in opposition to "carnal," which signifies the natural or unsanctified man. He was attempting to recover the ancient meaning of spiritual as opposed to later misunderstandings. What is spiritual, he says, is not what

4. Below, pp. 232 ff., where this communication of nature is said to be the "true" witness of the Spirit.

relates "to the spirit or soul of man, as the spiritual part of man, in opposition to the body"; [5] it is the self as a whole which is spiritual or is born of the Spirit. Moreover, what is spiritual does not have this character because it is incorporeal or because it has to do with immaterial things; the term "spiritual" means a relation of the integral self to God and not a special aspect or part of the self standing over against the body. Edwards thus gives expression to the principle just mentioned as forming a common background for all the signs. The Spirit dwells according to its own nature in those who are truly spiritual, and while the natural man may be subject to operations of the Spirit, he is in no sense an abode of the Spirit. Edwards makes use of his favorite figure of the *light* to express the meaning he has in mind.[6] The body which has no light except the light which shines upon it from outside itself cannot be called a "lightsome" body, but that body in which light is found as part of its internal constitution may properly be called a "lightsome" body. When it is said that the Spirit dwells in the sanctified in accordance with its own proper nature, the meaning is that the Spirit communicates its own *holiness* to the self. The activity of the Spirit upon the natural man does not involve this communication of nature. Thus there is a twofold difference between the natural and spiritual man; they differ both in their relation to the Spirit and in the manner in which the Spirit operates upon them.

Secondly, gracious affections are dependent on *supernatural* influences; the influences and the effects of God's Spirit are "above nature" and differ from everything natural in kind as well as in the manner in which they are communicated. Edwards introduces at this point an idea that plays a large part in the *Freedom of the Will:* the concept of a new inward perception or sensation, which must be regarded as a new creation just because it is not the result of any compounding of things natural.[7] The discontinuity between nature as the original creation and the new creation or grace in the form of a new perception is complete. With this new perception or new simple idea we shall have much to do in elaborating the

5. Below, p. 198.

6. Edwards stands squarely in the Augustinian tradition; this is manifested at many points, but chiefly in the illumination doctrine and the aesthetic significance of *order* and *proportion.*

7. Below, p. 205; Ramsey, ed., *Freedom of the Will,* p. 43.

other signs; at this point Edwards is concerned primarily to stress its status as supernatural. In many instances there seems to be no intelligible continuity between nature nad grace; the new perception has no intelligible connection with nature and it is put forth as the essence of an entirely new creation. Thus the new spiritual sense is said to be a second nature. But in other passages,[8] Edwards tells us "that not everything which in any respect appertains to spiritual affections, is new and entirely different from what natural man can conceive of . . . some things are common to gracious affections with other affections." And this would seem to introduce, in addition to the discontinuity of grace and nature, an acknowledgment of the participation of nature in grace.

Edwards claims that he does not intend a new faculty or faculties when he speaks of the new sense but rather a new foundation or principle for the exercise of our natural faculties. He says:

> So this new spiritual sense is not a new faculty of understanding, but it is a new foundation laid in the nature of the soul, for a new kind of exercises of the same faculty of understanding. So that new holy disposition of heart that attends this new sense, is not a new faculty of will, but a foundation laid in the nature of the soul, for a new kind of exercises of the same faculty of will.[9]

His insistence that there is no giving of a new understanding or will must be carefully interpreted. The change wrought by the Spirit is more fundamental than a change in some faculty or part of the self. A new foundation is laid which can be expressed through all the created powers of the self—understanding, will, affections—without destroying their essential natures. Edwards thus sides with the theological tradition holding that the finite can bear the infinite, that the Spirit can express itself through the created world. On the other hand, we must not suppose that the new foundation leaves the natural faculties exactly where they were before. If it is incorrect to speak of a new understanding or will, it is equally mistaken to forget that the natural man does not understand as the spiritual man understands; his affections differ, and he cannot will as the saints will. The central point, nevertheless, remains: the Spirit brings about a change in the self *as a whole*. It will not do to single

8. For example, p. 208.
9. Below, p. 206.

out a change in some special feature of the self. But if there is a change in the heart, we may expect it to be manifested in every aspect of the self; regeneration affects the total self and all its powers.[1]

The theological problem of the relation between nature and grace takes us beyond the *Affections,* but it is noteworthy that Edwards holds to a doctrine of continuity between the two. If at times he seems to stress their radical difference it is because of his need to have sure criteria for distinguishing the work of the Spirit from that of Satan in the revival. The more a genuine mark of the Spirit appears as something which fallen powers can neither produce nor counterfeit, the more readily can the genuine saints be discerned.[2]

The distinctions drawn in the first sign enable Edwards to argue against the abuses and delusions of the revival.[3] His main contention is that the extraordinary and "miraculous" happenings—vivid imagination, voices addressed to the self in a personal way, Scripture passages coming inexplicably to the mind at a crucial time, revelation of secret information, etc.—are unreliable signs of true affections because they neither require nor manifest a new nature or a new creation. What is remarkable or unexpected has no special religious significance. The mark of the divine takes us to another dimension altogether. Grace is a matter not of wizardry but of regeneration; Edwards was no enthusiast.

THE SECOND SIGN

This sign has occasioned much discussion because it has been taken to mean that self-love is excluded from the highest relationship between man and God. If, however, certain points are kept in view, the consistency of Edwards' position will be apparent, as will

1. JE always maintained the integrity of the self in all actions and affections. There are, of course, problems left over which involve explaining how the new nature bestowed in grace is related to the natural structures of the creature. The underlying theological problem, which takes us beyond the argument of the *Affections,* concerns the relation between the activity of God as Creator and as Redeemer. A consistent theology must show the compatibility of the two.

2. Below, p. 215.

3. It is interesting to note how the basically sermonic form survives within the work; in most cases a sign is first expounded and defended and then there is the "application" which consists in showing the bearing of the principle upon actual life.

its support of a great tradition in Christian theology—one that bases all on the sovereignty of God and the acknowledgment of the divine *gloria*. Edwards' chief aim is to single out those affections which arise because of the love the self has for the *excellence* of divine things simply grasped and contemplated. God and Christ, he emphasizes repeatedly, are to be viewed "in themselves," and apart from any consideration of the benefit they may bestow. Edwards does not minimize this benefit, but he denies that any "interest" the individual may have in loving God can be an essential factor in determining that love. Here Edwards stresses what Plato, for example, expressed in the *Euthyphro* when he urged that the good is to be loved because it is good and because of its own intrinsic nature. The same idea is to be found in Spinoza and Kant when they argued, each in his own way and context, that certain ultimate responses on the part of man—intellectual love and respect for the moral law—must be rooted in a grasp of the intrinsic nature of the object of love or respect for its own sake.

Similarly, Edwards holds that the genuine love of God can have no condition save that of the divine *gloria;* if any other consideration be introduced the love is not pure and the affections resulting are not gracious. " 'Tis unreasonable," says Edwards, "to think otherwise, than that the first foundation of a true love to God, is that whereby he is in himself lovely, or worthy to be loved." [4] This sums up the entire point of the second sign. The benefits of such love for the individual—his self-love or self-interest—are not ignored by Edwards, but he denies that this interest can be an initial determining ground. Self-love is a natural disposition or, more accurately, a disposition of the natural man, and as such it cannot be a determining ground of grace. Stated in another way, Edwards' point is that the love which the individual has for God cannot be *consequent* upon his belief that God loves him or has forgiven him.[5] The possibility of forgiveness follows from a love based upon the divine nature alone; it cannot be made into a ground of that love. True love is immediate in the sense of being determined by

4. Below, p. 242.

5. Below, pp. 248–9; where JE treats a seemingly contrary text, I John 4:19: "We love him, because he first loved us." The difficulty with JE's reply is that it refers to a time when we had no love to God; the problem is what meaning can be attached to that state in the case of the saints and on the doctrine of election which undergirds it.

the intrinsic nature of its object alone; the basic religious relationship thus excludes all elements of calculation on the part of the individual. Edwards allows for the self-love contained in our gratitude to God, but in every case he demands that it be preceded by the love which is unmixed.

THE THIRD SIGN

This sign is closely related to the previous one and actually does no more than make an important addition to it. In the section on the second sign the "amiableness" of God was made the chief ground of love; here is added the "loveliness of the moral excellency of divine things," as a further foundation.[6] The aesthetic element and its importance in Edwards' thought has been the subject of much discussion; some have tried to minimize it as running against the drift of Puritan piety, but there can be no doubt either of its presence or of its importance.[7] What Edwards refers to in this sign is identical with what the Bible describes as the "beauty of holiness." Holiness Edwards translates into "moral excellency" and explains its meaning through the distinction between *natural* and *moral* goods. His point is that moral good and evil must be understood as referring not to natural virtues in contrast to Christian virtues but to the goodness of God as distinct from his natural attributes, such as power, knowledge, etc. Thus moral excellency is rooted "in the heart or will of moral agents" [8] and it sums up the whole of moral perfection. The true believer loves this excellency for itself.

If holiness is moral perfection, we may well ask what Edwards understood by the *beauty* of holiness. Beauty is located in God and not in the eye of the believer, although Edwards believed that only the purified eye can apprehend it. In some passages he identifies the beauty of the divine nature with holiness and says that the beauty of the Christian religion resides in its having made holiness the paramount reality.[9] In other passages he speaks of the beauty of holiness as its "loveliness," a characteristic which is said to call forth both the delight and love of the beholder.

6. Below, p. 253.

7. We shall have occasion to return to this aspect more directly in discussion of the tenth sign; see below, pp. 38–9.

8. Below, p. 255.

9. But cf. p. 258.

It is clear that Edwards is trying to express the nature of God and at the same time to explain how the self is attracted to Him. The divine nature is always held up as the true foundation of the believer's response, but Edwards also places emphasis upon the capacity of the self to apprehend it. The reason behind this emphasis is that the "new sense"—the heart of the doctrine of affections—is the channel through which man lays hold of God. This sense is *not* one of the five "natural" senses; it is a *new creation,* given only to those regenerated by the Spirit. We shall be in no danger of exaggeration if we say that this new sense represents the unique contribution of the *Affections;* no idea in all of Edwards' works is more original and no doctrine was more far reaching in its influence upon the course of Puritan piety. Apprehending God through this sense, moreover, takes us to the depths of the individual soul; it is more than an awareness of God and certainly more than a belief in God. The new sense, as this sign makes plain, is a taste of the beauty of the divine *gloria.* In describing the beauty of holiness he says, "this kind of beauty is the quality that is the immediate object of this spiritual sense." [1] Since the beauty of holiness is not to be apprehended with "natural" equipment alone, he who apprehends it must do so in virtue of the activity of the Spirit. A love of God which does not include the taste and relish of the divine beauty is not the love which reveals the saints.

The individual may test his affections by this sign if he asks himself the following question: Is my affection arising from a grasp of the beauty of holiness, based on the consideration that it is something profitable for me (*bonum utile*), or does it find its ground in the divine holiness as a "beautiful good in itself" (*bonum formosum*)? The underlying principle of the third sign is thus made to stand out most clearly; those affections are not spiritual that are determined by the individual's concern for his welfare; the proper determining ground is the apprehension of the divine holiness as something good in itself.

THE FOURTH SIGN

Here is introduced the *spiritual understanding* at the root of all affections. The sign is closely connected with the next one, which points to the fruit of this understanding in the conviction that divine things are "real and certain." Together the two signs are

1. Below, p. 260.

among the most important of Edwards' doctrine of affections. They are, moreover, fraught with difficulties, because of the complex relations they disclose between understanding, the affections, and the will.

The main point is that gracious affections are those based upon a certain type of understandig or knowledge which is called "spiritual." And in this sign we have Edwards' rejection of the anti-intellectualist bias of much revival-type religion. In the *Affections* no less than in other writings he refused to oppose the religious conception of spirit to intellectual pursuits, and he did not join forces with popular revivalism, which sets understanding over against the "having of the spirit." "Holy affections," Edwards always held, "are not heat without light; but evermore arise from some information of the understanding, some spiritual instruction that the mind receives, some light or actual knowledge." [2] On the other hand, there are many affections entirely unrelated to such understanding, and of them he says, "it is a sure evidence that these affections are not spiritual, let them be ever so high." [3]

The question now arises: What sort of understanding is the spiritual understanding required for genuine affections? Edwards begins an answer by a sharp criticism of affections raised by "vain imaginings." Seeing a vivid image or a shining countenance, as many had claimed to do, is a far cry from the light in the mind that should precede genuine affections. In attacking uncontrolled imagination he was, of course, striking at the heart of popular piety, since many considered themselves confirmed in a right relation with God because of vivid experiences and visions. These Edwards rejected because they were devoid of both understanding and instruction. Similarly, he attacked affections based on texts of Scripture coming suddenly and miraculously to mind and giving people the idea that God was communicating his special favor to them individually. It is the meaning and understanding alone that forms a legitimate ground for affections; the extraordinary manner in which something comes to mind is of no account. When understanding is absent, affections are vain.

But exactly what sort of understanding does Edwards have in view? There is no doubt that the spiritual understanding differs from the understanding which is possible for the natural man.

2. Below, p. 266.
3. Below, pp. 266–7.

Understanding gained, he says, "merely by human teaching, with the common improvement of the faculties of the mind," [4] is not an understanding that is spiritual. The spiritual understanding "must consist in . . . a certain kind of ideas or sensations of the mind . . . the sensations of a new spiritual sense." [5] Spiritual understanding is identified with the *new spiritual sense* or the sense which apprehends the beauty and moral excellence of divine things. The nature of the understanding Edwards envisages stands out more clearly if we contrast it with what is called mere notional understanding. The difference between the two is crucial; it points up his attempt to introduce a *sensible* element into understanding, and thus to make it richer than a "dry light." [6] The notional understanding has mere information and grasps the meaning of terms without thereby inclining the self one way or the other; spiritual understanding contains within itself the new sense or new creation which has a "taste" for the beauty and moral excellence of divine things. Spiritual understanding involves the will and the heart. It retains its meaning as understanding so far as it grasps the nature of things and makes judgments about them, but it does so as a *participating* rather than as a merely *observing* or speculative power. Spiritual understanding means that the heart of the individual is intimately related to what is understood. When the heart is involved, the individual must be present also. There is a personal character about the sense of the heart; no man can have it for another, and to have it at all a man must experience it directly. In thus describing spiritual understanding, Edwards introduces a novel element into the Augustinian tradition. The enlightened mind now includes the presence of a new sense or taste; direct sensible perception is the channel of illumination.

Inclusion of the will and the heart within the understanding that is spiritual does not mean that the integrity of understanding is lost. Enlightenment means a genuine change in understanding; it is not a merely external addition made by the will to an understanding that remains untouched. Edwards does not mean that the natural and the spiritual man both understand the same things while the spiritual man alone believes or wills to accept them; the

4. Below, p. 269.
5. Below, p. 271.
6. The conception of a "spiritual sensation" developed by the Cambridge Platonist John Smith implies exactly the same point that Edwards is making.

natural man does not really understand the things of the Spirit on the basis of his natural understanding alone.[7] And his not understanding them aright is the reason for his failure to acknowledge their divine excellence.

The idea of the spiritual understanding helps us to see how Edwards' theory of affections was distorted both by his contemporaries and by his later commentators. Like Chauncy, almost everyone has tried to understand the view by starting with a vague and too simple contrast between the head and the heart. Within these terms some have defended one side or the other, but the general assumption has been that the two sides are both clear and exhaustive in their opposition. *But Edwards was trying to transcend that opposition.* His way of doing it was to describe the enlightened or spiritual understanding as already containing the new sense of the heart within itself.[8] The heart stands not for emotion or feeling or "commotions," as Chauncy and others thought, but for an apprehension which already has inclination or judgment in it.[9] Thus it was a great confusion when Chauncy identified reason or the head with judgment, and opposed it to imagination (of which Edwards generally takes a dim view) and emotion as representative of the heart. Edwards' chief purpose was to retain understanding in religion as furnishing a rational criterion, but also to redefine it as a *sensible* light involving direct sensible perception and the inclination of the heart. If this point is missed, the basic point of the *Affections* is lost and we shall be forced to rely upon that opposition between the head and the heart which bedeviled the polemics of the Revival and of Romanticism in later American life.

THE FIFTH SIGN

If the previous sign stressed the intellectual or apprehending aspect of the new sense, this one emphasizes the element of conviction. Genuine affections are those accompanied by an immediate certainty of the truth of religion. And Edwards did not shrink from admitting the complex and even paradoxical character of conviction; it carries with it both certainty and risk at the same time. On the one hand, the doctrines of the gospel are said to be "un-

7. Below, pp. 267–70.

8. Below, p. 271. JE was very clear in his criticism of any attempt to interpret the new sense as some form of enthusiasm.

9. Below, pp. 282–3, for the point that taste is the same as judgment.

doubted and indisputable" for those who have the new sense, but on the other hand the saints are described as "not afraid to venture their all" [1] on these truths. The certainty and the venture are seen as going together. Certainty of conviction wells up within the self, and this is, as Edwards says, no "predominating opinion" such as might be the probable outcome of speculation, but rather a direct apprehension. A man sees "that it is really so." But in addition to certainty there is the further awareness that the self trusts and depends upon religious truth and gives himself to it without reservation.

By conviction Edwards meant not a probable belief about this or that particular article of religion, but the engagement of the total self. As Charles Peirce once wrote, religion should not really be called belief, since belief implies a separation between the self and the item of belief, whereas religion defines the very being of the self.[2] Conviction is an immediate sight of divinity through the new sense; it grasps the person as a whole. What immediacy means, however, must not be misunderstood. It is not that the Spirit exercises some immediate forcing influence upon the will or inclination to accept what the understanding does not grasp.[3] Such a view would miss the point and distort all that Edwards has said about the nature and place of understanding. Conviction cannot arise except through the understanding. "The conviction of the judgment," he says, "arises from the illumination of the understanding: the passing of a right judgment on things, depends on an having a right apprehension or idea of things." [4] Where there is spiritual understanding, "then is the mind spiritual convinced of the divinity and truth of the great things of the gospel, when that conviction arises, either directly or remotely, from such a sense or view of their divine excellency and glory as is there exhibited." [5] There is a mystical element in this account, in virtue of the appeal to immediacy. And Edwards is most acute in seeing the relative character of that immediacy. It is not, he says in describing the man

1. Below, p. 291.

2. See my article "Religion and Theology in Peirce" in *Studies in the Philosophy of Charles Sanders Peirce,* ed. Wiener and Young (Cambridge, Harvard University Press, 1952), pp. 251–67.

3. One of the persistent problems for JE's entire theory is the relation of the new sense to the activity of reason.

4. Below, p. 296.

5. Below, p. 297.

of genuine piety, "that he judges the doctrines of the gospel to be from God, *without any argument or deduction at all;* but it is without any long chain of arguments." [6] The one step required is the apprehension by the spiritual understanding of the divine *gloria* in the things of religion; the resulting conviction of truth and certainty is mediated by this direct apprehension. The Augustinian tradition is thus carried on through Edwards' insistence that the ground of conviction must be something *internal* to the gospel itself and not in the surrounding circumstances. This internal quality is the moral excellence and beauty of the divine; Edwards' originality consists in his having taken it as something to be grasped by a new taste or sense.

THE SIXTH SIGN

No affections are genuine unless they are accompanied by what Edwards and his contemporaries called "evangelical humiliation." The point of this sign lies in the contrast between *legal* and *evangelical* humiliation. One aspect, at least, of the ancient theological problem concerning the relation between law and gospel is here introduced and interpreted in accordance with the doctrine of the new sense. He contrasts humility following from a sense of the greatness and awesome character of God with humility as a voluntary denial and renunciation of the self. Although Edwards expresses the distinction in several ways, the decisive feature is the quality of heart and will. He thinks of legal humiliation as forced or exacted from the self and thus as without that true acknowledgment of God's majesty to be found in the humility that grants all to God from the outset. Edwards is willing to allow that legal humiliation charges and convinces the conscience, but it does not go far enough. What is required is a *voluntary* [7] acknowledgment of God's sovereignty and moral excellence signifying not merely the conviction of the conscience but the change of inclination affecting the whole self.

6. Below, p. 298; my italics.

7. It is important to notice that in accordance with the doctrine set forth in the *Freedom of the Will,* this "voluntary" acknowledgment is really a necessary consequence of having received the new sense, and it cannot be given voluntarily until the new self is given. Like most Calvinists, JE holds not only that God offers himself to man, but that God also provides *all* the conditions of reception. Pressed to its conclusion, this position means that God both speaks and answers himself. Karl Barth has drawn this conclusion for contemporary theology.

In order to show how this sign may be used by the believer as a test, Edwards relates it to the Christian duty of self-denial. Denial has two parts or aspects; first, the denial of worldly inclinations or enjoyments, and secondly, the denial of the inclination to self-exaltation. The great danger accompanying each is that they may be carried out in a legal spirit. That is, the self may make a claim for what it takes to be its own achievement in humility and thus betray, in the very act, that it is not genuine. Spiritual pride is man's chief temptation, and the true danger lies in the fact that a pride of this order is a real possibility only for the man with religious concern. Hence the man who is anxious to do his Christian duty, in contrast to the lifeless and indifferent, will be all the more prone to compare himself with others to their disadvantage and his own glory. Spiritual pride is implicit in the judgment that one is better than others or that one has a just claim before God supported by spiritual attainments. True humility is inconsistent with both judgments. In stressing this point, Edwards was confronting a great deal of the popular piety of the revivals with a decisive test; not "spiritual attainments" or "great and overwhelming experiences" which may call forth pride and self-elevation, but the fundamental acknowledgment of the divine *gloria* called forth freely and in love. The true saint has his soul open to the vastness of the divine being and "the person is astonished to think how much it becomes him to love this God, and this glorious Redeemer, that has so loved man." [8] The result of this vision is a new sense of the smallness of man's greatest love in comparison with the divine love. Where a man tends to think first of himself and of his eminence among the saints, "he is certainly mistaken"; says Edwards, "he is no eminent saint; but under the great prevailings of a proud and self-righteous spirit." [9]

THE SEVENTH SIGN

It is curious that this sign expressing the foundation of the theory of affections should be buried in the middle of the list. That gracious affections are those attended by a *change of nature* is clear from all that has been said concerning the sense of the heart and the new creature. The reason for making the point in a separate sign is that Edwards wanted to give an explanation of conversion. In contemplating this topic, we must not be led to expect an analysis of the

8. Below, p. 324.
9. Below, p. 329.

soul by introspection aimed at tracking down the exact "moment" when the individual is saved. We find in fact nothing of the kind; Edwards has one point to make: it concerns the change of nature from which conversion derives its meaning. Conversion is literally [1] a turning toward God and away from corrupted nature. In Edwards' view the change must touch the nature of the self; there must be a new ground or principle for life. From the meaning he attached to the word "nature" we get a clue as to how this sign may be used as a test. "Nature," he says, "is an abiding thing" and this means that while the new nature does not "entirely root out the natural temper" it *must manifest, over a course of time and action, that it has some permanence.* Past sins and inclinations will not disappear, but their dominion is broken because they now stand related to a new self which, in virtue of its permanence, must reveal itself over a course of time. The Spirit does not actuate the self in or at a moment in an external manner; on the contrary, in dwelling within the self in accordance with its own nature it gives an enduring foundation. There is thus an important link between this sign and the twelfth, which emphasizes the *conduct* of the saints; true conversion is not evanescent but lasts over a course of life, so that in judging ourselves we must pay attention to our behavior. There is nothing sporadic about the transformation, and unless it has permanence it is not genuine. Affections expressing no more than the elevation or enthusiasm of an hour, and revealing nothing in the way of a new and abiding nature, are not gracious. Grace does not complete everything in an instant; Edwards speaks of it as having "proportions" and he describes its operation as a "continued conversion and renovation of nature." [2] There is thus a progress to perfection; nature has been overcome through the new basis which is given, but it remains to be overcome in detail through continuing historical life.

THE EIGHTH AND NINTH SIGNS

These two signs are straightforward in meaning and they occasion no difficulty. They may be taken together as further defining the type of life which must accompany genuine affections; they mark out further qualities of spirit to which such affections must

1. Both the Greek of the New Testament, ἐπιστρέφω, and its Latin equivalent, *converto* have the same connotation of a "turning."

2. Below, p. 343.

lead. The first of the two lays stress upon the Christlike character —love, meekness, quietness of spirit—and the second defines Christian tenderness or the heart of flesh. Here Edwards relies chiefly upon the beatitudes for his portrait of the Christian man and upon Christ as the head of the church. In no other part of the *Affections* is there so clear a description of the attitude with which the true believer should face the world, and how he should relate himself to others. The virtues cited here plus the account of Christian practice given in the final sign constitute the properly ethical part of the *Affections*. Whereas all the other signs (with the exception of the tenth which has an aesthetic turn) define the religious relationship, these express the moral aspect of Christian faith.

THE TENTH SIGN

Edwards' doctrine of affections is not without its aesthetic side. This sign gives the most explicit evidence of the fact. The characteristics of symmetry and proportion are to be found in the sanctified self and represent "God's workmanship." [3] In true piety there must be a uniformity and a balance among the various affections. Hope and fear, for example, should always accompany one another; the man who has a hope so confident that it obliterates all fear is sure to fall into an irreverent frame of mind. Hypocrites are bound to reveal a disharmony and disproportion in their affections which may take several forms.[4] It may mean, as in the above illustration, the predominance of one affection over another, or it may mean some essential deficiency in affections. Genuine piety continues to repent and to mourn for sin long after the first comfort of Christ has been received; hypocrites show their deficiency by supposing that repentance ceases to be necessary as soon as a sense of comfort is experienced. There is also another kind of disorder which Edwards calls a "strange partiality," wherein the same affection is subject to change in an unpredictable manner. A man may make a great show of his love to God and at the same time be envious and spiteful to his neighbor. Or he may show great kindness to his fellow men and have no love to God. Or, again, he may show love to those who accept him and reject others. All these disproportions are to be taken as signs of false affections, or rather

3. Below, p. 365.

4. The emphasis placed by Edwards on order and proportion is characteristic of the Augustinian tradition; Augustine's *De ordine* illustrates the point.

as indications that affections are not gracious. The application to the revival is obvious; those who are religious by "fits and starts," who are engaged only at certain times and seasons or who emphasize this or that virtue or sin to the neglect of everything else, fail to exhibit the symmetry which is the shape of the true religious life. The hypocrites, says Edwards in a magnificent figure, are like comets which appear for a time in a mighty blaze but have neither regularity in their movement nor constancy in their light, while the true saints are like fixed stars whose light is steady and sure.

THE ELEVENTH SIGN

The principle implicit in this sign is clear: gracious affections are such that the higher and purer they are, the more the appetite for God is increased; false affections are self-content and self-satisfied. Edwards' point is that the more clearly the divine excellence is grasped, the more obvious does the distance between God and man appear, and in true believers the greater is the desire to overcome the gulf. False affections, on the other hand, are those in which the individual rests as with a prize already attained, and there is no further appetite for the divine. Such is the state of men "secure in their conversion"; they feel safe in a salvation which is done once for all. "They live," says Edwards, "upon their first work, or some high experiences that are past," [5] and they suppose that striving is merely a means to a conversion which, once achieved, is a license for indolence. Implicit in the entire account is a principle that is required by Edwards' doctrine of affections. Affections are of the essence of the religious life, but they point beyond themselves to the God who is both their ground and their goal. Faith and love are not directed to the affections themselves, but to God. It would be tragic if Edwards' view were taken to mean that the affections are the object of faith. One is not to believe in affections; God alone is the object of faith, and affections are its fruits. Hence Edwards continually criticized those who found security in their "experiences" as ends in themselves. The basic assumption of the *Affections* is that it is possible to test the heart of the individual by testing his affections; this assumption would be mistaken if the affections were not *signs of something more ultimate*—God and the Spirit.

5. Below, p. 380.

THE TWELFTH SIGN

Edwards devoted more space to this sign than to any other; we cannot but conclude that it loomed largest in his mind. Moreover, he makes two claims which at once set it apart from the others. First, "it is," says Edwards, "the chief of all the signs of grace";[6] and secondly, the public character of practice makes it a sign whereby others are granted some insight into the sincerity of the believer. Edwards is most careful not to say that other men should use the sign and judge their neighbors; he confines himself instead to saying that practice is the best evidence of a man's godliness in the eyes of others. While it is true that the state of the believer is known but to God and the individual is subject to the divine judgment alone, the daily conduct of a man is not beyond the scrutiny and provisional judgment of his neighbors. Indeed if the established practice of accepting members into the church on the basis of a "public charity" was to have any meaning at all, it is difficult to see how judgment by others could have been avoided. The heart may have its hidden side, but since practice furnishes a genuine clue to its nature, it cannot remain entirely secret.[7]

The principle behind this sign is that holy affections must exert their influence in Christian practice; the deed is the most important "outward and visible sign of an inward and spiritual grace." Practice is a sure evidence of sincerity or, as Edwards says, "men's deeds are better and more faithful interpreters of their minds than their words."[8] But if practice is taken as a paramount sign, it becomes necessary to see that it is not also taken as a ground of grace. Practice is a reliable sign of holy affections but it points beyond to the center of the self from which it issues and to the Spirit which makes it possible.

The conduct of Christians in the world is to be guided by three demands. First, behavior must be in conformity with Christian rules; secondly, the "practice of religion" must be the chief occupation of life; and thirdly, one must persist in this practice till the end of his earthly days. As a principal means of establishing these demands, Edwards makes exhaustive use of biblical material. From all parts of both Testaments he culls illustrations supporting his

6. Below, p. 406; cf. "Christian practice is the *principal sign*." Ibid.
7. Below, p. 408.
8. Below, pp. 409–10.

thesis that true affections issue in universal obedience as the chief and enduring concern of life.

Critics of Edwards' interpretation of the revival have sometimes claimed that his view was inconsistent on the grounds that it is impossible to reconcile having a new nature with backsliding or the failure of Christian practice. If Edwards' doctrine of affections is correct, the argument runs, the true saints cannot fail in their Christian duty. In meeting this objection he claimed that "true saints may be guilty of some kinds and degrees of backsliding," [9] but that they cannot fall away from that earnestness toward God which stems from having the new sense of the heart. If a man's behavior shows that he no longer persists in making the love of God the chief business of his life, then we have a clear sign that he was never converted and his experiences are to no avail. On the other hand, since genuine piety consists in the new heart and the change in nature, true believers may fail in their moral duty and be convicted of sin through the law without falling away from God entirely.

We have before us a distinction between the heart or essential nature of a man and the fact of his day-to-day performance in the world. Genuine piety concerns the heart and not bare conformity to the law; practice, nevertheless, is supposed to provide some clue to the heart. The question is, how can practice be used as a test? The most obvious answer is that there are certain deeds to be done and others to be avoided, and that those who do not deviate from this standard are the true saints. Such an answer Edwards could not give. True religion consists not merely in conformity to rules but in the new heart; the use of practice as a sign, however, bids us try to understand how it can be a clue to the inner nature of the self from which it comes. This is the crux of the matter; taking conduct as a sign is a matter not merely of discovering whether it conforms to rules but of learning how and in what way it reveals the heart. Practice, then, cannot be viewed merely as a doing or abstaining,[1] for we must discover in a man's conduct the true affections of his heart. Accordingly, Edwards looked to the attitude behind practice, to the love and gratitude displayed, and to the persistence of the believer in seeking to obey the commands of religion over a course of time. It was his belief

9. Below, p. 390.

1. Below, pp. 423 ff., where JE makes this point very clearly himself.

that if a change of heart is genuine, its permanent character will continue to show itself through the whole of life.

Viewed in this light, the backsliding of the saints ceases to be the insuperable problem it first appeared to be. If genuine piety has to do not with a perfect conformity to the law but with the new heart at the basis of life, there will be no inconsistency in supposing that this new heart can exist side by side with moral failure and shortcomings.

The place of practice in the Christian life may be viewed from another perspective. The Spirit is said to dwell in the believer as a living power; the body, says Edwards, is a temple of life and not a tomb. As a principle of life, the Spirit shows itself in the true believer as a vital power; the form most appropriate to its nature is that of holy practice. What this means is that a man's conduct is something more than the moral consequence of the religious relationship; it means that practice takes on a religious dimension. It may take its place as the chief among the signs of gracious affections because it is the Holy Spirit revealing itself as life in the world.

The prominence given by Edwards to practice as a test of affections is of great moment not only for his own thought but for the driving force of American Protestantism as well. In setting up practice as a cardinal test, Edwards was no mere follower of tradition. Classical Protestantism had placed considerable emphasis upon the inner workings of the Spirit and upon the primacy of faith. Puritanism went even further in the direction of making religion into an affair of the interior life. While Edwards' doctrine of affections carried this trend forward, it also took a large step in the direction of making action a center of attention. American Protestantism has never been far from believing that the most reliable test of religious sincerity is the deed; seeing what a man will do is the best test of his heart.

In Edwards' time this was a bolder step than might be imagined. He was subordinating the traditional "immanent grace" to the power of the Spirit as expressed in overt behavior, and he did so without becoming involved in a doctrine of works. There is, he says, no justification in works: "I proceed to show that Christian practice . . . is . . . much to be preferred to the method of the first convictions, enlightenings and comforts in conversion, or any immanent discoveries or exercises of grace whatsoever, that begin and end in contemplation." [2] We need not follow Edwards through his tedious arguments in defense of the position; the conclusion to which they point is vastly more important. He was taking a long look at Protestantism's sacred domain—the inner life—and demanding that it be subjected to a public test. The ground of action, the new nature, is not displaced; in the order of essential things the sense of the heart is always prior. But from the standpoint of human knowing and testing the proof of the heart is to be found in the fruit it can produce in the world. The Holy Spirit not only dwells in the depths of the soul but is manifest in that power through which the face of nature is transformed.

The bearing of this doctrine on the relation between religion and technology in American life has still not been fully realized. American Protestantism has had no place for quietism; its robust sense of activity in the world can be traced to the strain of Puritan piety and not least to the interpretation of that piety by Jonathan Edwards. It is no small irony that a skillful and vigorous defense of the primacy of practice in religion should have found expression in a treatise on religious *affections.*

3. *Religion, Revivalism, and Religious Affections*

The details of Edwards' argument in the *Affections,* while important for revealing the subtlety of his mind, may prove more distracting than enlightening unless we can come to an understanding of the central contributions made by the work. We are bound, moreover, to ask for its relevance to our present situation. A work which attacks fundamental questions has perennial importance; it is the task of each age in confronting such a work to discover where that importance lies.

All about us at present are signs of renewed interest in the things of religion, and the past decade has witnessed not only a vigorous revival in theology but an even more vigorous upsurge of revivalism at the level of personal religion. But there are dissenting voices as well, those who view an increased emphasis upon religion with alarm, those who are convinced that morality is enough and that the idea of salvation is outmoded, those who believe that natural science alone gives reliable knowledge while all else is emotion and sentimental bias. Against such voices that of the revivalist in religion is raised even louder; the situation is urgent, secular society

2. Below, p. 426.

is godless, conversion is the answer to our ills, it is too late for discussion, the only course is to decide and have faith. We cannot, as we confront such a situation, avoid asking what light is shed upon our predicament by the thought of Jonathan Edwards. It would be strange indeed if one who labored so conscientiously in the revivalist vineyard and who thought so acutely about its problems should have nothing pertinent to say to us in the present hour.

What, then, can we find in Edwards' interpretation of heart religion that will provide us with a vantage point from which to understand and evaluate the current scene? There are three basic contributions made by the *Affections,* and each has a direct application to present religious thought and practice. Edwards recovered, through his doctrine of the new sense and the new nature, the distinctively religious dimension of life; he pointed the way to a form of understanding broad enough to retain its relation to the direct experience of the individual; he showed how piety, though ultimately rooted in the individual's relation to God, could be subject to rational scrutiny in the form of tests aimed at revealing its genuine or spurious character.

The first shows us the way to prevent the reduction of religion to something other than itself; the second makes it clear that understanding can be preserved within religion if it is not taken as a purely theoretical power which ignores the experience of the unique individual; the third gives us a basis for interpreting and evaluating the present concern over revivalistic religion. And in seeking to trace out the further implications of each of these points we do well to remember that if Edwards can aid us, our present religious situation enables us to understand him as perhaps never before. For we are falling or have fallen into some of the very pitfalls he sought to avoid; we are in a better position than any age since Edwards to understand the profundity of his contribution to theological thinking.

The properly religious aspect of man's life is always in danger of being obscured because of our tendency to identify it with something other than itself. Western society since the time of the Enlightenment has consistently manifested this misunderstanding. Religion has been taken as morality with emotional overtones or, even worse, has been made one with social and political idealisms, and thought of merely as an instrument of social change. Whatever form the corruption has assumed, loss of genuine religion has been the result. American Christianity has been especially vulnerable; the practical or pragmatic bent of much American life has led time and again to the reduction of religion to morality. The sincerity of the heart has been subordinated to action and, in its lowest terms, to appearing proper in the eyes of the world.

Edwards made no such mistake, and he can aid us in our attempts to overcome it. One of the clear declarations of the *Affections* is that religion has to do with the inner nature of a man, with the treasure on which his heart is set and with the love which supplies his life with purpose. There can be no identifying religion with morality or anything else; it is the deepest and most fundamental level of life and it goes to the *heart* of the matter. Religion, to be sure, issues in deeds, but it is not the same as right conduct. As Whitehead has pointed out in his arresting comparison between religion and arithmetic, "You use arithmetic, but you *are* religious." Edwards would have agreed. He was reviving the time-honored tradition of Augustine in finding religion in the whole man, in the fundamental inclination of his heart and in his love of the divine *gloria*. In recovering the religious dimension of life and in expressing it through the vivid idea of affections, Edwards is a guide. He has given us a means of exposing the pseudo-religions of moralism, sentimentality, and social conformity. For if religion concerns the essential nature of a man and the bent of his will, it cannot be made to coincide with moral rules, with fine sentiment, or with social respectability.

If our age has been plagued by its failure to comprehend what religion means, it has suffered no less from the acceptance of a false conception of the nature of human understanding. The dazzling successes of science, and their interpretation along wholly technological lines by pragmatically minded philosophers, have led to the conception of human understanding as a purely impersonal instrument aimed at finding objective and universal truths. We have acquiesced in that view of reason which sees in it only the abstractive intelligence fitted for expressing what is so true in general that it can have no bearing upon the life of the unique individual in particular. The rational self consequently has come to be understood as a spectator or as one who must put out the light of his own personal experience in order to gain that objective knowledge which alone is deemed worthy of concern. For religion the reduction of reason to science has meant that rationality is denied to religious truth and there is left to it nothing but the domain of emotion and caprice. Few have seen that this consequence is due to our view of what human understanding is and means; as understanding became narrower in scope it inevitably lost its capacity for dealing with dimensions other than science. Exclusive emphasis, moreover, upon understanding as dealing with the universal features of things has led to the disregard of individual experience; what can only be understood by personal experience has been subordinated to the knowledge that is gained by forgetting about yourself and attending to the universal law. What escapes the scientific net, we are told, is just on that account not a fish and need be considered no further as a possible object of rational understanding.

It is no secret that the philosophy known as existentialism in our time is dedicated to challenging the sufficiency of this scientific outlook for the whole of life. The attempt is being made, often in bizarre and unconventional ways, to bring the individual back to a sense of his own individuality and to the need for a broader conception of human understanding, one that does not eliminate everything but science from its concern.

With the *Affections* before us we are now in a position to see that Edwards, though by no stretch of imagination an existentialist, was wrestling with the same problem. He saw that an understanding which excludes first-person experience is doomed to be lost in abstraction and to forfeit its relevance for religion. To deal with the problem he reinterpreted human understanding so as to include a sensible element within it. He grasped the truth that sensible experience is always first-person experience; when we think in general concepts we pass beyond our own senses to a meaning common to many selves. But in using our own senses we are aware of grasping something that each individual must grasp for himself. If a man has never tasted honey, he cannot possibly know what is meant by calling it sweet and, similarly with Edwards' new sense, if a man has not actually tasted of the divine love no combination of general concepts will be adequate for conveying to him what it means.

Following the lead of the classical British experience-philosophy, Edwards placed primary emphasis upon first-person experience; in religion it took the form of the new sense or taste without which faith remains at the merely notional level. A spiritual understanding is not confined to the apprehension of universal concepts but includes within itself a sense which a man must experience directly.

If such experience is lacking, there is no way in which he can be made to understand the things of religion through general concepts alone. If, as Hegel said, the great principle of empiricism is that a man must see for himself and be in the presence of the thing he knows, the great principle of Edwards' spiritual understanding in religion is that a man must sense or taste for himself the divine love in order to understand what it means.

In the doctrine of the spiritual understanding Edwards was carrying on the tradition of Augustine and the Puritans, the tradition of the "light" in which, and through which, the things of God are to be grasped. But he qualified the purely rationalistic description of this light by bringing in the "sensible" factor. He had help in framing this conception not only from the English philosopher John Locke but from the English Puritans and the Cambridge Platonist John Smith. The latter was dissatisfied with the tendency of English Puritanism to overemphasize the purely intelligible aspect of the understanding; to correct the disbalance he developed the notion of a "spiritual sensation" or grasp of religious truth which is understanding and at the same time engagement of the individual heart. Edwards' "new sense" points in the same direction. It is the taste of the divine excellence which marks the difference between genuine piety and the merely conceptual grasp of religious doctrines that may lead a man to accept them as general truths without seeing and feeling their special bearing upon his own individual life and situation.

The doctrine of spiritual understanding shows a way in which both rationality and direct experience can be preserved within religion. It shows that understanding need not be a dry light which excludes individual experience. If, moreover, we follow Edwards in his view that understanding is a power of the whole man, we shall see that the heart and the will—the *inclination* of the self—are necessarily involved. A conception of understanding as a purely theoretical or observing power permits only what Edwards called a "speculative" approach: a man considers the problem abstractly but is not engaged. The theoretical attitude is inappropriate in religion because it leaves out the one thing which counts: the individual man and his destiny.

The contemporary relevance of these ideas is clear. If reason and understanding extend no further than the highly abstract knowledge to be found in the natural sciences, it becomes difficult to see how they can possibly have a legitimate function in religion. The original protest made by Kierkegaard against rationalism was directed against a reason which sets the individual self at a theoretical distance from everything it seeks to understand. The essence of the theoretical attitude is to ignore the peculiar bearing of what is known or contemplated upon the life and destiny of the one who knows.

Jonathan Edwards was dealing in his own way with the same problem. A merely notional understanding of Christianity is theoretical; it is inadequate because it leaves the individual soul outside as a spectator looking on at the feast. What is needed instead is engagement of the self and the inclination of the heart and will. But if we are to have such engagement and preserve understanding in religion at the same time, we shall need a conception of that power which neither shrinks it to the proportions of science nor identifies it with the theoretical grasp of general concepts. Understanding will have to be seen, as indeed Edwards viewed it, as a power of the integral self, a power related to the will and the heart. His skillful linking of the understanding to these other aspects of the self through the idea of the new sense opens up novel possibilities for attaining that broader doctrine of understanding so necessary at present.

Edwards' third contribution to the resolution of our modern predicament centers in his contention that affections can and must be subject to critical judgment. While he would not allow that there can be genuine piety which does not express itself in affections, he was equally insistent that they be put to the test. Affections do not test themselves and there can be, so to speak, no affectionate testing of affections. Critical examination calls for signs or marks that enable us to tell the true from the false. These criteria are provided by the New Testament picture of the Christian life as interpreted in a rational way.

A position seeking to recover immediate experience in religion and subject it at the same time to clearly announced tests is exactly what our present circumstance requires. It is a subtle position, one likely to be misunderstood, because it aims to combine what a one-sided way of thinking always sunders. But we must not be misled by the confusions of our forbears. Edwards' contemporaries failed to grasp the underlying consistency of the *Affections*. Some were confused by his double-barreled approach, while others were driven by frustration to anger. Edwards has declared himself for heart religion and against a narrow rationalism; to many this meant full support for revivalism even if it reached the bounds of enthusiasm and immediate revelation. But Edwards rejected enthusiasm and branded as false much of the popular piety resulting from the high tide of revivalist preaching. The heart, he contended, must be affected, for genuine religion is power and more than the verbal acceptance of doctrines. But the change of heart is not in the convulsion or the shout, the flowing tears or the inner voices. These external signs, the sensational marks of revivalism in every age, are no guarantee of genuine faith; there are other tests to be met.

The double-edged character of Edwards' doctrine gives it a peculiar relevance for the current situation because it holds out the possibility of bringing together in a fruitful way what many are concerned to separate. The present renewal of interest in religion often takes on a revivalistic form and thus stands in striking contrast to the underlying assumptions and conventions of our highly rationalistic, secular society. The opposition further widens the gap between faith and the rational disciplines. Rationalists, in order to eliminate, or at least minimize, the threat of revivalistic religion, tend to overestimate the power of reason and science while at the same time exaggerating the irrationality of all religion. On the other side many proponents of the religious revival preach the irrelevance of knowledge and the cultural disciplines, contrasting the critical attitude with the urgency of commitment and the theoretical approach with the immediate experience of the individual. The power of Edwards' doctrine of affections resides in its uncompromising demand that both sides be preserved and related in a fruitful way. The heart and the individual's direct perception are essential to genuine religion, but without critical and rational tests of the heart we cannot know when religion is genuine.

The motivation behind the revivalist in every period is a vivid sense of the personal character of religious faith. He sees that conventionalism is the death of religion and that each individual must confront the issues and make the decision for himself; there is no faith by proxy. He further sees that this truth itself may fall to the level of a general pronouncement and thus may fail to have the very impact it is meant to have in each individual case. His chief strategy for meeting the situation is to dramatize its urgency and seriousness. There is, he believes no time to stand off and survey the situation, no room for discussion and criticism. The object of faith stands before a man as a brute fact; if its importance is impressed upon him in a vivid and moving way, he will accept. For the majority of revivalists religion is as simple as that.

Edwards saw the element of truth in this position but he was too acute to fall prey to the errors that go with it. He saw well enough that where the individual is not touched at the heart there is no genuine religion. He would have joined hands with William James in believing that there can be no religion at second hand. Edwards' sense of the heart, his defense of the necessity of affections, and his doctrine of spiritual understanding underline the fact. But despite this avowal of heart religion he failed to fall in with revivalism at two crucial points; he denied that the urgency of believing provides any criterion for the truth of religion or the sincerity of the believer, and he was unwilling to follow the pattern of most revivalists and set the religious spirit over against learning and intellect. For Edwards the Word must come in truth as well as in power.

He was second to none in his sense of the seriousness and urgency with which the individual confronts the religious issues. He had repeatedly drummed the ears and laid it upon the consciences of his hearers that each man is judged according as he makes the "business of religion" central or peripheral to his life. But he did not suppose that the urgency by itself tells us what is to be believed, whether it is true, and to what extent the believer is sincere in his profession. Insight into these problems requires more than vivid preaching; the individual must have discipline, he must understand as well as hear, and behind it all must be the sense or "taste" of the beauty of holiness. No one of these essentials is furnished by the revivalist preacher armed with nothing more than the sense of urgency.

Edwards never tired of repeating the thesis that genuine affections are not heat without light. As even Chauncy acknowledged in Edwards' own time, this meant a refusal to accept the primitivism that has often attached itself to revivalist religion. He never was willing to represent himself as a simple soul able to understand the things of the spirit just because of a lack of "book learning." The great temptation of the revivalist is to come forward in this guise, to identify innocence with ignorance and to claim that only the soul uncorrupted by the studies and doctrines of the theologians is in a position to receive the gifts of the spirit. Edwards, on the contrary, was a scholar of the first rank, and he repeatedly criticized those who had neither the time nor the interest to give to the task of understanding their faith intelligently. He constantly urged his parishioners to study to the limit of their capacity, to avoid those who despised intellect in the belief that it is a power hostile to religion. The Bible is still the medium through which the ancient faith is preserved, and its treasures cannot be unlocked if learning is given up and interpretation becomes a matter of personal whim and individual vision. The recurrent error of the naive revivalist is to overlook the labor and the pains of learning; his conviction of the truth of his own immediate insight leads him to present the Bible as a book so clear in its import that he who runs may not only read but understand. Edwards never wavered in his repudiation of these ideas.

If, from the vantage point of the *Affections,* we view recent attempts to harvest souls in revivalist fashion, we shall lay hold of the enduring contribution of that treatise. In seeking for the signs that distinguish gracious affections from fleeting emotion and from the effects wrought by the rhetoric of an hour, Edwards was trying to penetrate beneath the surface of things. A genuine change must take place in the heart, and that change must show itself over a lifetime of work and worship in the world. As we contemplate the renewal of interest in religion, we must not fail to apply these criteria. What permanent change is taking place in the depths of the self and with what consistency will it show itself in practice? More likely than not the vast majority of cases will be unable to pass the test. And one of the principal reasons for the failure is to be found in our by now well-established tendency to view everything as a technique used by the human will to conquer nature and master history. Edwards had seen this source of corruptions, and he had attacked it through the doctrine of divine love as disinterested. Religion is genuine and has power only when rooted in a love which does not contemplate its own advantage. Religion becomes false at just the point when we attempt to make it into a device for solving problems. Faith does indeed move mountains, but only when it is informed by a love pure and unmixed, such as Edwards described in his fourth sign. Love of this kind overcomes the evil desires of the heart and proves itself in the Christian life, but if it is held forth as a panacea for all ills or as something to be *used* by an individual or a society to achieve benefits, its divine character is lost.

Edwards' calm word in the midst of "much noise about religion" is that religion must not be lifeless and it must be something more than doctrine or good conduct. True piety shows itself in the affections and in the fruits of the Spirit, but these must be put to the test so that we may know the gold coin from the counterfeit. To the revivalist in our time Edwards has a sobering word, one that is best expressed by biblical paraphrase: "Test the affections and see if they are of God, for many false affections have gone out into the earth."

4. *Learned Background: Edwards' Reading*

No other work of Edwards' is so heavily dotted with footnotes containing long extracts from the works of other theologians and divines. In addition to the writings of Solomon Stoddard, to which he had the easiest access, Edwards drew upon the works of sixteen other authors, mostly seventeenth-century English Puritans and dissenting clergy. The singular fact about the use of this material is that Edwards rarely enters directly into a dialogue with the author quoted; instead he uses his words as a support for the course of his own argument. There is no polemic or joining of issues, a fact which helps to explain why most quotations stand in the notes rather than in the text. The words of Shepard and Flavel, Preston and Perkins, stand as silent witnesses lending their own weight to the definition of Edwards' final position on the topic of conversion.

All writers cited, with the possible exception of Flavel and Jones, are well known to students of Puritanism. It seems likely, however, that their contribution to the formation of Edwards' thought has been underestimated. Previous editions of the *Affections* have omitted half the notes, no one has troubled to check the citations, and there has been an almost complete silence, in commentary touching the *Affections,* about the theologians and scholars Edwards had read.

The topic common to most passages cited is the nature of conversion, of sincerity, and of genuine piety. This was Edwards' central theme, and he chose his sources accordingly. But there are other ideas at work in the writings of the English Puritans with whom he was familiar. The influence of Locke and the British experience-philosophy upon Edwards have been described before, and there can be no question of their special relevance for the *Affections.*[3]

3. See esp. "Jonathan Edwards on the Sense of the Heart," *Harvard Theological Review, 41* (1948), 123–45. This article contains, in addition to introductory explanation by Miller, an edited text of Item No. 782 from the Yale Mss, containing JE's "Miscellanies." The number bears JE's title, "Ideas, Sense of the Heart, Spiritual Knowledge or Conviction. Faith."

But less well known is the part played by English intuitive-rationalist thought and the doctrine of illumination in shaping his opinions.[4] Many authors cited have as their main theme the concept of the Holy Spirit, and it is clear that Edwards was familiar with much that was being thought and written abroad about the working of the Spirit in individual and corporate piety.

Puritan Protestantism, in keeping with the importance it attached to individual experience, was attempting to bring again into prominence the much neglected Third Person of the Trinity. One of the powerful ideas behind this revival of thought about the Spirit was the doctrine of immediate apprehension or illumination, possible only for those to whom the divine light is given. This doctrine was central to the thought of the Cambridge Platonists, but it showed itself as well in the writings of Sibbes, Doddridge, Flavel, and especially John Owen. As the *Affections* shows, Edwards was familiar with the works of these men. In seeking to comprehend his doctrine of the new sense and the spiritual understanding, we must not neglect this theological contribution.

In preparing the following accounts, I have relied upon articles in *The Dictionary of National Biography* and upon the more detailed studies cited in the notes.

THOMAS SHEPARD (1605–49)[5]

Shepard was destined to exert immense influence upon the life and thought of New England. He was born in Northampton-

4. Recent studies of the doctrine of the Holy Spirit in English evangelical theology by G. F. Nuttall provide invaluable material. See his *The Holy Spirit in Puritan Faith and Experience,* Oxford, Blackwell, 1946; and *Visible Saints. The Congregational Way* 1640–1660, Oxford, Blackwell, 1957. Those theologians treated by Nuttall as most significant, including Richard Sibbes and John Owen, are among the authors read and cited by JE in the *Affections.*

5. See J. A. Albro, *The Life of Thomas Shepard,* Vol. 4 of *The Lives of the Chief Fathers of New England,* Boston, 1870. Albro makes use of the MS for an autobiography left by Shepard and first published in 1832. See also Perry Miller, *The New England Mind,* New York, Macmillan, 1939; *Orthodoxy in Massachusetts,* Cambridge, Harvard University Press, 1933. For a brief but illuminating note on Emmanuel College, Cambridge, where so many of the dissenting English clergy studied and in which Shepard was also educated, see M. M. Knappen, *Tudor Puritanism* (Chicago, University of Chicago Press, 1939), pp. 469–71. For a more complete account of Emmanuel College in this connection and of the Puritan influence of Cambridge University, see William Haller, *The Rise of Puritanism,* New York, Columbia University Press, 1938.

shire and fled to America in 1635. Like many other Puritan preachers and theologians, he was educated at Emmanuel College, Cambridge. His early years there were spent in a type of life ill-becoming a visible saint, but according to his autobiographical notes he was brought to himself through the preaching of John Preston, who had recently become master of Emmanuel. Shepard's later writings on conversion and salvation, especially on the idea of sincerity, were not without roots in his own experience.[6]

Edwards quoted more from Shepard than from any other writer, depending chiefly upon *The Parable of the Ten Virgins.* J. A. Albro noticed this fact and made the following observation:

> Our own Edwards, a man whose religious experience was as genuine and as deep as that of any divine whom New England or the world has produced, was more indebted to Shepard's sermons on the Parable of the Ten Virgins, in the preparation of his "Treatise concerning the Religious Affections," than to any other human production whatever, as is shown by the fact that out of one hundred and thirty-two quotations from all authors, upwards of seventy-five are from Mr. Shepard.[7]

The *Parable* was published posthumously from sermon notes left by Shepard; it appeared in England in 1660 under the editorship of Jonathan Mitchell and Shepard's son Thomas. As the title implies, the whole is a series of sermons on Matthew 25:1–14, the parable of the wise and foolish virgins.

The discussion is divided into two parts of equal length. The first concerns the preparation of the believer in the church to meet Christ (verses 1–5) and the second treats the coming forth of Christ to meet the true believers (verses 5–14). Shepard's brief summation of the application he wants to make is most helpful. The members of "some churches" at the time of Christ's coming will be "virgin professors," i.e. those who have already been stirred from worldly security and who are waiting in a "Covenant of Grace." They are "called out," but not all are finally "sealed in the Lord." Among these members, consequently, only a portion will be filled with the

6. See Frederick L. Gay, "Letter of Thomas Shepard, 1672," *Publications of the Colonial Society of Massachusetts, 14* (1911–13), 191–8, for Shepard's advice about idleness and drunkenness to his own son while a student at Harvard.

7. Albro, *Life,* pp. 318–19.

power of grace at the coming of Christ; the rest will "be found foolish." [8] The visible church is understood by Shepard as neither the kingdom of the third heaven nor the inner heart of grace in the true believer, for in neither place would there be foolish virgins. The visible church is a mixture of those who wait for Christ; some among them are wise and others foolish.

Shepard's description of the true believer shows the similarity between his main problem and that discussed by Edwards in the *Affections*. His account of faith as the supreme relation between Christ and the soul furnishes us with instructive parallels to Edwards' views. The sight of Christ is said to be prior in nature (if not always in time) to the act of faith. And this sight is not possible for the ordinary understanding alone. In passages remarkably similar to those in which Edwards described his idea of spiritual understanding, Shepard contrasts knowledge gained from historical report—from the Bible and the creeds—with a living knowledge that is also a saving knowledge.[9] Seeing something directly with the eye of the mind is contrasted with relative knowledge which comes through something else as a medium. The saints do not apprehend Christ perfectly in this spiritual vision, but what they do grasp is present in their own lives and does not represent a report at second-hand. Their grasp is, moreover, beyond the capacity of the unenlightened.

The stress placed upon direct apprehension through the understanding by Edwards and Shepard places them in the company of Sibbes, Owen, Goodwin, and other seventeenth-century English Puritans.[1] Shepard held that the decisive difference between the wise and foolish virgins lay in the nature of their understanding; the wise owe their wisdom to divine illumination.[2] "Folly or want of Divine

8. Shepard, *Parable* (London, 1660), Pt. I, p. 3.

9. We may note at this point, although virtually every Puritan writer would serve equally well, the incompleteness and even misleading character of the usual view that Protestantism substituted the Bible for the tradition and the church. The important point is that the Bible itself was for Protestants of the period one more piece of the tradition, or at least it could fall to this status unless it were animated by the Holy Spirit. The proper formula, as Edwards made clear enough, is the understanding of the Word through the Holy Spirit which illuminates it by transforming the eye and mind of the reader.

1. See Nuttall, *Holy Spirit*, pp. 23, 32 ff.

2. For an extended account of the Puritan theory of reason and illumination see Miller, *New England Mind*, ch. 7; also Haller, *Rise of Puritanism*, and Nuttall, *Holy Spirit*, ch. 2.

light made the one unready for Christ, wisdom or having of Divine light, made the other prepared for him."[3] In other places illumination is described as the "new mind, the eye and director of the whole man."[4]

Edwards' analysis is the more subtle of the two, largely because of the skillful way in which he brought sensible experience, understanding, and will together in the concept of affections. Shepard had a less complex view. In a passage remarkably similar to one in Plato's dialogue *Phaedrus,* Shepard writes: "The eye or mind of man sits like the coachman, and guides the headstrong affections; if now this (i.e. the mind or eye) be blind, there will be falls and deviations into crooked ways."[5] Here the term "affection" seems to mean what Edwards meant by a passion or emotion which overpowers the individual and reduces him to a passive being. An affection on the other hand was, for Edwards, not a lawless passion but a sensible exercise involving inclination and judgment together. Where Shepard saw a sharp opposition between sensibility and understanding, Edwards aimed at showing the continuity between the two. By exploiting the multiple meanings of the "sense of the heart," he was able to bring understanding and inclination together; the affections require both. By bringing sense within understanding, Edwards resolved some problems of long standing. Those who retained the more rationalistic conception of illumination found themselves unable to provide for the senses. For them there was always dualism in the self; the senses stand as lawless on one side and the law is provided by the understanding on the other. The two sides remain external to each other and are brought together only when one forces or subdues the other. Edwards had no such dualism and thus was better able to retain the integrity of the person.

Also of great importance for a reader of the *Affections* is the 18th chapter in the first part of Shepard's *Parable.* There it is maintained that the Holy Spirit dwells in the true believer as the principle of Holiness; this doctrine forms the substance of Edwards' eighth sign (see below, pp. 344 ff.).

In addition to the *Parable,* Edwards used Shepard's *The Sound*

3. Shepard, *Parable,* Pt. I, p. 143.

4. Shepard, *Parable,* Pt. I, p. 144. This section should be compared with Shepard's further discussion of illumination in sec. 2 of ch. 20. JE, it will be noticed, took some passages from this part; see pp. 214–15.

5. Ibid.

Believer and *The Sincere Convert.* The latter was one of the most widely read books of the period; it is a discourse on Matthew 7:14—"Straight is the gate . . ."—and a defense of "high Calvinism," as the following table of contents makes plain:

1. That there is a God, and this God is most glorious
2. That God made man in a blessed state
3. Man's misery by his fall
4. Christ, the only mediator by price
5. That few are saved and that with difficulty
6. That man's perdition is of himself

In the introduction Shepard lays it down that the understanding cannot entertain any truth concerning salvation unless the affections be "wrought upon." [6]

The Sound Believer addresses itself to the same problems as the *Affections.* Of special interest is Shepard's analysis of the soul's preparation for the reception of grace. There are three stages through which the soul must pass: *conviction* of sin, *compunction,* and *humiliation.* Conviction is described as an awareness of the understanding, whereas compunction is said to be a "pricking at the heart" [7] and a sense of sin finding its seat "in the affections and will." [8] Shepard holds that it is possible to have the conviction without the compunction, but that "in the elect" one always accompanies the other. Except for the fact that Edwards did not accept the idea of stages in the Spirit's working, their views are the same on this point.

SOLOMON STODDARD (1643–1729)

If Shepard's works, at least as regards the *Affections,* exercised the greatest theological influence upon Edwards, Stoddard must

6. This work has presented the most annoying of citation problems. Since the publication of the first edition, London, 1641, the work enjoyed the popularity of at least eight further editions by the end of the century, to say nothing of countless other printings, and this fact has made the location of passages cited both in the *Affections* and in the *Miscellanies* a very difficult one. I have been unable to discover which edition JE used. Curiously enough, along with his page references JE says "first edition" both in the *Affections* and the "Miscellanies"; not only do the pages fail to check for this edition, but I have been unable to locate any edition for which his references check. Consequently, I have cited the first edition. The passage quoted above in the text is the second paragraph in the introduction; this citation will enable a reader to find it in any edition, since in many editions the introduction is not paged.

7. Shepard, *Sound Believer* (Boston, 1742), p. 34; cf. p. 49.

8. Ibid., p. 34.

certainly have exerted the most powerful influence on Edwards' personal life. The full story of the relationship between Edwards and his ministerial grandfather need not be told here. We do, nevertheless, gain some insight into the theological relations between the two from the use made by Edwards in the *Affections* of Stoddard's works.

Stoddard was Boston born and a graduate of Harvard College in 1662; he served later as librarian of the College, a post he held until 1674. Four years earlier, in 1670, he had accepted the call to Northampton, where he remained until his death. Thus in 1670 began a dynasty which was to remain in power—first through the grandfather and then the grandson—until Edwards' dismissal in 1750, a period of eighty years.

With the exception of Shepard, Stoddard appears at greater length in Edwards' notes than any other writer. The most explicit comment in the *Affections* occurs in connection with the first sign of gracious affections and the witness of the Spirit.[9] Edwards notes that "Stoddard in younger time falling in with the opinion of some others" held to the view that godliness can be immediately revealed in particular cases through the testimony of the Spirit, but that later on he rejected this view in favor of a sounder one. Edwards quotes, in this connection, some paragraphs from *A Treatise Concerning Conversion* which first appeared in 1719.

Apart from this comment, quotations from Stoddard are given with implicit approval, and they are unaccompanied by further commentary. It is obvious that Edwards was pleased to have the support which the name of Stoddard obviously bestowed. In the statement and defense, for example, of the twelfth sign of gracious affections—"gracious and holy affections have their exercise and fruit in Christian practice"[1]—Edwards quotes several pages from Stoddard's sermon "The Way to Know Sincerity and Hypocrisy" (1719), bound together with *A Treatise Concerning Conversion.* This sermon makes obedience or practice—what was then called "carriage"—the chief sign of grace; consequently it provided Edwards with powerful support for his own view. Stoddard's thesis is that hypocrisy is revealed in a "course of life," whereas sincerity can

9. See below, p. 230, for Stoddard's view of conversion; also Miller, *The New England Mind: From Colony to Province* (Cambridge, Harvard University Press, 1953), pp. 282–3.

1. Below, pp. 383 ff.

be known only in "particular acts." This is a position very different from that of Edwards. In characteristic fashion, however, he pays no attention to these special distinctions, because he was more interested in the course of his own argument; he needed support for his general thesis that Christian obedience and practice represent the perfection of humility; Stoddard's sermon provided him with that support.

Further along in the discussion of the twelfth sign,[2] Edwards turns to Stoddard's sermon again, this time to support his contention that genuine saints can be guilty of backsliding in both kind and degree, but that their backsliding never goes so far as to destroy their being in a "way" or "manner" of universal obedience. Here Edwards' concept of a "way" or, as he expressed it in other places, a *habitus*, parallels Stoddard's concept of a "course of life" as distinct from singular acts taken one at a time.

Edwards' final use of Stoddard's "Way to Know Sincerity" provides an excellent illustration of empiricism or "experimental religion" in one of its more precise senses. Edwards argued that the acts of grace manifested in practice lead to greater assurance the more often and regularly they occur; it is as if the process shared the nature of induction from singular cases interpreted as increase in degree of confirmation with each new instance. He cites Stoddard's doctrine of the repeated renewal of the visible exercises of grace as a most dependable means of assurance.

Edwards' view was more critical than Stoddard's, but it also placed greater responsibility on men to discern the spirits through the application of criteria. In general, Stoddard's view leaned more in the direction of immediate apprehension without signs. Stoddard was fond of saying that grace is its own sign or that it shines by its own light, being an objective transformation of the self which the individual may come to know himself. Edwards, on the other hand, sought for a doctrine of signs according to which explicit criteria would be required, the presence of which under proper conditions could be interpreted as the presence of the Spirit.

Edwards' use of Stoddard's *Guide to Christ*, first published in 1714 (but cited by him in the edition of 1735), is singular; many of the passages are actually paraphrases strung together from different parts of the book. Edwards apparently felt secure enough in his understanding of the work and sufficiently familiar with its contents

2. Below, p. 390.

to use it in so free a way. The main theme is the necessity of humiliation and conviction of sin as a *prius* to faith; this Stoddard called "preparation." That Edwards did not hold this same view himself is not made clear in the reference to Stoddard in the *Affections*.[3] And again we have an excellent illustration of Edwards' use of a work for his own purposes; when he finds something in Stoddard to support him, he uses it, but there is no commitment to or even discussion of the main theme of the work. Of special importance to the *Affections* is Stoddard's idea that many signs which, under proper conditions, are legitimate signs of grace are falsely taken as assurances by natural men who have not been prepared to receive Christ and who consequently are in no position to exhibit the marks of grace at all. Edwards also quotes with approval Stoddard's idea that the failure of a man to specify the time of his conversion is no sufficient ground for the minister to draw the conclusion that he is rejected of God.

In addition to all of the above, Edwards used the *Treatise Concerning Conversion* (1719) and Stoddard's reply to Increase Mather on the subject of the Lord's Supper and who may be legitimately admitted to it: *An Appeal to the Learned,* first published in 1709. Edwards does not enter the controversy in which Stoddard was involved, and no passages used by him in the *Affections* are intended to raise that issue. He does, however, use Stoddard's argument against Mather to the effect that all visible signs may be common to both converted and unconverted men to support his own view that judging other men by outward appearances is at best uncertain.

A more complete account of the theological relations between the two men cannot be derived from a study of the material used by Edwards in the *Affections* alone. That something can be learned is evident, but the task of expanding and filling in the details remains to be done.

JOHN FLAVEL (1630–91) [4]

Flavel was a Presbyterian minister, educated at Oxford, and a student at University College. He was pastor to several congrega-

3. See "Miscellanies," No. 1019.

4. The name of Flavel does not occur in historical studies of seventeenth-century Puritanism as often as it should, and he is less well known than some contemporaries who wrote less and whose works were less influential among the

tions in England prior to 1656, when he settled at Dartmouth. The Act of Uniformity of 1662 drove him away from his post, although he was later allowed to return. His name will long be associated with Dartmouth not only because of the love and veneration of his parishioners there, but because of the risks and great sacrifices he made to return secretly to preach.

Many works of Flavel circulated vigorously in the latter part of the seventeenth century, and early in the following century his works were collected in several editions. For convenience I have cited the two-volume edition issued at Edinburgh in 1731 and in some cases I have also cited early separate editions. Edwards' citations give no clue to the editions he used.

Edwards, who referred to this man as "holy Mr. Flavel," quotes from five of his works: *Husbandry Spiritualized,* 1669; *Sacramental Meditations,* 1679; *The Touchstone of Sincerity,* 1679; *Preparations for Sufferings,* 1681; ΠΛΑΝΗΛΟΓΙΑ *or a Blow at the Root, A Discourse of the Causes and Cures of Mental Errors,* 1691.[5] The first three works were among his best known at the time and circulated widely. The use made by Edwards of each title is clear from the context, but it will be helpful to the reader to have before him a brief description of the theme of each work.

Husbandry Spiritualized is an excellent example of Puritan rhetoric which, as Haller and others have shown, was always for edification and never for "adornment," commencing with the view that earthly things are signs of heavenly things or the things of religion. Flavel uses the whole range of experience associated with the farmer's life as a set of similitudes containing within themselves spiritual truths. And as Miller has pointed out, Flavel's method is

---

common people. Edwards was nevertheless familiar with many of his books. For a recent treatment of Flavel see Miller, *The New England Mind: From Colony to Province,* pp. 404–5. There is a biographical sketch in Vol. 4 of Middleton's *Evangelical Biography* (pp. 48–64), but this account is more pious than informative, and a Life is attached to the Glasgow, 1754, edition of his collected works. The curious piece by E. Windeatt, "John Flavell: A Notable Dartmouth Puritan and His bibliography," contains a few important notes. This was reprinted "from the Trans. of the Devonshire association for the advancement of science, literature, and art," *43* (1911), 172–89. There is also a good article in the *DNB*.

5. The last item is a bibliographer's nightmare; it circulated under three titles, and many lists give us no indication of the fact. See below, p. 215.

rhetoric in reverse; instead of beginning with a general idea and expressing it in some figure or image, he begins with the concrete experience and finally arrives at the general idea. The portions quoted by Edwards are chiefly concerned with the similarity between the appearances of true believers and those who are not, and consequently with the difficulty of discerning, as Flavel says, "betwixt chaff and wheat." Edwards is criticizing those who claim to be able to discern with their own powers and standards the state of their fellows; he is arguing for the conclusion that Christ alone has the proper rule of true piety.[6]

The *Sacramental Meditations* consists of a series of twelve homilies on Scripture intended, as Flavel's title explains, to assist the reader in preparing his heart and exciting his affections for the solemn occasion of communion. Edwards was pleased to call attention to Flavel's claim in Meditation 4 that the "seal of the Spirit" can no longer be a witness to immediate revelation without the interpolation of the promises; the implication, reinforced by Flavel's illustrations, is that immediate sealing was possible within canonical times, but that revelation of this sort has now ceased. *The Touchstone of Sincerity* is an analysis of Revelation 3:17, 18; it deals with Edwards' main problem: how to distinguish the true recipients of grace from the hypocrites. The point for which Edwards would like to have support is that the opinions of *other men* and what is done in the public arena are not the proper touchstone of the saints.

Preparations for Sufferings is a "manual," as Flavel himself describes it, for preparing genuine Christians to endure the sufferings of the world. As in so many other cases, Edwards' use of the work fits his own purpose and the points singled out by him are not central to the drift of Flavel's discussion. The remaining work of Flavel quoted by Edwards is an elusive one because it circulated under at least three titles: ΠΛΑΝΗΛΟΓΙΑ, *A Blow at the Root,* and *The Causes and Cures of Mental Errors.*[7] The latter seems to have passed as the standard short title, but the others were also used. Flavel's aim in the work was to show that "the word of God . . . be the only test and touchstone to try and discover errors." In this case it happens that the use made by Edwards of the writing accords with its main theme.

6. See pp. 181, 186.

7. JE's "Catalogue" lists the work as *A Blow at the Root,* although he cites it in the *Affections* as *Causes and Cures,* etc.

JOHN PRESTON (1587–1628)[8]

There was no more eloquent defender of the covenant theology among English Puritans than John Preston of King's College, Cambridge.[9] Although originally a student at King's, he studied also at Queens' College and in 1622 became Master of Emmanuel. Into a relatively short life Preston crowded a great many accomplishments, including publication of several volumes of sermons and discourses, holding numerous university posts, and succeeding John Donne in the preachership at Lincoln's Inn.

Preston is to be distinguished from many Puritan divines by virtue of his considerable knowledge of Scholastic theology, particularly the system of Thomas Aquinas. He labored to show a continuity between reason and faith, and he was a strong supporter of the ancient doctrine that "faith is but the lifting up of the understanding." Moreover he laid great store by the certainty of the deliverances of the senses and held, as Edwards also did, that no one understands what it means to say that honey is sweet until he tastes it. To what extent Edwards was influenced by these ideas from Preston is difficult to say, since Edwards seems to have formed his ideas prior to study of Preston's works and especially because the material used by him in the *Affections* is of a different sort, exhibiting few of the ideas for which Preston is chiefly known. Edwards quotes from the *Treatise on Paul's Conversion,* 1637; *The Church's Carriage,* 1638; and the *Treatise of the Divine Love of Christ,* 1640.

The first of these writings is a discourse on the text of Acts 9:6 and has a subtitle, "The Right Way to Be Saved." The passages taken by Edwards are those in which Preston argues that a man

8. Preston is one of the most important of all Puritan divines, and consequently much has been written about him. In addition to his writings, our earliest source is John Ball's "Life of Dr. Preston" written in 1628 and preserved in Samuel Clarke, *A Generall Martyrologie,* London, 1651. It was edited and published in a critical edition by E. W. Harcourt in 1885. Extended discussion of Preston's thought is to be found in William Haller, *Rise of Puritanism,* esp. pp. 70 ff., and Miller, *The New England Mind,* pp. 22 ff. Haller's treatment is especially helpful because it refers to works of Preston used by JE in the *Affections.*

9. See Appendix B, "The Federal School of Theology," in Miller, *The New England Mind* (*The Seventeenth Century Background*), pp. 502–5, for a neat description of the covenant idea and a guide to the essential literature in which it was expressed.

can perform the commandments of God only after his humiliation. The natural man may do and refrain from doing some things, but he cannot surrender or give himself *absolutely* without the grace which works humility. The treatise entitled *The Church's Carriage* has as its theme the subjection of the church in its members to Christ, and especially the importance of obedience for the true Christian. Edwards uses this in support of his twelfth sign, the fruit of godliness in Christian practice. The work is of special significance because it outlines five tests, or what Edwards would call "signs," of sincerity: obedience to Christ, being obedient freely through love, concern and fear of God rather than of self in all offenses, willingness to be disobedient to others for the sake of the Lord, and the will to deny the sin dearest to the heart. A complete discussion would point out some interesting parallels between these tests and Edwards' signs of gracious affections, particularly with regard to Preston's first and third tests. The power to perfection in accordance with these signs is given, as Preston expressed it, through God's persuading "the heart by an inward enlightening, that it is best for the heart to be subject." [1]

The third work, in full dress title *The Onely Love of the Chiefest of Ten Thousand, or an Heavenly Treatise of the divine Love of Christ,* consists of a series of five sermons on the theme of love as an affection that is "planted in the will." These sermons are based on the text of I Corinthians 16:22: "If any man love not the Lord Jesus Christ, let him be had in execration."

JOHN CALVIN (1509–64)

Calvinists generally referred less to the actual writings of their theological master than might be expected. Edwards was no exception; the *Affections* makes but a few brief references to the *Institutes,* whereas dozens of pages are taken from Shepard, Stoddard, and Flavel. There are several possible ways of explaining this surprising fact. For one thing the main outlines of Calvinism and its principal points were well known to Edwards and his contemporaries; there seemed to be no need to return to the sources. As happens in every tradition, as soon as the rallying doctrines are reduced to commonplace formulas, the more subtle formulations of the founders may be neglected. Evangelical Puritanism, moreover, placed much more emphasis upon the inner life and religious

1. Preston, *The Church's Carriage,* p. 115.

experience of the isolated individual than Calvin did. As John McNeill has pointed out, Calvin was a "high" churchman; he revered the church as the one divine institution testifying to the grace of Christ. His interest accordingly was directed more to discerning and stating the true marks of the church—discipline, sacraments, and the preaching of the Word—than to discovering the distinguishing marks of a solitary piety. This is not to say that Edwards and other Calvinists were not concerned for the church; the fact remains, nevertheless, that conversion, sincerity, and humiliation—the marks of the inner life—were uppermost in their minds. For Calvin, theology was not yet that psychology of the Spirit it was to become for his later followers.

In citing the *Institutes,* Edwards does not indicate any edition; it is most likely that he made his own translation from whatever Latin edition was available. He provides us with the book, chapter, and section in each case.

WILLIAM PERKINS (1558–1602)

Perkins was a non-separatist Congregationalist whose reputation was based chiefly on his ability as a teacher of theology and lecturer at Cambridge University. His special importance for New England theology consists in the fact that his is the earliest expression of the Covenant or Federal theology. In the *Affections,* Edwards quotes only from one work, "A Discourse Concerning the State of a Christian," which is in reality a subsidiary treatise forming part of a larger work, *A Treatise Tending unto a Declaration, whether a Man Be in the Estate of Damnation, or in the Estate of Grace.*[2] The context in which Edwards uses this work is self-explanatory. His acquaintance with Perkins' works does not seem to have been very broad; it so happens that several references to Perkins in Edwards' manuscripts are to the same work quoted above.

JOHN SMITH (1618–52)

John Smith, one of the English philosophers known to us, along with Cudworth and More, as Cambridge Platonists, is the only writer quoted by Edwards who was not in the strict sense a theologian or divine. He was a student of Emmanuel College, Cambridge, where he distinguished himself in languages and philosophy and

2. Most writings in the collected works of Perkins have their own separate title page; this writing also has such a page and is dated London, 1608.

later became a fellow of Queens' College. Of his writings we have very little. Besides the *Select Discourses,* edited by Worthington in 1660 [3] and reprinted in 1673, we have *Commentaries on the Prophets* (1731) and the separate printing in 1745 of his ninth discourse "The Excellency and Nobleness of True Religion." The *Select Discourses* contains ten pieces, the eighth of which, "A Discovery of the Shortness and Vanity of a Pharisaical Righteousness," was used by Edwards, who took from it one of the longest single extracts quoted in the *Affections.* The passage is cited below from Worthington's edition, 1660. This discourse is based upon Matthew 19:20, 21, and further elaborates the theme running through all the essays and formulated in the ninth title, "The Excellency and Nobleness of True Religion": four points at which men are falsely led to believe that they have genuine religious faith when they do not. It is interesting that Edwards, in introducing the quoted passage, describes it as "remarkable" and so clearly expressive of his own view that, as he says, "I cannot forbear transcribing the whole of it."

It is impossible to estimate the true impact of Smith's thought upon Edwards' philosophy of religion. There is but one mention of Smith's name in the "Catalogue," [4] in a quotation recommending the *Discourses* as a work to be read and as having the power to raise "one's views above the world." Of very great interest is Smith's idea—expressed in the first discourse, "The True Way or Method of Attaining Divine Knowledge"—of a *spiritual sensation* by means of which the truths of religion are apprehended.[5] Smith's inclusion of the element of "sensation" in his doctrine of immediate knowing is strikingly similar to the idea expressed by Edwards, and at the same time different from the position held by other illumination-type rationalists whose "light" excluded the sensory element.

PHILIP DODDRIDGE (1702–51)

Edwards' "Catalogue" contains many entries citing theological and other scholarly works published abroad which were called to

3. The title means not that Worthington made a selection from among previously published discourses, but that he selected, from the manuscripts left at Smith's death, those he regarded as most significant. No other discourses were ever printed.

4. See p. 29, col. 2 f.

5. Smith's Greek formula for justifying the idea of a "spiritual sensation" is *γνῶσις εκάστων δι' ὁμοιότητος γίνεται.* It is important to notice that this is not the "dry" light of the understanding, but requires participation at the level of *sense.*

his attention by "Dr. Doddridge" in his *Family Expositor*. Doddridge was one of the nonconformist clergy of the eighteenth century; there are interesting parallels between his career and that of Edwards. Doddridge was educated in private schools, his religious convictions having made it impossible for him to matriculate at either Oxford or Cambridge. In 1729 he was asked to succeed his own teacher, John Jennings, as leader of a dissenting theological academy. In that same year Doddridge was called to the parish of Northampton and again he accepted, moving the academy with him. Recent studies have revealed the contribution made by this and other dissenting academies in the training of evangelical clergy. The spread of Baxter's theology was in large measure due to Doddridge's efforts.[6]

The work from which Edwards quotes in the *Affections*, namely *The Scripture Doctrine of Salvation* (1741), consists of two brief sermons on this theme. The text was available to him in Doddridge's *Practical Discourses on Regeneration* (1742) with which these two sermons were bound.[7]

WILLIAM AMES ("Amesius") (1576–1633)[8]

The writings of Ames were well known in New England from the outset; the *Medulla* and the *Cases* were as familiar to both students and preachers as Guffey's reader was to the average schoolboy

6. See G. F. Nuttall, *Richard Baxter and Philip Doddridge*, Oxford, Blackwell, 1951; Nuttall, ed., *Philip Doddridge, 1702–51; His Contribution to English Religion*, London, Independent Press, 1951. Further investigation is needed on the connection between Edwards and Doddridge, especially since the "Miscellanies" also contain references to other of his works. Lists of books "mentioned by Dr. Doddridge," as JE writes in the "Catalogue," should also be checked.

7. The 1742 Library in Yale University contains a copy of Doddridge's *Practical Discourses* (London, 1742), with which is bound the two sermons on the *Scripture Doctrine of Salvation*. These sermons have their own title page, London, 1741, and are separately paginated. Edwards' citation "Sermon I., p. 11" is correct. The British Museum catalogue does not, however, indicate that the sermons ever appeared separately, and with the kind assistance of Mr. A. W. Newton of the Department of Printed Books I located the British Museum copy and found it to be a duplicate of the Yale copy; it is virtually certain that the sermons did not appear separately and were available only with the *Discourses*. Since the Yale copy is marked "presented by the author" and was in the collection before the end of 1742, it is likely that it is the one Edwards used if he had not procured a copy of his own. The "Catalogue" (p. 10, column 2) mentions both the *Discourses* and the *Scripture Doctrine*, and JE says, "By Dr. Doddridge mentioned in his letter to Mr. Wadsworth an extract of which he sent me."

8. For Ames see Miller, *The New England Mind*, pp. 188 ff., 375; also Haller, *Rise of Puritanism*.

in the last century. Ames was born at Ipswich in 1576 and received his education at Christ's College, Cambridge, where he was a student of Perkins. His fame as a theologian rests on his *Medulla Theologiae* (1631, English translation 1642) and *De Conscientia* (1631, English translation as *Cases of Conscience,* 1643). The latter work is the one used by Edwards; it is cited by him as *Cases of Conscience* and passages are identified by book and chapter only.

As Ames informs us in the preface to that work, the plan of the book and the need for it were first suggested by the lectures of Perkins. It seemed to him that Protestant divines should have guidance in understanding and interpreting the experiences of their parishioners, especially where difficult cases of conscience and decision were involved. A large part of the value of this work for New England theology lay in its explication of the covenant idea, especially its emphasis upon the voluntary character of the covenant type of agreement. Edwards was, however, interested in it more for the light it threw upon the interpretation of individual experience as is shown by the fact that the few passages cited are drawn from discussion of the signs of sincerity and humility in the believer.

JOHN OWEN (1616–83)[9]

The breadth of Edwards' interest and reading can be seen when we reflect upon the presence in his list of authors of both a Doddridge and an Owen. Whereas Doddridge was a "broad" Calvinist in the Baxter line, Owen was generally described by his contemporaries as one of the "over-orthodox doctors." Many churchmen knew Owen after his break with the Presbyterians as a rigorous independent and as one of the less flexible Calvinists. In the temporal sphere, Owen was a figure of considerable influence. He occupied the post of Chaplain to Cromwell, became Dean of Christ Church, and served as Vice Chancellor of Oxford until the Restoration.

The work of Owen quoted by Edwards, Πνευματολογια *or A Discourse Concerning the Holy Spirit* (1674), is one of his mature and major works. It has for its aim a complete analysis of the nature of the Spirit and an interpretation of its central importance in the Christian religion. Owen wanted to show the difference between

9. See William Orme, *Memoirs of the Life of John Owen* (London, 1820) for a picture not only of Owen but also of the Puritan religious situation in England up to and including the reign of Cromwell. See also James Moffatt, *The Golden Book of John Owen,* London, 1904; and Nuttall, *Holy Spirit,* pp. 10 ff., 41–4, 71 ff.; *Visible Saints,* many references.

morality and religion; the difference, in Puritan language, between living a righteous and sober life and experiencing the special grace of God through the Holy Spirit. Edwards' excerpts are internally related to Owen's own argument as well as to the theme of the *Affections*. The passages quoted concern the difference between a common work of the Spirit as it operates "on the affections" and a spiritual operation in the proper sense. Edwards found himself in full agreement with Owen's contention that a gracious operation must "fix" the affections and "fill" them. The passages singled out by Edwards explain the meaning of these criteria for judging a work of the Spirit.[1]

RICHARD SIBBES (1577–1635)

Sibbes, an exceptionally popular preacher at Grey's Inn and other posts, was educated at St. John's College, Cambridge, and later became Master of St. Catherine's Hall. In addition to publishing works of his own, he took a leading part in the publication of the works of John Preston. It is impossible, as recent studies have shown, to overestimate the influence of Sibbes upon English Puritanism, especially as regards the doctrine of the Spirit. Nuttall has recently spelled out his contribution. He writes: "a large influence in directing the Puritan's attention to the doctrine of the Holy Spirit was the preaching of Richard Sibbes." [2] Edwards has but one quotation from his writings, and it is from his best known piece, *The Bruised Reede and the Smoaking Flax* (1630), the only one of his sermons to be published in his lifetime. This remarkable little work is based on Matthew 12:20 and has for its main theme the nature of conversion and the soul's awareness of its own condition. Its fame has been due in part at least to the fact that it was cited by Baxter as one of the chief influences in his own life.

Sibbes held a doctrine of the Spirit which is highly similar to the view expressed by Edwards in the *Affections*. Especially important is Sibbes' idea of the conjunction of the Word and the Spirit, as expressed in the following extract:

1. See below, pp. 250–51; 372–3. In JE's "Catalogue" there is the following entry: "Dr. Owen's recommended by Mr. Halyburton to the young students of divinity in the University of St. Andrews above all human writings for a true view of the mystery of the gospel" (p. 3, col. 2).

2. Nuttall, *Holy Spirit*, p. 14. See also Haller, *Rise of Puritanism*, pp. 65 ff., 93, 152. Other important sources are: Clarke's *Martyrologie* and the "Memoir" attached to Grosart's edition.

> God, joining with the soul and spirit of a man whom he intends to convert, besides that inbred light that is in the soul, causeth him to see a divine majesty shining forth in the Scriptures, so that there must be an infused establishing by the Spirit to settle the heart in this first principle . . . that the Scriptures are the word of God.
>
> As the spirits in the arteries quicken the blood in the veins, so the Spirit of God goes along with the word, and makes it work.
>
> The word is nothing without the Spirit; it is animated and quickened by the Spirit.[3]

The passage quoted by Edwards from *The Bruised Reed* is taken from a section near the end of the work in which Sibbes gives "some rules or directions how wee are to carry ourselves, that the judgment of Christ in us may indeed be victorious." No edition is cited by Edwards, and the book went through an amazing number of editions in a relatively short time, any one of which might have been used by him. The first edition appeared in 1630. I have not been able to examine this edition, but I have cited the passage quoted from the 6th edition (1638), where it appears on p. 263; it can also be found in the 4th edition (1632) on p. 279.

THEOPHILUS GALE (1628–78)[4]

Gale, a nonconformist tutor and a student of theology, was born in England and educated at Oxford, where he was a fellow of Magdalen College. He finally settled at Newington Green and established himself there as a tutor. At his death a considerable portion of his library was bequeathed to Harvard College. His scholarly life was devoted to the single idea of showing that all ancient languages and learning—particularly philosophical thought—derived from the Hebrew Scriptures. *The Court of the Gentiles,* Gale's great work and the one from which Edwards quoted, represents the outworking of this idea. Because it was a compendium of ancient learning, it was frequently referred to by scholars throughout the

3. These passages are quoted by Nuttall, *Holy Spirit,* pp. 23–4 (cf. p. 36), and are taken from Sibbes' *Works,* ed. A. B. Grosart (7 vols., Edinburgh, 1862–64), *3,* 427, 434; *5,* 427; *7,* 193, 199; *2,* 62. This view of the relation between the Spirit and the Bible should be compared with both "A Divine and Supernatural Light" and JE's sign in the *Affections,* below, pp. 291 ff.

4. See Miller, *The New England Mind,* pp. 98, 99, 374; Calamy's *Account* (1713), pp. 64 ff.

later seventeenth and eighteenth centuries. Edwards quotes a passage about the Pythagoreans and their spiritual pride; [5] this is one of the few places where he makes a special point of criticizing the pretensions of philosophers. Gale's *Court* began publication in 1669; it has four parts, sometimes referred to as volumes. The entire work was completed in 1677.

ANTHONY BURGESS (fl. 1652; d. 1664)

Burgess was an English Puritan who was educated at St. John's College, Cambridge, and later became a fellow of Emmanuel, the most important Puritan stronghold at Cambridge. He was pastor of the church at Sutton-Coldfield but was forced to relinquish his post after the Restoration. Besides *The Doctrine of Original Sin* (1659)—the work quoted by Edwards and Burgess' last published book—he wrote on the doctrine of justification against the Arminians and on antinomianism; finally he published sermons and commentary on Scripture.

Burgess' *Original Sin* is a most impressive analysis, although Edwards uses it only to support his own contention that the imagination is open to corruption and furnishes a constant source of temptation. Edwards quotes from a section headed "How prone it (imagination) is to receive the Devil's Impressions and Suggestions." It is an interesting fact and one which nicely illustrates Edwards' general practice with sources in the *Affections* that in a long section immediately preceding the section quoted, Burgess has a discussion about corruption of the affections. It is hard to see how a writer concerned to join issues with the authors he reads could have avoided discussion of the text at this most relevant point, but Edwards' silence may be explained on the ground that he had his own unique interpretation of the affections, whereas Burgess took the term in a more customary sense as being simply the sensual part of human nature in distinction from the understanding and the will. The pages cited by Edwards are correct for the first edition, London, 1659.

SAMUEL RUTHERFORD (1600–61) [6]

Rutherford, like Shepard, began his spiritual pilgrimage under the cloud of personal disgrace and lost his post as a result. He then decided to study theology under Ramsay and lived thereafter a life

5. See below, p. 316.

6. See J. T. McNeill, *The History and Character of Calvinism* (New York, Oxford University Press, 1954), p. 412.

of atonement, later becoming principal of St. Mary's College at St. Andrews and one of the leading figures at the Westminster Assembly. One of his early writings against Arminianism attracted a good deal of attention, and his *Lex Rex,* the work for which he is chiefly known, became one of the most important documents of political Calvinism, showing the illegitimacy of absolute royal claims.

Less well known than *Lex Rex* was Rutherford's *A Survey of the Spiritual Antichrist,* first published in 1648, a heavily weighted and compendious attack upon antinomianism, enthusiasm, and visionary religion. The quotation of this work by Edwards with approval gives further evidence that although he strongly defended the importance of affections and "heart religion," he did not countenance the enthusiasm and sectarianism frequently accompanying this type of piety.

The *Survey* contains large extracts from Luther's writings, and the passage used by Edwards is from a section called by Rutherford "Luther against Antinomians." It consists of many passages from Luther's Latin writings, brought together to show that Luther was an opponent of antinomianism and not, as the Jesuits claimed, the chief source of its views. The text contains excerpts in Latin from Luther in one column and his own English translation in the other. Edwards used the Latin passage from Rutherford's text but made his own translation, as a comparison between Rutherford's translation and the passage in the note will show.[7] The full citation of the original work of Luther is given in a note on the page where the quotation occurs.

Of some interest in connection with Rutherford is the following note from Edwards' "Catalogue": "Mr. Rutherford is spoken of as a great author by Mr. Ebenezer Erskine. Erskine's Sermons p. 142 and Mr. Noble of New York greatly commended the excellency of some of his writings as tending greatly to promote vital piety." [8]

7. See below, pp. 322–3. Rutherford's translation is certainly inferior; not only are words omitted, but nuances are missed. The Latin text has, for example, *Sic est vita Christiana, ut qui coeperit sibi videatur nihil habere,* but Rutherford reads, "So is the life of a Christian, that he who hath begun, may seem to have nothing," omitting the important reflexive *sibi*. JE translates this "seems to himself to have nothing." In view of the context and the centrality of self-knowledge and human pretension for Edwards' point, the reflexive takes on a special significance and certainly cannot be disregarded.

8. See p. 10, col. 2.

FRANÇOIS TURRETIN (1623–87)

Turretin (or Turretine) was born in Geneva, the son of Benoit Turretin, a professor of theology there in the early seventeenth century. The son was educated at Leyden and Paris, in addition to pursuing studies in his native city. In later years he served as pastor to the Italian congregation at Geneva and in 1650 was offered a chair of philosophy at the university. This he declined, but accepted several years later a chair of theology. Turretin represents the Calvinism of the Helvetian *Consensus* (1675), and his support of this confession was a major factor in its successful adoption.

His major work, the one quoted by Edwards,[9] *Institutio Theologiae Elencticae,* appeared in three volumes at Geneva from 1680 to 1683. It was famous as a handbook of systematic theology and passed through many editions, appearing in English translation as late as 1847 at Edinburgh.[1]

JEREMIAH JONES (1693–1724)

From Edwards' many writings as well as from the records of his background of reading, we come to see the formidable knowledge of the Bible he possessed. His familiarity with the major work of Jones gives further evidence of his standard of scholarship. Jones' *Canonical Authority of the New Testament* (3 vols. 1726–27) is cited by Edwards in connection with the interpretation of Peter's repentance, as recorded in Mark 14:72.[2] Jones was an Independent minister and theological scholar born in Wales.

5. *Note on the Text*

We possess no manuscript for Edwards' *Affections,* although, according to Dwight,[3] "it was a series of sermons, which he preached from his own desk." There is, however, a notebook in Edwards' hand which is clearly a workbook for the *Affections;* the document is part of the collection of Jonathan Edwards Manuscripts in the Yale University Library. It, like JE's sermon booklets, is stitched at the back and contains 20 sides (paged by JE, 1–20), 5″ × 6½″.

9. See below, p. 289.
1. McNeill, *History and Character,* p. 406.
2. See below, p. 335.
3. Dwight, *1,* 223.

The first sheet has "No. 7" at the top and in the body of the book reference is made to a "No. 9." JE apparently had a series of such workbooks before him in preparing the final text. In a brief section entitled "Authors to be looked into and cited" JE lists several of the writers whose works are actually cited in the *Affections,* including two references to the *Works* of Perkins that are identical with citations in the *Affections.* Although the notes on any given topic are sketchy, there are clear parallels between them and both the negative signs of Pt. II and several of the twelve signs of Pt. III. The idea of the "new sense" is clearly expressed, and JE stresses the point that it is entirely new and not to be derived from any "concurrence or composition" of natural sensations. There is considerable reference to counterfeit affections and to the delusions of imagination; both are rejected in language highly similar to that used in the *Affections.* The Christian practice of JE's twelfth sign comes in for some attention, and one passage suggests that the "main difference" between true and false grace is that one is practical and the other is not. On p. 19 of the booklet JE cites his own Miscellany No. 1000, which concerns the judging of others' sincerity. In a figure representative of the Puritan rhetoric at its best, JE points out the need for judging according to neither the leaves nor the blossoms but the fruit. The idea expressed in this Miscellany, and even the figure itself, is repeated by JE in Pt. II of the *Affections* and also in the Preface. The fragment from the Andover Collection is written on the reverse of a printed proclamation 12″ × 16½″, and folded so as to produce four writing sides. The contents show that it is part of a reply to criticism, largely about the doctrine of the divine Spirit in the *Affections,* but the circumstances remain unknown, since the fragment begins in the middle of a discussion and breaks off in the middle of a sentence at the end. The topics considered are, first, whether Christ died for all men or only for the saints, whether the assurance of salvation has reference primarily to human knowledge or to the fact itself as established in the divine will, the meaning of "nature" in JE's discussion of the new nature in the *Affections,* and a defense of his doctrine that the Spirit can communicate his nature to the saints. This latter point is one of the most important to be found in the fragments, and JE expands on the meaning of the concept of nature and further defends his view that when the divine Spirit communicates himself, he communicates not his *essence* but his holiness; the grace in the hearts of the saints is of the same nature as the divine, but infinitely less in degree. JE also reinforces his view that the new sense is not the bestowal of a new faculty.

There also exists in the Andover Collection a fragment of what appears to be a reply by Edwards in his own hand to some criticism raised against certain doctrines of the *Affections*. Apart from these manuscripts there is nothing remaining among the materials presently known that can in any way supplement the printed text. The first published edition is still our authoritative guide.

The text here reproduced is that of the first edition of the *Affections,* published by S. Kneeland "in Queen Street, over against the Prison" in Boston, 1746. It has been edited in accordance with the general principles of the Yale Edition;[4] most importantly, the amount of capitalization has been greatly reduced, some spellings have been modernized in accordance with Webster, and errata printed at the end of the first edition have been corrected silently, as have other obvious misprints both in the text and footnotes. Contractions current in the eighteenth century and earlier, though no longer in use—such as "ben't" for "be not" and "han't" for "have not" and "had not"—have been retained, and other expressions essential for rhetorical purposes—" 'em" for "them" and " 'tis" for "it is"—have been left unchanged. Apart from minor modifications made in the interest of presenting a more readable text, the initial edition has been reproduced faithfully.

The importance of retaining the reading of the first edition becomes apparent as soon as one makes a comparison between (a) the first edition of 1746, (b) Wesley's edition of 1801, (c) the Worcester edition of 1808, (d) the Dwight edition of 1829, (e) Loring's second edition of 1824, and (f) the American Tract Society abridgment by Ellerby of 1833. The following are samples representing the first two paragraphs of the work:

(a) *First edition, 1746*

In these words the Apostle represents the state of the minds of the Christians he wrote to, under the persecutions they were then the subjects of. These persecutions are what he has respect to, in the two preceding verses, when he speaks of the trial of their faith, and of their being in heaviness through manifold temptations.

(b) *Wesley, 1801*

In these words, the Apostle represents the state of mind of the Christians to whom he wrote, under the persecutions they then suffered. These persecutions are what he has respect to in the two preceding verses, when he speaks of "the trial of their faith," and of "their being in heaviness thro' manifold temptations."

4. See Vol. 1 of Ramsey, *Freedom of the Will,* pp. 118 ff.

Such trials are of threefold benefit to true religion: hereby the truth of it is manifested, and it appears to be indeed true religion: they, above all other things, have a tendency to distinguish between true religion and false, and to cause the difference between them evidently to appear. Hence they are called by the name of trials, in the verse next preceding the text, and in innumerable other places: they try the faith and religion of professors of what sort it is, as apparent gold is tried in the fire, and manifested, whether it be true gold or no. And the faith of true Christians being thus tried and proved to be true, "is found to praise, and honor, and glory"; as in that preceding verse.

Such trials are of threefold benefit to true Religion.

1. The truth of it is manifested by them. . . .
2. They serve to discover its *beauty* and amiableness . . .
3. They purify it from evil mixtures.

(c) *Worcester, 1808*

In these words, the apostle represents the state of the minds of the Christians he wrote to, under the persecutions they were then the subjects of. These persecutions are what he has respect to in the two preceding verses, when he speaks of *the trial of their faith,* and of *their being in heaviness through manifold temptations.*

Such trials are of threefold benefit to true religion. Hereby the truth of it is manifested, and it appears to be indeed true religion; they, above all other things, have a tendency to distinguish between true religion and false, and to cause the difference between them evidently to appear. Hence they are called by the name of *trials,* in the verse nextly preceding the text, and in innumerable other places; they try the faith and religion of professors, of what sort it is, as apparent gold is tried in the fire, and manifested, whether it be true gold or no. And the faith of true Christians

(d) *Dwight, 1829*

In these words, the apostle represents the state of the Christians to whom he wrote, under persecutions. To these persecutions he has respect, in the two preceding verses, when he speaks of *the trial of their faith,* and of *their being in heaviness* through manifold temptations.

Such trials are of threefold benefit to true religion. Hereby the *truth* of it is manifested, it appears to be indeed *true religion.* Trials, above all other things, have a tendency to distinguish true religion and false, and to cause the difference between them evidently to appear. Hence they are called by the name of *trials,* in the verse preceding the text, and innumerable other places.—They try the faith and religion of professors, of what sort it is, as apparent gold is tried in the fire, and manifested, whether it be true gold or not. And the faith of true Christians, being thus tried and

being thus tried and proved to be true, is "found to praise, and honor, and glory," as in that preceding verse.

proved to be true, is *found to praise, and honour, and glory.*

(e) *Loring, 1824*

The Christians to whom this epistle was addressed, were suffering from persecution; and in these words the Apostle represents the state of their minds under those painful circumstances. In the two verses immediately preceding, where he speaks of the trial of their faith, and their being in heaviness through manifold temptations, he has respect to these persecutions.

Such trials, though painful in themselves, are beneficial to religion. They are so in three respects:—Its TRUTH is thus manifested; its BEAUTY and AMIABLENESS are thus exhibited; and its PURITY and INCREASE are thus promoted.

(f) *American Tract Society, 1833*

The Apostle here describes the state of mind of the Christians he addressed, while they were suffering those persecutions and "manifold temptations" referred to in the preceding verses, as the "trial of their faith."

Such trials benefit religion. They try the faith of professors, and show whether it is genuine. They exhibit the *beauty, amiableness,* and *excellency* of true religion, which never appears so lovely as when it is most oppressed. They also tend to *purify* it from corrupt mixtures, establish and confirm it, and render it more lively and vigorous.

There were, to be sure, popular abridgments of the *Affections* made at various times and by various hands, including the London edition by Ellerby of 1817 which attempted to render Edwards' "language throughout more perspicuous and energetic" and to remove "the principal tautologies of the original." From such an edition [5] one does not expect much in the way of faithfulness to the

5. It is most unfortunate that the abridgment by Ellerby (London, 1817) was chosen by the American Tract Society for its publication of the *Affections* in popular form throughout the nineteenth century. The Tract Society publication, first issued in 1833, is actually a further abridgment of the Ellerby edition, although it was put forth with the claim that it had been emended on the basis of "a careful collation with the original work." That it is very different from the original is obvious from even the most cursory examination. The Tract Society edition was reprinted many times throughout the last century and its importance in tracing the history of the *Affections* stems from the fact that by 1875 some 75,000 copies of the text had been distributed. This means that most American readers who had read the work at all had probably read it in this

original, and perhaps even Wesley's edition can be excused along these lines, but one has a right to expect something better from the collected editions, especially since they did not claim to improve on Edwards' work. Worcester, though generally more reliable than Dwight, took as many liberties with the footnotes. For some unexplained reason almost everyone who had anything to do with the reprinting of the *Affections* fell into the same pattern of thinking; the work is very important as an evangelical tract; it ought to be read by everyone; it is too subtle for the average reader; it must be rewritten.

Particularly lamentable in the editorial practice of many previous editors has been the tampering with the notes and the quoted material they contain. In many editions they are omitted entirely and in others the notes are shortened, sometimes by the device of printing the beginning and end of the note while deleting material in the middle. Seventeen authors are quoted and more than thirty titles cited. Since most of these works are by seventeenth-century English Puritans—scarce books even then and guarded as treasures in every library—it is essential that Edwards' long quotations from them in his own footnotes be preserved without change. He was no doubt aware that the works he used would not be generally available to his readers; they are, if anything, even more difficult to obtain today. The present edition is the first in which these quotations have been located in the originals and the citations verified and corrected where necessary.

Apart from its appearance in the collected editions, the *Affections* has had a long history of reprinting as a separate volume.[6] It appeared frequently in America, England, and Scotland, and the long succession of editions and printings testifies to the continued popularity of the work; it has unquestionably been Edwards' most widely read book. The first edition of 1746 was the only one printed during his lifetime; it was followed by a second edition at Boston in 1768, with a New York printing of this edition appearing in the same year. The 1768 edition is a faithful reproduction of the original, with only minor editorial changes. In the meantime the first foreign edition was appearing at London in 1762 and with it the beginning

---

edition. Another and different abridgment of Ellerby's text appeared in 1821 at Boston, and again as "Loring's Second Edition" in 1824.

6. See Thomas H. Johnson, comp., *The Printed Writings of Jonathan Edwards, 1703–1758* (Princeton, Princeton University Press, 1940), pp. 33–43.

of the abridgments. This edition was shortened by William Gordon. Comparison with the first edition shows that Gordon reduced the size of the original by more than one-third, that he omitted many of the notes, and that he rewrote the text in hundreds of places. A hint of his purpose is furnished by a note attached to the first sign of gracious affections; after omitting Edwards' note on the preceding page, Gordon added a very long note of his own with the excuse that "our author under this first head is in some places too refined for common capacities" (p. 78 n.). The upshot is that the first foreign edition of the *Affections* was most unreliable. It was not until 1774 that a faithful text appeared in England.

In point of time, the next edition to appear was at Edinburgh in 1772. This is a faithful reproduction of the first edition. In view of the quality of the first London edition, it is clear that Edinburgh, 1772, represents the first accurate edition of the *Affections* abroad. Two years later, in 1774, the George Keith edition appeared at London, designated as the "Fourth Edition." This designation is correct if we ignore the Gordon abridgment and regard 1746, 1768, and the Edinburgh of 1772 as the three previous faithful texts. The George Keith edition is explicitly based upon the New York printing of the second edition, 1768, and is an accurate reproduction. Moreover, in using the American text as a basis, this edition bypasses London, 1762.

Of considerable interest theologically as well as textually is the edition of London, 1801, prepared by John Wesley. This, like the Gordon text, is an abridgment, but it represents an even more radical transformation of the original text. A comparison of Wesley's text with Gordon's points to the likelihood that Wesley worked from Gordon's edition rather than from the original. The probability that Wesley, working from an earlier edition and independently of Gordon, would have made so many of the same omissions and substitutions is certainly very small. And if we are correct in supposing that Wesley's abridgment was made from the first London edition, it becomes clear that his edition is even further removed from the original than any other edition, with the possible exception of Ellerby.

Fortunately, we do not have to guess at Wesley's aim in making the abridgment; he expressed it clearly in a signed note "To the Reader." Wesley's interpretation was that Edwards had subscribed in three earlier works to the view that the revival was a genuine work of the Spirit, but that by 1745 the evidences of backsliding were so great that in order for him to avoid what Wesley regarded as the damaging conclusion that "a true believer may 'make a shipwreck of the faith,'" he had to go on and prove that these believers were not genuine believers at all. In accordance with this interpretation, Wesley had to see in the *Affections* nothing but a heaping together of "so many curious, subtle, metaphysical distinctions as are sufficient to puzzle the brain" (p. 3), all for the purpose of avoiding a damaging conclusion. Despite this, Wesley followed what was by this time the standard practice of regarding the *Affections* as a good evangelical piece which should be read as soon as it was rewritten. Consequently, he aimed in his shortened version at a text that would enable the simple to be wise and in the process he hoped to separate the "wholesome food" from the "deadly poison." [7] Although the introductory note signed by Wesley is dated Sept. 1, 1773, there is evidence that the edition did not appear in his own lifetime.[8]

In addition to the above editions, a translation of the *Affections* into the Dutch language appeared at Utrecht in 1779, and a Welsh edition was issued in 1883. Many other editions and reprints were published throughout the nineteenth century, and these included volumes appearing in Boston, New York, Glasgow, Leeds, Dublin and Edinburgh.

Attention has already been called to the large amount of material quoted by Edwards from other writers in support of the position he adopted in the *Affections*. He quoted, for example, two entire pages from a discourse by John Smith, the Cambridge Platonist, and a total of more than two dozen pages from Thomas Shepard's *Parable of the Ten Virgins,* not to mention large extracts from the

7. This is no place to join the issue raised by Wesley, for, among other reasons, it is theologically very complex; but it seems clear that Wesley misunderstood the relation of the *Affections* to Edwards' previous writings on the revival. Whereas previously Edwards had treated the revival in what we may call its broad social aspect as part of the religious life of New England, in the *Affections* he attacked the underlying principle and raised the perennial problem of criteria for distinguishing genuine from false piety. There is nothing in the *Affections* which requires that Edwards modify his former view that the revival was a genuine work of the Spirit; on the contrary, he was prepared to assert that, on the basis of his own distinguishing signs, many genuine conversions had taken place. Moreover, there is no inconsistency involved in his concluding, upon the basis of the same signs, that many persons whom he had formerly regarded as sincere were not in fact genuinely converted.

8. See Johnson, *Printed Writings,* p. 37; No. 109.

writings of Stoddard, Flavel, and others. Edwards' practice in this regard has given rise to some editorial problems.

In a world of many books, excellent library facilities, and rapid communication we are able to maintain high standards in the use of published materials in our own writing. We expect that what appears between inverted commas will be an exact reproduction of an original and we demand accuracy in the citation of editions and page references. In the eighteenth century matters stood quite otherwise. Books, particularly those published abroad, were not readily available, and when a copy of some much sought-for work finally turned up it frequently happened that the book had to be passed on to others before accurate notes and references could be made. Consequently, it became necessary to rely upon memory and extracts copied somewhat hastily and stored up for use at a later time.

Very few of the direct quotations in the *Affections* are to be found in exactly the same form in the original editions, even though most changes are minor and do not materially affect the meaning involved. Edwards often paraphrased his source, and some of this paraphrased material appears within inverted commas along with direct quotation; the result is that the line between the two is difficult to draw. Edwards also made minor modifications, such as the changing of tenses or the dropping of an article or a pronoun, and he often strung together passages from different parts of a book, omitting material in between without use of ellipsis dots. What appears in some cases to be a sentence or paragraph from one page of a work is actually a construction from several pages, and it is identified by him in the citation only by the first page (or the last) from which the quotation is taken. The quotations in this edition are left as they appeared in the first edition, so that the interested student might be enabled to examine Edwards' own practice.

We must not suppose, however, that Edwards radically transformed his sources; it is rather that when he dipped into a work he invariably knew exactly what he wanted, and often he had to ignore some passages and stress others in order to achieve his purpose. He learned from others only insofar as he was willing to be taught, only insofar as he could see their contribution to the elaboration and defense of his own position.

An original source has been located for every quotation appearing in either the notes or text. Some have been located in the edition explicitly indicated by Edwards or, since in most cases no edition is given, in an edition published early enough for him to have used.

In identifying sources Edwards had a habit of presenting the reader with such vague indications as "ch. iv, towards the end" or "the last page but two." He was equally lax in specifying editions. Where it has been possible to ascertain the edition Edwards actually used, as it has been in the cases, for example, of Stoddard and Shepard, that edition has been cited. In cases where Edwards has either not indicated the edition (as when, for example, we are told no more than that a given passage is in Flavel's *Sacramental Meditations,* "Med. 4"), or where he has left us with insufficient information for determining it with accuracy, the first edition or other early edition published prior to 1746 has been cited. Thus in all cases an edition Edwards could have used has been cited. When an edition *other than* the first edition is cited, the date of the first edition of the work has been supplied in parenthesis. In the citation of Shepard's *Parable of the Ten Virgins,* for example, Edwards does not indicate the edition; his references, however, correlate in all cases with the London, 1695, edition, but not with the first edition, London, 1660. I have therefore cited the 1695 and noted the date of the first edition in parentheses.

As regards biblical quotations and citations, Edwards' own text has been reproduced without change except for obvious slips in the indication of chapters and verses. Thus, for example, if the first edition read "Isaiah 3:4" and the verse is in fact found at 3:6, the correction has been made silently (and similarly for chapter citations). Edwards used the King James version throughout, but his quotations often contain minor changes—for example, the dropping of "the" or "and" and the omission of parts of verses. No ellipses dots have been used for these minor omissions, but in cases where Edwards has strung together several verses, leaving out half a verse or more in the process, ellipses dots have been used.

Where reference is made in either the Introduction or the notes to other works of Edwards not published in the Yale Edition at the time of writing, the text of the Worcester edition (1808) has been followed.

6. *Acknowledgments*

I am pleased to take this opportunity to express my gratitude to those who so willingly gave their assistance to me in the preparation of this volume. I am especially grateful to Perry Miller for his incisive scrutiny and constructive criticism of the entire work. I have derived much from conversations with Paul Ramsey of Princeton University and I gratefully acknowledge his helpful suggestions. Richard Niebuhr of the Yale Divinity School was also kind enough to read the Introduction and I have profited from his commentary. Thomas Schafer of McCormick Theological Seminary, Chicago, not only contributed to my understanding of Edwards, but also kindly made available to me his transcriptions of hitherto unpublished manuscripts in Edwards' hand. To John Gerstner of the Pittsburgh-Xenia Theological Seminary I am indebted for many hours of conversation concerning ideas basic to Edwards' theology.

Alfred Stiernotte of Quinnipiac College painstakingly typed the text from the first printed edition and I am greatly indebted to him for his help in checking the text and for the location of some items cited in the notes. Marjorie Wynne, Librarian of the Rare Book Room at the Yale Library, has given of her time and knowledge without stint.

I wish also to thank Norman Pearson for helpful advice and Norman Donaldson of the Yale University Press for encouragement. To David Horne of the Yale Press I am especially grateful for valuable editorial assistance. Robert Tredwell kindly assisted in the checking of the text of the Gillespie correspondence against the original letters. Alburey Castell of the University of Oregon was kind enough to read the Introduction and I have greatly profited from his suggestions.

Above all, I am indebted to my wife for her patience and understanding in many readings and checking of the text and especially for her valuable suggestions on many points treated in the Introduction.

JOHN E. SMITH

New Haven
February 1959

AUTHOR'S PREFACE

THERE is no question whatsoever, that is of greater importance to mankind, and that it more concerns every individual person to be well resolved in, than this, what are the distinguishing qualifications of those that are in favor with God, and entitled to his eternal rewards? Or, which comes to the same thing, What is the nature of true religion? and wherein do lie the distinguishing notes of that virtue and holiness, that is acceptable in the sight of God. But though it be of such importance, and though we have clear and abundant light in the Word of God to direct us in this matter, yet there is no one point, wherein professing Christians do more differ one from another. It would be endless to reckon up the variety of opinions in this point, that divide the Christian world; making manifest the truth of that of our Saviour, "Strait is the gate, and narrow is the way, that leads to life, and few there be that find it."

The consideration of these things has long engaged me to attend to this matter, with the utmost diligence and care, and exactness of search and inquiry, that I have been capable of: it is a subject on which my mind has been peculiarly intent, ever since I first entered on the study of divinity. But as to the success of my inquiries, it must be left to the judgment of the reader of the following treatise.

I am sensible it is much more difficult to judge impartially of that which is the subject of this discourse, in the midst of the dust and smoke of such a state of controversy, as this land is now in, about things of this nature: as it is more difficult to write impartially, so it is more difficult to read impartially. Many will probably be hurt in their spirits, to find so much that appertains to religious affection, here condemned: and perhaps indignation and contempt will be excited in others, by finding so much here justified and approved. And it may be, some will be ready to charge me with inconsistence with myself, in so much approving some things, and so much condemning others; as I have found, this has always been objected to me by some, ever since the beginning of our late controversies about religion. 'Tis a hard thing to be a hearty zealous friend of what has been *good* and glorious, in the late extraordinary appearances, and to rejoice much in it; and at the same time, to see the evil and pernicious tendency of what has been *bad*, and earnestly to oppose that. But yet, I am humbly, but fully persuaded, we shall never be in the way of truth, nor go on in a way acceptable to God, and tending to the advancement of Christ's kingdom, till we do so. There is indeed something very mysterious in it, that so much good, and so much bad, should be mixed together in the church of God: as 'tis a mysterious thing, and what has puzzled and amazed many a good Christian, that there should be that which is so divine and precious, as the saving grace of God, and the new and divine nature, dwelling in the same heart, with so much corruption, hypocrisy and iniquity, in a particular saint. Yet neither of these, is more mysterious than real. And neither of 'em is a new or rare thing. 'Tis no new thing, that much false religion should prevail, at a time of great reviving of true religion; and that at such a time, multitudes of hypocrites should spring up among true saints. It was so in that great reformation, and revival of religion, that was in Josiah's time; as appears by Jer. 3:10 and 4:3–4 and also by the great apostasy that there was in the land, so soon after his reign. So it was in that great outpouring of the Spirit upon the Jews, that was in the days of John the Baptist; as appears by the great apostasy of that people, so soon after so general an awakening, and the temporary religious comforts and joys of many; "Ye were willing, for a season, to rejoice in his light" (John 5:35). So it was in those great commotions that were among the multitude, occasioned by the preaching of Jesus Christ: "Of the many that were then called, but few were chosen"; of the multitude that were roused and affected by his preaching, and at one time or other appeared mightily engaged, full of admiration of Christ, and elevated with joy, but few were true disciples, that stood the shock of the great trials that came afterwards, and endured to the end: many were like the stony ground, or thorny ground; and but few, comparatively, like the good ground: of the whole heap that was gathered, great part was chaff, that the wind afterwards drove away; and the heap of wheat that was left, was comparatively small; as appears abundantly, by the history of the New Testament. So it was in that great outpouring of the Spirit that was in the Apostle's days; as appears by Matt. 24:10–13, Gal. 3:1 and 4:11, 15; Philem. 2:21 and 3:18–19. And the two Epistles to the Corinthians, and many other parts of the New Testament. And so it was in the great Reformation from Popery. It appears plainly to have been in the visible church of God, in times of great reviving of religion, from time to time, as it is with the fruit trees in the spring; there are a multitude of blossoms; all of which appear fair and beautiful, and there is a promising appearance of young fruits; but many of 'em are but of short continuance, they soon fall off, and never come to maturity.

Not that it is to be supposed that it will always be so: for though there never will, in this world, be an entire purity; either in particular saints, in a perfect freedom from mixtures of corruption; or in the church of God, without any mixture of hypocrites with saints, and counterfeit religion, and false appearances of grace, with true religion and real holiness: yet, 'tis evident, that there will come a time of much greater purity in the church of God, than has been in ages past; it is plain by those texts of Scripture, Is. 52:1; Ezek. 44:6–7, 9; Joel 3:17; Zech. 14:21; Ps. 69:32, 35–36; Is. 35:8, 10; 4:3–4; Ezek. 20:38; Ps. 37:9–11, 29. And one great reason of it will be, that at that time, God will give much greater light to his people, to distinguish between true religion and its counterfeits; "And he shall sit as a refiner, and purifier of silver; and he shall purify the sons of Levi, and purge them as gold and silver; that they may offer to the Lord an offering in righteousness" (Mal. 3:3). With ver. 18, which is a continuation of the prophecy of the same happy times, "then shall ye return, and discern between the righteous and the wicked, between him that serveth God, and him that serveth him not."

'Tis by the mixture of counterfeit religion with true, not discerned and distinguished, that the devil has had his greatest advantage against the cause and kingdom of Christ, all along, hitherto. 'Tis plainly by this means, principally, that he has prevailed against all revivings of religion, that ever have been, since the first founding of the Christian church. By this, he hurt the cause of Christianity, in, and after the apostolic age, much more than by all the persecutions of both Jews and heathens: the apostles, in all their Epistles, show themselves much more concerned at the former mischief, than the latter. By this, Satan prevailed against the Reformation, begun by Luther, Zwingli, etc. to put a stop to its progress, and bring it into disgrace; ten times more, than by all those bloody, cruel, and before, unheard-of persecutions of the Church of Rome. By this principally, has he prevailed against revivals of religion, that have been in our nation since the Reformation. By this he prevailed against New England, to quench the love, and spoil the joy of her espousals, about an hundred years ago. And I think, I have had opportunity enough to see plainly, that by this, the devil has prevailed against the late, great revival of religion in New England, so happy and promising in its beginning: here most evidently has been the main advantage Satan has had against us; by this he has foiled us; 'tis by this means, that the daughter of Zion in this land, now lies on the ground, in such piteous circumstances, as we now behold her; with her garments rent, her face disfigured, her nakedness exposed, her limbs broken, and weltering in the blood of her own wounds, and in no wise able to arise; and this, so quickly after her late great joys and hopes: "Zion spreadeth forth her hands, and there is none to comfort her: the Lord hath commanded concerning Jacob, that his adversaries shall be round about him: Jerusalem is as a menstruous woman among them" (Lam. 1:17). I have seen the devil prevail the same way, against two great revivings of religion in this country. Satan goes on with mankind, as he began with them: he prevailed against our first parents, and cast 'em out of Paradise, and suddenly brought all their happiness and glory to an end, by appearing to be a friend to their happy paradisaic state, and pretending to advance it to higher degrees. So the same cunning serpent, that beguiled Eve through his subtlety, by perverting us from the simplicity that is in Christ, hath suddenly prevailed to deprive us of that fair prospect, we had a little while ago, of a kind of paradisaic state of the church of God in New England.

After religion has revived in the church of God, and enemies appear, people that are engaged to defend its cause, are commonly most exposed, where they are least sensible of danger. While they are wholly intent upon the opposition that appears openly before 'em, to make head against that, and do neglect carefully to look all round 'em, the devil comes behind 'em, and gives a fatal stab unseen; and has opportunity to give a more home stroke, and wound the deeper, because he strikes at his leisure, and according to his pleasure, being obstructed by no guard or resistance.

And so it is likely ever to be in the church, whenever religion revives remarkably, till we have learned well to distinguish between true and false religion, between saving affections and experiences, and those manifold fair shows, and glistering appearances, by which they are counterfeited; the consequences of which, when they are not distinguished, are often inexpressibly dreadful. By this means, the devil gratifies himself, by bringing it to pass, that that should be offered to God, by multitudes, under a notion of a pleasing acceptable service to him, that is indeed above all things abominable to him. By this means, he deceives great multitudes about the state of their souls; making them think they are something, when they are nothing; and so eternally undoes 'em: and not only so, but establishes many, in a strong confidence of their eminent holiness, who are in God's sight, some of the vilest of hypocrites. By this means, he many ways, damps and wounds religion in the hearts of the saints, obscures and deforms it by corrupt mixtures, causes their religious affections woefully to degenerate, and sometimes for a considerable time, to be like the manna, that bred worms and stank; and dreadfully ensnares and confounds the minds of others of the saints, and brings 'em into great difficulties and temptation, and entangles 'em in a wilderness, out of which they can by no means extricate themselves. By this means, Satan mightily encourages the hearts of open enemies of religion, and strengthens their hands, and fills them with weapons, and makes strong their fortresses; when at the same time, religion and the church of God lie exposed to 'em, as a city without walls. By this means, he brings it to pass, that men work wickedness under a notion of doing God service, and so sin without restraint, yea with earnest forwardness and zeal, and with all their might. By this means, he brings in, even the friends of religion, insensibly to themselves, to do the work of enemies, by destroying religion, in a far more effectual manner, than open enemies can do, under a notion of advancing it. By this means the devil scatters the flock of Christ, and sets 'em one against another, and that with great heat of spirit, under a notion of zeal for God; and religion by degrees, degenerates into vain jangling; and during the strife, Satan leads both parties far out of the right way, driving each to great extremes, one on the right hand, and the other on the left, according as he finds they are most inclined, or most easily moved and swayed, till the right path in the middle, is almost wholly neglected. And in the midst of this confusion, the devil has great opportunity to advance his own interest, and make it strong in ways innumerable, and get the government of all into his own hands, and work his own will. And by what is seen of the terrible consequences of this counterfeit religion, when not distinguished from true religion, God's people in general have their minds unhinged and unsettled, in things of religion, and know not where to set their foot, or what to think or do; and many are brought into doubts, whether there be anything at all in religion; and heresy, and infidelity, and atheism greatly prevail.

Therefore, it greatly concerns us to use our utmost endeavors clearly to discern, and have it well settled and established, wherein true religion does consist. Till this be done, it may be expected that great revivings of religion, will be but of short continuance: till this be done, there is but little good to be expected, of all our warm debates, in conversation and from the press, not knowing clearly and distinctly, what we ought to contend for.

My design is to contribute my mite, and use my best (however feeble) endeavors to this end, in the ensuing treatise: wherein it must be noted, that my design is somewhat diverse from the design of what I have formerly published, which was to show the distinguishing marks of a work of the Spirit of God, including both his common, and saving operations; but what I aim at now, is to show the nature and signs of the gracious operations of God's Spirit, by which they are to be distinguished from all things whatsoever that the minds of men are the subjects of, which are not of a saving nature. If I have succeeded in this my aim, in any tolerable measure, I hope it will tend to promote the interest of religion. And whether I have succeeded to bring any light to this subject, or no, and however my attempt may be reproached, in these captious, censorious times, I hope in the mercy of a gracious and righteous God, for the acceptance of the sincerity of my endeavors, and hope also, for the candor and prayers of the true followers of the meek and charitable Lamb of God.

PART ONE

Concerning the Nature of the Affections, and Their Importance in Religion

I PET. 1:8: *Whom having not seen, ye love: in whom, though now ye see him not, yet believing, ye rejoice with joy unspeakable, and full of glory.*

IN these words, the Apostle represents the state of the minds of the Christians he wrote to, under the persecutions they were then the subjects of. These persecutions are what he has respect to, in the two preceding verses, when he speaks of the trial of their faith, and of their being in heaviness through manifold temptations.

Such trials are of threefold benefit to true religion: hereby the truth of it is manifested, and it appears to be indeed true religion: they, above all other things, have a tendency to distinguish between true religion and false, and to cause the difference between them evidently to appear. Hence they are called by the name of trials, in the verse next preceding the text, and in innumerable other places: they try the faith and religion of professors of what sort it is, as apparent gold is tried in the fire, and manifested, whether it be true gold or no. And the faith of true Christians being thus tried and proved to be true, is found to praise, and honor, and glory; as in that preceding verse.

And then, these trials are of further benefit to true religion; they not only manifest the truth of it, but they make its genuine beauty and amiableness remarkably to appear. True virtue never appears so lovely, as when it is most oppressed: and the divine excellency of real Christianity, is never exhibited with such advantage, as when under the greatest trials: then it is that true faith appears much more precious than gold; and upon this account, is found to praise, and honor, and glory.

And again, another benefit that such trials are of to true religion, is, that they purify and increase it. They not only manifest it to be true, but also tend to refine it, and deliver it from those mixtures of that which is false, which encumber and impede it; that nothing may be left but that which is true. They tend to cause the amiableness of true religion to appear to the best advantage, as was before observed; and not only so, but they tend to increase its beauty, by establishing and confirming it, and making it more lively and vigorous, and purifying it from those things that obscured its luster and glory. As gold that is tried in the fire, is purged from its alloy and all remainders of dross, and comes forth more solid and beautiful; so true faith being tried as gold is tried in the fire, becomes more precious; and thus also is found unto praise, and honor, and glory. The Apostle seems to have respect to each of these benefits, that persecutions are of to true religion, in the verse preceding the text.

And in the text, the Apostle observes how true religion operated in the Christians he wrote to, under their persecutions, whereby these benefits of persecution appeared in them; or what manner of operation of *true* religion, in them, it was, whereby their religion, under persecution, was manifested to be true religion, and eminently appeared in the genuine beauty and amiableness of true religion, and also appeared to be increased and purified, and so was like to be found unto praise, and honor, and glory, at the appearing of Jesus Christ. And there were two kinds of operation, or exercise of true religion, in them, under their sufferings, that the Apostle takes notice of in the text, wherein these benefits appeared.

1. *Love to Christ;* "Whom having not seen, ye love." The world was ready to wonder, what strange principle it was, that influenced them to expose themselves to so great sufferings, to forsake the things that were seen, and renounce all that was dear and pleasant, which was the object of sense: they seemed to the men of the world about them, as though they were beside themselves, and to act as though they hated themselves; there was nothing in their view, that could induce them thus to suffer, and support them under, and carry them through such trials. But although there was nothing that was seen, nothing that the world saw, or that the Christians themselves ever saw with their bodily eyes, that thus influenced and supported 'em; yet they had a supernatural principle of love to something *unseen;* they loved Jesus Christ, for they saw him spiritually, whom the world saw not, and whom they themselves had never seen with bodily eyes.

2. *Joy in Christ.* Though their outward sufferings were very grievous, yet their inward spiritual joys were greater than their sufferings, and these supported them, and enabled them to suffer with cheerfulness.

There are two things which the Apostle takes notice of in the text concerning this joy. (1) The manner in which it rises, the way in which Christ, though unseen, is the foundation of it, viz. by faith; which is the evidence of things not seen; "In whom, though now ye see him not, yet believing, ye rejoice." (2) The nature of this joy; "unspeakable and full of glory." "Unspeakable" in the kind of it; very different from worldly joys, and carnal delights; of a vastly more pure, sublime and heavenly nature, being something supernatural, and truly divine, and so ineffably excellent; the sublimity, and exquisite sweetness of which, there were no words to set forth. Unspeakable also in degree; it pleasing God to give 'em this holy joy, with a liberal hand, and in large measure, in their state of persecution.

Their joy was "full of glory": although the joy was unspeakable, and no words were sufficient to describe it; yet something might be said of it, and no words more fit to represent its excellency, than these, that it was "full of glory"; or, as it is in the original, "glorified joy." In rejoicing with this joy, their minds were filled, as it were, with a glorious brightness, and their natures exalted and perfected: it was a most worthy, noble rejoicing, that did not corrupt and debase the mind, as many carnal joys do; but did greatly beautify and dignify it: it was a prelibation of the joy of heaven, that raised their minds to a degree of heavenly blessedness: it filled their minds with the light of God's glory, and made 'em themselves to shine with some communication of that glory.

Hence the proposition or doctrine, that I would raise from these words is this,

Doct. True religion, in great part, consists in holy affections.

We see that the Apostle, in observing and remarking the operations and exercises of religion, in the Christians he wrote to, wherein their religion appeared to be true and of the right kind, when it had its greatest trial of what sort it was, being tried by persecution as gold is tried in the fire, and when their religion not only proved true, but was most pure, and cleansed from its dross and mixtures of that which was not true, and when religion appeared in them most in its genuine excellency and native beauty, and was found to praise, and honor, and glory; he singles out the religious affections of love and joy, that were then in exercise in them: these are the exercises of religion he takes notice of, wherein their religion did thus appear true and pure, and in its proper glory.

Here I would, I. Show what is intended by the affections, II. Observe some things which make it evident, that a great part of true religion lies in the affections.

I. It may be inquired, what the affections of the mind are?

I answer, the affections are no other, than the more vigorous and sensible exercises of the inclination and will of the soul.

God has indued the soul with two faculties: one is that by which it is capable of perception and speculation, or by which it discerns and views and judges of things; which is called the understanding. The other faculty is that by which the soul does not merely perceive and view things, but is some way inclined with respect to the things it views or considers; either is inclined to 'em, or is disinclined, and averse from 'em; or is the faculty by which the soul does not behold things, as an indifferent unaffected spectator, but either as liking or disliking, pleased or displeased, approving or rejecting. This faculty is called by various names: it is sometimes called the *inclination:* and, as it has respect to the actions that are determined and governed by it, is called the *will:* and the *mind,* with regard to the exercises of this faculty, is often called the *heart.*

The exercises of this faculty are of two sorts; either those by which the soul is carried out towards the things that are in view, in approving of them, being pleased with them, and inclined to them; or those in which the soul opposes the things that are in view, in disapproving them, and in being displeased with them, averse from them, and rejecting them.

And as the exercises of the inclination and will of the soul are various in their kinds, so they are much more various in their degrees. There are some exercises of pleasedness or displeasedness, inclination or disinclination, wherein the soul is carried but a little beyond a state of perfect indifference. And there are other degrees above this, wherein the approbation or dislike, pleasedness or aversion, are stronger; wherein we may rise higher and higher, till the soul comes to act vigorously and sensibly, and the actings of the soul are with that strength that (through the laws of the union which the Creator has fixed between soul and body) the motion of the blood and animal spirits begins to be sensibly altered; whence oftentimes arises some bodily sensation, especially about the heart and vitals, that are the fountain of the fluids of the body: from whence it comes to pass, that the mind, with regard to the exercises of this faculty, perhaps in all nations and ages, is called the *heart.* And it is to be noted, that they are these more vigorous and sensible exercises of this faculty, that are called the *affections.*

The will, and the affections of the soul, are not two faculties; the affections are not essentially distinct from the will, nor do they differ from the mere actings of the will and inclination of the soul, but only in the liveliness and sensibleness of exercise.

It must be confessed, that language is here somewhat imperfect, and the meaning of words in a considerable measure loose and unfixed, and not precisely limited by custom, which governs the use of language. In some sense, the affection of the soul differs nothing at all from the will and inclination, and the will never is in any exercise any further than it is affected; it is not moved out of a state of perfect indifference, any otherwise than as it is affected one way or other, and acts nothing voluntarily [1] any further. But yet there are many actings of the will and inclination, that are not so commonly called affections: in everything we do, wherein we act voluntarily, there is an exercise of the will and inclination, 'tis our inclination that governs us in our actions: but all the actings of the inclination and will, in our common actions of life, are not ordinarily called affections. Yet, what are commonly called affections are not essentially different from them, but only in the degree and manner of exercise. In every act of the will whatsoever, the soul either likes or dislikes, is either inclined or disinclined to what is in view: these are not essentially different from those affections of love and hatred: that liking or inclination of the soul to a thing, if it be in a high degree, and be vigorous and lively, is the very same thing with the affection of love: and that disliking and disinclining, if in a great degree, is the very same with hatred. In every act of the will for, or towards something not present, the soul is in some degree inclined to that thing; and that inclination, if in a considerable degree, is the very same with the affection of desire. And in every degree of the act of the will, wherein the soul approves of something present, there is a degree of pleasedness; and that pleasedness, if it be in a considerable degree, is the very same with the affection of joy or delight. And if the will disapproves of what is present, the soul is in some degree displeased, and if that displeasedness be great, 'tis the very same with the affection of grief or sorrow.

1. "Voluntarily": JE indicated in the *Errata* to the first edition that this word should be deleted.

Such seems to be our nature, and such the laws of the union of soul and body, that there never is any case whatsoever, any lively and vigorous exercise of the will or inclination of the soul, without some effect upon the body, in some alteration of the motion of its fluids, and especially of the animal spirits. And on the other hand, from the same laws of the union of soul and body, the constitution of the body, and the motion of its fluids, may promote the exercise of the affections. But yet, it is not the body, but the mind only, that is the proper seat of the affections. The body of man is no more capable of being really the subject of love or hatred, joy or sorrow, fear or hope, than the body of a tree, or than the same body of man is capable of thinking and understanding. As 'tis the soul only that has ideas, so 'tis the soul only that is pleased or displeased with its ideas. As 'tis the soul only that thinks, so 'tis the soul only that loves or hates, rejoices or is grieved at what it thinks of. Nor are these motions of the animal spirits, and fluids of the body, anything properly belonging to the nature of the affections; though they always accompany them, in the present state; but are only effects or concomitants of the affections, that are entirely distinct from the affections themselves, and no way essential to them; so that an unbodied spirit may be as capable of love and hatred, joy or sorrow, hope or fear, or other affections, as one that is united to a body.

The *affections* and *passions* are frequently spoken of as the same; and yet, in the more common use of speech, there is in some respect a difference; and affection is a word, that in its ordinary signification, seems to be something more extensive than passion; being used for all vigorous lively actings of the will or inclination; but passion for those that are more sudden, and whose effects on the animal spirits are more violent, and the mind more overpowered, and less in its own command.

As all the exercises of the inclination and will, are either in approving and liking, or disapproving and rejecting; so the affections are of two sorts; they are those by which the soul is carried out to what is in view, cleaving to it, or seeking it; or those by which it is averse from it, and opposes it.

Of the former sort are love, desire, hope, joy, gratitude, complacence. Of the latter kind, are hatred, fear, anger, grief, and such like; which it is needless now to stand particularly to define.

And there are some affections wherein there is a composition of each of the aforementioned kinds of actings of the will; as in the affection of pity, there is something of the former kind, towards the person suffering, and something of the latter, towards what he suffers. And so in zeal, there is in it high approbation of some person or thing, together with vigorous opposition to what is conceived to be contrary to it.

There are other mixed affections that might be also mentioned, but I hasten to the

II. Second thing proposed, which was to observe some things that render it evident, that true religion, in great part, consists in the affections. And here,

1. What has been said of the nature of the affections, makes this evident, and may be sufficient, without adding anything further, to put this matter out of doubt: for who will deny that true religion consists, in a great measure, in vigorous and lively actings of the inclination and will of the soul, or the fervent exercises of the heart.

That religion which God requires, and will accept, does not consist in weak, dull and lifeless wouldings,[2] raising us but a little above a state of indifference: God, in his Word, greatly insists upon it, that we be in good earnest, fervent in spirit, and our hearts vigorously engaged in religion: "Be ye fervent in spirit, serving the Lord" (Rom. 12:11). "And now Israel, what doth the Lord thy God require of thee, but to fear the Lord thy God, to walk in all his ways, and to love him, and to serve the Lord thy God, with all thy heart, and with all thy soul?" (Deut. 10:12). And ch. 6:4–5: "Hear, O Israel; the Lord our God is one Lord; and thou shalt love the Lord thy God, with all thy heart, and with all thy soul, and with all thy might." 'Tis such a fervent, vigorous engagedness of the heart in religion, that is the fruit of a real circumcision of the heart, or true regeneration, and that has the promises of life; "And the Lord thy God will circumcise thine heart, and the heart of thy seed, to love the Lord thy God, with all thy heart, and with all thy soul, that thou mayest live" (Deut. 30:6).

If we ben't in good earnest in religion, and our wills and inclinations be not strongly exercised, we are nothing. The things of religion are so great, that there can be no suitableness in the exercises

2. "Wouldings": JE coined this word to refer to very weak inclinations which do not represent genuine convictions and do not issue in action; it is as if a man were always to say that he "would" believe or perform but never actually does. Cf. below, p. 448.

of our hearts, to their nature and importance, unless they be lively and powerful. In nothing, is vigor in the actings of our inclinations so requisite, as in religion; and in nothing is lukewarmness so odious. True religion is evermore a powerful thing; and the power of it appears, in the first place, in the inward exercises of it in the heart, where is the principal and original seat of it. Hence true religion is called the power of godliness, in distinction from the external appearances of it, that are the form of it, "Having a form of godliness, but denying the power of it" (II Tim. 3:5). The Spirit of God in those that have sound and solid religion, is a spirit of powerful holy affection; and therefore, God is said to have given them the spirit of power, and of love, and of a sound mind (II Tim. 1:7). And such, when they received the Spirit of God, in his sanctifying and saving influences, are said to be baptized with the Holy Ghost, and with fire; by reason of the power and fervor of those exercises the Spirit of God excites in their hearts, whereby their hearts, when grace is in exercise, may be said to burn within them; as is said of the disciples (Luke 24:32).

The business of religion is, from time to time, compared to those exercises, wherein men are wont to have their hearts and strength greatly exercised and engaged; such as running, wrestling or agonizing for a great prize or crown, and fighting with strong enemies that seek our lives, and warring as those that by violence take a city or kingdom.

And though true grace has various degrees, and there are some that are but babes in Christ, in whom the exercise of the inclination and will towards divine and heavenly things, is comparatively weak; yet everyone that has the power of godliness in his heart, has his inclinations and heart exercised towards God and divine things, with such strength and vigor, that these holy exercises do prevail in him above all carnal or natural affections, and are effectual to overcome them: for every true disciple of Christ, loves him above father or mother, wife and children, brethren and sisters, houses and lands; yea, than his own life. From hence it follows, that wherever true religion is, there are vigorous exercises of the inclination and will, towards divine objects: but by what was said before, the vigorous, lively and sensible exercises of the will, are no other than the affections of the soul.

2. The Author of the human nature has not only given affections to men, but has made 'em very much the spring of men's actions. As

the affections do not only necessarily belong to the human nature, but are a very great part of it; so (inasmuch as by regeneration, persons are renewed in the whole man, and sanctified throughout) holy affections do not only necessarily belong to true religion, but are a very great part of that. And as true religion is of a practical nature, and God has so constituted the human nature, that the affections are very much the spring of men's actions, this also shows, that true religion must consist very much in the affections.

Such is man's nature, that he is very inactive, any otherwise than he is influenced by some affection, either love or hatred, desire, hope, fear or some other. These affections we see to be the springs that set men agoing, in all the affairs of life, and engage them in all their pursuits: these are the things that put men forward, and carry 'em along, in all their worldly business; and especially are men excited and animated by these, in all affairs, wherein they are earnestly engaged, and which they pursue with vigor. We see the world of mankind to be exceedingly busy and active; and the affections of men are the springs of the motion: take away all love and hatred, all hope and fear, all anger, zeal and affectionate desire, and the world would be, in a great measure, motionless and dead; there would be no such thing as activity amongst mankind, or any earnest pursuit whatsoever. 'Tis affection that engages the covetous man, and him that is greedy of worldly profits, in his pursuits; and it is by the affections, that the ambitious man is put forward in his pursuit of worldly glory; and 'tis the affections also that actuate the voluptuous man, in his pursuit of pleasure and sensual delights: the world continues, from age to age, in a continual commotion and agitation, in a pursuit of these things; but take away all affection, and the spring of all this motion would be gone, and the motion itself would cease. And as in worldly things, worldly affections are very much the spring of men's motion and action; so in religious matters, the spring of their actions are very much religious affections: he that has doctrinal knowledge and speculation only, without affection, never is engaged in the business of religion.

3. Nothing is more manifest in fact, than that the things of religion take hold of men's souls, no further than they affect them. There are multitudes that often hear the Word of God, and therein hear of those things that are infinitely great and important, and that most nearly concern them, and all that is heard seems to be wholly ineffectual upon them, and to make no alteration in their disposi-

tion or behavior; and the reason is, they are not affected with what they hear. There are many that often hear of the glorious perfections of God, his almighty power, and boundless wisdom, his infinite majesty, and that holiness of God, by which he is of purer eyes than to behold evil, and cannot look on iniquity, and the heavens are not pure in his sight, and of God's infinite goodness and mercy, and hear of the great works of God's wisdom, power and Goodness, wherein there appear the admirable manifestations of these perfections; they hear particularly of the unspeakable love of God and Christ, and of the great things that Christ has done and suffered, and of the great things of another world, of eternal misery, in bearing the fierceness and wrath of almighty God, and of endless blessedness and glory in the presence of God, and the enjoyment of his dear love; they also hear the peremptory commands of God, and his gracious counsels and warnings, and the sweet invitation of the gospel; I say, they often hear these things, and yet remain as they were before, with no sensible alteration on them, either in heart or practice, because they are not affected with what they hear; and ever will be so till they are affected. I am bold to assert, that there never was any considerable change wrought in the mind or conversation of any one person, by anything of a religious nature, that ever he read, heard or saw, that had not his affections moved. Never was a natural man engaged earnestly to seek his salvation: never were any such brought to cry after wisdom, and lift up their voice for understanding, and to wrestle with God in prayer for mercy; and never was one humbled, and brought to the foot of God, from anything that ever he heard or imagined of his own unworthiness and deservings of God's displeasure; nor was ever one induced to fly for refuge unto Christ, while his heart remained unaffected. Nor was there ever a saint awakened out of a cold, lifeless frame, or recovered from a declining state in religion, and brought back from a lamentable departure from God, without having his heart affected. And in a word, there never was anything considerable brought to pass in the heart or life of any man living, by the things of religion, that had not his heart deeply affected by those things.

4. The Holy Scriptures do everywhere place religion very much in the affections; such as fear, hope, love, hatred, desire, joy, sorrow, gratitude, compassion and zeal.

The Scriptures place much of religion in godly fear; insomuch that 'tis often spoken of as the character of those that are truly religious persons, that they tremble at God's Word, that they fear before him, that their flesh trembles for fear of him, and that they are afraid of his judgments, that his excellency makes them afraid, and his dread falls upon them; and the like: and a compellation commonly given the saints in Scripture, is, fearers of God, or they that fear the Lord. And because the fear of God is a great part of true godliness, hence true godliness in general, is very commonly called by the name of the fear of God; as everyone knows, that knows anything of the Bible.

So hope in God and in the promises of his Word, is often spoken of in the Scripture, as a very considerable part of true religion. 'Tis mentioned as one of the three great things of which religion consists (I Cor. 13:13). Hope in the Lord is also frequently mentioned as the character of the saints: "Happy is he that hath the God of Jacob for his help, whose hope is in the Lord his God" (Ps. 146:5). "Blessed is the man that trusteth in the Lord, whose hope the Lord is" (Jer. 17:7). "Be of good courage, and he shall strengthen your heart, all ye that hope in the Lord" (Ps. 31:24). And the like in many other places. Religious fear and hope are, once and again, joined together, as jointly constituting the character of the true saints. "Behold the eye of the Lord is upon them that fear him, upon them that hope in his mercy" (Ps. 33:18). "The Lord taketh pleasure in them that fear him, in those that hope in his mercy" (Ps. 147:11). Hope is so great a part of true religion, that the Apostle says we are saved by hope (Rom. 8:24). And this is spoken of as the helmet of the Christian soldier, "and for an helmet, the hope of salvation" (I Thess. 5:8); and the sure and steadfast anchor of the soul, which preserves it from being cast away by the storms of this evil world, "which hope we have, as an anchor of the soul, both sure and steadfast, and which entereth into that within the veil" (Heb. 6:19) 'Tis spoken of as a great fruit and benefit which true saints receive by Christ's resurrection "Blessed be the God and Father of our Lord Jesus Christ, which according to his abundant mercy, hath begotten us again unto a lively hope, by the resurrection of Jesus Christ from the dead" (I Pet. 1:3).

The Scriptures place religion very much in the affection of love, in love to God, and the Lord Jesus Christ, and love to the people of God, and to mankind. The texts in which this is manifest, both in the Old Testament, and New, are innumerable. But of this more afterwards.

The contrary affection of hatred also, as having sin for its object, is spoken of in Scripture, as no inconsiderable part of true religion. It is spoken of as that by which true religion may be known and distinguished, Prov. 8:13: "The fear of the Lord is to hate evil." And accordingly the saints are called upon to give evidence of their sincerity by this, "Ye that fear the Lord hate evil" (Ps. 97:10). And the Psalmist often mentions it as an evidence of his sincerity; "I will walk within my house with a perfect heart; I will set no wicked thing before mine eyes: I hate the work of them that turn aside" (Ps. 101:2–3). "I hate every false way" (Ps. 119:104). So ver. 128. Again Ps. 139:21: "Do I not hate them, O Lord, that hate thee?"

So holy desire, exercised in longings, hungerings and thirstings after God and holiness, is often mentioned in Scripture as an important part of true religion; "The desire of our soul is to thy name, and to the remembrance of thee" (Is. 26:8). "One thing have I desired of the Lord, and that will I seek after; that I may dwell in the house of the Lord, all the days of my life, to behold the beauty of the Lord, and to enquire in his temple" (Ps. 27:4). "As the heart panteth after the water-brooks, so panteth my soul after thee, O God; my soul thirsteth for God, for the living God: when shall I come and appear before God?" (Ps. 42:1–2). "My soul thirsteth for thee; my flesh longeth for thee, in a dry and thirsty land, where no water is, to see thy power and thy glory, so as I have seen thee in the sanctuary" (Ps. 63:1–2). "How amiable are thy tabernacles, O Lord of hosts! My soul longeth, yea, even fainteth, for the courts of the Lord; my heart and my flesh crieth out for the living God" (Ps. 84:1–2). "My soul breaketh for the longing it hath unto thy judgments, at all times" (Ps. 119:20). So Ps. 73:25 and 143:6–7 and 130:6, Cant. 3:1–2 and 6:8. Such a holy desire and thirst of soul is mentioned, as one of those great things which renders or denotes a man truly blessed, in the beginning of Christ's Sermon on the Mount, "Blessed are they that do hunger and thirst after righteousness, for they shall be filled" (Matt. 5:6). And this holy thirst is spoken of, as a great thing in the condition of a participation of the blessings of eternal life, "I will give unto him that is athirst, of the fountain of the water of life freely" (Rev. 21:6).

The Scriptures speak of holy *joy*, as a great part of true religion. So it is represented in the text. And as an important part of religion, it is often exhorted to, and pressed, with great earnestness; "Delight thyself in the Lord, and he shall give thee the desires of thine heart"

(Ps. 37:4). "Rejoice in the Lord, ye righteous" (Ps. 97:12). So Ps. 33:1: "Rejoice in the Lord, O ye righteous." "Rejoice, and be exceeding glad" (Matt. 5:12). "Finally brethren, rejoice in the Lord" (Phil. 3:1). And ch. 4:4: "Rejoice in the Lord alway, and again I say rejoice." "Rejoice evermore" (I Thess. 5:16). "Let Israel rejoice in him that made him; let the children of Zion be joyful in their King" (Ps. 149:2). This is mentioned among the principal fruits of the spirit of grace, "The fruit of the spirit is love, joy," etc. (Gal. 5:22). The Psalmist mentions his holy joy, as an evidence of his sincerity, "I have rejoiced in the way of thy testimonies, as much as in all riches" (Ps. 119:14).

Religious *sorrow, mourning,* and *brokenness of heart,* are also frequently spoken of as a great part of true religion. These things are often mentioned as distinguishing qualities of the true saints, and a great part of their character; "Blessed are they that mourn; for they shall be comforted" (Matt. 5:4). "The Lord is nigh unto them that are of a broken heart, and saveth such as be of a contrite spirit" (Ps. 34:18). "The Lord hath anointed me . . . to bind up the broken-hearted, . . . to comfort all that mourn" (Is. 61:1–2). This godly sorrow, and brokenness of heart is often spoken of, not only, as a great thing in the distinguishing character of the saints, but that in them, which is peculiarly acceptable and pleasing to God; "The sacrifices of God are a broken spirit; a broken and a contrite heart, O God, thou wilt not despise" (Ps. 51:17). "Thus saith the high and lofty One that inhabiteth Eternity, whose name is Holy: I dwell in the high and holy place, with him also that is of a humble and contrite spirit, to revive the spirit of the humble, and to revive the heart of the contrite ones" (Is. 57:15). "To this man will I look, even to him that is poor, and of a contrite spirit" (ch. 66:2).

Another affection often mentioned, as that in the exercise of which much of true religion appears, is *gratitude;* especially as exercised in thankfulness and praise to God. This being so much spoken of in the Book of Psalms and other parts of the Holy Scriptures, I need not mention particular texts.

Again, the Holy Scriptures do frequently speak of *compassion* or *mercy,* as a very great and essential thing in true religion; insomuch that good men are in Scripture denominated from hence; and a merciful man, and a good man, are equivalent terms in Scripture; "The righteous perisheth, and no man layeth it to heart; and merciful men are taken away" (Is. 57:1). And the Scripture chooses out this quality, as that by which, in a peculiar manner, a righteous man is deciphered; "The righteous showeth mercy, and giveth" (Ps. 37:21); and ver. 26: "He is ever merciful, and lendeth." And Prov. 14:31: "He that honoureth the Lord, hath mercy on the poor." And Col. 3:12: "Put ye on, as the elect of God, holy and beloved, bowels of mercies," etc. This is one of those great things, by which those who are truly blessed are described by our Saviour, "Blessed are the merciful, for they shall obtain mercy" (Matt. 5:7). And this Christ also speaks of, as one of the weightier matters of the law, "Woe unto you, scribes and Pharisees, hypocrites; for ye pay tithe of mint, and anise, and cummin, and have omitted the weightier matters of the law, judgment, mercy, and faith" (Matt. 23:23). To the like purpose is that, "He hath showed thee, O man, what is good: and what doth the Lord require of thee, but to do justice, and love mercy, and walk humbly with thy God?" (Mic. 6:8). And also that, "For I desired mercy, and not sacrifice" (Hos. 6:6). Which seems to have been a text much delighted in by our Saviour, by his manner of citing it once and again (Matt. 9:13 and 12:7).

Zeal is also spoken of, as a very essential part of the religion of true saints. 'Tis spoken of as a great thing Christ had in view, in giving himself for our redemption; "Who gave himself for us, that he might redeem us from all iniquity, and purify unto himself a peculiar people, zealous of good works" (Titus 2:14). And is spoken of, as the great thing wanting in the lukewarm Laodiceans (Rev. 3:15–16, 19).

I have mentioned but a few texts, out of an innumerable multitude, all over the Scripture, which place religion very much in the affections. But what has been observed, may be sufficient to show that they who would deny that much of true religion lies in the affections, and maintain the contrary, must throw away what we have been wont to own for our Bible, and get some other rule, by which to judge of the nature of religion.

5. The Scriptures do represent true religion, as being summarily comprehended in *love,* the chief of the affections, and fountain of all other affections.

So our blessed Saviour represents the matter, in answer to the lawyer, who asked him, which was the great commandment of the law. "Jesus said unto him, Thou shalt love the Lord thy God, with all thy heart, and with all thy soul, and with all thy mind: this is the first, and great commandment; and the second is like unto it, Thou shalt love thy neighbour as thyself. On these two commandments hang all the law and the prophets" (Matt. 22:37–40). Which last words signify as much, as that these two commandments comprehend all the duty prescribed, and the religion taught in the law and the prophets. And the apostle Paul does from time to time make the same representation of the matter; as in Rom. 13:8: "He that loveth another, hath fulfilled the law." And ver. 10: "Love is the fulfilling of the law." And Gal. 5:14: "For all the law is fulfilled in one word, even in this, thou shalt love thy neighbor as thyself." So likewise in I Tim. 1:5: "Now the end of the commandment is charity, out of a pure heart," etc. So the same Apostle speaks of love, as the greatest thing in religion, and as the vitals, essence and soul of it; without which, the greatest knowledge and gifts, and the most glaring profession, and everything else which appertains to religion, are vain and worthless; and represents it as the fountain from whence proceeds all that is good, in I Cor. 13 throughout; for that which is there rendered "charity" in the original is αγάπη, the proper English of which is "love."

Now although it be true, that the love thus spoken of, includes the whole of a sincerely benevolent propensity of the soul, towards God and man; yet it may be considered, that it is evident from what has been before observed, that this propensity or inclination of the soul, when in sensible and vigorous exercise, becomes *affection,* and is no other than affectionate love. And surely it is such vigorous and fervent love which Christ speaks of, as the sum of all religion, when he speaks of loving God with all our hearts, with all our souls, and with all our minds, and our neighbor as ourselves, as the sum of all that was taught and prescribed in the law and the prophets.

Indeed it cannot be supposed, when this affection of love is here, and in other Scriptures, spoken of as the sum of all religion, that hereby is meant the act, exclusive of the habit, or that the exercise of the understanding is excluded, which is implied in all reasonable affection. But it is doubtless true, and evident from these Scriptures, that the essence of all true religion lies in holy love; and that in this divine affection, and an habitual disposition to it, and that light which is the foundation of it, and those things which are the fruits of it, consists the whole of religion.

From hence it clearly and certainly appears, that great part of true religion consists in the affections. For love is not only one of the affections, but it is the first and chief of the affections, and the fountain of all the affections. From love arises hatred of those things which are contrary to what we love, or which oppose and thwart us in those things that we delight in: and from the various exercises of love and hatred, according to the circumstances of the objects of these affections, as present or absent, certain or uncertain, probable or improbable, arise all those other affections of desire, hope, fear, joy, grief, gratitude, anger, etc. From a vigorous, affectionate, and fervent love to God, will necessarily arise other religious affections: hence will arise an intense hatred and abhorrence of sin, fear of sin, and a dread of God's displeasure, gratitude to God for his goodness, complacence and joy in God when God is graciously and sensibly present, and grief when he is absent, and a joyful hope when a future enjoyment of God is expected, and fervent zeal for the glory of God. And in like manner, from a fervent love to men, will arise all other virtuous affections towards men.

6. The religion of the most eminent saints we have an account of in the Scripture, consisted much in holy affections.

I shall take particular notice of three eminent saints, which have expressed the frame and sentiments of their own hearts, and so described their own religion, and the manner of their intercourse with God, in the writings which they have left us, that are a part of the sacred canon.

The first instance I shall take notice of, is David, that man after God's own heart; who has given us a lively portraiture of his religion, in the Book of Psalms. Those holy songs of his, he has there left us, are nothing else but the expressions and breathings of devout and holy affections; such as an humble and fervent love to God, admiration of his glorious perfections and wonderful works, earnest desires, thirstings and pantings of soul after God, delight and joy in God, a sweet and melting gratitude to God for his great goodness, an holy exultation and triumph of soul in the favor, sufficiency and faithfulness of God, his love to, and delight in the saints, the excellent of the earth, his great delight in the Word and ordinances of God, his grief for his own and others' sins, and his fervent zeal for God, and against the enemies of God and his church. And these expressions of holy affection, which the Psalms of David are everywhere full of, are the more to our present purpose, because those Psalms are not only the expressions of the religion of so eminent a saint, that God speaks of as so agreeable to his mind; but were also, by the direction of the Holy Ghost, penned for the use of the church of God in its public worship, not only in that age, but in after ages; as being fitted to express the religion of all saints, in all ages, as well as the religion of the Psalmist. And it is moreover to be observed, that David, in the Book of Psalms, speaks not as a private person, but as the psalmist of Israel, as the subordinate head of the church of God, and leader in their worship and praises; and in many of the Psalms, speaks in the name of Christ, as personating him in these breathings forth of holy affection, and in many other Psalms, he speaks in the name of the church.

Another instance I shall observe, is the apostle Paul; who was, in many respects, the chief of all the ministers of the New Testament; being above all others, a chosen vessel unto Christ, to bear his name before the Gentiles, and made the chief instrument of propagating and establishing the Christian church in the world, and of distinctly revealing the glorious mysteries of the gospel, for the instruction of the church in all ages; and (as has not been improbably thought by some) the most eminent servant of Christ, that ever lived, received to the highest rewards in the heavenly kingdom of his Master. By what is said of him in the Scripture, he appears to have been a person that was full of affection. And 'tis very manifest, that the religion he expresses in his Epistles, consisted very much in holy affections. It appears by all his expressions of himself, that he was, in the course of his life, inflamed, actuated and entirely swallowed up, by a most ardent love to his glorious Lord, esteeming all things as loss, for the excellency of the knowledge of him, and esteeming them but dung that he might win him. He represents himself, as overpowered by this holy affection, and as it were compelled by it to go forward in his service, through all difficulties and sufferings (II Cor. 5:14–15). And his Epistles are full of expressions of an overflowing affection towards the people of Christ: he speaks of his dear love to them (II Cor. 12:19; Phil. 4:1; II Tim. 1:2). Of his abundant love (II Cor. 2:4). And of his affectionate and tender love, as of a nurse towards her children, "But we were gentle among you; even as a nurse cherisheth her children; so being affectionately desirous of you, we were willing to have imparted unto you, not the gospel of God only, but also our own souls, because ye were dear unto us" (I Thess. 2:7–8). So also he speaks of his bowels of love (Phil. 1:8; Philem. ver. 12 and 20). So he speaks of his earnest care for others (II Cor. 8:16), and of his bowels of pity or mercy towards them (Phil. 2:1), and of his concern for others, even to anguish of heart, "For out of much affliction, and anguish of heart, I wrote unto you, with many tears; not that ye should be grieved; but that ye might know the love which I have more abundantly unto you" (II Cor. 2:4). He speaks of the great conflict of his soul for them (Col. 2:1). He speaks of great and continual grief that he had in his heart from compassion to the Jews (Rom. 9:2). He speaks of his mouth's being opened, and his heart enlarged towards Christians, "O ye Corinthians, our mouth is open unto you, our heart is enlarged"! (II Cor. 6:11). He often speaks of his affectionate and longing desires (I Thess. 2:8; Rom. 1:11; Phil. 1:8 and ch. 4:1; II Tim. 1:4). The same Apostle is very often, in his Epistles, expressing the affection of joy (II Cor. 1:12 and ch. 7:7 and ver. 9 and 16; Phil. 1:4, and ch. 2:1–2, and ch. 3:3; Col. 1:24; I Thess. 3:9). He speaks of his rejoicing with great joy (Phil. 4:10; Philem. 1:7), of his joying and rejoicing (Phil. 2:1, 7), and of his rejoicing exceedingly (II Cor. 7:13). And of his being filled with comfort, and being exceeding joyful (II Cor. 7:4). He speaks of himself as always rejoicing (II Cor. 6:10). So he speaks of the triumphs of his soul (II Cor. 2:14). And of his glorying in tribulation (II Thess. 1:4, and Rom. 5:3). He also expresses the affection of hope; in Phil. 1:20, he speaks of his earnest expectation, and his hope. He likewise expresses an affection of godly jealousy (II Cor. 11:2–3). And it appears by his whole history, after his conversion, in the Acts, and also by all his Epistles, and the accounts he gives of himself there, that the affection of zeal, as having the cause of his Master, and the interest and prosperity of his church, for its object, was mighty in him, continually inflaming his heart, strongly engaging to those great and constant labors he went through, in instructing, exhorting, warning and reproving others, travailing in birth with them; conflicting with those powerful and innumerable enemies who continually opposed him, wrestling with principalities and powers, not fighting as one who beats the air, running the race set before him, continually pressing forward through all manner of difficulties and sufferings; so that others thought him quite beside himself. And how full he was of affection, does further appear by his being so full of tears: in II Cor. 2:4 he speaks of his many tears, and so Acts 20:19. And of his tears that he shed continually, night and day, ver. 31.

Now if anyone can consider these accounts given in the Scripture of this great Apostle, and which he gives of himself, and yet not see that his religion consisted much in affection, must have a strange faculty of managing his eyes, to shut out the light which shines most full in his face.

The other instance I shall mention, is of the apostle John, that Beloved Disciple, who was the nearest and dearest to his Master of any of the twelve, and was by him admitted to the greatest privileges of any of them: being not only one of the three who were admitted to be present with him in the mount at his Transfiguration, and at the raising of Jairus' daughter, and whom he took with him when he was in his agony, and one of the three spoken of by the apostle Paul, as the three main pillars of the Christian church; but was favored above all, in being admitted to lean on his Master's bosom, at his Last Supper, and in being chosen by Christ, as the disciple to whom he would reveal his wonderful dispensations towards his church, to the end of time; as we have an account in the Book of Revelation: and to shut up the canon of the New Testament, and of the whole Scripture; being preserved much longer than all the rest of the apostles, to set all things in order in the Christian church, after their death.

It is evident by all his writings (as is generally observed by divines), that he was a person remarkably full of affection: his addresses to those whom he wrote to, being inexpressibly tender and pathetical, breathing nothing but the most fervent love; as though he were all made up of sweet and holy affection. The proofs of which can't be given without disadvantage, unless we should transcribe his whole writings.

7. He whom God sent into the world, to be the Light of the World, and Head of the whole church, and the perfect example of true religion and virtue, for the imitation of all, the shepherd whom the whole flock should follow wherever he goes, even the Lord Jesus Christ, was a person who was remarkably of a tender and affectionate heart; and his virtue was expressed very much in the exercise of holy affections. He was the greatest instance of ardency, vigor and strength of love, to both God and man, that ever was. It was these affections which got the victory, in that mighty struggle and conflict of his affections, in his agonies, when he prayed more earnestly, and offered strong crying and tears, and wrestled in tears and in blood. Such was the power of the exercises of his holy love, that they were stronger than death, and in that great struggle, over-

came those strong exercises of the natural affections of fear and grief, when he was sore amazed, and his soul was exceeding sorrowful, even unto death. And he also appeared to be full of affection, in the course of his life. We read of his great zeal, fulfilling that in the 69th Psalm: "The zeal of thine house hath eaten me up" (John 2:17). We read of his grief for the sins of men, "He looked round about on them with anger, being grieved for the hardness of their hearts" (Mark 3:5). And his breaking forth in tears and exclamations, from the consideration of the sin and misery of ungodly men, and on the sight of the city of Jerusalem, which was full of such inhabitants, "And when he was come near, he beheld the city, and wept over it, saying, if thou hadst known, even thou at least in this thy day, the things which belong unto thy peace! but now they are hid from thine eyes" (Luke 19:41–42). With ch. 13:34: "O Jerusalem, Jerusalem, which killeth the prophets, and stonest them that are sent unto thee, how often would I have gathered thy children together, as a hen doth gather her brood under her wings, and ye would not!" We read of Christ's earnest desire, "With desire have I desired to eat this passover with you, before I suffer" (Luke 22:15). We often read of the affection of pity or compassion in Christ (Matt. 15:32 and 18:34; Luke 7:13), and of his being moved with compassion (Matt. 9:36 and 14:14 and Mark 6:34). And how tender did his heart appear to be, on occasion of Mary's and Martha's mourning for their brother, and coming to him with their complaints and tears: their tears soon drew tears from his eyes: he was affected with their grief, and wept with them; though he knew their sorrow should so soon be turned into joy, by their brother's being raised from the dead; see John 11. And how ineffably affectionate was that last and dying discourse, which Jesus had with his eleven disciples the evening before he was crucified, when he told them he was going away, and foretold them the great difficulties and sufferings they should meet with in the world, when he was gone; and comforted and counseled 'em, as his dear little children, and bequeathed to them his holy Spirit, and therein his peace, and his comfort and joy, as it were in his last will and testament, in the 13th, 14th, 15th, and 16th chs. of John; and concluded the whole with that affectionate intercessory prayer for them, and his whole church, in ch. 17. Of all the discourses ever penned, or uttered by the mouth of any man, this seems to be the most affectionate, and affecting.

8. The religion of heaven consists very much in *affection*.

There is doubtless true religion in heaven, and true religion in its utmost purity and perfection. But according to the Scripture representation of the heavenly state, the religion of heaven consists chiefly in holy and mighty love and joy, and the expression of these in most fervent and exalted praises. So that the religion of the saints in heaven, consists in the same things with that religion of the saints on earth, which is spoken of in our text, viz. love, and joy unspeakable, and full of glory. Now it would be very foolish to pretend, that because the saints in heaven be not united to flesh and blood, and have no animal fluids to be moved (through the laws of union of soul and body), with those great emotions of their soul, that therefore their exceeding love and joy are no affections. We are not speaking of the affections of the body, but of the affections of the soul, the chief of which are love and joy. When these are in the soul, whether that be in the body or out of it, the soul is affected and moved. And when they are in the soul, in that strength in which they are in the saints in heaven, the soul is mightily affected and moved, or, which is the same thing, has great affections. 'Tis true, we don't experimentally know what love and joy are in a soul out of a body, or in a glorified body; i.e. we have not had experience of love and joy in a soul in these circumstances; but the saints on earth do know what divine love and joy in the soul are, and they know what love and joy are of the same kind, with the love and joy which are in heaven, in separate souls there. The love and joy of the saints on earth, is the beginning and dawning of the light, life, and blessedness of heaven, and is like their love and joy there; or rather, the same in nature, though not the same with it, or like to it, in degree and circumstances. This is evident by many Scriptures, as Prov. 4:18; John 4:14, and ch. 6:40, 47, 50–51, 54, 58; I John 3:15; I Cor. 13:8–12. 'Tis unreasonable therefore to suppose, that the love and joy of the saints in heaven, not only differ in degree and circumstances, from the holy love and joy of the saints on earth, but is so entirely different in nature, that they are no affections; and merely because they have no blood and animal spirits to be set in motion by them, which motion of the blood and animal spirits is not of the essence of these affections, in men on the earth, but the effect of them; although by their reaction they may make some circumstantial difference in the sensation of the mind. There is a sensation of the mind which loves and rejoices, that is antecedent to any effects on the fluids of the body; and this sensation of the mind, therefore don't depend on these motions in the body, and so may be in the soul without the body. And wherever there are the exercises of love and joy, there is that sensation of the mind, whether it be in the body, or out; and that inward sensation, or kind of spiritual sense, or feeling, and motion of the soul, is what is called affection; the soul when it thus feels, (if I may so say) and is thus moved, is said to be affected, and especially when this inward sensation and motion, are to a very high degree, as they are in the saints in heaven. If we can learn anything of the state of heaven from the Scripture, the love and joy that the saints have there, is exceeding great and vigorous; impressing the heart with the strongest and most lively sensation, of inexpressible sweetness, mightily moving, animating, and engaging them, making them like to a flame of fire. And if such love and joy be not affections, then the word "affection" is of no use in language. Will any say, that the saints in heaven, in beholding the face of their Father, and the glory of their Redeemer, and contemplating his wonderful works, and particularly his laying down his life for them, have their hearts nothing moved and affected, by all which they behold or consider?

Hence therefore the religion of heaven, consisting chiefly in holy love and joy, consists very much in affection: and therefore undoubtedly, true religion consists very much in affection. The way to learn the true nature of anything, is to go where that thing is to be found in its purity and perfection. If we would know the nature of true gold, we must view it, not in the ore, but when it is refined. If we would learn what true religion is, we must go where there is true religion, and nothing but true religion, and in its highest perfection, without any defect or mixture. All who are truly religious are not of this world, they are strangers here, and belong to heaven; they are born from above, heaven is their native country, and the nature which they receive by this heavenly birth, is an heavenly nature, they receive an anointing from above; that principle of true religion which is in them, is a communication of the religion of heaven; their grace is the dawn of glory; and God fits them for that world by conforming them to it.

9. This appears from the nature and design of the ordinances and duties, which God hath appointed, as means and expressions of true religion.

To instance in the duty of prayer: 'tis manifest, we are not appointed, in this duty, to declare God's perfections, his majesty, holiness, goodness, and allsufficiency, and our own meanness, emptiness, dependence, and unworthiness, and our wants and desires, to inform God of these things, or to incline his heart, and prevail with him to be willing to show us mercy; but suitably to affect our own hearts with the things we express, and so to prepare us to receive the blessings we ask. And such gestures, and manner of external behavior in the worship of God, which custom has made to be significations of humility and reverence, can be of no further use, than as they have some tendency to affect our own hearts, or the hearts of others.

And the duty of singing praises to God, seems to be appointed wholly to excite and express religious affections. No other reason can be assigned, why we should express ourselves to God in verse, rather than in prose, and do it with music, but only, that such is our nature and frame, that these things have a tendency to move our affections.

The same thing appears in the nature and design of the sacraments, which God hath appointed. God, considering our frame, hath not only appointed that we should be told of the great things of the gospel, and of the redemption of Christ, and instructed in them by his Word; but also that they should be, as it were, exhibited to our view, in sensible representations, in the sacraments, the more to affect us with them.

And the impressing divine things on the hearts and affections of men, is evidently one great and main end for which God has ordained, that his Word delivered in the Holy Scriptures, should be opened, applied, and set home upon men, in preaching. And therefore it don't answer the aim which God had in this institution, merely for men to have good commentaries and expositions on the Scripture, and other good books of divinity; because, although these may tend, as well as preaching, to give men a good doctrinal or speculative understanding of the things of the Word of God, yet they have not an equal tendency to impress them on men's hearts and affections. God hath appointed a particular and lively application of his Word, to men, in the preaching of it, as a fit means to affect sinners, with the importance of the things of religion, and their own misery, and necessity of a remedy, and the glory and sufficiency of a remedy provided; and to stir up the pure minds of the saints, and quicken their affections, by often bringing the great things of religion to their remembrance, and setting them before them in their proper colors, though they know them, and have been fully instructed in them already (II Pet. 1:12–13). And particularly, to promote those two affections in them, which are spoken of in the text, love and joy: Christ "gave some, apostles, and some, prophets; and some, evangelists; and some, pastors and teachers, that the body of Christ might be edified in love" (Eph. 4:11–12, 16). The Apostle, in instructing and counseling Timothy, concerning the work of the ministry, informs him that the great end of that Word which a minister is to preach, is *love* or *charity* (I Tim. 1:3–5). And another affection which God has appointed preaching as a means to promote in the saints, is *joy;* and therefore ministers are called helpers of their joy (II Cor. 1:24).

10. 'Tis an evidence that true religion, or holiness of heart, lies very much in the affection of the heart, that the Scriptures place the sin of the heart very much in hardness of heart. Thus the Scriptures do everywhere. It was hardness of heart, which excited grief and displeasure in Christ towards the Jews, "He looked round about on them with anger, being grieved for the hardness of their hearts" (Mark 3:5). It is from men's having such a heart as this, that they treasure up wrath for themselves. "After thy hardness and impenitent heart, treasurest up unto thy self wrath, against the day of wrath, and revelation of the righteous judgment of God" (Rom. 2:5). The reason given why the house of Israel would not obey God, was that they were hard-hearted, "But the house of Israel will not hearken unto thee; for they will not hearken unto me: for all the house of Israel are impudent and hard-hearted" (Ezek. 3:7). The wickedness of that perverse rebellious generation in the wilderness, is ascribed to the hardness of their hearts; "Today, if ye will hear my voice, harden not your heart, as in the provocation, and as in the day of temptation in the wilderness; when your fathers tempted me, proved me, and saw my work: forty years long was I grieved with this generation, and said it is a people that do err in their heart," etc. (Ps. 95:7–10). This is spoken of as to what prevented Zedekiah's turning to the Lord, "He stiffened his neck, and hardened his heart, from turning to the Lord God of Israel" (II Chron. 36:13). This principle is spoken of, as that from whence men are without the fear of God, and depart from God's ways: "O Lord, why has thou made us to err from thy ways, and hardened our heart from thy fear?" (Is. 63:17). And men's rejecting

Christ, and opposing Christianity, is laid to this principle; "But when divers were hardened, and believed not, but spake evil of that way before the multitude" (Acts 19:9); God's leaving men to the power of the sin and corruption of the heart, is often expressed by God's hardening their hearts; "Therefore hath he mercy on whom he will have mercy, and whom he will he hardeneth" (Rom. 9:18). "He hath blinded their mind, and hardened their hearts" (John 12:40). And the Apostle seems to speak of an evil heart, that departs from the living God, and a hard heart, as the same thing, "Harden not your heart, as in the provocation," etc. (Heb. 3:8). "Take heed brethren, lest there be in any of you an evil heart of unbelief in departing from the living God; but exhort one another daily, while it is called Today; lest any of you be hardened through the deceitfulness of sin" (ver. 12, 13). And that great work of God in conversion, which consists in delivering a person from the power of sin, and mortifying corruption, is expressed, once and again, by God's taking away the heart of stone, and giving an heart of flesh (Ezek. 11:19 and ch. 36:26).

Now by a hard heart, is plainly meant an unaffected heart, or a heart not easy to be moved with virtuous affections, like a stone, insensible, stupid, unmoved and hard to be impressed. Hence the hard heart is called a stony heart, and is opposed to an heart of flesh, that has feeling, and is sensibly touched and moved. We read in Scripture of a hard heart, and a tender heart: and doubtless we are to understand these, as contrary the one to the other. But what is a tender heart, but a heart which is easily impressed by what ought to affect it? God commends Josiah, because his heart was tender; and 'tis evident by those things which are mentioned as expressions and evidences of this tenderness of heart, that by his heart being tender is meant, his heart being easily moved with religious and pious affection; "Because thine heart was tender, and thou hast humbled thyself before the Lord, when thou heardst what I spake against this place, and against the inhabitants thereof, that they should become a desolation, and a curse, and hast rent thy clothes, and hast wept before me; I also have heard thee, saith the Lord" (II Kgs. 22:19). And this is one thing, wherein it is necessary we should become as little children, in order to our entering into the kingdom of God, even that we should have our hearts tender, and easily affected and moved in spiritual and divine things, as little children have in other things.

'Tis very plain in some places, in the texts themselves, that by hardness of heart is meant a heart void of affection. So to signify the ostrich's being without natural affection to her young, it is said, "She hardeneth her heart against her young ones, as though they were not hers" (Job 39:16). So a person having a heart unaffected in time of danger, is expressed by his hardening his heart, "Happy is the man that feareth alway; but he that hardeneth his heart shall fall into mischief" (Prov. 28:14).

Now therefore since it is so plain, that by a hard heart, in Scripture, is meant a heart destitute of pious affections, and since also the Scriptures do so frequently place the sin and corruption of the heart in hardness of heart; it is evident, that the grace and holiness of the heart, on the contrary, must, in a great measure, consist in its having pious affections, and being easily susceptive of such affection. Divines are generally agreed, that sin radically and fundamentally consists in what is negative, or privative, having its root and foundation in a privation or want of holiness. And therefore undoubtedly, if it be so that sin does very much consist in hardness of heart, and so in the want of pious affections of heart; holiness does consist very much in those pious affections.

I am far from supposing that all affections do show a tender heart: hatred, anger, vainglory, and other selfish and self-exalting affections, may greatly prevail in the hardest heart. But yet it is evident that hardness of heart, and tenderness of heart, are expressions that relate to the affections of the heart, and denote the heart's being susceptible of, or shut up against, certain affections, of which I shall have occasion to speak more afterwards.

Upon the whole, I think it clearly and abundantly evident, that true religion lies very much in the affections. Not that I think these arguments prove, that religion in the hearts of the truly godly, is ever in exact proportion to the degree of affection, and present emotion of the mind. For undoubtedly, there is much affection in the true saints which is not spiritual: their religious affections are often mixed; all is not from grace, but much from nature. And though the affections have not their seat in the body, yet the constitution of the body, may very much contribute to the present emotion of the mind. And the degree of religion is rather to be judged of by the fixedness and strength of the habit that is exercised in affection, whereby holy affection is habitual, than by the degree of the present exercise: and the strength of that habit is not always in proportion to outward effects and manifestations, or inward effects, in the hurry and vehemence, and sudden changes of the course of the thoughts of the mind. But yet it is evident, that religion consists so much in affection, as that without holy affection there is no true religion: and no light in the understanding is good, which don't produce holy affection in the heart; no habit or principle in the heart is good, which has no such exercise; and no external fruit is good, which don't proceed from such exercises.

Having thus considered the evidence of the proposition laid down, I proceed to some inferences.

1. We may hence learn how great their error is, who are for discarding all religious affections, as having nothing solid or substantial in them.

There seems to be too much of a disposition this way, prevailing in this land at this time. Because many who, in the late extraordinary season, appeared to have great religious affections, did not manifest a right temper of mind, and run into many errors, in the time of their affection, and the heat of their zeal; and because the high affections of many seem to be so soon come to nothing, and some who seemed to be mightily raised and swallowed with joy and zeal, for a while, seem to have returned like the dog to his vomit: hence religious affections in general are grown out of credit, with great numbers, as though true religion did not at all consist in them. Thus we easily, and naturally run from one extreme to another. A little while ago we were in the other extreme; there was a prevalent disposition to look upon all high religious affections, as eminent exercises of true grace, without much inquiring into the nature and source of those affections, and the manner in which they arose: if persons did but appear to be indeed very much moved and raised, so as to be full of religious talk, and express themselves with great warmth and earnestness, and to be filled, or to be very full, as the phrases were; it was too much the manner, without further examination, to conclude such persons were full of the Spirit of God, and had eminent experience of his gracious influences. This was the extreme which was prevailing three or four years ago. But of late, instead of esteeming and admiring all religious affections, without distinction, it is a thing much more prevalent, to reject and to discard all without distinction. Herein appears the subtlety of Satan. While he saw that affections were much in vogue, knowing the greater part of the land were not versed in such thigs, and had not had much experience of great religious affections, to enable them to judge well of 'em, and distinguish between true and false; then he knew he could best play his game, by sowing tares amongst the wheat, and mingling false affections with the works of God's Spirit; he knew this to be a likely way to delude and eternally ruin many souls, and greatly to wound religion in the saints, and entangle them in a dreadful wilderness, and by and by, to bring all religion into disrepute. But now, when the ill consequences of these false affections appear, and 'tis become very apparent, that some of those emotions which made a glaring show, and were by many greatly admired, were in reality nothing; the devil sees it to be for his interest to go another way to work, and to endeavor to his utmost to propagate and establish a persuasion, that all affections and sensible emotions of the mind, in things of religion, are nothing at all to be regarded, but are rather to be avoided, and carefully guarded against, as things of a pernicious tendency. This he knows is the way to bring all religion to a mere lifeless formality, and effectually shut out the power of godliness, and every thing which is spiritual, and to have all true Christianity turned out of doors. For although to true religion, there must indeed be something else besides affection; yet true religion consists so much in the affections, that there can be no true religion without them. He who has no religious affection, is in a state of spiritual death, and is wholly destitute of the powerful, quickening, saving influences of the Spirit of God upon his heart. As there is no true religion, where there is nothing else but affection; so there is no true religion where there is no religious affection. As on the one hand, there must be light in the understanding, as well as an affected fervent heart, where there is heat without light, there can be nothing divine or heavenly in that heart; so on the other hand, where there is a kind of light without heat, a head stored with notions and speculations, with a cold and unaffected heart, there can be nothing divine in that light, that knowledge is no true spiritual knowledge of divine things. If the great things of religion are rightly understood, they will affect the heart. The reason why men are not affected by such infinitely great, important, glorious, and wonderful things, as they often hear and read of, in the Word of God, is undoubtedly because they are blind; if they were not so, it would be impossible, and utterly inconsistent with human nature, that their hearts should be otherwise, than strongly impressed, and greatly moved by such things.

This manner of slighting all religious affections, is the way exceedingly to harden the hearts of men, and to encourage 'em in their stupidity and senselessness, and to keep 'em in a state of spiritual death as long as they live, and bring 'em at last to death eternal. The prevailing prejudice against religious affections at this day, in the land, is apparently of awful effect, to harden the hearts of sinners, and damp the graces of many of the saints, and stunt[3] the life and power of religion, and preclude the effect of ordinances, and hold us down in a state of dullness and apathy, and undoubtedly causes many persons greatly to offend God, in entertaining mean and low thoughts of the extraordinary work he has lately wrought in this land.

And for persons to despise and cry down all religious affections, is the way to shut all religion out of their own hearts, and to make thorough work in ruining their souls.

They who condemn high affections in others, are certainly not likely to have high affections themselves. And let it be considered, that they who have but little religious affection, have certainly but little religion. And they who condemn others for their religious affections, and have none themselves, have no religion.

There are false affections, and there are true. A man's having much affection, don't prove that he has any true religion: but if he has no affection, it proves that he has no true religion. The right way, is not to reject all affections, nor to approve all; but to distinguish between affections, approving some, and rejecting others; separating between the wheat and the chaff, the gold and the dross, the precious and the vile.

2. If it be so, that true religion lies much in the affections, hence we may infer, that such means are to be desired, as have much of a tendency to move the affections. Such books, and such a way of preaching the Word, and administration of ordinances, and such a way of worshiping God in prayer, and singing praises, is much to be desired, as has a tendency deeply to affect the hearts of those who attend these means.

Such a kind of means, would formerly have been highly approved

3. The original text reads "stund."

of and applauded by the generality of the people of the land, as the most excellent and profitable, and having the greatest tendency to promote the ends of the means of grace. But the prevailing taste seems of late strangely to be altered: that pathetical manner of praying and preaching, which would formerly have been admired and extolled, and that for this reason, because it had such a tendency to move the affections, now, in great multitudes, immediately excites disgust, and moves no other affections, than those of displeasure and contempt.

Perhaps, formerly the generality (at least of the common people) were in the extreme, of looking too much to an affectionate address, in public performances: but now, a very great part of the people, seem to have gone far into a contrary extreme. Indeed there may be such means, as may have a great tendency to stir up the passions of weak and ignorant persons, and yet have no great tendency to benefit their souls. For though they may have a tendency to excite affections, they may have little or none to excite gracious affections, or any affections tending to grace. But undoubtedly, if the things of religion, in the means used, are treated according to their nature, and exhibited truly, so as tends to convey just apprehensions, and a right judgment of them; the more they have a tendency to move the affections, the better.

3. If true religion lies much in the affections, hence we may learn, what great cause we have to be ashamed and confounded before God, that we are no more affected with the great things of religion. It appears from what has been said, that this arises from our having so little true religion.

God has given to mankind affections, for the same purpose which he has given all the faculties and principles of the human soul for, viz. that they might be subservient to man's chief end, and the great business for which God has created him, that is the business of religion. And yet how common is it among mankind, that their affections are much more exercised and engaged in other matters, than in religion! In things which concern men's worldly interest, their outward delights, their honor and reputation, and their natural relations, they have their desires eager, their appetites vehement, their love warm and affectionate, their zeal ardent; in these things their hearts are tender and sensible, easily moved, deeply impressed, much concerned, very sensibly affected, and greatly engaged; much depressed with grief at worldly losses, and highly raised with joy at worldly successes and prosperity. But how insensible and unmoved are most men, about the great things of another world! How dull are their affections! How heavy and hard their hearts in these matters! Here their love is cold, their desires languid, their zeal low, and their gratitude small. How they can sit and hear of the infinite height and depth and length and breadth of the love of God in Christ Jesus, of his giving his infinitely dear Son, to be offered up a sacrifice for the sins of men, and of the unparalleled love of the innocent, holy and tender Lamb of God, manifested in his dying agonies, his bloody sweat, his loud and bitter cries, and bleeding heart, and all this for enemies, to redeem them from deserved, eternal burnings, and to bring to unspeakable and everlasting joy and glory; and yet be cold, and heavy, insensible, and regardless! Where are the exercises of our affections proper, if not here? What is it that does more require them? And what can be a fit occasion of their lively and vigorous exercise, if not such an one as this? Can anything be set in our view, greater and more important? Anything more wonderful and surprising? Or more nearly concerning our interest? Can we suppose the wise Creator implanted such principles in the human nature as the affections, to be of use to us, and to be exercised on certain proper occasions, but to lie still on such an occasion as this? Can any Christian, who believes the truth of these things, entertain such thoughts?

If we ought ever to exercise our affections at all, and if the Creator han't unwisely constituted the human nature, in making these principles a part of it, when they are vain and useless; then they ought to be exercised about those objects which are most worthy of them. But is there anything, which Christians can find in heaven or earth, so worthy to be the objects of their admiration and love, their earnest and longing desires, their hope, and their rejoicing, and their fervent zeal, as those things that are held forth to us in the gospel of Jesus Christ? In which, not only are things declared most worthy to affect us, but they are exhibited in the most affecting manner. The glory and beauty of the blessed Jehovah, which is most worthy in itself, to be the object of our admiration and love, is there exhibited in the most affecting manner that can be conceived of, as it appears shining in all its luster, in the face of an incarnate, infinitely loving, meek, compassionate, dying Redeemer. All the virtues of the Lamb of God, his humility, patience, meekness, submission, obedience, love and compassion, are exhibited to our view, in a manner the most tending to move our affections, of any that can be imagined; as they all had their greatest trial, and their highest exercise, and so their brightest manifestation, when he was in the most affecting circumstances; even when he was under his last sufferings, those unutterable and unparalleled sufferings, he endured, from his tender love and pity to us. There also, the hateful nature of our sins is manifested in the most affecting manner possible; as we see the dreadful effects of them, in what our Redeemer, who undertook to answer for us, suffered for them. And there we have the most affecting manifestations of God's hatred of sin, and his wrath and justice in punishing it; as we see his justice in the strictness and inflexibleness of it, and his wrath in its terribleness, in so dreadfully punishing our sins, in One who was infinitely dear to him, and loving to us. So has God disposed things, in the affair of our redemption, and in his glorious dispensations, revealed to us in the gospel, as though everything were purposely contrived in such a manner, as to have the greatest, possible tendency to reach our hearts in the most tender part, and move our affections most sensibly and strongly. How great cause have we therefore to be humbled to the dust, that we are no more affected!

PART TWO

Shewing What Are No Certain Signs that Religious Affections Are Truly Gracious, or that They Are Not.

IF anyone, on the reading of what has been just now said, is ready to acquit himself, and say, "I am not one of those who have no religious affections; I am often greatly moved with the consideration of the great things of religion;" let him not content himself with this, that he has religious affections. For (as was observed before) as we ought not to reject and condemn all affections, as though true religion did not at all consist in affection; so on the other hand, we ought not to approve of all, as though everyone that was religiously affected, had true grace, and was therein the subject of the saving influences of the Spirit of God: and that therefore the right way is to distinguish among religious affections, between one sort and another. Therefore let us now endeavor to do this: and in order to it, I would do two things.

I. I would mention some things, which are no signs one way or the other, either that affections are such as true religion consists in, or that they are otherwise; that we may be guarded against judging of affections by false signs.

II. I would observe some things, wherein those affections which are spiritual and gracious, differ from those which are not so, and may be distinguished and known.

First, I would take notice of some things, which are no signs that affections are gracious, or that they are not.

1. 'Tis no sign one way or the other, that religious affections are very great, or raised very high.

Some are ready to condemn all high affections: if persons appear to have their religious affections raised to an extraordinary pitch, they are prejudiced against them, and determine that they are delusions, without further inquiry. But if it be as has been proved, that true religion lies very much in religious affections, then it follows, that if there be a great deal of true religion, there will be great religious affections; if true religion in the hearts of men, be raised to a great height, divine and holy affections will be raised to a great height.

Love is an affection; but will any Christian say, men ought not to love God and Jesus Christ in a high degree? And will any say, we ought not to have a very great hatred of sin, and a very deep sorrow for it? Or that we ought not to exercise a high degree of gratitude to God, for the mercies we receive of him, and the great things he has done for the salvation of fallen men? Or that we should not have very great and strong desires after God and holiness? Is there any who will profess, that his affections in religion are great enough; and will say, "I have no cause to be humbled, that I am no more affected with the things of religion than I am, I have no reason to be ashamed, that I have no greater exercises of love to God, and sorrow for sin, and gratitude for the mercies which I have received?" Who is there that will go and bless God, that he is affected enough with what he has read and heard, of the wonderful love of God to worms and rebels, in giving his only begotten Son to die for them, and of the dying love of Christ; and will pray that he mayn't be affected with them in any higher degree, because high affections are improper, and very unlovely in Christians, being enthusiastical, and ruinous to true religion?

Our text plainly speaks of great and high affections, when it speaks of rejoicing with joy unspeakable and full of glory: here the most superlative expressions are used, which language will afford. And the Scriptures often require us to exercise very high affections: thus in the first and great commandment of the law, there is an accumulation of expressions, as though words were wanting to express the degree, in which we ought to love God; "Thou shalt love the Lord thy God, with all thy heart, with all thy soul, with all thy mind, and with all thy strength." So the saints are called upon to exercise high degrees of joy: "Rejoice," says Christ to his disciples, "and be exceedingly glad" (Matt. 5:12). So it is said, "Let the righteous be glad; let them rejoice before God; yea, let them exceeding rejoice" (Ps. 68:3). So in the same Book of Psalms, the saints are often called upon to "shout for joy"; and in Luke 6:23 "to leap for joy." So they are abundantly called upon to exercise high degrees of gratitude for mercies, to praise God with all their hearts, with hearts lifted up in the ways of the Lord, and their souls magnifying the Lord, singing his praises, talking of his wondrous works, declaring his doings, etc.

And we find the most eminent saints in Scripture, often professing high affections. Thus the Psalmist speaks of his love, as if it were unspeakable; "Oh how love I thy Law!" (Ps. 119:97). So he expresses a great degree of hatred of sin; "Do I not hate them, O Lord, that hate thee? And am I not grieved with them that rise up against thee? I hate them with perfect hatred" (Ps. 139:21–22). He also expresses a high degree of sorrow for sin: he speaks of his sins going over his head, as an heavy burden, that was too heavy for him; and of his roaring all the day, and his moisture's being turned into the drought of summer, and his bones being as it were broken with sorrow. So he often expresses great degrees of spiritual desires, in a multitude of the strongest expressions which can be conceived of; such as his longing, his soul's thirsting as a dry and thirsty land where no water is, his panting, his flesh and heart crying out, his soul's breaking for the longing it hath, etc. He expresses the exercises of great and extreme grief for the sins of others, "Rivers of water run down mine eyes, because they keep not thy law" (Ps. 119:136). And ver. 53: "Horror hath taken hold upon me, because of the wicked that forsake thy law." He expresses high exercises of joy, "The king shall joy in thy strength and in thy salvation how greatly shall he rejoice!" (Ps. 21:1) "My lips shall greatly rejoice, when I sing unto thee" (Ps. 71:23). "Because thy loving-kindness is better than life, my lips shall praise thee. Thus will I bless thee, while I live: I will lift up my hands in thy name: my soul shall be satisfied as with marrow and fatness, and my mouth shall praise thee with joyful lips: when I remember thee upon my bed, and meditate on thee in the night watches; because thou hast been my help, therefore in the shadow of thy wings will I rejoice" (Ps. 63:3–7).

The apostle Paul expresses high exercises of affection. Thus he expresses the exercises of pity and concern for others' good, even to anguish of heart; a great, fervent and abundant love, and earnest and longing desires, and exceeding joy; and speaks of the exultation and triumphs of his soul, and his earnest expectation and hope, and his abundant tears, and the travails of his soul, in pity, grief, earnest desires, godly jealousy and fervent zeal, in many places that have been cited already, and which therefore I need not repeat. John the Baptist expressed great joy (John 3:39). Those blessed women that anointed the body of Jesus, are represented as in a very high exercise of religious affection, on occasion of Christ's resurrection; "And they departed from the sepulcher with fear and great joy" (Matt. 28:8).

'Tis often foretold of the church of God, in her future happy seasons here on earth, that they shall exceedingly rejoice; "They shall walk, O Lord, in the light of thy countenance: in thy name shall they rejoice all the day, and in thy righteousness shall they be exalted" (Ps. 89:15–16). "Rejoice greatly, O daughter of Zion, shout, O daughter of Jerusalem; behold thy King cometh," etc. (Zech. 9:9). The same is represented in innumerable other places. And because high degrees of joy are the proper and genuine fruits of the gospel of Christ, therefore the angel calls this gospel, "good tidings of great joy, that should be to all people."

The saints and angels in heaven, that have religion in its highest perfection, are exceedingly affected with what they behold and contemplate, of God's perfections and works. They are all as a pure heavenly flame of fire, in their love, and in the greatness and strength of their joy and gratitude: their praises are represented, as the voice of many waters, and as the voice of a great thunder. Now the only reason why their affections are so much higher than the holy affections of saints on earth, is, they see the things they are affected by, more according to their truth, and have their affections more conformed to the nature of things. And therefore, if religious affections in men here below, are but of the same nature and kind with theirs, the higher they are, and the nearer they are to theirs in degree, the better; because therein they will be so much the more conformed to truth, as theirs are.

From these things it certainly appears, that religious affections being in a very high degree, is no evidence that they are not such as have the nature of true religion. Therefore they do greatly err, who condemn persons as enthusiasts, merely because their affections are very high.

And on the other hand, 'tis no evidence that religious affections are of a spiritual and gracious nature, because they are great. 'Tis very manifest by the Holy Scripture, our sure and infallible rule to judge of things of this nature, that there are religious affections which are very high, that are not spiritual and saving. The apostle Paul speaks of affections in the Galatians, which had been exceedingly elevated, and which yet he manifestly speaks of, as fearing that they were vain, and had come to nothing, "Where is the blessedness you spake of? for I bear you record, that if it had been possible, you would have plucked out your own eyes, and have given them to me" (Gal. 4:15). And in the 11th verse he tells them, he was afraid of 'em, lest he had bestowed upon them labor in vain. So the children of Israel were greatly affected with God's mercy to 'em, when they had seen how wonderfully he wrought for them at the Red Sea, where they sang God's praise; though they soon forgat his works. So they were greatly affected again, at Mount Sinai, when they saw the marvelous manifestations God made of himself there; and seemed mightily engaged in their minds, and with great forwardness made answer, when God proposed his holy Covenant to them, saying, "All that the Lord hath spoken will we do, and be obedient." But how soon was there an end to all this mighty forwardness and engagedness of affection? How quickly were they turned aside after other gods, rejoicing and shouting around their golden calf? So great multitudes who were affected with the miracle of raising Lazarus from the dead, were elevated to a high degree, and made a mighty ado, when Jesus presently after entered into Jerusalem, exceedingly magnifying Christ, as though the ground were not good enough for the ass he rode to tread upon; and therefore cut down branches of palm trees, and strawed them in the way; yea pulled off their garments, and spread them in the way; and cried with loud voices, Hosanna to the Son of David, blessed is he that cometh in the name of the Lord, Hosanna in the highest; so as to make the whole city ring again, and put all into an uproar. We learn by the evangelist John, that the reason why the people made this ado, was because they were affected with the miracle of raising Lazarus (John 12:18). Here was a vast multitude crying "Hosanna" on this occasion, so that it gave occasion to the Pharisees to say: "Behold the world is gone after him" (John 12:19). But Christ had at that time but few true disciples. And how quickly was this ado at an end? All of this nature is quelled and dead, when this Jesus stands bound, with a mock robe and a crown of thorns, to be derided, spit upon, scourged, condemned and executed. Indeed there was a great and loud outcry concerning him, among the multitude then, as well as before; but of a very different kind: 'tis not then, "Hosanna, Hosanna," but "Crucify, Crucify."

And it is the concurring voice of all orthodox divines, that there may be religious affections, which are raised to a very high degree, and yet there be nothing of true religion.[1]

2. 'Tis no sign that affections have the nature of true religion, or that they have not, that they have great effects on the body.

All affections whatsoever, have in some respect or degree, an ef-

1. Mr. Stoddard observes, that common affections are sometimes stronger than saving. Solomon Stoddard, *A Guide to Christ* (Boston, 1735, 1st ed. 1714), p. 21. [JE cites the 1735 ed. For JE's use of Stoddard's writings see above, pp. 57–60.]

fect on the body. As was observed before, such is our nature, and such are the laws of union of soul and body, that the mind can have no lively or vigorous exercise, without some effect upon the body. So subject is the body to the mind, and so much do its fluids, especially the animal spirits, attend the motions and exercises of the mind, that there can't be so much as an intense thought, without an effect upon them. Yea, 'tis questionable, whether an embodied soul ever so much as thinks one thought, or has any exercise at all, but that there is some corresponding motion or alteration of motion, in some degree, of the fluids, in some part of the body. But universal experience shows, that the exercise of the affections, have in a special manner a tendency, to some sensible effect upon the body. And if this be so, that all affections have some effect on the body, we may then well suppose, the greater those affections be, and the more vigorous their exercise (other circumstances being equal) the greater will be the effect on the body. Hence it is not to be wondered at, that very great and strong exercises of the affections, should have great effects on the body. And therefore, seeing there are very great affections, both common and spiritual; hence it is not to be wondered at, that great effects on the body, should arise from both these kinds of affections. And consequently these effects are not signs, that the affections they arise from, are of one kind or the other.

Great effects on the body certainly are no sure evidences that affections are spiritual; for we see that such effects oftentimes arise from great affections about temporal things, and when religion is no way concerned in them. And if great affections about secular things that are purely natural, may have these effects, I know not by what rule we should determine, that high affections about religious things, which arise in like manner from nature, can't have the like effect.

Nor on the other hand, do I know of any rule any have to determine, that gracious and holy affections, when raised as high as any natural affections, and have equally strong and vigorous exercises, can't have a great effect on the body. No such rule can be drawn from reason: I know of no reason, why a being affected with a view of God's glory should not cause the body to faint, as well as a being affected with a view of Solomon's glory. And no such rule has as yet been produced from the Scripture: none has ever been found in all the late controversies which have been about things of this nature. There is a great power in spiritual affections; we read of the power which worketh in Christians,[2] and of the Spirit of God being in them, as the spirit of power,[3] and of the effectual working of his power in them [4] yea of the working of God's mighty power in them.[5] But man's nature is weak: flesh and blood are represented in Scripture as exceeding weak; and particularly with respect to its unfitness for great spiritual and heavenly operations and exercises (Matt. 26:41; I Cor. 15:43, and 50). The text we are upon speaks of "joy unspeakable, and full of glory." And who that considers what man's nature is, and what the nature of the affections are, can reasonably doubt but that such unutterable and glorious joys, may be too great and mighty for weak dust and ashes, so as to be considerably overbearing to it? It is evident by the Scripture, that true divine discoveries, or ideas of God's glory, when given in a great degree, have a tendency, by affecting the mind, to overbear the body; because the Scripture teaches us often, that if these ideas or views should be given to such a degree, as they are given in heaven, the weak frame of the body could not subsist under it, and that no man can, in that manner, see God and live. The knowledge which the saints have of God's beauty and glory in this world, and those holy affections that arise from it, are of the same nature and kind with what the saints are the subjects of in heaven, differing only in degree and circumstances: what God gives them here, is a foretaste of heavenly happiness, and an earnest of their future inheritance. And who shall limit God in his giving this earnest, or say he shall give so much of the inheritance, such a part of the future reward, as an earnest of the whole, and no more? And seeing God has taught us in his Word, that the whole reward is such, that it would at once destroy the body, is it not too bold a thing for us, so to set bounds to the sovereign God, as to say, that in giving the earnest of this reward in this world, he shall never give so much of it, as in the least to diminish the strength of the body, when God has nowhere thus limited himself?

The Psalmist speaking of vehement religious affections he had, speaks of an effect in his flesh or body, besides what was in his soul, expressly distinguishing one from the other, once and again, Ps. 84:2:

2. Eph. 3:7.
3. II Tim. 1:7.
4. II Tim. 1:7, 19.
5. Eph. 1:19.

"My soul longeth, yea even fainteth for the courts of the Lord, my heart and my flesh crieth out for the living God." Here is a plain distinction between the heart and the flesh, as being each affected. So Ps. 63:1: "My soul thirsteth for thee, my flesh longeth for thee, in a dry and thirsty land, where no water is." Here also is an evident designed distinction between the soul and the flesh.

The prophet Habakkuk speaks of his body's being overborne, by a sense of the majesty of God, "When I heard, my belly trembled, my lips quivered at the voice, rottenness entered into my bones, and I trembled in myself" (Hab. 3:16). So the Psalmist speaks expressly of his flesh trembling, "My flesh trembleth for fear of thee" (Ps. 119:120).

That such ideas of God's glory, as are sometimes given in this world, have a tendency to overbear the body, is evident, because the Scripture gives us an account, that this has sometimes actually been the effect of those external manifestations God has made of himself, to some of the saints, which were made to that end, viz. to give them an idea of God's majesty and glory. Such instances we have in the prophet Daniel, and the apostle John. Daniel giving an account of an external representation of the glory of Christ, says, "And there remained no strength in me, for my comeliness was turned into corruption, and I retained no strength" (Dan. 10:8). And the apostle John giving an account of a like manifestation made to him, says, "And when I saw him, I fell at his feet as dead" (Rev. 1:17). 'Tis in vain to say here, these were only external manifestations or symbols of the glory of Christ, which these saints beheld: for though it be true, that they were outward representations of Christ's glory, which they beheld with their bodily eyes; yet the end and use of these external symbols or representations, was to give to these prophets an idea of the thing represented, and that was the true divine glory and majesty of Christ, which is his spiritual glory; they were made use of only as significations of this spiritual glory, and thus undoubtedly they received them, and improved them, and were affected by them. According to the end, for which God intended these outward signs, they received by them a great and lively apprehension of the real glory and majesty of God's nature, which they were signs of; and thus were greatly affected, their souls swallowed up, and their bodies overborne. And I think, they are very bold and daring, who will say God cannot, or shall not give the like clear and affecting ideas and apprehensions of the same real glory and majesty of his nature, to none of his saints, without the intervention of any such external shadows of it.

Before I leave this head, I would farther observe, that 'tis plain the Scripture often makes use of bodily effects, to express the strength of holy and spiritual affections; such as trembling,[6] groaning,[7] being sick,[8] crying out,[9] panting,[1] and fainting.[2] Now if it be supposed, that these are only figurative expressions, to represent the degree of affection; yet I hope all will allow, that they are fit and suitable figures to represent the high degree of those spiritual affections, which the Spirit of God makes use of them to represent. Which I don't see how they would be, if those spiritual affections, let them be in never so high a degree, have no tendency to any such things; but that on the contrary, they are the proper effects, and sad tokens of false affections, and the delusion of the devil. I can't think, God would commonly make use of things which are very alien from spiritual affections, and are shrewd marks of the hand of Satan, and smell strong of the bottomless pit, as beautiful figures, to represent the high degree of holy and heavenly affections.

3. 'Tis no sign that affections are truly gracious affections, or that they are not, that they cause those who have them, to be fluent, fervent and abundant, in talking of the things of religion.

There are many persons, who if they see this in others, are greatly prejudiced against them. Their being so full of talk, is with them, a sufficient ground to condemn them, as Pharisees, and ostentatious hypocrites. On the other hand, there are many, who if they see this effect in any, are very ignorantly and imprudently forward, at once to determine that they are the true children of God, and are under the saving influences of his Spirit, and speak of it as a great evidence of a new creature: they say: "such an one's mouth is now opened: he used to be slow to speak; but now he is full and free: he is free now to open his heart, and tell his experiences, and declare the praises of God; it comes from him, as free as water from a fountain," and the like. And especially are they

6. Ps. 119:120; Ezra 9:4; Is. 66:2, 5; Hab. 3:16.
7. Rom. 8:26.
8. Cant. 2:5 and 5:8.
9. Ps. 84:2.
1. Ps. 38:10 and 42:1 and 119:131.
2. Ps. 84:2 and 119:81.

captivated into a confident and undoubting persuasion that they are savingly wrought upon, if they are not only free and abundant, but very affectionate and earnest in their talk.

But this is the fruit of but little judgment, a scanty and short experience; as events do abundantly show: and is a mistake, persons often run into, through their trusting to their own wisdom and discerning, and making their own notions their rule, instead of the Holy Scripture. Though the Scripture be full of rules, both how we should judge of our own state, and also how we should be conducted in our opinion of others; yet we have nowhere any rule, by which to judge ourselves or others to be in a good estate, from any such effect: for this is but the religion of the mouth and of the tongue, and what is in the Scripture represented by the leaves of a tree, which though the tree ought not to be without them, yet are nowhere given as an evidence of the goodness of the tree.

That persons are disposed to be abundant in talking of things of religion, may be from a good cause, and it may be from a bad one. It may be because their hearts are very full of holy affections; for "out of the abundance of the heart, the mouth speaketh": and it may be because persons' hearts are very full of religious affection which is not holy; for still out of the abundance of the heart the mouth speaketh. It is very much the nature of the affections, of whatever kind they be, and whatever objects they are exercised about, if they are strong, to dispose persons to be very much in speaking of that which they are affected with; and not only to speak much, but to speak very earnestly and fervently. And therefore persons talking abundantly and very fervently about the things of religion, can be an evidence of no more than this, that they are very much affected with the things of religion; but this may be (as has been already shown), and there be no grace. That which men are greatly affected with, while the high affection lasts, they will be earnestly engaged about, and will be likely to shew that earnestness in their talk and behavior; as the greater part of the Jews, in all Judea and Galilee, did for a while, about John the Baptist's preaching and baptism, when they were willing for a season to rejoice in his light: a mighty ado was made, all over the land, and among all sorts of persons, about this great prophet and his ministry. And so the multitude in like manner, often manifested a great earnestness, and mighty engagedness of spirit, in everything that was external, about Christ and his preaching and miracles, being astonished at his doctrine, anon with joy receiving the Word, following him, sometimes night and day, leaving meat, drink and sleep to hear him; once following him into the wilderness, fasting three days going, to hear him; sometimes crying him up to the clouds, saying, "Never man spake like this man!" being fervent and earnest in what they said. But what did these things come to, in the greater part of 'em?

A person may be overfull of talk of his own experiences; commonly falling upon it, everywhere, and in all companies; and when it is so, it is rather a dark sign than a good one. As a tree that is overfull of leaves seldom bears much fruit: and as a cloud, though to appearance very pregnant and full of water, if it brings with it overmuch wind, seldom affords much rain to the dry and thirsty earth: which very thing the Holy Spirit is pleased several times to make use of, to represent a great shew of religion with the mouth, without answerable fruit in the life: "Whoso boasteth himself of a false gift, is like clouds and wind without rain" (Prov. 25:14). And the apostle Jude, speaking of some in the primitive times, that crept in unawares among the saints, and having a great shew of religion, were for a while not suspected, "These are clouds (says he) without water, carried about of winds" (Jude 5:4 and 12). And the apostle Peter, speaking of the same, says, "These are clouds without water, carried with a tempest" (II Pet. 2:17).

False affections, if they are equally strong, are much more forward to declare themselves, than true. Because 'tis the nature of false religion, to affect shew and observation; as it was with the Pharisees.[3]

3. That famous experimental divine Mr. Shepard, says, "A Pharisee's trumpet shall be heard to the town's end; when simplicity walks through the town unseen. Hence a man will sometimes covertly commend himself (and "myself" ever comes in) and tells you a long story of conversion: and an hundred to one if some lie or other slip not out with it. Why the secret meaning is, I pray admire me. Hence complain of wants and weaknesses; pray think what a broken-hearted Christian I am." Thomas Shepard. *The Parable of the Ten Virgins* (London, 1695, 1st ed. 1660), Pt. I, pp. 179–80. [JE indicates no edition, but all his citations are consistent with the 1695 rather than with the 1660. For JE's relation to Shepard see above, pp. 53–7.]

And holy Mr. Flavel says thus, "O reader, if thy heart were right with God, and thou didst not cheat thyself with a vain profession, thou wouldst have frequent business with God, which thou wouldst be loath thy dearest friend, or the wife of thy bosom should be privy to. *Non est religio, ubi omnia patent.* Religion doth not lie open to all, to the eyes of men. Observed duties maintain our credit; but secret duties maintain our life. It was the saying of an heathen, about his secret correspondency with his friend, What need the world be ac-

4. 'Tis no sign that affections are gracious, or that they are otherwise, that persons did not make 'em themselves, or excite 'em of their own contrivance, and by their own strength.

There are many in these days, that condemn all affections which are excited in a way that the subjects of 'em can give no account of, as not seeming to be the fruit of any of their own endeavors, or the natural consequence of the faculties and principles of human nature, in such circumstances, and under such means; but to be from the influence of some extrinsic and supernatural power upon their minds. How greatly has the doctrine of the inward experience or sensible perceiving of the immediate power and operation of the Spirit of God, been reproached and ridiculed by many of late. They say the manner of the Spirit of God, is to cooperate in a silent, secret and undiscernible way, with the use of means, and our own endeavors; so that there is no distinguishing by sense, between the influences of the Spirit of God, and the natural operations of the faculties of our own minds.

And it is true, that for any to expect to receive the saving influences of the Spirit of God, while they neglect a diligent improvement of the appointed means of grace, is unreasonable presumption. And to expect that the Spirit of God will savingly operate upon their minds, without the Spirit's making use of means, as subservient to the effect, is enthusiastical. 'Tis also undoubtedly true, that the Spirit of God is very various in the manner and circumstances of his operations, and that sometimes he operates in a way more secret and gradual, and from smaller beginnings, than at others.

But if there be indeed a power, entirely different from and beyond our power, or the power of all means and instruments, and above the power of nature, which is requisite in order to the production of saving grace in the heart, according to the general profession of the country; then certainly, it is in no wise unreasonable to suppose that this effect should very frequently be produced after such a manner, as to make it very manifest, apparent, and sensible that it is so. If grace be indeed owing to the powerful and efficacious operation of an extrinsic agent, or divine efficient out of ourselves, why is it unreasonable to suppose, it should seem

---

quainted with it? Thou and I art theater enough to each other. There are enclosed pleasures in religion, which none but renewed spiritual souls do feelingly understand." John Flavel, *Touchstone of Sincerity* (London, 1679), ch. 2, sec. 2, p. 21. [See above, p. 62.]

to be so, to them who are the subjects of it? Is it a strange thing, that it should seem to be as it is? When grace in the heart, indeed is not produced by our strength, nor is the effect of the natural power of our own faculties, or any means or instruments, but is properly the workmanship and production of the spirit of the Almighty, is it a strange and unaccountable thing, that it should seem to them who are subjects of it agreeable to truth, and not right contrary to truth, so that if persons tell of effects that they are conscious to in their own minds, that seem to them not to be from the natural power or operation of their minds, but from the supernatural power of some other agent, it should at once be looked upon as a sure evidence of their being under a delusion, because things seem to them to be as they are? For this is the objection which is made: 'tis looked upon as a clear evidence that the apprehensions and affections that many persons have, are not really from such a cause, because they seem to them to be from that cause: they declare that what they are conscious of, seems to them evidently not to be from themselves, but from the mighty power of the Spirit of God; and others from hence condemn 'em, and determine what they experience is not from the Spirit of God, but from themselves, or from the devil. Thus unreasonably are multitudes treated at this day, by their neighbors.

If it be indeed so, as the Scripture abundantly teaches, that grace in the soul, is so the effect of God's power, that it is fitly compared to those effects, which are farthest from being owing to any strength in the subject, such as a generation, or a being begotten, and resurrection, or a being raised from the dead, and creation, or a being brought out of nothing into being, and that it is an effect wherein the mighty power of God is greatly glorified, and the exceeding greatness of his power is manifested; [4] then what account can be given of it, that the Almighty, in so great a work of his power, should so carefully hide his power, that the subjects of it should be able to discern nothing of it? Or what reason or revelation have any to determine that he does so? If we may judge by the Scripture, this is not agreeable to God's manner, in his operations and dispensations; but on the contrary, 'tis God's manner, in the great works of his power and mercy which he works for his people, to order things so, as to make his hand visible, and his power conspicuous, and men's dependence on him most evident, that no

4. Eph. 1:17–20.

flesh should glory in his presence,[5] that God alone might be exalted,[6] and that the excellency of the power might be of God and not of man,[7] and that Christ's power might be manifested in our weakness,[8] and none might say mine own hand hath saved me.[9] So it was in most of those temporal salvations which God wrought for Israel of old, which were types of the salvation of God's people from their spiritual enemies. So it was in the redemption of Israel, from their Egyptian bondage; he redeemed them with a strong hand, and an outstretched arm; and that his power might be the more conspicuous, he suffered Israel first to be brought into the most helpless and forlorn circumstances. So it was in the great redemption by Gideon; God would have his army diminished to a handful, and they without any other arms, than trumpets, and lamps, and earthen pitchers. So it was in the deliverance of Israel from Goliath, by a stripling, with a sling and a stone. So it was in that great work of God, his calling the Gentiles, and converting the heathen world, after Christ's ascension, after that the world by wisdom knew not God, and all the endeavors of philosophers had proved in vain, for many ages, to reform the world, and it was by everything, become abundantly evident that the world was utterly helpless, by anything else, but the mighty power of God. And so it was in most of the conversions of particular persons, we have an account of in the history of the New Testament: they were not wrought on in that silent, secret, gradual and insensible manner, which is now insisted on; but with those manifest evidences of a supernatural power, wonderfully and suddenly causing a great change, which in these days are looked upon as certain signs of delusion and enthusiasm.

The Apostle in Eph. 1:18–19 speaks of God's enlightening the minds of Christians, and so bringing them to believe in Christ, to the end, that they might know the exceeding greatness of his power to them who believe. The words are: "The eyes of your understanding being enlightened, that ye may know what is the hope of his calling, and what the riches of the glory of his inheritance in the saints, and what is the exceeding greatness of his power to us-ward,

5. I Cor. 1:27–29.
6. Is. 2:11–17.
7. II Cor. 4:7.
8. II Cor. 12:9.
9. Judg. 7:2.

who believe, according to the working of his mighty power," etc. Now when the Apostle speaks of their being thus the subjects of his power, in their enlightening and effectual calling, to the end, that they might know what his mighty power was to them who believe, he can mean nothing else, than that they might know by experience. But if the saints know this power by experience, then they feel it, and discern it, and are conscious of it; as sensibly distinguishable from the natural operations of their own minds, which is not agreeable to a notion of God's operating so secretly, and undiscernibly, that it can't be known that they are the subjects of the influence of any extrinsic power at all, any otherwise than as they may argue it from Scripture assertions; which is a different thing from knowing it by experience.

So that it is very unreasonable and unscriptural, to determine that affections are not from the gracious operations of God's Spirit, because they are sensibly not from the persons themselves, that are the subjects of them.

On the other hand, it is no evidence that affections are gracious, that they are not purposely produced by those who are the subjects of them, or that they arise in their minds in a manner they can't account for.

There are some who make this an argument in their own favor, when speaking of what they have experienced, they say: "I am sure I did not make it myself: it was a fruit of no contrivance or endeavor of mine; it came when I thought nothing of it; if I might have the world for it, I can't make it again when I please." And hence they determine, that what they have experienced, must be from the mighty influence of the Spirit of God, and is of a saving nature; but very ignorantly, and without grounds. What they have been the subjects of, may indeed, not be from themselves directly, but may be from the operation of an invisible agent, some spirit besides their own: but it does not thence follow, that it was from the Spirit of God. There are other spirits who have influence on the minds of men, besides the Holy Ghost. We are directed not to believe every spirit, but to try the spirits, whether they be of God. There are many false spirits, exceeding busy with men, who often transform themselves into angels of light, and do in many wonderful ways, with great subtlety and power, mimic the operations of the Spirit of God. And there are many of Satan's operations, which are very distinguishable from the voluntary exercises of men's own minds. They are so, in those dreadful and horrid suggestions, and blasphemous injections with which he follows many persons; and in vain and fruitless frights and terrors, which he is the author of. And the power of Satan may be as immediate, and as evident in false comforts and joys, as in terrors and horrid suggestions; and oftentimes is so in fact. 'Tis not in men's power to put themselves into such raptures, as the Anabaptists in Germany, and many other raving enthusiasts like them, have been the subjects of.

And besides, it is to be considered, that persons may have those impressions on their minds, which may not be of their own producing, nor from an evil spirit, but from the Spirit of God, and yet not be from any saving, but a common influence of the Spirit of God: and the subjects of such impressions, may be of the number of those we read of, "That are once enlightened, and taste of the heavenly gift, and are made partakers of the Holy Ghost, and taste the good Word of God, and the power of the world to come" (Heb. 6:4–5); and yet may be wholly unacquainted with those "better things that accompany salvation" spoken of ver. 9.

And where neither a good nor evil spirit have any immediate hand, persons, especially such as are of a weak and vapory habit of body, and the brain weak, and easily susceptive of impressions, may have strange apprehensions and imaginations, and strong affections attending them, unaccountably arising, which are not voluntarily produced by themselves. We see that such persons are liable to such impressions, about temporal things; and there is equal reason, why they should about spiritual things. As a person who is asleep, has dreams, that he is not the voluntary author of; so may such persons, in like manner, be the subjects of involuntary impressions, when they are awake.

5. 'Tis no sign that religious affections are truly holy and spiritual, or that they are not, that they come with texts of Scripture, remarkably brought to the mind.

'Tis no sign that affections are not gracious, that they are occasioned by Scriptures so coming to mind; provided it be the Scripture itself, or the truth which the Scripture so brought contains and teaches, that is the foundation of the affection, and not merely or mainly, the sudden and unusual manner of its coming to the mind.

But on the other hand, neither is it any sign that affections are gracious, that they arise on occasion of Scriptures brought suddenly and wonderfully to the mind; whether those affections be fear, or hope, joy, or sorrow, or any other. Some seem to look upon this, as a good evidence that their affections are saving; especially if the affections excited are hope or joy, or any other which are pleasing and delightful. They will mention it as an evidence that all is right, that their experience came with the Word, and will say: "There were such and such sweet promises brought to my mind: they came suddenly, as if they were spoke to me: I had no hand in bringing such a text to my own mind; I was not thinking of anything leading to it; it came all at once, so that I was surprised. I had not thought of it a long time before; I did not know at first that it was Scripture; I did not remember that ever I had read it." And it may be, they will add. "One Scripture came flowing in after another, and so texts all over the Bible, the most sweet and pleasant, and the most apt and suitable, which could be devised; and filled me full as I could hold: I could not but stand and admire: the tears flowed; I was full of joy, and could not doubt any longer." And thus, they think they have undoubted evidence, that their affections must be from God, and of the right kind, and their state good: but without any manner of grounds. How come they by any such rule, as that if any affections or experiences arise with promises, and comfortable texts of Scripture, unaccountably brought to mind, without their recollection, or if a great number of sweet texts follow one another in a chain, that this is a certain evidence their experiences are saving? Where is any such rule to be found in the Bible, the great and only sure directory in things of this nature?

What deceives many of the less understanding and considerate sort of people, in this matter, seems to be this; that the Scripture is the Word of God, and has nothing in it which is wrong, but is pure and perfect: and therefore, those experiences which come from the Scripture must be right. But then it should be considered, affections may arise on *occasion* of the Scripture, and not *properly come from* the Scripture, as the genuine fruit of the Scripture, and by a right use of it; but from an abuse of it. All that can be argued from the purity and perfection of the Word of God, with respect to experiences, is this, that those experiences which are agreeable to the Word of God, are right, and can't be otherwise; and not that those affections must be right, which arise on occasion of the Word of God, coming to the mind.

What evidence is there that the devil can't bring texts of Scripture to the mind, and misapply them, to deceive persons? There seems to be nothing in this which exceeds the power of Satan. 'Tis no work of such mighty power, to bring sounds or letters to persons' minds, that we have any reason to suppose; nothing short of omnipotence can be sufficient for it. If Satan has power to bring any words or sounds at all to persons' minds, he may have power to bring words contained in the Bible. There is no higher sort of power required in men, to make the sounds which express the words of a text of Scripture, than to make the sounds which express the words of an idle story or song. And so the same power in Satan, which is sufficient to renew one of those kinds of sounds in the mind, is sufficient to renew the other: the different signification, which depends wholly on custom, alters not the case, as to ability to make or revive the sounds or letters. Or will any suppose, that texts of Scripture are such sacred things, that the devil durst not abuse them, nor touch them? In this also they are mistaken. He who was bold enough to lay hold on Christ himself, and carry him hither and thither, into the wilderness, and into an high mountain, and to a pinnacle of the temple, is not afraid to touch the Scripture, and abuse that for his own purposes: as he shewed at the same time that he was so bold with Christ, he then brought one Scripture and another, to deceive and tempt him. And if Satan did presume, and was permitted, to put Christ himself in mind of texts of Scripture to tempt *him,* what reason have we to determine, that he dare not, or will not be permitted, to put wicked men in mind of texts of Scripture, to tempt and deceive *them?* And if Satan may thus abuse one text of Scripture, so he may another. Its being a very excellent place of Scripture, a comfortable and precious promise, alters not the case, as to his courage and ability. And if he can bring one comfortable text to the mind, so he may a thousand; and may choose out such Scriptures as tend most to serve his purpose; and may heap up Scripture promises, tending, according to the perverse application he makes of them, wonderfully to remove the rising doubts, and to confirm the false joy and confidence of a poor deluded sinner.

We know the devil's instruments, corrupt and heretical teachers, can and do pervert the Scripture, to their own and others' damnation (II Pet. 3:16). We see they have the free use of Scripture, in every part of it: there is no text so precious and sacred, but they are permitted to abuse it, to the eternal ruin of multitudes of souls: and there are no weapons they make use of with which they do more execution. And there is no manner of reason to determine, that the devil is not permitted thus to use the Scripture, as well as his instruments. For when the latter do it, they do it as his instruments and servants, and through his instigation and influence: and doubtless he does the same he instigates others to do: the devil's servants do but follow their master, and do the same work that he does himself.

And as the devil can abuse the Scripture, to deceive and destroy men, so may men's own folly and corruptions, as well. The sin which is in men, acts like its father. Men's own hearts are deceitful like the devil, and use the same means to deceive.

So that 'tis evident, that persons may have high affections of hope and joy, arising on occasion of texts of Scripture, yea precious promises of Scripture coming suddenly and remarkably to their minds, as though they were spoke to them, yea a great multitude of such texts, following one another in a wonderful manner, and yet all this be no argument that these affections are divine, or that they are any other than the effects of Satan's delusions.

And I would further observe, that persons may have raised and joyful affections, which may come with the Word of God, and not only so, but from the Word, and those affections not be from Satan, nor yet properly from the corruptions of their own hearts, but from some influence of the Spirit of God with the Word, and yet have nothing of the nature of true and saving religion in them. Thus the stony-ground hearers had great joy from the Word; yea which is represented as arising from the Word, as growth from a seed; and their affections had, in their appearance, a very great and exact resemblance with those represented by the growth on the good ground, the difference not appearing, until it was discovered by the consequences, in a time of trial: and yet there was no saving religion in these affections.[1]

1. Mr. Stoddard, in his *Guide to Christ,* speaks of it as a common thing, for persons while in a natural condition, and before they have ever truly accepted of Christ, to have Scripture promises come to them, with a great deal of refreshing; which they take as tokens of God's love, and hope that God has ac-

6. 'Tis no evidence that religious affections are saving, or that they are otherwise, that there is an appearance of love in them.

There are no professing Christians who pretend, that this is an argument against the truth and saving nature of religious affections. But on the other hand, there are some who suppose, it is a good evidence that affections are from the sanctifying and saving influences of the Holy Ghost. Their argument is, that Satan cannot love; this affection being directly contrary to the devil, whose very nature is enmity and malice. And it is true, that nothing is more excellent, heavenly and divine than a spirit of true Christian love to God and men; 'tis more excellent than knowledge, or prophecy, or miracles, or speaking with the tongue of men and angels. 'Tis the chief of the graces of God's Spirit, and the life, essence and sum of all true religion; and that by which we are most conformed to heaven, and most contrary to hell and the devil. But yet it is ill arguing from hence, that there are no counterfeits of it. It may be observed, that the more excellent anything is, the more will be the counterfeits of it. Thus there are many more counterfeits of silver and gold, than of iron and copper; there are many false diamonds and rubies, but who goes about to counterfeit common stones? Though the more excellent things are, the more difficult it is to make anything that shall be like them, in their essential nature and internal virtue; yet the more manifold will the counterfeits be, and the more will arts and subtlety be exercised and displayed, in an exact imitation of the outward appearance. Thus there is the greatest danger of being cheated in buying of medicines that are most excellent and sovereign, though it be most difficult to imitate 'em, with anything of the like value and virtue, and their counterfeits are good for nothing when we have them. So it is with Christian virtues and graces; the subtlety of Satan, and men's deceitful hearts, are wont chiefly to be exercised in counterfeiting those that are in highest repute. So there are perhaps no graces that have more counterfeits than love and humility; these being virtues wherein the beauty of a true Chrisitan does especially appear.

But with respect to love; it is plain by the Scripture, that persons may have a kind of religious love, and yet have no saving grace. Christ speaks of many professing Christians that have such

---

cepted them; and so are confident of their good estate. Stoddard, *Guide.* [A loose paraphrase of pp. 8–9. For JE's treatment of quoted material see above, pp. 80 ff.]

love, whose love will not continue, and so shall fail of salvation, "And because inquity shall abound, the love of many shall wax cold. But he that shall endure unto the end, the same shall be saved" (Matt. 24:12–13). Which latter words plainly shew, that those spoken of before, whose love should not endure to the end, but wax cold, should not be saved.

Persons may seem to have love to God and Christ, yea to have very strong and violent affections of this nature, and yet have no grace. For this was evidently the case with many graceless Jews, such as cried Jesus up so high, following him day and night, without meat, drink or sleep; such as said, "Lord I will follow thee whithersoever thou goest," and cried "Hosanna to the Son of David." [2]

The Apostle seems to intimate, that there were many in his days, who had a counterfeit love to Christ, in Eph. 6:24: "Grace be with all them that love the Lord Jesus Christ in sincerity." The last word, in the original, signifies "in incorruption"; which shews that the Apostle was sensible that there were many who had a kind of love to Christ, whose love was not pure and spiritual.

So also Christian love to the people of God may be counterfeited. 'Tis evident by the Scripture, that there may be strong affections of this kind, without saving grace; as there were in the Galatians towards the apostle Paul, when they were ready to pluck out their eyes and give 'em to him; although the Apostle expresses his fear that their affections were come to nothing, and that he had bestowed upon them labor in vain (Gal. 4:11, 15).

7. Persons having religious affections of many kinds, accompanying one another, is not sufficient to determine whether they have any gracious affections or no.

Though false religion is wont to be maimed and monstrous, and not to have that entireness and symmetry of parts, which is to be seen in true religion; yet there may be a great variety of false affections together, that may resemble gracious affections.

2. Agreeable to this Mr. Stoddard observes, in his *Guide to Christ,* that some sinners have pangs of affection, and give an account that they find a spirit of love to God, and of their aiming at the glory of God, having that which has a great resemblance of saving grace, and that sometimes their common affections are stronger than saving. And supposes that sometimes natural men may have such violent pangs of false affection to God, that they may think themselves willing to be damned. Stoddard, *Guide.* [A loose paraphrase of pp. 21 and 65.]

'Tis evident that there are counterfeits of all kinds of gracious affections; as of love to God, and love to the brethren, as has been just now observed: so of godly sorrow for sin, as in Pharaoh, Saul, and Ahab, and the children of Israel in the wilderness (Ex. 9:27; cf. I Sam. 24:16–17 and 26:21; I Kgs. 21:27; Num. 14:39–40); and of the fear of God, as in the Samaritans, who feared the Lord, and served their own gods at the same time (II Kgs. 17:32–33); and those enemies of God we read of Ps. 66:3 who through the greatness of God's power, submit themselves to him, or, as it is in the Hebrew, lie unto him, i.e. yield a counterfeit reverence and submission: so of a gracious gratitude, as in the children of Israel, who sang God's praise at the Red Sea (Ps. 106:12), and Naaman the Syrian, after his miraculous cure of his leprosy (II Kgs. 5:15, etc.).

So of spiritual joy, as in the stony-ground hearers (Matt. 13:20) and particularly many of John the Baptist's hearers (John 5:35). So of zeal, as in Jehu (II Kgs. 10:16), and in Paul before his conversion (Gal. 1:14; Phil. 3:6), and the unbelieving Jews (Acts 22:3; Rom. 10:2). So graceless persons may have earnest religious desires, which may be like Balaam's desires, which he expresses under an extraordinary view that he had of the happy state of God's people, as distinguished from all the rest of the world (Num. 23:9–10). They may also have a strong hope of eternal life, as the Pharisees had.

And as men, while in a state of nature, are capable of a resemblance of all kinds of religious affections, so nothing hinders but that they may have many of them together. And what appears in fact does abundantly evince that it is very often so indeed. It seems commonly to be so, that when false affections are raised high, there are many false affections attend each other. The multitude that attended Christ into Jerusalem, after that great miracle of raising Lazarus, seem to be moved with many religious affections at once, and all in a high degree. They seem to be filled with admiration, and there was a shew of an high affection of love, and also of a great degree of reverence, in their laying their garments on the ground, for Christ to tread upon; and also of great gratitude to him, for the great and good works he had wrought, praising him with loud voices for his salvation; and earnest desires of the coming of God's kingdom, which they supposed Jesus was now about to set up, and shewed great hopes and raised expectations of it, expecting it would immediately appear, and hence were filled with joy, by which they were so animated in their acclamations, as to make the whole city ring with the noise of them; and appeared great in their zeal and forwardness to attend Jesus, and assist him without further delay, now in the time of the great feast of the Passover, to set up his Kingdom. And it is easy, from nature, and the nature of the affections, to give an account why, when one affection is raised very high, that it should excite others; especially if the affection which is raised high, be that of counterfeit love, as it was in the multitude who cried "Hosanna." This will naturally draw many other affections after it. For, as was observed before, love is the chief of the affections, and as it were the fountain of them. Let us suppose a person who has been for some time in great exercise and terror through fear of hell, and his heart weakened with distress and dreadful apprehensions, and upon the brink of despair, and is all at once delivered, by being firmly made to believe, through some delusion of Satan, that God has pardoned him, and accepts him as the object of his dear love, and promises him eternal life: as suppose through some vision, or strong idea or imagination, suddenly excited in him, of a person with a beautiful countenance, smiling on him, and with arms open, and with blood dropping down, which the person conceives to be Christ, without any other enlightening of the understanding, to give a view of the spiritual divine excellency of Christ and his fullness, and of the way of salvation revealed in the gospel; or perhaps by some voice or words coming as if they were spoke to him, such as those, "Son, be of good cheer, thy sins be forgiven thee," or, "Fear not, it is the Father's good pleasure to give you the Kingdom," which he takes to be immediately spoken by God to him, though there was no preceding acceptance of Christ, or closing of the heart with him: I say, if we should suppose such a case, what various passions would naturally crowd at once, or one after another, into such a person's mind? It is easy to be accounted for, from mere principles of nature, that a person's heart, on such an occasion, should be raised up to the skies with transports of joy, and be filled with fervent affection, to that imaginary God or Redeemer, who he supposes has thus rescued him from the jaws of such dreadful destruction, that his soul was so amazed with the fears of, and has received him with such endearment, as a peculiar favorite; and that now he should be filled with admiration and gratitude, and his mouth should be opened, and be full of talk about what he has experienced; and that, for a while, he should think and speak of scarce anything else, and should seem to magnify that God who has done so much for him, and call upon others to rejoice with him, and appear with a cheerful countenance, and talk with a loud voice: and however, before his deliverance, he was full of quarrelings against the justice of God, that now it should be easy for him to submit to God, and own his unworthiness, and cry out against himself, and appear to be very humble before God, and lie at his feet as tame as a lamb; and that he should now confess his unworthiness, and cry out, "Why me? Why me?" (like Saul, who when Samuel told him that God had appointed him to be king, makes answer: "Am not I a Benjamite, of the smallest of the tribes of Israel, and my family the least of all the families of the tribe of Benjamin? Wherefore then speakest thou so to me?" Much in the language of David, the true saint, "Who am I, and what is my Father's house, that thou hast brought me hitherto!" II Sam. 7:18). Nor is it to be wondered at, that now he should delight to be with them who acknowledge and applaud his happy circumstances, and should love all such as esteem and admire him and what he has experienced, and have violent zeal against all such as would make nothing of such things, and be disposed openly to separate, and as it were to proclaim war with all who be not of his party, and should now glory in his sufferings, and be very much for condemning and censuring all who seem to doubt, or make any difficulty of these things; and while the warmth of his affections last, should be mighty forward to take pains, and deny himself, to promote the interest of the party who he imagines favor such things, and seem earnestly desirous to increase the number of them, as the Pharisees compassed sea and land to make one proselyte.[3] And so I might go on, and mention many other things, which will naturally arise in such circumstances. He must have but slightly considered human nature, who thinks such things as these can't arise in this manner, without any supernatural interposition of divine power.

As from true divine love flow all Christian affections, so from a counterfeit love in like manner, naturally flow other false affections. In both cases, love is the fountain, and the other affections are the

3. "Associating with godly men don't prove that a man has grace: Ahithophel was David's companion. Sorrows for the afflictions of the church, and desires for the conversion of souls, don't prove it. These things may be found in carnal men, and so can be no evidences of grace." Solomon Stoddard, *A Treatise Concerning Conversion* (Boston, 1719), p. 82.

streams. The various faculties, principles and affections of the human nature, are as it were many channels from one fountain: if there be sweet water in the fountain, sweet water will from thence flow out into those various channels; but if the water in the fountain be poisonous, then poisonous streams will also flow out into all those channels. So that the channels and streams will be alike, corresponding one with another; but the great difference will lie in the nature of the water. Or, man's nature may be compared to a tree, with many branches, coming from one root: if the sap in the root be good, there will also be good sap distributed throughout the branches, and the fruit that is brought forth will be good and wholesome; but if the sap in the root and stock be poisonous, so it will be in many branches (as in the other case), and the fruit will be deadly. The tree in both cases may be alike; there may be an exact resemblance in shape; but the difference is found only in eating the fruit. 'Tis thus (in some measure at least) oftentimes, between saints and hypocrites. There is sometimes a very great similitude between true and false experiences, in their appearance, and in what is expressed and related by the subjects of them: and the difference between them is much like the difference between the dreams of Pharaoh's chief butler and baker; they seemed to be much alike; insomuch that when Joseph interpreted the chief butler's dream, that he should be delivered from his imprisonment, and restored to the king's favor, and his honorable office in the palace, the chief baker had raised hopes and expectations, and told his dream also; but he was woefully disappointed; and though his dream was so much like the happy and well-boding dream of his companion, yet it was quite contrary in its issue.

8. Nothing can certainly be determined concerning the nature of the affections by this, that comforts and joys seem to follow awakenings and convictions of conscience, in a *certain order*.

Many persons seem to be prejudiced against affections and experiences, that come in such a method, as has been much insisted on by many divines; first, such awakenings, fears and awful apprehensions followed with such legal humblings, in a sense of total sinfulness and helplessness, and then, such and such light and comfort: they look upon all such schemes, laying down such methods and steps, to be of men's devising: and particularly if high affections of joy follow great distress and terror, it is made by many an argument against those affections. But such prejudices and objections are without reason or Scripture. Surely it can't be unreasonable to suppose, that before God delivers persons from a state of sin and exposedness to eternal destruction, he should give them some considerable sense of the evil he delivers from; that they may be delivered sensibly, and understand their own salvation, and know something of what God does for them. As men that are saved are in two exceeding different states, first a state of condemnation, and then in a state of justification and blessedness; and as God in the work of the salvation of mankind, deals with them suitably to their intelligent rational nature; so it seems reasonable, and agreeable to God's wisdom, that men who are saved, should be in these two states sensibly, first, that they should sensibly to themselves, be in a state of condemnation, and so in a state of woeful calamity and dreadful misery, and so afterwards sensibly in a state of deliverance and happiness; and that they should be first sensible of their absolute extreme necessity, and afterwards of Christ's sufficiency and God's mercy through him.

And that it is God's manner of dealing with men, to lead them into a wilderness, before he speaks comfortably to them, and so to order it, that they shall be brought into distress, and made to see their own helplessness, and absolute dependence on his power and grace, before he appears to work any great deliverence for them, is abundantly manifest by the Scripture. Then is God wont to repent himself for his professing people, when their strength is gone, and there is none shut up or left, and when they are brought to see that their false gods can't help them, and that the rock in whom they trusted is vain (Deut. 32:36–37). Before God delivered the children of Israel out of Egypt, they were prepared for it, by being made to see that they were in an evil case, and to cry unto God, because of their hard bondage (Ex. 2:23 and 5:19). And before God wrought that great deliverance for them at the Red Sea, they were brought into great distress, the wilderness had shut them in, they could not turn to the right hand nor the left, and the Red Sea was before them, and the great Egyptian host behind, and they were brought to see that they could do nothing to help themselves, and that if God did not help them, they should be immediately swallowed up; and then God appeared, and turned their cries into songs. So before they were brought to their rest, and to enjoy the milk and honey of Canaan, God led them through a great and terrible wilderness, that he might humble them, and teach them what was in their heart, and so do them good in their latter end (Deut. 8:2, 16). The woman that had the issue of blood twelve years, was not delivered, till she had spent all her living on earthly physicians, and could not be healed of any, and so was left helpless, having no more money to spend; and then she came to the great Physician, without any money or price, and was healed by him (Luke 8:43–44). Before Christ would answer the request of the woman of Canaan, he first seemed utterly to deny her, and humbled her, and brought her to own herself worthy to be called a dog; and then he showed her mercy, and received her as a dear child (Matt. 15:22, etc.). The apostle Paul, before a remarkable deliverance, was pressed out of measure, above strength, insomuch that he despaired even of life; but had the sentence of death in himself, that he might not trust in himself, but in God that raiseth the dead (II Cor. 1:8–10). There was first a great tempest, and the ship was covered with the waves, and just ready to sink, and the disciples were brought to cry to Jesus, "Lord, save us, we perish"; and then the winds and seas were rebuked, and there was a great calm; Matt. 8:24–26. The leper, before he is cleansed, must have his mouth stopped, by a covering on his upper lip, and was to acknowledge his great misery and utter uncleanness, by rending his clothes, and crying, "Unclean, unclean"; Lev. 13:45. And backsliding Israel, before God heals them, are brought to acknowledge that they have sinned, and have not obeyed the voice of the Lord, and to see that they lie down in their shame, and that confusion covers them, and that in vain is salvation hoped for from the hills, and from the multitude of mountains, and that God only can save them (Jer. 3:23–25). Joseph, who was sold by his brethren, and therein was a type of Christ, brings his brethren into great perplexity and distress, and brings them to reflect on their sin, and to say we are verily guilty; and at last to resign up themselves entirely into his hands for bondmen; and then reveals himself to them, as their brother and their savior.

And if we consider those extraordinary manifestations which God made of himself to saints of old, we shall find that he commonly first manifested himself in a way which was terrible, and then by those things that were comfortable. So it was with Abraham; first a horror of great darkness fell upon him, and then God revealed himself to him in sweet promises (Gen. 15:12–13). So it was with Moses at Mount Sinai; first God appeared to him in all the terrors of his dreadful majesty, so that Moses said, "I exceedingly fear and quake," and then he made all his goodness to pass before him, and proclaimed his name, the Lord God gracious and merciful, etc. So it was with Elijah; first, there is a stormy wind, and earthquake, and devouring fire, and then a still, small, sweet voice; I Kgs. 19. So it was with Daniel; he first saw Christ's countenance as lightning, that terrified him, and caused him to faint away; and then he is strengthened and refreshed with such comfortable words as these, "O Daniel, a man greatly beloved" (Dan. 10). So it was with the apostle John (Rev. 1). And there is an analogy observable in God's dispensations and deliverances which he works for his people, and the manifestation which he makes of himself to them, both ordinary and extraordinary.

But there are many things in Scripture which do more directly shew, that this is God's ordinary manner in working salvation for the souls of men, and in the manifestations God makes of himself and of his mercy in Christ, in the ordinary works of his grace on the hearts of sinners. The servant that owed his prince ten thousand talents, is first held to his debt, and the king pronounces sentence of condemnation upon him, and commands him to be sold, and his wife and children, and payment to be made; and thus he humbles him, and brings him to own the whole debt to be just, and then forgives him all. The prodigal son spends all he has, and is brought to see himself in extreme circumstances, and to humble himself, and own his unworthiness, before he is relieved and feasted by his father (Luke 15). Old inveterate wounds must be searched to the bottom, in order to healing: and the Scripture compares sin, the wound of the soul, to this, and speaks of healing this wound without thus searching of it, as vain and deceitful; Jer. 8:11. Christ, in the work of his grace on the hearts of men, is compared to rain on the mown grass, grass that is cut down with a scythe (Ps. 72:6), representing his refreshing, comforting influences on the wounded spirit. Our first parents, after they had sinned, were first terrified with God's majesty and justice, and had their sin, with its aggravations, set before them by their judge, before they were relieved, by the promise of the seed of the woman. Christians are spoken of as those that have fled for refuge, to lay hold on the hope set before them (Heb. 6:18), which representation implies great fear, and sense of danger preceding. To the like purpose, Christ is called a hiding place from the wind, and a covert from the tempest, and as rivers of water in a dry place, and as the shadow of a great rock in a weary land (Is. 32 at the beginning). And it seems to be the natural import of the word "gospel," glad tidings, that it is news of deliverance and salvation, after great fear and distress. There is all reason to suppose, that God deals with particular believers, as he dealt with his church, which he first made to hear his voice in the Law, with terrible thunders and lightnings, and kept her under that schoolmaster, to prepare her for Christ; and then comforted her with the joyful sound of the gospel from Mount Zion. So likewise John the Baptist came to prepare the way for Christ, and prepare men's hearts for his reception, by shewing them their sins, and by bringing the self-righteous Jews off from their own righteousness, telling them that they were a generation of vipers, and shewing them their danger of the wrath to come, telling them that the ax was laid at the root of the tree, etc.

And if it be indeed God's manner (as I think the foregoing considerations shew that it undoubtedly is) before he gives men the comfort of a deliverance from their sin and misery, to give them a considerable sense of the greatness and dreadfulness of those evils, and their extreme wretchedness by reason of them; surely it is not unreasonable to suppose, that persons, at least oftentimes, while under these views, should have great distress and terrible apprehensions of mind: especially if it be considered what these evils are, that they have a view of; which are no other than great and manifold sins, against the infinite majesty of the great Jehovah, and the suffering of the fierceness of his wrath to all eternity. And the more so still, when we have many plain instances in Scripture, of persons that have actually been brought into extreme distress, by such convictions, before they have received saving consolations: as the multitude at Jerusalem, who were pricked in their heart, and said unto Peter, and the rest of the apostles, "Men and brethren, what shall we do?" And the apostle Paul, who trembled and was astonished, before he was comforted; and the jailer, when he called for a light, and sprang in, and came trembling, and fell down before Paul and Silas, and said, "Sirs, what must I do to be saved?"

From these things it appears to be very unreasonable in professing Christians, to make this an objection against the truth and spiritual nature of the comfortable and joyful affections which any have, that they follow such awful apprehensions and distresses, as have been mentioned.

And on the other hand, it is no evidence that comforts and joys are right, because they succeed great terrors, and amazing fears of hell.[4] This seems to be what some persons lay great weight upon; esteeming great terrors an evidence of a great work of the law wrought on the heart, well preparing the way for solid comfort: not considering that terror, and a conviction of conscience, are different things. For though convictions of conscience do often cause terror; yet they don't consist in it; and terrors do often arise from other causes. Convictions of conscience, through the influences of God's Spirit, consist in conviction of sinfulness of heart and practice, and of the dreadfulness of sin, as committed against a God of terrible majesty, infinite holiness and hatred of sin, and strict justice in punishing of it. But there are some persons that have frightful apprehensions of hell, a dreadful pit ready to swallow them up, and flames just ready to lay hold of them, and devils around them ready to seize them; who at the same time seem to have very little proper enlightenings of conscience, really convincing them of their sinfulness of heart and life. The devil, if permitted, can terrify men as well as the Spirit of God: 'tis a work natural to him, and he has many ways of doing it, in a manner tending to no good. He may exceedingly affright persons, by impressing on them many external images and ideas, of a countenance frowning, a sword drawn, black clouds of vengeance, words of an awful doom pronounced,[5] hell gaping, devils coming, and the like; not to convince persons of things that are true, and revealed in the Word of God, but to lead them to vain and groundless determinations; as that their day is past, that they are reprobated, that God is implacable, that he has come to a resolution immediately to cut them off, etc.

And the terrors which some persons have, are very much owing to the particular constitution and temper they are of. Nothing is

4. Mr. Shepard speaks of men's "being cast down as low as hell by sorrow, and lying under chains, quaking in apprehension of terror to come, and then raised up to heaven in joy, not able to live; and yet not rent from lust . . . and such are objects of pity now, and are like to be objects of terror at the great day." Shepard, *Parable,* Pt. I, p. 125.

5. "The way of the Spirit's working, when it does convince men, is by enlightening natural conscience. The Spirit does not work by giving a testimony, but by assisting natural conscience to do its work. Natural conscience is the instrument in the hand of God, to accuse, condemn, terrify, and to urge to duty. The Spirit of God leads men into the consideration of their danger, and makes them to be affected therewith; Prov. 20:27: 'The spirit of man is the candle of the Lord, searching all the inward parts of the belly.'" Stoddard, *Guide,* p. 44.

more manifest, than that some persons are of such a temper and frame, that their imaginations are more strongly impressed with everything they are affected with, than others; and the impression on the imagination reacts on the affection, and raises that still higher; and so affection and imagination act reciprocally, one on another, till their affection is raised to a vast height, and the person is swallowed up, and loses all possession of himself.[6]

And some speak of a great sight they have of their wickedness, who really, when the matter comes to be well examined into and thoroughly weighed, are found to have little or no convictions of conscience. They tell of a dreadful hard heart, and how their heart lies like a stone; when truly they have none of those things in their minds or thoughts, wherein the hardness of men's heart does really consist. They tell of a dreadful load and sink of sin, a heap of black and loathsome filthiness within them; when, if the matter be carefully inquired into, they have not in view anything wherein the corruption of nature does truly consist, nor have they any thought of any particular thing wherein their hearts are sinfully defective, or fall short of what ought to be in them, or any exercises at all of corruption in them. And many think also they have great convictions of their actual sins, who truly have none. They tell how their sins are set in order before 'em, they see 'em stand encompassing them round in a row, with a dreadful frightful appearance; when really they have not so much as one of the sins they have been guilty of in the course of their lives, coming into view, that they are affected with the aggravations of.

And if persons have had great terrors, which really have been from the awakening and convincing influences of the Spirit of God, it don't thence follow that their terrors must needs issue in true comfort. The unmortified corruption of the heart may quench the Spirit of God (after he has been striving) by leading men to presumptuous, and self-exalting hopes and joys, as well as otherwise. 'Tis not every woman who is really in travail, that brings forth

6. The famous Mr. Perkins distinguishes between those sorrows that come through convictions of conscience, and melancholic passions rising only from mere imaginations, strongly conceived in the brain; which he says, "usually come on a sudden, like lightning into a house." [William Perkins, "A Dialogue of the State of a Christian," in *A Treatise Tending unto a Declaration, Whether a Man Be in the Estate of Damnation, or in the Estate of Grace,* in *Works* (3 vols. London, 1608–31), *1* (1608), 385.]

a real child; but it may be a monstrous production, without anything of the form or properties of human nature belonging to it. Pharaoh's chief baker, after he had lain in the dungeon with Joseph, had a vision that raised his hopes, and he was lifted up out of the dungeon, as well as the chief butler; but it was to be hanged.

But if comforts and joys do not only come after great terrors and awakenings, but there be an appearance of such preparatory convictions and humiliations, and brought about very distinctly, by such steps, and in such a method, as has frequently been observable in true converts; this is no certain sign that the light and comforts which follow are true and saving. And for these following reasons:

First, as the devil can counterfeit all the saving operations and graces of the Spirit of God, so he can counterfeit those operations that are preparatory to grace. If Satan can counterfeit those effects of God's Spirit which are special, divine and sanctifying; so that there shall be a very great resemblance, in all that can be observed by others; much more easily may he imitate those works of God's Spirit which are common, and which men, while they are yet his own children, are the subjects of. These works are in no wise so much above him as the other. There are no works of God that are so high and divine, and above the powers of nature, and out of the reach of the power of all creatures, as those works of his Spirit, whereby he forms the creature in his own image, and makes it to be a partaker of the divine nature. But if the devil can be the author of such resemblances of these as have been spoken of, without doubt he may of those that are of an infinitely inferior kind. And it is abundantly evident in fact, that there are false humiliations, and false submissions, as well as false comforts.[7] How far was Saul brought, though a very wicked man, and of a haughty spirit, when he (though a great king) was brought, in conviction of his sin, as it were to fall down, all in tears, weeping aloud, before David his own subject (and one that he had for a long time mortally hated, and

7. The venerable Stoddard observes, "A man may say, that now he can justify God however he deals with him, and not be brought off from his own righteousness; and that some men do justify God, from a partial conviction of the righteousness of their condemnation; conscience takes notice of their sinfulness, and tells them that they may be righteously damned; as Pharaoh, who justified God, Ex. 9:27. And they give some kind of consent to it, but many times it don't continue, they have only a pang upon them, that usually dies away after a little time." Stoddard, *Guide,* p. 71.

openly treated as an enemy), and condemn himself before him, crying out: "Thou art more righteous than I. Thou hast rewarded me good, whereas I have rewarded thee evil?" And at another time: "I have sinned, I have played the fool, I have erred exceedingly" (I Sam. 24:16–17 and ch. 26:21). And yet Saul seems then to have had very little of the influences of the Spirit of God, it being after God's Spirit had departed from him, and given him up, and an evil spirit from the Lord troubled him. And if this proud monarch, in a pang of affection, was brought to humble himself so low, before a subject that he hated, and still continued an enemy to; there doubtless may be appearances of great conviction and humiliation in men, before God, while they yet remain enemies to him, and though they finally continue so. There is oftentimes in men who are terrified through fears of hell, a great appearance of their being brought off from their own righteousness, when they are not brought off from it in all ways, although they are in many ways that are more plain and visible. They have only exchanged some ways of trusting in their own righteousness, for others that are more secret and subtle. Oftentimes a great degree of discouragement, as to many things they used to depend upon, is taken for humiliation: and that is called a submission to God, which is no absolute submission, but has some secret bargain in it, that it is hard to discover.

Secondly, if the operations and effects of the Spirit of God, in the convictions and comforts of true converts may be sophisticated, then the order of them may be imitated. If Satan can imitate the things themselves, he may easily put them one after another, in such a certain order. If the devil can make A, B, and C, 'tis as easy for him to put A first, and B next, and C next, as to range 'em in a contrary order. The nature of divine things is harder for the devil to imitate, than their order. He can't *exactly* imitate divine operations in their nature, though his counterfeits may be very much like them in external appearance; but he can exactly imitate their order. When counterfeits are made, there is no divine power needful in order to the placing one of them first, and another last. And therefore no order or method of operations and experiences, is any certain sign of their divinity. That only is to be trusted to, as a certain evidence of grace, which Satan cannot do, and which it is impossible should be brought to pass by any power short of divine.

Thirdly, we have no certain rule to determine how far God's own spirit may go in those operations and convictions which in themselves are not spiritual and saving, and yet the person that is the subject of them, never be converted, but fall short of salvation at last. There is no necessary connection in the nature of things, between anything that a natural man may experience, while in a state of nature, and the saving grace of God's Spirit. And if there be no connection in the nature of things, then there can be no known and certain connection at all, unless it be by divine revelation. But there is no revealed certain connection between a state of salvation, and anything that a natural man can be the subject of, before he believes in Christ. God has revealed no certain connection between salvation, and any qualifications in men, but only grace and its fruits. And therefore we don't find any legal convictions, or comforts following those legal convictions, in any certain method or order, ever once mentioned in the Scripture, as certain signs of grace, or things peculiar to the saints; although we do find gracious operations and effects themselves, so mentioned, thousands of times. Which should be enough with Christians, who are willing to have the Word of God, rather than their own philosophy, and experiences, and conjectures, as their sufficient and sure guide in things of this nature.

Fourthly, experience does greatly confirm, that persons seeming to have convictions and comforts following one another in such a method and order, as is frequently observable in true converts, is no certain sign of grace.[8] I appeal to all those ministers in this land, who have had much occasion of dealing with souls, in the late extraordinary season, whether there han't been many who don't prove well, that have given a fair account of their experiences, and have seemed to be converted according to rule, i.e. with convictions and affections, succeeding distinctly and exactly, in that order and method, which has been ordinarily insisted on, as the order of the operations of the Spirit of God in conversion.

And as a seeming to have this distinctness as to steps and method, is no certain sign that a person is converted; so a being without it, is no evidence that a person is not converted. For though it might be made evident to a demonstration, on Scripture principles, that

8. Mr. Stoddard, who had much experience of things of this nature, long ago observed, that converted and unconverted men can't be certainly distinguished by the account they give of their experience: the same relation of experiences being common to both, and that many persons have given a fair account of a work of conversion, that have carried well in the eye of the world for several years, but have not proved well at last. Solomon Stoddard, *An Appeal to the Learned* (Boston, 1709), pp. 75, 76.

a sinner can't be brought heartily to receive Christ as his Saviour, who is not convinced of his sin and misery, and of his own emptiness and helplessness, and his just desert of eternal condemnation; and that therefore such convictions must be some way implied in what is wrought in his soul; yet nothing proves it to be necessary, that all those things which are implied or presupposed in an act of faith in Christ must be plainly and distinctly wrought in the soul, in so many successive and separate works of the Spirit that shall be, each one, plain and manifest, in all who are truly converted. On the contrary (as Mr. Shepard observes), sometimes the change made in a saint, at first work, is like a confused chaos; so that the saints know not what to make of it. The manner of the Spirit's proceeding in them that are born of the Spirit, is very often exceeding mysterious and unsearchable: we, as it were, hear the sound of it, the effect of it is discernible; but no man can tell whence it came, or whither it went. And 'tis oftentimes as difficult to know the way of the Spirit in the new birth, as in the first birth: "Thou knowest not what is the way of the Spirit, or how the bones do grow in the womb of her that is with child: even so thou knowest not the work of God, that worketh all" (Eccles. 11:5). The ingenerating of a principle of grace in the soul, seems in Scripture to be compared to the conceiving of Christ in the womb (Gal. 4:19). And therefore the church is called Christ's mother (Cant. 3:11). And so is every particular believer (Matt. 12:49–50). And the conception of Christ in the womb of the blessed Virgin, by the power of the Holy Ghost, seems to be a designed resemblance of the conception of Christ in the soul of a believer, by the power of the same Holy Ghost. And we know not what is the way of the Spirit, nor how the bones do grow, either in the womb, or heart that conceives this holy child. The new creature may use that language in Ps. 139:14–15: "I am fearfully and wonderfully made. Marvelous are thy works: and that my soul knoweth right well. My substance was not hid from thee, when I was made in secret." Concerning the generation of Christ, both in his person, and also in the hearts of his people, it may be said, as in Is. 53:8: "Who can declare his generation." We know not the works of God, that worketh all. " 'Tis the glory of God to conceal a thing" (Prov. 25:2), and to have his path as it were in the mighty waters, that his footsteps may not be known: and especially in the works of his Spirit on the hearts of men, which are the highest and chief of his works. And therefore it is said, "Who hath directed the Spirit of the Lord, or being his counsellor hath taught him?" (Is. 40:13). 'Tis to be feared that some have gone too far towards directing the Spirit of the Lord, and marking out his footsteps for him, and limiting him to certain steps and methods. Experience plainly shows, that God's Spirit is unsearchable and untraceable, in some of the best of Christians, in the method of his operations, in their conversion. Nor does the Spirit of God proceed discernibly in the steps of a particular established scheme, one half so often as is imagined. A scheme of what is necessary, and according to a rule already received and established by common opinion, has a vast (though to many a very insensible) influence in forming persons' notions of the steps and method of their own experiences. I know very well what their way is; for I have had much opportunity to observe it. Very often, at first, their experiences appear like a confused chaos, as Mr. Shepard expresses it: but then those passages of their experience are picked out, that have most of the appearance of such particular steps that are insisted on; and these are dwelt upon in the thoughts, and these are told of from time to time, in the relation they give: these parts grow brighter and brighter in their view; and others, being neglected, grow more and more obscure: and what they have experienced is insensibly strained to bring all to an exact conformity to the scheme that is established. And it becomes natural for ministers, who have to deal with them and direct them that insist upon distinctness and clearness of method, to do so too. But yet there has been so much to be seen of the operations of the Spirit of God, of late, that they who have had much to do with souls, and are not blinded with a sevenfold veil of prejudice, must know that the Spirit is so exceeding various in the manner of his operating, that in many cases it is impossible to trace him, or find out his way.

What we have principally to do with, in our inquiries into our own state, or directions we give to others, is the nature of the effect that God has brought to pass in the soul. As to the steps which the Spirit of God took to bring that effect to pass, we may leave them to him. We are often in Scripture expressly directed to try ourselves by the *nature* of the fruits of the Spirit; but nowhere by the Spirit's *method* of producing them.[9] Many do greatly err in their notions of

9. Mr. Shepard, speaking of the soul's closing with Christ, says, "As a child cannot tell how his soul comes into it, nor it may be when; but afterwards it sees and feels that life; so that he were as bad as a beast, that should deny an immortal soul; so here." Shepard, *Parable,* Pt. II, p. 171.

"If the man do not know the time of his conversion, or first closing with

a clear work of conversion; calling that a clear work, where the successive steps of influence, and method of experience is clear: whereas that indeed is the clearest work (not where the order of doing is clearest, but), where the spiritual and divine nature of the work done, and effect wrought, is most clear.

9. 'Tis no certain sign that the religious affections which persons have are such as have in them the nature of true religion, or that they have not, that they dispose persons to spend much time in religion, and to be zealously engaged in the external duties of worship.

This has, very unreasonably, of late been looked upon as an argument against the religious affections which some have had, that they spend so much time in reading, praying, singing, hearing sermons, and the like. 'Tis plain from the Scripture that it is the tendency of true grace to cause persons very much to delight in such religious exercises. True grace had this effect on Anna the prophetess; "she departed not from the temple; but served God with fastings and prayers, night and day" (Luke 2:37). And grace had this effect upon the primitive Christians in Jerusalem; "And they continuing daily, with one accord in the temple, and breaking bread from house to house, did eat their meat with gladness, and singleness of heart, praising God" (Acts 2:46–47). Grace made Daniel delight in the duty of prayer, and solemnly to attend it three times a day: as it also did David; "Evening, morning and at noon will I pray" (Ps. 55:17). Grace makes the saints delight in singing praises to God: "Sing praises unto his name, for it is pleasant" (Ps. 135:3). And 147:1: "Praise ye the Lord, for it is good to sing praises unto our God, for it is pleasant, and praise is comely." It also causes them to delight to hear the Word of God preached: it makes the gospel a joyful sound to them (Ps. 89:15). And makes the feet of those who publish these good tidings, to be beautiful; "How beautiful upon the mountains are the feet of him that bringeth good tidings," etc. (Is. 52:7)!

Christ; the minister may not draw any peremptory conclusion from thence, that he is not godly." Stoddard, *Guide,* p. 83.

"Do not think there is no compunction, or sense of sin, wrought in the soul, because you cannot so clearly discern and feel it; nor the time of the working, and first beginning of it. I have known many that have come with their complaints, that they were never humbled, they never felt it so; yet there it hath been, and many times they have seen it, by the other spectacles, and blessed God for it." Thomas Shepard, *The Sound Believer* (Boston, 1742), p. 38.

It makes them love God's public worship; "Lord I have loved the habitation of thy house, and the place where thine honor dwelleth" (Ps. 26:8). And 27:4: "One thing have I desired of the Lord, that will I seek after, that I may dwell in the house of the Lord, all the days of my life; to behold the beauty of the Lord, and to inquire in his temple." "How amiable are thy tabernacles, O Lord of hosts! my soul longeth, yea even fainteth, for the courts of the Lord. . . . Yea the sparrow hath found an house, and the swallow a nest for herself, where she may lay her young, even thine altars, O Lord of hosts, my King and my God. Blessed are they that dwell in thine house; they will be still praising thee. Blessed is the man in whose heart are the ways of them, who passing through the valley of Baca . . . go from strength to strength, every one of them in Zion appeareth before God" (Ps. 84:1–2, etc.). "A day in thy courts is better than a thousand" (ver. 10).

This is the nature of true grace. But yet, on the other hand, persons being disposed to abound and to be zealously engaged in the external exercises of religion, and to spend much time in them, is no sure evidence of grace; because such a disposition is found in many that have no grace. So it was with the Israelites of old, whose services were abominable to God; they attended the new moons, and sabbaths, and calling of assemblies, and spread forth their hands, and made many prayers (Is. 1:2–15). So it was with the Pharisees; they made long prayers, and fasted twice a week. False religion may cause persons to be loud and earnest in prayer: "Ye shall not fast as ye do this day, to cause your voice to be heard on high" (Is. 58:4). That religion which is not spiritual and saving, may cause men to delight in religious duties and ordinances: "Yet they seek me daily, and delight to know my way; as a nation that did righteousness, and forsook not the ordinance of their God. They ask of me the ordinances of justice, they take delight in approaching to God" (Is. 58:2). It may cause them to take delight in hearing the Word of God preached; as it was with Ezekiel's hearers, "And they come unto thee as my people cometh, and they sit before thee as my people, and they hear thy words; but they will not do them: for with their mouth they shew much love; but their heart goeth after their covetousness. And lo, thou art unto them, as a very lovely song, of one that hath a pleasant voice, and can play well on an instrument: for they hear thy words, but they do them not" (Ezek. 33:31–32). So it was with Herod; he heard John the Baptist gladly (Mark 6:20).

So it was with others of his hearers, for a season, they rejoiced in his light (John 5:35). So the stony-ground hearers heard the word with joy.

Experience shows that persons, from false religion, may be inclined to be exceeding abundant in the external exercises of religion; yea, to give themselves up to them, and devote almost their whole time to them. Formerly a sort of people were very numerous in the Romish church, called recluses; who forsook the world, and utterly abandoned the society of mankind, and shut themselves up close, in a narrow cell, with a vow never to stir out of it, nor to see the face of any of mankind any more (unless that they might be visited in the case of sickness); to spend all their days in the exercises of devotion and converse with God. There were also in old time, great multitudes called hermits and anchorites, that left the world to spend all their days in lonesome deserts, to give themselves up to religious contemplations and exercises of devotion; some sorts of them having no dwellings, but the caves and vaults of the mountains, and no food, but the spontaneous productions of the earth. I once lived, for many months, next door to a Jew (the houses adjoining one to another), and had much opportunity daily to observe him; who appeared to me the devoutest person that ever I saw in my life; great part of his time being spent in the acts of devotion, at his eastern window, which opened next to mine, seeming to be most earnestly engaged, not only in the daytime, but sometimes whole nights.

10. Nothing can be certainly known of the nature of religious affections by this, that they much dispose persons with their mouths to praise and glorify God. This indeed is implied in what has been just now observed, of abounding and spending much time in the external exercises of religion, and was also hinted before; but because many seem to look upon it as a bright evidence of gracious affection, when persons appear greatly disposed to praise and magnify God, to have their mouths full of his praises, and affectionately to be calling on others to praise and extol him, I thought it deserved a more particular consideration.

No Christian will make it an argument against a person, that he seems to have such a disposition. Nor can it reasonably be looked upon as an evidence for a person, if those things that have been already observed and proved, be duly considered, viz. that persons, without grace, may have high affections towards God and Christ, and that their affections, being strong, may fill their mouths, and incline them to speak much, and very earnestly, about the things they are affected with, and that there may be counterfeits of all kinds of gracious affection. But it will appear more evidently and directly, that this is no certain sign of grace, if we consider what instances the Scripture gives us of it in those that were graceless. We often have an account of this, in the multitude that were present when Christ preached and wrought miracles; "And immediately he arose, took up his bed, and went forth before them all: insomuch that they were all amazed, and glorified God, saying, we never saw it on this fashion!" (Mark 2:12). So Matt. 9:8 and Luke 5:26. Also Matt. 15:31: "Insomuch that the multitude wondered, when they saw the dumb to speak, and the maimed to be whole, the lame to walk, and the blind to see; and they glorified the God of Israel." So we are told, that on occasion of Christ's raising the son of the widow of Nain, "There came a great fear on all; and they glorified God, saying, that a great prophet is risen up among us, and that God hath visited his people" (Luke 7:16). So we read of their glorifying Christ, or speaking exceedingly highly of him, "And he taught in their synagogues, being glorified of all" (Luke 4:15). And how did they praise him with loud voices, crying, "Hosanna to the son of David, Hosanna in the highest. Blessed is he that cometh in the name of the Lord," a little before he was crucified! And after Christ's ascension, when the apostles had healed the impotent man, we are told, that "all men glorified God for that which was done" (Acts 4:21). When the Gentiles in Antioch and Pisidia, heard from Paul and Barnabas, that God would reject the Jews, and take the Gentiles to be his people in their room, they were affected with this goodness of God to the Gentiles, and glorified the Word of the Lord: but all that did so were not true believers; but only a certain elect number of them; as is intimated in the account we have of it, "And when the Gentiles heard this, they were glad, and glorified the Word of the Lord; and as many as were ordained to eternal life, believed" (Acts 13:48). So of old, the children of Israel at the Red Sea, sang God's praise; but soon forgat his works. And the Jews in Ezekiel's time, with their mouth shewed much love, while their heart went after their covetousness. And 'tis foretold of false professors, and real enemies of religion, that they should show a forwardness to glorify God; "Hear ye the word of the Lord, ye that tremble at his word: your brethren that hated you, that cast you out for my name's sake, said, Let the Lord be glorified" (Is. 66:5).

'Tis no certain sign that a person is graciously affected, if in the midst of his hopes and comforts, he is greatly affected with God's unmerited mercy to him that is so unworthy, and seems greatly to extol and magnify free grace. Those that yet remain with unmortified pride and enmity against God, may, when they imagine that they have received extraordinary kindness from God, cry out of their unworthiness, and magnify God's undeserved goodness to them, from no other conviction of their ill-deservings, and from no higher principle, than Saul, had, who while he yet remained with unsubdued pride and enmity against David, was brought, though a king, to acknowledge his unworthiness, and cry out, "I have played the fool, I have erred exceedingly," and with great affection and admiration, to magnify and extol David's unmerited and unexampled kindness to him (I Sam. 25:16–19 and 26:21). And from no higher principle, than that from whence Nebuchadnezzar was affected with God's dispensations, that he saw and was the subject of, and praises, extols and honors the king of heaven; and both he, and Darius, in their high affections, call upon all nations to praise God (Dan. 3:28–30 and 4:1–3, 34–35, 37 and 6:25–27).

11. 'Tis no sign that affections are right, or that they are wrong, that they make persons that have them, exceeding confident that what they experience is divine, and that they are in a good estate.

It is an argument with some, against persons, that they are deluded if they pretend to be assured of their good estate, and to be carried beyond all doubting of the favor of God; supposing that there is no such thing to be expected in the church of God, as a full and absolute assurance of hope; unless it be in some very extraordinary circumstances; as in the case of martyrdom: contrary to the doctrine of Protestants, which has been maintained by their most celebrated writers against the Papists; and contrary to the plainest Scripture evidence. It is manifest that it was a common thing for the saints that we have a history, or particular account of in Scripture, to be assured. God in the plainest and most positive manner, revealed and testified his special favor to Noah, Abraham, Isaac, Jacob, Moses, Daniel, and others. Job often speaks of his sincerity and uprightness with the greatest imaginable confidence and assurance, often calling God to witness to it; and says plainly: "I know that my Redeemer liveth, and that I shall see him for myself, and not another" (Job 19:25, etc.). David, throughout the Book of Psalms, almost everywhere speaks without any hesitancy, and in the most positive manner of God as his God; glorying in him as his portion and heritage, his rock and confidence, his shield, salvation, and high tower, and the like. Hezekiah appeals to God, as one that knew that he had walked before him in truth and with a perfect heart (II Kgs. 20:3). Jesus Christ, in his dying discourse with his eleven disciples, in the 14th, 15th, and 16th chapters of John (which was as it were Christ's last will and testament to his disciples, and to his whole church), often declares his special and everlasting love to them, in the plainest and most positive terms; and promises them a future participation with him in his glory, in the most absolute manner; and tells them at the same time, that he does so, to the end, that their joy might be full; "These things have I spoken unto you, that my joy might remain in you, and that your joy might be full" (John 15:11). See also at the conclusion of his whole discourse, ch. 16:33: "These things have I spoken unto you, that in me ye might have peace. In the world ye shall have tribulation; but be of good cheer, I have overcome the world." Christ was not afraid of speaking too plainly and positively to them: he did not desire to hold them in the least suspense. And he concluded that last discourse of his, with a prayer in their presence, wherein he speaks positively to his Father of those eleven disciples, as having all of them savingly known him, and believed in him, and received and kept his word; and that they were not of the world; and that for their sakes he sanctified himself; and that his will was that they should be with him in his glory: and tells his Father, that he spake these things in his prayer, to the end, that his joy might be fulfilled in them (ver. 13). By these things it is evident, that 'tis agreeable to Christ's designs, and the contrived ordering and disposition Christ makes of things in his church, that there should be sufficient and abundant provision made, that his saints might have full assurance of their future glory.

The apostle Paul, through all his Epistles, speaks in an assured strain; ever speaking positively of his special relation to Christ, his Lord and Master and Redeemer, and his interest in, and expectation of the future reward. It would be endless to take notice of all places that might be enumerated; I shall mention but three or four, "Christ liveth in me, and the life which I now live in the flesh I live by the faith of the Son of God; who loved me, and gave himself for me" (Gal. 2:20). "For me to live is Christ, and to die is gain" (Phil. 1:21). "I know whom I have believed; and I am persuaded that he is able to keep that which I have committed to him, against that day" (II Tim. 1:12). "I have fought a good fight; I have finished my course; I have kept the faith: henceforth there is laid up for me a crown of righteousness, which the Lord, the righteous judge, will give me at that day" (II Tim. 1:8).

And the nature of the covenant of grace, and God's declared ends in the appointment and constitution of things in that covenant, do plainly show it to be God's design to make ample provision for the saints having an assured hope of eternal life, while living here upon earth. For so are all things ordered and contrived in that covenant, that everything might be made sure on God's part. The covenant is ordered in all things, and sure: the promises are most full, and very often repeated, and various ways exhibited; and there are many witnesses, and many seals; and God has confirmed his promises with an oath. And God's declared design in all this is, that the heirs of the promises might have an undoubting hope, and full joy, in an assurance of their future glory. "Wherein God willing, more abundantly to show to the heirs of promise, the immutability of his counsel, confirmed it by an oath; that by two immutable things, in which it was impossible for God to lie, we might have a strong consolation, who have fled for refuge, to lay hold on the hope set before us" (Heb. 6:17–18). But all this would be in vain, to any such purpose, as the saints' strong consolation, and hope of their obtaining future glory, if their interest in those sure promises in ordinary cases, was not attainable. For God's promises and oaths, let them be as sure as they will, can't give strong hope and comfort to any particular person, any further than he can know that those promises are made to him. And in vain is provision made in Jesus Christ, that believers might be perfect as pertaining to the conscience, as is signified (Heb. 9:9), if assurance of freedom from the guilt of sin is not attainable.

It further appears that assurance is not only attainable in some very extraordinary cases, that *all* Chrisians are directed to give all diligence to make their calling and election sure, and are told how they may do it (II Pet. 1:5–8). And 'tis spoken of as a thing very unbecoming of Christians, and an argument of something very blamable in them, not to know whether Christ be in them or no; "Know ye not your own selves, how that Jesus Christ is in you, except ye be reprobates?" (II Cor. 13:5). And 'tis implied that it is an argument of a very blamable negligence in Christians, if they practice Christianity after such a manner as to remain uncertain of the reward, in that "I therefore so run, as not uncertainly" (I Cor. 9:26). And to add no more, it is manifest, that Christians knowing their interests in the saving benefits of Christianity is a thing ordinarily attainable, because the apostles tell us by what means Christians (and not only apostles and martyrs) were wont to know this; "Now we have received, not the spirit of the world, but the Spirit which is of God, that we might know the things that are freely given to us of God" (I Cor. 2:12). And I John 2–3: "And hereby do we know that we know him, if we keep his commandments." And ver. 5: "Hereby know we that we are in him." "We know that we are passed from death to life, because we love the brethren" (ch. 3:14). "Hereby we know that we are of the truth, and shall assure our hearts before him" (ver. 19). "Hereby we know that he abideth in us, by the Spirit that he hath given us" (ver. 24). So ch. 4:13 and ch. 5:2 and ver. 19.

Therefore it must needs be very unreasonable to determine, that persons are hypocrites, and their affections wrong, because they seem to be out of doubt of their own salvation, and the affections they are the subjects of seem to banish all fears of hell.

On the other hand, it is no sufficient reason to determine that men are saints, and their affections gracious, because the affections they have are attended with an exceeding confidence that their state is good, and their affections divine.[1] Nothing can be certainly argued from their confidence, how great and strong soever it seems to be. If we see a man that boldly calls God his Father, and commonly speaks in the most bold, familiar and appropriating language in

1. "O professor, look carefully to your foundation: be not high-minded, but fear. You have it may be, done and suffered many things in and for religion; you have excellent gifts and sweet comforts; a warm zeal for God, and high confidence of your integrity: all this may be right, for aught that I, or (it may be) you know: but yet, it is possible it may be false also. You have sometimes judged yourselves, and pronounced yourselves upright; but remember your final sentence is not yet pronounced by your Judge. And what if God weigh you over again, in his more equal balance, and should say, *Mene, Tekel.* Thou art weighed in the balance, and art found wanting? What a confounded man wilt thou be, under such a sentence! *Quae splendent in conspectu hominis, sordent in conspectu judicis;* Things that are highly esteemed of men, are an abomination in the sight of God: he seeth not as man seeth. Thy heart may be false, and thou not know it: yea, it may be false, and thou strongly confident of its integrity." Flavel, *Touchstone of Sincerity* [above, p. 62], ch. 2, sec. 5, pp. 34–5.

"Some hypocrites are a great deal more confident than many saints." Solomon Stoddard, *The Way to Know Sincerity and Hypocrisy* (Boston, 1719), p. 128.

prayer, "My Father, my dear Redeemer, my sweet Saviour, my Beloved," and the like, and it is a common thing for him to use the most confident expressions before men, about the goodness of his state; such as: "I know certainly that God is my Father; I know so surely as there is a God in heaven, that he is my God; I know I shall go to heaven, as well as if I were there; I know that God is now manifesting himself to my soul, and is now smiling upon me": and seems to have done forever with my inquiry or examination into his state, as a thing sufficiently known, and out of doubt, and to condemn all that so much as intimate or suggest that there is some reason to doubt or fear whether all is right; such things are no signs at all that it is indeed so as he is confident it is.[2] Such an overbearing, high-handed and violent sort of confidence as this, so affecting to declare itself with a most glaring show, in the sight of men, which is to be seen in many, has not the countenance of a true Christian assurance: it savors more of the spirit of the Pharisees, who never doubted but that they were saints, and the most eminent of saints, and were bold to go to God, and come up near to him, and lift up their eyes, and thank him for the great distinction he had made between them and other men; and when Christ intimated that they were blind and graceless, despised the suggestion; "And some of the Pharisees which were with him, heard these words, and said unto him, Are we blind also?" (John 9:40). If they had more of the spirit of the Publican, with their confidence, who in a sense of his exceeding unworthiness, stood afar off, and durst not so much as lift up his eyes to heaven, but smote on his breast, and cried out of himself as a sinner, their confidence would have more of the aspect of the confidence of one that humbly trusts and hopes in Christ, and has no confidence in himself.

If we do but consider what the hearts of natural men are, what

2. "Doth the work of faith in some believers bear upon its top branches, the full ripe fruits of a blessed assurance? Lo, what strong confidence, and high-built persuasions of an interest in God, have sometimes been found in unsanctified ones. Yea, so strong may this false assurance be, that they dare boldly venture to go to the judgment seat of God, and there defend it. Doth the Spirit of God fill the heart of the assured believer with joy unspeakable and full of glory, giving them, through faith, a prelibation or foretaste of heaven itself, in those first fruits of it? How near to this comes what the Apostle supposes may be found in apostates!" John Flavel, *Husbandry Spiritualized* (3d ed. London, 1674, 1st ed. 1669), p. 110. Also *The Whole Works of Mr. John Flavel* (2 vols. Edinburgh, 1731), 2, 653.

principles they are under the dominion of, what blindness and deceit, what self-flattery, self-exaltation and self-confidence reigns there, we need not at all wonder that their high opinion of themselves, and confidence of their happy circumstances, be as high and strong as mountains, and as violent as a tempest, when once conscience is blinded, and convictions killed, with false, high affections, and those forementioned principles let loose, fed up and prompted by false joys and comforts, excited by some pleasing imaginations impressed by Satan, transforming himself into an angel of light.

When once a hypocrite is thus established in a false hope, he han't those things to cause him to call his hope in question, that oftentimes are the occasion of the doubting of true saints; as first, he han't that cautious spirit, that great sense of the vast importance of a sure foundation, and that dread of being deceived. The comforts of the true saints increase awakening and caution, and a lively sense how great a thing it is to appear before an infinitely holy, just and omniscient judge. But false comforts put an end to these things, and dreadfully stupefy the mind. Secondly, the hypocrite has not the knowledge of his own blindness, and the deceitfulness of his own heart, and that mean opinion of his own understanding, that the true saint has. Those that are deluded with false discoveries and affections, are evermore highly conceited of their light and understanding. Thirdly, the devil don't assault the hope of the hypocrite, as he does the hope of a true saint. The devil is a great enemy to a true Christian hope, not only because it tends greatly to the comfort of him that hath it, but also because it is a thing of a holy, heavenly nature, greatly tending to promote and cherish grace in the heart, and a great incentive to strictness and diligence in the Christian life. But he is no enemy to the hope of a hypocrite, which above all things establishes his interest in him that has it. A hypocrite may retain his hope without opposition, as long as he lives, the devil never disturbing it, nor attempting to disturb it. But there is perhaps no true Christian but what has his hope assaulted by him. Satan assaulted Christ himself, upon this, whether he were the Son of God or no: and the servant is not above his master, nor the disciple above his Lord; 'tis enough for the disciple, that is most privileged in this world, to be as his master. Fourthly, he who has a false hope has not that sight of his own corruptions, which the saint has. A true Christian has ten times so much to do with his heart, and its corruptions, as an hypocrite: and the sins of his heart and practice, appear to him in their blackness; they look dreadful; and it often appears a very mysterious thing that any grace can be consistent with such corruption, or should be in such a heart. But a false hope hides corruption, covers it all over, and the hypocrite looks clean and bright in his own eyes.

There are two sorts of hypocrites: one that are deceived with their outward morality and external religion; many of which are professed Arminians, in the doctrine of justification: and the other, are those that are deceived with false discoveries and elevations; which often cry down works, and men's own righteousness, and talk much of free grace; but at the same time make a righteousness of their discoveries, and of their humiliation, and exalt themselves to heaven with them. These two kinds of hypocrites Mr. Shepard, in his exposition of *The Parable of the Ten Virgins,* distinguishes by the names of *legal* and *evangelical* hypocrites; and often speaks of the latter as the worst. And 'tis evident that the latter are commonly by far the most confident in their hope, and with the most difficulty brought from it: I have scarcely known the instance of such an one, in my life, that has been undeceived. The chief grounds of the confidence of many of them, are the very same kind of impulses and supposed revelations (sometimes with texts of Scripture, and sometimes without), that so many of late have had concerning future events; calling these impulses about their good estate, the witness of the Spirit; entirely misunderstanding the nature of the witness of the Spirit, as I shall show hereafter. Those that have had visions and impulses about other things, it has generally been to reveal such things as they are desirous and fond of: and no wonder that persons who give heed to such things, have the same sort of visions or impressions about their own eternal salvation, to reveal to them that their sins are forgiven them, that their names are written in the Book of Life, that they are in high favor with God, etc., and especially when they earnestly seek, expect and wait for evidence of their election and salvation this way, as the surest and most glorious evidence of it. Neither is it any wonder, that when they have such a supposed revelation of their good estate, it raises in them the highest degree of confidence of it. 'Tis found by abundant experience that those who are led away by impulses and imagined revelations, are extremely confident: they suppose that the great Jehovah has declared these and those things to them; and having his immediate testimony, a strong confidence is the highest virtue.

Hence they are bold to say, "I know this or that; I know certainly; I am as sure as that I have a being," and the like: and they despise all argument and inquiry in the case. And above all things else, 'tis easy to be accounted for, that impressions and impulses about that which is so pleasing, so suiting their self-love and pride, as their being the dear children of God, distinguished from most in the world in his favor, should make them strongly confident: especially when with their impulses and revelations they have high affections, which they take to be the most eminent exercises of grace. I have known of several persons, that have had a fond desire of something of a temporal nature, through a violent passion that has possessed them, and they have been earnestly pursuing the thing they have desired should come to pass, and have met with great difficulty and many discouragements in it, but at last have had an impression or supposed revelation that they should obtain what they sought; and they have looked upon it as a sure promise from the Most High, which has made them most ridiculously confident, against all manner of reason to convince them to the contrary, and all events working against them. And there is nothing hinders, but that persons who are seeking their salvation, may be deceived by the like delusive impressions, and be made confident of that, the same way.

The confidence of many of this sort of hypocrites, that Mr. Shepard calls evangelical hypocrites, is like the confidence of some mad men, who think they are kings: they will maintain it against all manner of reason and evidence. And in one sense, it is much more immovable than a truly gracious assurance; a true assurance is not upheld, but by the soul's being kept in a holy frame, and grace maintained in lively exercise. If the actings of grace do much decay in the Christian, and he falls into a lifeless frame, he loses his assurance: but this kind of confidence of hypocrites will not be shaken by sin: they (at least some of them), will maintain their boldness in their hope, in the most corrupt frames and wicked ways: which is a sure evidence of their delusion.[3]

3. Mr. Shepard speaks of it, as a presumptuous peace, that is not interrupted and broke by evil works. And says, that the spirit will sigh, and not sing in that bosom, whence corrupt dispositions and passions break out. And that though men in such frames may seem to maintain the consolation of the Spirit, and not suspect their hypocrisy, under pretense of trusting the Lord's mercy; yet they can't avoid the condemnation of the Word. Shepard, *Parable,* Pt. I, p. 139.

Dr. Ames speaks of it as a thing, by which the peace of a wicked man may be distinguished from the peace of a godly man, "that the peace of a wicked man

And here I can't but observe, that there are certain doctrines often preached to the people, which need to be delivered with more caution and explanation than they frequently are; for as they are by many understood, they tend greatly to establish this delusion and false confidence of hypocrites. The doctrines I speak of are those of Christians living by faith, not by sight; their giving glory to God, by trusting him in the dark; living upon Christ, and not upon experiences; not making their good frames the foundation of their faith: which are excellent and important doctrines indeed, rightly understood, but corrupt and destructive, as many understand them. The Scripture speaks of living or walking by faith, and not by sight, in no other way than these, viz. a being governed by a respect to eternal things, that are the objects of faith, and are not seen, and not by a respect to temporal things, which are seen; and believing things revealed that we never saw with bodily eyes: and also living by faith in the promise of future things; without yet seeing or enjoying the things promised, or knowing the way how they can be fulfilled. This will be easily evident to anyone that looks over the Scriptures which speak of faith in opposition to sight; as II Cor. 4:18 and 5:7; Heb. 11:1, 8, 13, 17, 27, 29; Rom. 8:24; John 20:29. But this doctrine, as it is understood by many, is that Christians ought firmly to believe and trust in Christ, without spiritual sight or light, and although they are in a dark dead frame, and, for the present, have no spiritual experiences or discoveries. And it is truly the duty of those who are thus in darkness, to come out of darkness into light, and believe. But that they should confidently believe and trust, while they yet remain without spiritual light or sight, is an antiscriptural and absurd doctrine. The Scripture is ignorant of any such faith in Christ of the operation of God, that is not founded in a spiritual sight of Christ. That believing on Christ, which accompanies a title to everlasting life, is a seeing the Son, and believing on him, John 6:40. True faith in Christ is never exercised, any further than persons behold "as in a glass,

continues, whether he performs the duties of piety and righteousness or no; provided those crimes are avoided that appear horrid to nature itself." William Ames, *Conscience with the Power and Cases Thereof,* (Latin edition, 1631; first English ed., London, 1643), Bk. III, ch. 7, pp. 62–3. [The portion quoted by JE here differs from the English text cited; this means that JE is either paraphrasing or using a translation of his own from the original Latin edition. This latter possibility is the more likely because his own citation refers to "Lib. III." For JE's use of Ames' writings see above, pp. 67–8.]

the glory of the Lord," and have "the knowledge of the glory of God in the face of Jesus Christ" (II Cor. 3:18 and 4:6). They into whose minds "the light of the glorious gospel of Christ, who is the image of God," does not shine: they believe not (II Cor. 4:4). That faith, which is without spiritual light, is not the faith of the children of the light, and of the day; but the presumption of the children of darkness. And therefore to press and urge them to believe, without any spiritual light or sight, tends greatly to help forward the delusions of the prince of darkness. Men not only can't exercise faith without some spiritual light, but they can exercise faith only just in such proportion as they have spiritual light. Men will trust in God no further than they know him: and they can't be in the exercise of faith in him one ace further than they have a sight of his fulness and faithfulness in exercise. Nor can they have the exercise of trust in God, any further than they are in a gracious frame. They that are in a dead carnal frame, doubtless ought to trust in God; because that would be the same thing as coming out of their bad frame, and turning to God: but to exhort men confidently to trust in God, and so hold up their hope and peace, though they are not in a gracious frame, and continue still to be so, is the same thing in effect, as to exhort them confidently to trust in God, but not with a gracious trust: and what is that but a wicked presumption? It is just so impossible for men to have a strong or lively trust in God, when they have no lively exercises of grace, or sensible Christian experiences, as it is for them to be in the lively exercises of grace, without the exercises of grace.

'Tis true that it is the duty of God's people to trust in him, when in darkness, and though they remain still in darkness, in that sense, that they ought to trust in God when the aspects of his providence are dark, and look as though God had forsaken them, and did not hear their prayers, and many clouds gather, and many enemies surround them, with a formidable aspect, threatening to swallow them up, and all events of providence seem to be against them, all circumstances seem to render the promises of God difficult to be fulfilled, and God must be trusted out of sight, i.e. when we can't see which way it is possible for him to fulfill his Word, everything but God's mere Word makes it look unlikely, so that if persons believe, they must hope against hope. Thus the ancient patriarchs, and Job, and the Psalmist and Jeremiah, Daniel, Shadrach, Meshech and Abednego, and the apostle Paul gave glory to God by trusting in God in darkness. And we have many instances of such a glorious victorious faith in the eleventh of the Hebrews. But how different a thing is this, from trusting in God without spiritual sight, and being at the same time in a dead and carnal frame!

There is also such a thing as spiritual light's being let into the soul in one way, when it is not in another; and so there is such a thing as the saints trusting in God, and also knowing their good estate, when they are destitute of some kinds of experience. As for instance, they may have clear views of God's sufficiency and faithfulness, and so confidently trust in him, and know that they are his children; and at the same time, not have those clear and sweet ideas of his love, as at other times: for it was thus with Christ himself in his last passion. And they may have views of much of God's sovereignty, holiness and all-sufficiency,, enabling them quietly to submit to him, and exercise a sweet and most encouraging hope in God's fulness, when they are not satisfied of their own good estate. But how different things are these, from confidently trusting in God, without spiritual light or experience!

Those that thus insist on persons living by faith, when they have no experience, and are in very bad frames, are also very absurd in their notions of faith. What they mean by faith is, believing that they are in a good estate. Hence they count it a dreadful sin for them to doubt of their state, whatever frames they are in, and whatever wicked things they do, because 'tis the great and heinous sin of unbelief; and he is the best man, and puts most honor upon God, that maintains his hope of his good estate the most confidently and immovably, when he has the least light or experience; that is to say, when he is in the worst and wickedest frame and way; because, forsooth, that is a sign that he is strong in faith, giving glory to God, and against hope believes in hope. But what Bible do they learn this notion of faith out of, that it is a man's confidently believing that he is in a good estate? [4] If this be faith, the Pharisees had faith

4. "Men don't know that they are godly, by believing that they are godly. We know many things by faith, Heb. 11:3: 'By faith we understand that the worlds were made by the Word of God.' Faith is the evidence of things not seen; Heb. 11:1. Thus men know the trinity of persons of the Godhead; that Jesus Christ is the Son of God; that he that believes in him will have eternal life; the resurrection of the dead. And if God should tell a saint that he hath grace, he might know it by believing the Word of God. But it is not this way, that godly men do know that they have grace. It is not revealed in the Word; and the Spirit of God doth not testify it to particular persons." Stoddard, *Treatise,* pp. 83–4.

in an eminent degree; some of which, Christ teaches, committed the unpardonable sin against the Holy Ghost. The Scripture represents faith, as that by which men are *brought into* a good estate; and therefore it can't be the same thing, as believing that they are *already in* a good estate. To suppose that faith consists in persons believing that they are in a good estate, is in effect the same thing, as to suppose that faith consists in a person's believing that he has faith, or in believing that he believes.

Indeed persons doubting of their good estate, may in several respects arise from unbelief. It may be from unbelief, or because they have so little faith, that they have so little evidence of their good estate: if they had more experience of the actings of faith, and so more experience of the exercise of grace, they would have clearer evidence that their state was good; and so their doubts would be removed. And then their doubting of their state may be from unbelief thus, when though there be many things that are good evidences of a work of grace in 'em, yet they doubt very much whether they are really in a state of favor with God, because it is they, those that are so unworthy, and have done so much to provoke God to anger against them. Their doubts in such a case arise from unbelief, as they arise from want of a sufficient sense of, and reliance on the infinite riches of God's grace, and the sufficiency of Christ for the chief of sinners. They may also be from unbelief, when they doubt of their state, because of the mystery of God's dealings with them: they are not able to reconcile such dispensations with God's favor to them: or when they doubt whether they have any interest in the promises, because the promises from the aspects of providence, appear so unlikely to be fulfilled; the difficulties that are in the way, are so many and great. Such doubting arises from want of dependance upon God's almighty power, and his knowledge and wisdom, as infinitely above theirs. But yet, in such persons, their unbelief, and their doubting of their state, are not the same thing; though one arises from the other.

Persons may be greatly to blame for doubting of their state, on such grounds as these last mentioned; and they may be to blame, that they have no more grace, and no more of the present exercises and experiences of it, to be an evidence to 'em of the goodness of their state: men are doubtless to blame for being in a dead carnal frame; but when they are in such a frame, and have no sensible experience of the exercises of grace, but on the contrary, are very much under the prevalence of their lusts, and an unchristian spirit, they are not to blame for doubting of their state. 'Tis as impossible, in the nature of things, that a holy and Christian hope, should be kept alive, in its clearness and strength, in such circumstances, as it is to keep the light in the room, when the candle is put out; or to maintain the bright sunshine in the air, when the sun is gone down. Distant experiences, when darkened by present prevailing lust and corruption, will never keep alive a gracious confidence and assurance; but that sickens and decays upon it, as necessarily as a little child by repeated blows on the head with the hammer. Nor is it at all to be lamented that persons doubt of their state in such circumstances; but on the contrary, 'tis desirable and every way best that they should. 'Tis agreeable to that wise and merciful constitution of things, which God hath established, that it should be so. For so hath God contrived and constituted things, in his dispensations towards his own people, that when their love decays, and the exercises of it fail, or become weak, fear should arise; for then they need it to restrain them from sin, and to excite 'em to care for the good of their souls, and so to stir them up to watchfulness and diligence in religion: but God hath so ordered that when love rises, and is in vigorous exercise, then fear should vanish, and be driven away; for then they need it not, having a higher and more excellent principle in exercise, to restrain 'em from sin, and stir 'em up to their duty. There are no other principles, which human nature is under the influence of, that will ever make men conscientious, but one of these two, fear or love: and therefore, if one of these should not prevail, as the other decayed, God's people when fallen into dead and carnal frames, when love is asleep, would be lamentably exposed indeed. And therefore God has wisely ordained, that these two opposite principles of love and fear, should rise and fall, like the two opposite scales of a balance; when one rises, the other sinks. As light and darkness, necessarily and unavoidably succeed each other; if light prevails, so much does darkness cease, and no more; and if light decays, so much does darkness prevail; so it is in the heart of a child of God: if divine love decays and falls asleep, and lust prevails, the light and joy of hope goes out, and dark fear and doubting arises; and if on the contrary, divine love prevails, and comes into lively exercise, this brings in the brightness of hope, and drives away black lust, and fear with it. Love is the spirit of adoption, or the childlike principle; if that slumbers, men fall under fear, which is the spirit of bondage, or the servile principle: and so on the contrary. And if it be so, that love, or the spirit of adoption, be carried to a great height, it quite drives away all fear, and gives full assurance; agreeable to that of the Apostle, I John 4:18: "There is no fear in love, but perfect love casts out fear." These two opposite principles of lust and holy love, bring hope and fear into the hearts of God's children, in proportion as they prevail; that is, when left to their own natural influence, without something adventitious, or accidental intervening; as the distemper of melancholy, doctrinal ignorance, prejudices of education, wrong instruction, false principles, peculiar temptations, etc.

Fear is cast out by the Spirit of God, no other way than by the prevailing of love: nor is it ever maintained by his Spirit, when love is asleep. At such a time, in vain is all the saint's self-examinations, and poring on past experience, in order to establish his peace, and get assurance. For it is contrary to the nature of things, as God hath constituted them, that he should have assurance at such a time.

They therefore, do directly thwart God's wise and gracious constitution of things, who exhort others to be confident in their hope, when in dead frames; under a notion of living by faith, and not by sight, and trusting God in the dark, and living upon Christ, and not upon experiences; and warn them not to doubt of their good estate, lest they should be guilty of the dreadful sin of unbelief. And it has a direct tendency to establish the most presumptuous hypocrites, and to prevent their ever calling their state in question, how much soever wickedness rages, and reigns in their hearts, and prevails in their lives; under a notion of honoring God, by hoping against hope, and confidently trusting in God, when things look very dark. And doubtless vast has been the mischief, that has been done this way.

Persons can't be said to forsake Christ, and live on their experiences of the exercises of grace, merely because they take them and use them as evidences of grace; for there are no other evidences that they can or ought to take. But then may persons be said to live upon their experiences, when they make a righteousness of them; and instead of keeping their eye on God's glory, and Christ's excellency, they turn their eyes off these objects without them, on to themselves, to entertain their minds, by viewing their own attainments, and high experiences, and the great things they have met with, and are bright and beautiful in their own eyes, and are rich and increased with good, in their own apprehensions, and think that God has as admiring an esteem of them, on the same account, as they have of themselves: this is living on experiences, and not on Christ; and is more abominable in the sight of God, than the gross immoralities of those who make no pretenses to religion. But this is a far different thing from a mere improving experiences as evidences of an interest in a glorious Redeemer.

But to return from this digression, I would mention one thing more under the general head that I am upon.

12. Nothing can be certainly concluded concerning the nature of religious affections, that any are the subjects of, from this, that the outward manifestations of them, and the relation persons give of them, are very affecting and pleasing to the truly godly, and such as greatly gain their charity, and win their hearts.

The true saints have not such a spirit of discerning, that they can certainly determine who are godly, and who are not. For though they know experimentally what true religion is, in the internal exercises of it; yet these are what they can neither feel, nor see, in the heart of another.[5] There is nothing in others, that comes within their view but outward manifestations and appearances; but the Scripture plainly intimates that this way of judging what is in men by outward appearances, is at best uncertain, and liable to deceit; "The Lord seeth not as man seeth; for man looketh on the outward appearance, but the Lord looketh on the heart" (I Sam. 16:7). "He shall not judge after the sight of his eyes, neither reprove after the hearing of his ears" (Is. 11:3).[6] They commonly are but poor judges,

5. "Men may have the knowledge of their own conversion: the knowledge that other men have of it is uncertain; because no man can look into the heart of another, and see the workings of grace there." Stoddard, *Treatise,* p. 78.

6. Mr. Stoddard observes, that all visible signs are common to converted and unconverted men; and a relation of experiences among the rest. Stoddard, *Appeal to the Learned,* p. 75.

"O how hard is it for the eye of man to discern betwixt chaff and wheat! And how many upright hearts are now censured, whom God will clear! How many false hearts are now approved whom God will condemn! Men ordinarily have no convictive proofs, but only probable symptoms; which at most beget but a conjectural knowledge of another's state. And they that shall peremptorily judge either way, may possibly wrong the generation of the upright, or on the other side, absolve and justify the wicked. And truly, considering what hath been said,

and dangerous counsellors in soul cases, who are quick and peremptory in determining persons' states, vaunting themselves in their extraordinary faculty of discerning and distinguishing, in these great affairs; as though all was open and clear to them. They betray one of these three things; either that they have had but little experience; or are persons of a weak judgment; or that they have a great degree of pride and self-confidence, and so ignorance of themselves. Wise and experienced men will proceed with great caution in such an affair.

When there are many probable appearances of piety in others, it is the duty of the saints to receive them cordially into their charity, and to love them and rejoice in them, as their brethren in Christ Jesus. But yet the best of men may be deceived, when the appearances seem to them exceeding fair and bright, even so as entirely to gain their charity, and conquer their hearts. It has been a common thing in the church of God, for such bright professors, that are received as eminent saints, among the saints, to fall away and come to nothing.[7] And this we need not wonder at, if we consider the things that have been already observed; what things it has been shown, may appear in men who are altogether graceless. Nothing hinders but that all these things may meet together in men, and yet they be without a spark of grace in their hearts. They may have religious affections of many kinds together; they may have a sort of affection towards God, that bears a great

---

'tis no wonder that dangerous mistakes are so frequently made in this matter." John Flavel, *Husbandry Spiritualized,* p. 111. Also *The Whole Works of Mr. John Flavel, 2,* 653.

7. "Be not offended, if you see great cedars fall, stars fall from heaven, great professors die and decay: do not think they be all such: do not think that the elect shall fall. Truly, some are such, that when they fall, one would think a man truly sanctified might fall away, as the Arminians think. I John 2:19: 'They were not of us.' I speak this, because the Lord is shaking; and I look for great apostasies; for God is trying all his friends, through all the Christian world. In Germany what profession was there! Who would have thought it? The Lord who delights to manifest that openly, which was hid secretly, sends a sword and they fall." Shepard, *Parable,* Pt. I, pp. 117, 118.

"The saints may approve thee, and God condemn thee; Rev. 3:1: 'Thou hast a name that thou livest, and art dead.' Men may say, there is a true Nathanael; and God may say, there is a self-cozening Pharisee. Reader, thou hast heard of Judas, and Demas, of Ananias and Sapphira, of Hymeneus and Philetus, once renowned and famous professors, and thou hast heard how they proved at last." Flavel, *Touchstone,* ch. 2, sec. 5, p. 35.

resemblance of dear love to him; and so a kind of love to the brethren, and great appearances of admiration of God's perfections and works, and sorrow for sin, and reverence, submission, self-abasement, gratitude, joy, religious longings, and zeal for the interest of religion and the good of souls. And these affections may come after great awakenings and convictions of conscience; and there may be great appearances of a work of humiliation; and counterfeit love and joy, and other affections may seem to follow these, and one another, just in the same order, that is commonly observable in the holy affections of true converts. And these religious affections may be carried to a great height, and may cause abundance of tears, yea, may overcome the nature of those who are the subjects of them, and may make them affectionate, and fervent, and fluent in speaking of the things of God, and dispose them to be abundant in it; and may be attended with many sweet texts of Scripture, and precious promises, brought with great impression on their minds; and may dispose them with their mouths to praise and glorify God, in a very ardent manner, and fervently to call upon others to praise him, crying out of their unworthiness, and extolling free grace. And may, moreover, dispose them to abound in the external duties of religion, such as prayer, hearing the Word preached, singing, and religious conference; and these things attended with a great resemblance of a Christian assurance, in its greatest height, when the saints mount on eagles' wings, above all darkness and doubting. I think it has been made plain, that there may be all these things, and yet there be nothing more than the common influences of the Spirit of God, joined with the delusions of Satan, and the wicked and deceitful heart. To which I may add, that all these things may be attended with a sweet natural temper, and a good doctrinal knowledge of religion, and a long acquaintance with the saints' way of talking and of expressing their affections and experiences, and a natural ability and subtlety in accommodating their expressions and manner of speaking to the dispositions and notions of the hearers, and a taking decency of expression and behavior, formed by a good education. How great therefore may the resemblance be, as to all outward expressions and appearances, between an hypocrite and a true saint! Doubtless 'tis the glorious prerogative of the omniscient God, as the great searcher of hearts, to be able well to separate between sheep and goats. And what an indecent, self-exaltation, and arrogance is it, in poor fallible dark mortals, to pretend that they can determine and know, who are really sincere and upright before God, and who are not!

Many seem to lay great weight on that, and to suppose it to be what may determine them with respect to others' real piety, when they not only tell a plausible story, but when, in giving an account of their experiences, they make such a representation, and speak after such a manner, that they feel their talk; that is to say, when their talk seems to harmonize with their own experience, and their hearts are touched and affected and delighted, by what they hear them say, and drawn out by it, in dear love to them. But there is not that certainty in such things, and that full dependence to be had upon them, which many imagine. A true saint greatly delights in holiness: it is a most beautiful thing in his eyes; and God's work, in savingly renewing and making holy and happy, a poor, and before perishing soul, appears to him a most glorious work. No wonder therefore, that his heart is touched, and greatly affected, when he hears another give a probable account of this work, wrought on his own heart, and when he sees in him probable appearances of holiness; whether those pleasing appearances have anything real to answer them or no. And if he uses the same words, which are commonly made use of, to express the affections of true saints, and tells of many things following one another in an order, agreeable to the method of the experience of him that hears him, and also speaks freely and boldly, and with an air of assurance: no wonder that the other thinks his experiences harmonize with his own. And if besides all this, in giving his relation, he speaks with much affection; and above all, if in speaking, he seems to show much affection to him, to whom he speaks, such an affection as the Galatians did to the apostle Paul; these things will naturally have a powerful influence, to affect and draw his hearer's heart, and open wide the doors of his charity towards him. David speaks as one who had felt Ahithophel's talk, and had once a sweet savor and relish of it. And therefore exceedingly great was his surprise and disappointment, when he fell; it was almost too much for him. "It was not an enemy . . . then I could have borne it . . . but it was thou, a man, mine equal, my guide, and my acquaintance; we took sweet counsel together, and walked unto the house of God in company" (Ps. 55:12–14).

It is with professors of religion, especially such as become so in a time of outpouring of the Spirit of God, as it is with the blossoms in the spring;[8] there are vast numbers of them upon the trees, which all look fair and promising; but yet very many of them never come to anything. And many of those, that in a little time wither up, and drop off, and rot under the trees; yet for a while, look as beautiful and gay as others; and not only so, but smell sweet, and send forth a pleasant odor: so that we can't, by any of our senses, certainly distinguish those blossoms which have in them that secret virtue, which will afterwards appear in the fruit, and that inward solidity and strength which shall enable them to bear, and cause them to be perfected by the hot summer sun, that will dry up the others. 'Tis the mature fruit which comes afterwards, and not the beautiful colors and smell of the blossom, that we must judge by. So new converts (professedly so) in their talk about things of religion, may appear fair, and be very savory, and the saints may think they talk feelingly. They may relish their talk, and imagine they perceive a divine savor in it; and yet all may come to nothing.

'Tis strange how hardly men are brought to be contented with the rules and directions Christ has given them, but they must needs go by other rules, of their own inventing, that seem to them wiser and better. I know of no directions or counsels which Christ ever delivered more plainly, than the rules he has given us, to guide us in our judging of others' sincerity; viz. that we should judge of the tree chiefly by the fruit: but yet this won't do; but other ways are found out, which are imagined to be more distinguishing and certain. And woeful have been the mischievous consequences, of this arrogant setting up men's wisdom above the wisdom of Christ. I believe many saints have gone much out of the way of Christ's word, in this respect: and some of them have been chastised with whips, and (I had almost said) scorpions, to bring them back again. But many things which have lately appeared, and do now appear, may convince, that ordinarily, those who have gone furthest this way, that have been most highly conceited of their faculty of discerning, and have appeared most forward, peremptorily and suddenly to determine the state of men's souls, have been hypocrites, who have known nothing of true religion.

In the parable of the wheat and tares, it is said, "When the blade

8. A time of outpouring of the Spirit of God, reviving religion, and producing the pleasant appearances of it, in new converts, is in Scripture compared to this very thing, viz. the spring season, when the benign influences of the heavens, cause the blossoms to put forth (Cant. 2:11–12).

was sprung up, and brought forth fruit, then appeared the tares also" (Matt. 13:26). As though the tares were not discerned, nor distinguishable from the wheat, till then, as Mr. Flavel observes; [9] who mentions it as an observation of Jerome's, that wheat and tares are so much alike, till the blade of the wheat comes to bring forth the ear, that 'tis next to impossible to distinguish them. And then, Mr. Flavel adds: "How difficult soever it be to discern the difference between wheat and tares; yet doubtless the eye of sense can much easier discriminate them, than the most quick and piercing eye of man, can discern the difference between special and common grace. For all saving graces in the saints, have their counterfeits in hypocrites; there are similar works in those, which a spiritual and very judicious eye may easily mistake, for the saving and genuine effects of a sanctifying spirit."

As 'tis the ear or the fruit which distinguishes the wheat from the tares, so this is the true Shibboleth, that he who stands as judge at the passages of Jordan, makes use of to distinguish those that shall pass over Jordan into the true Canaan, from those that should be slain at the passages. For the Hebrew word "Shibboleth," signifies an ear of corn. And perhaps the more full pronunciation of Jephthah's friends, Shibboleth, may represent a full ear with fruit in it, typifying the fruits of the friends of Christ, the antitype of Jephthah; and the more lean pronunciation of the Ephraimites his enemies, may represent their empty ears, typifying the show of religion in hypocrites, without substance and fruit. This is agreeable to the doctrine we are abundantly taught in Scripture, viz. that he who is set to judge those that pass through death, whether they have a right to enter into the heavenly Canaan or no, or whether they should not be slain, will judge every man according to his works.

We seem to be taught the same things, by the rules given for the priests discerning the leprosy. In many cases it was impossible for the priest to determine whether a man had the leprosy, or whether he were clean, by the most narrow inspection of the appearances that were upon him, till he had waited to see what the appearances would come to, and had shut up the person who showed himself to him, one seven days after another; and when he judged, he was to determine by the hair, which grew out of the spot

9. Flavel, *Husbandry Spiritualized,* p. 109. Also *The Whole Works of Mr. John Flavel,* 2, 652.

that was shown him, which was as it were the fruit that it brought forth.

And here, before I finish what I have to say under this head, I would say something to a strange notion some have of late been led away with, of certainly knowing the good estate that others are in, as though it were immediately revealed to 'em from heaven, by their love flowing out to 'em in an extraordinary manner. They argue thus, that their love being very sensible and great, it may be certainly known by them who feel it, to be a true Christian love: and if it be a true Christian love, the Spirit of God must be the author of it: and inasmuch as the Spirit of God, who knows certainly whether others are the children of God or no, and is a Spirit of truth, is pleased, by an uncommon influence upon 'em, to cause their love to flow out, in an extraordinary manner, towards such a person, as a child of God; it must needs be that this infallible Spirit, who deceives none, knows that that person is a child of God. But such persons might be convinced of the falseness of their reasoning, if they would consider whether or no it be not their duty, and what God requires of 'em, to love those as the children of God, who they think are the children of God, and whom they have no reason to think otherwise of, from all that they can see in them, though God, who searches the hearts, know 'em not to be his children.

If it be their duty, then it is good, and the want of it sin; and therefore, surely the Spirit of God may be the author of it: the Spirit of God, without being a spirit of falsehood, may in such a case assist a person to do his duty, and keep him from sin. But then they argue from the uncommon degree and special manner, in which their love flows out to the person; which they think the Spirit of God never would cause, if he did not know the object to be a child of God. But then I would ask them, whether or no it is not their duty to love all such as they are bound to think are the children of God, from all that they can see in them, to a very great degree, though God, from other things which he sees, that are out of sight to them, knows 'em not to be so. 'Tis men's duty to love all whom they are bound in charity to look upon as the children of God, with a vastly dearer affection than they commonly do. As we ought to love Christ to the utmost capacity of our nature, so 'tis our duty to love those who we think are so near and dear to him as his members, with an exceeding dear affection, as Christ has loved us; and therefore it is sin in us not to love them so. We ought to pray to God that he would, by his Spirit keep us from sin, and enable us to do our duty: and may not his Spirit answer our prayers, and enable us to do our duty, in a particular instance, without lying? If he can't, then the Spirit of God is bound not to help his people to do their duty in some instances, because he can't do it without being a spirit of falsehood. But surely God is so sovereign as that comes to, that he may enable us to do our duty when he pleases, and on what occasion he pleases. When persons think others are his children, God may have other ends in causing their exceedingly endeared love to flow out to them, besides revealing to them whether their opinion of 'em be right or no: he may have that merciful end in it, to enable them to do their duty, and to keep them from that dreadful infinite evil, sin. And will they say God shall not show 'em that mercy in such a case? If I am at a distance from home, and hear, that in my absence, my house is burnt, but my family have, in some extraordinary manner, all escaped the flames; and everything in the circumstances of the story, as I hear it, makes it appear very credible; it would be sin in me, in such a case, not to feel a very great degree of gratitude to God, though the story indeed be not true. And is not God so sovereign, that he may if he pleases, show me that mercy on that occasion, and enable me to do my duty in a much further degree than I used to do it, and yet not incur the charge of deceitfulness, in confirming a falsehood?

'Tis exceeding manifest, that error or mistake may be the occasion of a gracious exercise, and consequently a gracious influence of the Spirit of God, by Rom. 14:6: "He that eateth to the Lord, he eateth, and giveth God thanks; and he that eateth not to the Lord, he eateth not, and giveth God thanks." The Apostle is speaking of those, who through erroneous and needless scruples, avoided eating legally unclean meats. By this it is very evident, that there may be true exercises of grace, a true respect to the Lord, and particularly, a true thankfulness, which may be occasioned, both by an erroneous judgment and practice. And consequently, an error may be the occasion of those truly holy exercises that are from the infallible Spirit of God. And if so, 'tis certainly too much for us to determine, to how great a degree the Spirit of God may give this holy exercise, on such an occasion.

This notion, of certainly discerning another's state, by love flowing out, is not only not founded on reason or Scripture, but it is antiscriptural, 'tis against the rules of Scripture; which say not a word of any such way of judging the state of others as this, but direct us to judge chiefly by the fruits that are seen in them. And it is against the doctrines of Scripture, which do plainly teach us that the state of others' souls towards God, cannot be known by us, as in Rev. 2:17: "To him that overcometh, will I give to eat of the hidden manna; and I will give him a white stone, and in the stone a new name written, which no man knoweth, saving he that receiveth it." And Rom. 2:29: "He is a Jew, which is one inwardly; and circumcision is that of the heart; in the spirit, and not in the letter; whose praise is not of men, but of God." That by this last expression, "whose praise is not of men, but of God," the Apostle has respect to the insufficiency of men to judge concerning him, whether he be inwardly a Jew or no (as they could easily see by outward marks, whether men were outwardly Jews) and would signify, that it belongs to God alone to give a determining voice in this matter, is confirmed by the same Apostle's use of the phrase, in I Cor. 4:5: "Therefore judge nothing before the time, until the Lord come; who both will bring to light the hidden things of darkness, and will make manifest the counsels of the hearts"; and then shall every man have praise to God. The Apostle, in the two foregoing verses, says: "But with me, it is a very small thing, that I should be judged of you, or of man's judgment: yea, I judge not mine own self, for I know nothing by my self, yet am I not hereby justified; but he that judgeth me is the Lord." And again, it is further confirmed, because the Apostle in this second chapter to the Romans, directs his speech especially to those who had a high conceit of their own holiness, made their boast of God, and were confident of their own discerning, and that they knew God's will, and approved the things which were excellent, or tried the things that differ (as it is in the margin), ver. 18. And were confident that they were guides of the blind, and a light to them which are in darkness, instructors of the foolish, teachers of babes; and so took upon them to judge others, see ver. 1, 17–20.

And how arrogant must the notion be, that they have, who imagine they can certainly know others' godliness, when that great apostle Peter pretends not to say any more concerning Silvanus, than that he was a faithful brother, as he supposed; I Pet. 5:12.

Though this Silvanus appears to have been a very eminent minister of Christ, and an evangelist, and a famous light in God's church at that day, and an intimate companion of the apostles. See II Cor. 1:19; I Thess. 1:1; and II Thess. 1:1.

PART THREE

Shewing What Are Distinguishing Signs of Truly Gracious and Holy Affections

I COME now to the second thing appertaining to the trial of religious affections, which was proposed, viz. to take notice of some things, wherein those affections that are spiritual and gracious, do differ from those that are not so.

But before I proceed directly to the distinguishing characters, I would previously mention some things which I desire may be observed, concerning the marks I shall lay down.

1. That I am far from undertaking to give such signs of gracious affections, as shall be sufficient to enable any certainly to distinguish true affection from false in others; or to determine positively which of their neighbors are true professors, and which are hypocrites. In so doing, I should be guilty of that arrogance which I have been condemning. Though it be plain that Christ has given rules to all Christians, to enable 'em to judge of professors of religion, whom they are concerned with, so far as is necessary for their own safety, and to prevent their being led into a snare by false teachers, and false pretenders to religion; and though it be also beyond doubt, that the Scriptures do abound with rules, which may be very serviceable to ministers, in counseling and conducting souls committed to their care, in things appertaining to their spiritual and eternal state; yet, 'tis also evident, that it was never God's design to give us any rules, by which we may certainly know, who of our fellow professors are his, and to make a full and clear separation between sheep and goats: but that on the contrary, it was God's design to reserve this to himself, as his prerogative. And therefore no such distinguishing signs as shall enable Christians or ministers to do this, are ever to be expected to the world's end: for no more is ever to be expected from any signs, that are to be found in the Word of God, or gathered from it, than Christ designed them for.

2. No such signs are to be expected, that shall be sufficient to enable those saints certainly to discern their own good estate, who are very low in grace, or are such as have much departed from God, and are fallen into a dead, carnal and unchristian frame. It is not agreeable to God's design (as has been already observed) that such

should know their good estate: nor is it desirable that they should; but on the contrary, every way best that they should not; and we have reason to bless God, that he has made no provision that such should certainly know the state that they are in, any other way, than by first coming out of the ill frame and way they are in.

Indeed it is not properly through the defect of the signs given in the Word of God, that every saint living, whether strong or weak, and those who are in a bad frame, as well as others, can't certainly know their good estate by them. For the rules in themselves are certain and infallible, and every saint has, or has had those things in himself, which are sure evidences of grace; for every, even the least act of grace is so. But it is through his defect to whom the signs are given. There is a twofold defect in that saint who is very low in grace, or in an ill frame, which makes it impossible for him to know certainly that he has true grace, by the best signs and rules which can be given him. First, a defect in the object, or the qualification to be viewed and examined. I don't mean an essential defect; because I suppose the person to be a real saint; but a defect in degree: grace being very small, cannot be clearly and certainly discerned and distinguished. Things that are very small, we can't clearly discern their form, or distinguish them one from another; though, as they are in themselves, their form may be very different. There is doubtless a great difference between the body of man, and the bodies of other animals, in the first conception in the womb: but yet if we should view the different embryos, it might not be possible for us to discern the difference, by reason of the imperfect state of the object; but as it comes to greater perfection, the difference becomes very plain. The difference between creatures of very contrary qualities, is not so plainly to be seen while they are very young, even after they are actually brought forth, as in their more perfect state. The difference between doves and ravens, or doves and vultures, when they first come out of the egg, is not so evident; but as they grow to their perfection, 'tis exceeding great and manifest. Another defect attending the grace of those I am speaking, is its being mingled with so much corruption, which clouds and hides it, and makes it impossible for it certainly to be known. Though different things that are before us, may have in themselves many marks thoroughly distinguishing them one from another; yet if we see them only in a thick smoke, it may nevertheless be impossible to distinguish them. A fixed star is easily distinguishable from a comet, in a clear sky; but if we view them through a cloud, it may be impossible to see the difference. When true Christians are in an ill frame, guilt lies on the conscience; which will bring fear, and so prevent the peace and joy of an assured hope.

Secondly, there is in such a case a defect in the eye. As the feebleness of grace and prevalence of corruption, obscures the object; so it enfeebles the sight; it darkens the sight as to all spiritual objects, of which grace is one. Sin is like some distempers of the eyes, that make things to appear of different colors from those which properly belong to them, and like many other distempers, that put the mouth out of taste, so as to disenable from distinguishing good and wholesome food from bad, but everything tastes bitter. Men in a corrupt and carnal frame, have their spiritual senses in but poor plight for judging and distinguishing spiritual things.

For these reasons, no signs that can be given, will actually satisfy persons in such a case: let the signs that are given, be never so good and infallible, and clearly laid down, they will not serve them. It is like giving a man rules, how to distinguish visible objects in the dark: the things themselves may be very different, and their difference may be very well and distinctly described to him; yet all is insufficient to enable him to distinguish them, because he is in the dark. And therefore many persons in such a case spend time in a fruitless labor, in poring on past experiences, and examining themselves by signs they hear laid down from the pulpit, or that they read in books; when there is other work for them to do, that is much more expected of them; which, while they neglect, all their self-examinations are like to be in vain, if they should spend never so much time in them. The accursed thing is to be destroyed from their camp, and Achan to be slain; and till this be done they will be in trouble. 'Tis not God's design that men should obtain assurance in any other way, than by mortifying corruption, and increasing in grace, and obtaining the lively exercises of it. And although self-examination be a duty of great use and importance, and by no means to be neglected; yet it is not the principal means, by which the saints do get satisfaction of their good estate. Assurance is not to be obtained so much by self-examination, as by action. The apostle Paul sought assurance chiefly this way, even by forgetting the things that were behind, and reaching forth unto those things that were before, pressing towards the mark for the prize of the high calling of God in Christ Jesus; if by any means he might attain unto the resurrection of the dead. And it was by this means chiefly that he obtained assurance, I Cor. 9:26: "I therefore so run, as not uncertainly." He obtained assurance of winning the prize, more by running, than by considering. The swiftness of his pace, did more towards his assurance of a conquest, than the strictness of his examination. Giving all diligence to grow in grace, by adding to faith, virtue, etc. is the direction that the apostle Peter gives us, for making our calling and election sure, and having an entrance ministered to us abundantly, into Christ's everlasting kingdom; signifying to us, that without this, our eyes will be dim, and we shall be as men in the dark, that cannot plainly see things past or to come, either the forgiveness of our sins past, or our heavenly inheritance that is future, and far off (II Pet. 1:5–11).[1]

Therefore, though good rules to distinguish true grace from counterfeit, may tend to convince hypocrites, and be of great use to the saints, in many respects; and among other benefits, may be very useful to them to remove many needless scruples, and establish their hope; yet I am far from pretending to lay down any such rules, as shall be sufficient of themselves, without other means, to enable all true saints to see their good estate, or as supposing they should be the principal means of their satisfaction.

3. Nor is there much encouragement, in the experience of present or past times, to lay down rules or marks to distinguish between true and false affections, in hopes of convincing any considerable number of that sort of hypocrites, who have been deceived with great false discoveries and affections, and are once settled in a false confidence, and high conceit of their own supposed great experiences and privileges. Such hypocrites are so conceited of their own wisdom, and so blinded and hardened with a very great self-righteousness (but very subtle and secret, under the disguise of great humility), and so invincible a fondness of their pleasing conceit, of their great exaltation, that it usually signifies nothing at all, to lay before them the most convincing evidences of their hypocrisy.

1. "The way to know your godliness, is to renew the visible exercises of grace. . . . The more the visible exercises of grace are renewed, the more certain you will be. The more frequently these actings are renewed, the more abiding and confirmed your assurance will be. . . . The more men's grace is multiplied, the more their peace is multiplied; II Pet. 1:2: 'Grace and peace be multiplied unto you, through the knowledge of God and Jesus Christ our Lord.'" Stoddard, *Sincerity and Hypocrisy,* pp. 139, 142–3.

Their state is indeed deplorable, and next to those that have committed the unpardonable sin, some of this sort of persons seem to be most out of the reach of means of conviction and repentance. But yet the laying down good rules may be a means of preventing such hypocrites, and of convincing many of other kinds of hypocrites: and God is able to convince even this kind, and his grace is not to be limited, nor means to be neglected. And besides, such rules may be of use to the true saints, to detect false affections, which they may have mingled with true. And be a means of their religion's becoming more pure, and like gold tried in the fire.

Having premised these things, I now proceed directly to take notice of those things in which true religious affections are distinguished from false.

I. Affections that are truly spiritual and gracious, do arise from those influences and operations on the heart, which are *spiritual, supernatural* and *divine.*

I will explain what I mean by these terms, whence will appear their use to distinguish between those affections which are spiritual, and those which are not so.

We find that true saints, or those persons who are sanctified by the Spirit of God, are in the New Testament called spiritual persons. And their being spiritual is spoken of as their peculiar character, and that wherein they are distinguished from those who are not sanctified. This is evident because those who are spiritual are set in opposition to natural men, and carnal men. Thus the spiritual man, and the natural man, are set in opposition one to another; "The natural man receiveth not the things of the Spirit of God, for they are foolishness unto him; neither can he know them; because they are spiritually discerned. But he that is spiritual judgeth all things" (I Cor. 2:14–15). The Scripture explains itself to mean an ungodly man, or one that has no grace, by a natural man: thus the apostle Jude, speaking of certain ungodly men, that had crept in unawares among the saints, ver. 4 of his Epistle, says, ver. 19: "These are sensual, having not the Spirit." This the Apostle gives as a reason why they behaved themselves in such a wicked manner as he had described. Here the word translated "sensual," in the original is ψυκικοι; which is the very same, which in those verses in I Cor. ch. 2 is translated "natural." In the like manner, in the continuation of the same discourse, in the next verse but one, spiritual men are opposed to carnal men: which the connection plainly shows mean the same, as spiritual men and natural men, in the foregoing verses; "and I, brethren, could not speak unto you, as unto spiritual, but as unto carnal"; i.e. as in a great measure unsanctified. That by carnal the Apostle means corrupt and unsanctified, is abundantly evident, by Rom. 7:25 and 8:1, 4–9, 12, 13; Gal. 5:16 to the end; cf. Col. 2:18. Now therefore, if by natural and carnal, in these texts, he intended "unsanctified"; then doubtless by spiritual, which is opposed thereto, is meant "sanctified" and gracious.

And as the saints are called spiritual in Scripture, so we also find that there are certain properties, qualities, and principles, that have the same epithet given them. So we read of a spiritual mind, Rom. 8:6–7 and of spiritual wisdom, Col. 1:9 and of spiritual blessings, Eph. 1:3.

Now it may be observed that the epithet "spiritual," in these and other parallel texts of the New Testament, is not used to signify any relation of persons or things to the spirit or soul of man, as the spiritual part of man, in opposition to the body, which is the material part: qualities are not said to be spiritual, because they have their seat in the soul, and not in the body: for there are some properties that the Scripture calls carnal or fleshly, which have their seat as much in the soul, as those properties that are called spiritual. Thus it is with pride and self-righteousness, and a man's trusting to his own wisdom, which the Apostle calls fleshly (Col. 2:18). Nor are things called spiritual, because they are conversant about those things that are immaterial, and not corporeal. For so was the wisdom of the wise men, and princes of this world, conversant about spirits, and immaterial beings; which yet the Apostle speaks of as natural men, totally ignorant of those things that are spiritual (I Cor. ch. 2). But it is with relation to the Holy Ghost, or Spirit of God, that persons or things are termed spiritual, in the New Testament. "Spirit," as the word is used to signify the third person in the Trinity, is the substantive, of which is formed the adjective "spiritual," in the Holy Scriptures. Thus Christians are called spiritual persons, because they are born of the Spirit, and because of the indwelling and holy influences of the Spirit of God in them. And things are called spiritual as related to the Spirit of God; "Which things also we speak, not in the words which man's wisdom teacheth, but which the Holy Ghost teacheth, comparing spiritual things with spiritual. But the natural man receiveth not the things of the Spirit of God" (I Cor. 2:13–14). Here the Apostle himself expressly signifies, that by spiritual things, he means the things of the Spirit of God, and things which the Holy Ghost teacheth. The same is yet more abundantly apparent by viewing the whole context. Again, "To be carnally minded is death: but to be spiritually minded is life and peace" (Rom. 8:6). The Apostle explains what he means by being carnally and spiritually minded, in what follows in the 9th verse, and shows that by being spiritually minded, he means a having the indwelling and holy influences of the Spirit of God in the heart. "But ye are not in the flesh, but in the Spirit, if so be the Spirit of God dwell in you. Now if any man have not the Spirit of Christ, he is none of his." The same is evident by all the context. But time would fail to produce all the evidence there is of this, in the New Testament.

And it must be here observed, that although it is with relation to the Spirit of God and his influences, that persons and things are called spiritual; yet not all those persons who are subject to any kind of influence of the Spirit of God, are ordinarily called spiritual in the New Testament. They who have only the common influences of God's Spirit, are not so called, in the places cited above, but only those, who have the special, gracious and saving influences of God's Spirit: as is evident, because it has been already proved, that by spiritual men is meant godly men, in opposition to natural, carnal and unsanctified men. And it is most plain, that the Apostle by spiritually minded, Rom. 8:6, means graciously minded. And though the extraordinary gifts of the Spirit, which natural men might have, are sometimes called spiritual, because they are from the Spirit; yet natural men, whatever gifts of the Spirit they had, were not, in the usual language of the New Testament, called spiritual persons. For it was not by men's having the gifts of the Spirit, but by their having the virtues of the Spirit, that they were called spiritual; as is apparent, by Gal. 6:1: "Brethren, if any man be overtaken in a fault, ye which are spiritual restore such an one in the spirit of meekness." Meekness is one of those virtues which the Apostle had just spoken of, in the verses next preceding, showing what are the fruits of the Spirit. Those qualifications are said to be spiritual in the language of the New Testament, which are truly gracious and holy, and peculiar to the saints.

Thus when we read of spiritual wisdom and understanding (as

in Col. 1:9: "We desire that ye may be filled with the knowledge of his will, in all wisdom and spiritual understanding"). Hereby is intended that wisdom which is gracious, and from the sanctifying influences of the Spirit of God. For doubtless, by spiritual wisdom, is meant that which is opposite to what the Scripture calls natural wisdom; as the spiritual man is opposed to the natural man. And therefore spiritual wisdom is doubtless the same with that wisdom which is from above, that the apostle James speaks of, "The wisdom that is from above, is first pure, then peaceable, gentle," etc. (Jas. 3:17), for this the Apostle opposes to natural wisdom, ver. 15: "This wisdom descendeth not from above, but is earthly, sensual," the last word in the original is the same that is translated "natural," in I Cor. 2:14.

So that although natural men may be the subjects of many influences of the Spirit of God, as is evident by many Scriptures, as Num. 24:2; I Sam. 10:10 and 11:6 and 16:14; I Cor. 13:1–3; Heb. 6:4–6 and many others; yet they are not in the sense of the Scripture, spiritual persons; either are any of those effects, common gifts, qualities or affections, that are from the influence of the Spirit of God upon them, called spiritual things. The great difference lies in these two things.

1. The Spirit of God is given to the true saints to dwell in them, as his proper lasting abode; and to influence their hearts, as a principle of new nature, or as a divine supernatural spring of life and action. The Scriptures represent the Holy Spirit, not only as moving, and occasionally influencing the saints, but as dwelling in them as his temple, his proper abode, and everlasting dwelling place (I Cor. 3:16; II Cor. 6:16; John 14:16–17). And he is represented as being there so united to the faculties of the soul, that he becomes there a principle or spring of new nature and life.

So the saints are said to live by Christ living in them (Gal. 2:20). Christ by his Spirit not only is in them, but lives in them; and so that they live by his life; so is his Spirit united to them, as a principle of life in them; they don't only drink living water, but this living water becomes a well or fountain of water, in the soul, springing up into spiritual and everlasting life (John 4:14), and thus becomes a principle of life in them; this living water, this Evangelist himself explains to intend the Spirit of God (ch. 7:38–39). The light of the Sun of Righteousness don't only shine upon them, but is so communicated to them that they shine also, and become little images of that Sun which shines upon them; the sap of the true vine is not only conveyed into them, as the sap of a tree may be conveyed into a vessel, but is conveyed as sap is from a tree into one of its living branches, where it becomes a principle of life. The Spirit of God being thus communicated and united to the saints, they are from thence properly denominated from it, and are called spiritual.

On the other hand, though the Spirit of God may many ways influence natural men; yet because it is not thus communicated to them, as an indwelling principle, they don't derive any denomination or character from it; for there being no union it is not their own. The light may shine upon a body that is very dark or black; and though that body be the subject of the light, yet, because the light becomes no principle of light in it, so as to cause the body to shine, hence that body don't properly receive its denomination from it, so as to be called a lightsome body. So the Spirit of God acting upon the soul only, without communicating itself to be an active principle in it, can't denominate it spiritual. A body that continues black, may be said not to have light, though the light shines upon it; so natural men are said not to have the Spirit, Jude 19: "sensual," or natural (as the word is elsewhere rendered) "having not the Spirit."

2. Another reason why the saints and their virtues are called spiritual (which is the principal thing), is that the Spirit of God, dwelling as a vital principle in their souls, there produces those effects wherein he exerts and communicates himself in his own proper nature. Holiness is the nature of the Spirit of God, therefore he is called in Scripture the Holy Ghost. Holiness, which is as it were the beauty and sweetness of the divine nature, is as much the proper nature of the Holy Spirit, as heat is the nature of fire, or sweetness was the nature of that holy anointing oil, which was the principal type of the Holy Ghost in the Mosaic dispensation; yea, I may rather say that holiness is as much the proper nature of the Holy Ghost, as sweetness was the nature of the sweet odor of that ointment. The Spirit of God so dwells in the hearts of the saints, that he there, as a seed or spring of life, exerts and communicates himself, in this his sweet and divine nature, making the soul a partaker of God's beauty and Christ's joy, so that the saint has truly fellowship with the Father, and with his Son Jesus Christ, in thus having the communion or participation of the Holy Ghost.

The grace which is in the hearts of the saints, is of the same nature with the divine holiness, as much as 'tis possible for that holiness to be, which is infinitely less in degree; as the brightness that is in a diamond which the sun shines upon, is of the same nature with the brightness of the sun, but only that it is as nothing to it in degree. Therefore Christ says, John 3:6: "That which is born of the Spirit is spirit"; i.e. the grace that is begotten in the hearts of the saints, is something of the same nature with that Spirit, and so is properly called a spiritual nature; after the same manner as that which is born of the flesh is flesh, or that which is born of corrupt nature is corrupt nature.

But the Spirit of God never influences the minds of natural men after this manner. Though he may influence them many ways, yet he never, in any of his influences, communicates himself to them in his own proper nature. Indeed he never acts disagreeably to his nature, either on the minds of saints or sinners: but the Spirit of God may act upon men agreeably to his own nature, and not exert his proper nature in the acts and exercises of their minds: the Spirit of God may act so, that his actions may be agreeable to his nature, and yet may not at all communicate himself in his proper nature, in the effect of that action. Thus, for instance, the Spirit of God moved upon the face of the waters, and there was nothing disagreeable to his nature in that action; but yet he did not at all communicate himself in that action, there was nothing of the proper nature of the Holy Spirit in that motion of the waters. And so he may act upon the minds of men many ways, and not communicate himself any more than when he acts on inanimate things.

Thus not only the manner of the *relation* of the Spirit, who is the operator, to the subject of his operations, is different; as the Spirit operates in the saints, as dwelling in them, as an abiding principle of action, whereas he doth not so operate upon sinners; but the influence and *operation itself* is different, and the effect wrought exceeding different. So that not only the persons are called spiritual, as having the Spirit of God dwelling in them; but those qualifications, affections and experiences that are wrought in them by the Spirit, are also spiritual, and therein differ vastly in their nature and kind from all that a natural man is or can be the subject of, while he remains in a natural state; and also from all that men or devils can be the authors of: 'tis a spiritual work in this high sense; and therefore above all other works is peculiar to the

Spirit of God. There is no work so high and excellent; for there is no work wherein God does so much communicate himself, and wherein the mere creature hath, in so high a sense, a participation of God; so that it is expressed in Scripture by the saints being made "partakers of the divine nature" (II Pet. 1:4), and having God dwelling in them, and they in God (I John 4:12, 15–16, and ch. 3:21), and having Christ in them (John 17:21; Rom. 8:10), being the temples of the living God (II Cor. 6:16), living by Christ's life (Gal. 2:20), being made partakers of God's holiness (Heb. 12:10), having Christ's love dwelling in them (John 17:26), having his joy fulfilled in them (John 17:13), seeing light in God's light, and being made to drink of the river of God's pleasures (Ps. 36:8–9), having fellowship with God, or communicating and partaking with him (as the word signifies) (I John 1:3). Not that the saints are made partakers of the essence of God, and so are "Godded" with God, and "Christed" with Christ, according to the abominable and blasphemous language and notions of some heretics; but, to use the Scripture phrase, they are made partakers of God's fullness (Eph. 3:17–19; John 1:16), that is, of God's spiritual beauty and happiness, according to the measure and capacity of a creature; for so it is evident the word "fullness" signifies in Scripture language. Grace in the hearts of the saints, being therefore the most glorious work of God, wherein he communicates of the goodness of his nature, it is doubtless his peculiar work, and in an eminent manner, above the power of all creatures. And the influences of the Spirit of God in this, being thus peculiar to God, and being those wherein God does, in so high a manner, communicate himself, and make the creature partaker of the divine nature (the Spirit of God communicating itself in its own proper nature). This is what I mean by those influences that are divine, when I say that truly gracious affections do arise from those influences that are spiritual and divine.

The true saints only have that which is spiritual; others have nothing which is divine, in the sense that has been spoken of. They not only have not these communications of the Spirit of God in so high a degree as the saints, but have nothing of that nature or kind. For the apostle James tell us, that natural men have not the Spirit; and Christ teaches the necessity of a new birth, or a being born of the Spirit, from this, that he that is born of the flesh, has only flesh, and no spirit (John 3:6). They have not the Spirit of God dwelling in them in any degree; for the Apostle teaches, that all who have the Spirit of God dwelling in them are some of his (Rom. 8:9–11). And an having the Spirit of God is spoken of as a certain sign that persons shall have the eternal inheritance; for 'tis spoken of as the earnest of it (II Cor. 1:22 and 5:5; Eph. 1:14), and an having anything of the Spirit is mentioned as a sure sign of being in Christ, "Hereby know we that we dwell in him, because he hath given us of his Spirit" (I John 4:30). Ungodly men, not only han't so much of the divine nature as the saints, but they are not partakers of it; which implies that they have nothing of it; for a being partaker of the divine nature is spoken of as the peculiar privilege of the true saints (II Pet. 1:4). Ungodly men are not partakers of God's holiness (Heb. 12:10). A natural man has no experience of any of those things that are spiritual: the Apostle teaches us that he is so far from it, that he knows nothing about them, he is a perfect stranger to them, the talk about such things is all foolishness and nonsense to him, he knows not what it means, "The natural man receiveth not the things of the Spirit of God; for they are foolishness to him; neither can he know them; because they are spiritually discerned" (I Cor. 2:14). And to the like purpose Christ teaches us that the world is wholly unacquainted with the Spirit of God, "Even the Spirit of truth, whom the world cannot receive; because it seeth him not, neither knoweth him" (John 14:17). And 'tis further evident, that natural men have nothing in them of the same nature with the true grace of the saints because the Apostle teaches us that those of them who go furthest in religion, have no charity, or true Christian love (I Cor. ch. 13). So Christ elsewhere reproves the Pharisees, those high pretenders to religion, that they had not the love of God in them (John 5:42). Hence natural men have no communion or fellowship with Christ, or participation with him (as these words signify), for this is spoken of as the peculiar privilege of the saints (I John 1:3, together with verses 6, 7, and I Cor. 1:8–9). And the Scripture speaks of the actual being of a gracious principle in the soul, though in its first beginning, as a seed there planted, as inconsistent with a man's being a sinner (I John 3:9). And natural men are represented in Scripture as having no spiritual light, no spiritual life, and no spiritual being; and therefore conversion is often compared to opening the eyes of the blind, raising the dead, and a work of creation (wherein creatures are made entirely new), and becoming newborn children.

From these things it is evident, that those gracious influences which the saints are subjects of, and the effects of God's Spirit which they experience, are entirely above nature, altogether of a different kind from anything that men find within themselves by nature, or only in the exercise of natural principles; and are things which no improvement of those qualifications, or principles that are natural, no advancing or exalting them to higher degrees, and no kind of composition of them, will ever bring men to; because they not only differ from what is natural, and from everything that natural men experience, in degree and circumstances; but also in kind; and are of a nature vastly more excellent. And this is what I mean by supernatural, when I say, that gracious affections are from those influences that are supernatural.

From hence it follows, that in those gracious exercises and affections which are wrought in the minds of the saints, through the saving influences of the Spirit of God, there is a new inward perception or sensation of their minds, entirely different in its nature and kind, from anything that ever their minds were the subjects of before they were sanctified. For doubtless if God by his mighty power produces something that is new, not only in degree and circumstances, but in its whole nature, and that which could be produced by no exalting, varying or compounding of what was there before, or by adding anything of the like kind; I say, if God produces something thus new in a mind, that is a perceiving, thinking, conscious thing; then doubtless something entirely new is felt, or perceived, or thought; or, which is the same thing, there is some new sensation or perception of the mind, which is entirely of a new sort, and which could be produced by no exalting, varying or compounding of that kind of perceptions or sensations which the mind had before; or there is what some metaphysicians call a new simple idea. If grace be, in the sense above described, an entirely new kind of principle; then the exercises of it are also entirely a new kind of exercises. And if there be in the soul a new sort of exercises which it is conscious of, which the soul knew nothing of before, and which no improvement, composition or management of what it was before conscious or sensible of, could produce, or anything like it; then it follows that the mind has an entirely new kind of perception or sensation; and here is, as it were, a new spiritual sense that the mind has, or a principle of new kind of perception or spiritual sensation, which is in its whole nature different from any former kinds of sensation of the mind, as tasting is diverse from any of the other senses; and something is perceived by a true saint, in the exercise of this new sense of mind, in spiritual and divine things, as entirely diverse from anything that is perceived in them, by natural men, as the sweet taste of honey is diverse from the ideas men get of honey by only looking on it, and feeling of it. So that the spiritual perceptions which a sanctified and spiritual person has, are not only diverse from all that natural men have, after the manner that the ideas or perceptions of the same sense may differ one from another, but rather as the ideas and sensations of different senses do differ. Hence the work of the Spirit of God in regeneration is often in Scripture compared to the giving a new sense, giving eyes to see, and ears to hear, unstopping the ears of the deaf, and opening the eyes of them that were born blind, and turning from darkness unto light. And because this spiritual sense is immensely the most noble and excellent, and that without which all other principles of perception, and all our faculties are useless and vain; therefore the giving this new sense, with the blessed fruits and effects of it in the soul, is compared to a raising the dead, and to a new creation.

This new spiritual sense, and the new dispositions that attend it, are no new faculties, but are new principles of nature. I use the word "principles," for want of a word of a more determinate signification. By a principle of nature in this place, I mean that foundation which is laid in nature, either old or new, for any particular manner or kind of exercise of the faculties of the soul; or a natural habit or foundation for action, giving a person ability and disposition to exert the faculties in exercises of such a certain kind; so that to exert the faculties in that kind of exercises, may be said to be his nature. So this new spiritual sense is not a new faculty of understanding, but it is a new foundation laid in the nature of the soul, for a new kind of exercises of the same faculty of understanding. So that new holy disposition of heart that attends this new sense, is not a new faculty of will, but a foundation laid in the nature of the soul, for a new kind of exercises of the same faculty of will.

The Spirit of God, in all his operations upon the minds of natural men, only moves, impresses, assists, improves, or some way acts upon natural principles; but gives no new spiritual principle. Thus when the Spirit of God gives a natural man visions, as he did Balaam, he only impresses a natural principle, viz. the sense of seeing, immediately exciting ideas of that sense; but he gives no new sense;

neither is there anything supernatural, spiritual or divine in it. So if the Spirit of God impresses on a man's imagination, either in a dream, or when he is awake, any outward ideas of any of the senses, either voices, or shapes and colors, 'tis only exciting ideas of the same kind that he has by natural principles and senses. So if God reveals to any natural man, any secret fact; as for instance, something that he shall hereafter see or hear; this is not infusing or exercising any new spiritual principle, or giving the ideas of any new spiritual sense; 'tis only impressing, in an extraordinary manner, the ideas that will hereafter be received by sight and hearing. So in the more ordinary influences of the Spirit of God on the hearts of sinners, he only assists natural principles to do the same work to a greater degree, which they do of themselves by nature. Thus the Spirit of God by his common influences may assist men's natural ingeniosity, as he assisted Bezaleel and Aholiab in the curious works of the tabernacle: so he may assist men's natural abilities in political affairs, and improve their courage, and other natural qualifications; as he is said to have put his Spirit on the seventy elders, and on Saul, so as to give him another heart: so God may greatly assist natural men's reason, in their reasoning about secular things, or about the doctrines of religion, and may greatly advance the clearness of their apprehensions and notions of things of religion in many respects, without giving any spiritual sense. So in those awakenings and convictions that natural men may have, God only assists conscience, which is a natural principle, to do that work in a further degree, which it naturally does. Conscience naturally gives men an apprehension of right and wrong, and suggests the relation there is between right and wrong, and a retribution: the Spirit of God assists men's consciences to do this in a greater degree, helps conscience against the stupefying influence of worldly objects and their lusts. And so there are many other ways might be mentioned wherein the Spirit acts upon, assists and moves natural principles; but after all, 'tis no more than nature moved, acted and improved; here is nothing supernatural and divine. But the Spirit of God in his spiritual influences on the hearts of his saints, operates by infusing or exercising new, divine and supernatural principles; principles which are indeed a new and spiritual nature, and principles vastly more noble and excellent than all that is in natural men.

From what has been said it follows, that all spiritual and gracious affections are attended with, and do arise from some apprehension, idea or sensation of mind, which is in its whole nature different, yea exceeding different from all that is or can be in the mind of a natural man; and which the natural man discerns nothing of, and has no manner of idea of (agreeable to I Cor. 2:14), and conceives of no more than a man without the sense of tasting can conceive of the sweet taste of honey, or a man without the sense of hearing can conceive of the melody of a tune, or a man born blind can have a notion of the beauty of the rainbow.

But here two things must be observed in order to the right understanding of this.

1. On the one hand it must be observed, that not everything which in any respect appertains to spiritual affections, is new and entirely different from what natural men can conceive of, and do experience; some things are common to gracious affections with other affections; many circumstances, appendages and effects are common. Thus a saint's love to God has a great many things appertaining to it, which are common with a man's natural love to a near relation: love to God makes a man have desires of the honor of God, and a desire to please him; so does a natural man's love to his friend make him desire his honor, and desire to please him: love to God causes a man to delight in the thoughts of God, and to delight in the presence of God, and to desire conformity to God, and the enjoyment of God; and so it is with a man's love to his friend; and many other things might be mentioned which are common to both. But yet that idea which the saint has of the loveliness of God, and that sensation, and that kind of delight he has in that view, which is as it were the marrow and quintessence of his love, is peculiar, and entirely diverse from anything that a natural man has, or can have any notion of. And even in those things that seem to be common, there is something peculiar: both spiritual love and natural, cause desires after the object beloved; but they be not the same sort of desires; there is a sensation of soul in the spiritual desires of one that loves God, which is entirely different from all natural desires: both spiritual love and natural love are attended with delight in the object beloved; but the sensations of delight are not the same, but entirely and exceedingly diverse. Natural men may have conceptions of many things about spiritual affections; but there is something in them which is as it were the nucleus, or kernel of them, that they have no more conceptions of, than one born blind has of colors.

It may be clearly illustrated by this: we will suppose two men;

one is born without the sense of tasting, the other has it; the latter loves honey and is greatly delighted in it because he knows the sweet taste of it; the other loves certain sounds and colors: the love of each has many things that appertain to it, which is common; it causes both to desire and delight in the object beloved, and causes grief when it is absent, etc.: but yet, that idea or sensation which he who knows the taste of honey, has of its excellency and sweetness, that is the foundation of his love, is entirely different from anything the other has or can have; and that delight which he has in honey, is wholly diverse from anything that the other can conceive of; though they both delight in their beloved objects. So both these persons may in some respects love the same object: the one may love a delicious kind of fruit, which is beautiful to the eye, and of a delicious taste; not only because he has seen its pleasant colors, but knows its sweet taste; the other, perfectly ignorant of this, loves it only for its beautiful colors: there are many things seem, in some respect, to be common to both; both love, both desire, and both delight; but the love, and desire, and delight of the one, is altogether diverse from that of the other. The difference between the love of a natural man and spiritual man is like to this; but only it must be observed, that in one respect it is vastly greater, viz. that the kinds of excellency which are perceived in spiritual objects, by these different kinds of persons, are in themselves vastly more diverse, than the different kinds of excellency perceived in delicious fruit, by a tasting and a tasteless man; and in another respect it may not be so great, viz. as the spiritual man may have a spiritual sense or taste, to perceive that divine and most peculiar excellency, but in small beginnings, and in a very imperfect degree.

2. On the other hand, it must be observed, that a natural man may have those religious apprehensions and affections, which may be in many respects very new and surprising to him, and what before he did not conceive of; and yet what he experiences be nothing like the exercises of a principle of new nature, or the sensations of a new spiritual sense: his affections may be very new, by extraordinarily moving natural principles, in a very new degree, and with a great many new circumstances, and a new cooperation of natural affections, and a new composition of ideas; this may be from some extraordinary powerful influence of Satan and some great delusion; but there is nothing but nature extraordinarily acted. As if a poor man, that had always dwelt in a cottage, and had never looked be-

yond the obscure village where he was born, should in a jest, be taken to a magnificent city and prince's court, and there arrayed in princely robes, and set in the throne, with the crown royal on his head, peers and nobles bowing before him, and should be made to believe that he was now a glorious monarch; the ideas he would have, and the affections he would experience, would in many respects be very new, and such as he had no imagination of before; but all is no more, than only extraordinarily raising and exciting natural principles, and newly exalting, varying and compounding such sort of ideas, as he has by nature; here is nothing like giving him a new sense.

Upon the whole, I think it is clearly manifest, that all truly gracious affections do arise from special and peculiar influences of the Spirit, working that sensible effect or sensation in the souls of the saints, which are entirely different from all that it is possible a natural man should experience, not only different in degree and circumstances, but different in its whole nature: so that a natural man not only cannot experience that which is individually the same, but can't experience anything but what is exceeding diverse, and immensely below it, in its kind; and that which the power of men or devils is not sufficient to produce the like of, or anything of the same nature.

I have insisted largely on this matter, because it is of great importance and use, evidently to discover and demonstrate the delusions of Satan, in many kinds of false religious affections, which multitudes are deluded by, and probably have been in all ages of the Christian church; and to settle and determine many articles of doctrine, concerning the operations of the Spirit of God, and the nature of true grace.

Now therefore, to apply these things to the purpose of this discourse.

From hence it appears that impressions which some have made on their imagination, or the imaginary ideas which they have of God, or Christ, or heaven, or anything appertaining to religion, have nothing in them that is spiritual, or of the nature of true grace. Though such things may attend what is spiritual, and be mixed with it, yet in themselves they have nothing that is spiritual, nor are they any part of gracious experience.

Here, for the sake of the common people, I will explain what is intended by impressions on the imagination, and imaginary ideas. The imagination is that power of the mind, whereby it can have a conception, or idea of things of an external or outward nature (that is, of such sort of things as are the objects of the outward senses), when those things are not present, and be not perceived by the senses. It is called imagination from the word "image"; because thereby a person can have an image of some external thing in his mind, when that thing is not present in reality, nor anything like it. All such kind of things as we perceive by our five external senses, seeing, hearing, smelling, tasting and feeling, are external things: and when a person has an idea, or image of any of these sorts of things in his mind, when they are not there, and when he don't really see, hear, smell, taste, nor feel them; that is to have an imagination of them, and these ideas are imaginary ideas: and when such kind of ideas are strongly impressed upon the mind, and the image of them in the mind is very lively, almost as if one saw them, or heard them, etc. that is called an impression on the imagination. Thus colors, and shapes, and a form of countenance, they are outward things; because they are that sort of things which are the objects of the outward sense of seeing: and therefore when any person has in his mind a lively idea of any shape, or color, or form of countenance; that is to have an imagination of those things. So if he has an idea of such sort of light or darkness, as he perceives by the sense of seeing; that is to have an idea of outward light, and so is an imagination. So if he has an idea of any marks made on paper, suppose letters and words written in a book; that is to have an external and imaginary idea of such kind of things as we sometimes perceive by our bodily eyes. And when we have the ideas of that kind of things which we perceive by any of the other senses, as of any sounds or voices, or words spoken; this is only to have ideas of outward things, viz. of such kind of things as are perceived by the external sense of hearing, and so that also is imagination: and when these ideas are livelily impressed, almost as if they were really heard with the ears, this is to have an impression on the imagination. And so I might go on, and instance in the ideas of things appertaining to the other three senses of smelling, tasting and feeling.

Many who have had such things have very ignorantly supposed them to be of the nature of spiritual discoveries. They have had lively ideas of some external shape, and beautiful form of countenance; and this they call spiritually seeing Christ. Some have had impressed upon them ideas of a great outward light; and this they call a spiritual discovery of God's or Christ's glory. Some have had ideas of Christ's hanging on the cross, and his blood running from his wounds; and this they call a spiritual sight of Christ crucified, and the way of salvation by his blood. Some have seen him with his arms open ready to embrace them; and this they call a discovery of the sufficiency of Christ's grace and love. Some have had lively ideas of heaven, and of Christ on his throne there, and shining ranks of saints and angels; and this they call seeing heaven opened to them. Some from time to time have had a lively idea of a person of a beautiful countenance smiling upon them; and this they call a spiritual discovery of the love of Christ to their souls, and tasting the love of Christ. And they look upon it as sufficient evidence that these things are spiritual discoveries, and that they see them spiritually, because they say they don't see these things with their bodily eyes, but in their hearts; for they can see them when their eyes are shut. And in like manner, the imaginations of some have been impressed with ideas of the sense of hearing; they have had ideas of words, as if they were spoke to them; sometimes they are the words of Scripture, and sometimes other words: they have had ideas of Christ's speaking comfortable words to them. These things they have called having the inward call of Christ, hearing the voice of Christ spiritually in their hearts, having the witness of the Spirit, and the inward testimony of the love of Christ, etc.

The common, and less considerate and understanding sort of people, are the more easily led into apprehensions that these things are spiritual things, because spiritual things being invisible, and not things that can be pointed forth with the finger, we are forced to use figurative expressions in speaking of them, and to borrow names from external and sensible objects to signify them by. Thus we call a clear apprehension of things spiritual by the name of light; and an having such an apprehension of such or such things, by the name of seeing such things; and the conviction of the judgment, and the persuasion of the will, by the word of Christ in the gospel, we signify by spiritually hearing the call of Christ: and the Scripture itself abounds with such like figurative expressions. Persons hearing these often used, and having pressed upon them the necessity of having their eyes opened, and having a discovery of spiritual things; and seeing Christ in his glory, and having the inward call, and the like, they ignorantly look and wait for some such external discoveries, and imaginary views as have been spoken of; and when they have them, are confident that now their eyes are opened, now Christ has discovered himself to them, and they are his children; and hence are exceedingly affected and elevated with their deliverance and happiness, and many kinds of affections are at once set in a violent motion in them.

But it is exceeding apparent that such ideas have nothing in them which is spiritual and divine, in the sense wherein it has been demonstrated that all gracious experiences are spiritual and divine. These external ideas are in no wise of such a sort, that they are entirely, and in their whole nature diverse from all that men have by nature, perfectly different from, and vastly above any sensation which 'tis possible a man should have by any natural sense or principle, so that in order to have them, a man must have a new spiritual and divine sense given him, in order to have any sensations of that sort: so far from this, that they are ideas of the same sort which we have by the external senses, that are some of the inferior powers of the humane nature; they are merely ideas of external objects, or ideas of that nature, of the same outward sensitive kind; the same sort of sensations of mind (differing not in degree, but only in circumstances) that we have by those natural principles which are common to us, with the beasts, viz. the five external senses. This is a low, miserable notion of spiritual sense, to suppose that 'tis only a conceiving or imagining that sort of ideas which we have by our animal senses, which senses the beasts have in as great perfection as we; it is, as it were, a turning Christ, or the divine nature in the soul, into a mere animal. There is nothing wanting in the soul, as it is by nature, to render it incapable of being the subject of all these external ideas, without any new principles. A natural man is capable of having an idea, and a lively idea of shapes and colors and sounds when they are absent, and as capable as a regenerate man is: so there is nothing supernatural in them. And 'tis known by abundant experience, that 'tis not the advancing or perfecting humane nature, which makes persons more capable of having such lively and strong imaginery ideas, but that on the contrary, the weakness of body and mind, and distempers of body, makes persons abundantly more susceptive of such impressions.[2]

2. "Conceits and whimseys abound most in men of weak reason; children, and such as are cracked in their understanding have most of them; strength of reason banishes them, as the sun does mists and vapors. But now the more rational any gracious person is, by so much more is he fixed and settled and satisfied in the grounds of religion: yea, there is the highest and purest reason in religion; and

As to a truly spiritual sensation, not only is the manner of its coming into the mind extraordinary, but the sensation itself is totally diverse from all that men have, or can have, in a state of nature, as has been shown. But as to these external ideas, though the way of their coming into the mind is sometimes unusual, yet the ideas in themselves are not the better for that; they are still of no different sort from what men have by their senses; they are of no higher kind, nor a whit better. For instance, the external idea a man has now of Christ hanging on the cross, and shedding his blood, is no better in itself, than the external idea that the Jews his enemies had, who stood round his cross and saw this with their bodily eyes. The imaginary idea which men have now, of an external brightness and glory of God, is no better than the idea the wicked congregation in the wilderness had of the external glory of the Lord at Mount Sinai, when they saw it with bodily eyes; or any better than that idea which millions of cursed reprobates will have of the external glory of Christ at the Day of Judgment, who shall see, and have a very lively idea of ten thousand times greater external glory of Christ, than ever yet was conceived in any man's imagination; [3] yea, the image of Christ, which men conceive in their imaginations, is not in its own nature, of any superior kind to the idea that the papists conceive of Christ, by the beautiful and affecting images of him which they see in their churches (though the way of their receiving the idea may not be so bad); nor are the affections they have, if built primarily on such imaginations, any better than the affections raised in the ignorant people, by the sight of those images, which oftentimes are very great; especially when these images, through

---

when this change is wrought upon men, it is carried on in a rational way, Is. 1:18; John 19:9." John Flavel, *Preparation[s] for Suffering,* London, 1682. *The Whole Works of Mr. John Flavel, 2,* 810.

3. "If any man should see, and behold Christ really, immediately, this is not the saving knowledge of him. I know the saints do know Christ as if immediately present; they are not strangers by their distance: if others have seen him more immediately, I will not dispute it. But if they have seen the Lord Jesus as immediately as if here on earth, yet Capernaum saw him so; nay some of them were disciples for a time, and followed him, John 6. And yet the Lord was hid from their eyes. Nay, all the world shall see him in his glory, which shall amaze them; and yet this is far short of having the saving knowledge of him, which the Lord doth communicate to the elect. So that though you see the Lord so really, as that you become familiar with him, yet Luke 13:26: 'Lord, have we not eat and drunk,' etc. . . . and so perish." Shepard, *Parable,* Pt. I, pp. 197–8.

the craft of the priests, are made to move, and speak, and weep, and the like.[4] Merely the way of persons receiving these imaginary ideas, don't alter the nature of the ideas themselves that are received: let them be received in what way they will, they are still but external ideas, or ideas of outward appearances, and so are not spiritual. Yea, if men should actually receive such external ideas by the immediate power of the most high God upon their minds, they would not be spiritual, they would be no more than a common work of the Spirit of God; as is evident in fact, in the instance of Balaam, who had impressed on his mind, by God himself, a clear and lively outward representation or idea of Jesus Christ, as the star rising out of Jacob, when he "heard the words of God, and knew the knowledge of the most High, and saw the vision of the Almighty, falling into a trance" (Num. 24:16–17). But yet had no manner of spiritual discovery of Christ; that day-star never spiritually rose in his heart, he being but a natural man.

And as these external ideas have nothing divine or spiritual in their nature, and nothing but what natural men, without any new principles, are capable of; so there is nothing in their nature which requires that peculiar, inimitable and unparalleled exercise of the glorious power of God, in order to their production, which it has been shown there is in the new production of true grace. There appears to be nothing in their nature above the power of the devil. 'Tis certainly not above the power of Satan to suggest thoughts to men; because otherwise he could not tempt them to sin. And if he can suggest any thoughts or ideas at all, doubtless imaginary ones, or ideas of things external are not above his power; [5] for the external

4. "Satan is transformed into an angel of light: and hence we have heard that some have heard voices; some have seen the very blood of Christ dropping on them, and his wounds in his side; some have seen a great light shining in the chamber; some wonderfully affected with their dreams; some in great distress have had inward witness, 'Thy sins are forgiven'; and hence such liberty and joy, that they are ready to leap up and down the chamber. O adulterous generation! This is natural and usual with men, they would fain see Jesus, and have him present to give them peace; and hence Papists have his images. . . . Woe to them that have no other manifested Christ, but such an one." Shepard, ibid., p. 198.

5. "Consider how difficult, yea and impossible it is to determine that such a voice, vision or revelation is of God, and that Satan cannot feign or counterfeit it; seeing he hath left no certain marks by which we may distinguish one spirit from another." John Flavel, *A Discourse of the Occasions, Causes, Nature, Rise, Growth, and Remedies of Mental Errors* (London, 1691), Cause 14. *The Whole Works of Mr. John Flavel, 1,* 440–1. [See above, p. 62.]

ideas men have are the lowest sort of ideas. These ideas may be raised only by impressions made on the body, by moving the animal spirits, and impressing the brain. Abundant experience does certainly show, that alterations in the body will excite imaginary or external ideas in the mind; as often, in case of a high fever, melancholy, etc. These external ideas are as much below the more intellectual exercises of the soul, as the body is a less noble part of man than the soul.

And there is not only nothing in the nature of these external ideas or imaginations of outward appearances, from whence we can infer that they are above the power of the devil; but it is certain also that the devil can excite, and often hath excited such ideas. They were external ideas which he excited in the dreams and visions of the false prophets of old, who were under the influence of lying spirits, that we often read of in Scripture, as Deut. 13:1; I Kgs. 22:22; Is. 28:7; Ezek. 13:7; Zech. 13:4. And they were external ideas that he often excited in the minds of the heathen priests, magicians and sorcerers in their visions and ecstasies; and they were external ideas that he excited in the mind of the man Christ Jesus, when he showed him all the kingdoms of the world with the glory of them, when those kingdoms were not really in sight.

And if Satan, or any created being, has power to impress the mind with outward representations, then no particular sort of outward representations can be any evidence of a divine power. Almighty power is no more requisite to represent the shape of man to the imagination, than the shape of anything else: there is no higher kind of power necessary to form in the brain one bodily shape or color than another: it needs a no more glorious power to represent the form of the body of man, than the form of a chip or block; though it be of a very beautiful human body, with a sweet smile in his countenance, or arms open, or blood running from hands, feet, and side: that sort of power which can represent black or darkness to the imagination, can also represent white and shining brightness: the power and skill which can well and exactly paint a straw, or a stick of wood, on a piece of paper or canvas; the same in kind, only perhaps further improved, will be sufficient to paint the body of a man, with great beauty and in royal majesty, or a magnificent city, paved with gold, full of brightness, and a glorious throne, etc. So 'tis no more than the same sort of power that is requisite to paint one as the other of these on the brain. The same sort of power that can put ink upon paper, can put on leaf-gold. So that it is evident to a demonstration, if we suppose it be in the devil's power to make any sort of external representation at all on the fancy (as without doubt it is, and never any one questioned it who believed there was a devil, that had any agency with mankind), I say, if so, it is demonstrably evident that a created power may extend to all kinds of external appearances and ideas in the mind.

From hence it again clearly appears, that no such things have anything in them that is spiritual, supernatural and divine, in the sense in which it has been proved that all truly gracious experiences have. And though external ideas, through man's make and frame, do ordinarily in some degree attend spiritual experiences, yet these ideas are no part of their spiritual experience, any more than the motion of the blood, and beating of the pulse, that attends experiences, are a part of spiritual experience. And though undoubtedly, through men's infirmity in the present state, and especially through the weak constitution of some persons, gracious affections which are very strong, do excite lively ideas in the imagination; yet 'tis also undoubted, that when persons' affections are founded on imaginations, which is often the case, those affections are merely natural and common, because they are built on a foundation that is not spiritual; and so are entirely different from gracious affections, which, as has been proved, do evermore arise from those operations that are spiritual and divine.

These imaginations do oftentimes raise the carnal affections of men to an exceeding great height: [6] and no wonder, when the sub-

6. There is a remarkable passage of Mr. John Smith, in his discourse on "The Shortness of a Pharisaic Righteousness" of his *Select Discourses,* describing that sort of religion which is built on such a foundation as I am here speaking of. I cannot forbear transcribing the whole of it. Speaking of a sort of Christians, whose life is nothing but a strong energy of fancy, he says: "Lest their religion might too grossly discover itself to be nothing else but a piece of art, there may be sometimes such extraordinary motions stirred up within them, which may prevent all their own thoughts, that they may seem to be a true operation of the divine life; when yet all this is nothing else but the energy of their own self-love, touched with some fleshly apprehensions of divine things, and excited by them. There are such things in our Christian religion, when a carnal, unhallowed mind takes the chair, and gets the expounding of them, may seem very delicious to the fleshly appetites of men; some doctrines and notions of free grace and justification, the magnificent titles of sons of God and heirs of heaven, ever flowing streams of joy and pleasure that blessed souls shall swim in to all eternity, a glorious Paradise in the world to come, always springing up with well-scented

jects of them have an ignorant, but undoubting persuasion, that they are divine manifestations, which the great Jehovah immediately makes to their souls, therein giving them testimonies, in an extraordinary manner, of his high and peculiar favor.

Again, it is evident from what has been observed and proved of the manner in which gracious operations and effects in the heart are spiritual, supernatural and divine, that the immediate suggesting of the words of Scripture to the mind, has nothing in it which is spiritual.

I have had occasion to say something of this already; and what has been said may be sufficient to evince it: but if the reader bears in mind what has been said concerning the nature of spiritual influences and effects, it will be more abundantly manifest that this is no spiritual effect. For I suppose there is no person of common understanding who will say or imagine, that the bringing words (let 'em be what words they will) to the mind, is an effect of that nature which it is impossible the mind of a natural man, while he remains in a state of nature, should be the subject of, or anything like it; or that it requires any new divine sense in the soul; or that the bringing

---

and fragrant beauties, a new Jerusalem paved with gold, and bespangled with stars, comprehending in its vast circuit such numberless varieties, that a busy curiosity may spend itself about to all eternity. I doubt not but that sometimes the most fleshly and earthly men, that fly in their ambition to the pomp of this world, may be so ravished with the conceits of such things as these, that they may seem to be made partakers of the powers of the world to come. I doubt not but that they might be much exalted with them, as the souls of crazed or distracted persons seem to be sometimes, when their fancies play with those quick and nimble spirits, which a distempered frame of body, and unnatural heat in their heads, beget within them. Thus may these blazing comets rise up above the moon, and climb higher than the sun; which yet, because they have no solid consistence of their own, and are of a base and earthly alloy, will soon vanish and fall down again, being only borne up by an external force. They may seem to themselves to have attained higher than those noble Christians, that are gently moved by the natural force of true goodness: they seem [to] be *pleniores Deo,* (i.e. more full of God) than those that are really informed and actuated by the divine Spirit, and do move on steadily and constantly in the way towards Heaven. As the seed that was sown in stony ground, grew up, and lengthened out its blade faster, than that which was sown in the good and fruitful soil. And as the motions of our sense and fancy and passions, while our souls are in this mortal condition, sunk down deeply into the body, are many times more vigorous, and make stronger impressions upon us, than those of the higher powers of the soul, which are more subtle, and remote from these mixed animal perceptions: that devotion which is there seated, may seem to have more energy and life in it, than

sounds or letters to the mind, is an effect of so high, holy and excellent a nature, that it is impossible any created power should be the cause of it.

As the suggesting words of Scripture to the mind, is only the exciting in the mind ideas of certain sounds or letters; so it is only one way of exciting ideas in the imagination; for sounds and letters are external things, that are the objects of the external senses of seeing and hearing. Ideas of certain marks upon paper, such as any of the twenty-four letters, in whatever order, or any sounds of the voice, are as much external ideas, as of any other shapes or sounds whatsoever: and therefore, by what has been already said concerning these external ideas, it is evident they are nothing spiritual; and if at any time the Spirit of God suggests these letters or sounds to the mind, this is a common, and not any special or gracious influence of that Spirit. And therefore it follows from what has been already proved, that those affections which have this effect for their foundation, are no spiritual or gracious affections. But let it be observed what it is that I say, viz. when this effect, even the immediate and extraordinary manner of words of Scripture's coming to the mind, is that which excites the affections, and is properly the foundation of them, then these affections are not spiritual. It may be so, that

that which gently, and with a more delicate kind of touch, spreads itself upon the understanding, and from thence mildly derives itself through our wills and affections. But however, the former may be more boisterous for a time, yet this is of a more consistent, spermatical and thriving nature. For that proceeding indeed from nothing but a sensual and fleshly apprehension of God and true happiness, is but of a flitting and fading nature; and as the sensible powers and faculties grow more languid, or the sun of divine light shines more brightly upon us, these earthly devotions, like our culinary fires, will abate their heat and fervor. But a true celestial warmth will never be extinguished, because it is of an immortal nature; and being once seated vitally in the souls of man, it will regulate and order all the motions of it in a due manner; as the natural heat, radicated in the hearts of living creatures, hath the dominion and economy of the whole body under it. True religion is no peace of artifice; it is no boiling up of our imaginative powers, nor the glowing heats of passion; though these are too often mistaken for it, when in our jugglings in religion we cast a mist before our own eyes: but it is a new nature, informing the souls of men; it is a godlike frame of spirit, discovering itself most of all in serene and clear minds, in deep humility, meekness, self-denial, universal love to God and all true goodness, without partiality, and without hypocrisy, whereby we are taught to know God, and knowing him to love him, and conform ourselves as much as may be to all that perfection which shines in him." John Smith, "A Discovery of the Shortness and Vanity of a Pharisaic Righteousness," *Select Discourses*, ed. J. Worthington (London, 1660), pp. 370–2. [See above, pp. 65–6.]

persons may have gracious affections going with Scriptures which come to their minds, and the Spirit of God may make use of those Scriptures to excite them; when it is some spiritual sense, taste or relish they have of the divine and excellent things contained in those Scriptures that is the thing which excites their affections, and not the extraordinary and sudden manner of words being brought to their minds. They are affected with the instruction they receive from the words, and the view of the glorious things of God or Christ, and things appertaining to them, that they contain and teach; and not because the words came suddenly, as though some person had spoken them to 'em, thence concluding that God did as it were immediately speak to 'em. Persons oftentimes are exceedingly affected on this foundation; the words of some great and high promises of Scripture come suddenly to their minds, and they look upon the words as directed immediately by God to them, as though the words that moment proceeded out of the mouth of God as spoken to them: so that they take it as a voice from God, immediately revealing to 'em their happy circumstances, and promising such and such great things to them: and this it is that affects and elevates them. There is no new spiritual understanding of the divine things contained in the Scripture, or new spiritual sense of the glorious things taught in that part of the Bible, going before their affection, and being the foundation of it: all the new understanding they have, or think they have, to be the foundation of their affection, is this, that the words are spoke to them, because they come so suddenly and extraordinarily. And so this affection is built wholly on the sand; because it is built on a conclusion for which they have no foundation. For, as has been shown, the sudden coming of the words to their minds, is no evidence that the bringing 'em to their minds in that manner, was from God. And if it was true that God brought the words to their minds, and they certainly knew it, that would not be spiritual knowledge; it may be without any spiritual sense: Balaam might know that the words which God suggested to him, were indeed suggested to him by God, and yet have no spiritual knowledge. So that these affections which are built on that notion, that texts of Scripture are sent immediately from God, are built on no spiritual foundation, and are vain and delusive. Persons who have their affections thus raised, if they should be enquired of, whether they have any new sense of the excellency of things contained in those Scriptures, would probably say, yes, without hesitation: but it is true no otherwise than thus, that when they have taken up that notion, that the words are spoken immediately to them, that makes them seem sweet to 'em, and they own the things which these Scriptures say to 'em, for excellent things, and wonderful things. As for instance, supposing these were the words which were suddenly brought to their minds, "Fear not . . . it is your Father's good pleasure to give you the kingdom"; they having confidently taken up a notion that the words were as it were immediately spoken from heaven to them, as an immediate revelation, that God was their Father, and had given the kingdom to them, they are greatly affected by it, and the words seem sweet to 'em; and oh, they say, they are excellent things that are contained in those words! But the reason why the promise seems excellent to 'em, is only because they think it is made to them immediately: all the sense they have of any glory in them, is only from self-love, and from their own imagined interest in the words: not that they had any view or sense of the holy and glorious nature of the kingdom of heaven, and the spiritual glory of that God who gives it, and of his excellent grace to sinful men, in offering and giving them this kingdom, of his own good pleasure, preceding their imagined interest in these things, and their being affected by them, and being the foundation of their affection, and hope of an interest in them. On the contrary, they first imagine they are interested, and then are highly affected with that, and then can own these things to be excellent. So that the sudden and extraordinary way of the Scriptures coming to their mind, is plainly the first foundation of the whole; which is a clear evidence of the wretched delusion they are under.

The first comfort of many persons, and what they call their conversion, is after this manner: after awakening and terrors, some comfortable sweet promise comes suddenly and wonderfully to their minds; and the manner of its coming makes 'em conclude it comes from God to them: and this is the very thing that is all the foundation of their faith, and hope, and comfort: from hence they take their first encouragement to trust in God and in Christ, because they think that God, by some Scripture so brought, has now already revealed to 'em that he loves 'em, and has already promised them eternal life: which is very absurd; for every one of common knowledge of the principles of religion, knows that it is God's manner to reveal his love to men, and their interest in the promises, after they have believed, and not before; because they must first believe, before they have any interest in the promises to be revealed. The Spirit of God is a spirit of truth, and not of lies: he don't bring Scriptures to men's minds to reveal to them that they have an interest in God's favor and promises, when they have none, having not yet believed: which would be the case, if God's bringing texts of Scripture to men's minds to reveal to them that their sins were forgiven, or that it was God's pleasure to give them the kingdom, or anything of that nature, went before, and was the foundation of their first faith. There is no promise of the covenant of grace belongs to any man, till he has first believed in Christ; for 'tis by faith alone that we become interested in Christ, and the promises of the new covenant made in him: and therefore whatever spirit applies the promises of that covenant to a person who has not first believed, as being already his, must be a lying spirit; and that faith which is first built on such an application of promises, is built upon a lie. God's manner is not to bring comfortable texts of Scripture to give men assurance of his love, and that they shall be happy, before they have had a faith of dependence.[7]

7. Mr. Stoddard, in his *Guide to Christ* says, that "sometimes men, after they have been in trouble a while, have some promises come to 'em, with a great deal of refreshing; and they hope God has accepted them. . . . In this case, the minister may tell them, that God never gives a faith of assurance, before he gives a faith of dependence; for he never manifests his love, till men are in a state of favor and reconciliation, which is by faith of dependence. When men have comfortable Scriptures come to them, they are apt to take them as tokens of God's love; but men must be brought into Christ, by accepting the offer of the gospel, before they are fit for such manifestations. God's method is, first to make the soul accept of the offers of grace, and then to manifest his good estate unto him." Stoddard, *A Guide to Christ,* p. 8. And speaking of them "that seem to be brought to lie at God's foot, and give an account of their closing with Christ, and that God has revealed Christ to them, and drawn their hearts to him, and that they do accept of Christ," he says, "in this case it is best to examine whether by that light that was given him, he saw Christ and salvation offered to him, or whether he saw that God loved him, or pardoned him: for the offer of grace and our acceptance goes before pardon, and therefore, much more, before the knowledge of it." Ibid., pp. 76–7.

Mr. Shepard, in his *Parable of the Ten Virgins,* says that "grace and the love of Christ (the fairest colors under the sun) may be pretended; but if you shall receive, under this appearance, that God witnesseth his love, first by an absolute promise, take heed there; for under this appearance, you may as well bring in immediate revelations, and from thence come to forsake the Scriptures." Shepard, *Parable,* Pt. II, p. 15. And in Pt. I he says, "Is Christ yours? Yes, I see it. How? By any word or promise! No: this is delusion." Ibid., Pt. I, p. 86. And speaking of them that have no solid ground of peace, he reckons, "Those that content

And if the Scripture which comes to a person's mind, be not so properly a promise, as an invitation; yet if he makes the sudden or unusual manner of the invitation's coming to his mind, the ground on which he believes that he is invited, it is not true faith; because it is built on that which is not the true ground of faith. True faith is built on no precarious foundation; but a determination that the words of such a particular text, were, by the immediate power of God, suggested to the mind, at such a time, as though then spoken and directed by God to him, because the words came after such a manner, is wholly an uncertain and precarious determination, as has been now shewn; and therefore is a false and sandy foundation for faith; and accordingly that faith which is built upon it is false. The only certain foundation which any person has to believe that he is invited to partake of the blessings of the gospel, is that the Word of God declares that persons so qualified as he is, are invited, and God who declares it is true and cannot lie. If a sinner be once convinced of the veracity of God, and that the Scriptures are his Word, he'll need no more to convince and satisfy him that he is invited; for the Scriptures are full of invitations to sinners, to the chief of sinners, to come and partake of the benefits of the gospel: he won't want any new speaking of God to him, what he hath spoken already will be enough with him.

As the first comfort of many persons, and their affections at the time of their supposed conversion, are built on such grounds as these which have been mentioned; so are their joys and hopes, and other affections, from time to time afterwards. They have often particular words of Scripture, sweet declarations and promises suggested to 'em, which by reason of the manner of their coming, they think are immediately sent from God to them, at that time; which they look upon as their warrant to take 'em; and which they actually make the main ground of their appropriating them to themselves, and of the comfort they take in them, and the confidence they

---

themselves with the revelation of the Lord's love, without the sight of any work, or not looking to it." Ibid., p. 136. And says presently after, "The testimony of the Spirit does not make a man more a Christian, but only evidenceth it; as 'tis the nature of a witness, not to make a thing to be true, but to clear and evidence it." Ibid., pp. 136–7. And speaking of them that say they have the witness of the Spirit, that makes a difference between them and hypocrites, he says, "The witness of the Spirit makes not the first difference: for first a man is a believer, and in Christ, and justified, called, and sanctified, before the Spirit does witness it; else the Spirit should witness to an untruth, and lie." Ibid., p. 140.

receive from them. Thus they imagine a kind of conversation is carried on between God and them; and that God, from time to time, does, as it were, immediately speak to 'em, and satisfy their doubts and testifies his love to 'em, and promises 'em supports and supplies, and his blessing in such and such cases, and reveals to 'em clearly their interest in eternal blessings. And thus they are often elevated, and have a course of a sudden and tumultuous kind of joys, mingled with a strong confidence, and high opinion of themselves; when indeed the main ground of these joys, and this confidence is not anything contained in, or taught by these Scriptures, as they lie in the Bible, but the manner of their coming to them; which is a certain evidence of their delusion. There is no particular promise in the Word of God that is the saint's, or is any otherwise made to him, or spoken to him, than all the promises of the covenant of grace are his, and are made to him, and spoken to him: [8] though it be true that some of these promises may be more peculiarly adapted to his case than others; and God by his Spirit may enable him better to understand some than others, and to have a greater sense of the preciousness, and glory, and suitableness of the blessings contained in them.

But here, some may be ready to say, what, is there no such thing as any particular spiritual application of the promises of Scripture by the Spirit of God? I answer, there is doubtless such a thing as a spiritual and saving application of the invitations and promises of Scripture to the souls of men: but it is also certain, that the nature of it is wholly misunderstood by many persons, to the great ensnaring of their own souls, and the giving Satan a vast advantage against them, and against the interest of religion, and the church of God. The spiritual application of a Scripture promise does not consist in its being immediately suggested to the thoughts by some extrinsic agent, and being borne into the mind with this strong apprehension,

8. Mr. Shepard, in his *Sound Believer,* says, "Embrace in thy bosom, not only some few promises, but all." And then he asks the question, "When may a Christian take a promise without presumption, as spoken to him?" He answers, "The rule is very sweet, but certain; when he takes all the Scripture, and embraces it as spoken unto him, he may then take any particular promise boldly. My meaning is, when a Christian takes hold, and wrestles with God for the accomplishment of all the promises of the New Testament, when he sets all the commands before him, as a compass and guide to walk after, when he applies all the threatenings to drive him nearer unto Christ the end of them. This no hypocrite can do; this the saints shall do; and by this they may know when the Lord speaks in particular unto them." Shepard, *Sound Believer,* p. 159.

that it is particularly spoken and directed to them at that time: there is nothing of the evidence of the hand of God in this effect, as events have proved in many notorious instances; and it is a mean notion of a spiritual application of Scripture; there is nothing in the nature of it at all beyond the power of the devil, if he ben't restrained by God; for there is nothing in the nature of the effect that is spiritual, implying any vital communication of God. A truly spiritual application of the Word of God is of a vastly higher nature: as much above the devil's power, as it is, so to apply the Word of God to a dead corpse, as to raise it to life; or to a stone, to turn it into an angel. A spiritual application of the Word of God consists in applying it to the heart, in spiritually enlightening, sanctifying influences. A spiritual application of an invitation or offer of the gospel consists in giving the soul a spiritual sense or relish of the holy and divine blessings offered, and also the sweet and wonderful grace of the offerer, in making so gracious an offer, and of his holy excellency and faithfulness to fulfill what he offers, and his glorious sufficiency for it; so leading and drawing forth the heart to embrace the offer; and thus giving the man evidence of his title to the thing offered. And so a spiritual application of the promises of Scripture, for the comfort of the saints, consists in enlightening their minds to see the holy excellency and sweetness of the blessings promised, and also the holy excellency of the promiser, and his faithfulness and sufficiency; thus drawing forth their hearts to embrace the promiser, and thing promised; and by this means, giving the sensible actings of grace, enabling them to see their grace, and so their title to the promise. An application not consisting in this divine sense and enlightening of the mind, but consisting only in the words being borne into the thoughts, as if immediately then spoken, so making persons believe, on no other foundation, that the promise is theirs; is a blind application, and belongs to the spirit of darkness, and not of light.

When persons have their affections raised after this manner, those affections are really not raised by the Word of God; the Scripture is not the foundation of them; 'tis not anything contained in those Scriptures which come to their minds, that raise their affections; but truly that effect, viz. the strange manner of the words being suggested to their minds, and a proposition from thence taken up by them, which indeed is not contained in that Scripture, nor any other; as that his sins are forgiven him, or that it is the Father's good pleasure to give him in particular the kingdom, or the like. There are propositions to be found in the Bible, declaring that persons of such and such qualifications are forgiven and beloved of God: but there are no propositions to be found in the Bible declaring that such and such particular persons, independent on any previous knowledge of any qualifications, are forgiven and beloved of God: and therefore when any person is comforted, and affected by any such proposition, it is by another word, a word newly coined, and not any Word of God contained in the Bible.[9] And thus many persons are vainly affected and deluded.

Again, it plainly appears from what has been demonstrated, that no revelation of secret facts by immediated suggestion, is anything spiritual and divine, in that sense wherein gracious effects and operations are so.

By secret facts I mean things that have been done, or are come to pass, or shall hereafter come to pass, which are secret in that sense that they don't appear to the senses, nor are known by any argumentation, or any evidence to reason, nor any other way, but only by that revelation by immediate suggestion of the ideas of them to the mind. Thus for instance, if it should be revealed to me that the next year this land would be invaded by a fleet from France, or that such and such persons would then be converted, or that I myself should then be converted; not by enabling me to argue out these events from anything which now appears in providence; but immediately suggesting and bearing in upon my mind, in an extraordinary manner, the apprehension or ideas of these facts, with a strong suggestion or impression on my mind, that I had no hand in myself, that these things would come to pass: or if it should be revealed to me, that this day there is a battle fought between the armies of such and such powers in Europe; or that such a prince in Europe was this

9. "Some Christians have rested with a work without Christ, which is abominable: but after a man is in Christ, not to judge by the work, is first not to judge from a word. For though there is a word, which may give a man a *dependence* on Christ, without feeling any work, nay when he feels none, as absolute promises; yet no word giving *assurance,* but that which is made to some work; "He that believeth, or is poor in spirit," etc., till that work is seen, has no assurance from that promise." Shepard, *Parable,* Pt. I, p. 86.

"If God should tell a saint that he has grace, he might know it by believing the Word of God: but it is not in this way that godly men do know that they have grace; it is not revealed in the Word, and the Spirit of God doth not testify it to particular persons." Stoddard, *Treatise,* pp. 83–4.

day converted, or is now in a converted state, having been converted formerly, or that one of my neighbors is converted, or that I myself am converted; not by having any other evidence of any of these facts, from whence I argue them, but an immediate extraordinary suggestion or excitation of these ideas, and a strong impression of 'em upon my mind: this is a revelation of secret facts by immediate suggestion, as much as if the facts were future; for the facts being past, present, or future alters not the case, as long as they are secret and hidden from my senses and reason, and not spoken of in Scripture, nor known by me any other way than by immediate suggestion. If I have it revealed to me, that such a revolution is come to pass this day in the Ottoman Empire, it is the very same sort of revelation, as if it were revealed to me that such a revolution would come to pass there this day come twelvemonth; because, though one is present and the other future, yet both are equally hidden from me, any other way than by immediate revelation. When Samuel told Saul that the asses which he went to seek were found, and that his father had left caring for the asses and sorrowed for him; this was by the same kind of revelation, as that by which he told Saul, that in the plain of Tabor, there should meet him three men going up to God to Bethel (I Sam. 10:2–3), though one of these things was future and the other was not. So when Elisha told the king of Israel the words that the king of Syria spoke in his bedchamber, it was by the same kind of revelation with that by which he foretold many things to come.

'Tis evident that this revelation of secret facts by immediate suggestion, has nothing of the nature of a spiritual and divine operation, in the sense forementioned: there is nothing at all in the nature of the perceptions or ideas themselves, which are excited in the mind, that is divinely excellent, and so, far above all the ideas of natural men; though the manner of exciting the ideas be extraordinary. In those things which are spiritual, as has been shown, not only the manner of producing the effect, but the effect wrought is divine, and so vastly above all that can be in an unsanctified mind. Now simply the having an idea of facts, setting aside the manner of producing those ideas, is nothing beyond what the minds of wicked men are susceptible of, without any goodness in 'em; and they all, either have or will have, the knowledge of the truth of the greatest and most important facts, that have been, are, or shall be.

And as to the extraordinary manner of producing the ideas or perception of facts, even by immediate suggestion, there is nothing in it, but what the minds of natural men, while they are yet natural men, are capable of; as is manifest in Balaam, and others spoken of in the Scripture. And therefore it appears that there is nothing appertaining to this immediate suggestion of secret facts that is spiritual, in the sense in which it has been proved that gracious operations are so. If there be nothing in the ideas themselves, which is holy and divine, and so nothing but what may be in a mind not sanctified, then God can put 'em into the mind by immediate power, without sanctifying it. As there is nothing in the idea of a rainbow itself, that is of a holy and divine nature; so that there is nothing hinders but that an unsanctified mind may receive that idea: so God if he pleases, and when he pleases, immediately, and in an extraordinary manner, may excite that idea in an unsanctified mind. So also, as there is nothing in the idea or knowledge that such and such particular persons are forgiven and accepted of God, and entitled to heaven, but what unsanctified minds may have and will have concerning many at the Day of Judgment; so God can if he pleases, extraordinarily and immediately suggest this to, and impress it upon an unsanctified mind now: there is no principle wanting in an unsanctified mind, to make it capable of such a suggestion or impression; nor is there anything in them to exclude, or necessarily to prevent such a suggestion.

And if these suggestions of secret facts be attended with texts of Scripture, immediately and extraordinarily brought to mind, about some other facts that seem in some respects similar, that don't make the operation to be of a spiritual and divine nature. For that suggestion of words of Scripture is no more divine, than the suggestion of the facts themselves; as has been just now demonstrated: and two effects together, which are neither of them spiritual, can't make up one complex effect, that is spiritual.

Hence it follows, from what has been already shown, and often repeated, that those affections which are properly founded on such immediate suggestions, or supposed suggestions of secret facts, are not gracious affections. Not but that it is possible that such suggestions may be the occasion, or accidental cause of gracious affections; for so may a mistake and delusion; but it is never properly the foundation of gracious affections: for gracious affections, as has been shown, are all the effects of an influence and operation which is spiritual, supernatural, and divine. But there are many affections, and high affections, which some have, that have such kind of suggestions or revelations for their very foundation: they look upon these as spiritual discoveries; which is a gross delusion; and this delusion is truly the spring whence their affections flow.

Here it may be proper to observe, that 'tis exceeding manifest from what has been said, that what many persons call the witness of the Spirit that they are the children of God, has nothing in it spiritual and divine; and consequently that the affections built upon it, are vain and delusive. That which many call the witness of the Spirit, is no other than an immediate suggestion and impression of that fact, otherwise secret, that they are converted, or made the children of God, and as that their sins are pardoned, and that God has given 'em a title to heaven. This kind of knowledge, viz. knowing that a certain person is converted, and delivered from hell, and entitled to heaven, is no divine sort of knowledge in itself. This sort of fact, is not that which requires any higher or more divine kind of suggestion, in order to impress it on the mind, than any other fact which Balaam had impressed on his mind. It requires no higher sort of idea or sensation, for a man to have the apprehension of his own conversion impressed upon him, than to have the apprehension of his neighbor's conversion, in like manner, impressed: but God, if he pleased, might impress the knowledge of this fact, that he had forgiven his neighbor's sins, and given him a title to heaven, as well as any other fact, without any communication of his holiness: the excellency and importance of the fact, don't at all hinder a natural man's mind being susceptible of an immediate suggestion and impression of it. Balaam had as excellent, and important, and glorious facts as this, immediately impressed on his mind, without any gracious influence; as particularly, the coming of Christ, and his setting up his glorious kingdom, and the blessedness of the spiritual Israel in his peculiar favor, and their happiness living and dying. Yea Abimelech, King of the Philistines, had God's special favor to a particular person, even Abraham, revealed to him (Gen. 20:6–7). So it seems that he revealed to Laban his special favor to Jacob, see Gen. 31:24 and Ps. 105:15. And if a truly good man should have an immediate revelation or suggestion from God, after the like manner, concerning his favor to his neighbor, or himself; it would be no higher kind of influence; it would be no more than a common sort of influence of God's Spirit; as the gift of prophecy, and all revelation by immediate suggestion is; see I Cor. 13:2. And though it be true, that it is not possible that a natural man should have that individual suggestion from the Spirit of God, that he is converted, because it is not true; yet that don't arise from the nature of the influence, or because that kind of influence which suggests such excellent facts, is too high for him to be the subject of; but purely from the defect of a fact to be revealed. The influence which immediately suggests this fact, when it is true, is of no different kind from that which immediately suggests other true facts: and so the kind and nature of the influence, is not above what is common to natural men, with good men.

But this is a mean ignoble notion of the witness of the Spirit of God given to his dear children, to suppose that there is nothing in the kind and nature of that influence of the Spirit of God, in imparting this high and glorious benefit but what is common to natural men, or which men are capable of, and be in the meantime altogether unsanctified, and the children of hell; and that therefore the benefit or gift itself has nothing of the holy nature of the Spirit of God in it, nothing of a vital communication of that Spirit. This notion greatly debases that high and most exalted kind of influence and operation of the Spirit, which there is in the true witness of the Spirit.[1] That which is called the witness of the Spirit (Rom. 8), is elsewhere in the New Testament called the seal of the Spirit (II Cor. 1:22; Eph. 1:13 and 4:13) alluding to the seal of princes, annexed

1. The late venerable Stoddard in his younger time, falling in with the opinion of some others, received this notion of the witness of the Spirit, by way of immediate suggestion; but in the latter part of his life, when he had more thoroughly weighed things, and had more experience, he entirely rejected it; as appears by his Treatise of the Nature of Saving Conversion, "The Spirit of God doth not testify to particular persons, that they are godly. Some think that the Spirit of God doth testify it to some; and they ground it on Rom. 8:16: 'The Spirit itself beareth witness with our spirit, that we are the children of God.' They think the Spirit reveals it by giving an inward testimony to it; and some godly men think they have had experience of it: but they may easily mistake; when the Spirit of God doth eminently stir up a spirit of faith, and sheds abroad the love of God in the heart, it is easy to mistake it for a testimony. And that is not the meaning of Paul's words. The Spirit reveals things to us, by opening our eyes to see what is revealed in the Word; but the Spirit doth not reveal new truths, not revealed in the Word. The Spirit discovers the grace of God in Christ, and thereby draws forth special actings of faith and love, which are evidential; but it doth not work in way of testimony. If God do but help us to receive the revelations in the Word, we shall have comfort enough without new revelations." Stoddard, *Treatise,* p. 84.

to the instrument, by which they advanced any of their subjects to some high honor and dignity, or peculiar privilege in the kingdom, as a token of their special favor. Which is an evidence that the influence of the Spirit of the Prince of princes, in sealing his favorites, is far from being of a common kind; and that there is no effect of God's Spirit whatsoever, which is in its nature more divine; nothing more holy, peculiar, inimitable and distinguishing of divinity: as nothing is more royal than the royal seal; nothing more sacred, that belongs to a prince, and more peculiarly denoting what belongs to him; it being the very end and design of it, to be the most peculiar stamp and confirmation of the royal authority, and great note of distinction, whereby that which proceeds from the king, or belongs to him, may be known from everything else. And therefore undoubtedly the seal of the great king of heaven and earth enstamped on the heart, is something high and holy in its own nature, some excellent communication from the infinite fountain of divine beauty and glory; and not merely a making known a secret fact by revelation or suggestion; which is a sort of influence of the Spirit of God, that the children of the devil have often been the subjects of. The seal of the Spirit is a kind of effect of the Spirit of God on the heart, which natural men, while such, are so far from a capacity of being the subjects of, that they can have no manner of notion or idea of it; agreeable to Rev. 2:17: "To him that overcometh, will I give to eat of the hidden manna; and I will give him a white stone, and in the stone a new name written, which no man knoweth, saving he that receiveth it." There is all reason to suppose that what is here spoken of, is the same mark, evidence, or blessed token of special favor, which is elsewhere called the seal of the Spirit.

What has misled many in their notion of that influence of the Spirit of God we are speaking of, is the word "witness," its being called the witness of the Spirit. Hence they have taken it, not to be any effect or work of the Spirit upon the heart, giving evidence, from whence men may argue that they are the children of God; but an inward immediate suggestion, as though God inwardly spoke to the man, and testified to him, and told him that he was his child, by a kind of a secret voice, or impression: not observing the manner in which the word "witness," or "testimony" is often used in the New Testament; where such terms often signify, not only a mere declaring and asserting a thing to be true, but holding forth evidence from whence a thing may be argued and proved to be true. Thus

(Heb. 2:4), God is said to bear witness, with signs and wonders, and diverse miracles, and gifts of the Holy Ghost. Now these miracles, here spoken of, are called God's witness, not because they are of the nature of assertions, but evidences and proofs. So: "Long time therefore, abode they speaking boldly in the Lord; which gave testimony unto the word of his grace; and granted signs and wonders to be done by their hands" (Acts 14:3). And: "But I have greater witness than that of John; for the works which the Father hath given me to finish, the same works that I do, bear witness of me, that the Father hath sent me" (John 5:36). Again, "The works that I do in my Father's name, they bear witness of me" (ch. 10:25). So the water and the blood are said to bear witness (I John 5:8), not that they spake or asserted anything, but they were proofs and evidences. So God's works of providence, in the rain and fruitful seasons, are spoken of as witnesses of God's being and goodness, i.e. they were evidences of these things. And when the Scripture speaks of the seal of the Spirit, it is an expression which properly denotes, not an immediate voice or suggestion, but some work or effect of the Spirit, that is left as a divine mark upon the soul, to be an evidence, by which God's children might be known. The seals of princes were the distinguishing marks of princes: and thus God's seal is spoken of as God's mark, "Hurt not the earth, neither the sea, nor the trees, till we have sealed the servants of our God in their foreheads" (Rev. 7:3); together with: "Set a mark upon the foreheads of the men that sign and cry for all the abominations that are done in the midst thereof" (Ezek. 9:4). When God sets his seal on a man's heart by his Spirit, there is some holy stamp, some image impressed and left upon the heart by the Spirit, as by the seal upon the wax. And this holy stamp, or impressed image, exhibiting clear evidence to the conscience, that the subject of it is the child of God, is the very thing which in Scripture is called the seal of the Spirit, and the witness, or evidence of the Spirit. And this image enstamped by the Spirit on God's children's hearts, is his own image: that is the evidence by which they are known to be God's children, that they have the image of their Father stamped upon their hearts by the spirit of adoption. Seals anciently had engraven on them two things, viz. the image and the name of the person whose seal it was. Therefore when Christ says to his spouse, "Set me as a seal upon thine heart, as a seal upon thine arm" (Cant. 8:6); it is as much as to say, let my name and image remain impressed there. The seals of princes were wont to bear their image; so that what they set their seal and royal mark upon, had their image left on it. It was the manner of princes of old to have their image engraven on their jewels and precious stones; and the image of Augustus engraven on a precious stone, was used as the seal of the Roman emperors, in Christ's and the apostles' times.[2] And the saints are the jewels of Jesus Christ, the great potentate, who has the possession of the empire of the universe: and these jewels have his image enstamped upon them, by his royal signet, which is the Holy Spirit. And this is undoubtedly what the Scripture means by the seal of the Spirit; especially when it is enstamped in so fair and clear a manner, as to be plain to the eye of conscience; which is what the Scripture calls our spirit. This is, truly an effect that is spiritual, supernatural, and divine. This is, in itself, of a holy nature, being a communication of the divine nature and beauty. That kind of influence of the Spirit which gives and leaves this stamp upon the heart is such that no natural man can be the subject of anything of the like nature with it. This is the highest sort of witness of the Spirit, which it is possible the soul should be the subject of: if there were any such thing as a witness of the Spirit by immediate suggestion or revelation, this would be vastly more noble and excellent, and as much above it as the heaven is above the earth. This the devil cannot imitate: as to an inward suggestion of the Spirit of God, by a kind of secret voice speaking, and immediately asserting and revealing a fact, he can do that which is a thousand times so like to this, as he can to that holy and divine effect, or work of the Spirit of God, which has been now spoken of.[3]

2. Ephraim Chambers, *Cyclopedia: or an Universal Dictionary of Arts and Sciences* (London, 1728), Vol. 1, under the word "Engraving."

3. Mr. Shepard is abundant in militating against the notion of men's knowing their good estate by an immediate witness of the Spirit, without judging by any effect or work of the Spirit wrought on the heart, as an evidence and proof that persons are the children of God. "Knowing your election of God. How so? Immediately? Some divines think angels see it not so, and that it is peculiar to God so to do; but mediately; for our Word came in power, and in much assurance, to make you enlarged for God, to turn you from idols unto God," etc. Shepard, *Parable*, Pt. I, p. 134. Again in the same page, "It's heaven to cleave to him in every command; it's death to depart from any command. Hereby know we that we are in him. If it were possible to ask of the angels, how they know they are not devils, they would answer, the Lord's will is ours. So here, how do you know you have not the nature of devils, and so in a state of devils, bound there till the judgment of the great day? Because God hath changed our vile natures, and made

Another thing which is a full proof that the seal of the Spirit is no revelation of any fact by immediate suggestion, but is grace itself in the soul, is that the seal of the Spirit is called the earnest

---

our wills like unto his glorious will." And Pt. I, p. 135, "The major is the Word, the minor experience, and the conclusion the Lord's Spirit's work, quickening your spirit to it. Now, say some, how do you know this? Thus you may be mistaken; for many have been deceived thus. Grant that; and shall a child not take bread when 'tis given him, though dogs snatch at it." And Pt. I, p. 137, "If you look to a spirit without a work, whilst you do seek consolation, you cannot avoid the condemnation of the Word. You say the Spirit has spoken peace to you; but do you love Christ? I look not to that; but to the Spirit. Why, the Word saith, 'He that loves him not, let him be anathema.' So, is the league between your sins and your souls broken? Ans. I look not to that. Why, John saith 'He that committeth sin is of the devil.' Are you new creatures? I look not to that. Why, the Word saith, 'unless you be born again,' you cannot enter into the kingdom of God." And Pt. I, pp. 176, 177, "A man saith, I have Christ; and so have not they. I ask, where is the Spirit? You have the deed; where is the seal? You have the testator; where is the executor? The Spirit in you? Yes, I have it; it has witnessed Christ is mine. Ans. It has witnessed; but what has it wrought? Where is the power of his death, killing thy lusts? Where is the life of the Spirit of Jesus in you? Where is the oil in your vessel? Truly I look for the bridegroom; but I regard not that; neither are others to regard it, in way of evidence. Then I say the chief evidence is destroyed in the churches. I have known many that have had assurances; yet never saw them prove right, till it witnessed this was here. What should be the causes of this, and that men should make blusters in the churches because of this, as though it was building on works? In several men they are several. 1. An aptness to outrun the truth, and to fall from one extreme to another. . . . 2. The apostasy of eminent professors, who have been deceived in their evidencing thus. . . . 3. Corrupt experience. . . . 4. A heart that never felt the bitterness and bondage of sin, as the greatest evil." Pt. I, pp. 215, 216, "The peace, and joy, and assurance of that glory, which eye never saw, in the saints, 'tis from the witness of the spirit of glory; not only because that God is their God, but because they are his people. 'Tis I say from the witness of God in his Word; not from themselves, nor from man only, that they approve me; nor from dreams, and diabolical breathings; but from the Spirit of God; he brings tidings of it; and from such a Spirit (that you may know it) that not only shews you God is your God, and so you rejoice, because of this; for thus 'tis with many a carnal heart, and he hath peace, being in horror, from this, the Lord loves me; but he makes you to rejoice, because you are the Lord's people, because he hath changed your heart: now the peace is sound, and joy is right: and here I would try the peace of any man." "All the heirs of the promises, as heirs that have legacies left them, they go to the will of the deceased father: and that comforts, that they hold to, that is sure; such an one shall have it, if his name be there. But if one shall say, such a One hath promised me such lands; is it in his will? No; but since he died, as I was taking a pipe, he came to me: Oh be not deceived!" Ibid., Pt. II, pp. 168–9.

Again in his *Sound Believer* there is a long discourse of sanctification as the of the Spirit, in the Scripture. 'Tis very plain, that the seal of the Spirit is the same thing with the earnest of the Spirit, by II Cor. 1:22: "Who hath also sealed us, and given the earnest of the Spirit in our hearts." And: "In whom, after that ye believed, ye were sealed

---

chief evidence of justification from p. 222, for many pages following, I shall transcribe but a very small part of it. "Tell me, how you will know that you are justified. You will say, by the testimony of the Spirit. And cannot the same Spirit shine upon your graces, and witness that you are sanctified, as well? I John 4:13, 24; I Cor. 2:12. Can the Spirit make the one clear to you, and not the other? Oh beloved, it is a sad thing, to hear such questions and such cold answers also, that sanctification possibly may be an evidence. May be! Is it not certain? Assuredly to deny it, is as bad as to affirm that God's own promises of favor are not true evidences thereof, and consequently that they are lies and untruths." Shepard, *Sound Believer,* p. 222.

Mr. Flavel also much opposes this notion of the witness of the Spirit by immediate revelation. *Sacramental Meditations,* Med. 4, speaking of the sealing of the Spirit, he says, "In sealing the believer, he doth not make use of an audible voice, nor the ministry of angels, nor immediate and extraordinary revelations; but he makes use of his own graces, implanted in our hearts, and his own promises, written in the Scripture: and in this method, he usually brings the doubting trembling heart of a believer to rest and comfort." . . . Again, "Assurance is produced in our souls by the reflexive acts of faith: the Spirit helps us to reflect upon what hath been done by him formerly upon our hearts; 'hereby we know that we know him,' I John 2:3. To know that we know, is a reflex act. Now it is impossible there should be a reflex, before there hath been a direct act. No man can have the evidence of his faith, before the habit is infused, and the vital act performed. The object matter, to which the Spirit seals, is his own sanctifying operation. . . . Afterwards, he says, "Immediate ways of the Spirit's sealing are ceased. No man may now expect, by any new revelation, or sign from heaven, by any voice, or extraordinary inspiration, to have his salvation sealed; but must expect that mercy in God's ordinary way and method, searching the Scriptures, examining our own hearts, and waiting on the Lord in prayer. The learned Gerson gives an instance of one that had been long upon the borders of despair, and at last sweetly assured and settled: he answered, *Non ex nova aliqua revelatione;* not by any new revelation, but by subjecting my understanding to, and comparing my heart with the written Word. And Mr. Roberts, in his *Treatise of the Covenants,* speaks of another, that so vehemently panted after the sealings and assurance of the love of God to his soul, that for a long time he earnestly desired some voice from heaven; and sometimes, walking in the solitary fields, earnestly desired some miraculous voice from the trees or stones there. This was denied him; but in time, a better was afforded, in a scriptural way." . . . Again, "This method of sealing, is beyond all other methods in the world. For in miraculous voices and inspirations, 'tis possible there may *subesse falsum,* be found some cheat, or impostures of the devil; but the Spirit's witness in the heart, suitable to the revelation in the Scripture, cannot deceive us." John Flavel, *Sacramental Meditations* (London, 1679), Med. 4, pp. 64 ff.

with that holy Spirit of promise; which is the earnest of our inheritance, until the redemption of the purchased possession, unto the praise of his glory" (Eph. 1:13–14). Now the earnest is part of the money agreed for, given in hand, as a token of the whole, to be paid in due time; a part of the promised inheritance, granted now, in token of full possession of the whole hereafter. But surely that kind of communication of the Spirit of God, which is of the nature of eternal glory, is the highest and most excellent kind of communication, something that is in its own nature spiritual, holy and divine, and far from anything that is common; and therefore high above anything of the nature of inspiration, or revelation of hidden facts by suggestion of the Spirit of God, which many natural men have had. What is the earnest and beginning of glory, but grace itself, especially in the more lively and clear exercises of it? 'Tis not prophecy, nor tongues, nor knowledge, but that more excellent divine thing, charity that never faileth, which is a prelibation and beginning of the light, sweetness, and blessedness of heaven, that world of love or charity. 'Tis grace that is the seed of glory, and dawning of glory in the heart, and therefore 'tis grace that is the earnest of the future inheritance. What is it that is the beginning or earnest of eternal life in the soul, but spiritual life? And what is that but grace? The inheritance that Christ has purchased for the elect, is the Spirit of God; not in any extraordinary gifts, but in his vital indwelling in the heart, exerting and communicating himself there, in his own proper, holy or divine nature: and this is the sum total of the inheritance that Christ purchased for the elect. For so are things constituted in the affair of our redemption, that the Father provides the Saviour, or purchaser, and the purchase is made of him; and the Son is the purchaser and the price; and the Holy Spirit is the great blessing or inheritance purchased, as is intimated Gal. 3:13–14, and hence the Spirit is often spoken of as the sum of the blessings promised in the gospel (Luke 24:49; Acts 1:4, and ch. 2:38–39; Gal. 3:14; Eph. 1:13). This inheritance was the grand legacy which Christ left his disciples and church, in his last will and testament (John chs. 14, and 15, and 16). This is the sum of the blessings of eternal life, which shall be given in heaven (Compare John 7:37–39 and John 4:14 with Rev. 21:6 and 22:1, 17). 'Tis through the vital communications and indwelling of the Spirit, that the saints have all their light, life, holiness, beauty and joy in heaven: and 'tis through the vital communications and indwelling of the same Spirit, that the saints have all light, life, holiness, beauty and comfort on earth; but only communicated in less measure. And this vital indwelling of the Spirit in the saints, in this less measure and small beginning, is the earnest of the Spirit, the earnest of the future inheritance, and the first fruits of the Spirit, as the Apostle calls it, Rom. 8:22 where, by the first fruits of the Spirit, the Apostle undoubtedly means the same vital gracious principle, that he speaks of in all the preceding part of the chapter, which he calls Spirit, and sets in opposition to flesh or corruption. Therefore this earnest of the Spirit, and first fruits of the Spirit, which has been shown to be the same with the seal of the Spirit, is the vital, gracious, sanctifying communication and influence of the Spirit, and not any immediate suggestion or revelation of facts by the Spirit.[4]

And indeed the Apostle, when in that Rom. 8:16 he speaks of the Spirit's bearing witness with our spirit, that we are the children of God, does sufficiently explain himself, if his words were but attended to. What is here expressed, is connected with the two preceding verses, as resulting from what the Apostle had said there, as every reader may see. The three verses together are thus: "For as many as are led by the Spirit of God, they are the sons of God: for ye have not received the spirit of bondage again to fear; but ye have received the spirit of adoption, whereby we cry, Abba, Father; the Spirit itself beareth witness with our spirits, that we are the children of God." Here, what the Apostle says, if we take it together, plainly shows, that what he has respect to, when he speaks of the Spirit's giving us witness or evidence that we are God's children; is his dwelling in us, and leading us, as a spirit of adoption, or spirit of a child, disposing us to behave towards God as to a Father. This is the witness or evidence the Apostle speaks of, that we are children, that we have the spirit of children, or spirit of adoption. And what is that, but the spirit of love? There are two kinds of spirits the Apostle speaks of, the spirit of a slave, or the

4. "After a man is in Christ, not to judge by the work, is not to judge by the Spirit. For the Apostle makes the earnest of the Spirit to be the seal. Now earnest is part of the money bargained for; the beginning of heaven, of the light and life of it. He that sees not that the Lord is his by that, sees no God his at all. Oh therefore, do not look for a Spirit, without a Word to reveal, nor a Word to reveal without seeing and feeling of some work first. I thank the Lord, I do but pity those that think otherwise. If a sheep of Christ, Oh, wander not." Shepard, *Parable,* Pt. I, p. 86.

spirit of bondage, that is fear; and the spirit of a child, or spirit of adoption, and that is love. The Apostle says, we han't received the spirit of bondage, or of slaves, which is a spirit of fear; but we have received the more ingenuous noble spirit of children, a spirit of love, which naturally disposes us to go to God, as children to a father, and behave towards God as children. And this is the evidence or witness which the Spirit of God gives us that we are children. This is the plain sense of the Apostle: and so undoubtedly the Apostle here is speaking of the very same way of casting out doubting, and fear, and the spirit of bondage, which the apostle John speaks of, viz. by the prevailing of love, that is the spirit of a child (I John 4:18). The spirit of bondage works by fear, the slave fears the rod; but love cries "Abba Father"; it disposes us to go to God, and behave ourselves towards God as children; and it gives us clear evidence of our union to God as his children, and so casts out fear. So that it appears that the witness of the Spirit the Apostle speaks of, is far from being any whisper, or immediate suggestion or revelation; but that gracious holy effect of the Spirit of God in the hearts of the saints, the disposition and temper of children, appearing in sweet childlike love to God, which casts out fear, or a spirit of a slave.

And the same thing is evident from all the context: 'tis plain the Apostle speaks of the Spirit, over and over again, as dwelling in the hearts of the saints, as a gracious principle, set in opposition to the flesh or corruption: and so he does in the words that immediately introduce this passage we are upon [Rom. 8:14–16], ver. 13: "For if ye live after the flesh, ye shall die; but if ye, through the Spirit do mortify the deeds of the flesh, ye shall live."

Indeed it is past doubt with me, that the Apostle has a more special respect to the spirit of grace, or the spirit of love, or spirit of a child, in its more lively actings: for 'tis perfect love, or strong love only, which so witnesses or evidences that we are children, as to cast out fear, and wholly deliver from the spirit of bondage. The strong and lively exercises of a spirit of childlike, evangelical, humble love to God, give clear evidence of the soul's relation to God, as his child; which does very greatly and directly satisfy the soul. And though it be far from being true, that the soul in this case, judges only by an immediate witness, without any sign or evidence; for it judges and is assured by the greatest sign and clearest evidence; yet in this case, the saint stands in no need of multiplied signs, or any long reasoning upon them. And though the sight of his relative union with God, and his being in his favor, is not without a medium, because he sees it by that medium, viz. his love; yet his sight of the union of his heart to God is immediate: love, the bond of union, is seen intuitively: the saint sees and feels plainly the union between his soul and God; it is so strong and lively, that he can't doubt of it. And hence he is assured that he is a child. How can he doubt whether he stands in a childlike relation to God, when he plainly sees a childlike union between God and his soul, and hence does boldly, and as it were, naturally and necessarily cry, "Abba Father"?

And whereas the Apostle says, the Spirit bears witness with our spirits; by "our spirit" here, is meant our conscience, which is called the spirit of man; "The spirit of man is the candle of the Lord, searching all the inward parts of the belly" (Prov. 20:27). We elsewhere read of the witness of this spirit of ours; "For our rejoicing is this, the testimony of our conscience" (II Cor. 1:12). And: "And hereby do we know that we are of the truth, and shall assure our hearts before him. For if our heart condemn us, God is greater than our heart, and knoweth all things. Beloved if our heart condemn us not, then have we confidence towards God" (I John 3:19–21). When the apostle Paul speaks of the Spirit of God bearing witness with our spirit, he is not to be understood of two spirits, that are two separate, collateral, independent witnesses; but 'tis by one, that we receive the witness of the other: the Spirit of God gives the evidence, by infusing and shedding abroad the love of God, the spirit of a child, in the heart; and our spirit, or our conscience, receives and declares this evidence for our rejoicing.

Many have been the mischiefs that have arisen from that false and delusive notion of the witness of the Spirit, that it is a kind of inward voice, suggestion, or declaration from God to a man, that he is beloved of him, and pardoned, elected, or the like, sometimes with, and sometimes without a text of Scripture; and many have been the false, and vain (though very high), affections that have arisen from hence. And 'tis to be feared that multitudes of souls have been eternally undone by it. I have therefore insisted the longer on this head.

But I proceed now to a second characteristic of gracious affections.

II. The first objective ground of gracious affections, is the transcendently excellent and amiable nature of divine things, as they are in themselves; and not any conceived relation they bear to self, or self-interest.

I say that the supremely excellent nature of divine things, is the first, or primary and original objective foundation of the spiritual affections of true saints; for I do not suppose that all relation which divine things bear to themselves, and their own particular interest, are wholly excluded from all influence in their gracious affections. For this may have, and indeed has, a secondary and consequential influence in those affections that are truly holy and spiritual; as I shall show how by and by.

It was before observed, that the affection of love is as it were the fountain of all affection; and particularly, that Christian love is the fountain of all gracious affections: now the divine excellency and glory of God, and Jesus Christ, the Word of God, the works of God, and the ways of God, etc. is the primary reason, why a true saint loves these things; and not any supposed interest that he has in them, or any conceived benefit that he has received from them, or shall receive from them, or any such imagined relation which they bear to his interest, that self-love can properly be said to be the first foundation of his love to these things.

Some say that all love arises from self-love; and that it is impossible in the nature of things, for any man to have any love to God, or any other being, but that love to himself must be the foundation of it. But I humbly suppose it is for want of consideration, that they say so. They argue, that whoever loves God, and so desires his glory, or the enjoyment of him, he desires these things as his own happiness; the glory of God, and the beholding and enjoying his perfections, are considered as things agreeable to him, tending to make him happy; he places his happiness in them, and desires them as things, which (if they were obtained) would be delightful to him, or would fill him with delight and joy, and so make him happy. And so, they say, it is from self-love, or a desire of his own happiness, that he desires God should be glorified, and desires to behold and enjoy his glorious perfections. But then they ought to consider a little further, and inquire how the man came to place his happiness in God's being glorified, and in contemplating and enjoying God's perfections. There is no doubt, but that after God's glory, and the beholding his perfections, are become so agreeable to him, that he places his highest happiness in these things, then he will desire them, as he desires his own happiness. But how came these things to be so agreeable to him, that he esteems it his highest happiness to glorify God, etc.? Is not this the fruit of love? A man must first love God, or have his heart united to him, before he will esteem God's good his own, and before he will desire the glorifying and enjoying of God, as his happiness. 'Tis not strong arguing, that because after a man has his heart united to God in love, as a fruit of this, he desires his glory and enjoyment as his own happiness, that therefore a desire of this happiness of his own, must needs be the cause and foundation of his love: unless it be strong arguing, that because a father begat a son, that therefore his son certainly begat him. If after a man loves God, and has his heart so united to him, as to look upon God as his chief good, and on God's good as his own, it will be a consequence and fruit of this, that even self-love, or love to his own happiness, will cause him to desire the glorifying and enjoying of God; it will not thence follow, that this very exercise of self-love, went before his love to God, and that his love to God was a consequence and fruit of that. Something else, entirely distinct from self-love might be the cause of this, viz. a change made in the views of his mind, and relish of his heart; whereby he apprehends a beauty, glory, and supreme good, in God's nature, as it is in itself. This may be the thing that first draws his heart to him, and causes his heart to be united to him, prior to all considerations of his own interest or happiness, although after this, and as a fruit of this, he necessarily seeks his interest and happiness in God.

There is such a thing, as a kind of love or affection, that a man may have towards persons or things, which does properly arise from self-love; a preconceived relation to himself, or some respect already manifested by another to him, or some benefit already received or depended on, is truly the first foundation of his love, and what his affection does wholly arise from; and is what precedes any relish of, or delight in the nature and qualities inherent in the being beloved, as beautiful and amiable. When the first thing that draws a man's benevolence to another, is the beholding those qualifications and properties in him, which appear to him lovely in themselves, and the subject of them, on this account, worthy of esteem and goodwill, love arises in a very different manner, than when it first arises from some gift bestowed by another, or depended on from him, as a judge loves and favors a man that has bribed him; or from the relation he supposes another has to him, as a man who loves another because he looks upon him as his child. When love to another arises thus, it does truly and properly arise from self-love.

That kind of affection to God or Jesus Christ, which does thus properly arise from self-love, cannot be a truly gracious and spiritual love; as appears from what has been said already: for self-love is a principle entirely natural, and as much in the hearts of devils as angels; and therefore surely nothing that is the mere result of it, can be supernatural and divine, in the manner before described.[5] Christ plainly speaks of this kind of love, as what is nothing beyond the love of wicked men, Luke 6:32: "If ye love them that love you, what thank have ye? For sinners also love those that love them." And the devil himself knew that that kind of respect to God which was so mercenary, as to be only for benefits received or depended on (which is all one), is worthless in the sight of God; otherwise he never would have made use of such a slander before God, against Job, as in Job 1:9–10: "Doth Job serve God for nought? Hast thou not made an hedge about him, and about his house?" etc. Nor would God ever have implicitly allowed the objection to have been good, in case the accusation had been true, by allowing that that matter should be tried, and that Job should be so dealt with, that it might appear in the event, whether Job's respect to God was thus mercenary or no, and by putting the proof of the sincerity and goodness of his respect, upon that issue.

'Tis unreasonable to think otherwise, than that the first foundation of a true love to God, is that whereby he is in himself lovely, or worthy to be loved, or the supreme loveliness of his nature. This is certainly what makes him chiefly amiable. What chiefly makes a man, or any creature lovely, is his excellency; and so what chiefly renders God lovely, and must undoubtedly be the chief ground of true love, is his excellency. God's nature, or the divinity, is infinitely excellent; yea 'tis infinite beauty, brightness, and glory itself. But how can that be true love of this excellent and lovely

5. "There is a natural love to Christ, as to one that doth thee good, and for thine own ends; and spiritual, for himself, whereby the Lord only is exalted." Shepard, *Parable*, Pt. I, p. 25.

nature, which is not built on the foundation of its true loveliness? How can that be true love of beauty and brightness, which is not for beauty and brightness' sake? How can that be a true prizing of that which is in itself infinitely worthy and precious, which is not for the sake of its worthiness and preciousness? This infinite excellency of the divine nature, as it is in itself, is the true ground of all that is good in God in any respect; but how can a man truly and rightly love God, without loving him for that excellency in him, which is the foundation of all that is in any manner of respect good or desirable in him? They whose affection to God is founded first on his profitableness to them, their affection begins at the wrong end; they regard God only for the utmost limit of the stream of divine good, where it touches them, and reaches their interest; and have no respect to that infinite glory of God's nature, which is the original good, and the true fountain of all good, the first fountain of all loveliness of every kind, and so the first foundation of all true love.

A natural principle of self-love may be the foundation of great affections towards God and Christ, without seeing anything of the beauty and glory of the divine nature. There is a certain gratitude that is a mere natural thing. Gratitude is one of the natural affections of the soul of man, as well as anger; and there is a gratitude that arises from self-love, very much in the same manner that anger does. Anger in men is an affection excited against another, or in opposition to another, for something in him that crosses self-love: gratitude is an affection one has toward another, for loving him, or gratifying him, or for something in him that suits self-love. And there may be a kind of gratitude, without any true or proper love; as there may be anger without any proper hatred, as in parents towards their children, that they may be angry with, and yet at the same time have a strong habitual love to them. This gratitude is the principle which is in exercise in wicked men, in that which Christ declares concerning them, in the 6th of Luke, where he says, "Sinners love those that love them" [Luke 6:32]; and which he declares concerning even the Publicans, who were some of the most carnal and profligate sort of men (Matt. 5:46). This is the very principle that is wrought upon by bribery, in unjust judges; and it is a principle that even the brute beasts do exercise: a dog will love his master that is kind to him. And we see in innumerable instances, that mere nature is sufficient to excite gratitude in men, or to affect their hearts with thankfulness to others for kindnesses received; and sometimes toward them, whom at the same time they have an habitual enmity against. Thus Saul was once and again greatly affected, and even dissolved with gratitude towards David, for sparing his life; and yet remained an habitual enemy to him. And as men, from mere nature, may be thus affected towards men; so they may towards God. There is nothing hinders, but that the same self-love may work after the same manner towards God, as towards men. And we have manifest instances of it in Scripture; as in the children of Israel, who sang God's praises at the Red Sea, but soon forgat God's works; and in Naaman the Syrian, who was greatly affected with the miraculous cure of his leprosy, so as to have his heart engaged thenceforward to worship the God that had healed him, and him only, excepting when it would expose him to be ruined in his temporal interest. So was Nebuchadnezzer greatly affected with God's goodness to him, in restoring him to his reason and kingdom, after his dwelling with the beasts.

Gratitude being thus a natural principle, it renders ingratitude so much the more vile and heinous; because it shows a dreadful prevalence of wickedness when it even overbears, and suppresses the better principles of human nature: as it is mentioned as an evidence of the high degree of the wickedness of many of the heathen, that they were without natural affection (Rom. 2:31). But that the want of gratitude, or natural affection, are evidences of an high degree of vice, is no argument that all gratitude and natural affection, has the nature of virtue, or saving grace.

Self-love, through the exercise of a mere natural gratitude, may be the foundation of a sort of love to God many ways. A kind of love may arise from a false notion of God, that men have been educated in, or have some way imbibed; as though he were only goodness and mercy, and no revenging justice; or as though the exercises of his goodness were necessary, and not free and sovereign; or as though his goodness were dependent on what is in them, and as it were constrained by them. Men on such grounds as these, may love a God of their own forming in their imaginations, when they are far from loving such a God as reigns in heaven.

Again, self-love may be the foundation of an affection in men towards God, through a great insensibility of their state with regard to God, and for want of conviction of conscience to make 'em sensible how dreadfully they have provoked God to anger; they have no sense of the heinousness of sin, as against God, and of the infinite and terrible opposition of the holy nature of God against it: and so having formed in their minds such a God as suits them, and thinking God to be such an one as themselves, who favors and agrees with them, they may like him very well, and feel a sort of love to him, when they are far from loving the true God. And men's affections may be much moved towards God, from self-love, by some remarkable outward benefits received from God; as it was with Naaman, Nebuchadnezzar, and the children of Israel at the Red Sea.

Again, a very high affection towards God, may, and often does arise in men, from an opinion of the favor and love of God to them, as the first foundation of their love to him. After awakenings and distress through fears of hell, they may suddenly get a notion, through some impression on their imagination, or immediate suggestion, with or without texts of Scripture, or by some other means, that God loves 'em, and has forgiven their sins, and made them his children; and this is the first thing that causes their affections to flow towards God and Jesus Christ: and then after this, and upon this foundation, many things in God may appear lovely to them, and Christ may seem excellent. And if such persons are asked, whether God appears lovely and amiable in himself? They would perhaps readily answer, Yes; when indeed, if the matter be strictly examined, this good opinion of God was purchased and paid for before ever they afforded it, in the distinguishing and infinite benefits they imagined they received from God; and they allow God to be lovely in himself, no otherwise, than that he has forgiven them, and accepted them, and loves them above most in the world, and has engaged to improve all his infinite power and wisdom in preferring, dignifying and exalting them, and will do for 'em just as they would have him. When once they are firm in this apprehension, 'tis easy to own God and Christ to be lovely and glorious, and to admire and extol them. 'Tis easy for them to own Christ to be a lovely person, and the best in the world, when they are first firm in it, that he, though Lord of the universe, is captivated with love to them, and has his heart swallowed up in them, and prizes 'em far beyond most of their neighbors, and loved 'em from eternity, and died for 'em, and will make 'em reign in eternal glory with him in heaven. When this is the case with carnal men, their very lusts will make him seem lovely: pride itself will prejudice them in favor of that which they call Christ: selfish proud man naturally calls that lovely that greatly contributes to his interest, and gratifies his ambition.

And as this sort of persons begin, so they go on. Their affections are raised from time to time, primarily on this foundation of self-love and a conceit of God's love to them. Many have a false notion of communion with God, as though it were carried on by impulses, and whispers, and external representations, immediately made to their imagination. These things they often have; which they take to be manifestations of God's great love to 'em, and evidences of their high exaltation above others of mankind; and so their affections are often renewedly set agoing.

Whereas the exercises of true and holy love in the saints arise in another way. They don't first see that God loves them, and then see that he is lovely; but they first see that God is lovely, and that Christ is excellent and glorious, and their hearts are first captivated with this view, and the exercises of their love are wont from time to time to begin here, and to arise primarily from these views; and then, consequentially, they see God's love; and great favor to them.[6] The saint's affections begin with God; and self-love has a hand in these affections consequentially, and secondarily only. On the contrary, those false affections begin with self, and an acknowledgment of an excellency in God, and an affectedness with it, is only consequential and dependent. In the love of the true saint God is the lowest foundation; the love of the excellency of his nature is the foundation of all the affections which come afterwards, wherein self-love is concerned as an handmaid: on the contrary, the hypocrite lays himself at the bottom of all, as the first foundation, and lays on God as the superstructure; and even his acknowledgment of God's glory itself, depends on his regard to his private interest.

Self-love may not only influence men, so as to cause them to be affected with God's kindness to them separately; but also with God's kindness to them, as parts of a community: as a natural principle of self-love, without any other principle, may be sufficient to make a man concerned for the interest of the nation to which he belongs: as for instance, in the present war, self-love may make

6. "There is a seeing of Christ after a man believes, which is Christ in his love, etc. But I speak of that first sight of him that precedes the second act of faith; and 'tis an intuitive, or real sight of him, as he is in his glory." Shepard, *Parable,* Pt. I, p. 74.

natural men rejoice at the successes of our nation, and sorry for their disadvantages, they being concerned as members of the body. So the same natural principles may extend further, and even to the world of mankind, and might be affected with the benefits the inhabitants of the earth have, beyond those of the inhabitants of other planets; if we knew that such there were, and knew how it was with them. So this principle may cause men to be affected with the benefits that mankind have received beyond the fallen angels. And hence men, from this principle, may be much affected with the wonderful goodness of God to mankind, his great goodness in giving his Son to die for fallen man, and the marvelous love of Christ in suffering such great things for us, and with the great glory they hear God has provided in heaven for us; looking on themselves as persons concerned and interested, as being some of this species of creatures, so highly favored: the same principle of natural gratitude may influence men here, as in the case of personal benefits.

But these things that I have said do by no means imply that all gratitude to God is a mere natural thing, and that there is no such thing as a spiritual gratitude, which is a holy and divine affection: they imply no more, than that there is a gratitude which is merely natural, and that when persons have affections towards God only or primarily for benefits received, their affection is only the exercise of a natural gratitude. There is doubtless such a thing as a gracious gratitude, which does greatly differ from all that gratitude which natural men experience. It differs in the following respects:

1. True gratitude or thankfulness to God for his kindness to us, arises from a foundation laid before, of love to God for what he is in himself; whereas a natural gratitude has no such antecedent foundation. The gracious stirrings of grateful affection to God, for kindness received, always are from a stock of love already in the heart, established in the first place on other grounds, viz. God's own excellency; and hence the affections are disposed to flow out, on occasions of God's kindness. The saint having seen the glory of God, and his heart overcome by it, and captivated into a supreme love to him on that account, his heart hereby becomes tender, and easily affected with kindnesses received. If a man has no love to another, yet gratitude may be moved by some extraordinary kindness; as in Saul towards David. But this is not the same kind of thing, as a man's gratitude to a dear friend, that his heart was be-

fore possessed with a high esteem of, and love to; whose heart by this means became tender towards him, and more easily affected with gratitude, and affected in another manner. Self-love is not excluded from a gracious gratitude; the saints love God for his kindness to them, "I love the Lord, because he hath heard the voice of my supplication" (Ps. 116:1). But something else is included; and another love prepares the way, and lays the foundation, for these grateful affections.

2. In a gracious gratitude, men are affected with the attribute of God's goodness and free grace, not only as they are concerned in it, or as it affects their interest, but as a part of the glory and beauty of God's nature. That wonderful and unparalleled grace of God, which is manifested in the work of redemption, and shines forth in the face of Jesus Christ, is infinitely glorious in itself, and appears so to the angels; 'tis a great part of the moral perfection and beauty of God's nature: this would be glorious, whether it were exercised towards us or no; and the saint who exercises a gracious thankfulness for it, sees it to be so, and delights in it as such; though his concern in it serves the more to engage his mind, and raise the attention and affection; and self-love here assists as an handmaid, being subservient to higher principles, to lead forth a mind to the view and contemplation, and engage and fix the attention, and heighten the joy and love: God's kindness to them is a glass that God sets before them, wherein to be behold the beauty of the attribute of God's goodness; the exercises and displays of this attribute, by this means, are brought near to them, and set right before them. So that in a holy thankfulness to God, the concern our interest has in God's goodness, is not the first foundation of our being affected with it; that was laid in the heart before, in that stock of love which was to God, for his excellency in himself, that makes the heart tender, and susceptive of such impressions from his goodness to us: nor is our own interest, or the benefits we have received, the only, or the chief objective ground of the present exercises of the affection; but God's goodness, as part of the beauty of his nature; although the manifestations of that lovely attribute, set immediately before our eyes, in the exercises of it for us, be the special occasion of the mind's attention to that beauty, at that time, and serves to fix the attention, and heighten the affection.

Some may perhaps be ready to object against the whole that has been said, that text, "We love him, because he first loved us" (I

John 4:19), as though this implied that God's love to the true saints were the first foundation of their love to him.

In answer to this I would observe, that the Apostle's drift in these words, is to magnify the love of God to us from hence, that he loved us, while we had no love to him; as will be manifest to anyone who compares this verse, and the two following, with the 9th, 10th and 11th verses. And that God loved us, when we had no love to him, the Apostle proves by this argument, that God's love to the elect, is the ground of their love to him. And that it is three ways: (1) The saints' love to God, is the fruit of God's love to them; as it is the gift of that love. God gave them a spirit of love to him, because he loved them from eternity. And in this respect God's love to his elect is the first foundation of their love to him, as it is the foundation of their regeneration, and the whole of their redemption. (2) The exercises and discoveries that God has made of his wonderful love to sinful men, by Jesus Christ, in the work of redemption, is one of the chief manifestations, which God has made of the glory of his moral perfection, to both angels and men; and so is one main objective ground of the love of both to God; in a good consistence with what was said before. (3) God's love to a particular elect person, discovered by his conversion, is a great manifestation of God's moral perfection and glory to him, and a proper occasion of the excitation of the love of holy gratitude, agreeable to what was before said. And that the saints do in these respects love God, because he first loved them, fully answers the design of the Apostle's argument in that place. So that no good argument can be drawn from hence, against a spiritual and gracious love in the saints, arising primarily from the excellency of divine things, as they are in themselves, and not from any conceived relation they bear to their interest.

And as it is with the love of the saints, so it is with their joy, and spiritual delight and pleasure: the first foundation of it, is not any consideration or conception of their interest in divine things; but it primarily consists in the sweet entertainment their minds have in the view or contemplation of the divine and holy beauty of these things, as they are in themselves. And this is indeed the very main difference between the joy of the hypocrite, and the joy of the true saint. The former rejoices in himself; self is the first foundation of his joy: the latter rejoices in God. The hypocrite has his mind pleased and delighted, in the first place, with his own privilege, and the happiness which he supposes he has attained, or shall attain. True saints have their minds, in the first place, inexpressibly pleased and delighted with the sweet ideas of the glorious and amiable nature of the things of God. And this is the spring of all their delights, and the cream of all their pleasures; 'tis the joy of their joy. This sweet and ravishing entertainment, they have in the view of the beautiful and delightful nature of divine things, is the foundation of the joy that they have afterwards, in the consideration of their being theirs. But the dependence of the affections of hypocrites is in a contrary order: they first rejoice, and are elevated with it, that they are made so much of by God; and then on that ground, he seems in a sort, lovely to them.

The first foundation of the delight a true saint has in God, is his own perfection; and the first foundation of the delight he has in Christ, is his own beauty; he appears in himself the chief among ten thousand, and altogether lovely: the way of salvation by Christ, is a delightful way to him, for the sweet and admirable manifestations of the divine perfections in it; the holy doctrines of the gospel, by which God is exalted and man abased, holiness honored and promoted, and sin greatly disgraced and discouraged, and free and sovereign love manifested; are glorious doctrines in his eyes, and sweet to his taste, prior to any conception of his interest in these things. Indeed the saints rejoice in their interest in God, and that Christ is theirs; and so they have great reason; but this is not the first spring of their joy: they first rejoice in God as glorious and excellent in himself, and then secondarily rejoice in it, that so glorious a God is theirs: they first have their hearts filled with sweetness, from the view of Christ's excellency, and the excellency of his grace, and the beauty of the way of salvation by him; and then they have a secondary joy, in that so excellent a Saviour, and such excellent grace is theirs.[7]

7. Dr. Owen, speaking of a common work of the Spirit, says, "The effects of this work on the mind, which is the first subject affected with it, proceeds not so far, as to give it delight, complacency and satisfaction in the lovely spiritual nature and excellencies of the things revealed unto it. The true nature of saving illumination consists in this, that it give the mind such a direct intuitive insight and prospect into spiritual things, as that in their own spiritual nature they suit, please, and satisfy it; so that it is transformed into them, cast into the mold of them, and rests in them; Rom. 6:17; 12:2; I Cor. 2:13–14; II Cor. 3:18; 4:6. This, the work we have insisted on, reacheth not unto. For notwithstanding any discovery that is made therein of spiritual things unto the mind, it finds not an im-

But that which is the true saint's superstructure, is the hypocrite's foundation. When they hear of the wonderful things of the gospel, of God's great love in sending his Son, of Christ's dying love to sinners, and the great things Christ has purchased, and promised to the saints, and hear these things livelily and eloquently set forth; they may hear with a great deal of pleasure, and be lifted up with what they hear: but if their joy be examined, it will be found to have no other foundation than this, that they look upon these things as theirs, all this exalts them, they love to hear of the great love of Christ so vastly distinguishing some from others; for self-love, and even pride itself, makes 'em affect great distinction from others: no wonder, in this confident opinion of their own good estate, that they feel well under such doctrine, and are pleased in the highest degree, in hearing how much God and Christ makes of 'em. So that their joy is really a joy in themselves, and not in God.

And because the joy of hypocrites is in themselves, hence it comes to pass, that in their rejoicings and elevations, they are wont to keep their eye upon themselves; having received what they call spiritual discoveries or experiences, their minds are taken up about them, admiring their own experiences: and what they are principally taken and elevated with, is not the glory of God, or beauty of Christ, but the beauty of their experiences. They keep thinking with themselves, what a good experience is this! What a great discovery is this! What wonderful things have I met with! And so they put their experiences in the place of Christ, and his beauty and fullness; and instead of rejoicing in Christ Jesus, they rejoice in their admirable experiences: instead of feeding and feasting their souls in the view of what is without them, viz. the innate, sweet, refreshing amiableness of the things exhibited in the gospel, their eyes are off from these things, or at least they view them only as it were sideways; but the object that fixes their contemplation, is their ex-

---

mediate, direct, spiritual excellency in them; but only with respect unto some benefit or advantage, which is to be attained by means thereof. It will not give such a spiritual insight into the mystery of God's grace by Jesus Christ, called his glory shining in the face of Christ, II Cor. 4:6, as that the soul, in its first direct view of it, should, for what it is in itself, admire it, delight in it, approve it, and find spiritual solace, with refreshment, in it. But such a light, such a knowledge, it communicates, as that a man may like it well in its effects, as a way of mercy and salvation." John Owen, *Pneumatologia or, A Discourse Concerning the Holy Spirit* (London, 1674), Bk. III, ch. 2, sec. 16, pp. 199–200. [For the influence of Owen's illumination doctrine see above, pp. 68–9.]

perience; and they are feeding their souls, and feasting a selfish principle with a view of their discoveries: they take more comfort in their discoveries than in Christ discovered, which is the true notion of living upon experiences and frames; and not a using experiences as the signs, on which they rely for evidence of their good estate, which some call living on experiences: though it be very observable, that some of them who do so, are most notorious for living upon experiences, according to the true notion of it.

The affections of hypocrites are very often after this manner; they are first, much affected with some impression on their imagination, or some impulse, which they take to be an immediate suggestion, or testimony from God, of his love and their happiness, and high privilege in some respect, either with or without a text of Scripture; they are mightily taken with this, as a great discovery; and hence arise high affections. And when their affections are raised, then they view those high affections, and call them great and wonderful experiences; and they have a notion that God is greatly pleased with those affections; and this affects them more; and so they are affected with their affections. And thus their affections rise higher and higher, till they sometimes are perfectly swallowed up: and self-conceit, and a fierce zeal rises withal; and all is built like a castle in the air, on no other foundation but imagination, self-love and pride.

And as the thoughts of this sort of persons are, so is their talk; for out of the abundance of their heart, their mouth speaketh. As in their high affections, they keep their eye upon the beauty of their experiences, and greatness of their attainments; so they are great talkers about themselves. The true saint, when under great spiritual affections, from the fullness of his heart, is ready to be speaking much of God, and his glorious perfections and works, and of the beauty and amiableness of Christ, and the glorious things of the gospel; but hypocrites, in their high affections, talk more of the discovery, than they do of the thing discovered; they are full of talk about the great things they have met with, the wonderful discoveries they have had, how sure they are of the love of God to them, how safe their condition is, and how they know they shall go to heaven, etc.

A true saint, when in the enjoyment of true discoveries of the sweet glory of God and Christ, has his mind too much captivated and engaged by what he views without himself, to stand at that time to view himself, and his own attainments: it would be a diversion and loss which he could not bear, to take his eye off from the ravishing object of his contemplation, to survey his own experience, and to spend time in thinking with himself, what an high attainment this is, and what a good story I now have to tell others. Nor does the pleasure and sweetness of his mind at that time, chiefly arise from the consideration of the safety of his state, or anything he has in view of his own qualifications, experiences, or circumstances; but from the divine and supreme beauty of what is the object of his direct view, without himself; which sweetly entertains, and strongly holds his mind.

As the love and joy of hypocrites, are all from the source of self-love; so it is with their other affections, their sorrow for sin, their humiliation and submission, their religious desires and zeal: everything is as it were paid for beforehand, in God's highly gratifying their self-love, and their lusts, by making so much of them, and exalting them so highly, as things are in their imagination. 'Tis easy for nature, as corrupt as it is, under a notion of being already some of the highest favorites of heaven, and having a God who does so protect 'em and favor 'em in their sins, to love this imaginary God that suits 'em so well, and to extol him, and submit to him, and to be fierce and zealous for him. The high affections of many are all built on the supposition of their being eminent saints. If that opinion which they have of themselves were taken away, if they thought they were some of the lower form of saints (though they should yet suppose themselves to be real saints), their high affections would fall to the ground. If they only saw a little of the sinfulness and vileness of their own hearts, and their deformity, in the midst of their best duties and their best affections, it would knock their affections on the head; because their affections are built upon self, therefore self-knowledge would destroy them. But as to truly gracious affections, they are built elsewhere: they have their foundation out of self, in God and Jesus Christ; and therefore a discovery of themselves, of their own deformity, and the meanness of their experiences, though it will purify their affections, yet it will not destroy them, but in some respects sweeten and heighten them.

III. Those affections that are truly holy, are primarily founded on the loveliness of the moral excellency of divine things. Or (to express it otherwise), a love to divine things for the beauty and sweetness of their moral excellency, is the first beginning and spring of all holy affections.

Here, for the sake of the more illiterate reader, I will explain what I mean by the moral excellency of divine things.

And it may be observed that the word "moral" is not to be understood here, according to the common and vulgar acceptation of the word, when men speak of morality, and a moral behavior; meaning an outward conformity to the duties of the moral law, and especially the duties of the second table; or intending no more at farthest, than such seeming virtues, as proceed from natural principles, in opposition to those virtues that are more inward, spiritual, and divine; as the honesty, justice, generosity, good nature, and public spirit of many of the heathen, are called moral virtues, in distinction from the holy faith, love, humility, and heavenly-mindedness of true Christians: I say the word "moral" is not to be understood thus in this place.

But in order to a right understanding what is meant, it must be observed, that divines commonly make a distinction between *moral* good and evil, and *natural* good and evil. By moral evil, they mean the evil of sin, or that evil which is against duty, and contrary to what is right and ought to be. By natural evil, they don't mean that evil which is properly opposed to duty; but that which is contrary to mere nature, without any respect to a rule of duty. So the evil of suffering is called natural evil, such as pain, and torment, disgrace, and the like: these things are contrary to mere nature, contrary to the nature of both bad and good, hateful to wicked men and devils, as well as good men and angels. So likewise natural defects are called natural evils, as if a child be monstrous, or a natural fool; these are natural evils, but are not moral evils, because they have not properly the nature of the evil of sin. On the other hand, as by moral evil, divines mean the evil of sin, or that which is contrary to what is right; so by moral good, they mean that which is contrary to sin, or that good in beings who have will and choice, whereby, as voluntary agents, they are, and act, as it becomes 'em to be and to act, or so as is most fit, and suitable, and lovely. By natural good they mean that good that is entirely of a different kind from holiness or virtue, viz. that which perfects or suits nature, considering nature abstractly from any holy or unholy qualifications, and without any relation to any rule or measure of right and wrong.

Thus pleasure is a natural good; so is honor; so is strength; so is speculative knowledge, human learning, and policy. Thus there is a distinction to be made between the natural good that men are possessed of, and their moral good; and also between the natural and moral good of the angels in heaven: the great capacity of their understandings, and their great strength, and the honorable circumstances they are in as the great ministers of God's kingdom, whence they are called thrones, dominions, principalities, and powers, is the natural good which they are possessed of; but their perfect and glorious holiness and goodness, their pure and flaming love to God, and to the saints, and one another, is their moral good. So divines make a distinction between the natural and moral perfections of God: by the moral perfections of God, they mean those attributes which God exercises as a moral agent, or whereby the heart and will of God are good, right, and infinitely becoming, and lovely; such as his righteousness, truth, faithfulness, and goodness; or, in one word, his holiness. By God's natural attributes or perfections, they mean those attributes, wherein, according to our way of conceiving of God, consists, not the holiness or moral goodness of God, but his greatness; such as his power, his knowledge whereby he knows all things, and his being eternal, from everlasting to everlasting, his omnipresence, and his awful and terrible majesty.

The moral excellency of an intelligent voluntary being, is more immediately seated in the heart or will of moral agents. That intelligent being whose will is truly right and lovely, he is morally good or excellent.

This moral excellency of an intelligent being, when it is true and real, and not only external, or merely seeming and counterfeit, is holiness. Therefore holiness comprehends all the true moral excellency of intelligent beings: there is no other true virtue, but real holiness. Holiness comprehends all the true virtue of a good man, his love to God, his gracious love to men, his justice, his charity, and bowels of mercies, his gracious meekness and gentleness, and all other true Christian virtues that he has, belong to his holiness. So the holiness of God in the more extensive sense of the word, and the sense in which the word is commonly, if not universally used concerning God in Scripture, is the same with the moral excellency of the divine nature, or his purity and beauty as a moral agent, comprehending all his moral perfections, his righteousness, faithfulness and goodness. As in holy men their charity, Christian kindness and mercy, belongs to their holiness; so the kindness and mercy of God, belongs to his holiness. Holiness in man, is but the image of God's holiness: there are not more virtues belonging to the image, than are in the original: derived holiness has not more in it, than is in that underived holiness, which is its fountain: there is no more than grace for grace, or grace in the image, answerable to grace in the original.

As there are two kinds of attributes in God, according to our way of conceiving of him, his moral attributes, which are summed up in his holiness, and his natural attributes, of strength, knowledge, etc. that constitute the greatness of God; so there is a twofold image of God in man, his moral or spiritual image, which is his holiness, that is the image of God's moral excellency (which image was lost by the Fall); and God's natural image, consisting in men's reason and understanding, his natural ability, and dominion over the creatures, which is the image of God's natural attributes.

From what has been said, it may easily be understood what I intend, when I say that a love to divine things for the beauty of their moral excellency, is the beginning and spring of all holy affections. It has been already shown, under the former head, that the first objective ground of all holy affections is the supreme excellency of divine things as they are in themselves, or in their own nature; I now proceed further, and say more particularly, that that kind of excellency of the nature of divine things, which is the first objective ground of all holy affections, is their moral excellency, or their holiness. Holy persons, in the exercise of holy affections, do love divine things primarily for their holiness: they love God, in the first place, for the beauty of his holiness or moral perfection, as being supremely amiable in itself. Not that the saints, in the exercise of gracious affections, do love God only for his holiness; all his attributes are amiable and glorious in their eyes; they delight in every divine perfection; the contemplation of the infinite greatness, power, and knowledge, and terrible majesty of God, is pleasant to them. But their love to God for his holiness is what is most fundamental and essential in their love. Here it is that true love to God begins: all other holy love to divine things flows from hence: this is the most essential and distinguishing thing that belongs to a holy love to God, with regard to the foundation of it. A love to God for the beauty of his moral attributes, leads to, and necessarily causes a delight in God for all his attributes; for his moral attributes can't be without his natural attributes: for infinite holiness supposes infinite wisdom, and an infinite capacity and greatness; and all the attributes of God do as it were imply one another.

The true beauty and loveliness of all intelligent beings does primarily and most essentially consist in their moral excellency or holiness. Herein consists the loveliness of the angels, without which, with all their natural perfections, their strength, and their knowledge, they would have no more loveliness than devils. 'Tis moral excellency alone, that is in itself, and on its own account, the excellency of intelligent beings: 'tis this that gives beauty to, or rather is the beauty of their natural perfections and qualifications. Moral excellency is the excellency of natural excellencies. Natural qualifications are either excellent or otherwise, according as they are joined with moral excellency or not. Strength and knowledge don't render any being lovely, without holiness; but more hateful: though they render them more lovely, when joined with holiness. Thus the elect angels are the more glorious for their strength and knowledge, because these natural perfections of theirs, are sanctified by their moral perfection. But though the devils are very strong, and of great natural understanding, they be not the more lovely: they are more terrible indeed, but not the more amiable; but on the contrary, the more hateful. The holiness of an intelligent creature, is the beauty of all his natural perfections. And so it is in God, according to our way of conceiving of the divine Being: holiness is in a peculiar manner the beauty of the divine nature. Hence we often read of the beauty of holiness (Ps. 29:2, Ps. 96:9, and 110:3). This renders all his other attributes glorious and lovely. 'Tis the glory of God's wisdom, that 'tis a holy wisdom, and not a wicked subtlety and craftiness. This makes his majesty lovely, and not merely dreadful and horrible, that it is a holy majesty. 'Tis the glory of God's immutability, that it is a holy immutability, and not an inflexible obstinacy in wickedness.

And therefore it must needs be, that a sight of God's loveliness must begin here. A true love to God must begin with a delight in his holiness, and not with a delight in any other attribute; for no other attribute is truly lovely without this, and no otherwise than as (according to our way of conceiving of God) it derives its loveliness from this; and therefore it is impossible that other attributes should appear lovely, in their true loveliness, till this is seen; and it is impossible that any perfection of the divine nature should be loved with true love, till this is loved. If the true loveliness of all God's perfections, arises from the loveliness of his holiness; then the true love of all his perfections, arises from the love of his holiness. They that don't see the glory of God's holiness, can't see anything of the true glory of his mercy and grace: they see nothing of the glory of those attributes, as any excellency of God's nature, as it is in itself; though they may be affected with them, and love them, as they concern their interest: for these attributes are no part of the excellency of God's nature, as that is excellent in itself, any otherwise than as they are included in his holiness, more largely taken; or as they are a part of his moral perfection.

As the beauty of the divine nature does primarily consist in God's holiness, so does the beauty of all divine things. Herein consists the beauty of the saints, that they are saints, or holy ones: 'tis the moral image of God in them, which is their beauty; and that is their holiness. Herein consists the beauty and brightness of the angels of heaven, that they are holy angels, and so not devils (Dan. 4:13, 17, 23; Matt. 25:31; Mark 8:38; Acts 10:22; Rev. 14:10). Herein consists the beauty of the Christian religion, above all other religions, that it is so holy a religion. Herein consists the excellency of the Word of God, that it is so holy; "Thy word is very pure, therefore thy servant loveth it" (Ps. 119:140). "I esteem all thy precepts, concerning all things, to be right; and I hate every false way" (ver. 128). "Thy testimonies, that thou hast commanded, are righteous, and very faithful" (ver. 138). And: "My tongue shall speak of thy word; for all thy commandments are righteousness" (ver. 172). And: "The law of the Lord is perfect, converting the soul: the testimony of the Lord is sure, making wise the simple: the statutes of the Lord are right, rejoicing the heart: the commandment of the Lord is pure, enlightening the eyes: the fear of the Lord is clean, enduring forever: the judgments of the Lord are true, and righteous altogether: more to be desired are they than gold, yea, than much fine gold; sweeter also than honey, and the honeycomb" (Ps. 19:7–10). Herein does primarily consist the amiableness and beauty of the Lord Jesus, whereby he is the chief among ten thousands and altogether lovely; even in that he is the holy One of God (Acts 3:14), and God's holy Child (Acts 4:27), and "he that is holy, and he that is true" (Rev. 3:7). All the spiritual beauty of his human nature, consisting in his meekness, lowliness, patience, heavenliness, love to God, love to men, condescension to the mean and vile, and compassion to the miserable, etc. all is summed up in his holiness. And the beauty of his divine nature, of which the beauty of his human nature is the image and reflection, does also primarily consist in his holiness. Herein primarily consists the glory of the gospel, that it is a holy gospel, and so bright an emanation of the holy beauty of God and Jesus Christ: herein consists the spiritual beauty of its doctrines, that they are holy doctrines, or doctrines according to godliness. And herein does consist the spiritual beauty of the way of salvation by Jesus Christ, that it [is] so holy a way. And herein chiefly consists the glory of heaven, that it is the holy city, the holy Jerusalem, the habitation of God's holiness, and so of his glory (Is. 63:15). All the beauties of the new Jerusalem, as it is described in the two last chapters of Revelation, are but various representations of this: see ch. 21:2, 10–11, 18, 21, 27; ch. 22: 1, 3.

And therefore it is primarily an account of this kind of excellency, that the saints do love all these things. Thus they love the Word of God, because it is very pure. 'Tis on this account they love the saints; and on this account chiefly it is, that heaven is lovely to them, and those holy tabernacles of God amiable in their eyes: 'tis on this account that they love God; and on this account primarily it is, that they love Christ, and that their hearts delight in the doctrines of the gospel, and sweetly acquiesce in the way of salvation therein revealed.[8]

Under the head of the first distinguishing characteristic of gracious affection, I observed that there is given to those that are regenerated, a new supernatural sense, that is as it were a certain divine spiritual taste, which is in its whole nature diverse from any former kinds of sensation of the mind, as tasting is diverse from any of the other five senses, and that something is perceived by a true saint in the

8. "To the right closing with Christ's person, this is also required, to taste the bitterness of sin, as the greatest evil: else a man will never close with Christ, for his holiness in him, and from him, as the greatest good. For we told you, that that is the right closing with Christ for himself, when it is for his holiness. For ask a whorish heart, what beauty he sees in the person of Christ; he will, after he has looked over his kingdom, his righteousness, all his works, see a beauty in them, because they do serve his turn, to comfort him only. Ask a virgin, he will see his happiness in all; but that which makes the Lord amiable, is his holiness, which is in him to make him holy too. As in marriage, it is the personal beauty draws the heart. And hence I have thought it reason that he that loves the brethren for a little grace, will love Christ much more." Shepard, *Parable,* Pt. I, p. 84.

exercise of this new sense of mind, in spiritual and divine things, as entirely different from anything that is perceived in them by natural men, as the sweet taste of honey is diverse from the ideas men get of honey by looking on it or feeling of it; now this that I have been speaking, viz. the beauty of holiness is that thing in spiritual and divine things, which is perceived by this spiritual sense, that is so diverse from all that natural men perceive in them: this kind of beauty is the quality that is the immediate object of this spiritual sense: this is the sweetness that is the proper object of this spiritual taste. The Scripture often represents the beauty and sweetness of holiness as the grand object of a spiritual taste, and spiritual appetite. This was the sweet food of the holy soul of Jesus Christ, "I have meat to eat, that ye know not of. . . . My meat is to do the will of him that sent me, and to finish his work" (John 4:32, 34). I know of no part of the Holy Scriptures, where the nature and evidences of true and sincere godliness, are so much of set purpose, and so fully and largely insisted on and delineated, as the 119th Psalm; the Psalmist declares his design in the first verses of the psalm, and he keeps his eye on this design all along, and pursues it to the end: but in this psalm the excellency of holiness is represented as the immediate object of a spiritual taste, relish, appetite and delight, God's law, that grand expression and emanation of the holiness of God's nature, and prescription of holiness to the creature, is all along represented as the food and entertainment, and as the great object of the love, the appetite, the complacence and rejoicing of the gracious nature, which prizes God's commandments above gold, yea, the finest gold, and to which they are sweeter than the honey, and honeycomb; and that upon account of their holiness, as I observed before. The same Psalmist declares, that this is the sweetness that a spiritual taste relishes in God's law, "The law of the Lord is perfect. . . . The commandment of the Lord is pure. . . . The fear of the Lord is clean. . . . The statutes of the Lord are right, rejoicing the heart. . . . The judgments of the Lord are true, and righteous altogether: more to be desired are they than gold, yea than much fine gold; sweeter also than honey and the honeycomb" (Ps. 19:7–10).

A holy love has a holy object: the holiness of love consists especially in this that it is the love of that which is holy, as holy, or for its holiness; so that 'tis the holiness of the object, which is the quality whereon it fixes and terminates. An holy nature must needs love that in holy things chiefly, which is most agreeable to itself; but surely that in divine things, which above all others is agreeable to holy nature, is holiness; because holiness must be above all other things agreeable to holiness; for nothing can be more agreeable to any nature than itself; holy nature must be above all things agreeable to holy nature; and so the holy nature of God and Christ, and the Word of God, and other divine things, must be above all other things, agreeable to the holy nature that is in the saints.

And again, an holy nature doubtless loves holy things, especially on the account of that, for which sinful nature has enmity against them: but that for which chiefly sinful nature is at enmity against holy things, is their holiness; it is for this, that the carnal mind is enmity against God, and against the law of God, and the people of God. Now 'tis just arguing from contraries; from contrary causes, to contrary effects; from opposite natures, to opposite tendencies. We know that holiness is of a directly contrary nature to wickedness: as therefore 'tis the nature of wickedness chiefly to oppose and hate holiness; so it must be the nature of holiness chiefly to tend to, and delight in holiness.

The holy nature in the saints and angels in heaven (where the true tendency of it best appears) is principally engaged by the holiness of divine things. This is the divine beauty which chiefly engages the attention, admiration and praise of the bright and burning seraphim; "One cried unto another, and said, Holy, holy, holy is the Lord of hosts; the whole earth is full of his glory" (Is. 6:3). And: "They rest not day and night, saying, Holy, holy, holy, Lord God almighty, which was, and is, and is to come" (Rev. 4:8). So the glorified saints, "Who shall not fear thee, O Lord, and glorify thy name, for thou only art holy?" (ch. 15:4).

And the Scriptures represent the saints on earth as adoring God primarily on this account, and admiring and extolling all God's attributes, either as deriving loveliness from his holiness, or as being a part of it. Thus when they praise God for his power, his holiness is the beauty that engages them: "O sing unto the Lord a new song, for he hath done marvellous things; his right hand and his holy arm hath gotten him the victory" (Ps. 98:1). So when they praise him for his justice and terrible majesty; "The Lord is great in Zion, and he is high above all people: let them praise thy great and terrible name, for it is holy" (Ps. 99:2–3). "Exalt ye the Lord our God, and worship at his footstool, for he is holy" (ver. 5). "Thou wast a God that forgavest them, though thou tookest vengeance of their inventions. Exalt ye the Lord our God, and worship at his holy hill; for the Lord our God is holy" (verses 8–9). So when they praise God for his mercy and faithfulness; "Light is sown for the righteous, and gladness for the upright in heart. Rejoice in the Lord ye righteous, and give thanks at the remembrance of his holiness" (Ps. 97:11–12). "There is none holy as the Lord; for there is none beside thee; neither is there any rock like our God" (I Sam. 2:2).

By this therefore all may try their affections, and particularly their love and joy. Various kinds of creatures show the difference of their natures, very much, in the different things they relish as their proper good, one delighting in that which another abhors. Such a difference is there between true saints, and natural men: natural men have no sense of the goodness and excellency of holy things; at least for their holiness; they have no taste of that kind of good; and so may be said not to know that divine good, or not to see it; it is wholly hid from them: but the saints, by the mighty power of God, have it discovered to them: they have that supernatural, most noble and divine sense given them, by which they perceive it: and it is this that captivates their hearts, and delights them above all things; 'tis the most amiable and sweet thing to the heart of a true saint, that is to be found in heaven or earth; that which above all others attracts and engages his soul; and that wherein, above all things, he places his happiness, and which he lots upon for solace and entertainment to his mind, in this world, and full satisfaction and blessedness in another. By this you may examine your love to God, and to Jesus Christ, and to the Word of God, and your joy in them, and also your love to the people of God, and your desires after heaven; whether they be from a supreme delight in this sort of beauty, without being primarily moved from your imagined interest in them, or expectations from 'em. There are many high affections, great seeming love and rapturous joys, which have nothing of this holy relish belonging to 'em.

Particularly, by what has been said you may try your discoveries of the glory of God's grace and love, and your affections arising from them. The grace of God may appear lovely two ways; either as *bonum utile,* a profitable good to me, that which greatly serves my interest, and so suits my self-love; or as *bonum formosum,* a beautiful good in itself, and part of the moral and spiritual excellency of the divine nature. In this latter respect it is that the true saints have their hearts affected, and love captivated by the free grace of God in the first place.

From the things that have been said, it appears, that if persons have a great sense of the natural perfections of God, and are greatly affected with them, or have any other sight or sense of God, than that which consists in, or implies a sense of the beauty of his moral perfections, it is no certain sign of grace: as particularly, men's having a great sense of the awful greatness, and terrible majesty of God; for this is only God's natural perfection, and what men may see, and yet be entirely blind to the beauty of his moral perfection, and have nothing of that spiritual taste which relishes this divine sweetness.

It has been shown already, in what was said upon the first distinguishing mark of gracious affections, that that which is spiritual, is entirely different in its nature, from all that it is possible any graceless person should be the subject of, while he continues graceless. But 'tis possible that those who are wholly without grace, should have a clear sight, and very great and affecting sense of God's greatness, his mighty power, and awful majesty; for this is what the devils have, though they have lost the spiritual knowledge of God, consisting in a sense of the amiableness of his moral perfections; they are perfectly destitute of any sense or relish of that kind of beauty, yet they have a very great knowledge of the natural glory of God (if I may so speak) or his awful greatness and majesty; this they behold, and are affected with the apprehension of, and therefore tremble before him. This glory of God all shall behold at the Day of Judgment; God will make all rational beings to behold it to a great degree indeed, angels and devils, saints and sinners: he will manifest his infinite greatness, and awful majesty to every one, in a most open, clear and convincing manner, and in a light that none can resist, when he shall come in the glory of his Father, and every eye shall see him; when they shall cry to the mountains to fall upon them, to hide them from the face of him that sits upon the throne, they are represented as seeing the glory of God's majesty (Is. 2:10, 19, 21). God will make all his enemies to behold this, and to live in a most clear and affecting view of it, in hell, to all eternity. God hath often declared his immutable purpose to make all his enemies to know him in this respect, in so often annexing these words to the threatenings he denounces against them, and they shall know that I am the Lord; yea, he hath sworn that all men shall see his glory in this respect; "As truly as I live, all the earth shall be filled with the glory of the Lord" (Num. 14:21). And this kind of manifestation of God is very often spoken of in Scripture, as made, or to be made, in the sight of God's enemies in this world (Ex. 9:16 and ch. 14:18 and 15:16; Ps. 66:3 and 46:10); and other places innumerable. This was a manifestation which God made of himself in the sight of that wicked congregation at Mount Sinai; deeply affecting them with it; so that all the people in the camp trembled. Wicked men and devils will see, and have a great sense of every thing that appertains to the glory of God, but only the beauty of his moral perfection. They will see his infinite greatness and majesty, his infinite power, and will be fully convinced of his omniscience, and his eternity and immutability; and they will see and know everything appertaining to his moral attributes themselves, but only the beauty and amiableness of them: they will see and know that he is perfectly just and righteous and true; and that he is a holy God, of purer eyes than to behold evil, who cannot look on iniquity, and they will see the wonderful manifestations of his infinite goodness and free grace to the saints; and there is nothing will be hid from their eyes, but only the beauty of these moral attributes, and that beauty of the other attributes, which arises from it. And so natural men in this world are capable of having a very affecting sense of everything else that appertains to God, but this only. Nebuchadnezzar had a great and very affecting sense of the infinite greatness and awful majesty of God, of his supreme and absolute dominion, and mighty and irresistible power, and of his sovereignty, and that he, and all the inhabitants of the earth were nothing before him; and also had a great conviction in his conscience of his justice, and an affecting sense of his great goodness (Dan. 4:1–3, 34–35, 37). And the sense that Darius had of God's perfections, seems to be very much like his (Dan. 6:25, etc.). But the saints and angels do behold the glory of God consisting in the beauty of his holiness: and 'tis this sight only, that will melt and humble the hearts of men, and wean them from the world, and draw them to God, and effectually change them. A sight of the awful greatness of God, may overpower men's strength, and be more than they can endure; but if the moral beauty of God be hid, the enmity of the heart will remain in its full strength, no love will be enkindled, all will not be effectual to gain the will, but that will remain inflexible; whereas the first glimpse of the moral and spiritual glory of God shining into the heart, produces all these effects, as it were with omnipotent power, which nothing can withstand.

The sense that natural men may have of the awful greatness of God may affect them various ways; it may not only terrify them, but it may elevate them, and raise their joy and praise, as their circumstances may be. This will be the natural effect of it, under the real or supposed receipt of some extraordinary mercy from God, by the influence of mere principles of nature. It has been shown already, that the receipt of kindness may, by the influence of natural principles, affect the heart with gratitude and praise to God; but if a person, at the same time that he receives remarkable kindness from God, has a sense of his infinite greatness, and that he is but nothing in comparison of him, surely this will naturally raise his gratitude and praise the higher, for kindness to one so much inferior. A sense of God's greatness had this effect upon Nebuchadnezzar, under the receipt of that extraordinary favor of his restoration, after he had been driven from men, and had his dwelling with the beasts: a sense of God's exceeding greatness raises his gratitude very high; so that he does, in the most lofty terms, extol and magnify God, and calls upon all the world to do it with him: and much more, if a natural man, at the same time that he is greatly affected with God's infinite greatness and majesty, entertains a strong conceit that this great God has made him his child and special favorite, and promised him eternal glory in his highest love; will this have a tendency, according to the course of nature, to raise his joy and praise to a great height.

Therefore, 'tis beyond doubt, that too much weight has been laid, by many persons of late, on discoveries of God's greatness, awful majesty, and natural perfection, operating after this manner, without any real view of the holy, lovely majesty of God. And experience does abundantly witness to what reason and Scripture declare as to this matter; there having been very many persons, who have seemed to be overpowered with the greatness and awful majesty of God, and consequentially elevated in the manner that has been spoken of, who have been very far from having appearances of a Christian spirit and temper, in any manner of proportion, or fruits in practice in any wise agreeable; but their discoveries have worked in a way contrary to the operation of truly spiritual discoveries.

Not that a sense of God's greatness and natural attributes is not exceeding useful and necessary. For, as I observed before, this is implied in a manifestation of the beauty of God's holiness. Though that be something beyond it, it supposes it, as the greater supposes the less. And though natural men may have a sense of the natural perfections of God; yet undoubtedly this is more frequent and common with the saints, than with natural men; and grace tends to enable men to see these things in a better manner, than natural men do. And not only enables them to see God's natural attributes, but that beauty of those attributes, which (according to our way of conceiving of God) is derived from his holiness.

IV. Gracious affections do arise from the mind's being enlightened, rightly and spiritually to understand or apprehend divine things.

Holy affections are not heat without light; but evermore arise from some information of the understanding, some spiritual instruction that the mind receives, some light or actual knowledge. The child of God is graciously affected, because he sees and understands something more of divine things than he did before, more of God or Christ and of the glorious things exhibited in the gospel; he has some clearer and better view than he had before, when he was not affected: either he receives some understanding of divine things that is new to him; or has his former knowledge renewed after the view was decayed; "Everyone that loveth . . . knoweth God" (I John 4:7). "I pray that your love may abound more and more, in knowledge and in all judgment" (I Phil. 1:9). "They have a zeal of God, but not according to knowledge" (Rom. 10:2). "The new man, which is renewed in knowledge" (Col. 3:10). "O send out thy light and thy truth; let them lead me, let them bring me into thy holy hill" (Ps.43:3–4). "It is written in the prophets, and they shall be all taught of God: every man therefore that hath heard and hath learned of the Father, cometh unto me" (John 6:45). Knowledge is the key that first opens the hard heart and enlarges the affections, and so opens the way for men into the kingdom of heaven; "Ye have taken away the key of knowledge" (Luke 11:52).

Now there are many affections which don't arise from any light in the understanding. And when it is thus, it is a sure evidence that these affections are not spiritual, let them be ever so high.[9] Indeed they have some new apprehensions which they had not before. Such is the nature of man, that it is impossible his mind should be affected, unless it be by something that he apprehends, or that his mind conceives of. But in many persons those apprehensions or conceptions that they have, wherewith they are affected, have nothing of the nature of knowledge or instruction in them. As for instance; when a person is affected with a lively idea, suddenly excited in his mind, of some shape, or very beautiful pleasant form of countenance, or some shining light, or other glorious outward appearance: here is something apprehended or conceived by the mind; but there is nothing of the nature of instruction in it: persons become never the wiser by such things, or more knowing about God, or a mediator between God and man, or the way of salvation by Christ, or anything contained in any of the doctrines of the gospel. Persons by these external ideas have no further acquaintance with God, as to any of the attributes or perfections of his nature; nor have they any further understanding of his word, or any of his ways or works. Truly spiritual and gracious affections are not raised after this manner: these arise from the enlightening of the under-

9. "Many that have had mighty strong affections at first conversion, afterwards become dry, and wither, and consume, and pine, and die away: and now their hypocrisy is manifest; if not to all the world, by open profaneness; yet to the discerning eye of living Christians, by a formal, barren, unsavory, unfruitful heart and course; because they never had light to conviction enough as yet. . . . 'Tis strange to see some people carried with mighty affection against sin and hell, and after Christ. And what is the hell you fear? A dreadful place. What is Christ? They scarce know so much as devils do; but that is all. Oh trust them not! Many have, and these will fall away to some lust, or opinion, or pride, or world; and the reason is, they never had light enough, John 5:35. John was a burning and shining light, and they did joy in him for a season; yet glorious as it was, they saw not Christ by it, especially not with divine light. It's rare to see Christians full both of light and affection. And therefore consider of this; many a man has been well brought up, and is of a sweet loving nature, mild and gentle, and harmless, likes and loves the best things, and his meaning, and mind, and heart is good, and has more in heart than in shew; and so hopes all shall go well with him. I say there may lie greatest hypocrisy under greatest affections; especially if they want light. You shall be hardened in your hypocrisy by them. I never liked violent affections and pangs, but only such as were dropped in by light; because those come from an external principle, and last not, but these do. Men are not affrighted by the light of the sun, though clearer than the lightning." Shepard, *Parable*, Pt. I, p. 146.

standing to understand the things that are taught of God and Christ, in a new manner, the coming to a new understanding of the excellent nature of God, and his wonderful perfections, some new view of Christ in his spiritual excellencies and fullness, or things opened to him in a new manner, that appertain to the way of salvation by Christ, whereby he now sees how it is, and understands those divine and spiritual doctrines which once were foolishness to him. Such enlightenings of the understanding as these, are things entirely different in their nature, from strong ideas of shapes and colors, and outward brightness and glory, or sounds and voices. That all gracious affections do arise from some instruction or enlightening of the understanding, is therefore a further proof, that affections which arise from such impression on the imagination, are not gracious affections, besides the things observed before, which make this evident.

Hence also it appears, that affections arising from texts of Scripture coming to the mind are vain, when no instruction received in the understanding from those texts, or anything taught in those texts, is the ground of the affection, but the manner of their coming to the mind. When Christ makes the Scripture a means of the heart's burning with gracious affection, 'tis by opening the Scriptures to their understandings; "Did not our heart burn within us, while he talked with us by the way, and while he opened to us the Scriptures?" (Luke 24:32). It appears also that the affection which is occasioned by the coming of a text of Scripture must be vain, when the affection is founded on something that is supposed to be taught by it, which really is not contained in it, nor in any other Scripture; because such supposed instruction is not real instruction, but a mistake, and misapprehension of the mind. As for instance, when persons suppose that they are expressly taught by some Scripture coming to their minds, that they in particular are beloved of God, or that their sins are forgiven, that God is their Father, and the like: this is a mistake or misapprehension; for the Scripture nowhere reveals the individual persons who are beloved, expressly; but only by consequence, by revealing the qualifications of persons that are beloved of God: and therefore this matter is not to be learned from Scripture any other way than by consequence, and from these qualifications: for things be not to be learned from the Scripture any other way than they are taught in the Scripture.

Affections really arise from ignorance, rather than instruction, in these instances which have been mentioned; as likewise in some others that might be mentioned. As some when they find themselves free of speech in prayer, they call it God's being with them; and this affects them more; and so their affections are set agoing and increased: when they look not into the cause of this freedom of speech; which may arise many other ways besides God's spiritual presence. So some are much affected with some apt thoughts that come into their minds about the Scripture, and call it the Spirit of God teaching them. So they ascribe many of the workings of their own minds, which they have a high opinion of, and are pleased and taken with, to the special immediate influences of God's Spirit; and so are mightily affected with their privilege. And there are some instances of persons, in whom it seems manifest that the first ground of their affection is some bodily sensation. The animal spirits, by some cause (and probably sometimes by the devil), are suddenly and unaccountably put into a very agreeable motion, causing persons to feel pleasantly in their bodies; the animal spirits are put into such a motion as is wont to be connected with the exhilaration of the mind; and the soul, by the laws of the union of soul and body, hence feels pleasure. The motion of the animal spirits don't first arise from any affection or apprehension of the mind whatsoever; but the very first thing that is felt, is an exhilaration of the animal spirits, and a pleasant external sensation, it may be in their breasts. Hence, through ignorance, the person being surprised, begins to think, surely this is the Holy Ghost coming into him. And then the mind begins to be affected and raised: there is first great joy; and then many other affections, in a very tumultuous manner, putting all nature, both body and mind, into a mighty ruffle. For though, as I observed before, 'tis the soul only that is the seat of the affections; yet this hinders not but that bodily sensations, may in this manner, be an occasion of affections in the mind.

And if men's religious affections do truly arise from some instruction or light in the understanding; yet the affection is not gracious, unless the light which is the ground of it be spiritual. Affections may be excited by that understanding of things, which they obtain merely by human teaching, with the common improvement of the faculties of the mind. Men may be much affected by knowledge of things of religion that they obtain this way; as some philosophers have been mightily affected, and almost carried beyond themselves, by the discoveries they have made in mathematics and natural philosophy. So men may be much affected from common illuminations of the Spirit of God, in which God assists men's faculties to a greater degree of that kind of understanding of religious matters, which they have in some degree, by only the ordinary exercise and improvement of their own faculties. Such illuminations may much affect the mind; as in many whom we read of in Scripture, that were once enlightened: but these affections are not spiritual.

There is such a thing, if the Scriptures are of any use to teach us anything, as a spiritual, supernatural understanding of divine things, that is peculiar to the saints, and which those who are not saints have nothing of. 'Tis certainly a kind of understanding, apprehending or discerning of divine things, that natural men have nothing of, which the Apostle speaks of, "But the natural man receiveth not the things of the Spirit of God; for they are foolishness unto him; neither can he know them, because they are spiritually discerned" (I Cor. 2:14). 'Tis certainly a kind of seeing or discerning spiritual things, peculiar to the saints, which is spoken of, "Whosoever sinneth hath not seen him, neither known him" (I John 3:6). "He that doeth evil hath not seen God" (III John 11). And "This is the will of him that sent me, that every one that seeth the Son, and believeth on him, may have everlasting life" (John 6:40). "The world seeth me no more; but ye see me" (ch. 14:19). "This is eternal life, that they might know thee the only true God, and Jesus Christ whom thou hast sent" (ch. 17:3). "No man knoweth the Son, but the Father; neither knoweth any man the Father, but the Son, and he to whomsoever the Son will reveal him" (Matt. 11:27). "He that seeth me, seeth him that sent me" (John 12:45). "They that know thy name, will put their trust in thee" (Ps. 9:10). "I count all things but loss, for the excellency of the knowledge of Christ Jesus my Lord" (Phil. 3:8). "That I may know him" (ver. 10). And innumerable other places there are, all over the Bible, which show the same. And that there is such a thing as an understanding of divine things, which in its nature and kind is wholly different from all knowledge that natural men have, is evident from this, that there is an understanding of divine things, which the Scripture calls spiritual understanding; "We do not cease to pray for you, and to desire that you may be filled with the knowledge of his will, in all wisdom, and spiritual understanding" (Col. 1:9). It has been already shown, that that which is spiritual, in the ordinary use of the word in the New Testament, is entirely different in nature and kind, from all which natural men are, or can be the subjects of.

From hence it may be surely inferred, wherein spiritual understanding consists. For if there be in the saints a kind of apprehension or perception, which is in its nature, perfectly diverse from all that natural men have, or that it is possible they should have, till they have a new nature; it must consist in their having a certain kind of ideas or sensations of mind, which are simply diverse from all that is or can be in the minds of natural men. And that is the same thing as to say, that it consists in the sensations of a new spiritual sense, which the souls of natural men have not; as is evident by what has been before, once and again observed. But I have already shown what that new spiritual sense is, which the saints have given them in regeneration, and what is the object of it. I have shown that the immediate object of it is the supreme beauty and excellency of the nature of divine things, as they are in themselves. And this is agreeable to the Scripture: the Apostle very plainly teaches that the great thing discovered by spiritual light, and understood by spiritual knowledge, is the glory of divine things, "But if our gospel be hid, it is hid to them that are lost; in whom the God of this world hath blinded the minds of them that believe not, lest the light of the glorious gospel of Christ, who is the image of God, should shine unto them" (II Cor. 4:3–4), together with: "For God who commanded the light to shine out of darkness, hath shined in our hearts, to give the light of the knowledge of the glory of God in the face of Jesus Christ" (ver. 6): and ch. 3:18 preceding: "But we all, with open face, beholding as in a glass, the glory of the Lord, are changed into the same image, from glory to glory, even as by the Spirit of the Lord." And it must needs be so, for as has been before observed, the Scripture often teaches that all true religion summarily consists in the love of divine things. And therefore that kind of understanding or knowledge, which is the proper foundation of true religion, must be the knowledge of the loveliness of divine things. For doubtless, that knowledge which is the proper foundation of love, is the knowledge of loveliness. What that beauty or loveliness of divine things is, which is the proper and immediate object of a spiritual sense of mind, was showed under the last head insisted on, viz. that it is the beauty of their moral perfection. Therefore it is in the view or sense of this, that Spiritual understanding does more immediately and primarily consist. And indeed it is plain it can be nothing else; for (as has been shown) there is nothing pertaining to divine things besides the beauty of their moral excellency, and those properties and qualities of divine things which this beauty is the foundation of, but what natural men and devils can see and know, and will know fully and clearly to all eternity.

From what has been said, therefore, we come necessarily to this conclusion, concerning that wherein spiritual understanding consists; viz. that it consists in a sense of the heart, of the supreme beauty and sweetness of the holiness or moral perfection of divine things, together with all that discerning and knowledge of things of religion, that depends upon, and flows from such a sense.

Spiritual understanding consists primarily in a sense of heart of that spiritual beauty. I say, a sense of heart; for it is not speculation merely that is concerned in this kind of understanding: nor can there be a clear distinction made between the two faculties of understanding and will, as acting distinctly and separately, in this matter. When the mind is sensible of the sweet beauty and amiableness of a thing, that implies a sensibleness of sweetness and delight in the presence of the idea of it: and this sensibleness of the amiableness or delightfulness of beauty, carries in the very nature of it, the sense of the heart; or an effect and impression the soul is the subject of, as a substance possessed of taste, inclination and will.

There is a distinction to be made between a mere notional understanding, wherein the mind only beholds things in the exercise of a speculative faculty; and the sense of the heart, wherein the mind don't only speculate and behold, but relishes and feels. That sort of knowledge, by which a man has a sensible perception of amiableness and loathsomeness, or of sweetness and nauseousness, is not just the same sort of knowledge with that, by which he knows what a triangle is, and what a square is. The one is mere speculative knowledge; the other sensible knowledge, in which more than the mere intellect is concerned; the heart is the proper subject of it, or the soul as a being that not only beholds, but has inclination, and is pleased or displeased. And yet there is the nature of instruction in it; as he that has perceived the sweet taste of honey, knows much more about it, than he who has only looked upon and felt of it.

The Apostle seems to make a distinction between mere speculative knowledge of the things of religion, and spiritual knowledge, in calling that the form of knowledge, and of the truth; "which has the form of knowledge, and of the truth in the law" (Rom. 2:20). The latter is often represented by relishing, smelling, or tasting; "Now thanks be to God, which always causeth us to triumph in Christ Jesus, and maketh manifest the savor of his knowledge, in every place" (II Cor. 2:14). "Thou savorest not the things that be of God, but those things that be of man" (Matt. 16:23). "As newborn babes, desire the sincere milk of the word, that ye may grow thereby; if so be ye have tasted that the Lord is gracious" (I Pet. 2:2–3). "Because of the savor of thy good ointment, thy name is as ointment poured forth; therefore do the virgins love thee" (Cant. 1:3); compared with: "But ye have an unction from the holy One, and ye know all things" (I John 2:20).

Spiritual understanding primarily consists in this sense, or taste of the moral beauty of divine things; so that no knowledge can be called spiritual, any further than it arises from this, and has this in it. But secondarily, it includes all that discerning and knowledge of things of religion, which depends upon, and flows from such a sense.

When the true beauty and amiableness of the holiness or true moral good that is in divine things, is discovered to the soul, it as it were opens a new world to its view. This shows the glory of all the perfections of God, and of everything appertaining to the divine being: for, as was observed before, the beauty of all arises from God's moral perfection. This shows the glory of all God's works, both of creation and providence: for 'tis the special glory of them, that God's holiness, righteousness, faithfulness and goodness are so manifested in them; and without these moral perfections, there would be no glory in that power and skill with which they are wrought. The glorifying of God's moral perfections, is the special end of all the works of God's hands. By this sense of the moral beauty of divine things, is understood the sufficiency of Christ as a mediator: for 'tis only by the discovery of the beauty of the moral perfection of Christ, that the believer is let into the knowledge of the excellency of his person, so as to know anything more of it than the devils do: and 'tis only by the knowledge of the excellency of Christ's person, that any know his sufficiency as a mediator; for the latter depends upon, and arises from the former. 'Tis by seeing the excellency of Christ's person, that the saints are made sensible of the preciousness of his blood, and its sufficiency to atone for sin: for therein consists the preciousness of Christ's blood, that 'tis the blood of so excellent and amiable a person. And on this depends the meritoriousness of his obedience, and sufficiency and prevalence of his intercession. By this sight of the moral beauty of divine things, is seen the beauty of the way of salvation by Christ: for that consists in the beauty of the moral perfections of God, which wonderfully shines forth in every step of this method of salvation, from beginning to end. By this is seen the fitness and suitableness of this way: for this wholly consists in its tendency to deliver us from sin and hell, and to bring us to the happiness which consists in the possession and enjoyment of moral good, in a way sweetly agreeing with God's moral perfections. And in the way's being contrived so as to attain these ends, consists the excellent wisdom of that way. By this is seen the excellency of the Word of God: take away all the moral beauty and sweetness in the Word, and the Bible is left wholly a dead letter, a dry, lifeless, tasteless thing. By this is seen the true foundation of our duty; the worthiness of God to be so esteemed, honored, loved, submitted to, and served, as he requires of us, and the amiableness of the duties themselves that are required of us. And by this is seen the true evil of sin: for he who sees the beauty of holiness, must necessarily see the hatefulness of sin, its contrary. By this men understand the true glory of heaven, which consists in the beauty and happiness that is in holiness. By this is seen the amiableness and happiness of both saints and angels. He that sees the beauty of holiness, or true moral good, sees the greatest and most important thing in the world, which is the fullness of all things, without which all the world is empty, no better than nothing, yea, worse than nothing. Unless this is seen, nothing is seen, that is worth the seeing: for there is no other true excellency or beauty. Unless this be understood, nothing is understood, that is worthy of the exercise of the noble faculty of understanding. This is the beauty of the Godhead, and the divinity of Divinity (if I may so speak), the good of the infinite Fountain of Good; without which God himself (if that were possible to be) would be an infinite evil: without which, we ourselves had better never have been; and without which there had better have been no being. He therefore in effect knows nothing, that knows not this: his knowledge is but the shadow of knowledge, or the form of knowledge, as the Apostle calls it. Well therefore may the Scripture represent those who are destitute of that spiritual sense, by which is perceived the beauty of holiness, as totally blind, deaf and senseless, yea dead. And well may regeneration, in which this divine sense is given to the soul by its Creator, be represented as opening the blind eyes, and raising the dead, and bringing a person into a new world. For if what has been said be considered, it will be manifest, that when a person has this sense and knowledge given him, he will view nothing as he did before; though before he knew all things after the flesh, yet henceforth he will know them so no more; and he is become "a new creature, old things are passed away, behold all things are become new"; agreeable to II Cor. 5:16–17.

And besides the things that have been already mentioned, there arises from this sense of spiritual beauty, all true experimental knowledge of religion; which is of itself, as it were a new world of knowledge. He that sees not the beauty of holiness, knows not what one of the graces of God's Spirit is; he is destitute of any idea or conception of all gracious exercises of soul, and all holy comforts and delights, and all effects of the saving influences of the Spirit of God on the heart: and so is ignorant of the greatest works of God, the most important and glorious effects of his power upon the creature: and also is wholly ignorant of the saints as saints; he knows not what they are: and in effect is ignorant of the whole spiritual world.

Things being thus, it plainly appears, that God's implanting that spiritual supernatural sense which has been spoken of, makes a great change in a man. And were it not for the very imperfect degree, in which this sense is commonly given at first, or the small degree of this glorious light that first dawns upon the soul; the change made by this spiritual opening of the eyes in conversion, would be much greater, and more remarkable, every way, than if a man, who had been born blind, and with only the other four senses, should continue so for a long time, and then at once should have the sense of seeing imparted to him, in the midst of the clear light of the sun, discovering a world of visible objects. For though sight be more noble than any of the other external senses; yet this spiritual sense which has been spoken of, is infinitely more noble than that, or any other principle of discerning that a man naturally has, and the object of this sense infinitely greater and more important.

This sort of understanding or knowledge is that knowledge of divine things from whence all truly gracious affections do proceed: by which therefore all affections are to be tried. Those affections that arise wholly from any other kind of knowledge, or do result from any other kind of apprehensions of mind, are vain.[1]

1. "Take heed of contenting yourselves with every kind of knowledge. Do not worship every image of your own heads; especially you that fall short of truth, or the knowledge of it. For when you have some, there may be yet that wanting,

From what has been said may be learned wherein the most essential difference lies between that light or understanding which is given by the common influences of the Spirit of God, on the hearts of natural men, and that saving instruction which is given to the saints. The latter primarily and most essentially lies in beholding the holy beauty that is in divine things; which is the only true moral good, and which the soul of fallen man is by nature totally blind to. The former consists only in a further understanding, through the assistance of natural principles, of those things which men may know, in some measure, by the alone ordinary exercise of their faculties. And this knowledge consists only in the knowledge of those things pertaining to religion, which are natural. Thus for instance, in those awakenings and convictions of conscience, that natural men are often subject to, the Spirit of God gives no knowledge of the true moral beauty which is in divine things; but only assists the mind to a clearer idea of the guilt of sin, or its relation to a punishment, and connection with the evil of suffering (without any sight of its true moral evil, or odiousness as sin) and a clearer idea of the natural perfections of God, wherein consists, not his holy beauty and glory, but his awful and terrible greatness. 'Tis a clear sight of this, that will fully awaken the consciences of wicked men at the Day of Judgment, without any spiritual light. And 'tis a lesser degree of the same, that awakens the consciences of natural

which may make you sincere. There are many men of great knowledge, able to teach themselves, and others too; and yet their hearts are unsound. How comes this to pass? Is it because they have so much light? No; but because they want much. And therefore content not yourselves with every knowledge. There is some knowledge which men have by the light of nature (which leaves them without excuse), from the book of creation; some by power of education; some by the light of the law, whereby men know their sin and evils; some by the letter of the gospel; and so men may know much, and speak well; and so in seeing, see not; some by the Spirit, and may see much, so as to prophesy in Christ's name, and yet bid depart; Matt. 7. Now there is a light of glory, whereby the elect see things in another manner: to tell you how, they cannot: it's the beginning of light in heaven: and the same Spirit that fills Christ, filling their minds, that they know, by this anointing, all things: which if ever you have, you must become babes and fools in your own eyes. God will never write his law in your minds, till all the scribblings of it are blotted out. Account all your knowledge loss for the gaining of this. 'Tis sad to see many a man pleasing himself in his own dreaming delusions; yet the poor creature in seeing, sees not; which is God's heavy curse upon men under greatest means, and which lays all waste and desolate." Shepard, *Parable,* Pt. I, p. 147.

men, without spiritual light, in this world. The same discoveries are in some measure given in the conscience of an awakened sinner in this world, which will be given more fully in the consciences of sinners at the Day of Judgment. The same kind of sight or apprehension of God, in a lesser degree, makes awakened sinners in this world, sensible of the dreadful guilt of sin, against so great and terrible a God, and sensible of its amazing punishment, and fills 'em with fearful apprehensions of divine wrath; that will thoroughly convince all wicked men, of the infinitely dreadful nature and guilt of sin, and astonish 'em with apprehensions of wrath, when Christ shall come in the glory of his power and majesty, and every eye shall see him, and all the kindreds of the earth shall wail because of him. And in those common illuminations, which are sometimes given to natural men, exciting in them some kind of religious desire, love and joy, the mind is only assisted to a clearer apprehension of the natural good that is in divine things. Thus sometimes, under common illuminations, men are raised with the ideas of the natural good that is in heaven; as its outward glory, its ease, its honor and advancement, a being there the objects of the high favor of God, and the great respect of men and angels, etc. So there are many things exhibited in the gospel, concerning God and Christ, and the way of salvation, that have a natural good in them, which suits the natural principle of self-love. Thus in that great goodness of God to sinners, and the wonderful dying love of Christ, there is a natural good, which all men love, as they love themselves; as well as a spiritual and holy beauty, which is seen only by the regenerate. Therefore there are many things appertaining to the Word of God's grace delivered in the gospel, which may cause natural men, when they hear it, anon with joy to receive it. All that love which natural men have to God, and Christ, and Christian virtues, and good men, is not from any sight of the amiableness of the holiness, or true moral excellency of these things; but only for the sake of the natural good there is in them. All natural men's hatred of sin, is as much from principles of nature, as men's hatred of a tiger for his rapaciousness, or their aversion to a serpent for his poison and hurtfulness: and all their love of Christian virtue, is from no higher principle than their love of a man's good nature, which appears amiable to natural men; but no otherwise than silver and gold appears amiable in the eyes of a merchant, or than the blackness of the soil is beautiful in the eyes of the farmer.

From what has been said of the nature of spiritual understanding, it appears that spiritual understanding does not consist in any new doctrinal knowledge, or in having suggested to the mind any new proposition, not before read or heard of: for 'tis plain that this suggesting of new propositions, is a thing entirely diverse from giving the mind a new taste or relish of beauty and sweetness.[2] 'Tis also evident that spiritual knowledge does not consist in any new doctrinal explanation of any part of the Scripture; for still, this is but doctrinal knowledge, or the knowledge of propositions; the doctrinal explaining of any part of Scripture, is only giving us to understand, what are the propositions contained or taught in that part of Scripture.

Hence it appears, that the spiritual understanding of the Scripture, don't consist in opening to the mind the mystical meaning of the Scripture, in its parables, types and allegories; for this is only a doctrinal explication of the Scripture. He that explains what is meant by the stony ground, and the seed's springing up suddenly, and quickly withering away, only explains what propositions or doctrines are taught in it. So he that explains what is typified by Jacob's ladder, and the angels of God ascending and descending on it, or what was typified by Joshua's leading Israel through Jordan, only shows what propositions are hid in these passages. And many men can explain these types, who have no spiritual knowledge. 'Tis possible that a man might know how to interpret all the types, parables, enigmas, and allegories in the Bible, and not have one beam of spiritual light in his mind; because he mayn't have the least degree of that spiritual sense of the holy beauty of divine things which has been spoken of, and may see nothing of this kind of glory in anything contained in any of these mysteries, or any other part of the Scripture. 'Tis plain, by what the Apostle says, that a man might understand all such mysteries, and have no saving grace; "And though I have the gift of prophecy, and understand all mysteries,

2. Calvin, in his *Institutes of the Christian Religion,* Bk. I, ch. 9, no. 1, says: "It is not the office of the Spirit that is promised us, to make new and before unheard of revelations, or to coin some new kind of doctrine, which tends to draw us away from the received doctrine of the gospel; but to seal and confirm to us that very doctrine which is by the gospel." And in the same place he speaks of some, that in those days maintained the contrary notion, pretending to be immediately led by the Spirit, as persons that were governed by a most haughty self-conceit; and not so properly to be looked upon as only laboring under a mistake, as driven by a sort of raving madness. [See above, pp. 64–5.]

and all knowledge, and have not charity, it profiteth me nothing" (I Cor. 13:2). They therefore are very foolish who are exalted in an opinion of their own spiritual attainments, from notions that come into their minds, of the mystical meaning of these and those passages of Scripture, as though it was a spiritual understanding of these passages, immediately given 'em by the Spirit of God, and hence have their affections highly raised: and what has been said shows the vanity of such affections.

From what has been said, it is also evident, that it is not spiritual knowledge, for persons to be informed of their duty, by having it immediately suggested to their minds, that such and such outward actions or deeds are the will of God. If we suppose that it is truly God's manner thus to signify his will to his people, by immediate inward suggestions, such suggestions have nothing of the nature of spiritual light. Such kind of knowledge would only be one kind of doctrinal knowledge; a proposition concerning the will of God, is as properly a doctrine of religion, as a proposition concerning the nature of God, or a work of God: and an having either of these kinds of propositions, or any other proposition, declared to a man, either by speech, or inward suggestion, differs vastly from an having the holy beauty of divine things manifested to the soul, wherein spiritual knowledge does most essentially consist. Thus there was no spiritual light in Balaam; though he had the will of God immediately suggested to him by the Spirit of God from time to time, concerning the way that he should go, and what he should do and say.

'Tis manifest therefore, that a being led and directed in this manner, is not that holy and spiritual leading of the Spirit of God, which is peculiar to the saints, and a distinguishing mark of the sons of God, spoken of Rom. 8:14: "For as many as are led by the Spirit of God, are the sons of God." "But if ye be led by the Spirit, ye are not under the law" (Gal. 5:18).

And if persons have the will of God concerning their actions, suggested to them by some text of Scripture, suddenly and extraordinarily brought to their minds, which text, as the words lay in the Bible before they came to their minds, related to the action and behavior of some other person, but they suppose, as God sent the words to them, he intended something further by them, and meant such a particular action of theirs; I say, if persons should have the will of God thus suggested to 'em with texts of Scripture, it alters not the case. The suggestion being accompanied with an apt text of

Scripture, don't make the suggestion to be of the nature of spiritual instruction. As for instance, if a person in New England, on some occasion, were at a loss whether it was his duty to go into some popish or heathenish land, where he was like to be exposed to many difficulties and dangers, and should pray to God that he would show him the way of his duty; and after earnest prayer, should have those words which God spake to Jacob, Gen. 46, suddenly and extraordinarily brought to his mind, as if they were spoken to him; "Fear not to go down into Egypt . . . and I will go with thee; and I will surely bring thee up again." In which words, though as they lay in the Bible before they came to his mind, they related only to Jacob, and his behavior; yet he supposes that God has a further meaning, as they were brought and applied to him; that thus they are to be understood in a new sense, that by Egypt is to be understood this particular country he has in his mind, and that the action intended is his going thither, and that the meaning of the promise is that God would bring him back into New England again. There is nothing of the nature of a spiritual or gracious leading of the Spirit in this; for there is nothing of the nature of spiritual understanding in it. Thus to understand texts of Scripture, is not to have a spiritual understanding of them. Spiritually to understand the Scripture, is rightly to understand what *is in* the Scripture, and what *was in* it before it was understood: 'tis to understand rightly, what used to be contained in the meaning of it; and not the making a new meaning. When the mind is enlightened spiritually and rightly to understand the Scripture, it is enabled to see that in the Scripture, which before was not seen, by reason of blindness. But if it was by reason of blindness; that is an evidence that the same meaning was in it before; otherwise it would have been no blindness not to see it: 'tis no blindness not to see a meaning which is not there. Spiritually enlightening the eyes to understand the Scripture, is to open the eyes, "Open thou mine eyes, that I may behold wondrous things out of thy law" (Ps. 119:18); which argues that the reason why the same was not seen in the Scripture before, was that the eyes were shut; which would not be the case, if the meaning that is now understood was not there before, but is now newly added to the Scripture, by the manner of the Scripture's coming to my mind. This making a new meaning to the Scripture, is the same thing as making a new Scripture: it is properly adding to the Word; which is threatened with so dreadful a curse. Spiritually to understand the Scripture, is to have the eyes of the mind opened, to behold the wonderful spiritual excellency of the glorious things contained in the true meaning of it, and that always were contained in it, ever since it was written; to behold the amiable and bright manifestations of the divine perfections, and of the excellency and sufficiency of Christ, and the excellency and suitableness of the way of salvation by Christ, and the spiritual glory of the precepts and promises of the Scripture, etc. Which things are, and always were in the Bible, and would have been seen before, if it had not been for blindness, without having any new sense added by the words being sent by God to a particular person, and spoken anew to him, with a new meaning.

And as to a gracious leading of the Spirit, it consists in two things; partly in *instructing* a person in his duty by the Spirit, and partly in powerfully *inducing* him to comply with that instruction. But so far as the gracious leading of the Spirit lies in instruction, it consists in a person's being guided by a spiritual and distinguishing taste of that which has in it true moral beauty. I have shown that spiritual knowledge primarily consists in a taste or relish of the amiableness and beauty of that which is truly good and holy: this holy relish is a thing that discerns and distinguishes between good and evil, between holy and unholy, without being at the trouble of a train of reasoning. As he who has a true relish of external beauty, knows what is beautiful by looking upon it: he stands in no need of a train of reasoning about the proportion of the features, in order to determine whether that which he sees be a beautiful countenance or no: he needs nothing, but only the glance of his eye. He who has a rectified musical ear, knows whether the sound he hears be true harmony: he don't need first to be at the trouble of the reasonings of a mathematician, about the proportion of the notes. He that has a rectified palate, knows what is good food, as soon as he tastes it, without the reasoning of a physician about it. There is a holy beauty and sweetness in words and actions, as well as a natural beauty in countenances and sounds, and sweetness in food; "Doth not the ear try words, and the mouth taste his meat?" (Job 12:11). When a holy and amiable action is suggested to the thoughts of a holy soul; that soul, if in the lively exercise of its spiritual taste, at once sees a beauty in it, and so inclines to it, and closes with it. On the contrary, if an unworthy unholy action be suggested to it, its sanctified eye sees no beauty in it, and is not pleased with it; its sanctified taste relishes no sweetness in it, but on the contrary, it is nauseous to it. Yea its holy taste and appetite leads it to think of that which is truly lovely, and naturally suggests it; as a healthy taste and appetite naturally suggests the idea of its proper object. Thus a holy person is led by the Spirit, as he is instructed and led by his holy taste, and disposition of heart; whereby, in the lively exercise of grace, he easily distinguishes good and evil, and knows at once, what is a suitable amiable behavior towards God, and towards man, in this case and the other; and judges what is right, as it were spontaneously, and of himself, without a particular deduction, by any other arguments than the beauty that is seen, and goodness that is tasted. Thus Christ blames the Pharisees, that they did not, even of their own selves judge what was right, without needing miracles to prove it (Luke 12:57). The Apostle seems plainly to have respect to this way of judging of spiritual beauty, in Rom. 12:2: "Be ye transformed by the renewing of your mind, that ye may prove what is that good, and perfect, and acceptable will of God."

There is such a thing as good taste of natural beauty (which learned men often speak of), that is exercised about temporal things, in judging of them; as about the justness of a speech, the goodness of style, the beauty of a poem, the gracefulness of deportment, etc. A late great philosopher of our nation, writes thus upon it:

> To have a *taste,* is to give things their real value, to be touched with the good, to be shocked with the ill; not to be dazzled with false lusters, but in spite of all colors, and everything that might deceive or amuse, to judge soundly.
>
> *Taste* and *judgment* then, should be the same thing; and yet 'tis easy to discern a difference. The judgment forms its opinions from reflection: the reason on this occasion fetches a kind of circuit, to arrive at its end; it supposes principles, it draws consequences, and it judges; but not without a thorough knowledge of the case; so that after it has pronounced, it is ready to render a reason of its decrees. Good taste observes none of these formalities; e'er it has time to consult, it has taken its side; as soon as ever the object is presented it, the impression is made, the sentiment formed, ask no more of it. As the ear is wounded with a harsh sound, as the smell is soothed with an agreeable odor, before ever the reason have meddled with those objects to judge of them, so the taste opens itself at once, and prevents all reflection. They may come afterwards to confirm it, and discover the secret reasons of its conduct; but it was not in its power to wait

for them. Frequently it happens not to know them at all, and what pains soever it uses, cannot discover what it was determined it to think as it did. This conduct is very different from that the judgment observes in its decisions: unless we choose to say, that good taste is as it were a first motion, or a kind of instinct of right reason, which hurries on with rapidity, and conducts more securely, than all the reasonings she could make: 'tis a first glance of the eye, which discovers to us the nature and relations of things in a moment.[3]

Now as there is such a kind of taste of the mind as this, which philosophers speak of, whereby persons are guided in their judgment of the natural beauty, gracefulness, propriety, nobleness and sublimity of speeches and actions, whereby they judge as it were by the glance of the eye, or by inward sensation, and the first impression of the object; so there is likewise such a thing as a divine taste, given and maintained by the Spirit of God, in the hearts of the saints, whereby they are in like manner led and guided in discerning and distinguishing the true spiritual and holy beauty of actions; and that more easily, readily and accurately, as they have more or less of the Spirit of God dwelling in them. And thus the sons of God are led by the Spirit of God, in their behavior in the world.

A holy disposition and spiritual taste, where grace is strong and lively, will enable a soul to determine what actions are right and becoming Christians, not only more speedily, but far more exactly, than the greatest abilities without it. This may be illustrated by the manner in which some habits of mind, and dispositions of heart, of a nature inferior to true grace, will teach and guide a man in his actions. As for instance, if a man be a very good-natured man, his good nature will teach him better how to act benevolently amongst mankind, and will direct him, on every occasion, to those speeches and actions, which are agreeable to rules of goodness, than the strongest reason will a man of a morose temper. So if a man's heart be under the influence of an entire friendship, and most endeared affection to another; though he be a man of an indifferent capacity, yet this habit of his mind will direct him, far more readily and exactly, to a speech and deportment, or manner of behavior, which shall in all respects be sweet and kind, and agreeable to a benevolent disposition of heart, than the greatest capacity without it. He has as it were a spirit within him, that guides him: the habit of his mind

3. Chambers, *Cyclopedia,* Vol. 2, under the word "Taste."

is attended with a taste, by which he immediately relishes that air and mien which is benevolent, and disrelishes the contrary, and causes him to distinguish between one and the other in a moment, more precisely, than the most accurate reasonings can find out in many hours. As the nature and inward tendency of a stone, or other heavy body, that is let fall from a loft, shows the way to the center of the earth, more exactly in an instant, than the ablest mathematician, without it, could determine, by his most accurate observations, in a whole day. Thus it is that a spiritual disposition and taste teaches and guides a man in his behavior in the world. So an eminently humble, or meek, or charitable disposition, will direct a person of mean capacity to such a behavior, as is agreeable to Christian rules of humility, meekness and charity, far more readily and precisely, than the most diligent study, and elaborate reasonings, of a man of the strongest faculties, who has not a Christian spirit within him. So also will a spirit of love to God, and holy fear and reverence towards God, and filial confidence in God, and an heavenly disposition, teach and guide a man in his behavior.

'Tis an exceeding difficult thing for a wicked man, destitute of Christian principles in his heart, to guide him, to know how to demean himself like a Christian, with the life, and beauty, and heavenly sweetness of a truly holy, humble, Christlike behavior. He knows not how to put on these garments; neither do they fit him; "A wise man's heart is at his right hand; but a fool's heart is at his left. Yea also, when he that is a fool, walketh by the way, his wisdom faileth him; and he saith to every one that he is a fool" (Eccles. 10:2–3); with: "The labor of the foolish, wearieth every one of them; because he knoweth not how to go to the city" (ver. 15). "The lips of the righteous know what is acceptable" (Prov. 10:32). "The tongue of the wise useth knowledge aright; but the mouth of fools poureth out foolishness" (ch. 15:2). And: "The heart of the righteous teacheth his mouth, and addeth learning to his lips" (ch. 16:23).

The saints in thus judging of actions by a spiritual taste, have not a particular recourse to the express rules of God's Word, with respect to every word and action that is before them, the good or evil of which they thus judge of: but yet their taste itself in general, is subject to the rule of God's Word, and must be tried by that, and a right reasoning upon it. As a man of a rectified palate judges of particular morsels by his taste: but yet his palate itself must be judged of, whether it be right or no, by certain rules and reasons. But a spiritual taste of soul, mightily helps the soul, in its reasonings on the Word of God, and in judging of the true meaning of its rules; as it removes the prejudices of a depraved appetite, and naturally leads the thoughts in the right channel, casts a light on the Word of God, and causes the true meaning, most naturally to come to mind, through the harmony there is between the disposition and relish of a sanctified soul, and the true meaning of the rules of God's Word. Yea, this harmony tends to bring the texts themselves to mind, on proper occasions; as the particular state of the stomach and palate, tends to bring such particular meats and drinks to mind, as are agreeable to that state. Thus the children of God are led by the Spirit of God in judging of actions themselves, and in their meditations upon, and judging of, and applying the rules of God's holy Word: and so God teaches them his statutes, and causes them to understand the way of his precepts; which the Psalmist so often prays for.

But this leading of the Spirit is a thing exceeding diverse from that which some call so; which consists not in teaching them God's statutes and precepts, that he has already given; but in giving them new precepts, by immediate inward speech or suggestion; and has in it no tasting the true excellency of things, or judging or discerning the nature of things at all. They don't determine what is the will of God by any taste or relish, or any manner of judgment of the nature of things, but by an immediate dictate concerning the thing to be done: there is no such thing as any judgment or wisdom in the case. Whereas in that leading of the Spirit which is peculiar to God's children, is imparted that true wisdom, and holy discretion, so often spoken of in the Word of God; which is high above the other way, as the stars are higher than a glowworm; and that which Balaam and Saul (who sometimes were led by the Spirit in that other way) never had, and no natural man can have, without a change of nature.

What has been said of the nature of spiritual understanding, as consisting most essentially in a divine supernatural sense and relish of the heart, not only shows that there is nothing of it in this falsely supposed leading of the Spirit, which has been now spoken of; but also shows the difference between spiritual understanding, and all kinds and forms of enthusiasm, all imaginary sights of God and Christ and heaven, all supposed witnessing of the Spirit, and testimonies of the love of God by immediate inward suggestion; and all impressions of future events, and immediate revelations of any secret facts whatsoever; all enthusiastical impressions and applications of words of Scripture, as though they were words now immediately spoken by God to a particular person, in a new meaning, and carrying something more in them, than the words contain as they lie in the Bible; and all interpretations of the mystical meaning of the Scripture, by supposed immediate revelation. None of these things consist in a divine sense and relish of the heart, of the holy beauty and excellency of divine things; nor have they anything to do with such a sense; but all consist in impressions in the head; all are to be referred to the head of impressions on the imagination, and consist in the exciting external ideas in the mind, either in ideas of outward shapes and colors, or words spoken, or letters written, or ideas of things external and sensible, belonging to actions done, or events accomplished, or to be accomplished. An enthusiastical supposed manifestation of the love of God, is made by the exciting an idea of a smiling countenance, or some other pleasant outward appearance, or by the idea of pleasant words spoken, or written, excited in the imagination, or some pleasant bodily sensation. So when persons have an imaginary revelation of some secret fact, 'tis by exciting external ideas; either of some words, implying a declaration of that fact, or some visible or sensible circumstances of such a fact. So the supposed leading of the Spirit, to do the will of God, in outward behavior, is either by exciting the idea of words (which are outward things) in their minds, either the words of Scripture, or other words, which they look upon as an immediate command of God; or else by exciting and impressing strongly the ideas of the outward actions themselves. So when an interpretation of a Scripture type or allegory, is immediately, in an extraordinary way, strongly suggested, it is by suggesting words, as though one secretly whispered, and told the meaning; or by exciting other ideas in the imagination.

Such sort of experiences and discoveries as these commonly raise the affections of such as are deluded by them, to a great height, and make a mighty uproar in both soul and body. And a very great part of the false religion that has been in the world, from one age to another, consists in such discoveries as these, and in the affections that flow from them. In such things consisted the experiences of the ancient Pythagoreans among the heathen, and many others among them, who had strange ecstasies and raptures, and pretended to a divine afflatus, and immediate revelations from heaven. In such things as these seem to have consisted the experiences of the Essenes, an ancient sect among the Jews, at and after the times of the Apostles. In such things as these consisted the experiences of many of the ancient Gnostics, and the Montanists, and many other sects of ancient heretics, in the primitive ages of the Christian church. And in such things as these consisted the pretended immediate converse, with God and Christ, and saints and angels of heaven, of the monks, anchorites, and recluses, that formerly abounded in the Church of Rome. In such things consisted the pretended high experiences, and great spirituality of many sects of enthusiasts, that swarmed in the world after the Reformation; such as the Anabaptists, Antinomians, and Familists, the followers of N. Stork, Th. Muncer, Jo. Becold, Henry Pfeifer, David George, Casper Schwenckfeld, Henry Nicolas, Johannes Agricola Eislebius; and the many wild enthusiasts that were in England in the days of Oliver Cromwell; and the followers of Mrs. Hutchinson, in New England; as appears by the particular and large accounts given of all these sects, by that eminently holy man, Mr. Samuel Rutherford in his *Display of the Spiritual Antichrist*. And in such things as these consisted the experiences of the late French prophets, and their followers. And in these things seems to lie the religion of the many kinds of enthusiasts of the present day. 'Tis by such sort of religion as this chiefly, that Satan transforms himself into an angel of light: and it is that which he has ever most successfully made use of to confound hopeful and happy revivals of religion, from the beginning of the Christian church to this day. When the Spirit of God is poured out, to begin a glorious work, then the old serpent, as fast as possible, and by all means introduces this bastard religion, and mingles it with the true; which has from time to time soon brought all things into confusion. The pernicious consequence of it is not easily imagined or conceived of, till we see and are amazed with the awful effects of it, and the dismal desolation it has made. If the revival of true religion be very great in its beginning, yet if this bastard comes in, there is danger of its doing as Gideon's bastard Abimelech did, who never left till he had slain all his threescore and ten true-born sons, excepting one, that was forced to flee. Great and strict therefore should be the watch and guard that ministers maintain against such things, especially at a time of great awakening: for men, especially the common people, are easily bewitched with such things; they having such a glaring and glittering show of high religion; and the devil hiding his own shape, and appearing as an angel of light, that men may not be afraid of him, but may adore him.

The imagination or phantasy seems to be that wherein are formed all those delusions of Satan, which those are carried away with, who are under the influence of false religion, and counterfeit graces and affections. Here is the devil's grand lurking place, the very nest of foul and delusive spirits. 'Tis very much to be doubted whether the devil can come at the soul of man, at all to affect it, or to excite any thought or motion, or produce any affect whatsoever in it, any other way, than by the phantasy; which is that power of the soul, by which it receives, and is the subject of the species, or ideas of outward and sensible things. As to the laws and means which the Creator has established, for the intercourse and communication of unbodied spirits, we know nothing about them; we don't know by what medium they manifest their thoughts to each other, or excite thoughts in each other. But as to spirits that are united to bodies, those bodies God has united 'em to, are their medium of communication: they have no other medium of acting on other creatures, or being acted on by them, than the body. Therefore it is not to be supposed that Satan can excite any thought, or produce any effect in the soul of man, any otherwise, than by some motion of the animal spirits, or by causing some motion or alteration in something which appertains to the body. There is this reason to think that the devil can't produce thoughts, in the soul immediately, or any other way, than by the medium of the body, viz. that he can't immediately see or know the thoughts of the soul: it is abundantly declared in the Scripture to be peculiar to the omniscient God to do that. But it is not likely that the devil can immediately produce an effect which is out of the reach of his immediate view. It seems unreasonable to suppose that his immediate agency, should be out of his own sight, or that it should be impossible for him to see what he himself immediately does. Is it not unreasonable to suppose that any spirit or intelligent agent, should by the act of his will, produce effects, according to his understanding, or agreeable to his own thoughts, and that immediately; and yet the effects produced, be beyond the reach of his understanding, or where he can have no immediate perception or discerning at all. But if this be so, that the devil can't produce thoughts in the soul immediately, or any other way than by the animal spirits, or by the body; then it follows, that he never brings to pass anything in the soul, but by the imagination or phantasy, or by exciting external ideas. For we know that alterations in the body, do immediately excite no other sort of ideas in the mind, but external ideas, or ideas of the outward senses, or ideas which are of the same outward nature. As to reflection, abstraction, reasoning, etc. and those thoughts and inward motions which are the fruits of these acts of the mind, they are not the next effects of impressions on the body. So that it must be only by the imagination, that Satan has access to the soul, to tempt and delude it, or suggest anything to it.[4] And this seems to be the reason why persons that are under the disease of melancholy, are commonly so visibly and remarkably subject to the suggestions and temptations of Satan: that being a disease which peculiarly affects the animal spirits, and is attended

4. "The imagination is that room of the soul, wherein the devil doth often appear. Indeed (to speak exactly) the devil hath no efficient power over the rational part of a man: he cannot change the will; he cannot alter the heart of a man. So that the utmost he can do, in tempting a man to sin, is by suasion and suggestion only. But then how doth the devil do this? Even by working upon the imagination. He observeth the temper, and bodily constitution of a man; and thereupon suggests to his fancy, and injects his fiery darts thereinto, by which the mind and will come to be wrought upon. The devil then, though he hath no imperious efficacy over the will, yet because he can thus stir and move thy imagination, and thou being naturally destitute of grace, canst not withstand these suggestions; hence it is that any sin in thy imagination, though but in the outward works of the soul, yet doth quickly lay hold on all. And indeed, by this means do arise those horrible delusions, that are in many erroneous ways of religion: all is because their imaginations are corrupted. Yea, how often are these diabolical delusions of the imagination, taken for the gracious operations of God's Spirit? . . . It is from hence that many have pretended to enthusiasms; . . . They leave the Scriptures, and wholly attend to what they perceive and feel within them." Anthony Burgess, *The Doctrine of Original Sin* (London, 1659), pp. 369–70. [See above, p. 71.]

The great Turretine, speaking on that question, "What is the power of angels," says, "As to bodies, there is no doubt, but that they can do a great deal upon all sorts of elementary and sublunary bodies, to move them locally, and variously to agitate them. 'Tis also certain, that they can act upon the external and internal senses, to excite them, or to bind them. But as to the rational soul itself, they can do nothing immediately upon that; for to God alone, who knows and searches the hearts, and who has them in his hands, does it also appertain to bow and move them whethersoever he will. But angels can act upon the rational soul, only mediately, by imaginations." François Turretine, *Institutio Theologiae Elencticae* (Geneva, 1680), Vol. *1*, Loc. VII, quest. 8, p. 591; (Geneva, 1734), p. 604. [See above, p. 73.]

with weakness of that part of the body which is the fountain of the animal spirits, even the brain, which is, as it were, the seat of the phantasy. 'Tis by impressions made on the brain, that any ideas are excited in the mind, by the motion of the animal spirits, or any changes made in the body. The brain being thus weakened and diseased, 'tis less under the command of the higher faculties of the soul, and yields the more easily to extrinsic impressions, and is overpowered by the disordered motions of the animal spirits; and so the devil has greater advantage to affect the mind, by working on the imagination. And thus Satan, when he casts in those horrid suggestions into the minds of many melancholy persons, in which they have no hand themselves, he does it by exciting imaginary ideas, either of some dreadful words or sentences, or other horrid outward ideas. And when he tempts other persons who are not melancholy, he does it by presenting to the imagination, in a lively and alluring manner, the objects of their lusts, or by exciting ideas of words, and so by them exciting thoughts; or by promoting an imagination of outward actions, events, circumstances, etc. Innumerable are the ways by which the mind might be led on to all kind of evil thoughts, by exciting external ideas in the imagination.

If persons keep no guard at these avenues of Satan, by which he has access to the soul, to tempt and delude it, they will be likely to have enough of him. And especially, if instead of guarding against him, they lay themselves open to him, and seek and invite him, because he appears as an angel of light, and counterfeits the illuminations and graces of the Spirit of God, by inward whispers, and immediate suggestions of facts and events, pleasant voices, beautiful images, and other impressions on the imagination. There are many who are deluded by such things, and are lifted up with them, and seek after them, that have a continued course of them, and can have 'em almost when they will; and especially when their pride and vainglory has most occasion for 'em, to make a shew of 'em before company. 'Tis with them, something as 'tis with those who are the professors of the art of telling where lost things are to be found, by impressions made on their imaginations; they laying themselves open to the devil, he is always at hand to give them the desired impression.

Before I finish what I would say on this head of imaginations, counterfeiting spiritual light, and affections arising from them, I would renewedly (to prevent misunderstanding of what has been said) desire it may be observed, that I am far from determining that no affections are spiritual which are attended with imaginary ideas. Such is the nature of man, that he can scarcely think of any thing intensely, without some kind of outward ideas. They arise and interpose themselves unavoidably, in the course of a man's thoughts; though oftentimes they are very confused, and are not what the mind regards. When the mind is much engaged, and the thoughts intense, oftentimes the imagination is more strong, and the outward idea more lively; especially in persons of some constitutions of body. But there is a great difference between these two things, viz. lively imaginations arising from strong affections, and strong affections arising from lively imaginations. The former may be, and doubtless often is, in case of truly gracious affections. The affections don't arise from the imagination, nor have any dependence upon it; but on the contrary, the imagination is only the accidental effect, or consequent of the affection, through the infirmity of human nature. But when the latter is the case, as it often is, that the affection arises from imagination, and is built upon it as its foundation, instead of a spiritual illumination or discovery; then is the affection, however elevated, worthless and vain. And this is the drift of what has been now said, of impressions on the imagination. Having observed this, I proceed to another mark of gracious affections.

V. Truly gracious affections are attended with a reasonable and spiritual conviction of the judgment, of the reality and certainty of divine things.

This seems to be implied in the text that was laid as the foundation of this discourse: "Whom having not seen, ye love; in whom, though now ye see him not, yet BELIEVING, ye rejoice with joy unspeakable and full of glory."

All those who are truly gracious persons have a solid, full, thorough and effectual conviction of the truth of the great things of the gospel. I mean that they no longer halt between two opinions; the great doctrines of the gospel cease to be any longer doubtful things, or matters of opinion, which, though probable, are yet disputable; but with them, they are points settled and determined, as undoubted and indisputable; so that they are not afraid to venture their all upon their truth. Their conviction is an effectual conviction; so that the great, spiritual, mysterious, and invisible things of the gospel have the influence of real and certain things upon them; they have the weight and power of real things in their hearts; and accordingly rule in their affections, and govern them through the course of their lives. With respect to Christ's being the Son of God, and Saviour of the world, and the great things he has revealed concerning himself, and his Father, and another world, they have not only a predominating opinion that these things are true, and so yield their assent, as they do in many other matters of doubtful speculation; but they see that it is really so: their eyes are opened, so that they see that really Jesus is the Christ, the Son of the living God. And as to the things which Christ has revealed, of God's eternal purposes and designs, concerning fallen man, and the glorious and everlasting things prepared for the saints in another world, they see that they are so indeed: and therefore these things are of great weight with them, and have a mighty power upon their hearts, and influence over their practice, in some measure answerable to their infinite importance.

That all true Christians have such a kind of conviction of the truth of the things of the gospel, is abundantly manifest from the Holy Scriptures. I will mention a few places of many; "But whom say ye that I am? Simon Peter answered and said, Thou art Christ, the Son of the living God. And Jesus answered, and said unto him, blessed art thou Simon Barjona: . . . my Father which is in heaven hath revealed it unto thee" (Matt. 16:15–17). "Thou has the words of eternal life: and we believe, and are sure that thou art that Christ, the Son of the living God" (John 6:68–69). "I have manifested thy name to the men which thou gavest me out of the world. . . . Now they have known that all things, whatsoever thou hast given me, are of thee: for I have given unto them, the words which thou gavest me; and they have received them, and have known surely that I came out from thee; and they have believed that thou didst send me" (John 17:6–8). "If thou believest with all thy heart, thou mayest" (Acts 8:37). "We which live, are always delivered unto death, for Jesus' sake: . . . Death worketh in us; . . . we having the spirit of faith; according as it is written, I believed, and therefore have I spoken; we also believe, and therefore speak: knowing that he which raised up the Lord Jesus, shall raise us up also by Jesus, and shall present us with you" (II Cor. 4:11–14). Together with: "For which cause, we faint not" (ver. 16). And: "While we look not at the things which are seen," etc. (ver. 18). And: "For we know that if our earthly house of this tabernacle were dissolved, we have a building of God" (ch. 5:1). And: "Therefore we are always confident; knowing that whilst we are at home in the body, we are absent from the Lord: for we walk by faith, not by sight; we are confident, I say, and willing rather to be absent from the body, and present with the Lord" (verses 6–8). "For the which cause, I also suffer these things: nevertheless, I am not ashamed; for I know whom I have believed; and I am persuaded that he is able to keep that which I have committed unto him, against that day" (II Tim. 1:12). "Whose house are we, if we hold fast the confidence, and the rejoicing of the hope, firm unto the end" (Heb. 3:6). "Now faith is the substance of things hoped for, and the evidence of things not seen" (Heb. 11:1): together with that whole chapter. "Hereby know we that we dwell in him, and he in us; because he hath given us of his Spirit; and we have seen, and do testify, that the Father sent the Son to be the Saviour of the world. Whosoever shall confess that Jesus is the Son of God, God dwelleth in him, and he in God. And we have known and believed the love that God hath to us" (I John 4:13–16). "For whatsoever is born of God, overcometh the world: and this is the victory that overcometh the world, even our faith. Who is he that overcometh the world, but he that believeth that Jesus is the Son of God?" (ch. 5:4–5).

Therefore truly gracious affections are attended with such a kind of conviction and persuasion of the truth of the things of the gospel, and sight of their evidence and reality, as these and other Scriptures speak of.

There are many religious affections, which are not attended with such a conviction of the judgment. There are many apprehensions and ideas which some have, that they call divine discoveries, which are affecting, but not convincing. Though for a little while, they may seem to be more persuaded of the truth of the things of religion, than they used to be, and may yield a forward assent, like many of Christ's hearers, who believed for a while; yet they have no thorough and effectual conviction; nor is there any great abiding change in them, in this respect, that whereas formerly they did not realize the great things of the gospel, now these things, with regard to reality and certainty, appear new to them, and they behold 'em quite in another view than they used to do. There are many persons who have been exceedingly raised with religious affections, and think they have been converted, they don't go about the world any more convinced of the truth of the gospel, than they used to be; or at least, there is no remarkable alteration: they are not men who live under the influence and power of a realizing conviction of the infinite and eternal things which the gospel reveals: if they were, it would be impossible for 'em to live as they do. Because their affections are not attended with a thorough conviction of the mind, they are not at all to be depended on; however great a show and noise they make, 'tis like the blaze of tow, or crackling of thorns, or like the forward flourishing blade on stony ground, that has no root, nor deepness of earth to maintain its life.

Some persons, under high affections, and a confident persuasion of their good estate, have that, which they very ignorantly call a seeing the truth of the Word of God, and which is very far from it, after this manner; they have some text of Scripture coming to their minds, in a sudden and extraordinary manner, immediately declaring to them (as they suppose) that their sins are forgiven or that God loves them, and will save them; and it may be have a chain of Scriptures coming one after another, to the same purpose; and they are convinced that it is truth; i.e. they are confident that it is certainly so, that their sins are forgiven, and God does love them, etc.; they say they know it is so; and when the words of Scripture are suggested to 'em, and as they suppose immediately spoken to 'em by God, in this meaning, they are ready to cry out, "Truth, truth! 'Tis certainly so! The Word of God is true!" And this they call a seeing the truth of the Word of God. Whereas the whole of their faith amounts to no more, than only a strong confidence of their own good estate, and so a confidence that those words are true, which they suppose tell 'em they are in a good estate: when indeed (as was shown before) there is no Scripture which declares that any person is in a good estate directly, or any other way than by consequence. So that this, instead of being a real sight of the Word of God, is a sight of nothing but a phantom, and is all over a delusion. Truly to see the truth of the Word of God, is to see the truth of the gospel; which is the glorious doctrine the Word of God contains, concerning God, and Jesus Christ, and the way of salvation by him, and the world of glory that he is entered into, and purchased for all them who believe; and not a revelation that such and such particular persons are true Christians, and shall go to heaven. Therefore those affections which arise from no other persuasion of the truth of the Word of God than this, arise from delusion, and not true conviction; and consequently are themselves delusive and vain.

But if the religious affections that persons have, do indeed arise from a strong persuasion of the truth of the Christian religion; their affections are not the better, unless their persuasion be a reasonable persuasion or conviction. By a reasonable conviction, I mean a conviction founded on real evidence, or upon that which is a good reason, or just ground of conviction. Men may have a strong persuasion that the Christian religion is true, when their persuasion is not at all built on evidence, but altogether on education, and the opinion of others; as many Mahometans are strongly persuaded of the truth of the Mahometan religion, because their fathers, and neighbors, and nation believe it. That belief of the truth of the Christian religion which is built on the very same grounds, with Mahometans' belief of the Mahometan religion, is the same sort of belief. And though the thing believed happens to be better; yet that don't make the belief itself, to be of a better sort: for though the thing believed happens to be true; yet the belief of it is not owing to this truth, but to education. So that as the conviction is no better than the Mahometans' conviction; so the affections that flow from it, are no better, in themselves, than the religious affections of Mahometans.

But if that belief of Christian doctrines, which persons' affections arise from, be not merely from education, but indeed from reasons and arguments which are offered, it will not from thence necessarily follow, that their affections are truly gracious: for in order to that, it is requisite, not only that the belief which their affections arise from, should be a reasonable, but also a spiritual belief or conviction. I suppose none will doubt but that some natural men do yield a kind of assent of their judgments to the truth of the Christian religion, from the rational proofs or arguments that are offered to evince it. Judas, without doubt, thought Jesus to be the Messiah, from the things which he saw and heard; but yet all along was a devil. So in John 2:23–25 we read of many that believed in Christ's name, when they saw the miracles that he did; whom yet Christ knew had not that within them, which was to be depended on. So Simon the Sorcerer believed, when he beheld the miracles and signs which were done; but yet remained in the gall of bitterness, and bond of iniquity, Acts 8:13, 23. And if there is such a belief or assent of the judgment in some natural men, none can doubt but that religious affections may arise from that assent or belief; as we read of some who believed for a while, that were greatly affected, and anon, with joy received the word.

'Tis evident that there is such a thing as a spiritual belief or conviction of the truth of the things of the gospel, or a belief that is peculiar to those who are spiritual, or who are regenerated, and have the Spirit of God, in his holy communications, and dwelling in them as a vital principle. So that the conviction they have, don't only differ from that which natural men have, in its concomitants, in that it is accompanied with good works; but the belief itself is diverse, the assent and conviction of the judgment is of a kind peculiar to those who are spiritual, and that which natural men are wholly destitute of. This is evident by the Scripture, if anything at all is so; "They have believed that thou didst send me" (John 17:8). "According to the faith of God's elect, and the acknowledging of the truth which is after godliness" (Titus 1:1). "The Father himself loveth you, because ye have loved me, and have believed that I came out from God" (John 16:27). "Whosoever shall confess that Jesus is the Son of God, God dwelleth in him, and he in God" (I John 4:15). "Whosoever believeth that Jesus is the Christ, is born of God" (ch. 5:1). "He that believeth on the Son of God, hath the witness in himself" (ver. 10).

What a spiritual conviction of the judgment is, we are naturally led to determine from what has been said already, under the former head of a spiritual understanding. The conviction of the judgment arises from the illumination of the understanding: the passing of a right judgment on things, depends on an having a right apprehension or idea of things. And therefore it follows, that a spiritual conviction of the truth of the great things of the gospel, is such a conviction, as arises from having a spiritual view or apprehension of those things in the mind. And this is also evident from the Scripture, which often represents, that a saving belief of the reality and divinity of the things proposed and exhibited to us in the gospel, is from the Spirit of God's enlightening the mind, to have right apprehensions of the nature of those things, and so as it were unveiling things, or revealing them, and enabling the mind to view them and see them as they are. "I thank thee, O Father, Lord of heaven and earth, that thou hast hid these things from the wise and prudent, and hast revealed them unto babes: even so Father, for so it seemed good in thy sight. All things are delivered unto me of my father; and no man knoweth who the Son is, but the Father, and who the Father is but the Son, and he to whom the Son will reveal him" (Luke 10:21–22). "And this is the will of him that sent me, that every one that seeth the Son, and believeth on him, may have everlasting life" (John 6:40). Where it is plain, that true faith arises from a spiritual sight of Christ. And: "I have manifested thy name unto the men which thou gavest me out of the world: . . . Now they have known that all things whatsoever thou hast given me, are of thee; for I have given unto them the words which thou gavest me, and they have received them, and known surely that I came out from thee, and they have believed that thou didst send me" (John 17:6–8). Where Christ's manifesting God's name to the disciples, or giving them a true apprehension and view of divine things, was that whereby they knew that Christ's doctrine was of God, and that Christ himself was of him, and was sent by him. "Simon Peter said, Thou art the Christ, the Son of the living God. And Jesus answered, and said unto him, Blessed art thou, Simon Barjona, for flesh and blood hath not revealed it unto thee, but my Father which is in heaven" (Matt. 16:16–17). "He that believeth on the Son of God, hath the witness in himself" (I John 5:10). "Being more exceedingly zealous of the traditions of my fathers. But when it pleased God, who separated me from my mother's womb, and called me by his grace, to reveal his Son in me, that I might preach him among the heathen, immediately I conferred not with flesh and blood" (Gal. 1:14–16).

If it be so, that that is a spiritual conviction of the divinity and reality of the things exhibited in the gospel, which arises from a spiritual understanding of those things; I have shown already what that is, viz. a sense and taste of the divine, supreme and holy excellency and beauty of those things. So that then is the mind spiritually convinced of the divinity and truth of the great things of the gospel, when that conviction arises, either directly or remotely, from such a sense or view of their divine excellency and glory as is there exhibited. This clearly follows from things that have been already said; and for this the Scripture is very plain and express. "But if our gospel be hid, it is hid to them that are lost: in whom the God of this world hath blinded the minds of them that believe not, lest the light of the glorious gospel of Christ, who is the image of God, should shine unto them. For we preach not ourselves, but Christ Jesus the Lord, and ourselves your servants for Jesus' sake. For God, who commanded the light to shine out of darkness, hath shined in our hearts, to give the light of the knowledge of the glory of God, in the face of Jesus Christ" (II Cor. 4:3–6). Together with the last verse of the foregoing chapter, which introduces this: "But we all with open face, beholding as in a glass, the glory of the Lord, are changed into the same image, from glory to glory, even as by the Spirit of the Lord." Nothing can be more evident then that a saving belief of the gospel, is here spoken of, by the Apostle, as arising from the mind's being enlightened, to behold the divine glory of the things it exhibits.

This view or sense of the divine glory, and unparalleled beauty of the things exhibited to us in the gospel, has a tendency to convince the mind of their divinity, two ways; directly; and more indirectly, and remotely.

1. A view of this divine glory directly, convinces the mind of the divinity of these things, as this glory is in itself a direct, clear, and all-conquering evidence of it; especially when clearly discovered, or when this supernatural sense is given in a good degree.

He that has his judgment thus directly convinced and assured of the divinity of the things of the gospel, by a clear view of their divine glory, has a reasonable conviction; his belief and assurance is altogether agreeable to reason; because the divine glory and beauty of divine things is in itself, real evidence of their divinity, and the most direct and strong evidence. He that truly sees the divine, transcendent, supreme glory of those things which are divine, does as it were know their divinity intuitively; he not only argues that they are divine, but he sees that they are divine; he sees that in them wherein divinity chiefly consists; for in this glory, which is so vastly and inexpressibly distinguished from the glory of artificial things, and all other glory, does mainly consist the true notion of divinity: God is God, and distinguished from all other beings, and exalted above 'em, chiefly by his divine beauty, which is infinitely diverse from all other beauty. They therefore that see the stamp of this glory in divine things, they see divinity in them, they see God in them, and so see 'em to be divine; because they see that in them wherein the truest idea of divinity does consist. Thus a soul may have a kind of intuitive knowledge of the divinity of the things exhibited in the gospel; not that he judges the doctrines of the gospel to be from God, without any argument or deduction at all; but it is without any long chain of arguments; the argument is but one, and the evidence direct; the mind ascends to the truth of the gospel but by one step, and that is its divine glory.

It would be very strange, if any professing Christian should deny it to be possible that there should be an excellency in divine things, which is so transcendent, and exceedingly different from what is in other things, that if it were seen, would evidently distinguish them. We can't rationally doubt, but that things that are *divine,* that appertain to the supreme Being, are vastly different from things that are *humane;* that there is a godlike, high, and glorious excellency in them, that does so distinguish them from the things which are of men, that the difference is ineffable; and therefore such, as, if seen, will have a most convincing, satisfying influence upon anyone, that they are what they are, viz. divine. Doubtless there is that glory and excellency in the divine being, by which he is so infinitely distinguished from all other beings, that if it were seen, he might be known by it. It would therefore be very unreasonable to deny that it is possible for God, to give manifestations of this distinguishing excellency, in things by which he is pleased to make himself known; and that this distinguishing excellency may be clearly seen in them. There are natural excellencies that are very evidently distinguishing of the subjects or authors, to any one who beholds them. How vastly is the speech of an understanding man different from that of a little child! And how greatly distinguished is the speech of some men of great genius, as Homer, Cicero, Milton, Locke, Addison, and others, from that of many other understanding men! There are no limits to be set to the degrees of manifestation of mental excellency, that there may be in speech. But the appearances of the natural perfections of God, in the manifestations he makes of himself, may doubtless be unspeakably more evidently distinguishing, than the appearances of those excellencies of worms of the dust, in which they differ one from another. He that is well acquainted with mankind, and their works, by viewing the sun, may know it is no human work. And 'tis reasonable to suppose, that when Christ comes at the end of the world, in the glory of his Father, it will be with such ineffable appearances of divinity, as will leave no doubt to the inhabitants of the world, even the most obstinate infidels, that he who appears is a divine person. But above all, do the manifestations of the moral and spiritual glory of the divine Being (which is the proper beauty of the Divinity) bring their own evidence, and tend to assure the heart. Thus the disciples were assured that Jesus was the Son of God, for "they beheld his glory, as the glory of the only begotten of the Father, full of grace and truth" (John 1:14). When Christ appeared in the glory of his transfiguration to his disciples, with that outward glory, to their bodily eyes, which was a sweet and admirable symbol and semblance of his spiritual glory, together with his spiritual glory itself, manifested to their minds; the manifestation of glory was such, as did perfectly, and with good reason, assure them of his divinity; as appears by what one of them, viz. the apostle Peter, says concerning it, "For we have not followed cunningly devised fables, when we made known unto you the power and coming of our Lord Jesus Christ, but were eye witnesses of his majesty: for he received from God the Father, honor and glory; when there came such a voice to him from the excellent glory, This is my beloved Son in whom I am well pleased. And this voice which came from heaven, we heard, when we were with him in the holy mount" (II Pet. 1:16–18). The Apostle calls that mount, the holy mount, because the manifestations of Christ which were there made to their minds, and which their minds were especially impressed and ravished with, was the glory of his holiness, or the beauty of his moral excellency; or, as another of these disciples, who saw it, expresses it, his glory, as full of grace and truth.

Now this distinguishing glory of the divine Being has its brightest appearance and manifestation, in the things proposed and exhibited to us in the gospel, the doctrines there taught, the word there spoken, and the divine counsels, acts and works there revealed. These things have the clearest, most admirable, and distinguishing representations and exhibitions of the glory of God's moral perfections, that ever were made to the world. And if there be such a distinguishing, evidential manifestation of divine glory in the gospel, 'tis reasonable to suppose that there may be such a thing as seeing it: what should hinder but that it may be seen? 'Tis no argument that it can't be seen, that some don't see it; though they may be discerning men in temporal matters. If there be such ineffable, distinguishing, evidential excellencies in the gospel, 'tis reasonable to suppose that they are such as are not to be discerned, but by the special influence and enlightenings of the Spirit of God. There is need of uncommon force of mind to discern the distinguishing excellencies of the works of authors of great genius: those things in Milton, which to mean judges, appear tasteless and imperfections, are his inimitable excellencies in the eyes of those who are of greater discerning, and better taste. And if there be a book, which God is the author of, 'tis most reasonable to suppose that the distinguishing glories of his Word are of such a kind, as that the sin and corruption of men's hearts, which above all things alienates men from the Deity, and makes the heart dull and stupid to any sense or taste of those things wherein the moral glory of the divine perfections consists; I say, 'tis but reasonable to suppose, that this would blind men from discerning the beauties of such a book; and that therefore they will not see them, but as God is pleased to enlighten them, and restore an holy taste, to discern and relish divine beauties.

This sense of the spiritual excellency and beauty of divine things, does also tend directly to convince the mind of the truth of the gospel, as there are very many of the most important things declared in the gospel, that are hid from the eyes of natural men, the truth of which does in effect consist in this excellency, or does so immediately depend upon it and result from it; that in this excellency's being seen, the truth of those things is seen. As soon as ever the eyes are opened to behold the holy beauty and amiableness that is in divine things, a multitude of most important doctrines of the gospel, that depend upon it (which all appear strange and dark to natural men), are at once seen to be true. As for instance, hereby appears the truth of what the Word of God declares concerning the exceeding evil of sin; for the same eye that discerns the transcendent beauty of holiness, necessarily therein sees the exceeding odiousness of sin: the same taste which relishes the sweetness of true moral good, tastes the bitterness of moral evil. And by this means a man sees his own sinfulness and loathsomeness; for he has now a sense to discern objects of this nature; and so sees the truth of what the Word of God declares concerning the exceeding sinfulness of mankind, which before he did not see. He now sees the dreadful pollution of his heart, and the desperate depravity of his nature, in a new manner; for his soul has now a sense given it to feel the pain of such a disease: and this shows him the truth of what the Scripture reveals concerning the corruption of man's nature, his original sin, and the ruinous undone condition man is in, and his need of a Saviour, his need of the mighty power of God to renew his heart and change his nature. Men by seeing the true excellency of holiness, do see the glory of all those things, which both reason and Scripture shew to be in the divine Being; for it has been shown that the glory of them depend on this: and hereby they see the truth of all that the Scripture declares concerning God's glorious excellency and majesty, his being the fountain of all good, the only happiness of the creature, etc. And this again shews the mind the truth of what the Scripture teaches concerning the evil of sin against so glorious a God; and also the truth of what it teaches concerning sin's just desert of that dreadful punishment which it reveals; and also concerning the impossibility of our offering any satisfaction, or sufficient atonement, for that which is so infinitely evil and heinous. And this again shews the truth of what the Scripture reveals concerning the necessity of a Saviour, to offer an atonement of infinite value for sin. And this sense of spiritual beauty that has been spoken of, enables the soul to see the glory of those things which the gospel reveals concerning the person of Christ; and so enables to see the exceeding beauty and dignity of his person, appearing in what the Gospel exhibits of his Word, works, acts and life: and this apprehension of the superlative dignity of his person, shews the truth of what the gospel declares concerning the value of his blood and righteousness, and so the infinite excellency of that offering he has made to God for us, and so its sufficiency to atone for our sins, and recommend us to God. And thus the Spirit of God discovers the way of salvation by Christ: thus the soul sees the fitness and suitableness of this way of salvation, the admirable wisdom of the contrivance, and the perfect answerableness of the provision that the gospel exhibits (as made for us), to our necessities. A sense of true divine beauty being given to the soul, the soul discerns the beauty of every part of the gospel scheme. This also shews the soul the truth of what the Word of God declares concerning man's chief happiness, as consisting in holy exercises and enjoyments. This shews the truth of what the gospel declares concerning the unspeakable glory of the heavenly state. And what the prophecies of the Old Testament, and the writings of the apostles declare concerning the glory of the Messiah's kingdom, is now all plain; and also what the Scripture teaches concerning the reasons and grounds of our duty. The truth of all these things revealed in the Scripture, and many more that might be mentioned, appear to the soul, only by imparting that spiritual taste of divine beauty, which has been spoken of. They being hidden things to the soul before.

And besides all this, the truth of all those things which the Scripture says about experimental religion, is hereby known; for they are now experienced. And this convinces the soul that one who knew the heart of man, better than we know our own hearts, and perfectly knew the nature of virtue and holiness, was the author of the Scriptures. And the opening to view, with such clearness, such a world of wonderful and glorious truth in the gospel, that before was unknown, being quite above the view of a natural eye, but now appearing so clear and bright, has a powerful and invincible influence on the soul to persuade of the divinity of the gospel.

Unless men may come to a reasonable solid persuasion and conviction of the truth of the gospel, by the internal evidences of it, in the way that has been spoken, viz. by a sight of its glory; 'tis impossible that those who are illiterate, and unacquainted with history, should have any thorough and effectual conviction of it at all. They may without this, see a great deal of probability of it; it may be reasonable for them to give much credit to what learned men, and historians tell 'em; and they may tell them so much, that it may look very probable and rational to them, that the Christian religion is true; and so much that they would be very unreasonable not to entertain this opinion. But to have a conviction, so clear, and evident, and assuring, as to be sufficient to induce them, with boldness, to sell all, confidently and fearlessly to run the venture of the loss of all things, and of enduring the most exquisite and long-continued torments, and to trample the world under foot, and count all things but dung, for Christ; the evidence they can have from history, cannot be sufficient. It is impossible that men, who have not something of a general view of the historical world, or the series of history from age to age, should come at the force of arguments for the truth of Christianity, drawn from history, to that degree, as effectually to induce them to venture their all upon it. After all that learned men have said to them, there will remain innumerable doubts on their minds: they will be ready, when pinched with some great trial of their faith, to say, How do I know this, or that? How do I know when these histories were written? Learned men tell me these histories were so and so attested in the day of them; but how do I know that there were such attestations then? They tell me there is equal reason to believe these facts, as any whatsoever that are related at such a distance; but how do I know that other facts which are related of those ages, ever were?

Those who have not something of a general view of the series of historical events, and of the state of mankind from age to age, cannot see the clear evidence from history, of the truth of facts, in distant ages; but there will endless doubts and scruples remain.

But the gospel was not given only for learned men. There are at least nineteen in twenty, if not ninety-nine in an hundred, of those for whom the Scriptures were written, that are not capable of any certain or effectual conviction of the divine authority of the Scriptures, by such arguments as learned men make use of. If men who have been brought up in heathenism, must wait for a clear and certain conviction of the truth of Christianity, till they have learning and acquaintance with the histories of politer nations, enough to see clearly the force of such kind of arguments; it will make the evidence of the gospel, to them, immensely cumbersome, and will render the propagation of the gospel among them, infinitely difficult. Miserable is the condition of the Houssatunnuck Indians, and others, who have lately manifested a desire to be instructed in Christianity; if they can come at no evidence of the truth of Christianity, sufficient to induce 'em to sell all for Christ, in no other way but this.

'Tis unreasonable to suppose, that God has provided for his people, no more than probable evidences of the truth of the gospel. He has with great care, abundantly provided, and given them, the most convincing, assuring, satisfying and manifold evidence of his faithfulness in the covenant of grace; and as David says, made a covenant, ordered in all things and sure. Therefore it is rational to suppose, that at the same time, he would not fail of ordering the matter so, that there should not be wanting, as great, and clear evidence, that this is his covenant, and that these promises are his promises; or which is the same thing, that the Christian religion is true, and that the gospel is his Word. Otherwise in vain are those great assurances he has given of his faithfulness in his covenant, by confirming it with his oath, and so variously establishing it by seals and pledges. For the evidence that it is his covenant, is properly the foundation on which all the force and effect of those other assurances do stand. We may therefore undoubtedly suppose and conclude, that there is some sort of evidence which God has given, that this covenant, and these promises are his, beyond all mere probability; that there are some grounds of assurance of it held forth, which, if we are not blind to them, tend to give an higher persuasion, than any arguing from history, human tradition, etc. which the illiterate, and unacquainted with history, are capable of; yea, that which is good ground of the highest and most perfect assurance, that mankind have in any case whatsoever; agreeable to those high expressions which the Apostle uses, "Let us draw near in full assurance of faith" (Heb. 10:22). And: "That their hearts might be comforted, being knit together in love, and unto all riches, of the full assurance of understanding, to the acknowledgment of the mystery of God, and of the Father, and of Christ" (Col. 2:2). It is reasonable to suppose, that God would give the greatest evidence, of those things which are greatest, and the truth of which is of greatest importance to us: and that we therefore, if we are wise, and act rationally, shall have the greatest desire of having full, undoubting, and perfect assurance of. But it is certain, that such an assurance is not to be attained, by the greater part of them who live under the gospel, by arguments fetched from ancient traditions, histories, and monuments.

And if we come to fact and experience, there is not the least reason to suppose, that one in an hundred of those who have been sincere Christians, and have had a heart to sell all for Christ, have come by their conviction of the truth of the gospel, this way. If we read over the histories of the many thousands that died martyrs for Christ, since the beginning of the Reformation, and have cheerfully undergone extreme tortures, in a confidence of the truth of the gospel, and consider their circumstances and advantages; how few of them were there, that we can reasonably suppose, ever came by their assured persuasion, this way; or indeed for whom it was possible, reasonably to receive so full and strong an assurance, from such arguments! Many of them were weak women and children, and the greater part of them illiterate persons, many of whom had been brought up in popish ignorance and darkness, and were but newly come out of it, and lived and died in times, wherein those arguments for the truth of Christianity from antiquity and history, had been but very imperfectly handled. And indeed, 'tis but very lately that these arguments have been set in a clear and convincing light, even by learned men themselves: and since it has been done, there never were fewer thorough believers, among those who have been educated in the true religion: infidelity never prevailed so much, in any age, as in this, wherein these arguments are handled to the greatest advantage.

The true martyrs of Jesus Christ, are not those who have only been strong in opinion that the gospel of Christ is true, but those that have seen the truth of it; as the very name of martyrs or witnesses (by which they are called in Scripture) implies. Those are very improperly called witnesses of the truth of anything, who only declare they are very much of opinion that such a thing is true. Those only are proper witnesses who can, and do testify that they have seen the truth of the thing they assert; "We speak that we do know, and testify that we have seen" (John 3:11). "And I saw, and bear record, that this is the Son of God" (John 1:34). "And we have seen, and do testify, that the Father sent the Son, to be the Saviour of the world" (I John 4:14). "The God of our fathers hath chosen thee, that thou should'st know his will, and see that just One, and should'st hear the voice of his mouth: for thou shalt be his witness unto all men, of what thou hast seen and heard" (Acts 22:14–15). But the true martyrs of Jesus Christ are called his witnesses: and all the saints, who by their holy practice under great trials, declare that faith, which is the substance of things hoped for, and the evidence of things not seen, are called witnesses (Heb. 11:1 and 12:1); because by their profession and practice, they declare their assurance of the truth and divinity of the gospel, having had the eyes of their minds enlightened, to see divinity in the gospel, or to behold that unparalleled, ineffably excellent, and truly divine glory shining in it, which is altogether distinguishing, evidential, and convincing: so that they may truly be said to have seen God in it, and to have seen that it is indeed divine: and so can speak in the style of witnesses; and not only say, that they think the gospel is divine, but say, that it is divine, giving it in as their testimony, because they have seen it to be so. Doubtless Peter, James, and John, after they had seen that excellent glory of Christ in the mount, would have been ready, when they came down, to speak in the language of witnesses, and to say positively that Jesus is the Son of God; as Peter says, they were eye-witnesses (II Pet. 1:16). And so all nations will be ready positively to say this, when they shall behold his glory at the Day of Judgment; though what will be universally seen, will be only his natural glory, and not his moral and spiritual glory, which is much more distinguishing. But yet, it must be noted, that among those who have a spiritual sight of the divine glory of the gospel, there is a great variety of degrees of strength of faith, as there is a vast variety of the degrees of clearness of views of this glory: but there is no true and saving faith, or spiritual conviction of the judgment, of the truth of the gospel, that has nothing in it, of this manifestation of its internal evidence, in some degree. The gospel of the blessed God don't go abroad a begging for its evidence, so much as some think; it has its highest and most proper evidence in itself. Though great use may be made of external arguments, they are not to be neglected, but highly prized and valued; for they may be greatly serviceable to awaken unbelievers, and bring them to serious consideration, and to confirm the faith of true saints: yea they may be in some respects subservient to the begetting of a saving faith in men. Though what was said before remains true, that there is no spiritual conviction of the judgment, but what arises from an apprehension of the spiritual beauty and glory of divine things: for, as has been observed, this apprehension or view has a tendency to convince the mind of the truth of the gospel, two ways; either directly or indirectly. Having therefore already observed how it does this directly, I proceed now

2. To observe how a view of this divine glory does convince the mind of the truth of Christianity, more indirectly.

First, it doth so as the prejudices of the heart against the truth of divine things are hereby removed, so that the mind thereby lies open to the force of the reasons which are offered. The mind of man is naturally full of enmity against the doctrines of the gospel; which is a disadvantage to those arguments that prove their truth, and causes them to lose their force upon the mind: but when a person has discovered to him the divine excellency of Christian doctrines, this destroys that enmity, and removes the prejudices, and sanctifies the reason, and causes it to be open and free. Hence is a vast difference, as to the force that arguments have to convince the mind. Hence was the very different effect, which Christ's miracles had to convince the disciples, from what they had to convince the Scribes and Pharisees: not that they had a stronger reason, or had their reason more improved; but their reason was sanctified, and those blinding prejudices, which the Scribes and Pharisees were under, were removed, by the sense they had of the excellency of Christ and his doctrine.

Secondly, it not only removes the hindrances of reason, but positively helps reason. It makes even the speculative notions more lively. It assists and engages the attention of the mind to that kind of objects; which causes it to have a clearer view of them, and more clearly to see their mutual relations. The ideas themselves, which otherwise are dim and obscure, by this means have a light cast upon them, and are impressed with greater strength; so that the mind can better judge of them, as he that beholds the objects on the face of the earth, when the light of the sun is cast upon them, is under greater advantage to discern them, in their true forms, and mutual relations, and to see the evidences of divine wisdom and skill in their contrivance, than he that sees them in a dim star light, or twilight.

What has been said, may serve in some measure to show the nature of a spiritual conviction of the judgment of the truth and reality of divine things; and so to distinguish truly gracious affections from others; for gracious affections are evermore attended with such a conviction of the judgment.

But before I dismiss this head, it will be needful to observe the ways whereby some are deceived, with respect to this matter; and take notice of several things, that are sometimes taken for a spiritual and saving belief of the truth of the things of religion, which are indeed very diverse from it.

(1) There is a degree of conviction of the truth of the great things of religion, that arises from the common enlightenings of the Spirit of God. That more lively and sensible apprehension of the things of religion, with respect to what is natural in them, such as natural men have who are under awakenings and common illuminations, will give some degree of conviction of the truth of divine things, beyond what they had before they were thus enlightened. For hereby they see the manifestations there are, in the revelation made in the Holy Scriptures, and things exhibited in that revelation, of the natural perfections of God; such as his greatness, power, and awful majesty; which tends to convince the mind, that this is the Word of a great and terrible God. From the tokens there are of God's greatness and majesty in his Word and works, which they have a great sense of, from the common influence of the Spirit of God, they may have a much greater conviction that these are indeed the Word and works of a very great invisible Being. And the lively apprehension of the greatness of God, which natural men may have, tends to make 'em sensible of the great guilt, which sin against such a God brings, and the dreadfulness of his wrath for sin. And this tends to cause them more easily and fully to believe the revelation the Scripture makes of another world, and of the extreme

misery it threatens, there to be inflicted on sinners. And so from that sense of the great natural good there is in the things of religion, which is sometimes given in common illuminations, men may be the more induced to believe the truth of religion. These things persons may have, and yet have no sense of the beauty and amiableness of the moral and holy excellency that is in the things of religion; and therefore no spiritual conviction of their truth. But yet such convictions are sometimes mistaken, for saving convictions, and the affections flowing from 'em, for saving affections.

(2) The extraordinary impressions which are made on the imaginations of some persons, in the visions, and immediate strong impulses and suggestions that they have, as though they saw sights, and had words spoken to 'em, may, and often do beget a strong persuasion of the truth of invisible things. Though the general tendency of such things, in their final issue, is to draw men off from the Word of God, and to cause 'em to reject the gospel, and to establish unbelief and atheism; yet for the present, they may, and often do beget a confident persuasion of the truth of some things that are revealed in the Scriptures; however their confidence is founded in delusion, and so nothing worth. As for instance, if a person has by some invisible agent, immediately and strongly impressed on his imagination, the appearance of a bright light, and glorious form of a person seated on a throne, with great external majesty and beauty, uttering some remarkable words, with great force and energy; the person who is the subject of such an operation, may be from hence confident, that there are invisible agents, spiritual beings, from what he has experienced, knowing that he had no hand himself in this extraordinary effect, which he has experienced: and he may also be confident that this is Christ, whom he saw and heard speaking: and this may make him confident that there is a Christ, and that Christ reigns on a throne in heaven, as he saw him; and may be confident that the words which he heard him speak are true, etc. In the same manner, as the lying miracles of the Papists, may for the present, beget in the minds of the ignorant deluded people, a strong persuasion of the truth of many things declared in the New Testament. Thus when the images of Christ, in popish churches, are on some extraordinary occasions, made by priestcraft to appear to the people as if they wept, and shed fresh blood, and moved, and uttered such and such words; the people may be verily persuaded that it is a miracle wrought by

Christ himself; and from thence may be confident there is a Christ, and that what they are told of his death and sufferings, and resurrection, and ascension, and present government of the world is true; for they may look upon this miracle, as a certain evidence of all these things, and a kind of ocular demonstration of them. This may be the influence of these lying wonders for the present; though the general tendency of them is not to convince that Jesus Christ is come in the flesh, but finally to promote atheism. Even the intercourse which Satan has with witches, and their often experiencing his immediate power, has a tendency to convince 'em of the truth of some of the doctrines of religion; as particularly the reality of an invisible world, or world of spirits, contrary to the doctrine of the Sadducees. The general tendency of Satan's influences is delusion; but yet he may mix some truth with his lies, that his lies mayn't be so easily discovered.

There are multitudes that are deluded with a counterfeit faith, from impressions on their imagination, in the manner which has been now spoken of. They say they know that there is a God, for they have seen him; they know that Christ is the Son of God, for they have seen him in his glory; they know that Christ died for sinners, for they have seen him hanging on the Cross, and his blood running from his wounds; they know there is a heaven and a hell, for they have seen the misery of the damned souls in hell, and the glory of saints and angels in heaven (meaning some external representations, strongly impressed on their imagination); they know that the Scriptures are the Word of God, and that such and such promises in particular, are his Word, for they have heard him speak 'em to them, they came to their minds suddenly and immediately from God, without their having any hand in it.

(3) Persons may seem to have their belief of the truth of the things of religion greatly increased, when the foundation of it is only a persuasion they have received, of their interest in 'em. They first, by some means or other, take up a confidence that, if there be a Christ and heaven, they are theirs; and this prejudices 'em more in favor of the truth of 'em. When they hear of the great and glorious things of religion, 'tis with this notion, that all these things belong to them; and hence easily become confident that they are true: they look upon it to be greatly for their interest that they should be true. 'Tis very obvious what a strong influence men's interest and inclinations have on their judgments. While a natural man thinks

that, if there be a heaven and hell; the latter, and not the former, belongs to him; then he'll be hardly persuaded that there is a heaven or hell: but when he comes to be persuaded, that hell belongs only to other folks, and not to him; then he can easily allow the reality of hell, and cry out of others' senselessness and sottishness in neglecting means of escape from it: and being confident that he is a child of God, and that God has promised heaven to him, he may seem strong in the faith of its reality, and may have a great zeal against that infidelity which denies it.

But I proceed to another distinguishing sign of gracious affections.

VI. Gracious affections are attended with evangelical humiliation.

Evangelical humiliation is a sense that a Christian has of his own utter insufficiency, despicableness, and odiousness, with an answerable frame of heart.

There is a distinction to be made between a *legal* and *evangelical* humiliation. The former is what men may be the subjects of, while they are yet in a state of nature, and have no gracious affection; the latter is peculiar to true saints: the former is from the common influence of the Spirit of God, assisting natural principles, and especially natural conscience; the latter is from the special influences of the Spirit of God, implanting and exercising supernatural and divine principles: the former is from the mind's being assisted to a greater sense of the things of religion, as to their natural properties and qualities, and particularly of the natural perfections of God, such as his greatness, terrible majesty, etc. which were manifested to the congregation of Israel, in giving the law at Mount Sinai; the latter is from a sense of the transcendent beauty of divine things in their moral qualities: in the former a sense of the awful greatness, and natural perfections of God, and of the strictness of his law, convinces men that they are exceeding sinful, and guilty, and exposed to the wrath of God, as it will wicked men and devils at the Day of Judgment; but they don't see their own odiousness on the account of sin; they don't see the hateful nature of sin; a sense of this is given in evangelical humiliation, by a discovery of the beauty of God's holiness and moral perfection. In a legal humiliation, men are made sensible that they are little and nothing before the great and terrible God, and that they are undone, and wholly insufficient to help themselves; as wicked men will be at the Day of Judgment: but they have not an answerable frame of heart, consisting in a disposition to abase themselves, and exalt God alone: this disposition is given only in evangelical humiliation, by overcoming the heart, and changing its inclination, by a discovery of God's holy beauty: in a legal humiliation, the conscience is convinced; as the consciences of all will be most perfectly at the Day of Judgment: but because there is no spiritual understanding the will is not bowed, nor the inclination altered: this is done only in evangelical humiliation. In legal humiliation men are brought to despair of helping themselves; in evangelical, they are brought voluntarily to deny and renounce themselves: in the former they are subdued and forced to the ground; in the latter, they are brought sweetly to yield, and freely and with delight to prostrate themselves at the feet of God.

Legal humiliation has in it no spiritual good, nothing of the nature of true virtue; whereas evangelical humiliation is that wherein the excellent beauty of Christian grace does very much consist. Legal humiliation is useful, as a means in order to evangelical; as a common knowledge of the things of religion is a means requisite in order to spiritual knowledge. Men may be legally humbled and have no humility; as the wicked at the Day of Judgment will be thoroughly convinced that they have no righteousness, but are altogether sinful, and exceeding guilty, and justly exposed to eternal damnation, and be fully sensible of their own helplessness, without the least mortification of the pride of their hearts: but the essence of evangelical humiliation consists in such humility, as becomes a creature, in itself exceeding sinful, under a dispensation of grace; consisting in a mean esteem of himself, as in himself nothing, and altogether contemptible and odious; attended with a mortification of a disposition to exalt himself, and a free renunciation of his own glory.

This is a great and most essential thing in true religion. The whole frame of the gospel, and everything appertaining to the new Covenant, and all God's dispensations towards fallen man, are calculated to bring to pass this effect in the hearts of men. They that are destitute of this, have no true religion, whatever profession they may make, and how high soever their religious affections may be; "Behold, his soul which is lifted up, is not upright in him; but the just shall live by his faith" (Hab. 2:4): i.e. he shall live by his faith on God's righteousness and grace, and not his own goodness and excellency. God has abundantly manifested in his Word, that this is what he has a peculiar respect to in his saints, and that nothing is acceptable to him without it; "The Lord is nigh unto them that are of a broken heart, and saveth such as be of a contrite spirit" (Ps. 34:18). "The sacrifices of God are a broken spirit; a broken and a contrite heart, O God, thou wilt not despise" (Ps. 51:17). "Though the Lord be high, he hath respect unto the lowly" (Ps. 138:6). "He giveth grace unto the lowly" (Prov. 3:34). "Thus saith the high and lofty One who inhabiteth eternity, whose name is holy, I dwell in the high and holy place, with him also that is of a contrite and humble spirit, to revive the spirit of the humble, and to revive the heart of the contrite ones" (Is. 57:15). "Thus saith the Lord, the heaven is my throne, and the earth is my footstool. . . . But to this man will I look, even to him that is poor, and of a contrite spirit, and trembleth at my Word" (Is. 66:1–2). "He hath showed thee, O Man, what is good; and what doth the Lord thy God require of thee, but to do justly, and to love mercy, and to walk humbly with thy God?" (Mic. 6:8). "Blessed are the poor in spirit: for theirs is the Kingdom of God" (Matt. 5:3). "Verily I say unto you, except ye be converted, and become as little children, ye shall not enter into the Kingdom of Heaven. Whosoever therefore shall humble himself as this little child, the same is greatest in the Kingdom of Heaven" (Matt. 18:3–4). "Verily I say unto you, whosoever shall not receive the Kingdom of God as a little child, he shall not enter therein" (Mark 10:15). The centurion, that we have an account of [in] Luke 7, acknowledged that he was not worthy that Christ should enter under his roof, and that he was not worthy to come to him. See the manner of the woman's coming to Christ that was a sinner, "And behold a woman in the city which was a sinner, when she knew that Jesus sat at meat in the Pharisee's house, brought an alabaster box of ointment, and stood at his feet behind him weeping, and began to wash his feet with her tears, and did wipe them with the hairs of her head" (Luke 7:37, etc.). She did not think the hair of her head, which is the natural crown and glory of a woman (I Cor. 11:15), too good to wipe the feet of Christ withal. Jesus most graciously accepted her, and says to her, "Thy faith hath saved thee, go in peace." The woman of Canaan submitted to Christ, in his saying, "It is not meet to take the children's bread, and to cast it to dogs," and did as it were own that she was worthy to be called a dog, whereupon Christ says unto her, "O woman, great is thy faith; be it unto thee, even as thou wilt" (Matt. 15:26–27). The Prodigal Son said: "I will arise and go to my father, and I will say unto him, Father, I have sinned against heaven, and before thee, and am no more worthy to be called thy son; make me as one of thy hired servants" (Luke 15:18, etc.). See also: "And he spake this parable unto certain that trusted in themselves that they were righteous, and despised others, etc. . . . The publican standing afar off, would not so much as lift up his eyes to heaven, but smote upon his breast, saying, God be merciful to me a sinner. I tell you, this man went down to his house justified, rather than the other: for every one that exalteth himself shall be abased, and he that humbleth himself shall be exalted" (Luke 18:9, etc.). "And they came, and held him by the feet, and worshiped him" (Matt. 28:9). "Put ye on, as the elect of God, . . . humbleness of mind" (Col. 3:12). "I will accept you with your sweet savor, when I bring you out from the people, etc. . . . And there shall ye remember your ways, and all your doings, wherein ye have been defiled; and ye shall loathe yourselves in your own sight, for all your evils that ye have committed" (Ezek. 20:41–43). "A new heart also will I give unto you, . . . and I will put my Spirit within you, and cause you to walk in my statutes," etc. "Then shall ye remember your own evil ways, and your doings that were not good, and shall loathe yourselves in your own sight, for your iniquities, and for your abominations" (ch. 36:26–27, 31). "That thou mayst remember and be confounded, and never open thy mouth any more, because of thy shame; when I am pacified toward thee, for all that thou hast done, saith the Lord" (ch. 16:63). "I abhor myself, and repent in dust and ashes" (Job 42:6).

As we would therefore make the Holy Scriptures our rule, in judging of the nature of true religion, and judging of our own religious qualifications and state; it concerns us greatly to look at this humiliation, as one of the most essential things pertaining to true Christianity.[5] This is the principal part of the great Chris-

5. Calvin in his *Institutes of the Christian Religion,* Bk. II, ch. 2, no. 11, says, "I was always exceedingly pleased with that saying of Chrysostom, 'The foundation of our philosophy is humility,' and yet more pleased with that of Augustine, 'as,' says he, 'the rhetorician, being asked, what was the first thing in the rules of eloquence, he answered, "pronunciation"; what was the second, "pronuncia-

tian duty of self-denial. That duty consists in two things, viz. first, in a man's denying his worldly inclinations, and in forsaking and renouncing all worldly objects and enjoyments; and secondly, in denying his natural self-exaltation, and renouncing his own dignity and glory, and in being emptied of himself; so that he does freely, and from his very heart, as it were renounce himself, and annihilate himself. Thus the Christian doth, in evangelical humiliation. And this latter is the greatest and most difficult part of self-denial: although they always go together, and one never truly is, where the other is not; yet natural men can come much nearer to the former than the latter. Many anchorites and recluses have abandoned (though without any true mortification) the wealth, and pleasures, and common enjoyments of the world, who were far from renouncing their own dignity and righteousness; they never denied themselves for Christ, but only sold one lust to feed another, sold a beastly lust to pamper a devilish one; and so were never the better, but their latter end was worse than their beginning; they turned out one black devil, to let in seven white ones, that were worse than the first, though of a fairer countenance. 'Tis inexpressible, and almost inconceivable, how strong a self-righteous, self-exalting disposition is naturally in man; and what he will not do and suffer, to feed and gratify it; and what lengths have been gone in a seeming self-denial in other respects, by Essenes and Pharisees among the Jews, and by Papists, many sects of heretics, and enthusiasts, among professing Christians; and by many Mahometans; and by Pythagorean philosophers, and others, among the heathen: and all to do sacrifice to this Moloch of spiritual pride or self-righteousness; and that they may have something wherein to exalt themselves before God, and above their fellow creatures.

That humiliation which has been spoken of, is what all the most glorious hypocrites, who make the most splendid show of mortification to the world, and high religious affection, do grossly fail in. Were it not that this is so much insisted on in Scripture, as a most essential thing in true grace; one would be tempted to think that many of the heathen philosophers were truly gracious, in whom was so bright an appearance of many virtues, and also great illumina-

tion"; what was the third, still he answered, "pronunciation." So if you should ask me concerning the precepts of the Christian religion, I would answer, firstly, secondly, and thirdly, and forever, humility.' "

tions, and inward fervors and elevations of mind, as though they were truly the subjects of divine illapses and heavenly communications.[6]

'Tis true that many hypocrites make great pretences to humility, as well as other graces; and very often there is nothing whatsoever which they make a higher profession of. They endeavor to make a great shew of humility in speech and behavior; but they commonly make bungling work of it; though glorious work in their own eyes. They can't find out what a humble speech and behavior is, or how to speak and act so that there may indeed be a savor of Christian humility in what they say and do: that sweet humble air and mien is beyond their art, being not led by the Spirit, or naturally guided to a behavior becoming holy humility, by the vigor of a lowly spirit within them. And therefore they have no other way, many of them, but only to be much in declaring that they be humble, and telling how they were humbled to the dust at such and such times, and abounding in very bad expressions which they use about themselves; such as: "I am the least of all saints, I am

6. "Albeit the Pythagoreans were thus famous for Judaic mysterious wisdom, and many moral, as well as natural accomplishments; yet were they not exempted from boasting and pride. Which was indeed a vice most epidemic, and as it were congenial, among all the philosophers; but in a more particular manner, among the Pythagoreans. So [Georgius] Hornius, Hist[oria] Philosoph[ia], line 3, ch. 11. The manners of the Pythagoreans were not free from boasting. They were all περιαυτολογοι such as abounded in the sense and commendation of their own excellencies, and boasting even almost to the degree of immodesty and impudence, as great Heinsius ad Horat has rightly observed. Thus indeed does proud nature delight to walk in the sparks of its own fire. And although many of these old philosophers could, by the strength of their own lights and heats, together with some common elevations and raisures of spirit (peradventure from a more than ordinary, though not special and saving assistance of the Spirit), abandon many grosser vices; yet they were all deeply immersed in that miserable cursed abyss of spiritual pride: so that all their natural and moral and philosophic attainments, did feed, nourish, strengthen, and render most inveterate, this hell-bred pest of their hearts. Yea those of them that seemed most modest, as the Academics, who professed they knew nothing, and the Cynics, who greatly decried, both in words and habits, the pride of others, yet even they abounded in the most notorious and visible pride. So connatural and morally essential to corrupt nature, is this envenomed root, fountain and plague of spiritual pride: especially where there is any natural, moral or philosophic excellence to feed the same. Whence Austin rightly judged all these philosophic virtues, to be but splendid sins." Theophilus Gale, *The Court of the Gentiles* (Oxford, 1671), Pt. II, Bk. II, ch. 9, par. 17, p. 204. [See above, p. 70.]

a poor vile creature, I am not worthy of the least mercy, or that God should look upon me! Oh, I have a dreadful wicked heart! my heart is worse than the devil! Oh, this cursed heart of mine," etc. Such expressions are very often used, not with a heart that is broken, not with spiritual mourning, not with the tears of her that washed Jesus' feet with her tears, not as remembering and being confounded, and never opening their mouth more, because of their shame, when God is pacified, as the expression is (Ezek. 16:63). But with a light air, with smiles in the countenance, or with a pharisaical affectation: and we must believe that they are thus humble, and see themselves so vile, upon the credit of their say so; for there is nothing appears in 'em of any savor of humility, in the manner of their deportment and deeds that they do. There are many that are full of expressions of their own vileness, who yet expect to be looked upon as eminent and bright saints by others, as their due; and 'tis dangerous for any, so much as to hint the contrary, or to carry it towards them any otherwise, than as if we looked upon 'em some of the chief of Christians. There are many that are much in crying out of their wicked hearts, and their great shortcomings, and unprofitableness, and speaking as though they looked on themselves as the meanest of the saints; who yet, if a minister should seriously tell 'em the same things in private, and should signify, that he feared they were very low and weak Christians, and thought they had reason solemnly to consider of their great barrenness and unprofitableness, and falling so much short of many others; it would be more than they could digest; they would think themselves highly injured; and there would be danger of a rooted prejudice in 'em against such a minister.

There are some that are abundant in talking against legal doctrines, legal preaching, and a legal spirit, who do but little understand the thing they talk against. A legal spirit is a more subtle thing than they imagine, it is too subtle for them. It lurks, and operates, and prevails in their hearts, and they are most notoriously guilty of it, at the same time, when they are inveighing against it. So far as a man is not emptied of himself, and of his own righteousness and goodness, in whatever form or shape, so far he is of a legal spirit. A spirit of pride of a man's own righteousness, morality, holiness, affection, experience, faith, humiliation, or any goodness whatsoever, is a legal spirit. It was no pride in Adam before the Fall, to be of a legal spirit: because of his circumstances, he might seek acceptance by his own righteousness. But a legal spirit in a fallen sinful creature, can be nothing else but spiritual pride; and reciprocally, a spiritually proud spirit is a legal spirit. There is no man living that is lifted up with a conceit of his own experiences and discoveries, and upon the account of them glisters in his own eyes, but what trusts in his experiences, and makes a righteousness of 'em; however he may use humble terms, and speak of his experiences as of the great things God has done for him, and it may be calls upon others to glorify God for them; yet he that is proud of his experiences, arrogates something to himself, as though his experiences were some dignity of his. And if he looks on them as his own dignity, he necessarily thinks that God looks on 'em so too; for he necessarily thinks his own opinion of 'em to be true; and consequently judges that God looks on them as he does; and so unavoidably imagines that God looks on his experiences as a dignity in him, as he looks on 'em himself; and that he glisters as much in God's eyes, as he does in his own. And thus he trusts in what is inherent in him, to make him shine in God's sight, and recommend him to God: and with this encouragement he goes before God in prayer; and this makes him expect much from God; and this makes him think that Christ loves him, and that he is willing to clothe him with his righteousness; because he supposes that he is taken with his experiences and graces. And this is a high degree of living on his own righteousness; and such persons are in the high road to hell. Poor deluded wretches, who think they look so glistering in God's eyes, when they are a smoke in his nose, and are many of 'em more odious to him, than the most impure beast in Sodom, that makes no pretense to religion! To do as these do, is to live upon experiences, according to the true notion of it; and not to do as those, who only make use of spiritual experiences, as evidences of a state of grace, and in that way receive hope and comfort from 'em.

There is a sort of men, who indeed abundantly cry down works, and cry up faith in opposition to works, and set up themselves very much as evangelical persons, in opposition to those that are of a legal spirit, and make a fair show of advancing Christ and the gospel, and the way of free grace; who are indeed some of the greatest enemies to the gospel way of free grace, and the most dangerous opposers of pure humble Christianity.[7]

7. "Take not every opinion and doctrine from men or angels, that bears a fair shew of advancing Christ; for they may be but the fruits of evangelical

There is a pretended great humiliation, and being dead to the law, and emptied of self, which is one of the biggest and most elated things in the world. Some there are, who have made great profession of experience of a thorough work of the law on their own hearts, and of being brought fully off from works; whose conversation has savored most of a self-righteous spirit, of any that ever I had opportunity to observe. And some who think themselves quite emptied of themselves, and are confident that they are abased in the dust, are full as they can hold with the glory of their own humility, and lifted up to heaven with an high opinion of their abasement. Their humility is a swelling, self-conceited, confident, showy, noisy, assuming humility. It seems to be the nature of spiritual pride to make men conceited and ostentatious of their humility. This appears in that first-born of pride, among the children of men, that would be called "His Holiness," even the man of sin, that exalts himself above all that is called God or is worshiped; he styles himself "servant of servants"; and to make a show of humility, washes the feet of a number of poor men at his inauguration.

For persons to be truly emptied of themselves, and to be poor in spirit, and broken in heart, is quite another thing, and has other effects, than many imagine. 'Tis astonishing how greatly many are deceived about themselves as to this matter, imagining themselves most humble, when they are most proud, and their behavior is really the most haughty. The deceitfulness of the heart of man appears in no one thing so much, as this of spiritual pride and self-righteousness. The subtlety of Satan appears in its height in

hypocrisy and deceit; that being deceived themselves, may deceive others too; Matt. 7:15: 'Beware of them, that come in sheep's clothing'; in the innocency, purity and meekness of Christ and his people, 'but inwardly are wolves,' proud, cruel, censorious, speaking evil of what they know not. 'By their fruit you shall know them.' Do not think beloved, that Satan will not seek to send delusions among us. And do you think these delusions will come out of the popish pack, whose inventions smell above ground here? No, he must come, and will come with more evangelical, fine spun devices. It's a rule observed amongst Jesuits, at this day, if they would conquer religion by subtlety, never oppose religion with a cross religion; but set it against itself: so oppose the gospel by the gospel. And look, as churches pleading for works, had new invented devised works; so when faith is preached, men will have their new inventions of faith. I speak not this against the doctrine of faith, where it is preached; but am glad of it: nor that I would have men content themselves with every form of faith; for I believe that most men's faith needs confirming or trying. But I speak to prevent danger on that hand." Shepard, *Parable,* Pt. I, p. 122.

his managing of persons with respect to this sin. And perhaps one reason may be, that here he has most experience: he knows the way of its coming in; he is acquainted with the secret springs of it; it was his own sin. Experience gives vast advantage in leading souls, either in good or evil.

But though spiritual pride be so subtle and secret an iniquity, and commonly appears under a pretext of great humility; yet there are two things by which it may (perhaps universally and surely) be discovered and distinguished.

1. The first thing is this; he that is under the prevalence of this distemper, is apt to think highly of his attainments in religion, as comparing himself with others. 'Tis natural for him to fall into that thought of himself, that he is an eminent saint, that he is very high amongst the saints, and has distinguishably good and great experiences. That is the secret language of his heart, "God, I thank thee, that I am not as other men" (Luke 18:11). And: "I am holier than thou" (Is. 65:5). Hence such are apt to put themselves forward among God's people, and as it were to take a high seat among them, as if there was no doubt of it but it belonged to them. They, as it were, naturally do that which Christ condemns (Luke 14:7, etc.), take the highest room. This they do, by being forward to take upon 'em the place and business of the chief: to guide, teach, direct and manage; they are confident that they are guides to the blind, a light of them which are in darkness, instructors of the foolish, teachers of babes (Rom. 2:19–20). 'Tis natural for them to take it for granted, that it belongs to them to do the part of dictators and masters in matters of religion; and so they implicitly affect to be called of men Rabbi, which is by interpretation master, as the Pharisees did (Matt. 23:6–7), i.e. they are apt to expect that others should regard 'em, and yield to 'em, as masters, in matters of religion.[8]

But he whose heart is under the power of Christian humility, is of a contrary disposition. If the Scriptures are at all to be relied on, such an one is apt to think his attainments in religion to be comparatively mean and to esteem himself low among the saints, and one of the least of saints. Humility, or true lowliness of mind, disposes persons to think others better than themselves; "In lowliness

8. "There be two things wherein it appears that a man has only common gifts, and no inward principle: 1. these gifts ever puff up, and make a man something in his own eyes, as the Corinthian knowledge did; and many a private man thinks himself fit to be a minister." Shepard, *Parable*, Pt. I, pp. 181–2.

of mind, let each esteem others better than themselves" (Phil. 2:3). Hence they are apt to think the lowest room belongs to them; and their inward disposition naturally leads them to obey that precept of our Saviour (Luke 14:10). 'Tis not natural to them to take it upon 'em to do the part of teachers; but on the contrary, they are disposed to think that they are not the persons, that others are fitter for it than they; as it was with Moses and Jeremiah (Ex. 3:11; Jer. 1:6) though they were such eminent saints, and of great knowledge. It is not natural to them to think that it belongs to them to teach, but to be taught: they are much more eager to hear, and to receive instruction from others, than to dictate to others; "Be ye swift to hear, slow to speak" (Jas. 1:19). And when they do speak, 'tis not natural to them to speak with a bold, masterly air; but humility disposes 'em rather to speak trembling. "When Ephraim spake trembling, he exalted himself in Israel; but when he offended in Baal, he died" (Hos. 13:1). They are not apt to assume authority, and to take upon 'em to be chief managers and masters; but rather to be subject to others; "Be not many masters" (Jas. 3:1–2). "All of you be subject one to another, and be clothed with humility" (I Pet. 5:5). "Submitting yourselves one to another, in the fear of God" (Eph. 5:21).

There are some persons' experiences that naturally work that way, to make them think highly of their experiences; and they do often themselves speak of their experiences as very great and extraordinary; they freely speak of the great things they have met with. This may be spoken, and meant in a good sense. In one sense, every degree of saving mercy is a great thing: it is indeed a thing great, yea, infinitely great, for God to bestow the least crumb of children's bread on such dogs as we are in ourselves; and the more humble a person is that hopes that God has bestowed such mercy on him, the more apt will he be to call it a great thing that he has met with, in this sense. But if by great things which they have experienced, they mean comparatively great spiritual experiences, or great compared with others' experiences, or beyond what is ordinary, which is evidently oftentimes the case; then for a person to say, I have met with great things, is the very same thing as to say, I am an eminent saint, and have more grace than ordinary: for to have great experiences, if the experiences be true and worth the telling of, is the same thing as to have great grace: there is no true experience, but the exercise of grace; and exactly according to the degree of true experience, is the degree of grace and holiness. The persons that talk thus about their experiences, when they give an account of them, expect that others should admire 'em. Indeed they don't call it boasting to talk after this manner about their experiences, nor do they look upon it as any sign of pride; because they say, they know that it was not they that did it, it was free grace, they are the great things that God has done for them, they would acknowledge the great mercy God has shown them, and not make light of it. But so it was with the Pharisee that Christ tells us of (Luke 18). He in words gave God the glory of making him to differ from other men; "God I thank thee," says he, "that I am not as other men." [9] Their verbally ascribing it to the grace of God, that they are holier than other saints, don't hinder their forwardness to think so highly of their holiness, being a sure evidence of the pride and vanity of their minds. If they were under the influence of an humble spirit, their attainments in religion would not be so apt to shine in their own eyes, nor would they be so much in admiring their own beauty. The Christians that are really the most eminent saints, and therefore have the most excellent experiences, and are greatest in the kingdom of heaven, humble themselves as a little child (Matt. 18:4). Because they look on themselves as but little children in grace, and their attainments to be but the attainments of babes in Christ, and are astonished at, and ashamed of the low degrees of their love, and their thankfulness, and their little knowledge of God. Moses when he had been conversing with God in the mount, and his face shone so bright in the eyes of others, as to dazzle their eyes, wist not that his face shone. There are some persons that go by the name of high professors, and some will own themselves to be high professors; but eminently humble saints, that will shine brightest in heaven, are not at all apt to profess high. I don't believe there is an eminent saint in the world that is a high professor. Such will be much more likely to profess themselves to be the least of all saints, and to think that every saint's attainments and experiences are higher than his.[1]

9. Calvin, in his *Institutes of the Christian Religion,* Bk. III, ch. 12, no. 7, speaking of this Pharisee, observes, "That in his outward confession he acknowledges that the righteousness that he has is the gift of God: but (says he) because he trusts that he is righteous, he goes away out of the presence of God, unacceptable and odious."

1. Luther, as his words are cited by Samuel Rutherford, *A Survey of the Spiritual Antichrist* (London, 1648), pp. 143–4, says thus, "So is the life of a Christian,

Such is the nature of grace, and of true spiritual light, that they naturally dispose the saints in the present state, to look upon their grace and goodness little, and their deformity great. And they that have the most grace and spiritual light, of any in this world, have most of this disposition. As will appear most clear and evident to anyone that soberly and thoroughly weighs the nature and reason of things, and considers the things following.

That grace and holiness is worthy to be called little, that is, little in comparison of what it ought to be. And so it seems to one that is truly gracious: for such an one has his eye upon the rule of his duty; a conformity to that is what he aims at; it is what his soul struggles and reaches after; and it is by that that he estimates and judges of what he does, and what he has. To a gracious soul, and especially to one eminently gracious, that holiness appears little, which is little of what it should be; little of what he sees infinite reason for, and obligation to. If his holiness appears to him to be at a vast distance from this, it naturally appears despicable in his eyes, and not worthy to be mentioned as any beauty or amiableness in him. For the like reason as a hungry man naturally accounts that which is set before him, but a little food, a small matter, not worth mentioning, that is nothing in comparison of his appetite. Or as the child of a great prince, that is jealous for the honor of his father, and beholds the respect which men show him, naturally looks on that honor and respect very little, and not worthy to be

---

that he that has begun, seems to himself to have nothing; but strives and presses forward, that he may apprehend. Whence Paul says, 'I count not myself to have apprehended.' For indeed nothing is more pernicious to a believer, than that presumption, that he has already apprehended, and has no further need of seeking. Hence also many fall back, and pine away in spiritual security and slothfulness. So Bernard says, 'To stand still in God's way, is to go back.' Wherefore this remains to him that has begun to be a Christian, to think that he is not yet a Christian, but to seek that he may be a Christian, that he may glory with Paul, 'I am not, but I desire to be'; a Christian not yet finished, but only in his beginnings. Therefore he is not a Christian, that is a Christian, that is, he that thinks himself a finished Christian, and is not sensible how he falls short. We reach after heaven, but are not in heaven. Woe to him that is wholly renewed that is, that thinks himself to be so. That man, without doubt, has never so much as begun to be renewed, nor did he ever taste what it is to be a Christian." [Rutherford reproduced a Latin text of the work of Luther which he is citing together with English translation; JE, however, does not use this translation but makes one of his own from the Latin. The Latin original can be found in: Luther, *Omnium Operum,* Tom. Quart. 1558, Annotationes in Cap. XIII. Matt. (1538), Fol. 343.]

regarded, which is nothing in comparison of that, which the dignity of his father requires.

But that is the nature of true grace and spiritual light, that it opens to a person's view the infinite reason there is that he should be holy in a high degree. And the more grace he has, the more this is opened to view, the greater sense he has of the infinite excellency and glory of the divine Being, and of the infinite dignity of the person of Christ, and the boundless length and breadth, and depth and height, of the love of Christ to sinners. And as grace increases, the field opens more and more to a distant view, till the soul is swallowed up with the vastness of the object, and the person is astonished to think how much it becomes him to love this God, and this glorious Redeemer, that has so loved man, and how little he does love. And so the more he apprehends, the more the smallness of his grace and love appears strange and wonderful: and therefore is more ready to think that others are beyond him. For wondering at the littleness of his own grace, he can scarcely believe that so strange a thing happens to other saints: 'tis amazing to him, that one that is really a child of God, and that has actually received the saving benefits of that unspeakable love of Christ, should love no more: and he is apt to look upon it as a thing peculiar to himself, a strange and exempt instance; for he sees only the outside of other Christians, but he sees his own inside.

Here the readers may possibly object, that love to God is really increased, in proportion as the knowledge of God is increased; and therefore how should an increase of knowledge in a saint, make his love appear less, in comparison of what is known? To which I answer, that although grace and the love of God in the saints, be answerable to the degree of knowledge or sight of God; yet it is not in proportion to the object seen and known. The soul of a saint, by having something of God opened to sight, is convinced of much more than is seen. There is something that is seen, that is wonderful; and that sight brings with it a strong conviction of something vastly beyond, that is not immediately seen. So that the soul, at the same time, is astonished at its ignorance, and that it knows so little, as well as that it loves so little. And as the soul, in a spiritual view, is convinced of infinitely more in the object, yet beyond sight; so it is convinced of the capacity of the soul, of knowing vastly more, if clouds and darkness were but removed. Which causes the soul, in the enjoyment of a spiritual view, to complain greatly of spiritual ignorance, and want of love, and long and reach after more knowledge, and more love.

Grace and the love of God in the most eminent saints in this world, is truly very little in comparison of what it ought to be. Because the highest love, that ever any attain to in this life, is poor, cold, exceeding low, and not worthy to be named in comparison of what our obligations appear to be, from the joint consideration of these two things; viz. 1. The reason God has given us to love him, in the manifestations he has made of his infinite glory, in his Word, and in his works; and particularly in the gospel of his Son, and what he has done for sinful man by him. 2. The capacity there is in the soul of man, by those intellectual faculties which God has given it, of seeing and understanding these reasons, which God has given us to love him. How small indeed is the love of the most eminent saint on earth, in comparison of what these things jointly considered do require! And this grace tends to convince men of; and especially eminent grace: for grace is of the nature of light, and brings truth to view. And therefore, he that has much grace, apprehends much more than others, that great height to which his love ought to ascend; and he sees better than others, how little a way he has risen towards that height. And therefore, estimating his love by the whole height of his duty, hence it appears astonishingly little and low in his eyes.

And the eminent saint, having such a conviction of the high degree in which he ought to love God, this shews him, not only the littleness of his grace, but the greatness of his remaining corruption. In order to judge how much corruption or sin we have remaining in us, we must take our measure from that height to which the rule of our duty extends: the whole of the distance we are at from that height, is sin: for failing of duty is sin; otherwise our duty is not our duty; and by how much the more we fall short of our duty, so much the more sin have we. Sin is no other than disagreeableness, in a moral agent, to the law, or rule of his duty. And therefore the degree of sin is to be judged of by the rule: so much disagreeableness to the rule, so much sin, whether it be in defect or excess. Therefore if men, in their love to God, don't come up half way to that height which duty requires, then they have more corruption in their hearts than grace; because there is more goodness wanting, than is there; and all that is wanting is sin: it is an abominable defect; and appears so to the saints, especially those that are eminent; it appears exceeding abominable to them, that Christ should be loved so little, and thanked so little for his dying love; it is in their eyes hateful ingratitude.

And then the increase of grace has a tendency another way, to cause the saints to think their deformity vastly more than their goodness: it not only tends to convince them that their corruption is much greater than their goodness; which is indeed the case: but it also tends to cause the deformity that there is in the least sin, or the least degree of corruption, to appear so great, as vastly to outweigh all the beauty there is in their greatest holiness: for this also is indeed the case. For the least sin against an infinite God, has an infinite hatefulness or deformity in it; but the highest degree of holiness in a creature, has not an infinite loveliness in it: and therefore the loveliness of it is as nothing, in comparison of the deformity of the least sin. That every sin has infinite deformity and hatefulness in it, is most demonstrably evident; because what the evil, or iniquity, or hatefulness of sin consists in, is the violating of an obligation, or the being or doing contrary to what we should be or do, or are obliged to. And therefore by how much the greater the obligation is that is violated, so much the greater is the iniquity and hatefulness of the violation. But certainly our obligation to love and honor any being, is in some proportion to his loveliness and honorableness, or to his worthiness to be loved and honored by us; which is the same thing. We are surely under greater obligation to love a more lovely being, than a less lovely: and if a being be infinitely lovely or worthy to be loved by us, then our obligations to love him, are infinitely great: and therefore, whatever is contrary to this love, has in it infinite iniquity, deformity and unworthiness. But on the other hand, with respect to our holiness or love to God, there is not an infinite worthiness in that. The sin of the creature against God, is ill-deserving and hateful in proportion to the distance there is between God and the creature: the greatness of the object, and the meanness and inferiority of the subject, aggravates it. But 'tis the reverse with regard to the worthiness of the respect of the creature to God; 'tis worthless, and not worthy, in porportion to the meanness of the subject. So much the greater the distance between God and the creature, so much the less is the creature's respect worthy of God's notice or regard. The great degree of superiority, increases the obligation on the inferior to regard the superior; and so makes the want of regard more hateful: but the great degree of inferiority diminishes the worth of the regard of the inferior; because the more he is inferior, the less is he worthy of notice, the less he is, the less is what he can offer worth; for he can offer no more than himself, in offering his best respect; and therefore as he is little, and little worth, so is his respect little worth. And the more a person has of true grace and spiritual light, the more will it appear thus to him; the more will he appear to himself infinitely deformed by reason of sin, and the less will the goodness that is in his grace, or good experience, appear in proportion to it. For indeed it is nothing to it: it is less than a drop to the ocean: for finite bears no proportion at all to that which is infinite. But the more a person has of spiritual light, the more do things appear to him, in this respect, as they are indeed. Hence it most demonstrably appears, that true grace is of that nature, that the more a person has of it, with remaining corruption, the less does his goodness and holiness appear, in proportion to his deformity; and not only to his past deformity, but to his present deformity, in the sin that now appears in his heart, and in the abominable defects of his highest and best affections, and brightest experiences.

The nature of many high religious affections, and great discoveries (as they are called) in many persons that I have been acquainted with, is to hide and cover over the corruption of their hearts, and to make it seem to them as if all their sin was gone, and to leave them without complaints of any hateful evil left in them (though it may be they cry out much of their past unworthiness); a sure and certain evidence that their discoveries (as they call them) are darkness and not light. 'Tis darkness that hides men's pollution and deformity; but light let into the heart discovers it, searches it out in its secret corners, and makes it plainly to appear; especially that penetrating, all-searching light of God's holiness and glory. 'Tis true that saving discoveries may for the present hide corruption in one sense; they restrain the positive exercises of it, such as malice, envy, covetousness, lasciviousness, murmuring, etc. but they bring corruption to light, in that which is privative, viz. that there is no more love, no more humility, no more thankfulness. Which defects appear most hateful, in the eyes of those who have the most eminent exercises of grace; and are very burdensome, and cause the saints to cry out of their leanness, and odious pride and ingratitude. And whatever positive exercises of corruption, at any time arise, and mingle themselves with eminent actings of grace, grace will exceedingly magnify the view of them, and render their appearance far more heinous and horrible.

The more eminent saints are, and the more they have of the light of heaven in their souls, the more do they appear to themselves, as the most eminent saints in this world do, to the saints and angels in heaven. How can we rationally suppose the most eminent saints on earth appear to them, if beheld any otherwise, than covered over with the righteousness of Christ, and their deformities swallowed up and hid in the coruscation of the beams of his abundant glory and love? How can we suppose our most ardent love and praises appear to them, that do behold the beauty and glory of God without a veil? How does our highest thankfulness for the dying love of Christ appear to them, who see Christ as he is, who know as they are known, and see the glory of the person of him that died, and the wonders of his dying love, without any cloud or darkness? And how do they look on the deepest reverence and humility, with which worms of the dust on earth approach that infinite majesty, which they behold? Do they appear great to them, or so much as worthy of the name of reverence and humility, in those that they see to be at such an infinite distance from that great and holy God, in whose glorious presence they are? The reason why the highest attainments of the saints on earth appear so mean to them, is because they dwell in the light of God's glory, and see God as he is. And it is in this respect with the saints on earth, as it is with the saints in heaven, in proportion as they are more eminent in grace.

I would not be understood that the saints on earth have, in all respects, the worst opinion of themselves, when they have most of the exercise of grace. In many respects 'tis otherwise. With respect to the positive exercises of corruption, they may appear to themselves freest and best when grace is most in exercise, and worst when the actings of grace are lowest. And when they compare themselves with themselves, at different times, they may know, when grace is in lively exercise, that 'tis better with them than it was before (though before, in the time of it, they did not see so much badness as they see now); and when afterwards they sink again in the frame of their minds, they may know that they sink, and have a new argument of their great remaining corruption, and a rational conviction of a greater vileness than they saw before; and may have more of a sense of guilt, and a kind of legal sense of their sinfulness, by far, than when in the lively exercise of grace. But yet it is true, and demonstrable from the forementioned considerations, that the children of God never have so much of a sensible and spiritual conviction of their deformity; and so great and quick and abasing a sense of their present vileness and odiousness, as when they are highest in the exercise of true and pure grace; and never are they so much disposed to set themselves low among Christians as then. And thus he that is greatest in the kingdom, or most eminent in the church of Christ, is the same that humbles himself, as the least infant among them; agreeable to that great saying of Christ (Matt. 18:4).

A true saint may know that he has some true grace: and the more grace there is, the more easily is it known; as was observed and proved before. But yet it does not follow, that an eminent saint is easily sensible that he is an eminent saint, when compared with others. I will not deny that it is possible, that he that has much grace, and is an eminent saint, may know it. But he won't be apt to know it: it won't be a thing obvious to him: that he is better than others, and has higher experiences and attainments, is not a foremost thought; nor is it that which, from time to time, readily offers itself: it is a thing that is not in his way, but lies far out of sight: he must take pains to convince himself of it: there will be need of a great command of reason, and a high degree of strictness and care in arguing, to convince himself. And if he be rationally convinced, by a very strict consideration of his own experiences, compared with the great appearances of low degrees of grace in some other saints, it will hardly seem real to him, that he has more grace than they: and he'll be apt to lose the conviction, that he has by pains obtained: nor will it seem at all natural to him to act upon that supposition. And this may be laid down as an infallible thing, *that the person who is apt to think that he, as compared with others, is a very eminent saint, much distinguished in Christian experience, in whom this is a first thought, that rises of itself, and naturally offers itself; he is certainly mistaken; he is no eminent saint; but under the great prevailings of a proud and self-righteous spirit*. And if this be habitual with the man, and is statedly the prevailing temper of his mind, he is no saint at all; he has not the least degree of any true Christian experience; so surely as the Word of God is true.

And that sort of experiences that appears to be of that tendency, and is found from time to time to have that effect, to elevate the subject of them with a great conceit of those experiences, is certainly vain and delusive. Those supposed discoveries that naturally blow up the person with an admiration of the eminency of his discoveries, and fill him with conceit, that now he has seen, and knows more than most other Christians, have nothing of the nature of true spiritual light in them. All true spiritual knowledge is of that nature, that the more a person has of it, the more is he sensible of his own ignorance; as is evident by I Cor 8:2: "He that thinketh he knoweth anything, he knoweth nothing yet, as he ought to know." Agur when he had a great discovery of God, and sense of the wonderful height of his glory, and of his marvelous works, and cries out of his greatness and incomprehensibleness; at the same time, had the deepest sense of his brutish ignorance, and looked upon himself the most ignorant of all the saints; "Surely I am more brutish than any man, and have not the understanding of a man: I neither learned wisdom, nor have the knowledge of the holy. Who hath ascended up into heaven, or descended? Who hath gathered the wind in his fists? Who hath bound the waters in a garment? Who hath established all the ends of the earth? What is his name? And what is his son's name? If thou canst tell" (Prov. 30:2–4).

For a man to be highly conceited of his spiritual and divine knowledge, is for him to be wise in his own eyes, if anything is. And therefore it comes under those prohibitions, "Be not wise in thine own eyes" (Prov. 3:7). "Be not wise in your own conceits" (Rom. 12:16). And brings men under that woe, "Woe unto them that are wise in their own eyes, and prudent in their own sight" (Is. 5:21). Those that are thus wise in their own eyes, are some of the least likely to get good of any in the world. Experience shews the truth of that, "Seest thou a man wise in his own conceit? There is more hope of a fool than of him" (Prov. 26:12).

To this some may object, that the Psalmist, when we must suppose that he was in a holy frame, speaks of his knowledge as eminently great, and far greater than that of other saints, "I have more understanding than all my teachers: for thy testimonies are my meditation. I understand more than the ancients: because I keep thy precepts" (Ps. 119:99–100).

To this I answer two things:

First, there is no restraint to be laid upon the Spirit of God as to what he shall reveal to a prophet, for the benefit of his church, who is speaking or writing under immediate inspiration. The Spirit of God may reveal to such an one, and dictate to him, to declare to others, secret things, that otherwise would be hard, yea impossible for him to find out. As he may reveal to him mysteries, that otherwise would be above the reach of his reason; or things in a distant place, that he can't see; or future events, that it would be impossible for him to know and declare, if they were not extraordinarily revealed to him. So the Spirit of God might reveal to David this distinguishing benefit he had received, by conversing much with God's testimonies; and use him as his instrument to record it for the benefit of others, to excite them to the like duty, and to use the same means to gain knowledge. Nothing can be gathered concerning the natural tendency of the ordinary gracious influences of the Spirit of God, from that, that David declares of his distinguishing knowledge under the extraordinary influences of God's Spirit, immediately dictating to him the divine mind by inspiration, and using David as his instrument to write what he pleased for the benefit of his church; any more than we can reasonably argue, that it is the natural tendency of grace to incline men to curse others, and with the most dreadful misery to 'em that can be thought of, because David, under inspiration, often curses others, and prays that such misery may come upon them.

Secondly, it is not certain that the knowledge David here speaks of, is spiritual knowledge, wherein holiness does fundamentally consist. But it may be that greater revelation which God made to him of the Messiah, and the things of his future kingdom, and the far more clear and extensive knowledge that he had of the mysteries and doctrines of the gospel, than others; as a reward for his keeping God's testimonies. In this, it is apparent by the Book of Psalms, that David far exceeded all that had gone before him.

Secondly, another thing that is an infallible sign of spiritual pride, is persons being apt to think highly of their humility. False experiences are commonly attended with a counterfeit humility. And it is the very nature of a counterfeit humility, to be highly conceited of itself. False religious affections have generally that tendency, especially when raised to a great height, to make persons think that their humility is great, and accordingly to take much notice of their great attainments in this respect, and admire them. But eminently gracious affections (I scruple not to say it) are evermore of a contrary tendency, and have universally a contrary effect, in those that have them. They indeed make them very sensible what reason there is that they should be deeply humbled, and cause 'em earnestly to thirst and long after it; but they make their present humility, or that which they have already attained to, to appear small; and their remaining pride great, and exceedingly abominable.

The reason why a proud person should be apt to think his humility great, and why a very humble person should think his humility small, may be easily seen, if it be considered, that it is natural for persons, in judging of the degree of their own humiliation, to take their measure from that which they esteem their proper height, or the dignity wherein they properly stand. That may be great humiliation in one, that is no humiliation at all in another: because the degree of honorableness or considerableness, wherein each does properly stand, is very different. For some great man, to stoop to loose the latchet of the shoes of another great man, his equal, or to wash his feet, would be taken notice of as an act of abasement in him; and he being sensible of his own dignity, would look upon it so himself. But if a poor slave is seen stooping to unloose the shoes of a great prince, nobody will take any notice of this, as any act of humiliation in him, or token of any great degree of humility: nor would the slave himself, unless he be horribly proud, and ridiculously conceited of himself: and if he after he had done it, he should, in his talk and behavior, shew that he thought his abasement great in it, and had his mind much upon it, as an evidence of his being very humble; would not everybody cry out upon him, "Who do you think yourself to be, that you should think this that you have done, such a deep humiliation?" This would make it plain to a demonstration, that this slave was swollen with a high degree of pride and vanity of mind, as much as if he declared in plain terms, "I think myself to be some great one." And the matter is no less plain and certain, when worthless, vile and loathsome worms of the dust, are apt to put such a construction on their acts of abasement before God, and to think it a token of great humility in them that they, under their affections, can find themselves so willing to acknowledge themselves to be so and so mean and unworthy, and to behave themselves as those that are so inferior. The very reason why such outward acts, and such inward exercises, look like great abasement in such an one, is because he has a high conceit of himself. Whereas if he thought of himself more justly, these things would appear nothing to him, and his humility in them worthy of no regard; but would rather be astonished at his pride, that one so infinitely despicable and vile, is brought no lower before God. When he says in his heart, "This is a great act of humiliation: it is certainly a sign of great humility in me, that I should feel thus, and do so"; his meaning is, "This is great humility for me, for such a one as I, that am so considerable and worthy." He considers how low he is now brought, and compares this with the height of dignity, on which, he in his heart thinks he properly stands, and the distance appears very great, and he calls it all mere humility, and as such admires it. Whereas, in him that is truly humble, and really sees his own vileness and loathsomeness before God, the distance appears the other way. When he is brought lowest of all, it does not appear to him, that he is brought below his proper station; but that he is not come to it: he appears to himself, yet vastly above it: he longs to get lower, that he may come to it; but appears at a great distance from it. And this distance he calls pride. And therefore his pride appears great to him, and not his humility. For although he is brought much lower than he used to be; yet it don't appear to him worthy of the name of humiliation, for him that is so infinitely mean and detestable, to come down to a place, which though it be lower than what he used to assume, is yet vastly higher than what is proper for him. As men would hardly count it worthy of the name of humility, in a contemptible slave, that formerly affected to be a prince, to have his spirit so far brought down, as to take the place of a nobleman; when this is still so far above his proper station.

All men in the world, in judging of the degree of their own and others' humility, as appearing in any act of theirs, consider two things; viz. the real degree of dignity they stand in; and the degree of abasement, and the relation it bears to that real dignity. Thus the complying with the same low place, or low act, may be an evidence of great humility in one, that evidences but little or no humility in another. But truly humble Christians have so mean an opinion of their own real dignity, that all their self-abasement, when considered with relation to that, and compared with that, appears very small to them. It don't seem to them to be any great humility, or any abasement to be made much of, for such poor, vile, abject creatures as they, to lie at the foot of God.

The degree of humility is to be judged of by the degree of abasement, and the degree of the cause for abasement: but he that is truly and eminently humble, never thinks his humility great, considering the cause. The cause why he should be abased appears so great, and the abasement of the frame of his heart so greatly short of it, that he takes much more notice of his pride than his humility.

Everyone that has been conversant with souls under conviction of sin, knows that those who are greatly convinced of sin, are not apt to think themselves greatly convinced. And the reason is this: Men judge of the degree of their own convictions of sin by two things jointly considered; viz. the degree of sense which they have of guilt and pollution, and the degree of cause they have for such a sense, in the degree of their real sinfulness. 'Tis really no argument of any great conviction of sin, for some men to think themselves to be very sinful, beyond most others in the world; because they are so indeed, very plainly and notoriously. And therefore a far less conviction of sin may incline such an one to think so than another: he must be very blind indeed not to be sensible of it. But he that is truly under great convictions of sin, naturally thinks this to be his case. It appears to him that the cause he has to be sensible of guilt and pollution, is greater than others have; and therefore he ascribes his sensibleness of this, to the greatness of his sin, and not to the greatness of his sensibility. 'Tis natural for one under great convictions to think himself one of the greatest of sinners in reality, and also that it is so very plainly and evidently; for the greater his convictions are, the more plain and evident it seems to be to him. And therefore it necessarily seems to him so plain and so easy to him to see it, that it may be seen without much conviction. That man is under great convictions, whose conviction is great in proportion to his sin. But no man that is truly under great convictions, thinks his conviction great in proportion to his sin. For if he does, 'tis a certain sign that he inwardly thinks his sins small. And if that be the case, that is a certain evidence that his conviction is small. And this, by the way, is the main reason, that persons when under a work of humiliation, are not sensible of it, in the time of it.

And as it is with conviction of sin, just so it is, by parity of reason, with respect to persons' conviction or sensibleness of their own meanness and vileness, their own blindness, their own impotence, and all that low sense that a Christian has of himself, in the exercise of evangelical humiliation. So that in a high degree of this, the saints are never disposed to think their sensibleness of their own meanness, filthiness, impotence, etc. to be great; because it never appears great to them, considering the cause.

An eminent saint is not apt to think himself eminent in any thing; all his graces and experiences are ready to appear to him to be comparatively small; but especially his humility. There is nothing that appertains to Christian experience, and true piety, that is so much out of his sight as his humility. He is a thousand times more quick-sighted to discern his pride, than his humility: that he easily discerns, and is apt to take much notice of, but hardly discerns his humility. On the contrary, the deluded hypocrite, that is under the power of spiritual pride, is so blind to nothing as his pride; and so quick-sighted to nothing, as the shews of humility that are in him.

The humble Christian is more apt to find fault with his own pride than with other men's. He is apt to put the best construction on others' words and behavior, and to think that none are so proud as himself. But the proud hypocrite is quick to discern the mote in his brother's eye, in this respect; while he sees nothing of the beam in his own. He is very often much in crying out of others' pride, finding fault with others' apparel and way of living; and is affected ten times as much with his neighbor's ring or ribband, as with all the filthiness of his own heart.

From the disposition there is in hypocrites to think highly of their humility, it comes to pass that counterfeit humility is forward to put forth itself to view. Those that have it, are apt to be much in speaking of their humiliations, and to set them forth in high terms, and to make a great outward shew of humility, in affected looks, gestures or manner of speech, or meanness of apparel, or some affected singularity. So it was of old with the false prophets (Zech. 13:4). So it was with the hypocritical Jews (Is. 57:5). And so Christ tells us it was with the Pharisees (Matt. 6:16). But it is contrariwise with true humility: they that have it, are not apt to display their eloquence in setting of it forth, or to speak of the degree of their abasement in strong terms.[2] It don't affect to shew itself in any singular outward meanness of apparel, or way of living; agreeable to what is implied in: "But thou, when thou fastest, anoint thine head, and wash thy face" (Matt. 6:17). "Which things have indeed a show of wisdom, in will-worship, and humility, and neglecting the body" (Col. 2:23). Nor is true humility a noisy thing; it is not loud and boisterous. The Scripture represents it as of a contrary nature.

2. It is an observation of Mr. Jones, in his excellent treatise of the canon of the New Testament, that the evangelist Mark, who was the companion of St. Peter, and is supposed to have written his gospel under the direction of that apostle; when he mentions Peter's repentance after his denying his Master, he don't use such strong terms to set it forth as the other evangelists, he only uses these words, "When he thought thereon he wept" (Mark 14:72), whereas the other evangelists say thus, "He went out and wept bitterly" (Matt. 26:75; Luke 22:62). Jeremiah Jones, *A New and Full Method of Settling the Canonical Authority of the New Testament* (3 vols. London, 1726–27), *3*, 81. [See above, p. 73.]

Ahab, when he had a visible humility, a resemblance of true humility, went softly (I Kgs. 21:27). A penitent, in the exercise of true humiliation, is represented as still and silent, "He sitteth alone, and keepeth silence, because he hath born it upon him" (Lam. 3:28). And silence is mentioned as what attends humility, "If thou hast done foolishly, in lifting up thyself, or if thou hast thought evil, lay thy hand upon thy mouth" (Prov. 30:32).

Thus I have particularly and largely shewn the nature of that true humility that attends holy affections, as it appears in its tendency to cause persons to think meanly of their attainments in religion, as compared with the attainments of others, and particularly, of their attainments in humility: and have shewn the contrary tendency of spiritual pride, to dispose persons to think their attainments in these respects to be great. I have insisted the longer on this matter, because I look upon it a matter of great importance, as it affords a certain distinction between true and counterfeit humility; and also as this disposition of hypocrites to look on themselves better than others, is what God has declared to be very hateful to him, a smoke in his nose, and a fire that burneth all the day (Is. 65:5). 'Tis mentioned as an instance of the pride of the inhabitants of that holy city (as it was called) Jerusalem, that they esteemed themselves far better than the people of Sodom, and so looked upon them worthy to be overlooked and disregarded by them; "For thy sister Sodom was not mentioned by thy mouth, in the day of thy pride" (Ezek. 16:56).

Let not the reader lightly pass over these things in application to himself. If you once have taken it in, that it is a bad sign for a person to be apt to think himself a better saint than others, there will arise a blinding prejudice in your own favor; and there will probably be need of a great strictness of self-examination, in order to determine whether it be so with you. If on the proposal of the question, you answer, "No, it seems to me, none are so bad as I." Don't let the matter pass off so; but examine again, whether or no you don't think yourself better than others on this very account, because you imagine you think so meanly of yourself. Haven't you a high opinion of this humility? And if you answer again, "No; I have not a high opinion of my humility; it seems to me I am as proud as the devil"; yet examine again, whether self-conceit don't rise up under this cover; whether on this very account, that you think yourself as proud as the devil, you don't think yourself to be very humble.

From this opposition that there is between the nature of a true, and of a counterfeit humility, as to the esteem that the subjects of them have of themselves, arises a manifold contrariety of temper and behavior.

A truly humble person, having such a mean opinion of his righteousness and holiness, is poor in spirit. For a person to be poor in spirit, is to be in his own sense and apprehension poor, as to what is in him, and to be of an answerable disposition. Therefore a truly humble person, especially one eminently humble, naturally behaves himself in many respects as a poor man. The poor useth entreaties, but the rich answereth roughly. A poor man is not disposed to quick and high resentment when he is among the rich: he is apt to yield to others, for he knows others are above him; he is not stiff and self-willed; he is patient with hard fare; he expects no other than to be despised, and takes it patiently; he don't take it heinously that he is overlooked, and but little regarded; he is prepared to be in low place; he readily honors his superiors; he takes reproofs quietly; he readily honors others as above him; he easily yields to be taught, and don't claim much to his understanding and judgment; he is not overnice or humorsome, and has his spirit subdued to hard things; he is not assuming, nor apt to take much upon him, but 'tis natural for him to be subject to others. Thus it is with the humble Christian. Humility is (as the great Mastricht expresses it) a kind of holy pusillanimity.

A man that is very poor is a beggar; so is he that is poor in spirit. This is a great difference between those affections that are gracious, and those that are false: under the former, the person continues still a poor beggar at God's gates, exceeding empty and needy; but the latter make men appear to themselves rich, and increased with goods, and not very necessitous; they have a great stock in their own imagination for their subsistence.[3]

A poor man is modest in his speech and behavior; so, and much more, and more certainly and universally, is one that is poor in

3. "This spirit ever keeps a man poor and vile in his own eyes, and empty. . . . When the man hath got some knowledge, and can discourse pretty well, and hath some tastes of the heavenly gift, some sweet illapses of grace, and so his conscience is pretty well quieted: and if he hath got some answer to his prayers, and hath sweet affections, he grows full: and having ease to his conscience, casts off sense, and daily groaning under sin. And hence the spirit of prayer dies: he loses his esteem of God's ordinances; feels not such need of 'em; or gets no good, feels no life or power by 'em. . . . This is the woeful condition of some: but yet they know it not. But now he that is filled with the Spirit, the Lord empties him:

spirit; he is humble and modest in his behavior amongst men. 'Tis in vain for any to pretend that they are humble, and as little children before God, when they are haughty, assuming and impudent in their behavior amongst men. The Apostle informs us that the design of the gospel is to cut off all glorying, not only before God, but also before men (Rom. 4:1–2). Some pretend to great humiliation, that are very haughty, audacious and assuming in their external appearance and behavior: but they ought to consider those Scriptures, "Lord, my heart is not haughty, nor my eyes lofty; neither do I exercise myself in great matters, or in things too high for me" (Ps. 131:1). "These six things doth the Lord hate, yea seven are an abomination unto him; a proud look," etc. (Prov. 6:16–17). "An high look, and a proud heart, are sin" (ch. 21:4). "Thou wilt bring down high looks" (Ps. 18:27). And: "Him that hath an high look, and a proud heart, will I not suffer" (Ps. 101:5). "Charity vaunteth not itself; doth not behave itself unseemly" (I Cor. 13:4). There is a certain amiable modesty and fear that belongs to a Christian behavior among men, arising from humility that the Scriptures often speaks of; "Be ready to give an answer to every man that asketh you . . . with meekness and fear" (I Pet. 3:15). "Fear, to whom fear" (Rom. 13:7). "Whilst he remembered the obedience of you all, how with fear and trembling ye received him" (II Cor. 7:15). "Servants be obedient to them which are your masters according to the flesh, with fear and trembling" (Eph. 6:5). "Servants be subject to your masters, with all fear" (I Pet. 2:18). "While they behold your chaste conversation, coupled with fear" (I Pet. 3:2). "That women adorn themselves in modest apparel, with shamefacedness and sobriety" (I Tim. 2:9). In this respect a Christian is like a little child; a little child is modest before men, and his heart is apt to be possessed with fear and awe amongst them.

The same spirit will dispose a Christian to honor all men. "Honor

---

and the more, the longer he lives. So that though others think he needs not much grace; yet he accounts himself the poorest." Shepard, *Parable,* Pt. II, p. 132.

"After all fillings, be ever empty, hungry and feeling need, and praying for more." Ibid., p. 151.

"Truly brethren, when I see the curse of God upon many Christians, that are now grown full of their parts, gifts, peace, comforts, abilities, duties, I stand adoring the riches of the Lord's mercy, to a little handful of poor believers; not only in making them empty, but in keeping them so all their days." Shepard, *Sound Believer,* pp. 158–9.

all men" (I Pet. 2:17). A humble Christian is not only disposed to honor the saints in his behavior; but others also, in all those ways that don't imply a visible approbation of their sins. Thus Abraham, the great pattern of believers, honored the children of Heth. "Abraham stood up, and bowed himself to the people of the land" (Gen. 23:11–12). This was a remarkable instance of a humble behavior towards them that were out of Christ, and that Abraham knew to be accursed; and therefore would by no means suffer his servant to take a wife to his son, from among them; and Esau's wives, being of these children of Heth, were a grief of mind to Isaac and Rebekah. So Paul honored Festus, "I am not mad, most noble Festus" (Acts 26:25). Not only will Christian humility dispose persons to honor those wicked men that are out of the visible church, but also false brethren and persecutors. As Jacob, when he was in an excellent frame, having just been wrestling all night with God, and received the blessing, honored Esau, his false and persecuting brother (Gen. 33:3): Jacob "bowed himself to the ground seven times, until he came near his brother" Esau. So he called him "Lord"; and commanded all his family to honor him in like manner.

Thus I have endeavored to describe the heart and behavior of one that is governed by a truly gracious humility, as exactly agreeable to the Scriptures, as I am able.

Now it is out of such a heart as this, that all truly holy affections do flow. Christian affections are like Mary's precious ointment, that she poured on Christ's head, that filled the whole house with a sweet odor. That was poured out of an alabaster box; so gracious affections flow out to Christ out of a pure heart. That was poured out of a broken box; till the box was broken the ointment could not flow, nor diffuse its odor: so gracious affections flow out of a broken heart. Gracious affections are also like those of Mary Magdalene (Luke 7 at the latter end) who also pours precious ointment on Christ, out of an alabaster broken box, anointing therewith the feet of Jesus, when she had washed 'em with her tears, and wiped them with the hair of her head. All gracious affections, that are a sweet odor to Christ, and that fill the soul of a Christian with an heavenly sweetness and fragrancy, are brokenhearted affections. A truly Christian love, either to God or men, is a humble brokenhearted love. The desires of the saints, however earnest, are humble desires: their hope is an humble hope; and their joy, even when it is unspeakable, and full of glory, is a humble, brokenhearted joy, and leaves the Christian more poor in spirit, and more like a little child, and more disposed to an universal lowliness of behavior.

VII. Another thing, wherein gracious affections are distinguished from others, is, that they are attended with a change of nature.

All gracious affections do arise from a spiritual understanding, in which the soul has the excellency and glory of divine things discovered to it, as was shown before. But all spiritual discoveries are transforming; and not only make an alteration of the present exercise, sensation and frame of the soul; but such power and efficacy have they, that they make an alteration in the very nature of the soul; "But we all, with open face, beholding as in a glass, the glory of the Lord, are changed into the same image, from glory to glory, even as by the Spirit of the Lord" (II Cor. 3:18). Such power as this is properly divine power, and is peculiar to the Spirit of the Lord: other power may make a great alteration in men's present frames and feelings; but 'tis the power of a Creator only that can change the nature, or give a new nature. And no discoveries or illuminations, but those that are divine and supernatural, will have this supernatural effect. But this effect all those discoveries have, that are truly divine. The soul is deeply affected by these discoveries and so affected as to be transformed.

Thus it is with those affections that the soul is the subject of in its conversion. The Scripture representations of conversion do strongly imply and signify a change of nature: such as being born again; becoming new creatures; rising from the dead; being renewed in the spirit of the mind; dying to sin, and living to righteousness; putting off the old man, and putting on the new man; a being ingrafted into a new stock; a having a divine seed implanted in the heart; a being made partakers of the divine nature, etc.

Therefore if there be no great and remarkable, abiding change in persons, that think they have experienced a work of conversion, vain are all their imaginations and pretenses, however they have been affected.[4] Conversion (if we may give any credit to the Scrip-

4. "I would not judge of the whole soul's coming to Christ, so much by sudden pangs, as by an inward bent. For the whole soul, in affectionate expressions and actions, may be carried to Christ; but being without this bent, and change of affections, is unsound." Shepard, *Parable*, Pt. I, p. 203.

ture) is a great and universal change of the man, turning him from sin to God. A man may be restrained from sin, before he is converted; but when he is converted, he is not only restrained from sin, his very heart and nature is turned from it, unto holiness: so that thenceforward he becomes a holy person, and an enemy to sin. If therefore, after a person's high affections, at his supposed first conversion, it comes to that in a little time, that there is no very sensible, or remarkable alteration in him, as to those bad qualities, and evil habits, which before were visible in him, and he is ordinarily under the prevalence of the same kind of dispositions that he used to be, and the same things seem to belong to his character, he appears as selfish, carnal, as stupid, and perverse, as unchristian, and unsavory as ever; it is greater evidence against him, than the brightest story of experiences that ever was told, is for him. For in Christ Jesus neither circumcision, nor uncircumcision, neither high profession, nor low profession, neither a fair story, nor a broken one, avails anything; but a new creature.

If there be a very great alteration visible in a person for a while; if it ben't abiding, but he afterwards returns, in a stated manner to be much as he used to be; it appears to be no change of nature. For nature is an abiding thing. A swine that is of a filthy nature may be washed; but the swinish nature remains. And a dove that is of a cleanly nature may be defiled, but its cleanly nature remains.[5]

Indeed allowances must be made for the natural temper: conversion don't entirely root out the natural temper: those sins which a man by his natural constitution was most inclined to before his conversion, he may be most apt to fall into still. But yet conversion will make a great alteration even with respect to these sins. Though grace, while imperfect, don't root out an evil natural temper; yet it is of great power and efficacy with respect to it, to correct it. The change that is wrought in conversion, is an universal change: grace changes a man with respect to whatever is sinful in him: the old man is put off and the new man put on: they are sanctified throughout: and the man becomes a new creature: old things are passed

5. " 'Tis with the soul, as with water; all the cold may be gone, but the native principle of cold remains still. You may remove the burning of lusts, not the blackness of nature. Where the power of sin lies, change of conscience from security to terror, change of life from profaneness to civility, and fashions of the world, to escape the pollutions thereof, change of lusts, nay quenching them for a time: but the nature is never changed, in the best hypocrite that ever was." Ibid., p. 194.

away, and all things are become new: all sin is mortified; constitution sins, as well as others. If a man before his conversion, was by his natural constitution, especially inclined to lasciviousness, or drunkenness, or maliciousness; converting grace will make a great alteration in him, with respect to these evil dispositions; so that however he may be still most in danger of these sins, yet they shall no longer have dominion over him; nor will they any more be properly his character. Yea, true repentence does in some respects, especially turn a man against his own iniquity; that wherein he has been most guilty, and has chiefly dishonored God. He that forsakes other sins, but saves his leading sin, the iniquity he is chiefly inclined to; is like Saul, when sent against God's enemies the Amalekites, with a strict charge to save none of them alive, but utterly to destroy them, small and great; who utterly destroyed inferior people, but saved the king, the chief of 'em all, alive.

Some foolishly make it an argument in favor of their discoveries and affections, that when they are gone, they are left wholly without any life or sense, or anything beyond what they had before. They think it an evidence that what they experienced was wholly of God, and not of themselves; because (say they) when God is departed, all is gone; they can see and feel nothing, and are no better than they used to be.

'Tis very true that all grace and goodness in the hearts of the saints is entirely from God: and they are universally and immediately dependent on him for it. But yet these persons are mistaken, as to the manner of God's communicating himself and his Holy Spirit, in imparting saving grace to the soul. He gives his Spirit to be united to the faculties of the soul, and to dwell there after the manner of a principle of nature; so that the soul, in being indued with grace, is indued with a new nature: but nature is an abiding thing. All the exercises of grace are entirely from Christ: but those exercises are not from Christ, as something that is alive, moves and stirs something that is without life, and yet remains without life; but as having life communicated to it; so as through Christ's power, to have inherent in itself, a vital nature. In the soul where Christ savingly is, there he lives. He don't only live without it, so as violently to actuate it; but he lives in it; so that that also is alive. Grace in the soul is as much from Christ, as the light in a glass, held out in the sunbeams, is from the sun. But this represents the manner of the communication of grace to the soul, but in part; because the glass remains as it was, the nature of it not being at all changed, it is as much without any lightsomeness in its nature as ever. But the soul of a saint receives light from the Sun of Righteousness, in such a manner, that its nature is changed, and it becomes properly a luminous thing: not only does the sun shine in the saints, but they also become little suns, partaking of the nature of the fountain of their light. In this respect, the manner of their derivation of light, is like that of the lamps in the tabernacle, rather than that of a reflecting glass; which though they were lit up by fire from heaven, yet thereby became, themselves burning shining things. The saints don't only drink of the water of life, that flows from the original fountain; but this water becomes a fountain of water in them, springing up there, and flowing out of them; cf. John 4:14 and ch. 7:38–39. Grace is compared to a seed implanted, that not only is in the ground, but has hold of it, has root there, and grows there, and is an abiding principle of life and nature there.

As it is with spiritual discoveries and affections given at first conversion, so it is in all illuminations and affections of that kind, that persons are the subjects of afterwards; they are all transforming. There is a like divine power and energy in them, as in the first discoveries: and they still reach the bottom of the heart, and affect and alter the very nature of the soul, in proportion to the degree in which they are given. And a transformation of nature is continued and carried on by them, to the end of life; till it is brought to perfection in glory. Hence the progress of the work of grace in the hearts of the saints, is represented in Scripture, as a continued conversion and renovation of nature. So the Apostle exhorts those that were at Rome, beloved of God, called to be saints, and that were the subjects of God's redeeming mercies, to be transformed by the renewing of their mind; "I beseech you therefore by the mercies of God, that ye present your bodies, a living sacrifice; . . . And be not conformed to this world; but be ye transformed, by the renewing of your mind" (Rom. 12:1–2). Compared with ch. 1:7. So the Apostle writing to the saints and faithful in Christ Jesus, that were at Ephesus (Eph. 1:1), and those who were once dead in trespasses and sins, but were now quickened, and raised up, and made to sit together in heavenly places in Christ, and created in Christ Jesus unto good works, that were once far off, but were now made nigh by the blood of Christ, and that were no more strangers and foreigners, but fellow citizens with the saints, and of the household of God, and that were built together for an habitation of God through the Spirit; I say, the Apostle writing to these, tells them, that he ceased not to pray for them, that God would give them the spirit of wisdom and revelation, in the knowledge of Christ; the eyes of their understanding being enlightened, that they might know, or experience, what was the exceeding greatness of God's power towards them that believe; according to the working of his mighty power, which he wrought in Christ when he raised him from the dead, and set him at his own right hand in the heavenly places (Eph. 1:16, to the end [of ch. 2]). In this the Apostle has respect to the glorious power and work of God in converting and renewing the soul: as is most plain by the sequel. So the Apostle exhorts the same persons to put off the old man, which is corrupt according to the deceitful lusts; and be renewed in the spirit of their minds; and put on the new man, which after God, is created in righteousness and true holiness (Eph. 4:22–24).

There is a sort of high affections that some have from time to time, that leave them without any manner of appearance of an abiding effect. They go off suddenly; so that from the very height of their emotion, and seeming rapture, they pass at once to be quite dead, and void of all sense and activity. It surely is not wont to be thus with high gracious affections; [6] they leave a sweet savor and relish of divine things on the heart, and a stronger bent of soul towards God and holiness. As Moses's face not only shone while he was in the mount, extraordinarily conversing with God; but it continued to shine after he came down from the mount. When men have been conversing with Christ in an extraordinary manner, there is a sensible effect of it remains upon them; there is something remarkable in their disposition and frame, which if we take knowledge of, and trace to its cause, we shall find it is because they have been with Jesus (Acts 4:13).

VIII. Truly gracious affections differ from those affections that are false and delusive, in that they tend to, and are attended with the lamblike, dovelike spirit and temper of Jesus Christ; or in other

6. "Do you think the Holy Ghost comes on a man, as on Balaam, by immediate acting, and then leaves him; and then he has nothing?" Shepard, *Parable,* Pt. I, p. 126.

words, they naturally beget and promote such a spirit of love, meekness, quietness, forgiveness and mercy, as appeared in Christ.

The evidence of this in the Scripture, is very abundant. If we judge of the nature of Christianity, and the proper spirit of the gospel, by the Word of God, this spirit is what may by way of eminency be called the Christian spirit; and may be looked upon as the true, and distinguishing disposition of the hearts of Christians, as Christians. When some of the disciples of Christ said something, through inconsideration and infirmity, that was not agreeable to such a spirit, Christ told them that knew not what manner of spirit they were of, Luke 9:55, implying that this spirit that I am speaking of, is the proper spirit of his religion and kingdom. All that are truly godly, and real disciples of Christ, have this spirit in them; and not only so but they are of this spirit; it is the spirit by which they are so possessed and governed, that it is their true and proper character. This is evident by what the wise man says (having respect plainly to such a spirit as this): "A man of understanding is of an excellent spirit" (Prov. 17:27); and by the particular description Christ gives of the qualities and temper of such as are truly blessed, that shall obtain mercy, and are God's children and heirs, "Blessed are the meek: for they shall inherit the earth. Blessed are the merciful: for they shall obtain mercy. Blessed are the peacemakers: for they shall be called the children of God" (Matt. 5:5, 7, 9). And that this spirit is the special character of the elect of God, is manifest by Col. 3:12–13: "Put on therefore, as the elect of God, holy and beloved, bowels of mercies, kindness, humbleness of mind, meekness, long-suffering; forbearing one another, and forgiving one another." And the Apostle speaking of that temper and disposition which he speaks of as the most excellent and essential thing in Christianity, and that without which none are true Christians, and the most glorious profession and gifts are nothing (calling this spirit by the name of charity) he describes it thus: "Charity suffereth long and is kind; charity envieth not; charity vaunteth not itself, is not puffed up; doth not behave itself unseemly; seeketh not her own; is not easily provoked; thinketh no evil" (I Cor. 13:4–5). And the same Apostle (Gal. 5), designedly declaring the distinguishing marks and fruits of true Christian grace, chiefly insists on the things that appertain to such a temper and spirit as I am speaking of, "The fruit of the spirit is love, joy, peace, long-suffering, gentleness, goodness, faith, meekness, temperance" (verses 22–23). And so does the apostle James, in describing true grace, or that wisdom that is from above, with that declared design, that others who are of a contrary spirit may not deceive themselves, and lie against the truth, in professing to be Christians, when they are not, "If ye have bitter envying and strife in your hearts, glory not, and lie not against the truth: this wisdom descendeth not from above; but is earthly, sensual, devilish. For where envying and strife is, there is confusion and every evil work. But the wisdom that is from above is first pure, then peaceable, gentle, easy to be intreated, full of mercy and good fruits" (Jas. 3:14–17).

Everything that appertains to holiness of heart, does indeed belong to the nature of true Christianity, and the character of Christians; but a spirit of holiness as appearing in some particular graces, may more especially be called the Christian spirit or temper. There are some amiable qualities and virtues, that do more especially agree with the nature of the gospel constitution, and Christian profession; because there is a special agreeableness in them, with those divine attributes which God has more remarkably manifested and glorified in the work of redemption by Jesus Christ, that is the grand subject of the Christian revelation; and also a special agreeableness with those virtues that were so wonderfully exercised by Jesus Christ towards us in that affair, and the blessed example he hath therein for us; and likewise because they are peculiarly agreeable to the special drift and design of the work of redemption, and the benefits we thereby receive, and the relation that it brings us into, to God and one another. And these virtues are such as humility, meekness, love, forgiveness, and mercy. These things therefore especially belong to the character of Christians, as such.

These things are spoken of as what are especially the character of Jesus Christ himself, the great head of the Christian church. They are so spoken of in the prophecies of the Old Testament; as in that cited Matt. 21:5: "Tell ye the daughter of Zion, behold thy king cometh unto thee, meek, and sitting upon an ass, and a colt the foal of an ass." So Christ himself speaks of 'em, "Learn of me; for I am meek and lowly in heart" (Matt. 11:29). The same appears by the name by which Christ is so often called in Scripture, viz. THE LAMB. And as these things are especially the character of Christ; so they are also especially the character of Christians. Christians are Christlike: none deserve the name of Christians that are not so, in their prevailing character. The new man is renewed, after the image of him that creates him (Col. 3:10). All true Christians behold as in a glass, the glory of the Lord, and are changed into the same image, by his Spirit (II Cor. 3:18). The elect are all predestinated to be conformed to the image of the Son of God, that he might be the first-born among many brethren (Rom. 8:29). As we have borne the image of the first man, that is earthly, so we must also bear the image of the heavenly: for as is the earthy, such are they also that are earthy; and as is the heavenly, such are they also that are heavenly (I Cor. 15:47–49). Christ is full of grace; and Christians all receive of his fullness, and grace for grace: i.e. there is grace in Christians answering to grace in Christ, such an answerableness as there is between the wax and the seal; there is character for character: such kind of graces, such a spirit and temper, the same things that belong to Christ's character, belong to theirs. That disposition wherein Christ's character does in a special manner consist, therein does his image in a special manner consist. Christians that shine by reflecting the light of the Sun of Righteousness, do shine with the same sort of brightness, the same mild, sweet and pleasant beams. These lamps of the spiritual temple, that are enkindled by fire from heaven, burn with the same sort of flame. The branch is of the same nature with the stock and root, has the same sap, and bears the same sort of fruit. The members have the same kind of life with the head. It would be strange if Christians should not be of the same temper and spirit that Christ is of; when they are his flesh and his bone, yea are one spirit (I Cor. 6:17), and live so, that it is not they that live, but Christ that lives in them. A Christian spirit is Christ's mark, that he sets upon the souls of his people; his seal in their foreheads, bearing his image and superscription. Christians are the followers of Christ: and they are so, as they are obedient to that call of Christ (Matt. 11:28–29). Come to me, and learn of me, for I am meek and lowly of heart. They follow him as the lamb; "These are they which follow the lamb whithersoever he goeth" (Rev. 14:14). True Christians are as it were clothed with the meek, quiet, and loving temper of Christ; for as many as are in Christ, have put on Christ. And in this respect the church is clothed with the Sun, not only by being clothed with his imputed righteousness, but also by being adorned with his graces (Rom. 13:14). Christ the great Shepherd, is himself a lamb, and believers are also lambs: all the flocks are lambs; "Feed my lambs"

(John 21:15). "I send you forth as lambs, in the midst of wolves" (Luke 10:3). The redemption of the church by Christ from the power of the devil was typified of old, by David's delivering the lamb, out of the mouth of the lion and the bear.

That such manner of virtue as has been spoken of is the very nature of the Christian spirit, or the Spirit that worketh in Christ and in his members, and the distinguishing nature of it, is evident by this, that the dove is the very symbol or emblem, chosen of God, to represent it. Those things are fittest emblems of other things, which do best represent that which is most distinguishing in their nature. The Spirit that descended on Christ, when he was anointed of the Father, descended on him like a dove. The dove is a noted emblem of meekness, harmlessness, peace and love. But the same Spirit that descended on the Head of the Church, descends to the members. God hath sent forth the Spirit of his Son into their hearts (Gal. 4:6). And if any man has not the Spirit of Christ, he is none of his (Rom. 8:9). There is but one Spirit to the whole mystical body, head and members (I Cor. 6:17; Eph. 4:4). Christ breathes his own Spirit on his disciples (John 20:22). As Christ was anointed with the Holy Ghost, descending on him like a dove, so Christians also have an anointing from the Holy One (I John 2:20, 27). And they are anointed with the same oil; 'tis the same precious ointment on the head, that goes down to the skirts of the garments: and on both it is a spirit of peace and love: "Behold how good, and how pleasant it is, for brethren to dwell together in unity! It is like the precious ointment upon the head, that ran down upon the beard, even Aaron's beard; that went down to the skirts of his garments" (Ps. 133:1–2). The oil on Aaron's garments, had the same sweet and inimitable odor, with that on his head; the smell of the same sweet spices. Christian affections, and a Christian behavior, is but the flowing out of the savor of Christ's sweet ointments. Because the church has a dovelike temper and disposition, therefore it is said of her that she has doves' eyes, "Behold thou art fair, my love; behold thou art fair: thou hast doves' eyes" (Cant. 1:15). And: "Behold thou art fair, my love; behold thou art fair: thou hast doves' eyes within thy locks" (ch. 4:1). The same that is said of Christ, "His eyes are as the eyes of doves" (ch. 5:12). And the church is frequently compared to a dove in Scripture, "O my dove, that art in the clefts of the rock" (Cant. 2:14). "Open to me my love, my dove" (ch. 5:2). And: "My dove, my undefiled, is but one" (ch. 6:9). "Ye shall be as the wings of a dove, covered with silver, and her feathers with yellow gold" (Ps. 68:13). And: "O deliver not the soul of thy turtle-dove unto the multitude of the wicked" (74:19). The dove that Noah sent out of the ark, that could find no rest for the sole of her foot, till she returned, was a type of a true saint.

Meekness is so much the character of the saints, that the meek and the godly, are used as synonymous terms in Scripture: so Ps. 37:10–11. The wicked and the meek are set in opposition one to another, as wicked and godly. "Yet a little while, and the wicked shall not be . . . but the meek shall inherit the earth." So: "The Lord lifteth up the meek: he casteth the wicked down to the ground" (Ps. 147:6).

'Tis doubtless very much on this account, that Christ represents all his disciples, all the heirs of heaven, as little children, "Suffer little children to come unto me, and forbid them not; for of such is the kingdom of heaven" (Matt. 19:14). "Whosoever shall give to drink unto one of these little ones, a cup of cold water, in the name of a disciple, verily I say unto you, he shall in no wise lose his reward" (Matt. 10:42). "Whoso shall offend one of these little ones," etc. (Matt. 18:6). "Take heed that ye despise not one of these little ones" (ver. 10). "It is not the will of your Father which is in heaven, that one of these little ones should perish" (ver. 14). "Little children, yet a little while am I with you" (John 13:33). Little children are innocent and harmless: they don't do a great deal of mischief in the world: men need not be afraid of them: they are no dangerous sort of persons: their anger don't last long: they don't lay up injuries in high resentment, entertaining deep and rooted malice. So Christians, in malice, are children (I Cor. 14:20). Little children are not guileful and deceitful; but plain and simple: they are not versed in the arts of fiction and deceit; and are strangers to artful disguises. They are yieldable and flexible, and not willful and obstinate; don't trust to their own understanding, but rely on the instructions of parents, and others of superior understanding. Here is therefore a fit and lively emblem of the followers of the Lamb. Persons being thus like little children, is not only a thing highly commendable, and what Christians approve of, and aim at, and which some of extraordinary proficiency do attain to; but it is their universal character, and absolutely necessary in order to entering the kingdom of heaven; unless Christ was mistaken; "Verily I say unto you, except ye be converted, and become as little children, ye shall not enter into the kingdom of heaven" (Matt. 18:3). "Verily I say unto you, whosoever shall not receive the kingdom of God as a little child, he shall not enter therein" (Mark 10:15).

But here some may be ready to say, is there no such thing as Christian fortitude, and boldness for Christ, being good soldiers in the Christian warfare, and coming out bold against the enemies of Christ and his people?

To which I answer, there doubtless is such a thing. The whole Christian life is compared to a warfare, and fitly so. And the most eminent Christians are the best soldiers, endowed with the greatest degrees of Christian fortitude. And it is the duty of God's people to be steadfast, and vigorous in their opposition to the designs and ways of such, as are endeavoring to overthrow the kingdom of Christ, and the interest of religion. But yet many persons seem to be quite mistaken concerning the nature of Christian fortitude. 'Tis an exceeding diverse thing from a brutal fierceness, or the boldness of beasts of prey. True Christian fortitude consists in strength of mind, through grace, exerted in two things; in ruling and suppressing the evil, and unruly passions and affections of the mind; and in steadfastly and freely exerting, and following good affections and dispositions, without being hindered by sinful fear, or the opposition of enemies. But the passions that are restrained and kept under, in the exercise of this Christian strength and fortitude, are those very passions that are vigorously and violently exerted, in a false boldness for Christ. And those affections that are vigorously exerted in true fortitude, are those Christian holy affections, that are directly contrary to 'em. Though Christian fortitude appears, in withstanding and counteracting the enemies that are without us; yet it much more appears, in resisting and suppressing the enemies that are within us; because they are our worst and strongest enemies, and have greatest advantage against us. The strength of the good soldier of Jesus Christ, appears in nothing more, than in steadfastly maintaining the holy calm, meekness, sweetness, and benevolence of his mind, amidst all the storms, injuries, strange behavior, and surprising acts and events of this evil and unreasonable world. The Scripture seems to intimate that true fortitude consists chiefly in this, "He that is slow to anger, is better than the mighty; and he that ruleth his spirit, than he that taketh a city" (Prov. 16:32).

The directest and surest way in the world, to make a right judgment, what a holy fortitude is, in fighting with God's enemies; is to look to the captain of all God's hosts, and our great leader and example; and see wherein his fortitude and valor appeared, in his chief conflict, and in the time of the greatest battle that ever was, or ever will be fought with these enemies, when he fought with them all alone, and of the people there was none with him, and exercised his fortitude in the highest degree that ever he did, and got that glorious victory that will be celebrated in the praises and triumphs of all the hosts of heaven, throughout all eternity: even to Jesus Christ in the time of his last sufferings; when his enemies in earth and hell made their most violent attack upon him, compassing him round on every side, like renting and roaring lions. Doubtless here we shall see the fortitude of a holy warrior and champion in the cause of God, in its highest perfection and greatest luster, and an example fit for the soldiers to follow, that fight under this captain. But how did he show his holy boldness and valor at that time? Not in the exercise of any fiery passions; not in fierce and violent speeches, and vehemently declaiming against, and crying out of the intolerable wickedness of opposers, giving 'em their own in plain terms; but in not opening his mouth when afflicted and oppressed, in going as a lamb to the slaughter, and as a sheep before his shearers, is dumb, not opening his mouth; praying that the Father would forgive his cruel enemies, because they knew not what they did; not shedding others' blood; but with all-conquering patience and love, shedding his own. Indeed one of his disciples, that made a forward pretense to boldness for Christ, and confidently declared he would sooner die with Christ than deny him, began to lay about him with a sword: but Christ meekly rebukes him, and heals the wound he gives. And never was the patience, meekness, love, and forgiveness of Christ, in so glorious a manifestation, as at that time. Never did he appear so much a lamb, and never did he show so much of the dovelike spirit, as at that time. If therefore we see any of the followers of Christ, in the midst of the most violent, unreasonable and wicked opposition, of God's and his own enemies, maintaining under all this temptation, the humility, quietness, and gentleness of a lamb, and the harmlessness, and love, and sweetness of a dove, we may well judge that here is a good soldier of Jesus Christ.

When persons are fierce and violent, and exert their sharp and bitter passions, it shows weakness, instead of strength and fortitude. "And I brethren, could not speak unto you, as unto spiritual, but as unto carnal, even as unto babes in Christ. . . . For ye are yet carnal: for whereas there is among you envying and strife, and divisions, are ye not carnal, and walk as men?" (I Cor. 3, at the beginning).

There is a pretended boldness for Christ that arises from no better principle than pride. A man may be forward to expose himself to the dislike of the world, and even to provoke their displeasure, out of pride. For 'tis the nature of spiritual pride to cause men to seek distinction and singularity; and so oftentimes to set themselves at war with those that they call carnal, that they may be more highly exalted among their party. True boldness for Christ is universal and overcomes all, and carries 'em above the displeasure of friends and foes; so that they will forsake all rather than Christ and will rather offend all parties, and be thought meanly of by all, than offend Christ. And that duty which tries whether a man is willing to be despised by them that are of his own party, and thought the least worthy to be regarded by them, is a much more proper trial of his boldness for Christ, than his being forward to expose himself to the reproach of opposers. The Apostle sought not glory, not only of heathens and Jews, but of Christians; as he declares (I Thess. 2:26).[7] He is bold for Christ, that has Christian fortitude enough, to confess his fault openly, when he has committed one that requires it, and as it were to come down upon his knees before opposers. Such things as these are a vastly greater evidence of holy boldness, than resolutely and fiercely confronting opposers.

As some are much mistaken concerning the nature of true boldness for Christ, so they are concerning Christian zeal. 'Tis indeed a flame, but a sweet one: or rather it is the heat and fervor of a sweet flame. For the flame of which it is the heat, is no other than that of divine love, or Christian charity; which is the sweetest and most benevolent thing that is, or can be, in the heart of man or angel. Zeal is the fervor of this flame, as it ardently and vigorously goes out towards the good that is its object, in desires of it, and pursuit after it: and so consequentially, in opposition to the evil that is contrary to it, and impedes it. There is indeed opposition, and

7. Mr. Shepard, speaking of hypocrites affecting applause, says: "hence men forsake their friends, and trample under foot the scorns of the world: they have credit elsewhere. To maintain their interest in the love of godly men, they will suffer much." Shepard, *Parable,* Pt. I, p. 180.

vigorous opposition, that is a part of it, or rather is an attendant of it; but it is against *things,* and not *persons.* Bitterness against the persons of men is no part of it, but is very contrary to it; insomuch that so much the warmer true zeal is, and the higher it is raised, so much the further are persons from such bitterness, and so much fuller of love, both to the evil and to the good. As appears from what has been just now observed, that it is no other, in its very nature and essence, than the fervor of a spirit of Christian love. And as to what opposition there is in it, to things, it is firstly and chiefly against the evil things in the person himself, who has this zeal; against the enemies of God and holiness, that are in his own heart (as these are most in his view, and what he is most to do with); and but secondarily against the sins of others. And therefore there is nothing in a true Christian zeal, that is contrary to that spirit of meekness, gentleness and love, that spirit of a little child, a lamb and dove, that has been spoken of; but it is entirely agreeable to it, and tends to promote it.

But to say something particularly concerning this Christian spirit I have been speaking of, as exercised in these three things, forgiveness, love and mercy; I would observe that the Scripture is very clear and express concerning the absolute necessity of each of these, as belonging to the temper and character of every Christian.

It is so as to a forgiving spirit, or a disposition to overlook and forgive injuries. Christ gives it to us both as a negative and positive evidence; and is express in teaching us, that if we are of such a spirit, 'tis a sign we are in a state of forgiveness and favor ourselves; and that if we are not of such a spirit, we are not forgiven of God; and seems to take special care that we should take good notice of it, and always bear it on our minds. "Forgive us our debts, as we forgive our debtors. . . . For if ye forgive men their trespasses, your heavenly Father will also forgive you: but if ye forgive not men their trespasses, neither will your Father forgive your trespasses" (Matt. 6:12, 14–15). Christ expresses the same again at another time (Mark 11:25–26 and again in Matt. 18:22, to the end), in the parable of the servant that owed his lord ten thousand talents, that would not forgive his fellow servant an hundred pence; and therefore was delivered to the tormentors. In the application of the parable Christ says, "So likewise shall my heavenly Father do . . . if ye from your heart forgive not every one his brother their trespasses" (ver. 35).

And that all true saints are of a loving, benevolent and beneficent temper, the Scripture is very plain and abundant. Without it the Apostle tells us, though we should speak with the tongues of men and angels, we are as a sounding brass or a tinkling cymbal: and that though we have the gift of prophecy, and understand all mysteries, and all knowledge; yet without this spirit we are nothing. And there is no one virtue or disposition of the mind, that is so often, and so expressly insisted on, in the marks that are laid down in the New Testament, whereby to know true Christians. 'Tis often given as a sign that is peculiarly distinguishing, by which all may know Christ's disciples, and by which they may know themselves: and is often laid down, both as a negative and positive evidence. Christ calls the law of love, by way of eminency, his commandment, "A new commandment I give unto you, that ye love one another, as I have loved you, that ye also love one another" (John 13:34). And: "This is my commandment, that ye love one another as I have loved you" (ch. 15:12). And: "These things I command you, that ye love one another" (ver. 17). And says, "By this shall all men know that ye are my disciples, if ye love one another" (ch. 13:35). And (still with a special reference to this which he calls *his* commandment): "He that hath my commandments, and keepeth them, he it is that loveth me" (ch. 14:21). The Beloved Disciple, who had so much of this sweet temper himself, abundantly insists on it, in his Epistles. There is none of the apostles, is so much in laying down express signs of grace, for professors to try themselves by, as he; and in his signs, he insists scarcely on anything else, but a spirit of Christian love, and an agreeable practice; "He that saith he is in the light, and hateth his brother, is in darkness even until now. He that loveth his brother abideth in the light, and there is none occasion of stumbling in him" (I John 2:9–10). "We know that we are passed from death to life, because we love the brethren. He that loveth not his brother abideth in death" (ch. 3:14). "My little children, let us not love in word and in tongue, but in deed and in truth. And hereby we know that we are of the truth, and shall assure our hearts before him" (verses 18–19). "This is his commandment, . . . that we should love one another. . . . And he that keepeth his commandments, dwelleth in him, and he in him: and hereby we know that he abideth in us, by the spirit which he hath given us" (verses 23–24). "Beloved, let us love one another; for love is of God; and everyone that loveth is born of God, and knoweth God: he that loveth not, knoweth not God; for God is love" (ch. 4:7–8). "No man hath seen God at any time: if we love one another, God dwelleth in us, and his love is perfected in us. Hereby know we that we dwell in him, because he hath given us of his spirit" (verses 12–13). "God is love: and he that dwelleth in love, dwelleth in God, and God in him" (ver. 16). "If a man say, I love God, and hateth his brother, he is a liar: for he that loveth not his brother that he hath seen, how can he love God whom he hath not seen?" (ver. 20).

And the Scripture is as plain as it is possible it should be, that none are true saints, but those whose true character it is, that they are of a disposition to pity and relieve their fellow creatures, that are poor, indigent and afflicted; "The righteous showeth mercy, and giveth" (Ps. 37:21): "He is evermerciful, and lendeth" (ver. 26). "A good man showeth favor, and lendeth" (Ps. 112:5). "He hath dispersed abroad, and given to the poor" (ver. 9). "He that honoreth God, hath mercy on the poor" (Prov. 14:31). "The righteous giveth, and spareth not" (Prov. 21:26). "He judged the cause of the poor and needy: then it was well with him: was not this to know me, saith the Lord?" (Jer. 22:16). "Pure religion and undefiled before God and the Father, is this, to visit the fatherless and widows in their affliction," etc. (Jas. 1:27). "For I desired mercy, and not sacrifice; and the knowledge of God, more than burnt-offerings" (Hos. 6:6). "Blessed are the merciful, for they shall obtain mercy" (Matt. 5:7). "I speak not by commandment, but by occasion of the forwardness of others, and to prove the sincerity of your love" (II Cor. 8:8). "For he shall have judgment without mercy, that hath shewed no mercy. . . . What doth it profit my brethren, though a man saith he hath faith, and have not works? Can faith save him? If a brother or sister be naked, and destitute of daily food, and one of you say unto them, depart in peace, be you warmed and filled; notwithstanding ye give them not those things which are needful for the body; what doth it profit?" (Jas. 2:13–16). "Whoso hath this world's goods, and seeth his brother have need, and shutteth up his bowels of compassion from him, how dwelleth the love of God in him?" (I John 3:17). Christ in that description he gives us of the Day of Judgment, Matt. 25 (which is the most particular that we have in all the Bible): represents that judgment will be passed at that day, according as men have been found to have been of a merciful spirit and practice, or otherwise. Christ's design in giving such a description of the process of that day, is plainly to possess all his followers with that apprehension, that unless this was their spirit and practice, there was no hope of their being accepted and owned by him, at that day. Therefore this is an apprehension that we ought to be possessed with. We find in Scripture that a "righteous man," and a "merciful man" are synonymous expressions; "The righteous perisheth, and no man layeth it to heart; and the merciful men are taken away, none considering that the righteous is taken away from the evil to come" (Is. 57:1).

Thus we see how full, clear and abundant, the evidence from Scripture is, that those who are truly gracious, are under the government of that lamblike, dovelike spirit of Jesus Christ. And that this is essentially and eminently the nature of the saving grace of the gospel, and the proper spirit of true Christianity. We may therefore undoubtedly determine that all truly Christian affections are attended with such a spirit; and that this is the natural tendency of the fear and hope, the sorrow and the joy, the confidence and the zeal of true Christians.

None will understand me that true Christians have no remains of a contrary spirit, and can never, in any instances, be guilty of a behavior disagreeable to such a spirit. But this I affirm, and shall affirm till I deny the Bible to be anything worth, that everything in Christians that belongs to true Christianity, is of this tendency, and works this way; and that there is no true Christian upon earth, but is so under the prevailing power of such a spirit, that he is properly denominated from it, and it is truly and justly his character: and that therefore ministers, and others have no warrant from Christ to encourage persons, that are of a contrary character and behavior, to think they are converted, because they tell a fair story of illuminations and discoveries. In so doing they would set up their own wisdom against Christ's, and judge without, and against that rule by which Christ has declared all men should know his disciples. Some persons place religion so much in certain transient illuminations and impressions (especially if they are in such a particular method and order) and so little in the spirit and temper persons are of, that they greatly deform religion, and form notions of Christianity quite different from what it is, as delineated in the Scriptures. The Scripture knows of no such true Christians, as of a sordid, selfish, cross and contentious spirit. Nothing can be invented that is a greater absurdity, than a morose, hard, close, high-spirited, spiteful true Christian. We must learn the way of bringing men to rules, and not rules to men, and so strain and stretch the rules of God's Word, to take in ourselves, and some of our neighbors, till we make them wholly of none effect.

'Tis true that allowances must be made for men's natural temper with regard to these things, as well as others. But not such allowances, as to allow men, that once were wolves and serpents, to be now converted, without any remarkable change in the spirit of their mind. The change made by true conversion, is wont to be most remarkable and sensible, with respect to that which before was the wickedness the person was most notoriously guilty of. Grace has as great a tendency to restrain and mortify such sins, as are contrary to the spirit that has been spoken of, as it has to mortify drunkenness or lasciviousness. Yea the Scripture represents the change wrought by gospel grace, as especially appearing in an alteration of the former sort; "The wolf shall dwell with the lamb; and the leopard shall lie down with the kid; and the calf, and the young lion, and the fatling together; and a little child shall lead them. And the cow, and the bear shall feed; their young ones shall lie down together: and the lion shall eat straw like the ox: and the sucking child shall play on the hole of the asp; and the weaned child shall put his hand on the cockatrice den. They shall not hurt nor destroy in all my holy mountain. For the earth shall be full of the knowledge of the Lord, as the waters cover the sea" (Is. 11:6–9). And to the same purpose is Is. 65:25. Accordingly we find that in the primitive times of the Christian church, converts were remarkably changed in this respect: "For we ourselves also were sometimes foolish, disobedient, deceived, serving divers lusts and pleasures; living in malice and envy, hateful, and hating one another. But after that the kindness and love of God our Saviour, toward men, appeared, . . . he saved us, by the washing of regeneration, and renewing of the Holy Ghost" (Titus 3:3 etc.). And: "In the which ye also walked, some time, when ye lived in them. But now you also put off all these; anger, wrath, malice, blasphemy, filthy communication out of your mouth" (Col. 3:7–8).

IX. Gracious affections soften the heart, and are attended and followed with a Christian tenderness of spirit.

False affections, however persons may seem to be melted by them while they are new, yet have a tendency in the end to harden the heart. A disposition to some kind of passions may be established; such as imply self-seeking, self-exaltation, and opposition to others. But false affections, with the delusion that attends them, finally tend to stupefy the mind, and shut it up against those affections wherein tenderness of heart consists: and the effect of 'em at last is, that persons in the settled frame of their minds, become less affected with their present and past sins, and less conscientious with respect to future sins, less moved with the warnings and cautions of God's Word, or God's chastisements in his providence, more careless of the frame of their hearts, and the manner and tendency of their behavior, less quick-sighted to discern what is sinful, less afraid of the appearance of evil, than they were while they were under legal awakenings and fears of hell. Now they have been the subjects of such and such impressions and affections, and have a high opinion of themselves, and look on their state to be safe; they can be much more easy than before, in living in the neglect of duties that are troublesome and inconvenient; and are much more slow and partial in complying with difficult commands; are in no measure so alarmed at the appearance of their own defects and transgressions; are emboldened to favor themselves more, with respect to the labor, and painful care and exactness in their walk, and more easily yield to temptations, and the solicitations of their lusts; and have far less care of their behavior, when they come into the holy presence of God, in the time of public or private worship. Formerly it may be, under legal convictions they took much pains in religion, and denied themselves in many things: but now they think themselves out of danger of hell, they very much put off the burden of the cross, and save themselves the trouble of difficult duties, and allow themselves more of the comfort of the enjoyment of their ease and their lusts.

Such persons as these, instead of embracing Christ as their *Saviour from sin,* they trust in him as the *Saviour of their sins:* instead of flying to him as their refuge from their spiritual enemies, they make use of him as the defense of their spiritual enemies, from God, and to strengthen them against him. They make Christ the minister of sin, and great officer and vicegerent of the devil, to strengthen his interest, and make him above all things in the world strong against JEHOVAH; so that they may sin against him with good courage, and without any fear, being effectually secured from restraints by his most solemn warnings and most awful threatenings. They trust in Christ to preserve to 'em the quiet enjoyment of their sins, and to be their shield to defend 'em from God's displeasure; while they come close to him, even to his bosom, the place of his children, to fight against him, with their mortal weapons, hid under their skirts.[8]

However some of these, at the same time, make a great profession of love to God, and assurance of his favor, and great joy in tasting the sweetness of his love.

8. "These are hypocrites that believe, but fail in regard of the use of the gospel, and of the Lord Jesus. And these we read of, Jude 4, viz. of some men 'that did turn grace into wantonness.' For therein appears the exceeding evil of a man's heart, that not only the law, but also the glorious gospel of the Lord Jesus, works in him all manner of unrighteousness. And 'tis too common for men at the first work of conversion, Oh then to cry for grace and Christ, and afterwards grow licentious, live and lie in the breach of the law, and take their warrant for their course from the gospel." Shepard, *Parable,* Pt. I, p. 126.

Again, Mr. Shepard speaks of such hypocrites as those "who like strange eggs, being put into the same nest, where honest men have lived, they have been hatched up; and when they are young, keep their nest, and live by crying and opening their mouths wide after the Lord and the food of his Word; but when their wings are grown, and they have got some affections, some knowledge, some hope of mercy, are hardened thereby to fly from God." And adds, "Can that man be good, whom God's grace makes worse?" Ibid., p. 232.

Again: "When men fly to Christ in times of peace, that so they may preserve their sins with greater peace of conscience; so that sin makes 'em fly to Christ, as well as misery; not that they may destroy and abolish sin, but that they may be preserved in their sins with peace; then men may be said to apprehend Christ only by a seeming faith. . . . Many an heart secretly saith this, if I can have my sin, and peace, and conscience quiet for the present, and God merciful to pardon it afterward; hence he doth rely (as he saith) only on the mercy of God in Christ: and now this hardens and blinds him, and makes him secure, and his faith is sermon proof, nothing stirs him. . . . And were it not for their faith they should despair, but this keeps 'em up. And now they think if they have any trouble of mind, the devil troubles 'em; and so make Christ and faith protectors of sin, not purifiers from sin; which is most dreadful; turning grace to wantonness, as they did sacrifice. So these would sin under the shadow of Christ, because the shadow is good and sweet, Mic. 3:11. They had subtle sly ends in good duties; for therein may lie a man's sin: yet they lean upon the Lord. . . . When money changers came into the temple, 'You have made it a den of thieves.' Thieves when hunted fly to their den or cave, and there they are secure against all searchers, and hue-and-cries: so here. But Christ whipped them out. So when men are pursued with cries and fears of conscience, away to Christ they go as to their den: not as saints to pray and lament out the life of their sin there; but to preserve their sin. This is vile: will the Lord receive such?" Ibid., Pt. II, p. 167.

After this manner they trusted in Christ, that the apostle Jude speaks of, who crept in among the saints unknown; but were really ungodly men, turning the grace of God into lasciviousness (Jude 4). These are they that trust in their being righteous; and because God has promised that the righteous shall surely live, or certainly be saved, are therefore emboldened to commit iniquity, whom God threatens in Ezek. 33:13: "When I shall say to the righteous, that he shall surely live; if he trust to his own righteousness, and commit iniquity; all his righteousness shall not be remembered; but for his iniquity that he hath committed, he shall die for it."

Gracious affections are of a quite contrary tendency; they turn a heart of stone more and more into a heart of flesh. An holy love and hope are principles that are vastly more efficacious upon the heart, to make it tender, and to fill it with a dread of sin, or whatever might displease and offend God, and to engage it to watchfulness and care and strictness, than a slavish fear of hell. Gracious affections, as was observed before, flow out of a contrite heart, or (as the word signifies) a bruised heart, bruised and broken with godly sorrow; which makes the heart tender, as bruised flesh is tender, and easily hurt. Godly sorrow has much greater influence to make the heart tender, than mere legal sorrow from selfish principles.

The tenderness of the heart of a true Christian, is elegantly signified by our Saviour, in his comparing such a one to a little child. The flesh of a little child is very tender: so is the heart of one that is new born. This is represented in what we are told of Naaman's cure of his leprosy, by his washing in Jordan, by the direction of the prophet; which was undoubtedly a type of the renewing of the soul, by washing in the laver of regeneration. We are told, that "he went down, and dipped himself seven times in Jordan, according to the saying of the man of God; and his flesh came again, like unto the flesh of a little child" (II Kgs. 5:14). Not only is the flesh of a little child tender, but his mind is tender. A little child has his heart easily moved, wrought upon and bowed: so is a Christian in spiritual things. A little child is apt to be affected with sympathy, to weep with them that weep, and can't well bear to see others in distress: so it is with a Christian (John 11:35; Rom. 12:15; I Cor. 12:26). A little child is easily won by kindness: so is a Christian. A little child is easily affected with grief at temporal evils, and has his heart melted, and falls a weeping: thus tender is the heart of a Christian, with regard to the evil of sin. A little child is easily affrighted at the appearance of outward evils. or anything that threatens its hurt: so is a Christian apt to be alarmed at the appearance of moral evil, and anything that threatens the hurt of the soul. A little child, when it meets enemies, or fierce beasts, is not apt to trust its own strength, but flies to its parents for refuge: so a saint is not self-confident in engaging spiritual enemies, but flies to Christ. A little child is apt to be suspicious of evil in places of danger, afraid in the dark, afraid when left alone, or far from home: so is a saint apt to be sensible of his spiritual dangers, jealous of himself, full of fear when he can't see his way plain before him, afraid to be left alone, and to be at a distance from God; "Happy is the man that feareth alway; but he that hardeneth his heart shall fall into mischief" (Prov. 28:14). A little child is apt to be afraid of superiors, and to dread their anger, and tremble at their frowns and threatenings: so is a true saint with respect to God; "My flesh trembleth for fear of thee, and I am afraid of thy judgments" (Ps. 119:120). "To this man will I look, even to him that is poor, and trembleth at my word" (Is. 66:2). "Hear ye the Word of the Lord, ye that tremble at his Word" (ver. 5). "Then were assembled unto me, everyone that trembled at the works of the God of Israel" (Ezra 9:4). "According to the counsel of my Lord, and of those that tremble at the commandment of our God" (ch. 10:3). A little child approaches superiors with awe: so do the saints approach God with holy awe and reverence. "Shall not his excellency make you afraid, and his dread fall upon you" (Job. 13:11). Holy fear is so much the nature of true godliness, that it is called in Scripture by no other name more frequently, than the fear of God.

Hence gracious affections don't tend to make men bold, forward, noisy and boisterous; but rather to speak trembling (Hos. 13:1: "When Ephraim spake trembling, he exalted himself in Israel; but when he offended in Baal, he died"); and to clothe with a kind of holy fear in all their behavior towards God and man; agreeable to Ps. 2:11; I Pet. 3:15; II Cor. 7:15; Eph. 6:5; I Pet. 3:2; Rom. 11:20.

But here some may object and say, is there no such thing as a holy boldness in prayer, and the duties of divine worship? I answer, there is doubtless such a thing; and it is chiefly to be found in eminent saints, persons of great degrees of faith and love. But this holy boldness is not in the least opposite to reverence; though it be to disunion and servility. It abolishes or lessens that disposition which arises from moral distance or alienation; and also distance of relation, as that of a slave: but not at all, that which becomes the natural distance, whereby we are infinitely inferior. No boldness in poor sinful worms of the dust, that have a right sight of God and themselves, will prompt 'em to approach to God with less fear and reverence, than spotless and glorious angels in heaven; who cover their faces before his throne (Is. 6 at the beginning). Rebecca (who in her marriage with Isaac, in almost all its circumstances, was manifestly a great type of the church, the spouse of Christ) when she meets Isaac, lights off from her camel, and takes a veil, and covers herself; although she was brought to him as his bride, to be with him, in the nearest relation, and most intimate union, that mankind are ever united one to another in.[9] Elijah, that great prophet, who had so much holy familiarity with God, at a time of special nearness to God, even when he conversed with him in the mount, wrapped his face in his mantle. Which was not because he was terrified with any servile fear, by the terrible wind, and earthquake, and fire; but after these were all over, and God spake to him as a friend, in a still small voice; "And after the fire, a still small voice: and it was so, when Elijah heard it, he wrapped his face in his mantle" (I Kgs. 19:12–13). And Moses, with whom God spake face to face, as a man speaks with his friend, and was distinguished from all the prophets, in the familiarity with God that he was admitted to; at a time when he was brought nearest of all, when God showed him his glory in that same mount, where he afterwards spake to Elijah; he made haste, and bowed his head towards the earth, and worshiped (Ex. 34:8). There is in some persons, a most unsuitable and unsufferable boldness, in their addresses to the great Jehovah, in an affectation of an holy boldness, and ostentation of eminent nearness and familiarity; the very thoughts of which would make 'em shrink into nothing, with horror and confusion, if they saw the distance that is between God and them. They are like the Pharisee, that boldly came up near, in a confidence of his own eminency in holiness. Whereas, if they saw their vileness, they would be more like the publican, that stood afar off, and durst not so much as lift up his eyes to heaven; but smote upon his breast saying, God be merciful to me a sinner. It becomes such sinful

9. Dr. Ames, in his *Cases of Conscience,* speaks of an holy modesty in the worship of God, as one sign of true humility. Ames, *Cases of Conscience,* Bk. III, ch. 4, pp. 53–4 [above, p. 68].

creatures as we, to approach a holy God (although with faith, and without terror, yet) with contrition, and penitent shame and confusion of face. It is foretold that this should be the disposition of the church, in the time of her highest privileges on earth, in her latter day of glory, when God should remarkably comfort her, by revealing his covenant mercy to her; "I will establish unto thee an everlasting covenant. Then thou shalt remember thy ways, and be ashamed. . . . And I will establish my covenant with thee; and thou shalt know that I am the Lord: that thou mayest remember, and be confounded, and never open thy mouth any more, because of thy shame, when I am pacified toward thee, for all that thou hast done; saith the Lord God" (Ezek. 16:60 to the end). The woman that we read of in the 7th chapter of Luke, that was an eminent saint, and had much of that true love which casts out fear, by Christ's own testimony (ver. 47), she approached Christ in an amiable, and acceptable manner, when she came with that humble modesty, reverence and shame, when she stood at his feet, weeping behind him, as not being fit to appear before his face, and washed his feet with her tears.

One reason why gracious affections are attended with this tenderness of spirit which has been spoken of, is that true grace tends to promote convictions of conscience. Persons are wont to have convictions of conscience before they have any grace: and if afterwards they are truly converted, and have true repentance, and joy, and peace in believing; this has a tendency to put an end to terrors, but has no tendency to put an end to convictions of sin, but to increase them. It don't stupefy a man's conscience; but makes it more sensible, more easily and thoroughly discerning the sinfulness of that which is sinful, and receiving a greater conviction of the heinous and dreadful nature of sin, susceptive of a quicker and deeper sense of it, and more convinced of his own sinfulness, and wickedness of his heart; and consequently it has a tendency to make him more jealous of his heart. Grace tends to give the soul a further and better conviction of the same things concerning sin, that it was convinced of under a legal work of the Spirit of God; viz. it's great contrariety to the will and law and honor of God, the greatness of God's hatred of it, and displeasure against it, and the dreadful punishment it exposes to and deserves. And not only so, but it convinces the soul of something further concerning sin, that it saw nothing of, while only under legal convictions; and that is the infinitely hateful nature of sin, and its dreadfulness upon that account. And this makes the heart tender with respect to sin; like David's heart, that smote him, when he had cut off Saul's skirt. The heart of a true penitent is like a burnt child, that dreads the fire. Whereas on the contrary, he that has had a counterfeit repentance, and false comforts and joys, is like iron that has been suddenly heated and quenched; it becomes much harder than before. A false conversion puts an end to convictions of conscience; and so either takes away, or much diminishes that conscientiousness, which was manifested under a work of the law.

All gracious affections have a tendency to promote this Christian tenderness of heart, that has been spoken of: not only a godly sorrow; but also a gracious joy; "Serve the Lord with fear, and rejoice with trembling" (Ps. 2:11). As also a gracious hope; "Behold the eye of the Lord is upon them that fear him, upon them that hope in his mercy" (Ps. 33:18). And: "The Lord taketh pleasure in them that fear him, and in them that hope in his mercy" (Ps. 147:11). Yea the most confident and assured hope, that is truly gracious, has this tendency. The higher an holy hope is raised, the more there is of this Christian tenderness. The banishing of a servile fear, by a holy assurance, is attended with a proportionable increase of a reverential fear. The diminishing of the fear of the fruits of God's displeasure in future punishment, is attended with a proportionable increase of fear of his displeasure itself: the diminishing of the fear of hell, with an increase of the fear of sin. The vanishing of jealousies of the person's state, is attended with a proportionable increase of jealousy of his heart, in a distrust of its strength, wisdom, stability, faithfulness, etc. The less apt he is to be afraid of natural evil, having "his heart fixed trusting in God, and so, not afraid of evil tidings"; the more apt is he to be alarmed with the appearance of moral evil, or the evil of sin. As he has more holy boldness, so he has less of self-confidence, and a forward assuming boldness, and more modesty. As he is more sure than others of deliverance from hell, so he has more of a sense of the desert of it. He is less apt than others to be shaken in faith; but more apt than others to be moved with solemn warnings, and with God's frowns, and with the calamities of others. He has the firmest comfort, but the softest heart: richer than others, but poorest of all in spirit: the tallest and strongest saint, but the least and tenderest child amongst them.

X. Another thing wherein those affections that are truly gracious and holy, differ from those that are false, is beautiful symmetry and proportion.

Not that the symmetry of the virtues, and gracious affections of the saints, in this life, is perfect: it oftentimes, is in many things defective, through the imperfection of grace, for want of proper instructions, through errors in judgment, or some particular unhappiness of natural temper, or defects in education, and many other disadvantages that might be mentioned. But yet there is, in no wise, that monstrous disproportion in gracious affections, and the various parts of true religion in the saints, that is very commonly to be observed, in the false religion, and counterfeit graces of hypocrites.

In the truly holy affections of the saints is found that proportion which is the natural consequence of the universality of their sanctification. They have the whole image of Christ upon them: they have "put off the old man, and have put on the new man" entire in all his parts and members. "It has pleased the Father that in Christ all fullness should dwell": there is in him every grace; he is full of grace and truth: and they that are Christ's, do of his fullness receive, and grace for grace (John 1:14, 16); i.e. there is every grace in them, which is in Christ: "grace for grace"; that is, grace answerable to grace: there is no grace in Christ, but there is its image in believers to answer it: the image is a true image; and there is something of the same beautiful proportion in the image, which is in the original; there is feature for feature, and member for member. There is symmetry and beauty in God's workmanship. The natural body, which God hath made consists of many members; and all are in a beautiful proportion: so it is in the new man, consisting of various graces and affections. The body of one that was born a perfect child, may fail of exact proportion through distemper, and the weakness and wounds of some of its members; yet the disproportion is in no measure like that of those that are born monsters.

It is with hypocrites, as it was with Ephraim of old, at a time when God greatly complains of their hypocrisy; "Ephraim is a cake not turned" (Hos. 7), half roasted and half raw: there is commonly no manner of uniformity in their affections.

There is in many of them a great partiality, with regard to the several kinds of religious affections: great affections in some things, and no manner of proportion in others. An holy hope and holy fear go together in the saints, as has been observed from Ps. 33:18 and 147:11. But in some of these is the most confident hope, while they are void of reverence, self-jealousy and caution, and to a great degree cast off fear. In the saints, joy and holy fear go together, though the joy be never so great; as it was with the disciples, in that joyful morning of Christ's resurrection, "And they departed quickly from the sepulcher, with fear and great joy" (Matt. 28:8).[1] But many of these rejoice without trembling: their joy is of that sort, that is truly opposite to godly fear.

But particularly, one great difference between saints and hypocrites is this, that the joy and comfort of the former is attended with godly sorrow and mourning for sin. They have not only sorrow to prepare 'em for their first comfort, but after they are comforted, and their joy established. As it is foretold of the church of God, that they should mourn and loathe themselves for their sins, after they were returned from the captivity, and were settled in the land of Canaan, the land of rest, and the land that flows with milk and honey, "And ye shall know that I am the Lord, when I shall bring you into the land of Israel, into the country for the which I lifted up mine hand, to give it to your fathers. And there shall ye remember your ways, and all your doings, wherein ye have been defiled; and ye shall loathe yourselves in your own sight, for all your evils that ye have committed" (Ezek. 20:42–43). As also in Ezek. 16:61–63. A true saint is like a little child in this respect; he never had any godly sorrow before he was born again; but since has it often in exercise: as a little child, before it is born, and while it remains in darkness, never cries; but as soon as ever it sees the light, it begins to cry; and thenceforward is often crying. Although Christ hath borne our griefs, and carried our sorrows, so that we are freed from the sorrow of punishment, and may now sweetly feed upon the comforts Christ hath purchased for us; yet that hinders not but that our feeding on these comforts should be attended with the sorrow of repentance. As of old, the children of Israel were commanded, evermore to feed upon the paschal lamb, with bitter herbs.[2]

1. "Renewed care and diligence follows the sealings of the Spirit. Now is the soul at the foot of Christ, as Mary was at the sepulcher, with fear and great joy. He that travels the road with a rich treasure about him, is afraid of a thief in every bush. Flavel, *Sacramental Meditations,* Med. 4, p. 77.

2. "If repentance accompanies faith, 'tis no presumption to believe. Many know

True saints are spoken of in Scripture, not only as those that have mourned for sin, but as those that do mourn, whose manner it is still to mourn; "Blessed are they that mourn, for they shall be comforted" (Matt. 5:4).

Not only is there often in hypocrites, an essential deficiency, as to the various kinds of religious affections; but also a strange partiality and disproportion, in the same affections, with regard to different objects.

Thus as to the affection of love, some make high pretenses, and a great shew of love to God and Christ, and it may be have been greatly affected with what they have heard or thought concerning

---

the sin; and hence believe in Christ, trust in Christ; and there is an end of their faith. But what confession and sorrow for sin? What more love to Christ follows this faith? Truly none. Nay, their faith is the cause why they have none. For they think, if I trust in Christ to forgive me, he will do it; and there is an end of the business. Verily this hedge-faith, this bramble-faith, that catches hold on Christ, and pricks and scratches Christ, by more impenitency, more contempt of him, is mere presumption; which shall one day be burnt up and destroyed by the fire of God's jealousy. Fie upon that faith, that serves only to keep a man from being tormented before his time! Your sins would be your sorrows, but that your faith quiets you. But if faith be accompanied with repentance, mourning for sin, more esteem of God's grace in Christ; so that nothing breaks thy heart more than the thoughts of Christ's unchangeable love to one so vile, and this love makes thee love much, and love him the more; as thy sin increaseth, so thou desirest thy love's increase; and now the stream of thy thoughts run, how thou mayest live to him that died for thee: this was Mary's faith, who sat at Christ's feet weeping, washing them with her tears, and loving much, because much was forgiven." Shepard, *Sound Believer,* pp. 128–9.

"You shall know godly sorrow (says Dr. Preston, in his "Discourse on Paul's Conversion") by the continuance of it: it is constant; but worldly sorrow is but a passion of the mind; it changes, it lasts not. Though for the present it may be violent and strong, and work much outwardly; yet it comes but by fits, and continues not: like a land flood, which violently, for the present, overflows the banks; but it will away again; it is not always thus. But godly sorrow is like a spring, that still keeps his running both winter and summer, wet and dry, in heat and cold, early and late. So this godly sorrow is the same in a regenerate man still; take him when you will, he is still sorrowing for sin. This godly sorrow stands like the center of the earth, which removes not, but still remains." John Preston, "Discourse on Paul's Conversion," *Remains of That Reverend and Learned Divine John Preston* (2d ed. London, 1637), p. 198.

"I am persuaded, many a man's heart is kept from breaking and mourning, because of this. He saith (it may be) that he is a vile sinner; but I trust in Christ, etc. If they do go to Christ to destroy their sin, this makes 'em more secure in their sin. For (say they) I cannot help it, and Christ must do all. Whereas faith makes the soul mourn after the Lord the more." Shepard, *Parable,* Pt. II, p. 168.

them: but they have not a spirit of love and benevolence towards men, but are disposed to contention, envy, revenge, and evil-speaking; and will, it may be, suffer an old grudge to rest in their bosoms towards a neighbor, for seven years together, if not twice seven years; living in real ill-will and bitterness of spirit towards him: and it may be in their dealings with their neighbors, are not very strict and conscientious in observing the rule of doing to others, as they would that they should do to them: "If a man say, I love God, and hateth his brother, he is a liar: for he that loveth not his brother, whom he hath seen, how can he love God whom he hath not seen?" (I John 4:20). And on the other hand, there are others, that appear as if they had a great deal of benevolence to men, are very good natured and generous in their way; but have no love to God.

And as to love to men, there are some that have flowing affections to some; but their love is far from being of so extensive and universal a nature, as a truly Christian love is. They are full of dear affections to some, and full of bitterness towards others. They are knit to their own party, them that approve of 'em, love 'em and admire 'em; but are fierce against those that oppose and dislike 'em. "Be like your Father which is in heaven: for he maketh his sun to rise on the evil and on the good. . . . For if ye love them which love you, what reward have ye? Do not even the publicans the same?" (Matt. 5:45–46). Some shew a great affection to their neighbors, and pretend to be ravished with the company of the children of God abroad; and at the same time are uncomfortable and churlish towards their wives and other near relations at home, and are very negligent of relative duties. And as to the great love to sinners and opposers of religion, and the great concern for their souls, that there is an appearance of in some, even to extreme distress and agony, singling out a particular person, from among a multitude, for its object, there being at the same time no general compassion to sinners, that are in equally miserable circumstances, but what is in a monstrous disproportion; this seems not to be of the nature of a gracious affection. Not that I suppose it to be at all strange, that pity to the perishing souls of sinners should be to a degree of agony, if other things are answerable; or that a truly gracious compassion to souls should be exercised much more to some persons than others that are equally miserable, especially on some particular occasions: there may many things happen to fix the mind, and affect the heart, with respect to a particular person, at such a juncture; and without doubt some saints have been in great distress for the souls of particular persons, so as to be as it were in travail for them: but when persons appear, at particular times, in wracking agonies for the soul of some single person, far beyond what has been usually heard or read of in eminent saints, but appear to be persons that have a spirit of meek and fervent love, charity, and compassion to mankind in general, in a far less degree than they; I say, such agonies are greatly to be suspected, for reasons already given; viz. that the Spirit of God is wont to give graces and gracious affections in a beautiful symmetry and proportion.

And as there is a monstrous disproportion in the love of some, in its exercises towards different persons, so there is in their seeming exercises of love towards the same persons. Some men shew a love to others as to their outward man, they are liberal of their worldly substance, and often give to the poor; but have no love to, or concern for the souls of men. Others pretend a great love to men's souls, that are not compassionate and charitable towards their bodies. The making a great shew of love, pity, and distress for souls, costs 'em nothing; but in order to shew mercy to men's bodies, they must part with money out of their pockets. But a true Christian love to our brethren, extends both to their souls and bodies. And herein is like the love and compassion of Jesus Christ. He shewed mercy to men's souls, by laboring for them in preaching the gospel to 'em; and shewed mercy to their bodies, in going about doing good, healing all manner of sickness and diseases among the people. We have a remarkable instance of Christ's having compassion at once both to men's souls and bodies, and shewing compassion by feeding both, in Mark 6:34 etc. "And Jesus, when he came out, saw much people, and was moved with compassion towards them; because they were as sheep not having a shepherd: and he began to teach them many things." Here was his compassion to their souls. And in the sequel, we have an account of his compassion to their bodies, because they had been a long while having nothing to eat: he fed five thousand of 'em with five loaves and two fishes. And if the compassion of professing Christians towards others don't work in the same ways, it is a sign that it is no true Christian compassion.

And furthermore, 'tis a sign that affections are not of the right sort, if persons seem to be much affected with the bad qualities of their fellow Christians, as the coldness and lifelessness of other saints, but are in no proportion affected with their own defects and corruptions. A true Christian may be affected with the coldness and unsavoriness of other saints, and may mourn much over it. But at the same time he is not so apt to be affected with the badness of anybody's heart, as his own. This is most in his view: this he is most quick-sighted to discern: this he sees most of the aggravations of, and is most ready to cry out of. And a lesser degree of virtue will bring him to pity himself, and be concerned at his own calamities, than rightly to be affected with others' calamities. And if men han't attained to the less, we may determine they never attained to the greater.

And here by the way, I would observe, that it may be laid down as a general rule, that if persons pretend that they come to high attainments in religion, but have never yet arrived to the lesser attainments, 'tis a sign of a vain pretense. As if persons pretend that they have got beyond mere morality, to live a spiritual and divine life; but really han't come to be so much as moral persons. Or pretend to be greatly affected with the wickedness of their hearts, and are not affected with the palpable violations of God's commands in their practice, which is a lesser attainment. Or if they pretend to be brought to be even willing to be damned for the glory of God, but have no forwardness to suffer a little in their estates and names and worldly convenience, for the sake of their duty. Or pretend that they are not afraid to venture their souls upon Christ, and commit their all to God, trusting to his bare word, and the faithfulness of his promises, for their eternal welfare; but at the same time, han't confidence enough in God, to dare to trust him with a little of their estates, bestowed to pious and charitable uses: I say, when it is thus with persons, their pretenses are manifestly vain. He that is in a journey, and imagines he has got far beyond such a place in his road, and never yet came to it, must be mistaken; and he is not yet arrived to the top of the hill, that never yet got halfway thither. But this by the way.

The same that has been observed of the affection of love, is also to be observed of other religious affections. Those that are true, extend in some proportion, to the various things that are their due and proper objects: but when they are false, they are commonly strangely disproportionate. So it is with religious desires and longings: these in the saints, are to those things that are spiritual and excellent in general, and that in some proportion to their excellency, importance or necessity, or their near concern in them: but in false longings, 'tis often far otherwise. They will strangely run, with an impatient vehemence, after something of less importance, when other things of greater importance are neglected. Thus for instance, some persons, from time to time, are attended with a vehement inclination, and unaccountably violent pressure, to declare to others what they experience, and to exhort others; when there is at the same time, no inclination, in any measure equal to it, to other things, that true Christianity has as great, yea, a greater tendency to; as the pouring out the soul before God in secret earnest prayer and praise to him, and more conformity to him, and living more to his glory, etc. We read in Scripture of groanings that cannot be uttered, and soul-breakings for the longing it hath, and longings, thirstings, and pantings, much more frequently to these latter things, than the former.

And so as to hatred and zeal; when these are from right principles, they are against sin in general, in some proportion to the degree of sinfulness; "I hate every false way" (Ps. 119:104). So verse 128. But a false hatred and zeal against sin, is against some particular sin only. Thus some seem to be very zealous against profaneness, and pride in apparel, who themselves are notorious for covetousness, closeness, and it may be backbiting, envy towards superiors, turbulency of spirit towards rulers, and rooted ill will to them that have injured them. False zeal is against the sins of others, while men have no zeal against their own sins. But he that has true zeal exercises it chiefly against his own sins: though he shews also a proper zeal against prevailing and dangerous iniquity in others. And some pretend to have a great abhorrence of their own sins of heart, and cry out much of their inward corruption; and yet make light of sins in practice, and seem to commit them without much restraint or remorse; though these imply sin, both in heart and life.

As there is a much greater disproportion in the exercises of false affections, than of true, as to different objects; so there is also, as to different times. For although true Christians are not always alike; yea, there is very great difference, at different times, and the best have reason to be greatly ashamed of their unsteadiness; yet there is in no wise that instability and inconstancy in the hearts of those who are true virgins, that follow the lamb whithersoever he goeth, which is in false-hearted professors. The righteous man is truly said to be one whose heart is fixed, trust in God (Ps. 112:7), and to have his heart established with grace (Heb. 13:9), and to hold on his way. "The righteous shall hold on his way, and he that hath clean hands shall wax stronger and stronger" (Job 17:9). 'Tis spoken of as a note of the hypocrisy of the Jewish church, that they were as a swift dromedary, traversing her ways.

If therefore persons are religious only by fits and starts; if they now and then seem to be raised up to the clouds in their affections, and then suddenly fall down again, lose all, and become quite careless and carnal, and this is their manner of carrying on religion; if they appear greatly moved, and mightily engaged in religion, only in extraordinary seasons, in the time of a remarkable outpouring of the Spirit, or other uncommon dispensation of providence, or upon the real or supposed receipt of some great mercy, when they have received some extraordinary temporal mercy, or suppose that they are newly converted, or have lately had what they call a great discovery; but quickly return to such a frame, that their hearts are chiefly upon other things, and the prevailing bent of their hearts and stream of their affections is ordinarily towards the things of this world; when they are like the children of Israel in the wilderness, who had their affections highly raised by what God had done for 'em at the Red Sea, and sang his praise, and soon fell a lusting after the fleshpots of Egypt, but then again when they came to Mount Sinai, and saw the great manifestations God made of himself there, seemed to be greatly engaged again, and mighty forward to enter into covenant with God, saying, "All that the Lord hath spoken will we do, and be obedient," but then quickly made 'em a golden calf; I say, when it is thus with persons, 'tis a sign of the unsoundness of affections.[3]

3. Dr. Owen (on the *Spirit*) speaking of a common work of the Spirit, says, "This work operates greatly on the affections: we have given instances, in fear, sorrow, joy, and delight, about spiritual things, that are stirred up and acted thereby: but yet it comes short in two things, of a thorough work upon the affections themselves. For 1st, it doth not *fix* them. And 2ndly, it doth not *fill* them. 1. It is required that our affections be fixed on heavenly and spiritual things: and true grace will effect it; Col. 3:1–2: 'If ye be risen with Christ, seek those things which are above, where Christ sitteth on the right hand of God. Set your affections on things above.' The joys, the fears, the hopes, the sorrows, with reference unto spiritual and eternal things, which the work before-mentioned doth produce, are evanid, uncertain, unstable, not only as to the degrees, but as to the very being of them. Sometimes they are as a river ready to overflow its banks, men cannot but be pouring them out on all occasions; and sometimes as

They are like the waters in the time of a shower of rain, which during the shower, and a little after, run like a brook, and flow abundantly; but are presently quite dry: and when another shower comes, then they will flow again. Whereas a true saint is like a stream from a living spring; which though it may be greatly increased by a shower of rain, and diminished in time of drought; yet constantly runs (John 4:14: "The water that I shall give him, shall be in him, a well of water springing up," etc.): or like a tree planted by such a stream, that has a constant supply at the root, and is always green, even in time of the greatest drought. "Blessed is the man that trusteth in the Lord, and whose hope the Lord is. For he shall be as a tree planted by the waters, and that spreadeth out her roots by the river; and shall not see when heat cometh; but her leaf shall be green; and shall not be careful in the year of drought; neither shall cease from yielding fruit" (Jer. 17:7–8). Many hypocrites are like comets, that appear for a while with a mighty blaze; but are very unsteady and irregular in their motion (and are therefore called wandering stars, Jude 13), and their blaze soon disappears, and they appear but once in a great while. But the

---

waters that fail, no drop comes from them. Sometimes they are hot, and sometimes cold; sometimes up, and sometimes down; sometimes all heaven, and sometimes all world; without equality, without stability. But true grace fixeth the affections on spiritual things. As to the degrees of their exercise, there may be, and is in them a great variety, according as they may be excited, aided, assisted by grace and the means of it; or obstructed and impeded, by the interposition of temptations and diversions. But the constant bent and inclination of renewed affections, is unto spiritual things; as the Scripture everywhere testifieth, and as experience doth confirm." Owen, *Pneumatologia,* Bk. III, ch. 2, sec. 18, pp. 200–1.

"There is," says Dr. Preston, "a certain love, by fits, which God accepts not; when men come and offer to God great promises, like the waves of the sea, as big as mountains: Oh, they think, they will do much for God! But their minds change; and they become as those high waves, which at last fall level with the other waters. If a man should profer thee great kindnesses; and thou shouldst afterwards come to him to make use of him, and he should look strangely upon thee, as if he were never acquainted with thee; how wouldst thou esteem of such love? If we are now on, now off, in our love, God will not esteem of such love." John Preston, *The Onely Love of the Chiefest of Ten Thousand, or an Heavenly Treatise of the Divine Love of Christ* (London, 1640), pp. 157–8.

Mr. Flavel, speaking of these changeable professors, says, "These professors have more of the moon than of the sun; little light, less heat, and many changes. They deceive many, yea, they deceive themselves, but cannot deceive God. They want that ballast and establishment in themselves, that would have kept them tight and steady." Flavel, *Touchstone,* ch. 2, sec. 2, pp. 18–19.

true saints are like the fixed stars, which, though they rise and set, and are often clouded, yet are steadfast in their orb, and may truly be said to shine with a constant light. Hypocritical affections are like a violent motion; like that of the air that is moved with winds (Jude 12). But gracious affections are more a natural motion, like the stream of a river; which though it has many turns hither and thither, and may meet with obstacles, and run more freely and swiftly in some places than others; yet in the general, with a steady and constant course, tends the same way, till it gets to the ocean.

And as there is a strange unevenness and disproportion in false affections, at different times; so there often is in different places. Some are greatly affected from time to time, when in company; but have nothing that bears any manner of proportion to it, in secret, in close meditation, secret prayer, and conversing with God, when alone, and separated from all the world.[4] A true Christian doubtless delights in religious fellowship, and Christian conversation, and finds much to affect his heart in it: but he also delights at times to retire from all mankind, to converse with God in solitary places. And this also has its peculiar advantages for fixing his heart, and engaging its affections. True religion disposes persons to be much alone, in solitary places, for holy meditation and prayer. So it wrought in Isaac (Gen. 24:63). And which is much more, so it wrought in Jesus Christ. How often do we read of his retiring into mountains and solitary places, for holy converse with his Father? 'Tis difficult to conceal great affections, but yet gracious affections are of a much more silent and secret nature, than those that are counterfeit. So it is with the gracious sorrow of the saints. So it is

4. "The Lord is neglected secretly, yet honored openly; because there is no wind in their chambers to blow their sails; and therefore there they stand still. Hence many men keep their profession, when they loose their affection. They have by the one a name to live (and that is enough), though their hearts be dead. And hence so long as you love and commend them, so long they love you; but if not, they will forsake you. They were warm only by another's fire, and hence having no principle of life within, soon grow dead. This is the water that turns a Pharisee's mill." Shepard, *Parable,* Pt. I, p. 180.

"The hypocrite," says Mr. Flavel, "is not for the closet, but the synagogue; Matt. 6:5–6: 'Tis not his meat and drink to retire from the clamor of the world, to enjoy God in secret." Flavel, *Touchstone,* ch. 7, sec. 2, p. 148.

Dr. Ames, in his *Cases of Conscience,* speaks of it as a thing by which sincerity may be known, "That persons be obedient in the absence, as well as in the presence of lookers-on; in secret, as well, yea more than in public"; alleging Phil. 2:12 and Matt. 6:6. Ames, *Cases of Conscience,* Bk. III, ch. 5, p. 55.

with their sorrow for their own sins.[5] Thus the future gracious mourning of true penitents, at the beginning of the latter day glory, is represented as being so secret, as to be hidden from the companions of their bosom; "And the land shall mourn, every family apart. The family of the house of David apart, and their wives apart. The family of the house of Nathan apart, and their wives apart. The family of the house of Levi apart, and their wives apart. The family of Shimei apart, and their wives apart. All the families that remain, every family apart, and their wives apart" (Zech. 12:12–14). So it is with their sorrow for the sins of others. The saints' pains and travailing for the souls of sinners is chiefly in secret places; "If ye will not hear it, my soul shall weep in secret places for your pride. And mine eye shall weep for, and run down with tears; because the Lord's flock is carried away captive" (Jer. 13:17). So it is with gracious joys: they are hidden manna, in this respect, as well as others (Rev. 2:17). The Psalmist seems to speak of his sweetest comforts, as those that were to be had in secret; "My soul shall be satisfied as with marrow and fatness, and my mouth shall praise thee with joyful lips; when I remember thee upon my bed, and meditate upon thee in the night watches" (Ps. 63:5). Christ calls forth his spouse, away from the world, into retired places, that he may give her his sweetest love; "Come my beloved, let us go forth into the field, let us lodge in the villages . . . there will I give thee my love" (Cant. 7:11–12). The most eminent divine favors that the saints obtained, that we read of in Scripture, were in their retirement. The principal manifestations that God made of himself, and his covenant mercy to Abraham, were when he was alone, apart from his numerous family; as anyone will judge that carefully reads his history. Isaac received that special gift of God to him, Rebekah, who was so great a comfort to him, and by whom he obtained the promised seed, walking alone, meditating in the field. Jacob was retired for secret prayer, when Christ came to him, and he wrestled with him, and obtained the blessing. God revealed himself to Moses in the bush, when he was in a solitary place in the desert, in Mount Horeb (Ex. 3 at the beginning). And afterwards, when God shewed him his glory, and he was admitted to the highest degree of com-

5. Mr. Flavel, in reckoning up those things, wherein the sorrow of saints is distinguished from the sorrow of hypocrites, about their sins, says, "Their troubles for sin are more private and silent troubles than others are; their sore runs in the night." Flavel, *Touchstone*, ch. 6, sec. 5, pp. 123–4.

munion with God that ever he enjoyed; he was alone, in the same mountain, and continued there forty days and forty nights, and then came down with his face shining. God came to those great prophets, Elijah and Elisha, and conversed freely with them, chiefly in their retirement. Elijah conversed alone with God at Mount Sinai, as Moses did. And when Jesus Christ had his greatest prelibation of his future glory, when he was transfigured it was not when he was with the multitude, or with the twelve disciples, but retired into a solitary place in a mountain, with only three select disciples, charging them that they should tell no man, till he was risen from the dead. When the angel Gabriel came to the blessed virgin, and when the Holy Ghost came upon her, and the power of the highest overshadowed her, she seems to have been alone, and to be in this matter hid from the world; her nearest and dearest earthly friend Joseph, that had betrothed her (though a just man), knew nothing of the matter. And she that first partook of the joy of Christ's resurrection, was alone with Christ at the sepulcher (John 20). And when the Beloved Disciple was favored with those wonderful visions of Christ, and his future dispensations towards the church and the world, he was alone in the isle of Patmos. Not but that we have also instances of great privileges that the saints have received when with others; or that there is not much in Christian conversation, and social and public worship, tending greatly to refresh and rejoice the hearts of the saints. But this is all that I aim at by what has been said, to shew that it is the nature of true grace, that however it loves Christian society in its place, yet it in a peculiar manner delights in retirement, and secret converse with God. So that if persons appear greatly engaged in social religion, and but little in the religion of the closet, and are often highly affected when with others, and but little moved when they have none but God and Christ to converse with, it looks very darkly upon their religion.

XI. Another great and very distinguishing difference between gracious affections and others is, that gracious affections, the higher they are raised, the more is a spiritual appetite and longing of soul after spiritual attainments, increased. On the contrary, false affections rest satisfied in themselves.[6]

6. "Truly there is no work of Christ that's right," says Mr. Shepard, "but it carries the soul to long for more of it." Shepard, *Parable,* Pt. I, p. 136.

And again, "There is in true grace an infinite circle: a man by thirsting re-

The more a true saint loves God with a gracious love, the more he desires to love him, and the more uneasy is he at his want of love to him: the more he hates sin, the more he desires to hate it, and laments that he has so much remaining love to it: the more he mourns for sin, the more he longs to mourn for sin: the more his heart is broke, the more he desires it should be broke: the more he thirsts and longs after God and holiness, the more he longs to long, and breathe out his very soul in longings after God: the kindling and raising of gracious affections is like kindling a flame; the higher it is raised, the more ardent it is; and the more it burns, the more vehemently does it tend and seek to burn. So that the spiritual appetite after holiness, and an increase of holy affections, is much more lively and keen in those that are eminent in holiness, than others; and more when grace and holy affections are in their most lively exercise, than at other times. 'Tis as much the nature of one that is spiritually new born, to thirst after growth in holiness, as 'tis the nature of a newborn babe, to thirst after the mother's breast; who has the sharpest appetite, when best in health; "As newborn babes, desire the sincere milk of the word, that ye may grow thereby; if so be that ye have tasted that the Lord is gracious" (I Pet. 2:2–3). The most that the saints have in this world, is but a taste, a prelibation of that future glory which is their proper fulness; 'tis only an earnest of their future inheritance in their hearts (II Cor. 1:22 and 5:5 and Eph. 1:14). The most eminent saints in this state are but children, compared with their future, which is their proper state of maturity and perfection, as the Apostle observes (I Cor. 13:10–11). The greatest eminency and perfection, that the saints arrive to in this world, has no tendency to satiety, or to abate their desires after more; but on the contrary, makes 'em more eager to press forwards; as is evident by the Apostle's words, "Forgetting the things which are behind, and reaching forth

---

ceives, and receiving thirsts for more. But hence the Spirit is not poured out abundantly on churches; because men shut it out, by shutting in, and contenting themselves with their common graces and gifts; Matt. 7:29. Examine if it be not so." Ibid., p. 182.

And he says, "This I say, true grace as it comforts, so it never fills, but puts an edge on the appetite: more of that grace, Lord! Thus Paul, Phil. 3:13–14. Thus David; out of my poverty I have given, etc. I Chron. 29:3, 17–18. It's a sure way never to be deceived in lighter strokes of the Spirit, to be thankful for any, but to be content with no measure of it. And this cuts the thread of difference, between a superficial lighter stroke of the Spirit, and that which is sound." Ibid., p. 210.

unto those things which are before, I press toward the mark. . . . Let us therefore, as many as be perfect, be thus minded" (Phil. 3:13–15).

The reasons of it are, that the more persons have of holy affections, the more they have of that spiritual taste which I have spoken of elsewhere; whereby they perceive the excellency, and relish the divine sweetness of holiness. And the more grace they have, while in this state of imperfection, the more they see their imperfction and emptiness, and distance from what ought to be; and so the more do they see their need of grace; as I shewed at large before, when speaking of the nature of evangelical humiliation. And besides grace, as long as it is imperfect, is of a growing nature, and in a growing state. And we see it to be so with all living things, that while they are in a state of imperfection, and in their growing state, their nature seeks after growth; and so much the more, as they are more healthy and prosperous. Therefore the cry of every true grace, is like that cry of true faith, "Lord I believe, help thou my unbelief" (Mark 9:24). And the greater spiritual discoveries and affections the true Christian has, the more does he become of an earnest beggar for grace, and spiritual food, that he may grow; and the more earnestly does he pursue after it, in the use of proper means and endeavors: for true and gracious longings after holiness, are no idle ineffectual desires.

But here some may object and say, how is this consistent with what all allow, that spiritual enjoyments are of a soul-satisfying nature?

I answer, its being so, will appear to be not at all inconsistent with what has been said, if it be considered in what manner spiritual enjoyments are said to be of a soul-satisfying nature. Certainly they are not so in that sense, that they are of so cloying a nature, that he who has anything of them, though but in a very imperfect degree, desires no more. But spiritual enjoyments are of a soul-satisfying nature in the following respects, (1) They in their kind and nature, are fully adapted to the nature, capacity and need of the soul of man. So that those who find them, desire no other kind of enjoyments; they sit down fully contented with that kind of happiness which they have, desiring no change, nor inclining to wander about any more, saying who will show us any good? The soul is never cloyed, never weary; but perpetually giving up itself, with all its powers, to this happiness. But not that those who have something of this happiness, desire no more of the same. (2) They are satisfying also in this respect, that they answer the expectation of the appetite. When the appetite is high to anything, the expectation is consequently so. Appetite to a particular object, implies expectation in its nature. This expectation is not satisfied by worldly enjoyments, the man expected to have a great accession of happiness, but he is disappointed. But it is not so with spiritual enjoyments; they fully answer and satisfy the expectation. (3) The gratification and pleasure of spiritual enjoyments is permanent. 'Tis not so with worldly enjoyments. They in a sense satisfy particular appetites; but the appetite in being satisfied, is glutted, and then the pleasure is over: and as soon as that is over, the general appetite of human nature after happiness returns; but is empty, and without anything to satisfy it. So that the glutting of a particular appetite, does but take away from, and leave empty, the general thirst of nature. (4) Spiritual good is satisfying, as there is enough in it, to satisfy the soul, as to degree, if obstacles were but removed, and the enjoying faculty duly applied. There is room enough here for the soul to extend itself; here is an infinite ocean of it. If men ben't satisfied here, in degree of happiness, the cause is with themselves; 'tis because they don't open their mouths wide enough.

But these things don't argue that a soul has no appetite excited after more of the same, that has tasted a little; or that his appetite will not increase, the more he tastes, till he comes to fullness of enjoyment: as bodies that are attracted to the globe of the earth, tend to it more strongly, the nearer they come to the attracting body, and are not at rest out of the center. Spiritual good is of a satisfying nature; and for that very reason, the soul that tastes, and knows its nature, will thirst after it, and a fullness of it, that it may be satisfied. And the more he experiences, and the more he knows this excellent, unparalleled, exquisite, and satisfying sweetness, the more earnestly will he hunger and thirst for more, till he comes to perfection. And therefore this is the nature of spiritual affections, that the greater they be, the greater the appetite and longing is, after grace and holiness.

But with those joys, and other religious affections, that are false and counterfeit, it is otherwise. If before, there was a great desire, of some sort, after grace; as these affections rise, that desire ceases, or is abated. It may be before, while the man was under legal convictions, and much afraid of hell, he earnestly longed that he might obtain spiritual light in his understanding, and faith in Christ, and love to God: but now, when these false affections are risen, that deceive him, and make him confident that he is converted, and his state good, there are no more earnest longings after light and grace: for his end is answered; he is confident that his sins are forgiven him, and that he shall go to heaven; and so he is satisfied. And especially when false affections are raised very high, do they put an end to longings after grace and holiness. The man now is far from appearing to himself, a poor empty creature: on the contrary, he is rich, and increased with goods; and hardly conceives of anything more excellent, than what he has already attained to.

Hence there is an end to many persons' earnestness in seeking, after they have once obtained that which they call their conversion: or at least, after they have had those high affections, that make them fully confident of it. Before, while they looked upon themselves as in a state of nature, they were engaged in seeking after God and Christ, and cried earnestly for grace, and strove in the use of means: but now they act as though they thought their work was done: they live upon their first work, or some high experiences that are past; and there is an end to their crying, and striving after God and grace.[7] Whereas the holy principles that actuate a true saint, have a far more

7. "It is usual to see a false heart most diligent in seeking the Lord, when he has been worst, and most careless when 'tis best. Hence many at first conversion, sought the Lord earnestly: afterwards affections and endeavors die; that now they are as good as the Word can make 'em. . . . An hypocrite's last end is to satisfy himself: hence he has enough. A saint's is to satisfy Christ: hence he never has enough." Shepard, *Parable,* Pt. I, p. 157.

"Many a man, it may be, may say, I have nothing in myself, and all is in Christ; and comfort himself there; and so falls asleep. Hands off! And touch not this ark, lest the Lord slay thee: a Christ of clouts would serve your turn as well." Ibid., p. 71.

"An hypocrite's light goes out, and grows not. Hence many ancient standers take all their comfort from their first work, and droop when in old age." Ibid., p. 77.

And Mr. Shepard, mentioning the characters of those that have a dead hope, says, "They that content themselves with any measure of holiness and grace, they look not for Christ's coming and company. For saints that do look for him, though they have not that holiness and grace they would have, yet they rest not satisfied with any measure; I John 3:3: 'He that hath this hope, purifieth himself as he is pure.' . . . The saints content not themselves with any drossings, till made glorious; and so fit for fellowship with that spouse. . . . When a man leaves not, till he gets such a measure of faith and grace, and now when he has got this,

powerful influence to stir him up to earnestness in seeking God and holiness, than servile fear. Hence seeking God is spoken of as one of the distinguishing characters of the saints; and those that seek God, is one of the names by which the godly are called in Scripture; "This is the generation of them that seek him, that seek thy face, O Jacob" (Ps. 24:6). "Let not those that seek thee be confounded for my sake" (Ps. 69:6). "The humble shall see this and be glad, and your heart shall live that seek God" (ver. 32). And: "Let all those that seek thee rejoice, and be glad in thee; and let such as love thy salvation say continually, the Lord be magnified" (74:4) And the Scriptures

---

contents himself with this, as a good sign that he shall be saved, he looks not for Christ. Or when men are heavily laden with sin; then close with Christ; and then are comforted, sealed, and have joy that fills them; and now the work is done. . . . And when men shall not content themselves with any measure; but wish they had more, if grace would grow, while they tell clocks and sit idle; and so God must do all; but do not purge themselves, and make work of it." Ibid., pp. 93–4.

Again, "There is never a hypocrite living, but closeth with Christ for his own ends: for he cannot work beyond his principle. Now when men have served their own turns out of another man, away they go, and keep that which they have. An hypocrite closeth with Christ, as a man with a rich shop: he will not be at cost to buy all the shop, but so much as serves his turn. Commonly men in horror, seek so much of Christ as will ease them; and hence profess, and hence seek for so much of Christ as will credit them; and hence their desires after Christ are soon satisfied. *Appetitus finis est infinitus.*" Ibid., p. 109.

"Woe to thee that canst paint such a Christ in thy head, and receive such a Christ into thy heart, as must be a pander to your sloth. The Lord will revenge this wrong done to his glory, with greater sorrows than ever any felt: to make Christ not only meat and drink to feed, but clothes to cover your sloth. . . . Why what can we do? What can we do? . . . Why as the first Adam conveys not only guilt, but power; so the second conveys both righteousness and strength." Ibid., p. 158.

"When the Lord hath given some light and affection, and some comfort, and some reformation, now a man grows full here. Saints do for God; and carnal hearts do something too; but a little fills them, and quiets them, and so damns them. And hence men at the first work upon them, are very diligent in the use of means; but after that, they be brought to neglect prayer, sleep out sermons, and to be careless, sapless, lifeless." Ibid., p. 210.

"It is an argument of want of grace, when a man saith to himself, as the glutton said to his soul, take they rest, for thou hast goods laid up for many years. So thou hast repentance, and grace, and peace enough for many years: and hence the soul takes its rest, grows sluggish and negligent. Oh, if you die in this case, this night thy soul shall be taken away to hell." Ibid., p. 227.

everywhere represent the seeking, striving and labor of a Christian, as being chiefly after his conversion, and his conversion as being but the beginning of his work. And almost all that is said in the New Testament, of men's watching, giving earnest heed to themselves, running the race that is set before them, striving and agonizing, wrestling not with flesh and blood, but principalities and powers, fighting, putting on the whole armor of God, and standing, having done all to stand, pressing forward, reaching forth, continuing instant in prayer, crying to God day and night; I say, almost all that is said in the New Testament of these things, is spoken of, and directed to the saints. Where these things are applied to sinners seeking conversion once, they are spoken of the saints' prosecution of the great business of their high calling ten times. But many in these days have got into a strange antiscriptural way, of having all their striving and wrestling over before they are converted; and so having an easy time of it afterwards, to sit down and enjoy their sloth and indolence; as those that now have a supply of their wants, and are become rich and full. But when the Lord fills the hungry with good things, these rich are like to be sent away empty (Luke 1:53).

But doubtless there are some hypocrites, that have only false affections, who will think they are able to stand this trial; and will readily say, that they desire not to rest satisfied with past attainments, but to be pressing forward, they do desire more, they long after God and Christ, and desire more holiness, and do seek it. But the truth is, their desires are not properly the desires of appetite after holiness, for its own sake, or for the moral excellency and holy sweetness that is in it; but only for by-ends. They long after clearer discoveries, that they may be better satisfied about the state of their souls; or because in great discoveries, self is gratified, in being made so much of by God, and so exalted above others, they long to taste the love of God (as they call it) more than to have more love to God. Or, it may be, they have a kind of forced, fancied or made longings; because they think they must long for more grace, otherwise it will be a dark sign upon them. But such things as these are far different from the natural, and as it were necessary appetite and thirsting of the new man, after God and holiness. There is an inward burning desire that a saint has after holiness, as natural to the new creature, as vital heat is to the body. There is a holy breathing and panting after the Spirit of God, to increase holiness, as natural to a holy nature, as breathing is to a living body. And holiness or sanctification is more directly the object of it, than any manifestation of God's love and favor. This is the meat and drink that is the object of the spiritual appetite; "My meat is to do the will of him that sent me, and to finish his work" (John 4:34). Where we read in Scripture of the desires, longings and thirstings of the saints, righteousness and God's laws are much more frequently mentioned, as the object of them, than anything else. The saints desire the sincere milk of the Word, not so much to testify God's love to them, as that they may grow thereby in holiness. I have shewn before that holiness is that good which is the immediate object of a spiritual taste. But undoubtedly the same sweetness that is the chief object of a spiritual taste, is also the chief object of a spiritual appetite. Grace is the godly man's treasure; "The fear of the Lord is his treasure" (Is. 33:6). Godliness is the gain that he is covetous and greedy of (I Tim. 6:6). Hypocrites long for discoveries, more for the present comfort of the discovery, and the high manifestation of God's love in it, than for any sanctifying influence of it. But neither a longing after great discoveries, or after great tastes of the love of God, nor longing to be in heaven, nor longing to die, are in any measure so distinguishing marks of true saints, as longing after a more holy heart, and living a more holy life.

But I am come now to the last distinguishing mark of holy affections that I shall mention.

XII. Gracious and holy affections have their exercise and fruit in Christian practice. I mean, they have that influence and power upon him who is the subject of 'em, that they cause that a practice, which is universally conformed to, and directed by Christian rules, should be the practice and business of his life.

This implies three things; (1) That his behavior or practice in the world, be universally conformed to, and directed by Christian rules. (2) That he makes a business of such a holy practice above all things; that it be a business which he is chiefly engaged in, and devoted to, and pursues with highest earnestness and diligence: so that he may be said to make this practice of religion eminently his work and business. And (3) That he persists in it to the end of life: so that it may be said, not only to be his business at certain seasons, the business of Sabbath days, or certain extraordinary times, or the business of a month, or a year, or of seven years, or his business under certain circumstances; but the business of his life; it being that business which he perseveres in through all changes, and under all trials, as long as he lives.

The necessity of each of these, in all true Christians, is most clearly and fully taught in the Word of God.

1. 'Tis necessary that men should be universally obedient: [8]

8. "He that pretends to godliness, and turns aside to crooked ways, is an hypocrite: for those that are really godly, do live in a way of obedience; Ps. 119:1–3: 'Blessed are the undefiled in the way, that walk in the law of the Lord. . . . They also do no iniquity.' Luke 1:6: 'They were both righteous before God, walking in all the commandments of the Lord blameless.' But such as live in ways of sin, are dissemblers; for all such will be rejected in the Day of Judgment; Matt. 7:23: 'Depart from me, ye that work iniquity.' The like we have Luke 13:27. If men live in a way of disobedience, they don't love God; for love will make men keep God's commandments; I John 5:3: 'Herein is love, that we keep his commandments, and his commandments are not grievous.' If men live in a way of disobedience, they have not a spirit of faith; for faith sanctifies men; Acts 26:18: 'Sanctified by faith that is in me.' If men live in a way of disobedience, they are not Christ's sheep; for his sheep hear his voice; John 10:27. Men that live in a way of disobedience are not born of God; I John 3:9: 'He that is born of God sinneth not.' Men that live in a way of disobedience are the servants of sin; John 8:34: 'He that committeth sin is the servant of sin.'

"A course of external sin is an evidence of hypocrisy; whether it be a sin of omission or commission. If men live in the neglect of known duties, or in the practice of known evils, that will be their condemnation; let the sin be what it will; let it be profaneness, uncleanness, lying or injustice. . . . If men allow themselves in malice, envy, wanton thoughts, profane thoughts, that will condemn them; though those corruptions don't break out in any scandalous way. These thoughts are an evidence of a rotten heart; Titus 3:3: 'We ourselves were sometimes foolish, disobedient, deceived, serving divers lusts and pleasures, living in malice, and envy, hateful, and hating one another.' If a man allows himself, though he thinks he doth not, in malice and envy, he is an hypocrite: though his conscience disallows it, yet if his heart allows it, he is no saint. . . . Some make pretenses to godliness, whereby they do not only deceive others, but (which is a great deal worse) deceive themselves also: but this will condemn them, that they live in a course of sin, and so must go with ungodly men; Ps. 125:5: 'As for such as turn aside unto their crooked ways, the Lord will lead them forth with the workers of iniquity.' If there be a great change in a man's carriage, and he be reformed in several particulars, yet if there be one evil way, the man is an ungodly man: where there is piety there is universal obedience. A man may have great infirmities, yet be a godly man. So it was with Lot, David, and Peter: but if he lives in a way of sin, he don't render his godliness only suspicious, but it is full evidence against him. Men that are godly have respect to all God's commandments; Ps. 119:6. There be a great many commands, and if there be one of

"Every man that hath this hope in him, purifieth himself, even as he is pure. . . . And ye know that he was manifested to take away our sins, and in him was no sin. Whosoever abideth in him, sinneth not. Whosoever sinneth, hath not seen him, neither known him. . . . He that doth righteousness, is righteous, even as he is righteous. He that commiteth sin, is of the devil" (I John 3:3, etc.). "We know that whosoever is born of God, sinneth not; but he that is begotten of God, keepeth himself, and that wicked one toucheth him not" (ch. 5:18). "Ye are my friends, if ye do whatsoever I command you" (John 15:14). "Whosoever shall keep the whole law, and yet offend in one point, he is guilty of all" (Jas. 2:10). "Know ye not that the unrighteous shall not inherit the kingdom of God. Be not deceived, neither fornicators, nor idolators, . . . shall inherit the kingdom of God" (I Cor. 6:9). "Now the works of the flesh are manifest, which are these, adultery, fornication, uncleanness, lasciviousness, idolatry, witchcraft, hatred, variance, emulations, wrath, strife, envyings, murders, drunkenness, revelings, and such like: of the which I tell you before, as I have also told you in time past, that they which

---

them that a man has not respect unto, he will be put to shame another day. If a man lives in one evil way, he is not subject to God's authority: but then he lives in rebellion; and that will take off all his pleas, and at once cut off all his pretenses; and he will be condemned in the Day of Judgment. . . . One way of sin is exception enough against the man's salvation.

"Though the sin that he lives in be but small: such persons won't be guilty of perjury, stealing, drunkenness, fornication; they look upon them to be heinous things, and they are afraid of them; but they do not much matter it, if they oppress a little in a bargain, if they commend a thing too much which they are about to sell, if they break a promise, if they spend the Sabbath unprofitably, if they neglect secret prayer, if they talk rudely and reproach others; they think these are but small things: if they can keep clear of great transgression, they hope that God will not insist upon small things. But indeed all the commands of God are established by divine authority: a small shot may kill a man, as well as a cannon bullet: a small leak may sink a ship. If a man lives in small sins, that shews he has no love to God, no sincere care to please and honor God. Little sins are of a damning nature, as well as great: if they don't deserve so much punishment as greater, yet they do deserve damnation. There is a contempt of God in all sins; Matt. 5:19: 'He that shall break one of the least of these commands, and shall teach men so, shall be called the least in the kingdom of God.' Prov. 19:16: 'He that keepeth the commandment, keepeth his own soul; but he that despiseth his way, shall die.' If a man says, this is a great command, and so lays weight on it, and another is a little commandment, and so don't regard it, but will allow himself to break it, he is in a perishing condition." Stoddard, *Sincerity and Hypocrisy,* pp. 122–3, 124–5, 129–31.

do such things, shall not inherit the kingdom of God" (Gal. 5:19–20). Which is as much as to say, they that do any sort of wickedness. "Is not destruction to the wicked, and a strange punishment to the workers of iniquity? Doth not he see my ways, and count all my steps? Let me be weighed in an even balance, that God may know my integrity. If my step hath turned out of the way, and mine heart walked after mine eyes, and if any blot hath cleaved to mine hands," etc. (Job 34:3–7). "If he walk in the statutes of life, without committing iniquity, he shall surely live" (Ezek. 33:15). If one member only be corrupt and we don't cut it off, it will carry the whole body to hell (Matt. 5:29–30). Saul was commanded to slay all God's enemies, the Amalekites; and he slew all but Agag, and the saving him alive proved his ruin. Caleb and Joshua entered into God's promised rest, because they wholly followed the Lord (Num. 14:24 and 32:11–12; Deut. 1:36; Josh. 14:6–9, 14). Naaman's hypocrisy appeared in that, however he seemed to be greatly affected with gratitude to God for healing his leprosy, and engaged to serve him, yet in one thing he desired to be excused. And Herod, though he feared John, and observed him, and heard him gladly, and did many things; yet was condemned, in that in one thing he would not hearken to him, even in parting with his beloved Herodias. So that it is necessary that men should part with their dearest iniquities, which are as their right hand and right eyes, sins that most easily beset them, and which they are most exposed to by their natural inclinations, evil customs, or particular circumstances, as well as others. As Joseph would not make known himself to his brethren, who had sold him, till Benjamin, the beloved child of the family, that was most hardly parted with, was delivered up; no more will Christ reveal his love to us, till we part with our dearest lusts, and till we are brought to comply with the most difficult duties, and those that we have the greatest aversion to.

And it is of importance, that it should be observed, that in order to a man's being truly said to be universally obedient, his obedience must not only consist in negatives, or in universally avoiding wicked practices, consisting in sins of commission; but he must also be universal in the positives of religion. Sins of omission are as much breaches of God's commands, as sins of commission. Christ, in Matt. 25, represents those on the left hand, as being condemned and cursed to everlasting fire, for sins of omission, "I was an hungered and ye gave me no meat," etc. A man therefore can't be said to be universally obedient, and of a Christian conversation, only because he is no thief, nor oppressor, nor fraudulent person, nor drunkard, nor tavern-haunter, nor whoremaster, nor rioter, nor nightwalker, nor unclean, nor profane in his language, nor slanderer, nor liar, nor furious, nor malicious, nor reviler: he is falsely said to be of a conversation that becomes the gospel, who goes thus far and no farther; but in order to this, it is necessary that he should also be of a serious, religious, devout, humble, meek, forgiving, peaceful, respectful, condescending, benevolent, merciful, charitable and beneficent walk and conversation. Without such things as these, he don't obey the laws of Christ, and laws that he and his apostles did abundantly insist on, as of greatest importance and necessity.

2. In order to men's being true Christians, it is necessary that they prosecute the business of religion, and the service of God with great earnestness and diligence, as the work which they devote themselves to, and make the main business of their lives. All Christ's peculiar people, not only do good works, but are zealous of good works (Titus 2:14). No man can do the service of two masters at once. They that are God's true servants, do give up themselves to his service, and make it as it were their whole work, therein employing their whole hearts, and the chief of their strength; "This one thing I do" (Phil. 3:13). Christians in their effectual calling, are not called to idleness, but to labor in God's vineyard, and spend their day in doing a great and laborious service. All true Christians comply with this call (as is implied in its being an effectual call), and do the work of Christians; which is everywhere in the New Testament compared to those exercises, wherein men are wont to exert their strength, with the greatest earnestness, as running, wrestling, fighting. All true Christians are good and faithful soldiers of Jesus Christ, and fight the good fight of faith: for none but those who do so, do ever lay hold on eternal life. Those who fight as those that beat the air, never win the crown of victory. They that run in a race, run all; but one wins the prize; and they that are slack and negligent in their course, do not so run, as that they may obtain. The kingdom of heaven is not to be taken but by violence. Without earnestness there is no getting along, in that narrow way that leads to life; and so no arriving at that state of glorious life and happiness which it leads to. Without earnest labor, there is no ascending the steep and high

hill of Zion; and so no arriving at the heavenly city on the top of it. Without a constant laboriousness, there is no stemming the swift stream in which we swim, so as ever to come to that fountain of water of life, that is at the head of it. There is need that we should watch and pray always, in order to our escaping those dreadful things, that are coming on the ungodly, and our being counted worthy to stand before the Son of Man. There is need of our putting on the whole armor of God, and doing all to stand, in order to our avoiding a total overthrow, and being utterly destroyed by the fiery darts of the devil. There is need that we should forget the things that are behind, and be reaching forth to the things that are before, and pressing towards the mark for the prize of the high calling of God, in Christ Jesus our Lord, in order to our obtaining that prize. Slothfulness in the service of God, in his professed servants, is as damning, as open rebellion: for the slothful servant, is a wicked servant, and shall be cast into outer darkness, among God's open enemies (Matt. 25:26–28). They that are slothful, are not followers of them, who through faith and patience inherit the promises. "And we desire that every one of you do shew the same diligence, to the full assurance of hope, unto the end: that ye be not slothful; but followers of them, who through faith and patience inherit the promises" (Heb. 6:11–12). And all they who follow that cloud of witnesses that are gone before to heaven, do lay aside every weight, and the sin that easily besets them, and do run with patience the race that is set before them (Heb. 12:1). That true faith, by which persons rely on the righteousness of Christ, and the work that he hath done for them, and do truly feed and live upon him, is evermore accompanied with such a spirit of earnestness in the Christian work and course. Which was typified of old, by the manner of the children of Israel's feeding on the paschal lamb: who were directed to eat it, as those that were in haste, with their loins girded, their shoes on their feet, and staff in their hand; "And thus shall ye eat it; with your loins girded, your shoes on your feet, and your staff in your hand, and ye shall eat it in haste: it is the Lord's passover" (Ex. 12:11).

3. Every true Christian perseveres in this way of universal obedience, and diligent and earnest service of God, through all the various kinds of trials that he meets with, to the end of life. That all true saints, all those that do obtain eternal life, do thus persevere in the practice of religion, and the service of God, is a doctrine so abundantly taught in the Scripture, that particularly to rehearse all the texts which imply

it would be endless. I shall content myself with referring to some in the margin.[9]

But that in perseverance in obedience, which is chiefly insisted on in the Scripture, as a special note of the truth of grace, is the continuance of professors in the practice of their duty, and being steadfast in an holy walk, through the various trials that they meet with.

By trials, here I mean, those things that occur, and that a professor meets with in his course, that do especially render his continuance in his duty, and faithfulness to God, difficult to nature. These things are from time to time called in Scripture by the name of trials, or temptations (which are words of the same signification). These are of various kinds: there are many things that render persons' continuance in the way of their duty difficult, by their tendency to cherish and foment, or to stir up and provoke their lusts and corruptions. Many things make it hard to continue in the way of duty, by their being of an alluring nature, and having a tendency to entice persons to sin; or by their tendency to take off restraints, and embolden 'em in iniquity. Other things are trials of the soundness and steadfastness of professors, by their tendency to make their duty appear terrible to 'em, and so to affright and drive 'em from it: such as the sufferings which their duty will expose 'em to; pain, ill will, contempt, and reproach, or loss of outward possessions and comforts. If persons, after they have made a profession of religion, live any considerable time, in this world which is so full of changes, and so full of evil, it can't be otherwise, than that they should meet with many trials of their sincerity and steadfastness. And besides, 'tis God's manner, in his providence, to bring trials on his professing friends and servants designedly, that he may manifest them, and may exhibit sufficient matter of conviction of the state which they are in, to their own consciences; and oftentimes, to the world. As appears by innumerable Scriptures; some are referred to the margin.[1]

9. Deut. 5:29; Deut. 32:18–20; I Chron. 28:9; Ps. 78:7–8, 10–11, 35–37, 41–42, 56, etc.; Ps. 106:3, 12–15; Ps. 125:4–5; Prov. 26:11; Is. 64:5; Jer. 17:13; Ezek. 3:20, and 18:24, and 33:12–13; Matt. 10:22; Matt. 13:4–8, 19–23; Matt. 25:8; Matt. 24:12–13; Luke 9:62; 12:35, etc.; 22:28; 17:32; John 8:30–31; 15:6–9, 10, 16; Rom. 2:7; 11:22; Col. 1:22–23; Heb. 3:6, 12, 14; 6:11–12; 10:35, etc.; Jas. 1:25; Rev. 2:13, 26; 2:10; I Tim. 2:15; II Tim. 4:4–8.

1. Gen. 22:1; Ex. 15:25; 16:4; Deut. 8:2, 15–16; 13:3; Judg. 2:22; 3:1, 4; Job 23:10; Ps. 66:10–11; Ezek. 3:20; Dan. 12:10; Zech. 13:9; Matt. 8:19–20; 18:21–22; Luke 1:35; I Cor. 11:19; II Cor. 8:8; Jas. 1:12; I Pet. 4:12; I John 2:19; Heb. 11:17; Rev. 3:10.

True saints may be guilty of some kinds and degrees of backsliding, and may be soiled by particular temptations, and may fall into sin, yea great sins: but they can never fall away so, as to grow weary of religion, and the service of God, and habitually to dislike it and neglect it; either on its own account, or on account of the difficulties that attend it: as is evident by Gal. 6:9; Rom. 2:7; Heb. 10:36; Is. 43:22; Mal. 1:13. They can never backslide, so as to continue no longer in a way of universal obedience; or so, that it shall cease to be their manner to observe all the rules of Christianity, and do all duties required, even the most difficult, and in the most difficult circumstances.[2] This is abundantly manifest by the things that have been observed already. Nor can they ever fall away so, as habitually to be more engaged in other things, than in the business of religion; or so that it should become their way and manner to serve something else more than God; or so as statedly to cease to serve God, with such earnestness and diligence, as still to be habitually devoted and given up to the business

2. "One way of sin is exception enough against men's salvation . . . though their temptations be great. Some persons delight in iniquity; they take pleasure in rudeness, and intemperate practices: but there be others, that don't delight in sin; when they can handsomely avoid it, they don't choose it; except they be under some great necessity, they will not do it. They are afraid to sin; they think it is dangerous, and have some care to avoid it: but sometimes they force themselves to sin; they are reduced to difficulties, and can't tell how well to avoid it; it is a dangerous thing not to do it. If Naaman don't bow himself in the house of Rimmon, the king will be in a rage with him, take away his office, it may be take away his life, and so he complies; II Kgs. 5:18. . . . So Jeroboam forced himself to set up the calves at Dan and Bethel: he thought that if the people went up to Jerusalem to worship, they would return to Rehoboam, and kill him; therefore he must think of some expedient to deliver himself in this strait; I Kgs. 12:27–28. . . . He was driven by appearing necessity to take this wicked course. So the stony ground hearers were willing to retain the profession of the true religion; but the case was such, that they thought they could not well do it; Matt. 13:21: 'When tribulation or persecution ariseth because of the Word, by and by he is offended.' . . . So Achan and Gabazi had singular opportunities to get an estate; if they live twenty years they are not like to have such an advantage; and they force themselves to borrow a point, and break the law of God. They lay a necessity on estate and liberty and life, but not upon obedience. If a man be willing to serve God in ordinary cases, but excuse himself when there be great difficulties, he is not godly. It is a small matter to serve God when men have no temptation; but Lot was holy in Sodom, Noah was righteous in the old world. Temptations try men, but they don't force men to sin: and grace will establish the heart in a day of temptation. They are blessed that do endure temptation, Jas. 1:12. But they are cursed that fall away in a day of temptation." Stoddard, *Sincerity and Hypocrisy*, pp. 130, 132–3.

of religion. Unless those words of Christ can fall to the ground, "Ye cannot serve two masters," and those of the Apostle, "He that will be a friend of the world, is the enemy of God"; and unless a saint can change his God, and yet be a true saint. Nor can a true saint ever fall away so, that it shall come to this, that ordinarily there shall be no remarkable difference in his walk and behavior since his conversion, from what was before. They that are truly converted are new men, new creatures; new, not only within, but without; they are sanctified throughout, in spirit, soul and body; old things are passed away, all things are become new; they have new hearts, and new eyes, new ears, new tongues, new hands, new feet; i.e. a new conversation and practice; and they walk in newness of life, and continue to do so to the end of life. And they that fall away, and cease visibly to do so, 'tis a sign they never were risen with Christ.[3] And especially when men's opinion of their being converted, and so in a safe estate, is the very cause of their coming to this, it is a most evident sign of their hypocrisy.[4] And that, whether their falling away be into their former sins, or into some new kind of wickedness; having the corruption of nature only turned into a new channel, instead of its being mortified. As when persons that think themselves converted, though they do not

3. "Hence we learn what verdict to pass and give in, concerning those men that decay and fall off from the Lord. They never had oil in the vessel; never had a dram of grace in their heart. Thus I John 2:19: 'If they had been of us, they would no doubt have continued with us.' It seems they were such men, which were so eminent and excellent, as that there were no brands nor marks upon them, to give notice to the churches, that they were marked out for apostasy; but were only discovered to be unsound, by their apostasy; and this was argument good enough." Shepard, *Parable,* Pt. I, p. 226.

4. "When a man's rising is the cause of his fall, or seals a man up in his fall, or at least the cause through his corruption, e.g. time was, a man lived a loose, careless, carnal life; by the ministry of some word, or reading of some book, or speaking with some friend, he comes to be convinced of his misery and woeful condition, and sees no good nor grace in himself; he hath been even hitherto deceived: at last he comes to get some light, some taste, some sorrows, some heart to use the means, some comfort and mercy and hope of life: and when it is thus with him, now he falls; he grows full and falls; and this rising is the cause of his fall; his light is darkness and death to him; and grows to a form of knowledge; his rising makes him fall to formality, and then to profaneness; and so his tasting satisfies him; his sorrows empty his heart of sorrow for sin; and his sorrows for his falls harden his heart in his falls; and all the means of recovering him harden him. . . . Look as it is in diseases; if the physic and meat turns to be poison, then there is no hope of recovery; a man is sick to death now. The saint's little measure makes him forget what is behind." Ibid., p. 226.

return to former profaneness and lewdness; yet from the high opinion they have of their experiences, graces and privileges, gradually settle more and more in a self-righteous and spiritually proud temper of mind, and in such a manner of behavior and conversation, as naturally arises therefrom. When it is thus with men, however far they may seem to be from their former evil practices, this alone is enough to condemn 'em, and may render their last state far worse than the first. For this seems to be the very case of the Jews of that generation that Christ speaks of (Matt. 12:43–45), who having been awakened by John the Baptist's preaching, and brought to a reformation of their former licentious courses, whereby the unclean spirit was as it were turned out, and the house swept and garnished; yet being empty of God and of grace, became full of themselves, and were exalted in an exceeding high opinion of their own righteousness and eminent holiness, and became habituated to an answerably self-exalting behavior; so changing the sins of publicans and harlots, for those of the Pharisees; and in the issue, had seven devils, worse than the first.

Thus I have explained what exercise and fruit I mean, when I say that gracious affections have their exercise and fruit in Christian practice.

The reason why gracious affections have such a tendency and effect, appears from many things that have already been observed, in the preceding parts of this discourse.

The reason of it appears from this, that gracious affections do arise from those operations and influences which are spiritual, and that the inward principle from whence they flow, is something divine, a communication of God, a participation of the divine nature, Christ living in the heart, the Holy Spirit dwelling there, in union with the faculties of the soul, as an internal vital principle, exerting his own proper nature, in the exercise of those faculties. This is sufficient to show us why true grace should have such activity, power and efficacy. No wonder that which is divine, is powerful and effectual; for it has omnipotence on its side. If God dwells in the heart, and be vitally united to it, he will shew that he is a God, by the efficacy of his operation. Christ is not in the heart of a saint, as in a sepulcher, or as a dead Saviour, that does nothing; but as in his temple, and as one that is alive from the dead. For in the heart where Christ savingly is, there he lives, and exerts himself after the power of that endless life, that he received at his resurrection. Thus every saint that is the subject of the benefit of Christ's sufferings, is made to know and experience the power of his resurrection. The spirit of Christ, which is the immediate spring of grace in the heart, is all life, all power, all act; "In demonstration of the Spirit, and of power" (II Cor. 2:4). "Our gospel came not unto you in word only, but also in power, and in the Holy Ghost" (I Thess. 1:5). "The kingdom of God is not in word, but in power" (I Cor. 4:20). Hence saving affections, though oftentimes they don't make so great a noise and show as others; yet have in them a secret solidity, life and strength, whereby they take hold of, and carry away the heart, leading it into a kind of captivity (II Cor. 10:5), gaining a full and steadfast determination of the will for God and holiness; "Thy people shall be willing in the day of thy power" (Ps. 110:3). And thus it is that holy affections have a governing power in the course of a man's life. A statue may look very much like a real man, and a beautiful man; yea it may have, in its appearance to the eye, the resemblance of a very lively, strong and active man; but yet an inward principle of life and strength is wanting; and therefore it does nothing, it brings nothing to pass, there is no action or operation to answer the shew. False discoveries and affections don't go deep enough, to reach and govern the spring of men's actions and practice. The seed in stony ground had not deepness of earth, and the root did not go deep enough to bring forth fruit. But gracious affections go to the very bottom of the heart, and take hold of the very inmost springs of life and activity. Herein chiefly appears the power of true godliness, viz. in its being effectual in practice. And the efficacy of godliness in this respect, is what the Apostle has respect to, when he speaks of the power of godliness (II Tim. 3:5), as is very plain; for he there is particularly declaring, how some professors of religion would notoriously fail in the practice of it; and then in the fifth verse observes, that in being thus of an unholy practice, they deny the power of godliness, though they have the form of it. Indeed the power of godliness is exerted in the first place within the soul, in the sensible, lively exercise of gracious affections there. Yet the principal evidence of this power of godliness, is in those exercises of holy affections that are practical, and in their being practical; in conquering the will, and conquering the lusts and corruptions of men, and carrying men on in the way of holiness, through all temptation, difficulty and opposition.

Again, the reason why gracious affections have their exercise and effect in Christian practice, appears from this (which has also been before observed) that the first objective ground of gracious affections, is the transcendently excellent and amiable nature of divine things, as they are in themselves, and not any conceived relation they bear to self, or self-interest. This shews why holy affections will cause men to be holy in their practice universally. What makes men partial in religion is, that they seek themselves, and not God, in their religion, and close with religion, not for its own excellent nature, but only to serve a turn. He that closes with religion only to serve a turn, will close with no more of it than he imagines serves that turn: but he that closes with religion for its own excellent and lovely nature closes with all that has that nature: he that embraces religion for its own sake, embraces the whole of religion. This also shows why gracious affections will cause men to practice religion perseveringly, and at all times. Religion may alter greatly in process of time, as to its consistence with men's private interest, in many respects; and therefore he that complies with it only from selfish views, is liable, in change of times, to forsake it: but the excellent nature of religion, as it is in itself, is invariable; it is always the same, at all times, and through all changes; it never alters in any respect.

The reason why gracious affections issue in holy practice, also further appears from the kind of excellency of divine things, that it has been observed is the foundation of all holy affection, viz. their moral excellency, or the beauty of their holiness. No wonder that a love to holiness, for holiness' sake, inclines persons to practice holiness, and to practice everything that is holy. Seeing holiness is the main thing that excites, draws and governs all gracious affections, no wonder that all such affections tend to holiness. That which men love, they desire to have and to be united to, and possessed of. That beauty which men delight in, they desire to be adorned with. Those acts which men delight in, they necessarily incline to do.

And what has been observed of that divine teaching and leading of the Spirit of God, which there is in gracious affections, shows the reason of this tendency of such affections to an universally holy practice. For as has been observed, the Spirit of God in this his divine teaching and leading, gives the soul a natural relish of the sweetness of that which is holy, and of everything that is holy, so far as it comes in view, and excites a disrelish and disgust of everything that is unholy.

The same also appears from what has been observed of the nature of that spiritual knowledge, which is the foundation of all holy affection, as consisting in a sense and view of that excellency in divine things, which is supreme and transcendent. For hereby these things appear above all others, worthy to be chosen and adhered to. By the sight of the transcendent glory of Christ, true Christians see him worthy to be followed; and so are powerfully drawn after him: they see him worthy that they should forsake all for him: by the sight of that superlative amiableness, they are thoroughly disposed to be subject to him, and engaged to labor with earnestness and activity in his service, and made willing to go through all difficulties for his sake. And 'tis the discovery of this divine excellency of Christ, that makes 'em constant to him: for it makes a deep impression upon their minds, that they cannot forget him; and they will follow him whithersoever he goes, and it is in vain for any to endeavor to draw them away from him.

The reason of this practical tendency and issue of gracious affections, further appears, from what has been observed of such affections being attended with a thorough conviction of the judgment, of the reality and certainty of divine things. No wonder that they who were never thoroughly convinced that there is any reality in the things of religion, will never be at the labor and trouble of such an earnest, universal and persevering practice of religion, through all difficulties, self-denials and sufferings, in a dependence on that, which they are not convinced of. But on the other hand, they who are thoroughly convinced of the certain truth of those things, must needs be governed by them in their practice; for the things revealed in the Word of God are so great, and so infinitely more important, than all other things, that it is inconsistent with the human nature, that a man should fully believe the truth of them, and not be influenced by them above all things, in his practice.

Again, the reason of this expression and effect of holy affections in the practice, appears from what has been observed of a change of nature, accompanying such affections. Without a change of nature, men's practice will not be thoroughly changed. Till the tree be made good, the fruit will not be good. Men don't gather grapes of thorns, nor figs of thistles. The swine may be washed, and appear clean for a little while, but yet, without a change of nature, he will still wallow in the mire. Nature is a more powerful principle of action, than anything that opposes it: though it may be violently restrained for a while, it will finally overcome that which restrains it: 'tis like the stream of a river, it may be stopped a while with a dam, but if nothing be done to dry the fountain, it won't be stopped always; it will have a course, either in its old channel, or a new one. Nature is a thing more constant and permanent, than any of those things that are the foundation of carnal men's reformation and righteousness. When a natural man denies his lust, and lives a strict, religious life, and seems humble, painful and earnest in religion, 'tis not natural, 'tis all a force against nature; as when a stone is violently thrown upwards; but that force will be gradually spent; yet nature will remain in its full strength, and so prevails again, and the stone returns downwards. As long as corrupt nature is not mortified, but the principle left whole in a man, 'tis a vain thing to expect that it should not govern. But if the old nature be indeed mortified, and a new and heavenly nature infused; then may it well be expected, that men will walk in newness of life, and continue to do so to the end of their days.

The reason of this practical exercise and effect of holy affections, may also be partly seen, from what has been said of that spirit of humility which attends them. Humility is that wherein a spirit of obedience does much consist. A proud spirit is a rebellious spirit, but a humble spirit is a yieldable, subject, obediential spirit. We see among men, that the servant who is of a haughty spirit, is not apt in everything to be submissive and obedient to the will of his master; but it is otherwise with that servant who is of a lowly spirit.

And that lamblike, dovelike spirit, that has been spoken of, which accompanies all gracious affections, fulfills (as the Apostle observes, Rom. 13:8–10 and Gal. 5:14) all the duties of the second table of the law; wherein Christian practice does very much consist, and wherein the external practice of Christianity chiefly consists.

And the reason why gracious affections are attended with that strict, universal and constant obedience which has been spoken of, further appears, from what has been observed of that tenderness of spirit, which accompanies the affections of true saints, causing in them so quick and lively a sense of pain, through the presence of moral evil, and such a dread of the appearance of evil.

And one great reason why the Christian practice which flows from gracious affections, is universal, and constant, and persevering, appears from what has been observed of those affections themselves, from whence this practice flows, being universal and constant, in all kinds of holy exercises, and towards all objects, and in all circumstances, and at all seasons, in a beautiful symmetry and proportion.

And much of the reason why holy affections are expressed and manifested in such an earnestness, activity, and engagedness and perseverance in holy practice, as has been spoken of, appears from what has been observed, of the spiritual appetite and longing after further attainments in religion, which evermore attends true affection, and don't decay, but increases, as those affections increase.

Thus we see how the tendency of holy affections to such a Christian practice as has been explained, appears from each of those characteristics of holy affection, that have been before spoken of.

And this point may be further illustrated and confirmed, if it be considered, that the Holy Scriptures do abundantly place sincerity and soundness in religion, in making a full choice of God as our only Lord and portion, forsaking all for him, and in a full determination of the will for God and Christ, on counting the cost; in our hearts closing and complying with the religion of Jesus Christ, with all that belongs to it, embracing it with all its difficulties, as it were hating our dearest earthly enjoyments, and even our own lives, for Christ; giving up ourselves, with all that we have, wholly and forever, unto Christ, without keeping back anything or making any reserve; or in one word, in the great duty of self-denial for Christ; or in denying, i.e. as it were disowning and renouncing ourselves for him, making ourselves nothing that he may be all. See the texts to this purpose referred to in the margin.[5] Now surely having an heart to forsake all for Christ, tends to actually forsaking all for him, so far as there is occasion, and we have the trial. An having an heart to deny ourselves for Christ, tends to a denying ourselves in deed, when Christ and self-interest stand in competition. A giving up ourselves, with all that we have in our hearts, without making any reserve there, tends to our behaving ourselves universally as his, as subject to his will, and devoted to his ends. Our hearts entirely closing with the religion of Jesus, with all that belongs to it, and as attended with all its difficulties, upon a deliberate counting the cost, tends to an universal closing with the same in act and deed, and actually going through all the difficulties that we meet with in the way of religion, and so holding out with patience and perseverance.

5. Matt. 5:29–30; 6:24; 8:19–22; 4:18–22; 10:37–39; 13:44–46; 16:24–26; 18:8–9; 19:21, 27–29; Luke 5:27–28; 10:42; 12:33–34; 14:16–20, 25–33; 16:13; Acts 4:34–35; 5:1–11; Rom. 6:3–8; Gal. 2:20; 6:14; Phil. 3:7–10; Jas. 1:8–10; 4:4; I John 2:15; Rev. 14:4; Gen. 12:1–4 with Heb. 11:8–10; Gen. 22:12 and Heb. 11:17; Heb. 11:24–27; Deut. 13:6 and 33:9; Ruth 1:6–16 with Ps. 45:10–11 and II Sam. 15:19–22; Ps. 73:25; 16:5–6; Lam. 3:24; Jer. 10:16.

The tendency of grace in the heart to holy practice, is very direct, and the connection most natural close and necessary. True grace is not an unactive thing; there is nothing in heaven or earth of a more active nature; for 'tis life itself, and the most active kind of life, even spiritual and divine life. 'Tis no barren thing; there is nothing in the universe that in its nature has a greater tendency to fruit. Godliness in the heart has as direct a relation to practice, as a fountain has to a stream, or as the luminous nature of the sun has to beams sent forth, or as life has to breathing, or the beating of the pulse, or any other vital act; or as a habit or principle of action has to action: for 'tis the very nature and notion of grace, that 'tis a principle of holy action or practice. Regeneration, which is that work of God in which grace is infused, has a direct relation to practice; for 'tis the very end of it, with a view to which the whole work is wrought: all is calculated and framed, in this mighty and manifold change wrought in the soul, so as directly to tend to this end: "For we are his workmanship, created in Christ Jesus, unto good works" (Eph. 2:10). Yea 'tis the very end of the redemption of Christ; "Who gave himself for us, that he might redeem us from all iniquity, and purify unto himself a peculiar people, zealous of good works" (Titus 2:14). "He died for all, that they which live, should not henceforth live unto themselves, but unto him who died, and rose again" (II Cor. 5:15). "How much more shall the blood of Christ, who through the eternal Spirit, offered up himself without spot to God, purge your consciences from dead works, to serve the living God?" (Heb. 9:14). "And you that were sometimes alienated, and enemies in your minds by wicked works, yet now hath he reconciled, in the body of his flesh, through death, to present you holy and unblamable, and unreprovable in his sight" (Col. 1:21–22). "For as much as ye know that ye were not redeemed with corruptible things, as silver and gold, from your vain conversation" (I Pet. 1:18). "That he would grant us, that we being delivered out of the hands of our enemies, might serve him without fear, in holiness and righteousness before him, all the days of our lives" (Luke 1:74–75). God often speaks of holy practice, as the end of that great typical redemption, the redemption from Egyptian bondage; as Exod. 4:23: "Let my son go, that he may serve me." So ch. 4:23 and 7:16 and 8:1, 20 and 9:1, 13 and 10:3. And this is also declared to be the end of election; "Ye have not chosen me; but I have chosen you, and ordained you, that you go and bring forth fruit, and that your fruit should remain" (John 15:13). "According as he hath chosen us in him, before the foundation of the world, that we should be holy, and without blame before him, in love" (Eph. 1:4). "Created unto good works; which God hath foreordained that we should walk in them" (ch. 2:10). Holy practice is as much the end of all that God does about his saints, as fruit is the end of all the husbandman does about the growth of his field or vineyard: as the matter is often represented in Scripture (Matt. 3:10; ch. 13:8, 23, 24–30, 38; ch. 21:19, 33–34; Luke 13:6; John 15:1, 2, 4–6, 8; I Cor. 3:9; Heb. 6:7–8; Is. 5:1–8; Cant. 8:11–12; Is. 27:2–3).[6] And therefore everything in a true Christian is calculated to reach this end. This fruit of holy practice, is what every grace, and every discovery, and every individual thing, which belongs to Christian experience, has a direct tendency to.[7]

6. "To profess to know much is easy; but to bring your affections into subjection, to wrestle with lusts, to cross your wills and yourselves, upon every occasion, this is hard. The Lord looketh, that in our lives we should be serviceable to him, and useful to men. That which is within, the Lord and our brethren are never better for it: but the outward obedience, flowing thence, glorifieth God and does good to men. The Lord will have this done. What else is the end of our planting and watering, but that the trees may be filled with sap? And what is the end of that sap, but that the trees may bring forth fruit? What careth the husbandman for leaves, and barren trees?" John Preston, *The Church's Carriage, The Golden Scepter with the Church's Marriage and the Church's Carriage in Three Treatises* (London, 1638), pp. 101–2. [The treatises are separately paged.]

7. "What is the end of every grace, but to mollify the heart, and make it pliable to some command or other? Look, how many commandments, so many graces there are in virtue and efficacy, although not so many several names are given them. The end of every such grace is to make us obedient: as the end of temperance is chastity, to bow the heart to these commands, Be ye sober, etc. not in chambering and wantonness, etc. When the Lord commandeth us not to be angry with our brother, the end of meekness, and why the Lord infuseth it, is to keep us from unadvised rash anger. So faith, the end of it is to take Jesus Christ, to make us obedient to the command of the gospel, which commands us to believe in him. So as all graces do join together, but to frame and fashion the soul to obedience; then so much obedience as is in your lives, so much grace in your hearts, and no more. Therefore ask your hearts, how subject you are to the Lord in your lives? It was the counsel that Francis Spira gave to them about him, saith he, learn all of me to take heed of severing faith and obedience; I taught justification by faith, but neglected obedience; and therefore is this befallen me. I have known some godly men, whose comfort on their deathbeds hath been not from the inward acts of their minds, which apart considered, might be subject to misapprehension, but from the course of obedience in their lives, issuing thence. Let Christians look to it, that in all their conversation, as they stand in every

The constant and indissoluble connection that there is between a Christian principle and profession in the true saints, and the fruit of holy practice in their lives, was typified of old in the frame of the golden candlestick in the temple. 'Tis beyond doubt that that golden candlestick, with its seven branches and seven lamps, was a type of the church of Christ. The Holy Ghost himself, has been pleased to put that matter out of doubt, by representing his church by such a golden candlestick, with seven lamps, in the fourth chapter of Zechariah, and representing the seven churches of Asia by seven golden candlesticks, in the first chapter of the Revelation. That golden candlestick in the temple was everywhere, throughout its whole frame, made with knops and flowers (Ex. 25:31, to the end, and ch. 37:17–24). The word translated "knop" in the original signifies apple or pomegranate. There was a knop and a flower, a knop and a flower: wherever there was a flower, there was an apple or pomegranate with it: the flower and the fruit were constantly connected without fail. The flower contained the principles of the fruit, and a beautiful promising appearance of it; and it never was a deceitful appearance: the principle or shew of fruit, had evermore real fruit attending it, or succeeding it. So it is in the church of Christ: there is the principle of fruit in grace in the heart; and there is an amiable profession, signified by the open flowers of the candlestick; and there is answerable fruit, in holy practice, constantly attending this principle and profession. Every branch of the golden candlestick, thus composed of golden apples and flowers, was crowned with a burning, shining lamp on the top of it. For 'tis by this means that the saints shine as lights in the world. By making a fair and good profession of religion, and having their profession evermore joined with answerable fruit in practice: agreeable to that of our Saviour, "Neither do men light a candle, and put it under a bushel, but on a candlestick; and it giveth light unto all that are in the house. Let your light so shine before men, that they may SEE YOUR GOOD WORKS, and glorify your Father which is in heaven" (Matt. 5:15–16). A fair and beautiful profession, and golden fruits accompanying one another, are the amiable ornaments of the true church of Christ. Therefore we find that apples and flowers were not only the ornaments of the candlestick in the temple, but

---

relation, as scholars, tradesmen, husbands, wives, look to this, that when they come to die, they have been subject in all things. This will yield comfort." Ibid., pp. 102–3.

of the temple itself, which is a type of the church; which the Apostle tells us is the temple of the living God. See I Kgs. 6:18: "And the cedar of the house within, was carved with knops and open flowers." The ornaments and crown of the pillars, at the entrance of the temple were of the same sort: they were lilies and pomegranates, or flowers and fruits mixed together (I Kgs. 7:18–19). So it is with all those that are as pillars in the temple of God, who shall go no more out, or never be ejected as intruders; as it is with all true saints; "Him that overcometh will I make a pillar in the temple of my God, and he shall go no more out" (Rev. 3:12).

Much the same things seems to be signified by the ornaments on the skirt of the ephod, the garment of Aaron the high priest; which were golden bells and pomegranates. That these skirts of Aaron's garment represent the church, or the saints (that are as it were the garment of Christ) is manifest; for they are evidently so spoken of, "Behold, how good and how pleasant it is for brethren to dwell together in unity! It is like the precious ointment upon the head, that ran down upon the beard, even Aaron's beard, that went down to the skirts of his garments" (Ps. 133:1–2). That ephod of Aaron signified the same with the seamless coat of Christ our great high priest. As Christ's coat had no seam, but was woven from the top throughout, so it was with the ephod (Ex. 39:22). As God took care in his providence, that Christ's coat should not be rent; so God took special care that the ephod should not be rent (Ex. 28:32 and ch. 39:23). The golden bells on this ephod, by their precious matter and pleasant sound, do well represent the good profession that the saints make; and the pomegranates, the fruit they bring forth. And as in the hem of the ephod, bells and pomegranates were constantly connected, as is once and again observed, there was a golden bell and a pomegranate, a golden bell and a pomegranate (Ex. 28:34 and ch. 39:26). So it is in the true saints; their good profession and their good fruit, do constantly accompany one another: the fruit they bring forth in life, evermore answers the pleasant sound of their profession.

Again, the very same thing is represented by Christ, in his description of his spouse, "Thy belly is like a heap of wheat, set about with lilies" (Cant. 7:2). Here again are beautiful flowers, and good fruit, accompanying one another. The lilies were fair and beautiful flowers, and the wheat was good fruit.

As this fruit of Christian practice is evermore found in true saints, according as they have opportunity and trial, so it is found in them only; none but true Christians do live such an obedient life, so universally devoted to their duty, and given up to the business of a Christian, as has been explained. All unsanctified men are workers of inquity: they are of their father the devil, and the lusts of their father they will do. There is no hypocrite that will go through with the business of religion, and both begin and finish the tower: they will not endure the trials God is wont to bring on the professors of religion, but will turn aside to their crooked ways: they will not be thoroughly faithful to Christ in their practice, and follow him whithersoever he goes. Whatever lengths they may go in religion in some instances, and though they may appear exceeding strict, and mightily engaged in the service of God for a season; yet they are servants to sin; the chains of their old taskmasters are not broken: their lusts yet have a reigning power in their hearts; and therefore to these masters they will bow down again.[8] "Many shall be purified

8. "No unregenerate man, though he go never so far, let him do never so much, but he lives in some one sin or other, secret or open, little or great. Judas went far, but he was covetous: Herod went far, but he loved his Herodias. Every dog hath his kennel; every swine hath his swill; and every wicked man his lust." Thomas Shepard, *The Sincere Convert* (London, 1641), p. 139.

"There is never an unsound heart in the world, but as they say of witches, they have some familiar that sucks them, so they have some lust that is beloved of them, some beloved there is, they have given a promise to never to forsake." Shepard, *Parable,* Pt. I, p. 15.

"No man that is married to the law, but his fig leaves cover some nakedness. All his duties ever brood some lust. There is some one sin or other the man lives in; which either the Lord discovers, and he will not part with, as the young man; or else is so spiritual, he cannot see all his lifetime. Read through the strictest of all, and see this, Matt. 23: [27], 'painted sepulchers.' Paul that was blameless, yet (Eph. 2:3; Titus 3:3) 'served divers lusts and pleasures.' And the reason is, the law is not the ministration of the Spirit, II Cor. 3:8–9, which breaks off from every sin. There is no law that can give life, Gal. 3:21, and hence many men have strong resolutions, and break all again. Hence men sin and sorrow, and pray again, and then go with more ease in their sin. Examine thyself; is there any living lust with thy righteousness? 'Tis sure, 'tis a righteousness thou art married to, and never wert yet matched to Christ." Ibid., pp. 19–20.

"No hypocrite, though he closeth with Christ, and for a time grow up in knowledge of, and communion with Christ, but he hath at that time hidden lusts and thorns that overgrow his growings, and choke all at last, and in conclusion mediates a league between Christ and his lusts, and seeks to reconcile 'em together." Ibid., p. 109.

"Their faith is in such a party, as never was yet thoroughly rent from sin. And here is the great wound of the most cunning hypocrites living. . . . Let a man be

and made white and tried: but the wicked will do wickedly: and none of the wicked shall understand" (Dan. 12:10). "Let favor be shewed to the wicked, yet will he not learn righteousness; in the land of uprightness will he deal unjustly" (Is. 26). "And an highway shall be there, and a way, and it shall be called the way of holiness,

---

cast down as low as hell with sorrow, and lie under chains, quaking in apprehension of terror to come; let a man then be raised up to heaven in joy, not able to live; let a man reform and shine like an earthly angel; yet if not rent from lust, that either you did never see it, or if so, you have not followed the Lord to remove it, but proud, dogged, worldly, sluggish still, false in your dealings, cunning in your tradings, devils in your families, images in your churches; you are objects of pity now, and shall be of terror at the great day. For where sin remains in power, it will bring faith, and Christ, and joy into bondage and service of itself." Ibid., p. 125.

"Methinks it is with the best hypocrites, as 'tis with divers old merchants: they prize and desire the gain of merchandise; but to be at the trouble to prepare the ship, to put themselves upon the hazards and dangers of the ship, to go and fetch the treasure that they prize, this they will never do. So many prize and desire earnestly the treasures of heaven; but to be at the trouble of a heaven voyage to fetch this treasure, to pass through the valley of *Baca,* tears, temptations, the powers of darkness, the breaches, opposition and contradictions of a sinful unbelieving heart, good and evil report, to pass from one depth and wave to another, this the best hypocrite fails in; and hence loses all at last. And this I conceive to be one of the great differences between the strong desires and esteems of hypocrites and saints. . . . Look, as 'tis with men that have two trades, or two shops; one is as much as ever they can follow or tend; they are forced at last to put off one, and they must neglect one; so here. . . . That spirit of sloth and slumber, which the Lord ever leaves the best hypocrite to, so mightily oppresseth all their senses, that they cannot use effectually all means to accomplish their ends. And hence a man desires the end, but has it not; Prov. 13:4." Ibid., pp. 150–1.

"Read through all the Scripture; constantly, never any hypocrites but they had this brand, Matt. 7:23: 'you workers of iniquity.'" Ibid., p. 195.

"A carnal man may hit upon some good duty that God commands, and refrain some sin that God forbids; but to go through, he cannot: to take up reproach and disgrace, to lose his credit, to forsake his friends, to lose honor, and riches and pleasures; this he will not do, till he be humbled." Preston, *Remains,* p. 206.

"So it is with men, because they want humiliation. Therefore their profession and they do not continue, but part willingly one from another. They will do some things, but not all things: and they will forego some things, but not all things. And therefore our Saviour saith, Luke 14 [The text has simply "Luke 14" whereas the passage quoted is a combination of Luke 14:33 and Matt. 10:38.]: 'He that will not forsake all for my sake, is not worthy of me.' He is not worth the saving, that prizes not me above all things whatsoever. And a man will not prize Christ, nor forsake all things for Christ, till he be humbled." Ibid., p. 239.

the unclean shall not pass over it" (Is. 35:8). "The ways of the Lord are right, and the just shall walk in them; but the transgressors shall fall therein" (Hos. 14:9). "What is the hope of the hypocrite? . . . Will he delight himself in the Almighty? Will he always call upon God?" (Job 27:8–10). An unsanctified man may hide his sin, and may in many things and for a season refrain from sin; but he will not be brought finally to renounce his sin, and give it a bill of divorce: sin is too dear to him, for him to be willing for that: wickedness is sweet in his mouth; and therefore he hides it under his tongue; he spares it and forsakes it not; but keeps it still within his mouth (Job 20:12–13). Herein chiefly consists the straightness of the gate, and the narrowness of the way that leads to life; upon the account of which, carnal men will not go in thereat, viz that it is a way of utterly denying, and finally renouncing all ungodliness, and so a way of self-denial or self-renunciation.

Many natural men, under the means that are used with them, and God's strivings with them to bring them to forsake their sins, do by their sins, as Pharaoh did by his pride and covetousness, which he gratified by keeping the children of Israel in bondage, when God strove with him to bring him to let the people go. When God's hand pressed Pharaoh sore, and he was exercised with fears of God's future wrath, he entertained some thoughts of letting the people go, and promised he would do it; but from time to time he broke his promises, when he saw there was respite. When God filled Egypt with thunder and lightning, and the fire ran along the ground, then Pharaoh is brought to confess his sin with seeming humility, and to have a great resolution to let the people go, "And Pharaoh sent and called for Moses and Aaron, and said unto them, I have sinned this time; the Lord is righteous, and I and my people are wicked: intreat the Lord (for it is enough) that there be no more mighty thunderings and hail, and I will let you go, and ye shall stay no longer" (Ex. 9:27–28). So sinners are sometimes, by thunders and lightnings, and great terrors of the law, brought to a seeming work of humiliation, and to appearance to part with their sins; but are no more thoroughly brought to a disposition to dismiss them, than Pharaoh was to let the people go. Pharaoh in the struggle that was between his conscience and his lusts, was for contriving that God might be served, and he enjoy his lusts that were gratified by the slavery of the people, too. Moses insisted that Israel's God should be served and sacrificed to: Pharaoh was willing to consent to that; but would have it done without his parting with the people: "Go sacrifice to your God in the land," says he (Ex. 8:25). So many sinners are for contriving to serve God, and enjoy their lusts too. Moses objected against complying with Pharaoh's proposal, that serving God, and yet continuing in Egypt under their taskmasters, did not agree together, and were inconsistent one with another (there is no serving God, and continuing slaves to such enemies of God at the same time). After this Pharaoh consented to let the people go, provided they would not go far away: he was not willing to part with them finally, and therefore would have them within reach. So do many hypocrites with respect to their sins. Afterwards Pharaoh consented to let the men go, if they would leave the women and children (Ex. 10:8–10). And then after that, when God's hand was yet harder upon him, he consented that they should go, even women and children, as well as men, provided they would leave their cattle behind: but he was not willing to let them go, and all that they had (Ex. 10:24). So it oftentimes is with sinners: they are willing to part with some of their sins; but not all: they are brought to part with the more gross acts of sin; but not to part with their lusts, in lesser indulgences of 'em. Whereas we must part with all our sins, little and great; and all that belongs to 'em, men, women, children, and cattle: they must all be let go, with their young, and with their old, with their sons, and with their daughters, with their flocks, and with their herds; there must not be an hoof left behind: as Moses told Pharaoh, with respect to the children of Israel. At last, when it came to extremity, Pharaoh consented to let the people all go, and all that they had; but he was not steadfastly of that mind: he soon repented, and pursued after them again: and the reason was, that those lusts of pride and covetousness, that were gratified by Pharaoh's dominion over the people, and the gains of their service, were never really mortified in him, but only violently restrained. And thus, he being guilty of backsliding, after his seeming compliance with God's commands was destroyed without remedy. Thus there may be a forced parting with ways of disobedience to the commands of God, that may seem to be universal, as to what appears, for a little season: but because 'tis a mere force, without the mortification of the inward principle of sin, they will not persevere in it; but will return as the dog to his vomit; and so bring on themselves dreadful and remediless destruction. There were many false disciples in Christ's time, that followed him for a while;

but none of them followed him to the end; but some on one occasion, and some on another, went back and walked no more with him.[9]

From what has been said it is manifest, that Christian practice or a holy life is a great and distinguishing sign of true and saving grace. But I may go further, and assert, that it is the chief of all the signs of grace, both as an evidence of the sincerity of professors unto others, and also to their own consciences.

But then it is necessary that this be rightly taken, and that it be well understood and observed, in what sense and manner Christian practice is the greatest sign of grace. Therefore, to set this matter in a clear light, I will endeavor particularly and distinctly to prove, that Christian practice is the *principal sign* by which Christians are

9. "The counterfeit and common grace of foolish virgins, after some time of glorious profession, will certainly go out and be quite spent. It consumes in the using and shining and burning. . . . Men that have been most forward, decay; their gifts decay, life decays. . . . It is so, after some time of profession: for at first, it rather grows than decays and withers: but afterward they have enough of it, it withers and dies. . . . The Spirit of God comes upon many hypocrites, in abundant and plentiful measure of awakening grace; it comes upon them, as it did upon Balaam, and as it is in overflowing waters, which spread far, and grow very deep, and fill many empty places. . . . Though it doth come upon them so, yet it doth never rest within, so as to dwell there, to take up an eternal mansion for himself. . . . Hence it doth decay by little and little; till at last it is quite gone. As ponds filled with rain water, which comes upon them; not spring water, that riseth up within them; it dries up by little and little, until quite dry." Shepard, *Parable,* Pt. II, pp. 58–9.

"Some men may apprehend Christ, neither out of fear of misery, nor only to preserve some sin; but God lets in light and heat of the blessed beams of the glorious gospel of the Son of God: and therefore there is mercy, rich, free, sweet, for damned, great, vile sinners: good Lord, saith the soul, what a sweet ministry, Word, God and gospel is this! and there rests. This was the frame of the stony ground; which heard the Word, and received it with joy, and for a time believed. And this is the case of thousands, that are much affected with the promise and mercy of Christ, and hang upon free grace for a time: but as 'tis with sweet smells in a room, they continue not long; or as flowers, they grow old and withered, and then fall. In time of temptation, lust, and world, and sloth is more sweet than Christ, and all his gospel is." Ibid., p. 168.

"Never any carnal heart, but some root of bitterness did grow up at last in this soil." Ibid., Pt. I, p. 195.

"We shall see in experience: take the best professors living; though they may come, as they and others judge, to the Lord, and follow the Lord; yet they will in time depart. . . . The Spirit never was given effectually to draw them; nor yet to keep them." Ibid., p. 205.

to judge, both of their own and others' sincerity of godliness; withal observing some things that are needful to be particularly noted, in order to a right understanding of this matter.

1. I shall consider Christian practice and an holy life, as a manifestation and sign of the sincerity of a professing Christian, to the eye of his neighbors and brethren.

And that this is the chief sign of grace in this respect, is very evident from the Word of God. Christ, who knew best how to give us rules to judge of others, has repeated it and inculcated it, that we should know them by their fruits; "Ye shall know them by their fruits" (Matt. 7:16). And then after arguing the point, and giving clear reasons why it must needs be, that men's fruits must be the chief evidence of what sort they are, in the following verses, he closes by repeating the assertion; "Wherefore by their fruits ye shall know them" (ver. 20). Again, "Either make the tree good, and his fruit good; or else make the tree corrupt, and his fruit corrupt" (ch. 12:33). As much as to say, 'tis a very absurd thing, for any to suppose that the tree is good, and yet the fruit bad, that the tree is of one sort, and the fruit of another; for the proper evidence of the nature of the tree is its fruit. Nothing else can be intended by that last clause in the verse, "for the tree is known by its fruit," than that the tree is chiefly known by its fruit, that this is the main and most proper diagnostic by which one tree is distinguished from another. So Luke 6:44: "Every tree is known by his own fruit." Christ nowhere says, ye shall know the tree by its leaves or flowers, or ye shall know men by their talk, or ye shall know them by the good story they tell of their experiences, or ye shall know them by the manner and air of their speaking, and emphasis and pathos of expression, or by their speaking feelingly, or by making a very great show by abundance of talk, or by many tears and affectionate expressions, or by the affections ye feel in your hearts towards them: but by their fruits shall ye know them; the tree is known by its fruit; every tree is known by its own fruit. And as this is the evidence that Christ has directed us mainly to look at in others, in judging of them, so it is the evidence that Christ has mainly directed us to give to others, whereby they may judge of us; "Let your light so shine before men, that others seeing your good works, may glorify your Father which is in heaven" (Matt. 5:16). Here Christ directs us to manifest our godliness to others. Godliness is as it were a light that shines in the soul: Christ directs that this light should not only shine within, but that it should shine out before men, that they may see it. But which way shall this be? 'Tis by our good works. Christ don't say, that others hearing your good words, your good story, or your pathetical expressions; but that others seeing your good works, may glorify your Father which is in heaven. Doubtless when Christ gives us a rule how to make our light shine, that others may have evidence of it, his rule is the best that is to be found. And the apostles do mention a Christian practice, as the principal ground of their esteem of persons as true Christians. As the apostle Paul, in the 6th chapter of Hebrews. There the Apostle in the beginning of the chapter, speaks of them that have great common illuminations, that have been enlightened, and have tasted of the heavenly gift, and were made partakers of the Holy Ghost, and have tasted the good Word of God, and the powers of the world to come, that afterwards fall away, and are like barren ground, that is nigh unto cursing, whose end is to be burned: and then immediately adds in the 9th verse (expressing his charity for the Christian Hebrews, as having that saving grace, which is better than all these common illuminations): "But beloved, we are persuaded better things of you, and things that accompany salvation; though we thus speak." And then in the next verse, he tells 'em what was the reason he had such good thoughts of 'em: he don't say, that it was because they had given him a good account of a work of God upon their souls, and talked very experimentally; but it was their work, and labor of love; "For God is not unrighteous, to forget your work, and labor of love, which ye have shewed towards his name, in that ye have ministered to the saints, and do minister." And the same Apostle speaks of a faithful serving God in practice, as the proper proof to others of men's loving Christ above all, and preferring his honor to their private interest, "For all seek their own, not the things which are Jesus Christ's: but ye know the proof of him, that as a son with the father, he hath served with me in the gospel" (Phil. 2:21–22). So the apostle John expresses the same, as the ground of his good opinion of Gaius, "For I rejoiced greatly, when the brethren came and testified of the truth that is in thee" (III John 3–6). But how did the brethren testify of the truth that was in Gaius? And how did the Apostle judge of the truth that was in him? It was not because they testified that he had given 'em a good account of the steps of his experiences, and talked like one that felt what he said, and had the very language of a Christian; but they testified, that he walked in the truth; as it follows, "even as thou walkest in the truth. I have no greater joy, than to hear that my children walk in the truth. Beloved, thou dost faithfully, whatsoever thou dost to the brethren and to strangers; which have borne witness of thy charity before the church." Thus the Apostle explains what the brethren had borne witness of, when they came and testified of his walking in the truth. And the Apostle seems in this same place, to give it as a rule to Gaius how he should judge of others; in verse 10, he mentions one Diotrephes, that did not carry himself well, and led away others after him; and then in the 11th verse he directs Gaius to beware of such, and not to follow them; and gives him a rule whereby he may know them, exactly agreeable to that rule Christ had given before, "By their fruits ye shall know 'em"; says the Apostle: "Beloved, follow not that which is evil, but that which is good. He that doth good is of God; but he that doth evil hath not seen God." And I would further observe that the apostle James, expressly comparing that way of showing others our faith and Christianity by our practice or works, with other ways of showing our faith without works, or not by works, does plainly and abundantly prefer the former; "Yea a man may say, thou hast faith and I have works: Show me thy faith without thy works, and I will show thee my faith by my works" (Jas. 2:18). A manifestation of our faith without works, or in a way diverse from works, is a manifestation of it in words, whereby a man professes faith. As the Apostle says, "What doth it profit, my brethren, though a man SAY he hath faith?" (ver. 14). Therefore here are two ways of manifesting to our neighbor what is in our hearts; one by what we *say*, and the other by what we *do*. But the Apostle abundantly prefers the latter as the best evidence. Now certainly all accounts we give of ourselves in words, our saying that we have faith, and that we are converted, and telling the manner how we came to have faith, and the steps by which it was wrought, and the discoveries and experiences that accompanied it, are still but manifesting our faith by what we say; 'tis but showing our faith by our words; which the Apostle speaks of as falling vastly short of manifesting of it by what we do, and showing our faith by our works.

And as the Scripture plainly teaches that practice is the best evidence of the sincerity of professing Christians; so reason teaches the same thing. Reason shows that men's deeds are better and more faithful interpreters of their minds, than their words. The common sense of all mankind, through all ages and nations, teaches 'em to judge of men's hearts chiefly by their practice, in other matters: as whether a man be a loyal subject, a true lover, a dutiful child, or a faithful servant. If a man professes a great deal of love and friendship to another, reason teaches all men, that such a profession is not so great an evidence of his being a real and hearty friend, as his appearing a friend in deeds; being faithful and constant to his friend, in prosperity and adversity, ready to lay out himself, and deny himself, and suffer in his personal interest, to do him a kindness. A wise man will trust to such evidences of the sincerity of friendship, further than a thousand earnest professions and solemn declarations, and most affectionate expressions of friendship in words. And there is equal reason why practice should also be looked upon as the best evidence of friendship towards Christ. Reason says the same that Christ said, in John 14:21: "He that hath my commandments, and keepeth them, he it is that loveth me." Thus if we see a man, who in the course of his life, seems to follow and imitate Christ, and greatly to exert and deny himself for the honor of Christ and to promote his kingdom and interest in the world; reason teaches that this is an evidence of love to Christ, more to be depended on, than if a man only says he has love to Christ, and tells of the inward experiences he has had of love to him, what strong love he felt, and how his heart was drawn out in love at such and such a time, when it may be there appears but little imitation of Christ in his behavior, and he seems backward to do any great matter for him, or to put himself out of his way for the promoting of his kingdom, but seems to be apt to excuse himself, whenever he is called to deny himself for Christ. So if a man in declaring his experiences, tells how he found his heart weaned from the world, and saw the vanity of it, so that all looked as nothing to him, at such and such times, and professes that he gives up all to God, and calls heaven and earth to witness to it; but yet in his practice is violent in pursuing the world, and what he gets he keeps close, is exceeding loath to part with much of it to charitable and pious uses, it comes from him almost like his heart's blood. But there is another professing Christian, that says not a great deal, yet in his behavior appears ready at all times to forsake the world, whenever it stands in the way of his duty, and is free to part with it at any time, to promote religion and the good of his fellow creatures;

reason teaches that the latter gives far the most credible manifestation of an heart weaned from the world. And if a man appears to walk humbly before God and men, and to be of a conversation that savors of a broken heart, appearing patient and resigned to God under affliction, and meek in his behavior amongst men; this is a better evidence of humiliation, than if a person only tells how great a sense he had of his own unworthiness, how he was brought to lie in the dust, and was quite emptied of himself, and saw himself nothing and all over filthy and abominable, etc., etc.; but yet acts as if he looked upon himself one of the first and best of saints, and by just right the head of all the Christians in the town, and is assuming, self-willed, and impatient of the least contradiction or opposition; we may be assured in such a case, that a man's practice comes from a lower place in his heart, than his profession. So (to mention no more instances) if a professor of Christianity manifests in his behavior a pitiful tender spirit towards others in calamity, ready to bear their burdens with them, willing to spend his substance for them, and to suffer many inconveniences in his worldly interest to promote the good of others' souls and bodies; is not this a more credible manifestation of a spirit of love to men, than only a man's telling what love he felt to others at certain times, how he pitied their souls, how his soul was in travail for 'em, and how he felt a hearty love and pity to his enemies; when in his behavior he seems to be of a very selfish spirit, close and niggardly, all for himself and none for his neighbors, and perhaps envious and contentious? Persons in a pang of affection may think they have a willingness of heart for great things, to do much and to suffer much, and so may profess it very earnestly and confidently; when really their hearts are far from it. Thus many in their affectionate pangs, have thought themselves willing to be damned eternally for the glory of God. Passing affections easily produce words; and words are cheap; and godliness is more easily feigned in words than in actions. Christian practice is a costly laborious thing. The self-denial that is required of Christians, and the narrowness of the way that leads to life, don't consist in words, but in practice. Hypocrites may much more easily be brought to talk like saints, than to act like saints.

Thus it is plain that Christian practice is the best sign or manifestation of the true godliness of a professing Christian, to the eye of his neighbors.

But then the following things should be well observed, that this matter may be rightly understood.

First, it must be observed, that when the Scripture speaks of Christian practice, as the best evidence to others, of sincerity and truth of grace, a profession of Christianity is not excluded, but supposed. The rules mentioned were rules given to the followers of Christ, to guide them in their thoughts of professing Christians, and those that offered themselves as some of their society, whereby they might judge of the truth of their pretenses, and the sincerity of the profession they made; and not for the trial of heathens, or those that made no pretense to Christianity, and that Christians had nothing to do with. This is as plain as is possible in that great rule which Christ gives in the 7th of Matthew, "By their fruits ye shall know them." He there gives a rule how to judge of those that professed to be Christians, yea that made a very high profession, "false prophets, who come in sheep's clothing," as ver. 15. So it is also with that of the apostle James, "Show me thy faith without thy works, and I will show thee my faith by my works" (ch. 2:18). 'Tis evident that both these sorts of persons, offering to give these diverse evidences of their faith, are professors of faith: this is implied in their offering each of them to give evidences of the faith they professed. And 'tis evident by the preceding verses, that the Apostle is speaking of professors of faith in Jesus Christ. So it is very plain that the apostle John, in those passages that have been observed in his third Epistle, is speaking of professing Christians. Though in these rules, the Christian practice of professors be spoken of as the greatest and most distinguishing sign of their sincerity in their profession, much more evidential than their profession itself; yet a profession of Christianity is plainly presupposed: it is not the main thing in the evidence, nor anything distinguishing in it; yet 'tis a thing requisite and necessary in it. As the having an animal body, is not anything distinguishing of a man, from other creatures, and is not the main thing in the evidence of human nature; yet 'tis a thing requisite and necessary in the evidence. So that if any man should say plainly that he was not a Christian, and did not believe that Jesus was the Son of God, or a person sent of God; these rules of Christ and his apostles don't at all oblige us to look upon him as a sincere Christian, let his visible practice and virtues, be what they will. And not only do these rules take no place with respect to a man that explicitly denies Christianity, and is a professed deist,

Jew, heathen, or open infidel; but also with respect to a man that only forbears to make a profession of Christianity: because these rules were given us only to judge of professing Christians: fruits must be joined with open flowers; bells and pomegranates go together.

But here will naturally arise this inquiry, viz. when a man may be said to profess Christianity, or what profession may properly be called a profession of Christianity?

I answer in two things;

(1) In order to a man's being properly said to make a profession of Christianity, there must undoubtedly be a profession of all that is necessary to his being a Christian, or of so much as belongs to the essence of Christianity. Whatsoever is essential in Christianity itself, the profession of that is essential in the profession of Christianity. The profession must be of the thing professed. For a man to profess Christianity is for him to declare that he has it. And therefore so much as belongs to a thing, so as to be necessary in order to its being truly denominated *that* thing; so much is essential to the declaration of that thing, in order to its being truly denominated a declaration of that thing. If we take only a part of Christianity, and leave out a part that is essential to it, what we take is not Christianity; because something that is of the essence of it is wanting. So if we profess only a part, and leave out a part that is essential, that which we profess is not Christianity. Thus in order to a profession of Christianity, we must profess that we believe that Jesus is the Messiah; for this reason, because such a belief is essential to Christianity. And so we must profess, either expressly or implicitly, that Jesus satisfied for our sins, and other essential doctrines of the gospel; because a belief of these things also are essential to Christianity. But there are other things as essential to religion, as an orthodox belief; which it is therefore as necessary that we should profess, in order to our being truly said to profess Christianity. Thus it is essential to Christianity that we repent of our sins, that we be convinced of our own sinfulness, and that we are sensible we have justly exposed ourselves to God's wrath, and that our hearts do renounce all sin, and that we do with our whole hearts embrace Christ as our only Saviour, and that we love him above all, and are willing for his sake to forsake all, and that we do give up ourselves to be entirely and forever his, etc. Such things as these do as much belong to the essence of Christianity, as the

belief of any of the doctrines of the gospel: and therefore the profession of them does as much belong to a Christian profession. Not that in order to a being professing Christians, 'tis necessary that there should be an explicit profession of every individual thing that belongs to Christian grace or virtue: but certainly, there must be a profession, either express or implicit, of what is of the essence of religion. And as to those things that Christians should express in their profession, we ought to be guided by the precepts of God's Word, or by Scripture examples of public professions of religion, God's people have made from time to time. Thus they ought to profess their repentance of sin: as of old, when persons were initiated as professors, they came confessing their sins, manifesting their humiliation for sin (Matt. 3:6). And the baptism they were baptized with, was called the baptism of repentance (Mark 1:3). And John, when he had baptized them, exhorted them to bring forth fruits meet for repentance (Matt. 3:8), i.e. agreeable to that repentance which they had professed; encouraging them, that if they did so, they should escape the wrath to come, and be gathered as wheat into God's garner (Matt. 3:7–10, 12). So the apostle Peter says to the Jews, "Repent, and be baptized" (Acts 2:38): which shows that repentance is a qualification that must be visible in order to baptism; and therefore ought to be publicly professed. So when the Jews that returned from captivity, entered publicly into covenant, it was with confession, or public profession of repentance of their sins (Neh. 9:2). This profession of repentance should include or imply a profession of conviction that God would be just in our damnation: see Neh. 9:33 together with ver. 35 and the beginning of the next chapter. They should profess their faith in Jesus Christ, and that they embrace Christ, and rely upon him as their Saviour, with their whole hearts, and that they do joyfully entertain the gospel of Christ. Thus Philip, in order to baptizing the eunuch, required that he should profess that he believed with all his heart: and they that were received as visible Christians, at that great outpouring of the Spirit, which began at the day of Pentecost, appeared gladly to receive the gospel; "Then they that gladly received the word, were baptized, and the same day there were added unto them about three thousand souls" (Acts 2:41). They should profess that they rely only on Christ's righteousness and strength, and that they are devoted to him, as their only Lord and Saviour, and that they rejoice in him as their only righteousness and portion. It is foretold that all nations should be brought publicly to make this profession, "Look to me, and be ye saved, all the ends of the earth; for I am God, and there is none else. I have sworn by myself the word is gone out of my mouth in righteousness, and shall not return, that unto me every knee shall bow, every tongue shall swear. Surely shall one say, in the Lord have I righteousness and strength. Even to him shall men come: and all that are incensed against him shall be ashamed. In the Lord shall all the seed of Israel be justified, and shall glory" (Is. 45:22, to the end). They should proceed to give up themselves entirely to Christ, and to God through him; as the children of Israel, when they publicly recognized their covenant with God; "Thou hast avouched the Lord this day to be thy God, and to walk in his ways, and to keep his statutes, and his commandments, and his judgments, and to hearken unto his voice" (Deut. 26:17). They ought to profess a willingness of heart to embrace religion with all its difficulties, and to walk in a way of obedience to God universally and perseveringly (Ex. 19:8 and 24:3, 7; Deut. 26:16–18; II Kgs. 23:3; Neh. 10:28–29; Ps. 119:57, 106). They ought to profess that all their hearts and souls are in these engagements to be the Lord's, and for ever to serve him (II Chron. 15:12–14). God's people swearing to God, and swearing by his name, or to his name, as it might be rendered (by which seems to be signified their solemnly giving up themselves to him in covenant, and vowing to receive him as their God, and to be entirely his, to obey and serve him), is spoken of as a duty to be performed by all God's visible Israel (Deut. 6:13 and 10:20; Ps. 63:11; Is. 19:18, ch. 45:23–24 compared with Rom. 14:11 and Phil. 2:10–11; Is. 48:1–2 and 65:15–16; Jer. 4:2 and 5:7 and 12:16; Hos. 4:15 and 10:4). Therefore, in order to persons being entitled to full esteem and charity, with their neighbors, as being sincere professors of Christianity; by those forementioned rules of Christ and his apostles, there must be a visibly holy life, with a profession, either expressing, or plainly implying such things as those which have been now mentioned. We are to know them by their fruits; that is, we are by their fruits to know whether they be what they profess to be; not that we are to know by their fruits, that they have something in them, which they don't so much as pretend to.

And moreover,

(2) That profession of these things, which is properly called a Christian profession, and which must be joined with Christian

practice, in order to persons' being entitled to the benefit of those rules, must be made (as to what appears) understandingly: that is, they must be persons that appear to have been so far instructed in the principles of religion, as to be in an ordinary capacity to understand the proper import of what is expressed in their profession. For sounds are no significations or declarations of anything, any further than men understand the meaning of their own sounds.

But in order to persons making a proper profession of Christianity, such as the Scripture directs to, and such as the followers of Christ should require, in order to the acceptance of the professors with full charity, as of their society; 'tis not necessary they should give an account of the particular steps and method, by which the Holy Spirit, sensibly to them, wrought and brought about those great essential things of Christianity in their hearts. There is no footstep in the Scripture of any such way of the apostles, or primitive ministers and Christians requiring any such relation, in order to their receiving and treating others, as their Christian brethren, to all intents and purposes, or of their first examining them, concerning the particular method and order of their experiences. They required of them a profession of the things wrought; but no account of the manner of working was required of them. Nor is there the least shadow in the Scripture of any such custom in the church of God, from Adam to the death of the apostle John.

I am far from saying that it is not requisite that persons should give any sort of account of their experiences to their brethren. For persons to profess those things wherein the essence of Christianity lies, is the same thing as to profess that they experience those things. Thus for persons solemnly to profess, that, in a sense and full conviction of their own utter sinfulness, misery, and impotence, and totally undone state as in themselves, and their just desert of God's utter rejection and eternal wrath, without mercy, and the utter insufficiency of their own righteousness, or anything in them, to satisfy divine justice, or recommend 'em to God's favor, they do only and entirely depend on the Lord Jesus Christ and his satisfaction and righteousness; that they do with all their hearts believe the truth of the gospel of Christ; and that in a full conviction and sense of his sufficiency and perfect excellency as a savior, as exhibited in the gospel, they do with their whole souls cleave to him, and acquiesce in him, as the refuge and rest of their souls, and fountain of their comfort; that they repent of their sins, and utterly renounce all sin, and give up themselves wholly to Christ, willingly subjecting themselves to him as their king; that they give him their hearts and their whole man; and are willing and resolved to have God for their whole and everlasting portion; and in a dependence on his promises of a future eternal enjoyment of him in heaven, to renounce all the enjoyments of this vain world, selling all for this great treasure and future inheritance, and to comply with every command of God, even the most difficult and self-denying, and devote their whole lives to God's service; and that in forgiveness of those that have injured them, and a general benevolence to mankind, their hearts are united to the people of Jesus Christ as their people, to cleave to them and love them as their brethren, and worship and serve God and follow Christ in union and fellowship with them, being willing and resolved to perform all those duties that belong to them, as members of the same family of God and mystical Body of Christ; I say, for persons solemnly to profess such things as these, as in the presence of God, is the same thing, as to profess that they are conscious to, or do experience such things in their hearts.

Nor is it what I suppose, that persons giving an account of their experience of particular exercises of grace, with the times and circumstances, gives no advantage to others in forming a judgment of their state; or that persons may not fitly be inquired of concerning these in some cases, especially cases of great importance, where all possible satisfaction concerning persons' piety is especially to be desired and sought after, as in the case of ordination or approbation of a minister. It may give advantage in forming a judgment, in several respects; and among others, in this, that hereby we may be better satisfied that the professor speaks honestly and understandingly, in what he professes; and that he don't make the profession in mere formality. In order to a profession of Christianity being accepted to any purpose, there ought to be good reason, from the circumstances of the profession, to think that the professor don't make such a profession out of a mere customary compliance with a prescribed form, using words without any distinct meaning, or in a very lax and ambiguous manner, as confessions of faith are often subscribed; but that the professor understandingly and honestly signifies what he is conscious of in his own heart; otherwise his profession can be of no significance, and no more to be regarded than the sound of things without life. But indeed (whatever advantage an account of particular exercises may give in judging of this) it must be owned that the professor having been previously thoroughly instructed by his teachers, and giving good proof of his sufficient knowledge, together with a practice agreeable to his profession, is the best evidence of this.

Nor do I suppose, but that, if a person that is inquired of about particular passages, times and circumstances of his Christian experience, among other things, seems to be able to give a distinct account of the manner of his first conversion, in such a method as has been frequently observable in true conversion, so that things seem sensibly and distinctly to follow one another, in the order of time, according to the order of nature; it is an illustrating circumstance, that among other things, adds luster to the evidence he gives his brethren of the truth of his experiences.

But the thing that I speak of as unscriptural, is the insisting on a particular account of the distinct method and steps, wherein the Spirit of God did sensibly proceed, in first bringing the soul into a state of salvation, as a thing requisite in order to receiving a professor into full charity as a real Christian; or so, as for the want of such relation, to disregard other things in the evidence persons give to their neighbors of their Christianity, that are vastly more important and essential.

Secondly, that we may rightly understand how Christian practice is the greatest evidence that others can have of the sincerity of a professing Christian, 'tis needful that what was said before, showing what Christian practice is, should be borne in mind; and that it should be considered how far this may be visible to others. Merely that a professor of Christianity is what is commonly called an honest man, and a moral man (i.e. we have no special transgression or iniquity to charge him with, that might bring a blot on his character), is no great evidence of the sincerity of his profession. This is not making his light shine before men. This is not that work and labor of love showed towards Christ's Name, which gave the Apostle such persuasion of the sincerity of the professing Hebrews (Heb. 6:9–10). It may be so, that we may see nothing in a man, but that he may be a good man, there may appear nothing in his life and conversation inconsistent with his being godly, and yet neither may there be any great positive evidence that he is so. But there may be great positive appearances of holiness in men's visible behavior: their life may appear to be a life of the service of

God: they may appear to follow the example of Jesus Christ, and come up in a great measure to those excellent rules in the 5th, 6th, and 7th chapters of Matthew, and 12th of Romans, and many other parts of the New Testament: there may be a great appearance of their being universal in their obedience to Christ's commands and the rules of the gospel. They may appear to be universal in the performance of the duties of the first table, manifesting the fear and love of God: and also universal in fulfilling rules of love to men, love to saints, and love to enemies; rules of meekness and forgiveness, rules of mercy and charity, and looking not only at our own things, but also at the things of others; rules of doing good to men's souls and bodies, to particular persons and to the public; rules of temperance and mortification, and of an humble conversation; rules of bridling the tongue, and improving it to glorify God and bless men, showing that in their tongues is the law of kindness. They may appear to walk as Christians in all places, and at all seasons, in the house of God, and in their families, and among their neighbors, on Sabbath days, and every day, in business and in conversation, towards friends and enemies, towards superiors, inferiors and equals. Persons in their visible walk may appear to be very earnestly engaged in the service of God and mankind, much to labor and lay out themselves in this work of a Christian, and to be very constant and steadfast in it, under all circumstances and temptations. There may be great manifestations of a spirit to deny themselves, and suffer for God and Christ, and the interest of religion, and the benefit of their brethren. There may be great appearances in a man's walk, of a disposition to forsake anything, rather than to forsake Christ, and to make everything give place to his honor. There may be great manifestations in a man's behavior of such religion as this being his element, and of his placing the delight and happiness of his life in it: and his conversation may be such, that he may carry with him a sweet odor of Christian graces and heavenly dispositions, wherever he goes. And when it is thus in the professors of Christianity, here is an evidence to others of their sincerity in their profession, to which all other manifestations are not worthy to be compared.

There is doubtless a great variety in the degrees of evidence that professors do exhibit of their sincerity, in their life and practice; as there is a variety in the fairness and clearness of accounts persons give of the manner and method of their experiences: but undoubtedly such a manifestation as has been described, of a Christian spirit in practice, is vastly beyond the fairest and brightest story of particular steps and passages of experience, that ever was told. And in general a manifestation of the sincerity of a Christian profession in practice, is far better than a relation of experiences.

But yet,

Thirdly, it must be noted, agreeable to what was formerly observed, that no external manifestations and outward appearances whatsoever, that are visible to the world, are infallible evidences of grace. These manifestations that have been mentioned, are the best that mankind can have; and they are such as to oblige Christians entirely to embrace professors as saints, and love 'em and rejoice in 'em as the children of God, and are sufficient to give them as great satisfaction concerning them, as ever is needful to guide them in their conduct, or for any intent and purpose that needs to be answered in this world. But nothing that appears to them in their neighbor, can be sufficient to beget an absolute certainty concerning the state of his soul: for they see not his heart, nor can they see all his external behavior; for much of it is in secret, and hid from the eye of the world: and 'tis impossible certainly to determine, how far a man may go in many external appearances and imitations of grace, from other principles. Though undoubtedly, if others could see so much of what belongs to men's practice, as their own consciences may see of it, it might be an infallible evidence of their state, as will appear from what follows:

Having thus considered Christian practice as the best evidence of the sincerity of professors to others, I now proceed,

2. To observe that the Scripture also speaks of Christian practice as a distinguishing and sure evidence of grace to persons' own consciences. This is very plain in I John 2:3: "Hereby we do know that we know him, if we keep his commandments." And the testimony of our consciences, with respect to our good deeds, is spoken of as that which may give us assurance of our own godliness; "My little children, let us not love in word, neither in tongue, but in deed (in the original it is εργῳ 'in work') and in truth. And hereby we know that we are of the truth, and shall assure our hearts before him" (I John 3:18–19). And the apostle Paul, in Heb. 6 speaks of "the work and labor of love," of the Christian Hebrews, as

that which both gave him a persuasion that they had something above the highest common illuminations, and also as that evidence which tended to give them the highest assurance of hope concerning themselves; ver. 9, etc.: "But beloved, we are persuaded better things of you, and things that accompany salvation, though we thus speak. For God is not unrighteous, to forget your work, and labor of love, which ye have showed towards his name; in that ye have ministered to his saints, and do minister. And we desire that every one of you do show the same diligence, to the full assurance of hope, unto the end." So the Apostle directs the Galatians to examine their behavior or practice, that they might have rejoicing in themselves in their own happy state; "Let every man prove his own work; so shall he have rejoicing in himself, and not in another" (Gal. 6:4). And the Psalmist says, "Then shall I not be ashamed, when I have respect to all thy commandments" (Ps. 119:6), i.e. then shall I be bold and assured and steadfast in my hope. And in that of our Saviour, "Every tree that bringeth not forth good fruit is hewn down and cast into the fire: wherefore by their fruits ye shall know them" (Matt. 7:19–20). Though Christ gives this firstly, as a rule by which we should judge of others, yet in the words that next follow he plainly shews, that he intends it also as a rule by which we should judge ourselves; "not every one that saith unto me Lord, Lord, shall enter into the kingdom of heaven, but he that doth the will of my Father, which is in heaven. Many will say unto me in that day, Lord, Lord," etc., "and then I will profess unto them, I never knew you; depart from me ye that work iniquity. Therefore whosoever heareth these sayings of mine, and DOTH them, I will liken him to a wise man, which built his house upon a rock. . . . And every one that heareth these sayings of mine and DOTH THEM NOT, shall be likened unto a foolish man, which built his house upon the sand." I shall have occasion to mention other texts that show the same thing, hereafter.

But for the greater clearness in this matter, I would first, shew how Christian practice, doing good works, or keeping Christ's commandments, is to be taken, when the Scripture represents it as a sure sign to our own consciences, that we are real Christians. And secondly, will prove that this is the chief of all evidences that men can have of their own sincere godliness.

First, I would shew how Christian practice, or keeping Christ's commandments, is to be taken, when the Scripture represents it as a sure evidence to our own consciences, that we are sincere Christians.

And here I would observe, that we can't reasonably suppose that when the Scripture in this case speaks of good works, good fruit, and keeping Christ's commandments; that it has respect merely to what is external, or the motion and action of the body, without including anything else, having no respect to any aim or intention of the agent, or any act of his understanding or will. For consider men's action so, and they are no more good works or acts of obedience, than the regular motions of a clock; nor are they considered as the actions of the men, or any human actions at all. The actions of the body, taken thus, are neither acts of obedience, nor disobedience; any more than the motions of the body in a convulsion. But the obedience and fruit that is spoken of, is the obedience and fruit of the man; and therefore not only the acts of the body, but the obedience of the soul, consisting in the acts and practice of the soul. Not that I suppose that when the Scripture speaks, in this case of gracious works and fruit and practice that in these expressions is included all inward piety and holiness of heart, both principle and exercise, both spirit and practice: because then, in these things being given as signs of a gracious principle in the heart, the same thing would be given as a sign of itself, and there would be no distinction between root and fruit. But only the gracious exercise, and holy act of the soul is meant, and given as the sign of the holy principle, and good estate. Neither is every kind of inward exercise of grace meant; but the practical exercise, that exercise of the soul, and exertion of inward holiness, which there is in an obediential act; or that exertion of the mind, and act of grace, which issues and terminates in what they call the imperate acts of the will; in which something is directed and commanded by the soul to be done, and brought to pass in practice.

Here for a clearer understanding, I would observe, that there are two kinds of exercises of grace. (1) There are those that some call immanent acts: that is, those exercises of grace that remain within the soul, that begin and are terminated there, without any immediate relation to anything to be done outwardly, or to be brought to pass in practice. Such are the exercises of grace, which the saints often have in contemplation: when the exercise that is in the heart, don't directly proceed to, or terminate in anything beyond the thoughts of the mind; however they may tend to practice (as all exercises of grace do) more remotely. (2) There is another kind of acts of grace, that are more strictly called practical, or effective exercises; because they immediately respect something to be done. They are the exertions of grace in the commanding acts of the will, directing the outward actions. As when a saint gives a cup of cold water to a disciple, in and from the exercise of the grace of charity; or voluntarily endures persecution, in the way of his duty, immediately from the exercise of a supreme love to Christ. Here is the exertion of grace producing its effect in outward actions. These exercises of grace are practical and productive of good works, not only in this sense, that they are of a productive nature (for so are all exercises of true grace), but they are the producing acts. This is properly the exercise of grace in the act of the will; and this is properly the practice of the soul. And the soul is the immediate actor of no other practice but this: the motions of the body follow from the laws of union between the soul and body, which God, and not the soul has fixed, and does maintain. The act of the soul, and the exercise of grace, that is exerted in the performance of a good work, is the good work itself, so far as the soul is concerned in it, or so far as it is the soul's good work. The determinations of the will, are indeed our very actions, so far as they are properly ours, as Dr. Doddridge observes.[1] In this practice of the soul, is included the aim and intention of the soul which is the agent. For not only should we not look on the motions of a statue, doing justice or distributing alms by clockwork, as any acts of obedience to Christ in that statue; but neither would anybody call the voluntary actions of a man, externally and materially agreeable to a command of Christ, by the name of obedience to Christ, if he had never heard of Christ, or any of his commands, or had no thought of his commands in what he did. If the acts of obedience and good fruits spoken of, be looked upon, not as mere motions of the body, but as acts of the soul; the whole exercise of the spirit of the mind, in the action, must be taken in, with the end acted for, and the respect the soul then has to God, etc.; otherwise they are no acts of denial of ourselves, or obedience to God, or service done to him, but something else. Such effective exercises of grace as these that I have now described, many of the martyrs have ex-

1. Phillip Doddridge, "The Scripture Doctrine of Salvation," *Practical Discourses on Regeneration,* Philadelphia, 1794.

perienced in a high degree. And all true saints live a life of such acts of grace as these; as they all live a life of gracious works, of which these operative exertions of grace are the life and soul. And this is the obedience and fruit that God mainly looks at, as he looks at the soul, more than the body; as much as the soul, in the constitution of the human nature, is the superior part. As God looks at the obedience and practice of the man, he looks at the practice of the soul; for the soul is the man in God's sight; for the Lord seeth not as man seeth, for he looketh on the heart.

And thus it is, that obedience, good works, good fruit, are to be taken, when given in Scripture as a sure evidence to our own consciences of a true principle of grace; even as including the obedience and practice of the soul, as preceding and governing the actions of the body. When practice is given in Scripture as the main evidence of our true Christianity to others, then is meant that in our practice which is visible to them, even our outward actions: but when practice is given as a sure evidence of our real Christianity to our own consciences, then is meant that in our practice which is visible to our own consciences; which is not only the motion of our bodies, but the exertion and exercise of the soul, which directs and commands that motion; which is more directly and immediately under the view of our own consciences, than the act of the body. And that this is the intent of the Scripture, not only does the nature and reason of the thing show, but it is plain by the Scripture itself. Thus it is evident that when Christ, at the conclusion of his Sermon on the Mount, speaks of doing or practicing those sayings of his, as the grand sign of professors being true disciples, without which he likens 'em to a man that built his house upon the sand, and with which, to a man that built his house upon a rock; he has a respect, not only to the outward behavior, but to the inward exercise of the mind in that behavior: as is evident by observing what those preceding sayings of his are, that he refers to, when he speaks of our doing or practicing them: and we shall find they are such as these; "Blessed are the poor in spirit, blessed are they that mourn, blessed are the meek, blessed are they that do hunger and thirst after righteousness, blessed are the merciful, blessed are the pure in heart, whosoever is angry with his brother without a cause," etc., "whosoever looketh on a woman to lust after her," etc., "love your enemies, take no thought for your life," and others of the like nature, which imply inward exercises: and when Christ says, "He that hath my commandments and keepeth them, he it is that loveth me" (John 14:21); he has evidently a special respect to that command several times repeated in the same discourse (which he calls, by way of eminence, his commandment) "that they should love one another, as he had loved them" (see ch. 13:34–35 and ch. 15:10, 12–14). But this command respects chiefly an exercise of the mind or heart, though exerted in practice. So when the apostle John says, "Hereby we do know that we know him, if we keep his commandments" (I John 2:3); he has plainly a principal respect to the same command, as appears by what follows (verses 7–11, and 2nd Epistle verses 5–6). And when we are told in Scripture that men shall at the last day be judged according to their works, and all shall receive according to the things done in the body; it is not to be understood only of outward acts; for if so, why is God so often spoken of as searching the hearts and trying the reins, that he may render to everyone according to his works? as Rev. 2:23: "And all the churches shall know that I am he that searcheth the reins and the hearts; and I will give unto everyone according to his works." "I the Lord search the hearts, I try the reins; even to give every man according to his ways, and according to the fruit of his doings" (Jer. 17:9–10). But if by "his ways" and "the fruit of his doings," is meant only the actions of his body, what need of "searching the heart" and "reins," in order to know them? Hezekiah in his sickness pleads his practice as an evidence of his title to God's favor, as including, not only his outward actions, but what was in his heart, Is. 38:3: "Remember now, O Lord, I beseech thee, how I have walked before thee, in truth, and with a perfect heart."

Though in this great evidence of sincerity that the Scripture gives us, what is inward is of greatest importance; yet what is outward is included and intended, as connected with the practical exertion of grace in the will, directing and commanding the actions of the body. And hereby are effectually cut off all pretensions that any man can have to evidences of godliness, who externally lives wickedly: because the great evidence lies in that inward exercise and practice of the soul, which consists in the act of the will, commanding outward acts. But 'tis known that these commanding acts of the will are not one way, and the actions of the bodily organs another: for the unalterable law of nature is, that they should be united, as long as soul and body are united, and the organs are not so destroyed as to be incapable of those motions that the soul commands. Thus it would be ridiculous for a man to plead, that the commanding act of his will was to go to the public worship, while his feet carry him to a tavern or brothel house; or that the commanding act of his will was to give such a piece of money he had in his hand, to a poor beggar, while his hand at the same instant, kept it back, and held it fast.

Secondly, I proceed to show that Christian practice, taken in the sense that has been explained, is the chief of all the evidences of a saving sincerity in religion, to the consciences of the professors of it; much to be preferred to the method of the first convictions, enlightenings and comforts in conversion, or any immanent discoveries or exercises of grace whatsoever, that begin and end in contemplation.[2] The evidence of this appears by the following arguments.

Argument 1. Reason plainly shews that those things which put it to the proof what men will actually cleave to and prefer in their practice, when left to follow their own choice and inclinations, are

2. "Look upon John, Christ's beloved disciple and bosom companion; he had received the anointing to know him that is true, and he knew that he knew him, I John 2:3. But how did he know that? He might be deceived (as 'tis strange to see what a melancholy fancy will do, and the effects of it; as honest men are reputed to have weak brains, and never saw the depths of the secrets of God) what's his *last* proof? Because we keep his commandments." Shepard, *Parable,* Pt. I, p. 131.

"A man may know his present union to the Lord Jesus, by a work; I John 2:4: 'He that saith I know him, and keeps not his commandments, is a liar.' . . . Yes that is true negatively; but may a man, ought a man, to see or know his union positively by this? Ans. verse 5. Many said they did know and love the Lord, but he that keeps his words. O they are sweet! It's heaven to cleave to him in every command; it is death to depart from any command: 'Hereby know we that we are in him.' If it were possible to ask of angels, how they know they are not devils, they would answer, the Lord's will is ours." Ibid., p. 134.

"If the question be, whom doth the Lord Jesus love; you need not go to heaven for it, the Word is nigh thee, 'Those that love Christ'? Who are those? 'Those that keep his commandments.'" Ibid., p. 138.

"Will you have Christ sit in heaven, and not look that he subdue your lusts by the work of his grace, and so sway your hearts? You despise his kingdom then. Do you seek for pardon in the blood of Christ, and never look for the virtue and end of that blood to wash you and make you without spot, etc.? You despise his priesthood and blood then. Do you look for Christ to do work for you, and you not do Christ's work, and bring forth fruit to him? You despise his honor then, John 15:8. If I were to discover a hypocrite, or a false heart, this I would say, it is he that shall set up Christ, but loathe his work." Ibid., pp. 139–140.

the proper trial what they do really prefer in their hearts. Sincerity in religion, as has been observed already, consists in setting God highest in the heart, in choosing him before other things, in having a heart to sell all for Christ, etc. But a man's actions are the proper trial what a man's heart prefers. As for instance, when it is so that God and other thing things come to stand in competition, God is as it were set before a man on one hand, and his worldly interest or pleasure on the other (as it often is so in the course of a man's life), his behavior in such case, in actually cleaving to the one and forsaking the other, is the proper trial which he prefers. Sincerity consists in forsaking all for Christ in heart; but to forsake all for Christ in heart, is the very same thing as to have an heart to forsake all for Christ: but certainly the proper trial whether a man has an heart to forsake all for Christ, is his being actually put to it, the having Christ and other things coming in competition, that he must actually or practically cleave to one and forsake the other. To forsake all for Christ in heart, is the same thing as to have an heart to forsake all for Christ when called to it: but the highest proof to ourselves and others, that we have an heart to forsake all for Christ when called to it, is actually doing it when called to it, or so far as called to it. To follow Christ in heart, is to have an heart to follow him. To deny ourselves in heart for Christ, is the same thing as to have an heart to deny ourselves for him in fact. The main and most proper proof of a man's having an heart to anything, concerning which he is at liberty to follow his own inclinations, and either to do or not to do as he pleases, is his doing of it. When a man is at liberty whether to speak or keep silence, the most proper evidence of his having an heart to speak, is his speaking. When a man is at liberty whether to walk or sit still, the proper proof of his having an heart to walk, is his walking. Godliness consists not in an heart to intend to do the will of God, but in an heart to do it. The children of Israel in the wilderness had the former, of whom we read, "Go thou near, and hear all that the Lord our God shall say; and speak thou unto us all that the Lord our God shall speak unto thee; and we will hear it and do it. And the Lord heard the voice of your words, when ye spake unto me; and the Lord said unto me, I have heard the voice of the words of this people, which they have spoken unto thee: they have well said all that they have spoken: O that there were such an HEART in them, that they would fear me, and keep all my commandments always, that it might be well with them, and with their children forever" (Deut. 5:27–29). The people manifested that they had a heart to intend to keep God's commandments, and to be very forward in those intentions; but God manifests that this was far from being the thing that he desired, wherein true godliness consists, even an heart actually to keep them.

'Tis therefore exceeding absurd, and even ridiculous, for any to pretend that they have a good heart, while they live a wicked life, or don't bring forth the fruit of universal holiness in their practice. For 'tis proved in fact, that such men don't love God above all. 'Tis foolish to dispute against plain fact and experience. Men that live in ways of sin, and yet flatter themselves that they shall go to heaven, or expect to be received hereafter as holy persons, without a holy life and practice, act as though they expected to make a fool of their Judge. Which is implied in what the Apostle says (speaking of men's doing good works, and living an holy life, thereby exhibiting evidence of their title to everlasting life): "Be not deceived; God is not mocked: for whatsoever a man soweth, that shall he also reap" (Gal. 6:7). As much as to say, "Don't deceive yourselves with an expectation of reaping life everlasting hereafter, if you don't sow to the Spirit here; 'tis in vain to think that God will be made a fool of by you, that he will be shamed and baffled with shadows instead of substance, and with vain pretenses, instead of that good fruit which he expects, when the contrary to what you pretend, appears plainly in your life, before his face." In this manner the word "mock" is sometimes used in Scripture. Thus Delilah says to Samson: "Behold, thou hast mocked me, and told me lies" (Judg. 16:10, 13), i.e. "thou hast baffled me, as though you would make a fool of me, as if I might be easily turned off with any vain pretense, instead of the truth." So it is said that Lot, when he told his sons-in-law that God would destroy that place, "he seemed as one that mocked to his sons-in-law" (Gen. 19:14), i.e. he seemed as one that would make a game of them, as though they were such credulous fools as to regard such bugbears. But the great Judge, whose eyes are as a flame of fire, will not be mocked or baffled with any pretenses, without a holy life. If in his name men have prophesied and wrought miracles, and have had faith, so that they could remove mountains, and cast out devils, and however high their religious affections have been, however great resemblances they have had of grace, and though their hiding place has been so dark and deep, that no human skill nor search could find them out; yet if they are workers or practicers of iniquity, they can't hide their hypocrisy from their Judge; "There is no darkness, nor shadow of death, where the workers of iniquity may hide themselves" (Job. 34:22). Would a wise prince suffer himself to be fooled and baffled by a subject, who should pretend that he was a loyal subject, and should tell his prince that he had an entire affection to him and that at such and such a time he had experience of it, and felt his affections strongly working towards him, and should come expecting to be accepted and rewarded by his prince, as one of his best friends on that account, though he lived in rebellion against him, following some pretender to his crown, and from time to time stirring up sedition against him? Or would a master suffer himself to be shamed and gulled by a servant, that should pretend to great experiences of love and honor towards him in his heart, and a great sense of his worthiness and kindness to him, when at the same time he refused to obey him, and he could get no service done by him?

Argument 2. As reason shows that those things which occur in the course of life that put it to the proof whether men will prefer God to other things in practice, are the proper trial of the uprightness and sincerity of their hearts; so the same are represented as the proper trial of the sincerity of professors, in the Scripture. There we find that such things are called by that very name, trials or temptations (which I before observed are both words of the same signification). The things that put it to the proof whether men will prefer God to other things in practice, are the difficulties of religion, or those things which occur that make the practice of duty difficult and cross to other principles besides the love of God; because in them, God and other things are both set before men together, for their actual and practical choice; and it comes to this, that we can't hold to both, but one or the other must be forsaken. And these things are all over the Scripture called by the name of trials or proofs.[3] And they are called by this name, because hereby professors are tried and proved of what sort they be, whether they be really what they profess and appear to be; and because in them, the reality of a supreme love to God is brought to the test of experiment and fact; they are the proper proofs, in which it is truly de-

3. II Cor. 8:2; Heb. 11:36; I Pet. 1:7; 4:12; Gen. 22:1; Deut. 8:2, 16; 13:3; Ex. 15:25 and 16:4; Judg. 2:22; 3:1, 4; Ps. 66:10–11; Dan. 12:10; Rev. 3:10; Job 23:10; Zech. 13:9; Jas. 1:12; Rev. 2:10; Luke 8:13; Acts 20:19; Jas. 1:2–3; I Pet. 1:6.

termined by experience, whether men have a thorough disposition of heart to cleave to God or no; "And thou shalt remember all the way which the Lord thy God led thee, these forty years in the wilderness, to humble thee, and to prove thee, whether thou wouldst keep his commandments or no" (Deut. 8:2). "I also will not henceforth drive out any from before them, of the nations which Joshua left when he died; that through them I may prove Israel, whether they will keep the way of the Lord" (Judges 2:21–22). So ch. 3:1, 4 and Ex. 16:4. And the Scripture, when it calls these difficulties of religion by the name of temptations or trials, explains itself to mean thereby, the trial or experiment of their faith, "My brethren, count it all joy when ye fall into divers temptations, knowing this, that the trying of your faith worketh patience" (Jas. 1:2–3). "Now for a season ye are in heaviness, through manifold temptations; that the trial of your faith, being much more precious than of gold," etc. (I Pet. 1:6–7). So the apostle Paul speaks of that expensive duty of parting with our substance to the poor, as the proof of the sincerity of the love of Christians (II Cor. 8:8): And the difficulties of religion are often represented in Scripture as being the trial of professors, in the same manner that the furnace is the proper trial of gold and silver; "Thou, O God, hast proved us, thou hast tried us, as silver is tried: thou broughtest us into the net; thou laidst affliction upon our loins" (Ps. 66:10–11), "And I will bring the third part of them through the fire: and I will refine them as silver is refined; and I will try them as gold is tried" (Zech. 13:9). That which has the color and appearance of gold is put into the furnace to try whether it be what it seems to be, real gold or no. So the difficulties of religion are called trials, because they try those that have the profession and appearance of saints, whether they are what they appear to be, real saints. If we put true gold into the furnace, we shall find its great value and preciousness: so the truth and inestimable value of the virtues of a true Christian appear, when under these trials; "That the trial of your faith, being much more precious than of gold that perisheth, might be found unto praise, and honor, and glory" (I Pet. 1:7). True and pure gold will come out of the furnace in full weight: so true saints when tried come forth as gold (Job 23:10). Christ distinguishes true grace from counterfeit by this, that it is "gold tried in the fire" (Rev. 3:17–18). So that it is evident that these things are called trials in Scripture, principally as they try or prove the sincerity of professors. And from what has been now observed, 'tis evident that they are the most proper trial or proof of their sincerity; inasmuch as the very meaning of the word "trial," as it is ordinarily used in Scripture, is the difficulty occurring in the way of a professor's duty, as the trial or experiment of his sincerity. If "trial of sincerity" be the proper name of these difficulties of religion, then doubtless these difficulties of religion are properly and eminently the trial of sincerity: for they are doubtless eminently what they are called by the Holy Ghost: God gives things their name from that which is eminently their nature. And if it be so, that these things are the proper and eminent trial, proof or experiment of the sincerity of professors; then certainly the result of the trial or experiment (that is persons' behavior or practice under such trials) is the proper and eminent evidence of their sincerity. For they are called trials or proofs, only with regard to the result, and because the effect is eminently the proof, or evidence. And this is the most proper proof and evidence to the conscience of those that are the subjects of these trials. For when God is said by these things to try men, and prove them, to see what is in their hearts, and whether they will keep his commandments or no; we are not to understand, that it is for his own information, or that he may obtain evidence himself of their sincerity (for he needs no trials for his information); but chiefly for their conviction, and to exhibit evidence to their consciences.[4] Thus when God is said to prove Israel by the difficulties they met with in the wilderness, and by the difficulties they met with from their enemies in Canaan, to know what was in their hearts, whether they would keep his commandments or no; it must be understood that it was to discover them to themselves, that they might know what was in their own hearts. So when God tempted or tried Abraham with that difficult command of offering up his son, it was not for his satisfaction, whether he feared God or no, but for Abraham's own greater satisfaction and comfort, and the more clear manifestation of the favor of God to him. When Abraham had proved faithful under this trial, God says to him, "Now I know that thou fearest God, seeing thou hast not withheld thy son, thine only son

4. "I am persuaded, as Calvin is, that all the several trials of men, are to shew them to themselves, and to the world, that they be but counterfeits; and to make saints known to themselves, the better. . . . Rom. 5:3–4: 'Tribulation works trial, and that hope.' Prov. 17:3. If you will know whether it will hold weight, the trial will tell you." Shepard, *Parable*, Pt. I, p. 191.

from me." Which plainly implies that in this practical exercise of Abraham's grace under this trial, was a clearer evidence of the truth of his grace, than ever was before; and the greatest evidence to Abraham's conscience; because God himself gives it to Abraham as such, for his comfort and rejoicing; and speaks of it to him, as what might be the greatest evidence to his conscience, of his being upright in the sight of his Judge. Which proves what I say, that holy practice under trials is the highest evidence of the sincerity of professors to their own consciences. And we find that Christ from time to time took the same method to convince the consciences of those that pretended friendship to him, and to shew them what they were. This was the method he took with the rich young man (Matt. 19:16, etc.). He seemed to shew a great respect to Christ; he came kneeling to him, and called him "Good Master," and made a great profession of obedience to the commandments; but Christ tried him by bidding him go and sell all that he had, and give to the poor, and come and take up his cross, and follow him; telling him that then he should have treasure in heaven. So he tried another that we read of Matt. 8:20. He made a great profession of respect to Christ: says he: "Lord, I will follow thee whithersoever thou goest." Christ immediately puts his friendship to the proof, by telling him that the foxes had holes, and the birds of the air had nests, but that the Son of Man had not where to lay his head. And thus Christ is wont still to try professed disciples in general, in his providence. So the seed sown in every kind of ground, stony ground, thorny ground, and good ground, which in all appears alike, when it first springs up; yet is tried, and the difference made to appear, by the burning heart of the sun.

Seeing therefore that these are the things that God makes use of to try us, 'tis undoubtedly the surest way for us to pass a right judgment on ourselves, to try ourselves by the same things. These trials of his are not for his information, but for ours; therefore we ought to receive our information from thence. The surest way to know our gold, is to look upon it and examine it in God's furnace, where he tries it for that end that we may see what it is. If we have a mind to know whether a building stands strong or no, we must look upon it when the wind blows. If we would know whether that which appears in the form of wheat, has the real substance of wheat, or be only chaff, we must observe it when it is winnowed. If we would know whether a staff be strong, or a rotten broken reed, we must observe it when it is leaned on, and weight is borne upon it. If we would weigh ourselves justly, we must weigh ourselves in God's scales, that he makes use of to weigh us.[5] These trials in

5. Dr. Sibbes says, in his *Bruised Reed,* "When Christ's will cometh in competition with any worldly loss or gain, yet if then, in that particular case, the heart will stoop to Christ, it is a true sign. For the truest trial of the power of grace, is in such particular cases as touch us nearest; for there our corruption maketh the greatest head. When Christ came home to the young man in the gospel, he lost a disciple of him." Richard Sibbes, *The Bruised Reede and Smoaking Flax* (6th ed. London, 1638, 1st ed. 1630), p. 263.

Mr. Flavel speaks of a holy practice under trials, as the greatest evidence of grace: "No man," says he, "can say what he is, whether his graces be true or false, till they be tried and examined by those things, which are to them as fire is to gold." Flavel, *Touchstone,* ch. 4, sec. 1, p. 62. Again, speaking of great difficulties and sufferings in the way of duty, wherein a person must actually part with what is dearest of a worldly nature, or with his duty; he says, "That such sufferings as these will discover the falseness and rottenness of men's hearts, cannot be doubted; if you consider, that this is the fire designed by God for this very use and purpose, to separate the gold from the dross. So you will find it, I Pet. 4:12: 'Beloved, think it not strange concerning the fiery trial that is to try you,' i.e. the very design and aim of Providence in permitting and ordering them, is to try you. Upon this account you find the hour of persecution (in a suitable notion) called the hour of temptation or probation, Rev. 3:10. For then professors are sifted to the very bran, searched to the very bottom principles. 'This is the day that burns as an oven; all that do wickedly shall be as stubble,' Mal. 4:1. For in that day the predominant interest must appear and be discovered, it can be concealed no longer. 'No man can serve two masters,' saith Christ, Luke 16:13. A man may serve many masters, if they all command the same thing or things subordinate to each other; but he cannot serve two masters if their commands clash and interfere with each other: and such are the commands of Christ and the flesh in a suffering hour: thus the two interests come in full opposition. And now have but patience and wait a little, and you will discern which is predominant. A dog follows two men, while they both walk one way, and you know not which of the two is his master: stay but a little, till their path parts, and then you shall quickly see who is his master: so it is in this case." Ibid., ch. 8, sec. 3, pp. 169–70. And in another chapter he says, "Great numbers of persons are deceived and destroyed by trusting to seeming untried grace. This was the miserable condition of the Laodicean professors: they reckoned themselves rich, but were really poor: all is not gold that glisters: their gold (as they accounted it) was never tried in the fire. If a man's whole estate lay in some precious stone, suppose a rich diamond, how is he concerned to have it thoroughly tried, to see whether it will bear a smart stroke with the hammer, or fly like a Bristol diamond!" Ibid., ch. 10, sec. 3, p. 200. Again in the same place, "The promises of salvation are made over to tried grace, and that only as will endure the trial." Ibid., p. 200.

"The Lord will try you. God hath his trying times: and they were never sent, but to discover who were dross, who were gold. And the main end of all God's

the course of our practice are as it were the balances in which our hearts are weighed, or in which Christ and the world, or Christ and his competitors, as to the esteem and regard they have in our hearts, are weighed, or are put into opposite scales, by which there is opportunity to see which preponderates. When a man is brought to the dividing of paths, the one of which leads to Christ, and the other to the objects of his lusts, to see which way he will go, or is brought, and as it were set between Christ and the world, Christ on the right hand, and the world on the left, so that if he goes to one he must leave the other, to see which his heart inclines most to, or which preponderates in his heart; this is just the same thing as laying Christ and the world in two opposite scales: and his going to the one, and leaving the other, is just the same thing, as the sinking of one scale, and rising of the other. A man's practice therefore, under the trials of God's providence, are as much the proper experiment and evidence of the superior inclination of his heart, as the motion of the balance, with different weights, in opposite scales, is the proper experiment of the superior weight.

Argument 3. Another argument, that holy practice, in the sense which has been explained, is the highest kind of evidence of the truth of grace to the consciences of Christians, is, that in practice, grace, in Scripture style, is said to be made perfect, or to be finished. So the apostle James says (Jas. 2:22): "Seest thou how faith wrought with his works, and by works was faith made perfect, or finished" (as the word in the original properly signifies). So the love of God is said to be made perfect, or finished, in keeping his commandments; "He that saith, I know him, and keepeth not his commandments, is a liar, and the truth is not in him; but whoso keepeth his word, in him verily is the love of God perfected" (I John 2:4–5). The commandment of Christ, which the Apostle has especial respect to, when he here speaks of our keeping his commandments, is (as I

---

trials, is to discover this truth that I now am pressing upon you. Some have a thorough work; and now the trial discovers the truth, as in Abraham, Heb. 11:17. Some have a superficial work, and they fall in trial, as in Saul; and it doth discover it was but an overly work. For this is the question God makes, is it thorough or no? Ay, saith the carnal heart; yes, saith a gracious heart. Hence it is strange to see what men will do when a trial comes." Shepard, *Parable,* Pt. I, p. 219.

"There is an hour of temptation which tries men, which will discover men indeed." Ibid., Pt. II, p. 60.

observed before) that great commandment of his, which respects deeds of love to our brethren; as appears by the following verses. Again, the love of God is said to be perfected, in the same sense, "If we love one another, God dwelleth in us, and his love is perfected in us" (ch. 4:12). Here doubtless the Apostle has still respect to loving one another, in the same manner that he had explained in the preceding chapter, speaking of loving one another, as a sign of the love of God, "Whoso hath this world's goods, and shutteth up his bowels . . . how dwelleth the love of God in him? My little children, let us not love in word, neither in tongue, but in deed" (or in work), "and in truth" (verses 17–18). By thus loving in work, the Apostle says the love of God is perfected in us. Grace is said to be perfected or finished in holy practice, as therein it is brought to its proper effect, and to that exercise which is the end of the principle; the tendency and design of grace, herein is reached, and its operation completed and crowned. As the tree is made perfect in the fruit: 'tis not perfected in the seeds being planted in the ground; it is not perfected in the first quickening of the seed, and in its putting forth root and sprout; nor is it perfected when it comes up out of the ground; nor is it perfected in bringing forth leaves; nor yet in putting forth blossoms: but when it has brought forth good ripe fruit, then it is perfected, therein it reaches its end, the design of the tree is finished: all that belongs to the tree is completed and brought to its proper effect in the fruit: so is grace in its practical exercises. Grace is said to be made perfect or finished in its work or fruit, in the same manner as 'tis said of sin, "When lust hath conceived, it bringeth forth sin; and sin, when it is finished, bringeth forth death" (Jas. 1:15). Here are three steps; first, sin in its principle or habit, in the being of lust in the heart; and nextly, here is its conceiving, consisting in the immanent exercises of it in the mind; and lastly, here is the fruit that was conceived actually brought forth, in the wicked work and practice. And this the Apostle calls the finishing or perfecting of sin: for the word in the original is the same that is translated "perfected" in those forementioned places.

Now certainly if it be so, if grace be in this manner made perfect, in its fruit, if these practical exercises of grace are those exercises wherein grace is brought to its proper effect and end, and the exercises wherein whatsoever belongs to its design, tendency and operation is completed and crowned; then these exercises must be the highest evidences of grace, above all other exercises. Certainly the proper nature and tendency of every principle, must appear best and most fully, in its most perfect exercises, or in those exercises wherein its nature is most completely exerted, and its tendency most fully answered and crowned, in its proper effect and end. If we would see the proper nature of anything whatsoever, and see it in its full distinction from other things; let us look upon it in the finishing of it. The apostle James says, "by works is faith made perfect"; and introduces this as an argument to prove that works are the chief evidence of faith, whereby the sincerity of the professors of faith is justified (Jas. 2). And the apostle John, after he had once and again told us, that love was made perfect in keeping Christ's commandments, observes, "that perfect love casteth out fear" (I John 4:18). Meaning (at least in part) love made perfect in this sense; agreeable to what he had said in the foregoing chapter, "that by loving in deed, or work, we know that we are of the truth, and shall assure our hearts (verses 18–19).

Argument 4. Another thing which makes it evident that holy practice is the principal evidence that we ought to make use of in judging both of our own and others' sincerity, is, that this evidence is above all others insisted on in Scripture. A common acquaintance with the Scripture, together with a little attention and observation, will be sufficient to show to anyone, that this is ten times more insisted on as a note of true piety, throughout the Scripture, from the beginning of Genesis to the end of Revelations, than anything else. And in the New Testament, where Christ and his apostles do expressly, and of declared purpose, lay down signs of true godliness, this is almost wholly insisted on. It may be observed, that Christ and his apostles do not only often say those things, in their discoursing on the great doctrines of religion, which do show what the nature of true godliness must be, or from whence the nature and signs of it may be inferred by just consequence, and often occasionally mention many things which do appertain to godliness; but they do also often, of set purpose, give signs and marks for the trial of professors, putting them upon trying themselves by the signs they give, introducing what they say with such like expressions as these: "By this you shall know that you know God; by this are manifest the children of God and the children of the devil; he that hath this, builds on a good foundation; he that hath it not, builds on the sand; hereby we shall assure our hearts; he is the man that loveth Christ," etc. But I can find no place, where either Christ or his apostles do in this manner give signs of godliness (though the places are many), but where Christian practice is almost the only thing insisted on. Indeed in many of these places, love to the brethren is spoken of as a sign of godliness; and (as I have observed before) there is no one virtuous affection or disposition so often expressly spoken of as a sign of true grace, as our having love one to another: but then the Scriptures explain themselves to intend chiefly this love as exercised and expressed in practice, or in deeds of love. So does the apostle John (who above all others insists on love to the brethren as a sign of godliness) most expressly explain himself, in that I John 3:14, etc.: "We know that we have passed from death to life, because we love the brethren. He that loveth not his brother abideth in death. . . . Whoso hath this world's good, and seeth his brother have need, and shutteth up his bowels of compassion from him, how dwelleth the love of God in him? My little children, let us love, not in word, neither in tongue, but in deed" (i.e. in deeds of love), "and in truth, and hereby we know that we are of the truth, and shall assure our hearts before him." So that when the Scripture so much insists on our loving one another, as a great sign of godliness, we are not thereby to understand the immanent workings of affection which men feel one to another, so much as the soul's practicing all the duties of the second table of the law; all which the New Testament tells us again and again, a true love one to another comprehends (Rom. 13:8, and 10; Gal. 5:14; Matt. 22:39–40). So that really, there is no place in the New Testament, where the declared design is to give signs of godliness, but that holy practice, and keeping Christ's commandments, is the mark chosen out from all others to be insisted on. Which is an invincible argument that it is the chief of all the evidences of godliness: unless we suppose that when Christ and his apostles on design, set themselves about this business of giving signs, by which professing Christians in all ages might determine their state, they did not know how to choose signs so well as we could have chosen for 'em. But if we make the word of Christ our rule, then undoubtedly those marks which Christ and his apostles did chiefly lay down, and give to us, that we might try ourselves by them, those same marks we ought especially to receive, and chiefly to make use of, in the trial of ourselves.[6] And surely those things which Christ and his

6. "It is a sure rule," says Dr. Preston, "that what the Scriptures bestow much words on, we should have much thoughts on; and what the Holy Ghost urgeth most, we should prize most." Preston, *The Church's Carriage,* p. 89.

apostles chiefly insisted on in the rules they gave, ministers ought chiefly to insist on in the rules they give. To insist much on those things that the Scripture insists little on, and to insist very little on those things on which the Scripture insists much, is a dangerous thing; because it is going out of God's way, and is to judge ourselves, and guide others, in an unscriptural manner. God knew which way of leading and guiding souls was safest and best for them: he insisted so much on some things, because he knew it to be needful that they should be insisted on; and let other things more alone, as a wise God, because he knew it was not best for us, so much to lay the weight of the trial there. As the Sabbath was made for man, so the Scriptures were made for man; and they are by infinite wisdom fitted for our use and benefit. We should therefore make them our guide in all things, in our thoughts of religion, and of ourselves. And for us to make that great which the Scripture makes little, and that little which the Scripture makes great, tends to give us a monstrous idea of religion; and (at least indirectly and gradually) to lead us wholly away from the right rule, and from a right opinion of ourselves, and to establish delusion and hypocrisy.

Argument 5. Christian practice is plainly spoken of in the Word of God, as the main evidence of the truth of grace, not only to others, but to men's own consciences. It is not only more spoken of and insisted on than other signs, but in many places where it is spoken of, it is represented as the chief of all evidences. This is plain in the manner of expression from time to time. If God were now to speak from heaven to resolve our doubts concerning signs of godliness, and should give some particular sign, that by it all might know whether they were sincerely godly or not, with such emphatical expressions as these, the man that has such a qualification or mark, "That is the man that is a true saint, that is the very man, by this you may know, this is the thing by which it is manifest who are saints and who are sinners, such men as these are saints indeed"; should not we look upon it as a thing beyond doubt, that this was given as a special, and eminently distinguishing note of true godliness? But this is the very case with respect to the sign of grace I am speaking of; God has again and again uttered himself in his Word in this very manner, concerning Christian practice; as John 14: "He that hath my commandments and keepeth them, he it is that loveth me." This Christ in this place gives to the disciples, not so much to guide 'em in judging of others, but to apply to themselves for their own comfort after his departure, as appears by every word of the context. And by the way I would observe, that not only the emphasis with which Christ utters himself is remarkable, but also his so much insisting on, and repeating the matter, as he does in the context; "If ye love me, keep my commandments" (ver. 15). "If a man love me, he will keep my words" (ver. 23). And: "He that loveth me not, keepeth not my sayings" (ver. 24). And in the next chapter over and over; "Every branch in me that beareth not fruit, he taketh away; and every branch that beareth fruit, he purgeth" (ver. 2). "Herein is my Father glorified, that ye bear much fruit, so shall ye be my disciples" (ver. 8). "Ye are my friends, if ye do whatsoever I command you" (ver. 14). We have this mark laid down with the same emphasis again, "If ye continue in my word, then are ye my disciples indeed" (John 8:31). And again, "Hereby we do know that we know him, if we keep his commandments" (I John 2:3). And "Whoso keepeth his Word, in him verily is the love of God perfected; hereby know we that we are in him" (ver. 5). And: "Let us love in deed and in truth, hereby we know that we are of the truth" (ch. 3:18–19). What is translated "hereby," would have been a little more emphatical, if it had been rendered more literally from the original, "by this we do know . . ." And how evidently is holy practice spoken of as the grand note of distinction between the children of God and the children of the devil, in ver. 10 of the same chapter? "In this the children of God are manifest, and the children of the devil." Speaking of a holy, and a wicked practice, as may be seen in all the context: as ver. 3: "Every man that hath this hope in him, purifieth himself, even as he is pure." "Whosoever abideth in him sinneth not; whosoever sinneth hath not seen him nor known him. Little children, let no man deceive you; he that doth righteousness is righteous, even as he is righteous; he that committeth sin is of the Devil. . . . Whosoever is born of God sinneth not . . . Whosoever doth not righteousness is not of God" (verses 6–10). So we have the like emphasis: "This is love, that we walk after his commandments" (II John 6). That is (as we must understand it), this is the proper evidence of love. So I John 5:3: "This is the love of God, that we keep his commandments." So the apostle James, speaking of the proper evidences of true and pure religion, says, "Pure religion, and undefiled before God and the Father, is this, to visit the fatherless and widows in their affliction, and to keep himself unspotted from the world" (Jas. 1:27). We have the like emphatical expressions used about the same thing in the Old Testament; "And unto man he said, Behold the fear of the Lord, that is wisdom, and to depart from evil is understanding" (Job 28:28). "Did not thy father eat and drink, and do judgment and justice? . . . He judged the cause of the poor and needy; . . . was not this to know me? saith the Lord" (Jer. 22:15–16). "Come ye children unto me, and I will teach you the fear of the Lord. . . . Keep thy tongue from evil, and thy lips from speaking guile; depart from evil, and do good, seek peace, and pursue it" (Ps. 34:11, etc.). Ps. 15 at the beginning: "Who shall abide in thy tabernacle? Who shall dwell in his holy hill? He that walketh uprightly," etc. "Who shall ascend into the hill of the Lord? And who shall stand in thy holy place? He that hath clean hands, and a pure heart," etc. (Ps. 24:3–4). "Blessed are the undefiled in the way, who walk in the law of the Lord" (Ps. 119:1). "Then shall I not be ashamed when I have respect to all thy commandments" (ver. 6). "The fear of the Lord is to hate evil" (Prov. 8:13).

So the Scripture never uses such emphatical expressions concerning any other signs of hypocrisy, and unsoundness of heart, as concerning an unholy practice. So Gal. 6:7: "Be not deceived, God is not mocked: for whatsoever a man soweth, that shall he also reap." "Be not deceived, neither fornicators, nor idolaters, etc. shall inherit the kingdom of God" (I Cor. 6:9–10). "For this know, that no whoremonger, nor unclean person, etc. hath any inheritance in the kingdom of Christ and of God: let no man deceive you with vain words" (Eph. 5:5–6). "Little children, let no man deceive you; he that doth righteousness is righteous, even as he is righteous: he that commiteth sin is of the devil" (I John 3:7–8). "He that saith, I know him, and keepeth not his commandments, is a liar, and the truth is not in him" (ch. 2:4). And: "If we say we have fellowship with him, and walk in darkness, we lie, and do not the truth" (ch. 1:6). "If any man among you seem to be religious, and bridleth not his tongue, but deceiveth his own heart, this man's religion is vain" (Jas. 1:27). "If ye have bitter envying and strife in your hearts, glory not, and lie not against the truth: this wisdom descendeth not from above, but is earthly, sensual, devilish" (ch. 3:14–15). "As for such as turn aside to their crooked ways, the Lord shall lead them forth with the workers of iniquity" (Ps. 125:5). "An highway shall be there, and it shall be called the way of holiness; the unclean shall not pass over it" (Is. 35:8). "And there shall in no wise enter into it, whatsoever worketh abomination or maketh a lie" (Rev.

21:27). And in many places: "Depart from ye, I know you not, ye that work iniquity."

Argument 6. Another thing which makes it evident, that holy practice is the chief of all the signs of the sincerity of professors, not only to the world, but to their own consciences, is, that this is the grand evidence which will hereafter be made use of, before the judgment seat of God; according to which his judgment will be regulated, and the state of every professor of religion unalterably determined. In the future judgment, there will be an open trial of professors; and evidences will be made use of in the judgment. For God's future judging of men, in order to their eternal retribution, will not be his trying, and finding out, and passing a judgment upon the state of men's hearts, in his own mind; but it will be a declarative judgment: and the end of it will be, not God's forming a judgment within himself, but the manifestation of his judgment, and the righteousness of it, to men's own consciences, and to the world. And therefore the Day of Judgment is called the day of the revelation of the righteous judgment of God (Rom. 2:5). And the end of God's future trial and judgment of men, as to the part that each one in particular is to have in the judgment, will be especially the clear manifestation of God's righteous judgment, with respect to him, to his conscience: as is manifest by Matt. 18:31, to the end; ch. 20:8–15, ch. 22:11–13, ch. 25:19–30, and ver. 35, to the end; Luke 19:15–23. And therefore though God needs no medium, whereby to make the truth evident to himself, yet evidences will be made use of in his future judging of men. And doubtless the evidences that will be made use of in their trial, will be such as will be best fitted to serve the ends of the judgment; viz. the manifestation of the righteous judgment of God, not only to the world, but to men's own consciences. But the Scriptures do abundantly teach us, that the grand evidences which the Judge will make use in the trial, for these ends, according to which the judgment of every one shall be regulated, and the irreversible sentence passed, will be men's works, or practice, here in this world: "And I saw the dead, small and great, stand before God; and the books were opened . . . and the dead were judged out of those things which were written in the books, according to their works" (Rev. 20:12). So ver. 13: "And the sea gave up the dead which were in it, and death and hell gave up the dead which were in them; and they were judged, every man, according to their works." "For we must all appear before the judgment seat of Christ, that every one may receive the things done in the body, whether it be good or bad" (II Cor. 5:10). So men's practice is the only evidence, that Christ represents the future judgment as regulated by, in that most particular description of the Day of Judgment, which we have in the holy Bible, Matt. 25, at the latter end. See also Rom. 2:6–13; Jer. 17:10; Job 34:11; Prov. 24:12; Jer. 32:19; Rev. 22:12; Matt. 16:27; Rev. 2:23; Ezek. 33:20; I Pet. 1:17. The Judge at the Day of Judgment, won't (for the conviction of men's own consciences, and to manifest 'em to the world) go about to examine men, as to the method of their experiences, or set every man to tell his story of the manner of his conversion; but his works will be brought forth, as evidences of what he is, what he has done in darkness and in light; "For God will bring every work into judgment, with every secret thing, whether it be good, or whether it be evil" (Eccles. 12:14). In the trial that professors shall be the subjects of, in the future judgment, God will make use of the same evidences, to manifest 'em to themselves and to the world, which he makes use of to manifest them, in the temptations or trials of his providence here, viz. their practice, in cases wherein Christ and other things come into actual and immediate competition. At the Day of Judgment, God, for the manifestation of his righteous judgment, will weigh professors in a balance that is visible. And the balance will be the same that he weighs men in now; which has been already described.

Hence we may undoubtedly infer, that men's works (taken in the sense that has been explained) are the highest evidences, by which they ought to try themselves. Certainly that which our supreme Judge will chiefly make use of, to judge us by, when we come to stand before him, we should chiefly make use of, to judge ourselves by.[7] If it had not been revealed in what manner, and by what evidence the Judge would proceed with us hereafter; how natural would it be for one to say: "O that I knew what token God will chiefly look for and insist upon in the last and decisive judgment; and which he expects that all should be able to produce who would then be accepted of him, and according to which sentence shall be passed; that I might know what token or evidence especially to look at and

7. "That which God maketh a rule of his own judgment, as that by which he judgeth of every man, that is a sure rule for every man to judge himself by. That which we shall be judged by at the last day, is a sure rule to apply to ourselves for the present. Now by our obedience and works, he judgeth us. 'He will give to every man according to his works.'" Preston, *The Church's Carriage*, p. 99.

seek after now, as I would be sure not to fail then." And seeing God has so plainly and abundantly revealed what this token or evidence is; surely if we act wisely, we shall regard it as of the greatest importance.

Now from all that has been said, I think it to be abundantly manifest, that Christian practice is the most proper evidence of the gracious sincerity of professors, to themselves and others; and the chief of all the marks of grace, the sign of signs, and evidence of evidences, that which seals and crowns all other signs. I had rather have the testimony of my conscience, that I have such a saying of my supreme Judge on my side, as that, "He that hath my commandments and keepeth them, he it is that loveth me" (John 14:21); than the judgment, and fullest approbation, of all the wise, sound and experienced divines, that have lived this thousand years, on the most exact and critical examination of my experiences, as to the manner of my conversion. Not that there are no other good evidences of a state of grace but this. There may be other exercises of grace, besides these efficient exercises, which the saints may have in contemplation, that may be very satisfying to them: but yet this is the chief and most proper evidence. There may be several good evidences that a tree is a fig tree; but the highest and most proper evidence of it, is that it actually bears figs. 'Tis possible that a man may have a good assurance of a state of grace, at his first conversion, before he has had opportunity to gain assurance, by this great evidence I am speaking of. If a man hears that a great treasure is offered him, in a distant place, on condition that he will prize it so much, as to be willing to leave what he possesses at home, and go a journey for it, over the rocks and mountains that are in the way, to the place where it is; 'tis possible the man may be well assured, that he values the treasure to the degree spoken of, as soon as the offer is made him; he may feel a willingness to go for the treasure, within him, beyond all doubt: but yet, this don't hinder but that his actual going for it is the highest and most proper evidence of his being willing, not only to others, but to himself. But then as an evidence to himself, his outward actions, and the motions of his body in his journey, are not considered alone, exclusive of the actions of his mind, and a consciousness within himself, of the thing that moves him, and the end he goes for; otherwise, his bodily motion is no evidence to him, of his prizing the treasure. In such a manner is Christian practice the most proper evidence of a saving value of the pearl of great price, and treasure hid in the field.

Christian practice is the sign of signs, in this sense that it is the great evidence, which confirms and crowns all other signs of godliness. There is no one grace of the Spirit of God, but that Christian practice is the most proper evidence of the truth of it. As it is with the members of our bodies, and all our utensils, the proper proof of the soundness and goodness of 'em, is in the use of 'em; so it is with our graces (which are given to be used in practice, as much as our hands and feet, or the tools with which we work, or the arms with which we fight) the proper trial and proof of them is in their exercise in practice. Most of the things we use, are serviceable to us, and so have their serviceableness proved, in some pressure, straining, agitation, or collision. So it is with a bow, a sword, an ax, a saw, a cord, a chain, a staff, a foot, a tooth, etc. And they that are so weak, as not to bear the strain or pressure we need to put them to, are good for nothing. So it is with all the virtues of the mind. The proper trial and proof of them, is in being exercised under those temptations and trials that God brings us under, in the course of his providence, and in being put to such service as strains hard upon the principles of nature.

Practice is the proper proof of the true and saving knowledge of God; as appears by that of the Apostle already mentioned, "Hereby do we know that we know him, that we keep his commandments." 'Tis in vain for us to profess that we know God, if in works we deny him (Titus 1:16). And if we know God, but glorify him not as God; our knowledge will only condemn us, and not save us (Rom. 1:21). The great note of that knowledge which saves and makes happy, is that it is practical; "If ye know these things, happy are ye if ye do them" (John 13:17). "To depart from evil is understanding" (Job 28:28).

Holy practice is the proper evidence of repentance. When the Jews professed repentance, when they came confessing their sins to John, preaching the baptism of repentance for the remission of sins; he directed 'em to the right way of getting and exhibiting proper evidences of the truth of their repentance, when he said to 'em: "Bring forth fruits meet for repentance" (Matt. 3:8). Which was agreeable to the practice of the apostle Paul; see Acts 26:20. Pardon and mercy are from time to time promised to him who has this evidence of true repentance, that he forsakes his sin (Prov. 28:13 and Is. 55:7; and many other places).

Holy practice is the proper evidence of a saving faith. 'Tis evident that the apostle James speaks of works, as what does eminently justify faith, or (which is the same thing) justify the professors of faith, and vindicate and manifest the sincerity of their profession, not only to the world, but to their own consciences: as is evident by the instance he gives of Abraham (Jas. 2:21–24). And in verses 20 and 26, he speaks of the practical and working nature of faith, as the very life and soul of it; in the same manner, that the active nature and substance, which is in the body of a man, is the life and soul of that. And if so, doubtless practice is the proper evidence of the life and soul of true faith, by which it is distinguished from a dead faith. For doubtless, practice is the most proper evidence of a practical nature, and operation the most proper evidence of an operative nature.

Practice is the best evidence of a saving belief of the truth. That is spoken of as the proper evidence of the truth's being in a professing Christian, that "he walks in the truth," "I rejoiced greatly, when the brethren came and testified of the truth that is in thee, even as thou walkest in the truth" (III John 3).

Practice is the most proper evidence of a true coming to Christ, and accepting of, and closing with him. A true and saving coming to Christ, is (as Christ often teaches) a coming so, as to forsake all for him. And as was observed before, to forsake all for Christ in heart, is the same thing as to have a heart actually to forsake all; but the proper evidence of having a heart actually to forsake all, is indeed actually to forsake all, so far as called to it. If a prince makes suit to a woman in a far country, that she would forsake her own people, and father's house, and come to him, to be his bride; the proper evidence of the compliance of her heart with the king's suit, is her actually forsaking her own people, and father's house, and coming to him. By this, her compliance with the king's suit, is made perfect, in the same sense, that the apostle James says, "by works is faith made perfect." [8] Christ promises us eternal life, on condition of our coming to him: but it is such a coming as he directed the

8. "Our real taking of Christ, appears in our actions and works; Is. 1:19: 'If ye consent and obey, ye shall eat the good things of the land.' That is, if ye will consent to take Jehovah for your Lord and king: 'if ye give consent'; there is the first thing: but that is not enough; 'but if ye also obey.' The consent that standeth in the inward act of the mind, the truth of it will be seen in your obedience, in the acts of your lives. 'If ye consent and obey, ye shall eat the good things of the land'; that is, you shall take of all that he hath that is convenient for you: for then you are married to him in truth, and have an interest in all his goods." Preston, *The Church's Carriage,* pp. 99–100.

young man to, who came to inquire, what he shall do, that he might have eternal life; Christ bid him go, and sell all that he had, and come to him, and follow him. If he had consented in his heart to the proposal (and had therein come to Christ in his heart), the proper evidence of it would have been his doing of it: and therein his coming to Christ would have been made perfect. When Christ called Levi the publican, when sitting at the receipt of custom, and in the midst of his worldly gains; the closing of Levi's heart with this invitation of his Saviour, to come to him, was manifested, and made perfect, by his actually rising up, leaving all, and following him (Luke 5:27–28). Christ and other things, are set before us together, for us practically to cleave to one, and forsake the other: in such a case, a practical cleaving to Christ, is a practical acceptance of Christ; as much as a beggar's reaching out his hand, and taking a gift that is offered, is his practical acceptance of the gift. Yea that act of the soul that is in cleaving to Christ in practice, is itself the most perfect coming of the soul to Christ.

Practice is the most proper evidence of trusting in Christ for salvation. The proper signification of the word "trust," according to the more ordinary use of it, both in common speech, and in the Holy Scriptures, is the emboldening and encouragement of a person's mind, to run some venture in practice, or in something that he does, on the credit of another's sufficiency and faithfulness. And therefore the proper evidence of his trusting, is the venture he runs in what he does. He is not properly said to run any venture, in a dependence on anything, that does nothing on that dependence, or whose practice is no otherwise than if he had no dependence. For a man to run a venture, on a dependence on another, is for him to do something from that dependence, by which he seems to expose himself, and which he would not do, were it not for that dependence. And therefore it is in complying with the difficulties, and seeming dangers of Christian practice, in a dependence on Christ's sufficiency and faithfulness to bestow eternal life, that persons are said to venture themselves upon Christ, and trust in him for happiness and life. They depend on such promises as that, "He that loseth his life for my sake, shall find it" (Matt. 10:39). And so they part with all, and venture their all, in a dependence on Christ's sufficiency and truth. And this is the Scripture notion of trusting in Christ, in the exercise of a saving faith in him. Thus Abraham, the father of believers, trusted in Christ, and by faith, forsook his own country, in a reliance on the covenant of grace God established with him (Heb. 11:8–9). Thus also "Moses, by faith, refused to be called the son of Pharoah's daughter, choosing rather to suffer affliction with the people of God, than to enjoy the pleasures of sin for a season" (Heb. 11:23, etc.). So by faith, others exposed themselves to be stoned, and sawn in sunder, or slain with the sword; endured the trial of cruel mockings and scourgings, bonds and imprisonments, and wandered about in sheepskins and goatskins, being destitute, afflicted, tormented. And in this sense the apostle Paul, by faith, trusted in Christ, and committed himself to him, venturing himself, and his whole interest, in a dependence on the ability and faithfulness of his Redeemer, under great persecutions, and in suffering the loss of all things; "For the which cause I also suffer these things, nevertheless I am not ashamed; for I know whom I have believed; and I am persuaded, that he is able to keep that which I have committed to him, against that day" (II Tim. 1:12).

If a man should have word brought him from the king of a distant land, that he intended to make him his heir, if upon receiving the tidings, he immediately leaves his native land, and friends, and all that he has in the world, to go to that country, in a dependence on what he hears; then he may be said to venture himself, and all he has in the world upon it. But if he only sits still, and hopes for the promised benefit, inwardly pleasing himself with the thoughts of it; he can't properly be said to venture himself upon it; he runs no venture in the case; he does nothing, otherwise than he would do, if he had received no such tidings, by which he would be exposed to any sufferings, in case all should fail. So he that on the credit of what he hears of a future world, and in a dependence on the report of the gospel, concerning life and immortality, forsakes all, or does so at least so far as there is occasion, making everything entirely give place to his eternal interest; he, and he only, may properly be said to venture himself on the report of the gospel. And this is the proper evidence of a true trust in Christ for salvation.

Practice is the proper evidence of a gracious love, both to God and men. The texts that plainly teach this, have been so often mentioned already, that it is needless to repeat them.

Practice is the proper evidence of humility. That expression and manifestation of humility of heart, which God speaks of, as the great expression of it, that he insists on; that, we should look upon as the proper expression and manifestation of it: but this is walking humbly; "He hath shewed thee, O man, what is good, and what doth the Lord require of thee, but to do justly, to love mercy, and to walk humbly with thy God?" (Mic. 6:8).

This is also the proper evidence of the true fear of God. "The fear of the Lord is to hate evil" (Prov. 8:13). "Come ye children, hearken unto me, and I will teach you the fear of the Lord. . . . Keep thy tongue from evil, and thy lips from speaking guile; depart from evil and do good, seek peace, and pursue it" (Ps. 34:11, etc.). "Fear the Lord, and depart from evil" (Prov. 3:7). "By the fear of the Lord, men depart from evil" (Prov. 16:6). "Hast thou considered my servant Job . . . a perfect and an upright man, one that feareth God, and escheweth evil?" (Job 1:8). "Hast thou considered my servant Job . . . a perfect and an upright man, one that feareth God, and escheweth evil? And still he holdeth fast his integrity, although thou movedst me against him" (ch. 2:3). "The transgression of the wicked, saith within my heart, there is no fear of God before his eyes" (Ps. 36:1).

So practice, in rendering again according to benefits received, is the proper evidence of true thankfulness. "What shall I render to the Lord, for all his benefits towards me?" (Ps. 116:12). "But Hezekiah rendered not again according to the benefit done unto him" (II Chron. 32:25). Paying our vows unto God, and ordering our conversation aright, seem to be spoken of, as the proper expression and evidence of true thankfulness, in the 50th Psalm, ver. 14: "Offer unto God thanksgiving, and pay thy vows unto the most High." Verse 23: "Whoso offereth praise, glorifieth me; and to him that ordereth his conversation aright, will I shew the salvation of God."

So the proper evidence of gracious desires and longings, and that which distinguishes them from those that are false and vain, is that they are not idle wishes and wouldings,[9] like Balaam's; but effectual in practice, to stir up persons earnestly and thoroughly to seek the things they long for. "One thing have I desired of the Lord, that will I seek after" (Ps. 27:4). "O God, thou art my God; early will I seek thee: my soul thirsteth for thee; my flesh longeth for thee, in a dry and thirsty land, where no water is, to see thy power and thy glory" (Ps. 63:1–2). "My soul followeth hard after thee" (ver. 8). "Draw me, we will run after thee" (Cant. 1:4).

Practice is the proper evidence of a gracious hope. "Every man that hath this hope in him, purifieth himself, even as he is pure" (I John

9. For the meaning of this term see above, p. 99.

3:3). Patient continuance in well doing, through the difficulties and trials of the Christian course, is often mentioned as the proper expression and fruit of a Christian hope. "Remembering without ceasing, your work of faith, and labor of love, and patience of hope" (I Thess. 1:3). "Wherefore, gird up the loins of your mind, be sober, and hope to the end, for the grace that is to be brought unto you, at the revelation of Jesus Christ, as obedient children," etc. (I Pet. 1:13–14). "Lord, I have hoped in thy salvation, and done thy commandments" (Ps. 119–166). "That they might set their hope in God, and not forget the works of the Lord, but keep his commandments" (Ps. 78:7).

A cheerful practice of our duty and doing the will of God, is the proper evidence of a truly holy joy. "Thou meetest him that rejoiceth, and worketh righteousness" (Is. 64:5). "Thy testimonies have I taken for my heritage forever, for they are the rejoicing of my heart: I have inclined my heart to perform thy statutes alway, even unto the end" (Ps. 119:111–112). "I have rejoiced in the way of thy testimonies, as much as in all riches" (ver. 14). "Charity rejoiceth not in iniquity, but rejoiceth in the truth" (I Cor. 13:6). "The abundance of their joy, abounded to the riches of their liberality" (II Cor. 8:2).

Practice also is the proper evidence of Christian fortitude. The trial of a good soldier, is not in his chimney corner, but in the field of battle (I Cor. 9:25–26; II Tim. 2:3–5).

And as the fruit of holy practice is the chief evidence of the truth of grace; so the degree in which experiences have influence on a person's practice, is the surest evidence of the degree of that which is spiritual and divine in his experiences. Whatever pretenses persons may make to great discoveries, great love and joys, they are no further to be regarded, than they have influence on their practice. Not but that allowances must be made for the natural temper. But that don't hinder, but that the degree of grace is justly measured, by the degree of the effect in practice. For the effect of grace is as great, and the alteration as remarkable, in a person of a very ill natural temper, as another. Although a person of such a temper, will not behave himself so well, with the same degree of grace, as another; the diversity from what was before conversion, may be as great; because a person of a good natural temper, did not behave himself so ill, before conversion.

Thus I have endeavored to represent the evidence there is, that

Christian practice is the chief of all the signs of saving grace. And before I conclude this discourse, I would say something briefly, in answer to two objections, that may possibly be made by some, against what has been said upon this head.

Object. I. Some may be ready to say, this seems to be contrary to that opinion, so much received among good people; that professors should judge of their state, chiefly by their inward experience, and that spiritual experiences are the main evidence of true grace.

I answer, 'tis doubtless a true opinion, and justly much received among good people, that professors should chiefly judge of their state by their experience. But it is a great mistake, that what has been said is at all contrary to that opinion. The chief sign of grace to the consciences of Christians, being Christian practice, in the sense that has been explained, and according to what has been shewn to be the true notion of Christian practice, is not at all inconsistent with Christian experience being the chief evidence of grace. Christian or holy practice is spiritual practice; and that is not the motion of a body, that knows not how, nor when, nor wherefore it moves: but spiritual practice in man, is the practice of a spirit and body jointly, or the practice of a spirit, animating, commanding and actuating a body, to which it is united, and over which it has power given it by the Creator. And therefore the main thing in this holy practice, is the holy acts of the mind, directing and governing the motions of the body. And the motions of the body are to be looked upon as belonging to Christian practice, only secondarily, and as they are dependent and consequent on the acts of the soul. The exercises of grace that Christians find, or are conscious to, within themselves, are what they experience within themselves; and herein therefore lies Christian experience: and this Christian experience, consists as much in those operative exercises of grace in the will, that are immediately concerned in the management of the behavior of the body, as in other exercises. These inward exercises, are not the less a part of Christian experience, because they have outward behavior immediately connected with them. A strong act of love to God, is not the less a part of spiritual experience, because it is the act that immediately produces and effects some self-denying and expensive outward action, which is much to the honor and glory of God.

To speak of Christian experience and practice, as if they were two things, properly and entirely distinct, is to make a distinction without consideration or reason. Indeed all Christian experience is not properly called practice; but all Christian practice is properly experience. And the distinction that is made between them, is not only an unreasonable, but an unscriptural distinction. Holy practice is one kind or part of Christian experience; and both reason and Scripture represent it as the chief, and most important, and most distinguishing part of it. So it is represented in Jer. 22:15–16: "Did not thy father eat and drink, and do justice and judgment? . . . He judged the cause of the poor and needy: . . . was not this to know me? saith the Lord." Our inward acquaintance with God, surely belongs to the head of experimental religion; but this God represents, as consisting chiefly in that experience which there is in holy practice. So the exercises of those graces of the love of God, and the fear of God, are a part of experimental religion; but these the Scripture represents as consisting chiefly in practice, in those forementioned texts. "This is the love of God, that we keep his commandments" (I John 5:3). "This is love, that we walk after his commandments" (II John 6). "Come, ye children, and I will teach you the fear of the Lord: . . . Depart from evil, and do good" (Ps. 34:11, etc.). Such experiences as these Hezekiah took comfort in chiefly, on his sick bed: when he said: "Remember, O Lord, I beseech thee, how I have walked before thee, in truth, and with a perfect heart." And such experiences as these, the Psalmist chiefly insists upon, in the 119th Psalm and elsewhere. Such experiences as these, the apostle Paul mainly insists upon, when he speaks of his experiences in his Epistles; as Rom. 1:9: "God is my witness, whom I serve with my spirit, in the gospel of his son"; "For our rejoicing is this, the testimony of our conscience, that . . . by the grace of God, we have had our conversation in the world" (II Cor. 1:12). "We having the same spirit of faith: according as it is written, I have believed, and therefore have I spoken; we also believe, and therefore speak" (ch. 4:13). "We walk by faith, not by sight" (ch. 5:7). "The love of Christ constraineth us" (ver. 14). "In all things approving ourselves as the ministers of God, in much patience, in afflictions, in necessities, in distresses . . . in labors, in watchings, in fastings; by pureness, by knowledge, by kindness, by the Holy Ghost, by love unfeigned . . . by the power of God" (ch. 6:4–7). "I am crucified with Christ. Nevertheless, I live; yet not I; but Christ liveth in me. And the life which I now live in the flesh, I live by the faith of the Son of God" (Gal. 2:20). "But what things were gain to me, those I counted loss for Christ: yea doubtless, and

I count all things but loss for the excellency of the knowledge of Christ Jesus my Lord, and do count them but dung that I may win Christ" (Phil. 3:7–8). "Whereunto I also labor, striving, according to his working, which worketh in me mightily" (Col. 1:29). "We are bold in our God, to speak unto you the gospel of God, with much contention" (I Thess. 2:2). "Being affectionately desirous of you, we were willing to have imparted unto you, not the gospel of God only, but also our own souls; because ye were dear unto us. For ye remember brethren, our labor and travail, laboring night and day. . . . Ye are witnesses, and God also, how holily, and justly, and unblameably we behaved ourselves among you" (verses 8–10). And such experiences as these, they were, that this blessed Apostle chiefly comforted himself in the consideration of, when he was going to martyrdom, "For I am now ready to be offered, and the time of my departure is at hand. I have fought a good fight: I have finished my course: I have kept the faith" (II Tim. 4:6–7).

And not only does the most important and distinguishing part of Christian experience, lie in spiritual practice; but such is the nature of that sort of exercises of grace, wherein spiritual practice consists, that nothing is so properly called by the name of experimental religion. For that experience which is in these exercises of grace, that are found, and prove effectual, at the very point of trial, wherein God proves which we will actually cleave to, whether Christ or our lusts, are as has been shown already, the proper *experiment* of the truth and power of our godliness; wherein its victorious power and efficacy, in producing its proper effect, and reaching its end, is found by experience. This is properly Christian experience, wherein the saints have opportunity to see, by actual *experience* and *trial,* whether they have a heart to do the will of God, and to forsake other things for Christ, or no. As that is called experimental philosophy, which brings opinions and notions to the test of fact; so is that properly called experimental religion, which brings religious affections and intentions, to the like test.

There is a sort of external religious practice, wherein is no inward experience; which no account is made of in the sight of God; but it is esteemed good for nothing. And there is what is called experience, that is without practice, being neither accompanied, nor followed with a Christian behavior; and this is worse than nothing. Many persons seem to have very wrong notions of Christian experience, and spiritual light and discoveries. Whenever a person finds within him, an heart to treat God as God, at the time that he has the trial, and finds his disposition effectual in the experiment, that is the most proper, and most distinguishing experience. And to have at such a time that sense of divine things, that apprehension of the truth, importance and excellency of the things of religion, which then sways and prevails, and governs his heart and hands; this is the most excellent spiritual light, and these are the most distinguishing discoveries. Religion consists much in holy affection; but those exercises of affection which are most distinguishing of true religion, are these practical exercises. Friendship between earthly friends consists much in affection; but yet those strong exercises of affection, that actually carry them through fire and water for each other, are the highest evidences of true friendship.

There is nothing in what has been said, contrary to what is asserted by some divines; when they say, that there are no sure evidences of grace, but the acts of grace. For that don't hinder but that these operative, productive acts, those exercises of grace that are effectual in practice, may be the highest evidences, above all other kinds of acts of grace. Nor does it hinder but that, when there are many of these acts and exercises, following one another in a course, under various trials, of every kind, the evidence is still heightened; as one act confirms another. A man by once seeing his neighbor, may have good evidence of his presence: but by seeing him from day to day, and conversing with him in a course, in various circumstances, the evidence is established. The disciples, when they first saw Christ, after his resurrection, had good evidence that he was alive: but by conversing with him for forty days, and his shewing himself to 'em alive, by many infallible proofs, they had yet higher evidence.[1]

1. "The more these visible exercises of grace are renewed, the more certain you will be. The more frequently these actings are renewed, the more abiding and confirmed your assurance will be. A man that has been assured of such visible exercises of grace, may quickly after be in doubt, whether he was not mistaken. But when such actings are renewed again and again, he grows more settled and established about his good estate. If a man see a thing once, that makes him sure: but if afterwards he fear he was deceived, when he comes to see it again, he is more sure he was not mistaken. If a man read such passages in a book, he is sure it is so. Some months after, some may bear him down, that he was mistaken, so as to make him question it himself: but when he looks, and reads it again, he is abundantly confirmed. The more men's grace is multiplied, the more their peace is multiplied; II Pet. 1:2: 'Grace and peace be multiplied unto you, through the knowledge of God and Jesus our Lord.'" Stoddard, *Sincerity and Hypocrisy*, pp. 142–3.

The witness or seal of the Spirit that we read of, doubtless consists in the effect of the Spirit of God in the heart, in the implantation and exercises of grace there, and so consists in experience. And it is also beyond doubt, that this seal of the Spirit, is the highest kind of evidence of the saints' adoption, that ever they obtain. But in these exercises of grace in practice, that have been spoken of, God gives witness, and sets to his seal, in the most conspicuous, eminent and evident manner. It has been abundantly found to be true in fact, by the experience of the Christian church; that Christ commonly gives, by his Spirit, the greatest, and most joyful evidences to his saints, of their sonship, in those effectual exercises of grace, under trials, which have been spoken of; as is manifest in the full assurance, and unspeakable joys of many of the martyrs. Agreeable to that, I Pet. 4:14: "If ye are reproached for the name of Christ, happy are ye; for the spirit of glory, and of God resteth upon you." And that in Rom. 5:2–3: "We rejoice in hope of the glory of God, and glory in tribulations." And agreeable to what the apostle Paul often declares of what he experienced in his trials. And when the apostle Peter, in my text, speaks of the "joy unspeakable, and full of glory," which the Christians to whom he wrote, experienced; he has respect to what they found under persecution, as appears by the context. Christ's thus manifesting himself, as the friend and Saviour of his saints, cleaving to him under trials, seems to have been represented of old, by his coming and manifesting himself, to Shadrach, Meshach, and Abednego, in the furnace. And when the Apostle speaks of the witness of the spirit, in Rom. 8:15–17; he has a more immediate respect to what the Christians experienced, in their exercises of love to God, in suffering persecution; as is plain by the context. He is, in the foregoing verses, encouraging the Christian Romans under their suffering, that though their bodies be dead, because of sin, yet they should be raised to life again. But it is more especially plain by the verse immediately following, ver. 18: "For I reckon that the sufferings of this present time, are not worthy to be compared with the glory that shall be revealed in us." So the Apostle has evidently respect to their persecutions, in all that he says to the end of the chapter. So when the Apostle speaks of the "earnest of the Spirit," which God had given to him, in II Cor. 5:5; the context shews plainly that he has respect to what was given him in his great trials and sufferings. And in that promise of the white stone, and new name, to him that overcomes (Rev. 2:17); 'tis evident

Christ has a special respect to a benefit that Christians should obtain, by overcoming, in the trial they had, in that day of persecution. This appears by ver. 13, and many other passages in this Epistle to the seven churches of Asia.

Object. II. Some also may be ready to object against what has been said of Christian practice being the chief evidence of the truth of grace, that this is a legal doctrine; and that this making practice a thing of such great importance in religion, magnifies works, and tends to lead men to make too much of their own doings, to the diminution of the glory of free grace, and does not seem well to consist with that great gospel doctrine of justification by faith alone.

But this objection is altogether without reason. Which way is it inconsistent with the freeness of God's grace, that holy practice should be a sign of God's grace? 'Tis our works being the price of God's favor, and not their being the sign of it, that is the thing which is inconsistent with the freeness of that favor. Surely the beggar's looking on the money he has in his hands, as a sign of the kindness of him who gave it to him, is in no respect, inconsistent with the freeness of that kindness. 'Tis his having money in his hand as the price of a benefit, that is the thing which is inconsistent with the free kindness of the giver. The notion of the freeness of the grace of God to sinners, as that is revealed and taught in the gospel, is not that no holy and amiable qualifications or actions in us shall be a fruit, and so a sign of that grace; but that it is not the worthiness or loveliness of any qualification or action of ours which recommends us to that grace; that kindness is shown to the unworthy and unlovely; that there is great excellency in the benefit bestowed, and no excellency in the subject as the price of it; that goodness goes forth and flows out, from the fullness of God's nature, the fullness of the Fountain of Good, without any amiableness in the object to draw it. And this is the notion of justification without works (as this docrine is taught in the Scripture) that it is not the worthiness or loveliness of our works, or anything in us, which is in any wise accepted with God, as a balance for the guilt of sin, or a recommendation of sinners to his acceptance as heirs of life. Thus we are justified only by the righteousness of Christ, and not by our righteousness. And when works are opposed to faith in this affair, and it is said that we are justified by faith and not by works; thereby is meant, that it is not the worthiness or amiableness of our works, or anything in us, which recommends us to an interest in Christ and his benefits;

but that we have this interest only by faith, or by our souls receiving Christ, or adhering to, and closing with him. But that the worthiness or amiableness of nothing in us recommends and brings us to an interest in Christ, is no argument that nothing in us is a sign of an interest in Christ.

If the doctrines of free grace, and justification by faith alone, be inconsistent with the importance of holy practice as a sign of grace; then they are equally inconsistent with the importance of anything whatsoever in us as a sign of grace, and holiness, or any grace that is in us, or any of our experiences of religion: for 'tis as contrary to the doctrines of free grace and justification by faith alone, that any of these should be the righteousness which we are justified by, as that holy practice should be so. 'Tis with holy works, as it is with holy qualifications: 'tis inconsistent with the freeness of gospel grace, that a title to salvation should be given to men for the loveliness of any of their holy qualifications, as much as that it should be given for the holiness of their works. It is inconsistent with the gospel doctrine of free grace, that an interest in Christ and his benefits should be given for the loveliness of a man's true holiness, for the amiableness of his renewed, sanctified, heavenly heart, his love to God, and being like God, or his experience of joy in the Holy Ghost, self-emptiness, a spirit to exalt Christ above all, and to give all glory to him, and a heart devoted unto him: I say, it is inconsistent with the gospel doctrine of free grace, that a title to Christ's benefits should be given out of regard to the loveliness of any of these, or that any of these should be our righteousness in the affair of justification. And yet this don't hinder the importance of these things as evidences of an interest in Christ. Just so it is with respect to holy actions and works. To make light of works, because we ben't justified by works, is the same thing in effect, as to make light of all religion, all grace and holiness, yea, true evangelical holiness, and all gracious experience: for all is included, when the Scripture says, we are not justified by works: for by works in this case, is meant all our own righteousness, religion, or holiness, and everything that is in us, all the good we do, and all the good which we are conscious of, all external acts, and all internal acts and exercises of grace, and all experiences, and all those holy and heavenly things wherein the life and power, and the very essence of religion do consist, all those great things which Christ and his apostles mainly insisted on in their preaching, and endeavored to promote, as of the greatest consequence in the hearts and lives of men, and all good dispositions, exercises and qualifications of every kind whatsoever; and even faith itself, considered as a part of our holiness. For we are justified by none of these things: and if we were, we should, in a Scripture sense, be justified by works. And therefore if it ben't legal, and contrary to the evangelical doctrine of justification without works, to insist on any of these, as of great importance, as evidences of an interest in Christ; then no more is it thus, to insist on the importance of holy practice. It would be legal to suppose that holy practice justifies by bringing us to a title to Christ's benefits, as the price of it, or as recommending to it by its preciousness or excellence; but it is not legal to suppose, that holy practice justifies the sincerity of a believer, as the proper evidence of it. The apostle James did not think it legal to say, that Abraham our father was justified by works in this sense. The Spirit that indited the Scripture did not think the great importance and absolute necessity of holy practice, in this respect, to be inconsistent with the freeness of grace; for it commonly teaches 'em both together; as in Rev. 21:6–7, God says: "I will give unto him that is athirst, of the fountain of the water of life freely": and then adds, in the very next words: "He that overcometh shall inherit all things." As though behaving well in the Christian race and warfare, were the condition of the promise. So in the next chapter, in the 14th, and 15th verses, Christ says: "Blessed are they that do his commandments, that they may have right to the tree of life, and enter in through the gates, into the city": and then declares in the 15th verse, how they that are of a wicked practice shall be excluded; and yet in the two verses next following, does with very great solemnity, give forth an invitation to all to come and take of the water of life freely; "I am the root and the offspring of David, the bright and morning star: and the Spirit and the bride say, come, and let him that heareth say, come, and let him that is athirst, come, and whosoever will, let him come and take of the water of life freely." So ch. 3:20–21: "Behold I stand at the door and knock: if any man hear my voice, and open the door, I will come in to him, and sup with him, and he with me"; but then it is added in the next words: "To him that overcometh, will I grant to sit with me on my throne." And in that great invitation of Christ, "Come unto me, all ye that labor and are heavy laden, and I will give you rest" (Matt. 11, latter end); Christ adds in the next words: "Take my yoke upon you, and learn of me, for I am meek and lowly of heart, and ye shall find rest unto your souls: for my yoke is easy, and my burden is light": as though taking the burden of Christ's service, and imitating his example, were necessary in order to the promised rest. So in that great invitation to sinners to accept of free grace, "Ho, every one that thirsteth! come ye to the waters: and he that hath no money, come ye, buy and eat; yea, come, buy wine and milk, without money and without price": even there, in the continuation of the same invitation, the sinner's forsaking his wicked practice is spoken of as necessary to the obtaining mercy" (Is. 55). "Let the wicked forsake his way, and the unrighteous man his thoughts, and let him return unto the Lord, and he will have mercy upon him, and to our God, and he will abundantly pardon" (ver. 7). So the riches of divine grace, in the justification of sinners, is set forth, with the necessity of holy practice, "Wash ye, make you clean; put away the evil of your doings, from before mine eyes: cease to do evil, learn to do well; seek judgment, relieve the oppressed, judge the fatherless, plead for the widow: come now, let us reason together, saith the Lord, though your sins be as scarlet, they shall be as white as snow; though they be red like crimson, they shall be as wool" (Is. 1:15, etc.). And in that most solemn invitation of wisdom, Prov. 9, after it is represented what great provision is made, and how that all things were ready, the house built, the beasts killed, the wine mingled, and the table furnished, and the messengers sent forth to invite the guests; then we have the free invitation, "Whoso is simple, let him turn in hither; as for him that wanteth understanding" (i.e. has no righteousness), "she saith to him, come, eat of my bread, and drink of the wine which I have mingled": but then in the next breath it follows, "Forsake the foolish, and live, and go in the way of understanding" (verses 4–6): as though forsaking sin, and going in the way of holiness, were necessary in order to life. So that the freeness of grace, and the necessity of holy practice, which are thus from time to time joined together in Scripture, are not inconsistent one with another. Nor does it at all diminish the honor and importance of faith, that the exercises and effects of faith in practice, should be esteemed the chief signs of it; any more than it lessens the importance of life, that action and motion are esteemed the chief signs of that.

So that in what has been said of the importance of holy practice, as the main sign of sincerity; there is nothing legal, nothing derogatory to the freedom and sovereignty of gospel grace, nothing in the least clashing with the gospel doctrine of justification by faith alone, without the works of the law, nothing in the least tending to lessen the glory of the mediator, and our dependence on his righteousness, nothing infringing on the special prerogatives of faith in the affair of our salvation, nothing in any wise detracting from the glory of God and his mercy, or exalting man, or diminishing his dependence and obligation. So that if any are against such an importance of holy practice as has been spoken of, it must be only from a senseless aversion to the letters and sound of the word "works"; when there is no reason in the world to be given for it, but what may be given with equal force, why they should have an aversion to the words "holiness," "godliness," "grace," "religion," "experience," and even "faith" itself: for to make a righteousness of any of these, is as legal, and as inconsistent with the way of the new covenant, as to make a righteousness of holy practice.[2]

'Tis greatly to the hurt of religion, for persons to make light of, and insist little on, those things which the Scriptures insist most upon, as of the most importance in the evidence of our interest in Christ (under a notion that to lay weight on these things is legal, and an old covenant way); and so to neglect the exercises, and effectual operations of grace in practice, and insist almost wholly on discoveries, and the method and manner of the immanent exercises of conscience and grace in contemplation; depending on an ability to make nice distinctions in these matters, and a faculty of accurate discerning in them, from philosophy or experience. It is in vain to seek for any

2. "You say you know Christ, and the love and goodwill of Christ towards you, and that he is the propitiation for your sins. How do you know this? 'He that saith I know him, and keepeth not his commandments, is a liar, I John 2:4. True, might some reply, he that keeps not the commands of Christ, hath thereby a sure evidence that he knows him not, and that he is not united to him; but is this any evidence that we do know him, and that we are united to him, if we do keep his commandments? Yes verily, saith the Apostle, 'Hereby we do know that we know him, if we keep his commandments.' And again, ver. 5: 'Hereby knew we that we are in him.' What can be more plain? What a vanity is it to say, that this is running upon a convenant of works? . . . O beloved, it is a sad thing to hear such questions, and such cold answers also, that sanctification possibly may be an evidence. May be? Is it not certain? Assuredly to deny it, is as bad as to affirm that God's own promises of favor are not sure evidence thereof, and consequently that they are lies and untruths. . . . Our Saviour, who was no legal preacher, pronounceth, and consequently evidenceth blessedness, by eight or nine promises, expressly made to such persons, as had inherent graces, Matt. 5:3–4, etc." Shepard, *Sound Believer,* pp. 221–2, 222–3.

better, or any further signs, than those that the Scriptures have most expressly mentioned, and most frequently insisted on, as signs of godliness. They who pretend to a greater accuracy in giving signs, or by their extraordinary experience, or insight into the nature of things, to give more distinguishing marks, which shall more thoroughly search out, and detect the hypocrite; are but subtle to darken their own minds, and the minds of others; their refinings, and nice discerning, is in God's sight, but refined foolishness, and sagacious delusion. Here are applicable those words of Agur, "Every Word of God is pure; he is a shield to them that put their trust in him: add thou not unto his words, lest he reprove thee, and thou be found a liar" (Prov. 30:5–6). Our wisdom and discerning, with regard to the hearts of men, is not much to be trusted. We can see but a little way into the nature of the soul, and the depths of man's heart. The ways are so many whereby persons' affections may be moved without any supernatural influence, the natural springs of the affections are so various and so secret, so many things have oftentimes a joint influence on the affections, the imagination (and that in ways innumerable and unsearchable), natural temper, education, the common influences of the Spirit of God, a surprising concourse of affecting circumstances, an extraordinary coincidence of things in the course of men's thoughts, together with the subtle management of invisible malicious spirits; that no philosophy or experience will ever be sufficient to guide us safely through this labyrinth and maze, without our closely following the clue which God has given us in his Word. God knows his own reasons why he insists on some things, and plainly sets them forth as the things that we should try ourselves by, rather than others. It may be it is because he knows that these things are attended with less perplexity, and that we are less liable to be deceived by them than others. He best knows our nature; and he knows the nature and manner of his own operations; and he best knows the way of our safety: he knows what allowances to make for different states of his church, and different tempers of particular persons, and varieties in the manner of his own operations, how far Nature may resemble Grace, and how far Nature may be mixed with Grace, what affections may arise from imagination, and how far imagination may be mixed with spiritual illumination. And therefore 'tis our wisdom not to take his work out of his hands; but to follow him, and lay the stress of the judgment of ourselves there, where he has directed us. If we do otherwise, no wonder if we are bewildered, confounded and fatally deluded. But if we had got into the way of looking chiefly at those things, which Christ and his apostles and prophets chiefly insisted on, and so in judging of ourselves and others, chiefly regarding practical exercises and effects of grace, not neglecting other things; it would be of manifold happy consequence; it would above all things tend to the conviction of deluded hypocrites, and to prevent the delusion of those whose hearts were never brought to a thorough compliance with the strait and narrow way which leads to life; it would tend to deliver us from innumerable perplexities, arising from the various inconsistent schemes that are about methods and steps of experience; it would greatly tend to prevent professors neglecting strictness of life, and tend to promote their engagedness and earnestness in their Christian walk; and it would become fashionable for men to shew their Christianity, more by an amiable distinguished behavior, than by an abundant and excessive declaring their experiences; and we should get into the way of appearing lively in religion, more by being lively in the service of God and our generation, than by the liveliness and forwardness of our tongues, and making a business of proclaiming on the house tops, with our mouths, the holy and eminent acts and exercises of our own hearts; and Christians that are intimate friends, would talk together of their experiences and comforts, in a manner better becoming Christian humility and modesty, and more to each other's profit; their tongues not running before, but rather going behind their hands and feet, after the prudent example of the blessed Apostle, II Cor. 12:6; and many occasions of spiritual pride would be cut off; and so a great door shut against the devil; and a great many of the main stumbling blocks against experimental and powerful religion would be removed; and religion would be declared and manifested in such a way, that instead of hardening spectators, and exceedingly promoting infidelity and atheism, would above all things tend to convince men that there is a reality in religion, and greatly awaken them, and win them, by convincing their consciences of the importance and excellency of religion. Thus the light of professors would so shine before men, that others seeing their good works, would glorify their Father which is in heaven.

RELATED CORRESPONDENCE

Introduction

THE letters here reproduced between Edwards and Thomas Gillespie of Carnock, Scotland, are interesting both for the questions they raise and for the opportunity they afforded Edwards to expand some points maintained in the *Affections*. Moreover, they are indicative of the interest stirred up by Edwards' writings abroad, and they emphasize his connections with the evangelical movement in Scotland. The four letters, two from the pen of each man, are reproduced together in one place for the first time. Each has been printed before, but those editions that included the letters as an appendix to the *Affections* printed only Edwards' replies, leaving the reader in the dark as to the queries behind the correspondence. The Worcester edition does not contain any letters as an appendix to the *Affections,* but the Dwight edition has Edwards' two letters appended to the *Affections* volume with Gillespie's letters inserted in the first volume as part of Dwight's *Life*. There is, however, no indication in the *Affections* appendix that Gillespie's letters appear elsewhere in the edition. The Leeds edition (1806–11; Volume 4, 1808, containing the *Affections*) was the first to include Edwards' two letters as an appendix. The separate editions of the *Affections* do not include the letters.

According to Dwight [1] the entire correspondence was first printed in the *Edinburgh Quarterly Magazine;* the letters will be found distributed throughout Volume 1 (1798) of that periodical as follows:

Gillespie to Edwards (Nov. 24, 1746), No. 1, March 1798, pp. 29–41
Edwards to Gillespie (Sept. 4, 1747), No. 2, June 1798, pp. 109–24
Gillespie to Edwards (Sept. 19, 1748), No. 3, Sept. 1798, pp. 181–95
Edwards to Gillespie (April 2, 1750), No. 4, Dec. 1798, pp. 337–54

The Andover Collection of Edwards manuscripts contains all four letters either in the original or as copies. The first letter from Edwards (Sept. 4, 1747) is in his own hand and has the original ad-

1. Vol. 5, p. 322.

dress and seal on the reverse of the last sheet; there can be little doubt that it is the letter actually sent, since Edwards says twice in the body of his second letter that he "kept no copy" of the first. Edwards' second letter (April 2, 1750) is also in his own hand, and again it is most probably the letter actually sent. Unlike its predecessor, however, there is neither address nor seal on the reverse of the last sheet. The two letters from Gillespie in the Andover Collection are copies (the originals are most likely to have been returned to Scotland) and they are in rather poor condition. Consequently, I have reproduced these two letters as they appeared in the *Edinburgh Quarterly Magazine;* where it has been possible to compare them with the handwritten copies, I have found no significant differences. The two letters of Edwards have been edited from the originals in the Andover Collection. It is fortunate that we have them preserved in this form, since Dwight took some liberties with them, and in view of the fact that the Leeds edition is scarce, the reader already familiar with the correspondence has probably made his acquaintance with it through Dwight's edition.

Thomas Gillespie (1708–74) is best described as a "Scottish Evangelical" [2] and he is best known as one of the founders of the "Presbytery of Relief," a protest body which was later to combine with others in the formation of what is now the United Presbyterian Church. Gillespie originally matriculated at Edinburgh University, but left without completing his course to attend the Academy at Northampton which was then under the guidance of Philip Doddridge.[3] Gillespie's name stood at the head of the list of scholars at the Academy in 1741. His career as a student gives us some indication of the importance of the educational work Doddridge was doing and also provides us with some evidence of the role

2. An excellent picture of Gillespie's work is to be found in an address entitled "Scottish Evangelicals of the Seventeenth Century," delivered by Professor John Foster of the University of Glasgow at the Gillespie Bicentenary Celebration in 1952. It is printed in *The London Quarterly and Holborn Review, 21* (1952), 259 ff. There are some interesting parallels between the work of the Scottish evangelical ministers of the period and the activities of Jonathan Edwards in New England. I am indebted to Professor Foster for having sent to me a copy of his article and for having given some valuable hints concerning Gillespie's relation to the Scottish church. The reader should also consult Gavin Struthers' histories of the Relief Church in Scotland, and William Lindsay's *Life and Times of the Rev. Thomas Gillespie,* Edinburgh, 1849.

3. See above, Intro., pp. 66–7.

of the dissenting academies in preparing men for the ministry at a time when the leading universities were either in academic decline or hostile to the interests of evangelically inclined students.

The Presbytery of Relief was formed as a result of Gillespie's ouster by the General Assembly in 1752 after he had refused to assent to the ordination of a patron's candidate for the church of Inverkeithing. Gillespie and others joined hands against both the patronage system and the control exercised by the Scottish ecclesiastical courts.

Edwards was in correspondence not only with Gillespie but with Gillespie's colleagues, McCulloch, Robe, and especially John Erskine.[4] The extent of Edwards' influence upon the religious situation in Scotland was considerable and it seems not to be generally known.

As regards the substance of the letters themselves, the reader should find little difficulty in following the discussion, because Gillespie's comments are specific and directed to clearly identified passages in the text. There is, however, one point calling for clarification and commentary.

Gillespie's first question concerns Edwards' insistence that confident believing and trusting in God is impossible "without spiritual light or sight." Gillespie takes this frequently repeated doctrine of Edwards' to mean that there are some, i.e. those in a dead or carnal state, who are thereby relieved of their duty to believe in God, whereas he holds that every man stands at all times under the command to love and trust God as surely as he is under the command not to kill or steal. Edwards' reply to this first point is curious. He begins by expressing the wish that Gillespie had read through the whole before making his comment,[5] and then proceeds to agree with him by saying that his words were never intended to assert or imply that anyone is freed from the duty to believe. Edwards, however, arguing in a way reminiscent of the *Freedom of the Will,* proceeds to draw a distinction which is to settle the issue; it is difficult to say whether this distinction is oversubtle or even whether Edwards is entitled to draw it on his view. His reply is simply this: there is a great difference between it being a man's duty when he

4. See *Freedom of the Will,* ed. Ramsey, pp. 2–7, 115–17.

5. JE has no clear ground in Gillespie's letter for assuming that because his question concerns a point made early in the discussion Gillespie had not yet gone through the whole before commenting.

is *without spiritual light* to believe, and it being his duty to *believe without spiritual light.* The distinction is not obvious on its face. The clue to understanding is given in the fact that the expression "without spiritual light," though used in the same sense both times, has nevertheless two different connections. When it describes the *man,* as in the first alternative, Edwards wants to say only what he has already admitted, namely that *everyone* (including those "without spiritual light") has a duty to believe in God. When, as in the second alternative, the expression has to do with the act of *believing* and not with the description of the man, Edwards' point is that it makes no sense to say that anyone has a duty to believe without the very thing that is needed for believing, namely spiritual light.

Even if we allow that the second alternative is legitimate and perfectly consistent with Edwards' view, the question remaining is, what meaning can be attached to the first alternative? What does it mean to say that someone (in this case a man "without spiritual light") has a duty to perform something when the very description of the person shows that it is *impossible* for him to perform it? It would seem that if it is impossible to believe without spiritual light, it is equally impossible for a man without spiritual light to believe. It would have been more defensible if Edwards had said not that it is the duty of the man without the light to believe in God, but that it is his duty to obtain whatever it is that will *enable* him to believe in God. Since the light is the enabling factor, it would then be his duty to obtain the light. Unfortunately, the problem would then be to understand what it would mean to say that a man has the duty to obtain what cannot, on Edwards' view, be obtained by an act of will at all. The reply which both he and Gillespie seem prepared to accept, namely that "ability is not the rule of duty," does not consistently solve the problem. In the first place, what is meant by "ability" remains vague; secondly (and decisively), Edwards has already maintained that it is a contradiction to say that a man has the duty to *believe* without spiritual light on the ground that we would then be asking him to do what he *cannot* do just because he lacks one of the enabling conditions. Apparently, then, ability is, if not the rule of duty, at least a relevant factor in determining whether it makes sense to say that someone has a duty to do this or that.

The underlying question, and Edwards certainly avoids it in this correspondence, concerns the contribution which the will of the creature makes to the acceptance and reception of the divine grace. The point is that the more one stresses, as the Calvinistic tradition always has, the doctrine that God not only bestows grace in justification and sanctification but further provides all the conditions for grasping and receiving this grace, the more difficult it becomes to understand what can be meant by saying that a man has a *duty* to do this or that in connection with believing in God.

Gillespie fastens upon just this point in his second letter and expresses uncertainty over the distinction by which Edwards proposed to resolve the problem. He says many acute things about faith and the act of believing which are not taken up by Edwards in the succeeding letter. In fact, Edwards' final word in the letter of 1750 is to the effect that there are none but verbal differences between himself and Gillespie concerning believing and the spiritual light. This would seem to justify allowing the correspondence to speak here for itself. It is noteworthy that in his second letter Edwards makes more explicit the practical reason behind his doctrine of the need for spiritual light. Much harm, he writes, has been done in America by those who have insisted that a man ought to believe and be confident without paying any attention to whether he has the essentials for believing. Here again, it must be said that Edwards is right in pointing out what faith involves and requires in his understanding of true religion, but he avoids at this juncture the more basic problem of what it means to speak of duty in relation to what is impossible for the created will.

It is clear that the line of discussion here begun must inevitably lead to the problems dealt with in the *Freedom of the Will*. The Gillespie correspondence may thus be interpreted as forming something of a link between the *Affections* and Edwards' masterpiece of later years.

Letter 1. Gillespie to Edwards

Carnock, Nov. 24, 1746

Very dear Sir,

I have ever honored you for your works' sake, and what the great Shepherd made you the instrument of, from the time you published the then very extraordinary account of the Revival of Religion at Northampton, I think in the year 1735. The two performances you published on the subject of the late glorious work in New England, well adapted to that in Scotland, gave me great satisfaction, especially the last of them, for peculiar reasons. This much I think myself bound to say. I have many a time, for some years, designed to claim humbly the privilege of correspondence with you. What has made me defer doing it so long, when some of my brethren and good acquaintances have been favored with it, for a considerable time, it is needless now to mention. I shall only say, I have blamed myself for neglect in that matter. I do now earnestly desire a room in your prayers and friendship, and a letter from you sometimes, when you have occasion to write to Scotland; and I shall wish to be as regular as I can, in making a return. With your permission, I propose to trouble you now and then with the proposal of doubts and difficulties that I meet with, and am exercised by; as for other reasons, so because some solutions in the two mentioned performances were peculiarly agreeable to me, and I find from these discourses, that wherein I have differed in some things from many others, my sentiments harmonized with Mr. Edwards. This especially was the case in some things contained in your *Thoughts concerning the Revival of Religion in New England.* All the apology I make for using such freedom, though altogether unacquainted, is that you will find from my short attestation in Mr. Robe's Narrative, I am no enemy to you, or to the work you have been engaged in, and which you have defended in a way I could not but much approve of. Also my friend and countryman, the Rev. Mr. Robert Abercrombie, will inform you about me, if you have occasion to see him or hear from him.

I longed much to see somewhat about impressions respecting

facts and future events, etc. whether by Scripture texts or otherwise, made on the minds of good people, and supposed to be from the Lord; for I have had too good occasion to know the hurtful, yea, pernicious tendency of this principle, as commonly managed, upon many persons in manifold instances and various respects. It has indeed surprised me much, that wise, holy and learned divines, as well as others, have supposed this a spiritual experience, an answer of prayers, an evidence of being highly favored by the Lord, etc. and I was exceeding glad, that the Lord had directed you to give so seasonable a caveat against what I am assured you had the best reason to term, "A handle in the hand of the devil, etc." I was only sorry your then design had not permitted you to say more on that point. It merits a volume; and the proper full discussion of it would be one of the most seasonable and effectual services done the church of Christ, and interest of vital religion through the world, that I know of. I rejoice to find there is a good deal more on that subject interspersed in your *Treatise of Religious Affections,* which I have got, but could not as yet regularly peruse. I humbly think the Lord calls you, dear Sir, to consider every part of that point in the most critical manner, and to represent fully the consequences resulting from the several principles in that matter, good people, as well as others, have been so fond of. And as (if I don't mistake) Providence has already put that in your hand as a part of your generation-work, so it will give me, as well as others, vast satisfaction to find more said on the subject by you, if you don't find what is in the mentioned treatises sufficient, as to which I can form no judgment, because, for myself, I have not as yet considered it. If any other author has treated that subject, I don't remember to have met with it, and I believe hell has been no less delighted than surprised that a regular attack has not been made on them on that side before now. I doubt not they dread the consequences of such assault with exquisite horror, the neglect or oversight, if not the mistakes of so many learned authors, who have insisted on doctrines that bear similitude of relation to this matter, while it was passed over, I humbly think should teach us humility, and some other useful lessons I need not name to Mr. Edwards.

I hope, dear Sir, it will not offend you, that I humbly offer some remarks, with all due deference, upon what I have observed in looking into your *Treatise on Religious Affections,* and, upon farther perusal, shall frankly represent what I may find difficulty about, if any such passage should cast up; expecting you will be so good as to set me right, if I shall mistake or not perceive your meaning.

Pages 175 and 176, there are several passages I do not well understand. Page 175, line 26 *ad finem,* you say, "That they should confidently believe and trust, while they yet remain without spiritual light or sight, is an antiscriptural and absurd doctrine you are refuting." But this doctrine, as it is understood by many, is, that Christians ought firmly to believe and trust in Christ without light or sight, and though they are in a dark, dead frame, and for the present having no spiritual experiences and discoveries. Had you said they could not, or would not believe or trust without spiritual light or sight, this is what could not be doubted; but I humbly apprehend, the position will not hold as you have laid it, whether it is applied to a sinner or a saint, as I suppose you understand it; for though the sinner never will believe on the Lord Jesus till he has received a saving manifestation of his glory by the work of the Spirit, yet every sinner, we know, is indispensably bound, at all seasons, by the divine authority, to believe instantly in the Lord Jesus. The command of the Lord, I John 3:23 that we should believe on the name of his Son Jesus Christ, no less binds the sinner to immediate performance than the command not to kill, to keep the Sabbath day or any other duty as to the present performance of which, in way of duty, all agree, the sinner is bound. I suppose none of us think we are authorized or will adventure to preach, that the sinner should delay to attempt to believe in the Saviour, till he finds light from heaven shining into his mind, or has got a saving sight or discovery of the Lord Jesus, though it is certain he cannot believe, nor will do it effectually, till favored with such light or sight; because we should, in that event, put in a qualification where the apostle Paul and Silas did put none; such is their exhortation to the jailor (Acts 16:31). Also, as it may be the last call the sinner is to receive, in dispensation of the word, we are bound to require him instantly to believe, whatever he does, or does not feel in himself. If you did intend not the sinner, but the saint, in the before mentioned positions, as I am apt to think your scope plainly intimates, still I apprehend these your assertions are not tenable; for I humbly suppose the Christian is bound to trust the divine faithfulness plighted in the promise for needful blessings, be his case with respect to light or darkness, sight, etc. what it will; and that no situation the saint can be in, looses him from obligation to glorify the Lord on all occasions, by trusting in him and expecting the fulfilment of his word suiting his case. Also I would imagine in Is. 1:10 the saint is required to believe, in the precise circumstances mentioned in your assertion above mentioned. Pardon my freedom. You do indeed say, "It is truly the duty of those who are thus in darkness to come out of darkness into light and believe," p. 175, line 25; but how to reconcile that with the mentioned assertion that immediately follows, or with Is. 1:10 or other Scriptures, or said assertions, and the other, of which before, I am indeed at a loss. Sometimes I think it is not believing the promise, or trusting the Lord, and trusting in him, you mean in the positions I have cited; but the belief of the goodness of one's state that he is a saint. If that was what you intended, I heartily wish you had said so much in the book; but as this is not ordinarily what is meant by believing in Scripture, I must suppose it was not the idea affixed to your words; and an expression of yours seems to make it evident. Had you plainly stated the distinction betwixt the impossibility of one's actually believing and its yet being his duty to believe, in the circumstances you mentioned, danger of mistake and a handle for cavil had been cut off.

Page 176, line 7, etc. you say, "To press and urge them to believe, without any spiritual light or sight, tends greatly to help forward the delusions of the prince of darkness." Had you said, to press them to believe the Lord was their God, when going on a course of sin, or when sinning presumptuously, was of such tendency, which probably was in part what you designed, it would in my humble apprehension, have been much more safe, for reasons given. Also, as it is ordinarily and justly observed, that they who are most humbled think they are least so, when under a saving work of the Spirit, perhaps in like manner, spiritual light and sight may, in some instances, be mistaken or not duly apprehended; in which case, the person, upon admitting and proceeding upon your suppositions, may perhaps be apt to give way to unbelief, and to say, if I am not to be urged by the Lord's servants to believe in my present circumstances, it would surely be presumptuous in me to entertain thoughts of attempting it. Or, it may be, he shall think he has not that degree of spiritual light or sight that is absolutely necessary in order to his believing, and thus the evil heart of unbelief shall make him depart from the living God, and neglect to set to his seal that he is true, perhaps from the apprehension that it is his duty to remain as he is, or at least in the persuasion it would be in vain to essay to believe till matters be otherwise with him. If I have deduced consequences from your work and manner of reasoning which you think they do not justly bear, I will be glad to be rectified by you, dear Sir, and would be satisfied to know from you how the practice you remark upon in the forementioned passage tends to help forward the delusions of Satan. I am apt to believe the grounds upon which you proceeded in the whole paragraph I have mentioned, is, that you have with you, real Antinomians, who teach things about faith and believing subversive of new obedience and gospel-holiness, and inconsistent with the Scripture doctrines concerning them. But as we have few, if any such at all (I believe I might say more), in this country, and at the same time have numbers who would have the most accurate and judicious evangelical preachers to insist a great deal more upon *doing,* and less upon *believing* (Mark 10: 17–23), for what reasons you will perceive, I am afraid your words will be misrepresented by them, and a sense put on your expressions which you was far from intending. I expect a mighty clamor by the Seceders, if the book shall fall into their hands. All I shall say about what is expressed by you, p. 175, line 21, etc. is, I have frequently heard it taught by them accounted the most orthodox, that the believer was bound to trust in the Lord in the very worst frame he could be in, and that the exercise of faith was the way to be delivered from darkness, deadness, backsliding, etc. It is impossible one should err who follows the course prescribed by the Lord in his Word. I suppose no person is bound or allowed to defer believing one single moment, because he finds himself in a bad situation, because the Spirit breathes not on him, or he finds not an actual influence from heaven communicated to him at that season, rendering him capable or meet for it; for this reason, that not our ability or fitness, but the Lord's command, is the rule of duty, etc. It merits consideration whether the believer should ever doubt of his state on any account whatever; because doubting, as opposed to believing, is absolutely sinful. I know the opposite has been prescribed when the saint is plunged in prevailing iniquity; but does not doubting strengthen corruption? is not unbelief the leading sin, as faith is the leading grace? Page 390. You cite as an authority Mr. Stoddard affirming, note 2, "One way of sin is exception enough against men's salvation, though their temptations be great." I well remember the singularly judicious Dr. Owen somewhere says to this effect, "Prevalence of a particular sin over a person for a considerable time shows him to be no saint, except when under the power of a strong temptation." I would suppose such texts as Is. 64:6; Ps. 65:3, etc. warranted the Doctor to assert as he did. It is, I own, no small difficulty to steer the middle course betwixt affording hypocrites ground unwarrantably to presume on the one hand, and wounding the Lord's dear children on the other; and all the little knowledge of the Scriptures I would hope the Lord has given me, makes me think Mr. Shepherd, good and great man as he was, verged not a little to the last extreme, with whom, if I mistake not, Mr. Stoddard symbolizes in the above assertion; for such as I have mentioned I apprehend is the drift and tendency of Mr. Shepherd's principles. In some instances, daily experience and observation confirms me still more, we should be very cautious and modest when asserting on that head, and should take care to go no farther in the matter than we have plain Scripture to bear us out. The consideration, that indwelling sin sometimes certainly gets such ascendant, that the new creature is, for the time the Lord sees meet, as fire burned under ashes, undiscerned and inactive, lays foundation, in my humble apprehension, for saying somewhat stronger on that point, than I would choose to utter in public teaching, and how long a saint may have been in the case now hinted, I suppose it belongs not to us precisely to determine.

Page 391, you say, "Nor can a true saint ever fall away, so that it shall come to this, that ordinarily there shall be no remarkable difference in his walk and behavior since his conversion, from what was before." I do not remember that the Scripture anywhere mentions that David or Solomon were sanctified from the womb. I think the contrary may be presumed; and it is evident for a considerable time, with the first ordinarily, and for a long time, in the case of the latter ordinarily, there was a remarkable difference to the worse on the walk and behavior of both of them, when we are sure they were saints, from what it appears it had been in their younger years. Besides, let us suppose a person of a good natural disposition, bred up in aversion to all vicious practices by a religious education and example, and virtuous inclination thus cultivated in him (II Pet. 2:20), and he is converted when come to maturity, and afterwards corruption in him meets with peculiar temptations; I doubt much if there would be a remarkable difference betwixt his then conversation and walk and that in irregeneracy. The contrary I think is found in experience, and the principles laid down leave room to suppose it.

I own in what I have above said I have perhaps gone farther than becomes a man of my standing in writing to one of Mr. Edwards' experience, and am heartily sorry my first letter to you is in such a strain, and on such a subject. But love to you, dear Sir, and concern lest you should be thought to patronize what I am sure you do not, and to oppose what is your sentiments, made me write with such freedom and break over restraints, modesty, decency, etc. should otherwise have laid me under, that you might have an opportunity to know in what light these things I mention to you appear to some who are your real friends in this country. A valuable minister, in looking into what is noticed in pp. 175 and 176 said to me, it would be right some should write you about it, and I take this first opportunity, that you may have access to judge of the matter, and what it may be proper for you to do, or not to do in it.

I will expect an answer with your convenience. I hope you will deal freely with me; for I can say, I would sit down and learn at your feet, dear Sir, accounting myself as a child in knowledge of the Scriptures, when compared with others I will not name, and the longer I live I see the greater advantage in improvements of that kind. Conceal nothing that you think will tend to put me right if you find my views are not just. I proposed in the beginning of this letter to trouble you with some questions or doubts, and shall mention one or two at present. What should one do who is incessantly harassed by Satan; can by no means keep him out of his mind; has used all means prescribed in Scripture and suggested by divines for resistance, known to him, in vain; it may be for a long time has cried to Christ, but he hears not, seems not to regard him; all his efforts are swallowed up in the deluge of the foe; do what he will, seems to gain no ground against the powers of darkness; is apt to dread he shall sink under the load, and never shall be delivered in this world? what would you advise such a person to do? what construction, think you, should he put on the sovereign conduct and dispensation of Heaven toward him? I have occasion to be conversant about this case practically demonstrated, of many years continuance, without interruption; and will therefore be glad to have your mind about it in a particular manner, and as much at large as you conveniently can. It is said, all things work for good, etc. As degrees of glory will be in proportion to those of grace, how can it be made appear it is for one's good what sometimes happens to saints, their being permitted to fall under backslidings and spiritual decays, and to die in that state, perhaps after continuing in it a considerable while, and when their situation has been attended with the melancholy circumstances and consequences that sometimes have place in that state of matters? The solution of this I would gladly receive from you.

Are the works of great Mr. Boston known in your country, viz. the Fourfold State of Man, View of the Covenant of Grace, and a Discourse on Afflictions, and Church communion, etc. If not, inform me by your letter. I have now need to own my fault in troubling you with so long a letter, and so I shall end, etc.

Letter 2. Edwards to Gillespie

Northampton, Sept. 4, 1747

Rev. and dear Sir,

I received your letter of Nov. 24, 1746, though very long after it was written. I thank you for it, and for your offering me a correspondence with you. Such an offer I shall gladly embrace, and esteem it a great privilege, more especially from the character I have received of you from Mr. Abercrombie, who I perceive was intimately acquainted with you.

As to the objections you make against some things contained in my late book on *Religious Affections,* I am sorry you did not read the book through, before you made them; if you had, perhaps the difficulties would not have appeared quite so great. As to what is contained in the 175th and 176th pages, I suppose there is not the least difference of opinion between you and me, unless it be concerning the signification and propriety of expressions. I am fully of your mind, and always was without the least doubt of it: "That every one, both saint and sinner, is indispensably bound, at all seasons, by the divine authority, to believe instantly on the Lord Jesus, and that the command of the Lord (I John 3:23), that we should believe on the name of his Son Jesus Christ, as it is a prescription of the moral law, no less binds the sinner to immediate performance, than the commandment not to kill, to keep the Sabbath day, or any other duty, as to the *present* performance of which, in way of duty, all agree the sinner is bound; and that men are bound to trust the divine faithfulness, be their case with respect to light and darkness, sight, etc. what it will; and that no situation they can be in, looses them from obligation to glorify the Lord at all seasons, and expecting the fulfilment of his words; and that the sinner that is without spiritual light or sight is bound to believe, and that it is a duty *at that very time* incumbent on him to believe." But I conceive that there is a great deal of difference between these two things, viz. its being a man's duty that is without spiritual light or sight to believe, and its being his duty to believe without spiritual light or sight, or to believe while he yet remains without spiritual light or sight. Just the same difference that is between these two things, viz. its being *his* duty that has no faith to believe, and its being his duty to believe without faith, or to believe without believing. I trust there is none will assert the latter, because of the contradiction that it implies. As it is not proper to say, it is a man's duty to believe without faith, because it implies a contradiction, so I think it equally improper to say it is a man's duty to believe without these things that are essentially implied in faith, because that also implies a contradiction. But a spiritual sight of Christ or knowledge of Christ is essentially implied in the very nature and notion of faith, and therefore it is absurd to talk of believing on Christ without spiritual light or sight. It is the duty of a man that is without these things, that essentially belong to faith, to believe, and it is the duty of a man that is without these things that essentially belong to love, to love God; because it is an indispensable obligation that lies on all men at all times, and in all circumstances, to love God: but yet it is not a duty to love God without loving him, or continuing without those things that essentially belong to his love. It is the duty of those that have no sense of the loveliness of God and have no esteem of him, to love him, and they be not in the least excused by the want of this sense and esteem, in not loving him one moment; but yet it would be properly nonsense to say it is their duty to love him without any sense of his loveliness or any esteem of him. It is indeed their duty this moment to come out of their disesteem and stupid wicked insensibility of his loveliness, and to love him. I made the distinction, (I thought), very plainly , in the midst of those sentences you quote as exceptionable. I say expressly, p. 175, "It is truly the duty of those who are in darkness to come out of darkness into light and believe; but, that they should confidently believe and trust, while they yet remain without spiritual light or sight, is an antiscriptural and absurd doctrine." The misunderstanding between us, dear Sir, I suppose to be in the different application of the particle *without,* in my use of it, and your understanding of it, or what we understand as spoken of and supposed in the expression, *without spiritual light or sight.* As I use it, I apply it to the act of believing, and I suppose it to be very absurd to talk of an act of faith, *without* spiritual light and sight, wherein I suppose you will allow me to be in the right. As you understand it, it is applied to duty or obligation, and you suppose it to be not at all absurd to talk of an obligation to believe without spiritual light or sight, but that the obligation remains full where there is no spiritual light or sight, wherein I allow you are in the right. I think, Sir, if you read what I have said in my book on this head again, it will be exceeding apparent to you, that it is thus that I apply the preposition *without,* and not as you before understood it. I thought I had very plainly manifested that what I meant by *being in darkness* was a being in spiritual blindness, and so in a dead, stupid, carnal and unchristian frame and way, and not what is commonly called a being without the light of God's countenance, under the hidings of his face. We have a great number of people in these parts that go on that supposition in their notions and practice, that there really is such a thing as such a manner of believing, such a kind of faith as this, viz, a confident believing and firm trusting in God in the dark, in the sense mentioned, that is to be sought after and is the subject matter of divine prescription, and which many actually have; and indeed there are inummerable instances of such as are apparently in a most senseless, careless, negligent, apostate, and every way unchristian and wicked frame, that yet, encouraged by this principle, do retain an exceeding strong confidence of their good state, and count that herein they do their duty and give much glory to God, under the notion of trusting God in the dark, and hoping against hope, and not trusting on their own righteousness; and they suppose it would show a legal spirit to do otherwise. I thought it would be manifest to every reader that I was arguing against such a sort of people.

You say, "It merits consideration whether the believer should ever doubt of his state, on any account whatever, because doubting, as opposed to believing, is absolutely sinful." Here, Sir, you seem to suppose that a person's doubting of his own good estate, is the proper opposite of faith, and these and some other expressions in your letter seem to suppose that doubting of one's good estate and unbelief is the same thing, and so, that being confident of one's good estate and faith are the same thing. This I acknowledge I don't understand; I don't take faith, and a person's believing that they have faith, to be the same thing. Nor do I take unbelief, or being without faith and doubting whether they have it, to be the same thing, but entirely different. I should have been glad either that you had taken a little more notice of what I say on this head, pp. 177, 178, or that you had said something to convince me that I am wrong in this point. *The exercise of faith is doubtless the way to be delivered from darkness, deadness, backsliding, etc.* or rather is the deliverance; as forsaking sin is the way to deliverance from sin, and is the deliverance itself. The exercise of grace is doubtless the way to deliverance from a graceless frame, that consists in the want of the exercise of grace. But as to what you say, or seem to intimate, of a person's being confident of his own good estate, as being the way to be delivered from darkness, deadness, backsliding and prevailing iniquity, I think, whoever supposes this to be God's method of delivering his saints, when sunk into an evil, careless, carnal and unchristian frame, first to assure them of their good estate and his favor, while they yet remain in such a frame, and to make *that* the means of their deliverance, does surely mistake God's method of dealing with such persons. Among all the multitudes I have had opportunity to observe, I never knew one dealt with after this manner. I have known many brought back from great declension, that appeared to me to be true saints, but it was in a way very diverse from this. *In the first place,* conscience has been awakened, and they have been brought into great fear of the wrath of God, having his favor hid, and they have been the subjects of a kind of new work of humiliation, brought to a great sense of their deserving of God's wrath, even while they have yet feared it, before God has delivered them from the apprehension of it, and comforted them with a renewed sense of his favor.

As to what I say of the necessity of universal obedience, or one way of known sin, (i.e. so as properly to be said to be the way and manner of the man), being exception enough against a man's salvation; I should have known better what to have said further about it, if you had briefly shown how the Scriptures that I mention, and the argument I deduce from them, are insufficient for the proof of this point. I confess they appear to me to prove it as fully as any thing concerning the necessary qualifications of a true saint can be proved from Scripture.

You object against my saying, p. 391, "Nor can a true saint ever fall away, so that it shall come to this, that ordinarily there shall be no remarkable difference in his walk and behavior since his conversion, from what was before." This, I think, implies no more than that his walk over the same ground, in like circumstances, and under like trials, will have a remarkable difference. As to the instance you mention of David and Solomon, I don't know that the Scriptures give us anywhere so much of a history of their walk and behavior before their conversion, as to put us into any proper capacity of comparing their after walk with their former. These examples are uncertain. But I think those doctrines of the Scripture are not uncertain, which I mention in the place you cite, to confirm the point, which teach that converts are new men, new creatures, that they are renewed not only within but without, that old things are passed away, and all things become new, that they walk in newness of life, that the members of their bodies are new, that whereas they before were the servants of sin, and yielded their members servants of iniquity, now they yield them servants of righteousness unto holiness.

As to those doubts and cases of difficulty you mention, I should think it very needless for a divine of your character, to apply yourself to me for a solution of difficulties, for whom it would be more proper to learn of you. However, since you are pleased to insist on my giving my mind upon them, I would observe, as to the first case you mention, of a person incessantly harassed by Satan, etc. you don't say of what nature the temptations are that he is harassed with. But I think it impossible to give proper advice and directions without knowing this. Satan is to be resisted in a very different manner, in different kinds of onsets. When persons are harassed with those strange, horrid injections, that melancholic persons are often subject to, he is to be resisted in a very different manner, from what is proper in case of violent temptation to gratify some worldly lust. In the former case, I should by no means advise a person to resist the devil by entering the lists with him, and vehemently engaging their mind in an earnest dispute and violent struggle with the grand adversary, but rather by diverting the mind from his frightful suggestions, by going on steadfastly and diligently in the ordinary course of duty, without allowing themselves time and leisure to attend to the devil's sophistry, or viewing his frightful representations, committing themselves to God by prayer in this way, without anxiety about what had been suggested. That is the best way of resisting the devil, that crosses his design most; and he more effectually disappoints him in such cases, that treats him with neglect, than he that attends so much to him, as to engage in a direct conflict, and goes about to try his strength and skill with him, in a violent dispute or combat. The latter course rather gives him advantage, than anything else. It is what he would; if he can get persons thus engaged in a violent struggle, he gains a great point. He knows that melancholic persons are not fit for it. By this he gains that point of diverting and taking off the person from the ordinary course of duty, which is one great thing he aims at; and by this, having gained the person's attention to what he says, he has opportunity to use all his craft and subtlety, and by this struggle he raises melancholic vapors to a greater degree, and further weakens the person's mind, and gets him faster and faster in his snares, deeper and deeper in the mire. He increases the person's anxiety of mind, which is the very thing by which mainly he fulfills all his purposes with such persons.

Concerning the other difficulty you mention relating to the verifying of Rom. 8:20, "All things shall work together for good," etc. in a saint that falls under backsliding and spiritual decay, etc. it seems to be a matter of some difficulty to understand exactly how this is to be taken, and how far it may from hence be inferred, that the temptations the saints meet with from Satan, and an evil world, and their own declensions and sins, shall surely work for their good. However, since you desire my thoughts, I would express them, such as they are, as follows.

In order rightly to state this matter, there are two things may be laid down, as positions of certain and indubitable truth concerning this doctrine of the Apostle.

First, the meaning cannot be that God's dispensations and disposals towards each saint are the best for him, most tending to his happiness *of all that are possible;* or that all things that are ordered for him, or done by God with respect to him, are in all respects better for him than anything else that God could have ordered or done, issuing in the highest good and happiness, that it is possible he should be brought to; for that would be as much as to say, that God will bestow on every one of his elect, as much happiness as he can, in the utmost exercise of his omnipotence, and this sets aside all these different degrees of grace and holiness here, and glory hereafter, which he bestows according to his sovereign pleasure.

All things may work together for good to the saints. All may be of benefit to them, and may have a concurring tendency to their happiness, and may all finally issue in it, and yet not tend to, or issue in the highest degree of good and happiness possible. There is a certain measure of holiness and happiness, that each one of the elect is eternally appointed to, and all things that relate to him, work together to bring to pass *this appointed measure of good.* The text and context speak of God's *eternal purpose* of good to the elect, predestinating them to a conformity to his Son in holiness and happiness; and the implicit reasoning of the Apostle leads us to suppose that all things will surely concur to bring to effect God's eternal purpose. And therefore from his reasoning it may be inferred, that all things will tend to, and work together to bring to pass, that degree of good that God has purposed to bestow upon them, and not any more. And indeed it would be in itself unreasonable to suppose anything else but this; inasmuch as God is the supreme orderer of all things, doubtless all things shall be so ordered, that with one consent, they shall help to bring to pass his ends, aims and purposes; but surely not to bring to pass what he does not aim at, and never intended. God in his government of the world, is carrying on his own designs in everything; but he is not carrying on that which is not his design, and therefore there is no need of supposing, that all the circumstances, means and advantages of every saint, are the best in every respect that God could have ordered for him, or that there could have been no circumstances or means that he could have been the subject of, that would with God's usual blessing have issued in his greater good. Every saint is as it were a living stone, that in this present state of preparation, is fitting for the place appointed for him in the heavenly temple. And in this sense all things undoubtedly work together for good to every one that is called according to God's purpose. He is, all the while he lives in this world, by all the dispensations of Providence towards him, fitting for the particular mansion in glory, that is appointed and prepared for him, or hewing for his appointed place in the heavenly building.

Secondly, another thing which is no less certain and demonstrable than the position that has been already laid down, and indeed follows from it, is this. When it is said, "all things work together for good," etc. hereby cannot be intended that all things, *both positive and negative, are best for them,* or that it is so universally, that not only every positive thing that the saints are the subjects of, or are concerned in, will work for their good, but also that where anything is absent or withheld from them by God in his providence, that absence or withholding is also for their good in that sense, or to be better for them than the presence or bestowment would have been; for this would have the same absurd consequence that was mentioned before, viz. that God makes every saint as happy as possibly he can. And besides, if so, it would follow that God's withholding greater degree of the sanctifying influences of his Spirit is for the saints' good, and that it is held for them to live and die so low in grace as they do, which would be as much as to say that it is for their good to have no more good, or that it is for their happiness to have no more happiness here and hereafter. If we take good notice of the Apostle's discourse in Rom. 8 it will be apparent that his words imply no such thing. All God's creatures, and all that God does in disposing of them, is for the good of the saint. But it will not thence follow, that all God's forbearing to do is also for his good, or that it is best for him, that God does no more for him.

Therefore, the following things I humbly conceive to be the truth, concerning the sins and temptations of the saints being for their good.

1. That all things, whatsoever, are for the good of the saints, things negative as well as positive, in this sense, that *God intends that some benefit to them shall arise from every thing,* so that something of the grace and love of God, will hereafter be seen to have been exercised towards them in everything. At the same time, the sovereignty of God will also be seen, with regard to the measure of the good or benefit aimed at, in that some other things, if God had seen cause to order them, would have produced an higher benefit. And with regard to negative disposals, consisting not in God's doing, but forbearing to do, not in giving, but withholding, some benefit in some respect or other, will ever accrue to the saints, even from these; though sometimes the benefit will not be equal to the benefit withheld, if it had been bestowed. As for instance, when a saint lives and dies comparatively low in grace. There is some good improvement shall be made, even of this, in the eternal state of the saint, whereby he shall receive a real benefit, though the benefit shall not be equal to the benefit of an higher degree of holiness, if God had bestowed it.

2. God carries on a design of love to his people, and to each individual saint, not only in all things that they are the subjects of while they live, but also in all his works and disposals, and in all his acts from eternity to eternity.

3. That the sin, in general, of the saints, is for their good, and for the best in this respect, viz. that it is a thing that, through the sovereign grace of God, and his infinite wisdom, will issue in a high advancement of their eternal happiness, that they have been sinful, fallen creatures, and not from the beginning perfectly innocent and holy, as the elect angels; and that they shall obtain some additional good on occasion of all the sin they have been the subjects of, or have committed, beyond what they would have had, if they never had been fallen creatures.

4. The sin of the saints in this sense cannot be for their good, that it should finally be best for them, that while they lived in this world, their restoration and recovery from the corruption they became subject to by the fall, was no greater, the mortification of sin, and spiritual vivification of their soul carried on to no greater degree, that they remained so sinfully deficient, as to love to God, Christian love to men, humility, heavenly-mindedness, and that they were so barren, and did so few good works, and consequently, that in general, they had so much sin, and of the exercises of it, and not more holiness, and of the exercises and fruits of that, for in proportion as one of these is more, the other will be less, as infallibly, as darkness is more or less, in proportion to the diminution or increase of light. It cannot finally be better for the saints, that in general, while they live, they had so much sin of heart and life, rather than more holiness of heart and life. Because the reward of all at last will be according to their works, and he that sowed sparingly shall reap sparingly, and he that sowed bountifully, shall reap also bountifully, and he that builds wood, hay and stubble, shall finally suffer loss, and have a less reward, than if he had built gold, silver and precious stones, though he himself shall be saved. But notwithstanding this,

5. The sins and falls of the saints, may be for their good, and for the better, in this respect, that the issue may be better than if the temptation had not happened, and so the occasion not given, either for the sin of yielding to the temptation, or the virtue of overcoming it: and yet not in the respect (with regard to their sins or falls in general), that it should be better for them in the issue, that they have yielded to the temptation offered, than if they had overcome. For the fewer victories they obtain over temptation, the fewer are their good works, and particularly of that kind of good works to which a distinguished reward is promised in Rev. 2 and 3 and in many other parts of Scripture. The Word of God represents the work of a Christian in this world as a warfare, and it is evident in the Scripture that he who acquits himself as the best soldier shall win the greatest prize. Therefore, when the saints are brought into backslidings and decays, by being overcome by temptations, the issue of their backslidings may be some good to them, they may receive some benefit by occasion of it, beyond what they would have received if that temptation had never happened; and yet their backslidings in general may be a great loss to them in that respect,

viz., that they shall have much less reward, than if the temptations had been overcome, and they notwithstanding had persevered in spiritual vigor and diligence. But yet this don't hinder but that,

6. It may be so ordered by a sovereign and all-wise God, that the saints' falls and backslidings, through their being overcome by temptation in some particular instances, may prove best for them; not only that the issue may be greater good to them, than they would have received if the temptation had not happened, but even greater in that instance, than if the temptation had been overcome. It may be so ordered that their being overcome by that temptation, shall be an occasion of their having greater strength, and in the whole, obtaining more and greater victories, than if they had not fallen in that instance. But this is nowhere promised, nor can it be so, that, in the general, it should prove better for them that they are foiled so much, and do overcome so little, in the course of their lives, and that finally their decay is so great, or their progress so small. From these things it appears,

7. That the saying of the apostle, "all things work together for good to them that love God," though it be fulfilled in some respect to all saints, and at all times, and in all circumstances, yet is fulfilled more especially and eminently to the saints continuing in the exercise of love to God, not falling from the exercises, or failing of the fruits of divine love in times of trial: then temptations, enemies and suffering, such as be will be best for them, working that which is most for their good every way; and they shall be more than conquerors over tribulation, distress, persecution, famine, nakedness, peril and sword (Rom. 8:35–37).

8. As God is carrying on a design of love to each individual saint, in all his works and disposals whatsoever, as was observed before, so the particular design of love to them that he is carrying on, is to fit them for, and bring them to their appointed place in the heavenly temple, or to that individual, precise happiness and glory in heaven, that his eternal love designed for them, and no other (for God's design of love or of happiness to them, is only just what it is, and is not different from itself). And to fulfill this particular design of love, everything that God does, or in any respect disposes, whether it be positive, privative or negative, contributes, because doubtless everything that God does, or in any respect offers, tends to fulfill his aims and designs. Therefore, undoubtedly,

9. All the while the saint lives in the world, he is fitting for his

appointed mansion in glory, and hewing for his place in the heavenly building. And all his temptations, though they may occasion, for the present, great spiritual wounds, yet at last, they shall be an occasion of his being more fitted for his place in glory. And, therefore, we may determine, that however the true saint may die in some respects, under decays, under the decay of comfort, and of the exercise of some religious affections, yet every saint dies at that time when his habitual fitness for his place in the heavenly temple is most complete, because otherwise, all things that happen to him while he lives, would not work together to fit him for that place.

10. God brings his saints at the end of their lives to this greatest fitness for their place in heaven, not by diminishing grace in their hearts, but by increasing it, and carrying on the work of grace in their souls. If it be not so, that cannot be true, that where God has begun a good work he will perform it, or carry it on to the day of Christ, for if they die with a less degree of grace than they had before, then it ceases to be carried on before the day of Christ comes. If grace is finally diminished, then Satan so far finally obtains the victory. He finally prevails to diminish the fire in the smoking flax, and then how is that promise verified, that God will not quench the smoking flax, till he bring forth judgment unto victory? So that it must needs be, that although saints may die under decay in some respects, yet they never die under a real habitual decay of the work of grace in general. If they fall, they shall rise again before they die, and rise higher than before, if not in joy, and some other affections, yet in greater degrees of spiritual knowledge, self-emptiness, trust in God, and solidity and ripeness of grace.

If these things that have been observed are true, then we may infer from them these corollaries.

1st, that notwithstanding the truth of that saying of the Apostle, Rom. 8:28, the saints have cause to lament their leanness and barrenness, and that they are guilty of so much sin, not only as it is to the dishonor of God, but also as that which is like to be to their own eternal loss and damage.

2dly, that nothing can be inferred from the forementioned promise tending to set aside, or make void the influence of motives to earnest endeavors to avoid all sin, to increase in holiness, and abound in good works, from an aim at an high and eminent degree of glory and happiness in the future world.

3dly, that though it is to the eternal damage of the saints, ordinarily, when they yield to, and are overcome by temptations, yet Satan and other enemies of the saints by whom these temptations come, are always wholly disappointed in their temptations, and baffled in their design to hurt the saints, inasmuch as the temptation and the sin that comes by it, is for the saints' good, and they receive a greater benefit in the issue, than if the temptation had not been, and yet less than if the temptation had been overcome.

As to Mr. Boston's view of the covenant of grace, I have had some opportunity with it, and I confess I did not understand his scheme delivered in that book. I have read his *Fourfold State of Man,* and liked it exceeding well. I think he herein shows himself to be a truly great divine.

Hoping that you will accept my letter with candor, and remember me in your prayers, I subscribe myself, your

affectionate and obliged Brother
and Servant,
JONATHAN EDWARDS

Letter 3. Gillespie to Edwards

Sept. 19, 1748

Rev. very dear Sir,

I had the favor of yours in spring last, for which I heartily thank you. I did not want inclination to make you a return long ago, as I prize your correspondence, but some things concurred that effectually prevented me, which has given me concern.

It was desire to be informed, and inclination to make you understood by some others, your real friends and well wishers in this country, that determined me to presume to offer you some few remarks on the passages mentioned in my former letter, and desire of further information, engages me now, with all respect, to make some observations upon some things in your letter. I hope you will pardon my freedom, and bear with me in it, and set me right wherein you may find me to misapprehend your meaning, or to mistake in any other respect.

You say, "You conceive that there is a great difference between these two things, viz. its being a man's duty, that is without 'spiritual light' or sight to believe, and its being *his* duty to believe *without* spiritual light or sight, or to believe while he yet remains without spiritual light or sight: it is not proper to say, it is a man's duty to believe *without* faith," etc. Now, dear Sir, the difference here, I am not able to conceive; for all are bound to believe the divine testimony and to trust in Christ, which you acknowledge, and the want of spiritual light or sight does not loose from the obligation one is laid under by the divine command to believe instantly on Christ, and at all seasons, the promise, as his circumstances shall require, nor does it excuse him in any degree for not believing. I own that a person who has no spiritual light or sight cannot eventually believe, if by light or sight is meant the influence and grace of the Spirit, by which one's mind is irradiated to take up the object and grounds of faith, so as to be made to have a spiritual sight of Christ, and to act that grace; yet still, even when one wants this, it is his duty, and he is bound to believe, for we know it is a maxim, "ability is not the rule of duty." I also acknowledge, that no person who is, and always has been, without spiritual light or sight, is bound, nor is it his duty to believe, that he has actually believed, or to conclude he is really a partaker of the faith of God's elect. I have some apprehension this is all you meant by the expressions I have noticed, and the reasoning in consequence of them; or else certainly different ideas are affixed to words with you and among us. There is indeed a great deal of difference betwixt its being one's duty to believe, or to act faith, and its being his duty to believe he has believed, or has acted divine faith, i.e. you say *you* apply the particle *without,* respecting spiritual light or sight, to the act of believing, by which I suppose you intend, "all *should* believe," or none *do* really believe *without* spiritual light or sight; in which I entirely agree with you. The word *duty* indeed, which you use when treating that matter, is ordinarily supposed to signify the obligation the person is under by the divine authority to believe, as applied to the *matter* of faith, and not to the *act* of faith, put forth in consequence of such obligation. Had I not supposed you plainly meant by the expressions I quoted from the book, the *duty* or *obligation* to believe, and not an act of faith exerted, I should have made no remarks on them. It is indeed as absurd for one to conclude he has really believed without spiritual light or sight, as to say one should believe he had believed, without these things that are essentially implied in faith. But I must differ from you in thinking it is very proper to say, it is man's duty to believe *without* faith, i.e. while he yet remains without spiritual light or sight, or to put forth an act of faith on the Saviour, however void of spiritual light or sight; for if this was not the truth, the finally impenitent sinner could not be condemned for unbelief, as the Holy Ghost declares he will be (John 3:19–20, 24), and that notwithstanding the power of the Spirit of faith must make him believe. I should be glad to know the precise idea you affix to the words *faith* and *believing.* I do not remember a person's reflecting on his act of faith anywhere in Scripture termed belief. You remark, "That I seem to suppose that a person's doubting of his good estate is the proper opposite of faith," and I own, as it is a believer's duty to expect salvation through Christ, which, in other words, is to believe his good estate (Acts 15:11; Gal. 2:20; Eph. 2:4; Job 19:25), doubting of it must be his sin, an effect of unbelief, a part of it, and thus the proper opposite of faith, considered in its full compass and latitude. Once doubting of his good estate by a true believer, and unbelief in one branch of it, or one part and manner of its acting, are the same thing. Faith and unbelief are opposed in Scripture, and what is the opposite of one ingredient in unbelief must be faith in one part of it—one thing that belongs to its exercise. A person's believing the Lord will never leave nor forsake him who is in a gracious state (Heb. 13:5) is owned to be his indispensable duty, and this comprehends or supposes his being confident of his good estate, and is properly divine faith, because it has the divine testimony now cited, on which it bottoms (Jer. 3:19), the Lord says, "Thou shalt call me my father, and shalt not turn away from me," which is evidently faith, and no less manifestly belief of one's good estate, or being confident of it, because the expression must denote the continued exercise of faith, in not turning away from the Lord. Crying "Abba father," Rom. 8:15 is faith in the Lord as one's father, which must have, a being confident of one's good estate inseparable from it, or rather enwrapped in it. I suppose what I have mentioned is very consistent with what you say, "That faith, and persons believing that they have faith, are not the same"; for one's believing that he has faith, simply and by itself, has for its object the man's inward frame, or the actings and exercises of his spirit, and not a divine testimony; this is not divine faith, but as I have laid the matter, a being confident of one's good estate has for its foundation the word of God (Heb. 13:5, etc.) ultimately—at least to be sure, this is *one* way in which faith is acted, or one thing in its exercise. I am far from thinking unbelief, or being without faith, and doubting whether they have faith, to be the same thing in an unconverted sinner, whom your words "being without faith," must mean, and therein we entirely agree. But I must think, as to the believer, his doubting, whether or not he has faith is sinful, because it is belying the Holy Ghost, denying his work in him, so there is no sin to which that doubting can so properly be reduced as unbelief. You know, dear Sir, doubting and believing are opposed in Scripture (Matt. 14:31: 21:21; Mark 11:23), and I cannot exclude from the idea of doubting, a questioning the truth and reality of a work of grace on one's soul, for the Holy Ghost requires us to believe the reality of his work in us, in all its parts, just as it is, and never would allow us, much less call us to sin, or to believe a falsehood, that one is void of grace, when he has it, that good might come of it, i.e. that the person might be awakened from security, etc.: "Every man that hath this hope in him purifieth himself, as he is pure" (I John 3:3); I think intimates, that in proportion to the degree of one's hope, that the Lord is his father, will be his aim after sanctification, and his attainment of it; if so, to renounce this hope, to throw it up at any season, on any account, must be unlawful; whence I infer, for the believer to doubt of his gracious state, to call it in question for any reason whatever, so as to raze it, it is simply sinful, "I write unto you, little children, because your sins are forgiven you, viz. love not the world" (I John 2:12, 15). Here forgiveness of sin is used as a motive or incitement not to love the world, and this reasoning of the Apostle would lose all its force, was it incumbent on a believer at some seasons to think he was not within the bond of the new covenant thus he is bound ever to hold that conclusion fixed. The exhortation, not to cast away one's confidence, certainly comprehends a call to persevere in believing interest in the Lord, and to practice it at all seasons (Heb. 10:35). Job's friends endeavored to make him question whether the root of the matter was in him, and to conclude that he was an hypocrite. He resolved, though the Lord should slay him, he would trust in him (ch. 13:15), being confident of his own good estate, "All the while my breath is in me" (ch. 27:3, 5), and "Till I die, I will not remove my integrity from me" (ver. 5), and we see, from the whole tenor of his book, what there he resolved, he actually did practice, he never entertained the thought of supposing the Lord was not his God, notwithstanding the grievous eruptions of iniquity in him, in quarreling sovereignty, etc. And in the end, the Lord condemned his friends for speaking of him "the things that were not right," and pronounced that Job his servant had said of him the thing "that is right" (Job 4:1); from which it is to be presumed he was approved in guarding against razing his state. Also II Cor. 1:12 what the Apostle terms there, "his rejoicing," was what supposed his being confident of his good estate, that he was participant of a principle of grace, which made him capable of acting, as he did, with godly sincerity. All which, with other considerations, do satisfy me, that a believer never should raze his state on any account whatever; and that, as has been mentioned, doubting of his gracious state is sinful, one way of unbelief, its acting in him, though not the direct and immediate opposite of that acting of faith by which a person renounces his own righteousness and closes with Christ, yet the opposite of the posterior exercise of faith *in* him, and *upon* the promise, in certain respects. Your book is now lent, and therefore I cannot take notice, as you wish and I incline, of what you say on this head, pp. 177, 178 more particularly than I have done. However, I have, I think, touched the precise point in difference between us.

You observe, I seem to intimate, "A person's being confident of his own good estate is the way to be delivered from darkness, deadness, backsliding, and prevailing iniquity." And you add, that "you think whoever supposes this to be God's method of delivering his saints, when sunk into an evil, careless, carnal, and unchristian frame, first to assure them of their good estate and his favor, while they yet remain in such a frame, and so to make *that* the means of their deliverance, does surely mistake God's method of dealing with such persons." Here I think you represent the case too strong; for the words in my letter to which you refer, were, "I have heard it taught that the believer was bound to trust in the Lord in the very worst frame he could be in, and that the exercise of faith was the way to be delivered from darkness, deadness, backsliding," etc. And afterwards I said, when questioning whether the believer should ever doubt of his estate on any account whatever, "I know the opposite has been prescribed, when the saint is plunged in the mire of prevailing iniquity." Now, as a believer may be thus plunged, and yet sin at that instant his grief and burden (Rom. 7:24), and he may have the hope and expectation of being relieved from it even then (Ps. 15:3), I do not think my words convey the idea you affix to them. Also you will observe, I do not say that a person's being confident of his own good estate is the way to be delivered from, etc. but "that the believer was bound to trust the Lord in the worst of frame," etc. This I mention, precisely to state my words, and they are, I think, very defensible; for the believer is called "to trust in the Lord forever" (Is. 26:4). If so, when in the situation mentioned; for this is a trusting in the Lord as one's God. The woman, with the issue of blood, her touching Christ, and the success, is, I suppose, a call and encouragement to touch him by faith for having the worst soul-maladies healed (Mark 5:25). Trusting in the Lord for needful blessings, in the situation mentioned, gives him the glory of his faithfulness, and engages him to act in the believer's behalf; thus to do, it is both duty and interest. Jonah, when in a course of grievous rebellion, and under awful chastisement for it, when perhaps he had actually disclaimed interest in the Lord, or was in danger of it, said, "he would look again toward the Lord's holy temple" (ch. 2:4), evidently in exercise of faith in the Lord as his God, the Lord assuring him of his good estate and his favor, by the operation of the Spirit causing him to act, and to be conscious of it, and "when my soul fainted within me, I remembered the Lord, and my prayer came in unto thee, into thine holy temple" (ver. 7). Here is my assertion exemplified in practice, by a believer, I may venture to say in an evil frame, when the Spirit breathed upon him. Though a prophet, he deliberately disobeyed the express instructions of his great Lord (ch. 1:2–3), in a careless frame, for he sleeped securely in the sides of the ship during a tempest raised for his sake, and the heathen mariners every one called upon his god (ch. 1:5–6). So far was he from dreading, as he had reason to do, that the Lord would plead a controversy with him for the part he acted, that dismal security, awful carelessness, and a carnal frame had seized him; for he declared to the Lord, "he said to him in his country he would repent of the evil he had said he would do to the Ninevites, if they turned from their evil way," and assigned that for the reason why he fled to Tarshish (ch. 4:2), thus would rather that the Lord should want the honor that would redound to his name by the repentance, though only outward, of the Ninevites, and that the whole city should be destroyed, one of the largest the sun shone upon, and the most populous, and that himself should lose the honor and comfort of being the instrument of its preservation, than that he should fall under the imputation of being a false prophet, for which there would yet have been no foundation. Horrid carnality this! for as it was dreadful selfishness, it may, in that view, be termed carnality—astonishing pride! thus "filthiness of the spirit," worse than that of the flesh, and, all circumstances of his conduct considered, he was not only in an ungodly frame, but in an inhumane one, and he sinned presumptuously in one of the highest degrees, we may suppose, in which it is possible for a believer so to act, notwithstanding it appears the happy turn was begun in him, under the influence of the Spirit, by renewing his faith in the Lord as his God, and being confident of his good estate, upon which he prayed, as already mentioned, and was heard by his God (see ver. 7–8), was delivered out of his then dismal and dangerous circumstances (ch. 11:12). —Thus I have done more than I was bound to, and have proved the point not only in the manner in which I expressed it, but in the strong light your words, a comment on mine, had set it; for one plain Scripture instance, such certainly as that I have given, is sufficient, as agreed, to prove anything. It is so far from being a mistaking God's method of dealing with such persons, as you suggest (pardon me, dear Sir), to say, that it is, "the Lord's method of delivering his saints when in a backsliding, etc. condition, first to assure them of their good estate and his favor, and so, to make that the means of their deliverance," that I give you the words of the Holy Ghost, for these are as express and full as anything possibly can be, Jer. 3:12–14; ver. 14: "Turn, O backsliding children, saith the Lord, for I am married unto you." This was, to be sure, the Lord's intimating the new covenant relation in which he stood on the spiritual Israel among them; and (ver. 22 of that chapter), the Lord says, "Return, ye backsliding *children,* and I will heal your backslidings"; and in the close of the verse, we have the Lord's thus assuring them of their good estate and his favor, shown to be the effectual mean of their backsliding being healed: "Behold we come unto thee; for thou art the Lord our God." "O Israel, return unto the Lord thy God, for thou hast fallen by thine iniquity" (Hos. 14:1). Here the first words of the Lord's message to his spiritual Israel, are, that "the Lord was their God," and the expression, "fallen by iniquity," conveys a very strong idea, when applied to a believer, perhaps as strong, as is comprehended in your words, "evil, etc. frame"; and I must think this verse is so expressed, to work on holy ingenuity in them, for its revival when under the ashes of corruption. It would perhaps be no difficult matter to multiply Scripture testimonies of such kind; but these adduced are, I think, full proof of the point, for confirmation of which they are brought. The love of Christ constrains the believer to return from folly as well as to other things in other respect (II Cor. 5:14). I might argue here from the efficacy of the love of God apprehended, the genius of the new creature, and nature in believers, and a variety of other topics, but choose, without expatiating, to confine myself to precise Scripture testimonies. As to what you say, that "among all the multitudes you have had opportunity to observe you never knew one dealt with in this manner, but have known many brought back from great declensions, that appeared to be true saints, but it was in a very diverse way from this: first, conscience awakened; they brought into great fear of the wrath of God; his favor hid; the subjects of a kind of new work of humiliation; brought to great sense of deserving God's wrath, while they yet feared it, before God has delivered from apprehension of it, and comforted with a renewed sense of his favor." All I observe upon this is, that the way I have laid down, is obviously that the Lord declares in his Word, he takes, for bringing back his people from declensions, and thus in it that mercy is to be expected, whatever the Lord may be pleased to do in sovereignty, and he will not be limited; also, persons do not perceive everything that passes within them, far less are they capable to give a full distinct account of every thing of each kind. Experiences of Christians are to be brought to the touchstone of the infallible bar, and to stand or fall by it; the Bible is not to be brought to their test and judged of by them. I own we may mistake the sense of Scripture, but it is so obvious in the passages I have quoted, that I cannot see how it can be misapprehended.

I cannot say anything now about the other remarks I made on your book, touched on in your letter, because I have not now the book to look into. I understand the passages about prevalence of sin, so as to demonstrate a person not in a gracious state, better, by what you have wrote; and, if any difficulty shall remain after comparing your book and letter, I may come to propose it to you afterwards.

What you wrote about the case of temptation was very agreeable, and I thank you for it. I shall now state the case more plainly, because I want much your further thoughts upon it; it is precisely this. A person finds himself beset by evil angels (what if I remember right *Voetius* terms *obsessio,* and one in that situation *obsessus*); they incessantly break into his body and mind, sometimes by vain, at other seasons by vile thoughts, now by the thoughts of a business neglected, which was a thing seasonable to be done, then by a Scripture text, or an engaging thought of some spiritual truth, when entrance is not to be had another way, and by a variety of other methods. They do all they can, perpetually to seize, defile and discourage; he is conscious of the whole transaction, and finds his spirit broken by it, and goes not about to reason with Satan, knows the inexpediency of this course, is aware Satan wants no better, than that he pray much and long against his temptations, and so won't pray himself out of breath, by his instigation, is convinced the remedy is to get them kept out of body and mind, trusts, in dependence on the Lord, to the use of medical, moral and religious means for that end, because experience shows all of them are expedient and advantageous in their place; but all is in vain, no relief for him, relish of divine things wore off the mind, no comfort, it rendered callous by cruel constant buffetings, he cries, but the Lord hears not. By what I understand, this is a just representation of the case, and will lead you to the knowledge of other circumstances in it; what would you advise such a person to do? how shall he recover favor of spiritual truths and objects?

I wondered you said nothing in your letter about what I mentioned in mine, respecting *supposed immediate revelations of facts and future events,* as special favors conferred on some special favorites of heaven. I give in to your sentiments on that point, expressed in the three treatises you have published, and greatly like what Mr. Brainerd said on the subject, as mentioned, I think by you, in the funeral sermon on him, which I perused with a great deal of pleasure, and shall now mention some things, said in favor of that principle, of which people are very tenacious, that I may have your answers to them, which will be a singular favor done me for certain reasons, e.g. John 16:13 is affirmed to be an express promise of such a thing; —it is urged, the thing is not contrary to Scripture, and therefore, *may be;* —it is urged (John 13:24–27 is an example of it), an intimation what the Lord will do in such kind when it pleaseth him, till the end of time. It is pretended, and indeed this is the strength of the cause, that the thing is a matter of fact, has nothing to do with the Bible, therefore nothing about it is to be expected in Scripture, and simply to deny it in all cases, is daringly to limit sovereignty. The Lord has not said he will *not* grant it, and how dare any say it cannot be? it is reasoned, there are numbers of well attested instances of the thing in different ages and places, facts are stubborn things, and to deny them all is shocking, an overturning all moral evidence. It is insisted on, that the thing *has been* formerly; it is confessed, and why may it not be now? We are told, a considerable time before a thing happened, that it has been impressed on the mind in all its circumstances, which exactly happened in every point; if when asked, what one can say to this, he says, perhaps it was from Satan, to this it is answered, does *he* know future contingent events? the reply is at hand, it is not above him to figure a thing on the fancy long before, which he is resolved by some means to bring about; but to all this it is answered by advocates for immediate revelations, such reasoning tends to sap one of the main pillars of evidence of the divinity of the Scripture prophecies.

I have, by what I remember, given you the force of the argument, to establish what has had, I too well know, very bad effects, as commonly managed, in Britain, as well as in New England, a history of instances of them, would not be without its use, and materials for it are not wanting. I will long much to see what you say in way of reply to all this. I am sure you cannot employ time better than in framing it. I should have mentioned, that the authority of eminent divines is brought to bear upon them, whose stomachs stand at swallowing things, like additions to the Bible—Mr. Fleming, in *the Fulfilling of the Scriptures*. Dr. Goodwin, etc. But on this, it has been pleasantly observed, that the authority of the worthies in the eleventh of the Hebrews, would have done a good deal better. I have some apprehension this is a point of truth, which the Lord is to clear up in this age.

I have read your *Humble Attempt,* and with much satisfaction, was charmed with the Scripture of the latter day glory set in one point of light. Do think humbly your observations on Lowman have great strength of reason. The killing of the witnesses, as yet to come, has been to me a grievous temptation; for which reason, I perused with peculiar pleasure what you say on that subject; but if you answer the objection, "it would appear the seventh trumpet is to sound soon after the resurrection of the witnesses, and the kingdoms of the world, etc. but that has not happened, therefore the witnesses are not killed": I say, if this your answer, I have forgot. —I should have also mentioned, that it seems evident, the doctrine of immediate revelations must be simply denied as unscriptural, and thus well-founded in *no* case, or it must be allowed in its full compass and latitude, let the consequences of it be what they will, for if the thing is allowed *possible,* reasonings about its effects will not conclude nor avail; I can see no middle way between the two things. That principle taken for granted, by almost all in all times past, is, as I mentioned in my last letter, to me a surprising thing.

Mr. Whitefield arrived at Edinburgh, Wednesday last, and was to preach on Thursday evening, but as I am fifteen miles from the city, of which two miles by sea, I have not yet heard of the effects of his preaching, or the number of the audiences; I wish they may be as frequent as when he was last here. May divine power specially attend his ministrations! We need it much, as we are generally fallen under great deadness. I believe he will find use for all his prudence and patience in dealing with us, for different reasons. With great pleasure, friends to vital religion, and to him, are informed he is to make no collections at this time. I was glad to hear you write, he labored with success in New England, in rectifying mistakes he had favored, about intimations made by the Lord to his people, etc. and heartily wish he may be directed to apply an antidote here, where it is also needed.

I have tired you with a long epistle, and shall therefore now break off. What you was pleased to favor me with, upon the difficulty stated from Rom. 8:28 was very acceptable, and I thank you much for it. I will expect a letter from you first opportunity after this comes to hand; and in it all the news of New England, particularly some account of the state of religion with you. It gives me pleasure to think, I may write you my sentiments on everything without reserve. Please take the trouble to make my affectionate compliments to my friend, Mr. Abercrombie, when you see him, or write to him, and tell him, I remember I am in his debt for a letter. I hope the ship I am informed of, for carrying this, is not failed, and therefore it will not be so long in coming to your hand, after being writ, as my last.

I am, etc.

Letter 4. Edwards to Gillespie

Northampton, April 2, 1750

Rev. and dear Sir,

I received your favor of Sept. 19, 1748, the last summer, and would now heartily thank you for it. I suppose it might come in the same ship with letters I had from my other correspondents in Scotland, which I answered the last summer; but it did not come to hand till a long time after most of the others, and after I had finished and sent away my answers to them, and that opportunity for answering was past. I have had no leisure or opportunity to write any letters to Scotland from that time till now, by reason of my peculiar and very extraordinary circumstances on account of the controversy that has arisen between me and my people concerning the profession that ought to be made by persons that come to Christian sacraments, which is likely speedily to issue in a separation between me and my congregation. This controversy, in the progress of it, has proved not only a controversy between me and my people, but between me and a great part of New England; there being many far and near that are warmly engaged in it. This affair has unavoidably engaged my mind, and filled up my time, and taken me off from other things. I need the prayers of my friends, that God would be with me, and direct and assist me in such a time of trial, and mercifully order the issue.

As to the epistolary controversy, dear Sir, between you and me, about faith and doubting, I am sorry it should *seem* to be greater than it is, through misunderstanding of one another's meaning, and that the *real* difference between us is so great, as it is, in some part of the controversy.

As to the dispute about believing without spiritual light or sight, I thought I expressed my meaning in my last letter very plainly, but I kept no copy, and it might perhaps be owing to my dullness that I thought so. However I perceive I was not understood. I cannot find out by anything you say to me on this head, that we really differ in sentiments, but only in words. I acknowledge with you that "all are bound to believe the divine testimony, and trust in

Christ; and that the want of spiritual light or sight does not loose from the obligation one is laid under by the divine command, to believe instantly on Christ, and at all seasons, nor excuse him, in any degree, for not believing. Even when one wants the influence and grace of the Spirit, still he is bound to believe. Ability is not the rule of duty." I think the obligation to believe, lies on a person *who is remaining without spiritual light or sight,* or even in darkness. No darkness, no blindness, no carnality or stupidity, excuses him a moment from having a strong and lively faith and love as ever was exercised by the apostle Paul, or rather renders it not sinful in him that he is at that same moment without such a faith and love;—and yet I believe it is absurd, and of very hurtful consequence, to urge persons to believe in the dark, in the manner and in the sense in which many hundreds have done in *America,* who plainly intend, a believing strongly with such a sort of strong faith or great confidence as is consistent with continuing still, even in the time of these strong acts of faith, without spiritual light, carnal, stupid, careless, and senseless. Their doctrine evidently comes to this, both in sense and effect, that it is a mere duty strongly to believe with a lightless and sightless faith, or to have a confident, although a blind, dark, and stupid faith. And such a faith has indeed been promoted exceedingly by their doctrine; and has prevailed with its dreadful effects, answerable to the nature of the cause. We have had, and have to this day, multitudes of such strong believers, whose bold, proud and stupid confidence, attended with a very wicked behavior, has given the greatest wound to the cause of truth and vital religion that ever it suffered in America.

As to what follows in your letter, concerning a person's believing himself to be in a good estate, its being properly of the nature of faith; In this there seems to be some real difference between us. But perhaps there would be none, if distinctness were well observed in the use of words. If by a man's believing that he is in a good estate, be meant no more than his believing that he does believe in Christ, does love God, etc., I think there is nothing of the nature of faith in it; because knowing it or believing it depends on our own immediate sensation or consciousness, and not on divine testimony. True believers, in the hope they entertain of salvation, make use of the following syllogism: *whosoever believes, shall be saved; I believe, therefore,* etc. Assenting to the major proposition is properly of the nature of faith; because the ground of my assent to that is divine testimony. But my assent to the minor proposition, I humbly conceive, is not of the nature of faith, because that is not grounded on divine testimony, but my own consciousness. The testimony that is the proper ground of faith is in the Word of God, "Faith cometh by hearing, and hearing by the word of God" (Rom. 10:17). There is such a testimony given us in the Word of God, that *he that believes shall be saved:* But there is no such testimony in the word of God, as that such an individual person, in such a town in Scotland or New England, believes. There is such a proposition in the Scripture, as that *Christ loves those that love him;* and therefore that everyone is bound to believe; and a firm believing it on divine testimony is properly of the nature of faith; and for any one to doubt of it, is properly the heinous sin of unbelief: But there is no such proposition in Scripture, or that is any part of the gospel of Christ, that such an individual person in Northampton loves Christ. If I know I have complacence in Christ, I know it the same way that I know I have complacence in my wife and children, viz. by the testimony of my own heart, or inward consciousness. Evangelical faith has the gospel of Christ for its foundation; but that *I love Christ* is a proposition not contained in the gospel of Christ.

And therefore, that we mayn't dispute in the dark, 'tis necessary, that we will explain what we mean by a person's believing he is in a good estate. If thereby we mean only believing the minor of the foregoing syllogism (or such like syllogism), *I believe* or *I love God,* 'tis not of the nature of faith; But if by a man's believing himself to be in a good estate, be understood his believing not only the minor, but the consequence, *therefore I shall be saved,* or *therefore God will never leave nor forsake me;* then a man's believing his good estate, partakes of the nature of faith; for these consequences depend on divine testimony in the Word of God and gospel of Jesus Christ. Yea, I would observe farther, that a man's judging of the faith or love he finds in himself, whether they are that sort of faith and love which he finds to be saving, may depend on his reliance on Scripture rules and marks, which are divine testimonies, which he may be tempted not to rely upon from the consideration of his great unworthiness. But his judging that he has those individual inward acts of understanding, and exercises of heart that he has, depends on inward sensation, and not on any testimony of the word of God. The knowing present acts depends on immediate consciousness, and the knowing past acts depends on memory. And therefore the fullness of my satisfaction that I now have such an inward act or exercise of mind, depends on the strength of the sensation; and my satisfaction, that I have had them heretofore, depends on the clearness of my memory, and not on the strength of my reliance on any divine testimony; and so my doubting whether I have, or have had, such individual inward acts, is not of the nature of unbelief, though, it may arise from unbelief *indirectly;* because, if I had had more faith, the actings of it would have been more sensible, and the memory of them more clear, and so I should have been better satisfied that I had them.

God seems to have given Abraham's servant, a revelation, that the damsel in whom he found such marks, viz. coming to draw water with a pitcher to that well, her readiness to give him and his camels drink, etc. should be Isaac's wife, and therefore his assenting to *this* was of the nature of faith, having divine testimony for its foundation. But his believing that Rebekah was the damsel that had these individual marks, his knowing that she came to draw water, and that she let down her pitcher, etc. was not of the nature of faith. His knowing *this* was not from divine testimony, but from the testimony of his own senses. Vide Gen. 24.

You speak of "a saint's doubting of his good estate as a part of unbelief, and the opposite of faith, considered in its full compass and latitude, as one branch of unbelief, one ingredient in unbelief; and of assurance of a man's good estate, as one thing that belongs to the exercise of faith." I do not know whether I take your meaning in these expressions. If you mean, that a person's believing himself to be in a good estate is one thing that appertains to the essence of saving faith, or that saving faith, in all that belongs to its essence, as its perfection, cannot be without implying it, I must humbly ask leave to differ from you. That a believing that I am in a good estate, is no part or ingredient in the essence of saving faith, is evident by this, that the essence of saving faith, must be complete in me, before it can be true, that I am in a good estate. If I have not as yet acted faith, yea if there be anything wanting in me to make up the essence of saving faith, then I am not as yet in a state of salvation, and therefore can have no ground to believe that I am so. Anything that belongs to the essence of saving faith is prior, in the order of nature, to a man's being in a state of salvation, because it is saving faith that brings him into such a state. And therefore believing that he is in such a state cannot be one thing that is essential or necessary in order to his being in such a state; for that would imply a contradition. It would be to suppose a man's believing that he is in a good estate to be prior, in the order of nature, to his being in a good estate. But a thing cannot be both prior and posterior, antecedent and consequent, with respect to the very same thing. The real truth of a proposition is in the order of nature first, before its being believed to be true. But till a man has already all that belongs to the essence of saving faith, that proposition, *that he is in a good estate,* is not as yet true. All the propositions contained in the gospel, all divine testimonies that we have in God's words, are true already, are already laid for a foundation for faith, and were laid long ago. But that proposition, *I am in a good estate,* not being one of them, is not true till I have first believed; and therefore this proposition cannot be believed to be true, till saving faith be first complete. Therefore the completeness of the act of saving faith will not make it take in a belief of this proposition, nor will the strength or perfection of the act cause it to imply this. If a man, in his first act of faith, has ever so great a conviction of God's sufficiency and faithfulness, and let his reliance on the divine testimony in the gospel be ever so strong and perfect, all will have no tendency to make him believe this proposition, *I am in a good estate,* to be true, till it be true, which it is not till the first act of faith is complete, and has made it true. A belief of divine testimony in the first act of faith, may be to any assignable degree of strength and perfection, without believing that proposition, for there is no such divine testimony then extant, nor is there any such truth extant, but in consequence of the first act of faith. Therefore (as I said), saving faith may be, with all that belongs to its essence, and that in the highest perfection, without implying a belief of my own good estate. I do not say it can be without having this immediate *effect.* But it is rather the *effect* of faith, than a *part, branch,* or *ingredient* of faith. And so I don't dispute whether a man's doubting of his good estate may be a consequence of unbelief (I doubt not but it is so in those who *are* in a good estate); because, if men had the exercise of faith in such a degree as they ought to have, it could not but be very sensible and plain that they had it. But yet I think this doubting of a good estate is entirely a different thing from the sin of unbelief itself, and has nothing of the nature of unbelief in it, i.e. if we take doubting one's good estate in the sense in which I have before explained it, viz. for doubting whether I have such individual principles and acts in my soul. Take it in a complex sense, and it may have the sin of unbelief in it; e.g. if, although I doubt not that I have such and such qualifications, I yet doubt of those consequences, for which I have divine testimony or promise; as when a person that doubts not that he *loves Christ,* yet doubts whether *he shall receive a crown of life.* The doubting of this consequence is properly the sin of unbelief.

You say, dear Sir, "The Holy Ghost requires us to believe the reality of his work in us in all its parts just as it is"; and a little before, "The believer's doubting whether or not he has faith, is sinful; because it is belying the Holy Ghost, denying his work in him; so there is no sin to which that doubting can so properly be reduced as unbelief."

Here I would ask leave thus to express my thoughts in a diversity from yours. I think, if it be allowed to be sinful for a believer to doubt whether he has faith, that doubting is not the sin of unbelief on any such account as you mention, viz. as belying or denying any testimony of the Holy Ghost. There is difference between doubting of the being of some *work* of the Holy Ghost, and denying the *testimony* of the Holy Ghost, as there is a difference between doubting concerning some other works of God, and denying the testimony of God. 'Tis the work of God to give a man great natural abilities; and if we suppose God *requires* such a man *to believe the reality of his work, in all its parts, just as it is;* and so that 'tis sinful for him at all to doubt of his natural abilities being just as good as they are; yet this is no belying any testimony of God (though it be doubting of a work of God) and so is diverse from the sin of unbelief. So, if we suppose a very eminent saint is to blame in doubting whether he has so much grace as he really has; he indeed *don't believe the reality of God's work in him, in all its parts, just as it is:* yet he is not therein guilty of the sin of unbelief, against any testimony of God, any more than the other.

I acknowledge, that for a true saint in a carnal and careless frame, to doubt of his good estate, is sinful, as it were mediately and indirectly, as the cause of it is sinful, viz. the lowness and insensibility of the actings of grace in him, and the prevalence of carnality and stupidity. 'Tis sinful to be without assurance, or (as we say), *'tis his own fault,* he sinfully deprives himself of it, or foregoes it, as a servant's being without his tools is his sin, when he has carelessly lost 'em, or as 'tis his sin to be without strength of body, or without the sight of his eyes, when he has deprived himself of these by intemperance; not that weakness or blindness of body, in their own nature, are sin, for they are qualities of the body, and not of mind, the subject in which sin is inherent. 'Tis indirectly the duty of a true saint always to rejoice in the light of God's countenance, because sin is the cause of his being without this joy at any time, and therefore it was indirectly David's sin that he was not rejoicing in the light of God's countenance, at that time when he was in the bed of adultery with Bathsheba. But yet 'tis not directly a believer's duty to rejoice in the light of God's countenance, when God hides his face. But it rather then becomes him to be troubled and to mourn: So there are perhaps many other privileges of saints that are their duty indirectly, and the want of 'em is sinful, not simply but completely considered. Of this kind I take the want of assurance of one's good estate to be.

I think no words of mine either in my book or letter implied that a person's deliverance from a bad frame, don't begin with renewed acts of faith or trusting in God: If they did, they implied what I never intended. Doubtless if a saint comes out of an ill frame, wherein grace is asleep and inactive, it must be by renewed actings of grace: 'Tis very plainly impossible, that grace should begin to cease to be inactive, in any other way, than by its beginning to be active. It must begin with the renewed actings of some grace or other, and I know nothing that I have said to the contrary, but that the grace that shall first begin sensibly to revive shall be faith, and that this shall lead the way to the renewed acting of all other graces, and to the farther acting of faith itself. But a person's coming out of a carnal, careless, dead frame, by, or in the reviving of grace in his soul, is quite another thing from a saint's having a strong exercise of faith, or strong hope, or strong exercise of any other grace, while yet remaining in a carnal, careless, dead frame; or, in other words, in a frame wherein grace is so far from being in strong exercise that it is asleep and in a great measure without exercise.

There is a *holy hope,* a truly *Christian hope,* that the Scripture speaks of, that is reckoned among the graces of the Spirit. And I think I should never desire or seek any other hope but such an one; for I believe no other hope has any holy or good tendency. Therefore *this* hope, *this* grace of hope alone, can properly be called a duty. But 'tis just as absurd to talk of the exercise of this holy hope, the strong exercise of this holy hope, the strong exercise of this grace of the Spirit, in a carnal, stupid, careless frame, *such a frame yet remaining,* as it would be to talk of the strong exercises of love to God, or heavenly-mindedness, or any other grace, remaining in such a frame. It is doubtless proper, earnestly to exhort those who are in such a frame to come out of it, in and by the strong exercises of all grace; but I should not think it proper to press a man earnestly to maintain strong hope, *notwithstanding* the prevailing and continuance of great carnality and stupidity (which is plainly the case of the people I opposed). For this is plainly to press people to an unholy hope, a strong hope that is no Christian grace; and that is strong wicked presumption; and the promoting of this has most evidently been the effect of such a method of dealing with souls, in innumerable multitudes of awful instances.

You mean, Sir, to suppose pp. 6 and 7 of your letter that 'tis God's manner of dealing with his saints, while in a *secure, careless* frame, first to give 'em assurance of their good estate, while they remain in such a frame, and to make use of that assurance as a mean to bring 'em out of such a frame. Here, again I must crave leave to differ from you, and to think, that none of the instances of texts you adduce from Scripture, do at all prove the point. I think it is God's manner first to awaken their consciences, and to bring 'em to reflect upon themselves, and to bring 'em to feel their own calamity which they have brought upon themselves by so departing from God (by which an end is put to their carelessness and security), and again earnestly and carefully to seek God's face before they find him, and before God restores the comfortable and joyful sense of his favor; and I think this is abundantly evident both by Scripture and experience. You much insist on Jonah as a clear instance of the thing you lay down. You observe that he says, "I said I am cast out of thy sight, yet will I look again towards thy holy temple" (ch. 2:4). "When my soul fainteth within me, I remembered the Lord, and my prayer came in unto thee, even into thine holy temple" (ver. 7). You speak of these words as "demonstrating an assurance of his good estate and of God's favor" (I will not now dispute whether they do or no); and you speak of this exercise of assurance, etc. as *his practice in an evil frame, and in a careless frame; for he slept securely in the sides of the ship,* manifesting *dismal security, awful carelessness in a carnal frame.* That Jonah was in a careless, secure frame when he was asleep in the sides of the ship, I don't deny. But, dear Sir, does that prove that he remained still in a careless, secure frame, when in his heart he said these things in the fish's belly (ch. 2:4, 7)? Does it prove that he remained careless after he was awakened, and saw the furious storm, and owned it was the fruit of God's anger towards him for his sins? and does it prove, that he still remained careless after the whale had swallowed him, when he seemed to himself to be *in the belly of hell?* when *the water compassed him about, even to the soul;* and, as he says, *all God's waves and billows passed* over him, and he was ready to despair; when he went down to the bottoms of the mountains, was ready to think God had cast him out of his sight, and imprisoned in a prison, that he could never escape, *the earth with her bars was about me, forever, and his soul fainted within him.* He was brought into this condition after his sleeping securely in the sides of the ship, before he said, *I will look again towards thine holy temple, etc.* He was evidently first awakened out of carelessness and security, and brought into distress, before he was comforted.

The other place you also much insist on, concerning the people of Israel, is very much like this: Before God comforted them with the testimonies of his favor, after their backslidings, he first, by severe chastisements, together with the awakening influences of his Spirit, brought them out of their *carelessness* and carnal *security.* It appears by many Scriptures, that this was God's way of dealing with that people. So Hos. ch. 2., God first *hedged up her way with thorns, and made a wall that she could not find her paths; And took away her corn and wine and wool and flax, destroyed her vines and fig trees, and caused her mirth to cease;* and, by this means, brought her to herself, brought out of her security, carelessness and deep sleep, very much as the prodigal son was brought to himself. God *brought her first into the wilderness,* before *he spake comfortably to her,* and opened to her *a door of hope;* By her distress first brought her to say, I will go and return to my first husband; and then, when God spake comfortably to her, she called him, "Ishi, my husband"; and God did as it were renewedly betroth her unto him. That 2 of Hosea is very parallel with Jer. 3. One place serves well to illustrate and explain the other, and that it was God's way of dealing with his people Israel, after their apostasy and carnal security, first to awaken them, and under a sense of their sin and misery, to bring them solicitously to seek his face, before he gave them sensible evidence of his favor; and not to awaken out of security, by first making manifest his favor to 'em, is evident by many Scriptures; as, Lev. 26:40–42; Deut. 32:36–39; I Kgs. 8:47–51; Jer. 29:12–14; 30:12–22; 50:4–8; Ezek. 20:35–37; Hos. 5:15; 6:1–3; 13:9–10; ch. 14 throughout.

And besides I would observe, that in Jer. 3 the prophecy is not concerning the recovery of backsliding saints or the mystical church, which though she had corrupted herself, still continued to be God's wife; But concerning apostate Israel, that had forsaken and renounced her husband, and gone after other lovers, and whom God had renounced, put away, and given her a bill of divorce (ver. 8); so that her recovery could not be by giving her assurance of her good estate as still remaining his wife, and that God was already married unto her; for that was not true, and is not consistent with the context. And whereas it is said, "Return, O backsliding children, saith the Lord; for I am married unto you, and I will take you one of a city," etc. (ver. 14). Indeed, "I am married," in the Hebrew, is in the preterperfect tense; but you know, Sir, that in the language of prophecy, the preter tense is very commonly put for the future; and whereas it is said, "How shall I put thee among the children? And I said, Thou shalt call me my father" (ver. 19). I acknowledge this expression here, "my Father," and that Rom. 8:15 is the language of faith. It is so two ways, 1st, it is such language of the soul as is the immediate effect of a lively faith. I acknowledge, that the lively exercises of faith do naturally produce satisfaction of a good estate *as their immediate effect.* 2d, it is language which, in another sense, does properly and naturally *express* the very act of faith itself, yea, the first act of faith in a sinner, before which he never was in a good estate. As thus, supposing a man in distress pursued by his enemies that sought his life, should have the gates of several fortresses set open before him, and should be called to from each of them to fly thither for refuge; and viewing them all, and one appearing to him strong and safe, but the rest insufficient, he should accept the invitation to that one, and fly thither with this language, *This is my fortress, this is my refuge. In vain is salvation looked for from the other. Behold I come to thee; this is my sure defense.* Not that he means that he is already within the fortress, and so in a good and safe estate. But this is my chosen fortress, in the strength of which I trust, and to which I betake myself for safety. So if a woman were at once solicited by many lovers, to give herself to them in a married state, and beholding the superior excellencies of one far above all the rest, should betake herself to him, with this language, "This is my husband, behold I come unto thee. Thou art my spouse." Not that she means that she is already married to him, but that he is her chosen husband, etc. Thus God offers himself to sinners as their Saviour, God and Father; and the language of the heart of him that accepts the offer by a true faith, is, *Thou art my Saviour;* in vain is salvation hoped for from others that offer themselves, *Thou art my God and Father.* Not that he is already his child, but he chooses him, and comes to him, that he may be one of his children, as in Jer. 3:19, Israel calls God her Father, as the way to be *put among the children,* and be one of them, and not as being one already; and in ver. 21–23 she is not brought out of a careless and secure state by knowing that the Lord is her God; but she is first brought to consideration and sense of her sin and misery, weeping and supplications for mercy and conviction of the vanity of other saviors and refuges, not only before she has assurance of her good estate, but before she is brought to fly to God for refuge that she may be in a good estate.

As to the instance of Job, I would only say that I think he, while in his state of sore affliction, though he had some great exercises of infirmity and impatience under his extreme trials, yet was very far from being in such a frame as I intended, when I spoke of a *secure, careless, carnal* frame, etc. I doubt not, nor did I ever question it, that the saints' hope and knowledge of their good estate, is in many cases of excellent benefit, to help them against temptation and exercises of corruption.

With regard to the case of extraordinary temptation, and buffeting of Satan, which you mention, I don't very well know what to say further. I have often found my own insufficiency as a counsellor in such like cases, wherein melancholy and bodily distemper have so great a hand, and give Satan so great advantage, as appears to me in the case you mention: If the Lord do not help, whence should we help? If some Christian friends of such afflicted and (as it were) possessed persons, would, from time to time, pray and fast for them, it might be a proper exercise of Christian charity, and the likeliest way I know for relief. I kept no copy of my former letter to you, and so don't remember fully what I have already said concerning this case. But this I have often found with such melancholy people, that the greatest difficulty don't lie in giving them good advice, but in persuading them to take it. One thing I think of great importance, which is, that such persons should go on in a steady course of performance of all duties, born of their general and particular calling, without suffering themselves to be diverted from it by any violence of Satan, or specious pretense of his whatsoever, properly ordering, proportioning and timing all sorts of duties, duties to God, public, private and secret, and duties to man, relative duties, of business and conversation, family duties, duties of friendship and good neighborhood, duly proportioning labor and rest, intentness and relaxation, without suffering one duty to crowd out or intrench upon another. If such persons could be persuaded to this, I think, in this way, they would be best guarded against the devil, and he would soonest be discouraged, and a good state of body would be most likely to be gained, and persons would act most as if they trusted and rested in God, and would be most in the way of his help and blessing.

With regard to what you write concerning immediate revelations, I have thought of it, and I find I cannot say anything to purpose, without drawing out this letter to a very extraordinary length, and I am already got to such length, that I had need to ask your excuse. I have written enough to tire your patience.

It has indeed been with great difficulty that I have found time to write so much. If you knew any extraordinary circumstances, I doubt not, you would excuse my not writing any more. I acknowledge the subject you mention is very important. Probably, if God spares my life, and gives me opportunity, I may write largely upon it. I know not how Providence will dispose of me, I am going to be cast on the wide world, with my large family of ten children.—I humbly request your prayers for me under my difficulties and trials.

As to the state of religion in this place and this land, it is at present very sorrowful and dark. But I must, for a more particular account of things, refer you to my letter to Mr. McLaurin of Glasgow, and Mr. Robe. So, asking a remembrance in your prayers, I must conclude, by subscribing myself, with much esteem and respect, your obliged brother and servant,

JONATHAN EDWARDS

P.S. July 3, 1750. Having had no leisure to finish the preparation of my letters to Scotland before this time, by reason of the extraordinary troubles, hurries and confusions of my unusual circumstances,

I can now inform you, that the controversy between me and my people, that I mentioned in the beginning of my letter, has issued in a separation between me and my people. An ecclesiastical council was called on the affair; who sat here the week before last, who, by a majority of one voice, determined an immediate separation to be necessary; and according my pastoral relation to my people was dissolved on June 22. If I can procure the printed accounts from Boston of the proceedings of the council, I will give order to my friend there to enclose them with this letter, and direct them to you. —I desire your prayers that I may take a suitable notice of the frowns of heaven on me and this people (between whom was once so great an union), in the bringing to pass such a separation between us; and that these troubles may be sanctified to me, that God would overrule this event for his own glory (which doubtless many adversaries will rejoice and triumph in), that God would open a door for my future usefulness, and provide for me and my numerous family, and take a fatherly care of us in our present unsettled, uncertain circumstances, being cast on the wide world.

J. E.

INDEX